Meinem Nachbarn
Sitzreihe von St. Elisabeth
Paul Drobec
zugeeignet, um den Einblick
in mein Leben zu gewinnen....

6.6.2024

Letters to My Grandchildren

Reinhold Knoll

Translated by
Kenneth Quandt

2022

Letters to My Grandchildren

Reinhold Knoll

Translated by
Kenneth Quandt

2022

Academica Press
Washington~London

Library of Congress Cataloging-in-Publication Data

Names: Knoll, Reinhold (author) | Quandt, Kenneth (translator)
Title: Letters to my grandchildren | Knoll, Reinhold. Kenneth Quandt
Description: Washington : Academica Press, 2022. | Includes references.
Identifiers: LCCN 2022941204 | ISBN 9781680538748 (hardcover) |
9781680538755 (e-book)

Table of Contents

Foreword

The pandemic held the year 2021 in a firm grip. Vienna's respite from the floods of traffic and tourism drew an eerie contrast with the worldwide infection. At the same time the limiting of visits with family and friends was straining. There was nothing left to me than to write my grandchildren: to see them and talk with them I could not do. And so the first letter was addressed to a school child. It was very uppity of me to impose upon Nina the question *why* 2 x 2 = 4! The circle of addressees soon came to include all the grandchildren, and the topics of the letters became more and more challenging significant.

The original purpose of the project had changed. No longer was I writing in a "child-friendly" way to children. I wrote about my ideas, my experiences, and my observations – the things that have formed my life. In these the socio-historical turning points of my country – 1945, 1955, 1970, 1995, from National Socialism to joining the European Union – played an important role.

With the publication of these letters every reader immediately enters my life. Soon the combining and juxtaposition of subjects becomes evident. The excuse for this is easy: it is a indeed a review of social science and history, art and political observations, music and religion. Every reader will automatically become skeptical: Why should my life be of interest to him, already a life of yesterday? These "documents" are no "memoir" about birth, background, and career. Rather they present a view of an "Austrian" world. And they have much to say to the USA, not just about Mozart and Sigmund Freud!

It says a lot that it was "Americans" who reconstructed Austrian history after 1945 – from Alfred Diamant to Carl E. Schorske, and Charles A. Gulick to William Johnston. The unexpected publication of these letters in the USA is a gesture of my thanks. Publishing them in Austria would in any case be viewed askance. This is how bad things are at present. To this day the aftermath of National Socialism has poisoned all sincerity. Changing the accent of political affiliation and party is powerless against this: we need a broader change of emphasis. It is the overall sense of these letters to give to the next generation a panorama of what has happened, what is needed, and what is possible. And when the propositions of science become arid, it is architecture, painting, music, and literature that provide the complement to the picture. It is a perennial feature of Austria to think in terms of the possible – at least this was the case just before and just after 1918.

From this "panorama" stems an inspiration to defeat the monocularity of the several sciences. Kant once called it "cyclopean." The objection is against specialization in the sciences. The warning against it is needed now more than ever. To prevent the pictures drawn in the letters lead to a feeling of pessimism humor serves as a necessary antidote. It was retained here on principle: indeed humor was once the distinguishing mark of what is Austrian, in the social criticism from Johann Nestroy to Billy Wilder to Thomas Bernhard.

In the later letters wishes for the future become more and more important. With the current increase in belligerence and aggressiveness around 2020, wishes might seem groundless. These days it is common to anticipate a tendency toward the worse. Wishes have no place in this. So there is a general prejudice against them. It lies with the next generation to contradict the putative "logic" of history. The wish is, "Arise, Abel!"

– Reinhold Knoll, Vienna January 7, 2022.

Apology of the Translator

It appears to be the lot of our species to see the most important things "through a glass darkly." Attempts to ameliorate this condition rather than submit to its mystery characterize modernity since the Enlightenment, whether by seeking refuge within our own thought horizon all else transcendent, by replacing what is nascently organic with a systematization that makes its living foregone and unnecessary, or by chastening the fancies of our consciousness under the sophomoric schoolmarm of ordinary language. Such attempts have only enslaved us to our weakness. Phenomenology finally rebelled, not with enlightenment or a solution but a cry for authenticity, its strength being in its weakness; yet now we surrender our thought, unbeknownst, to the cybernetic dictates of a computer that knows us only to rob us.

This is the *fil directeur* running through these letters, an admonition for the future, which the Reader will perforce find obscure. Let him remember that at times even the prophets did not understand what they were saying. I have translated them because of their truth, and could not have been confident of my translation without the extensive help of Professor Knoll's student, Francesca Bisanti, whose redoubtable linguistic skills have removed most of my errors but whose empathy for their author has succeeded to preserve the texture, paradox, indirect humor, and occasional high tone of his writing.

Kenneth Quandt
San Francisco, March 15, 2022.

1.
The First Step in Science

Dear Nina,

I wish you a pleasant day – free of troubles and full of new things. I hope that school will add to your store of facts, and that you can make good use of them. Of course, the things you learn set you a path of their own: they can be strengthened by experiences and at the same time can be corrected and improved by contradictions, which will always come up. The things we learn are not settled forever but have an ongoing life in our thinking.

What I am here writing to you is the beginning of a philosophy of science: Would you be amused just thinking whether your teachers might have some use for it?

All the best, Your R.

2.
How Knowledge Builds

Dear Nina,

Last time I wrote you about learning facts, how one takes possession of them or, we might say, organizes the facts through one's experience. Please note the different ways of talking about it: one can be taught facts in school, but alternatively one might gather them from experience. Factual knowledge has a way of very soon taking on its own form, its own structure; that is, the facts soon fit together with each other and become a body of understanding. It is only as the knowledge of facts advances toward such understanding that one gets the sense of gaining real insight. In this way insight is the first test of the facts, an empirical test of what we thought we knew: the factual knowledge we have gotten has a kind of not-knowing attached to it. Only when we have completed such tests and have shown similar outcomes in parallel researches can we then begin to speak of gaining insight through such experiences.

For example I see a black stone. When I pick it up in my hands they get dirty. Someone tells me I can burn this stone in a furnace and that it is called coal. I proceed to do this, and the stone gives out heat. Next I come to know of several such black stones and I compare them. I weigh them and see that coal is somewhat lighter than another kind of stone (e.g., pitchblende); the coal breaks up in my fingers but the other stones do not; the other stones cannot be set on fire. Next, I inquire into the chemical properties of coal: I discover it comes from plants, and that millions of years ago it was wood. Quite gradually I have come to understand that what I at first picked up is a material transformed from wood to stone. From now on, I have gained insight.

Loving greetings – stay with me! Your R.

3.

The Reality of
Nature and the Reality of Society

Dear Nina,

We started with the facts one assembles in the course of one's life. These also enable a person to perform tasks, so that a knowledge of facts can prove helpful and needful. But understanding is something more. As I said last time, these helpful and necessary insights have a role in a wide variety of areas, in our life and in the world around us. In fact they are of decisive importance for our existence.

So, we must be careful. We often take claims we have heard to be insights; after all they are very good at explaining things we had hadn't understood. That the earth "orbits" the sun is an insight that was reached not by ourselves but rather by astronomers and physicists. We believe them, and thus share in the understanding. We do this all the time. We are able to do this if the insight comes with high credentials. But at this point we must be doubly careful, for a strict scientist will say that this conclusion in astronomy was an assumption that might indeed explain many things well, but may in the end be incorrect. Is this possible? Yes, it is possible. From science we know that we only revise our understanding when it is ousted by deeper and more valuable understanding. And this goes on continually, as long as science goes on. Thus we learn that our assertions are at bottom assumptions that achieve what credibility they enjoy merely from the current state of our understanding.

That however is just one area of understanding, the one concerned with the broad field of the natural sciences and technical knowledge. As to what concerns us, about ourselves as humans, we must achieve another kind of understanding. We are able to say that there also exists an understanding of the realm of society, or the economy, or the relations between men – a kind of understanding that can be formulated in an entirely different way from that of the natural sciences. We have often made the mistake of drawing an analogy between these two areas and of relying on similarities between them in ways that are unwarranted. The basic fact is that man – his dealings and his outlook and his plans – stem from a variety of motives that cannot be deduced only from considering him as a natural being.

Really to understand them I have to take into account many men in order to achieve insights. And with this concept of understanding I move into an entirely different category of analyzing, interpreting, and reading the signs. As you surely know, the history of mankind consists of many many facets, of many events, that do not simply follow a chain of cause and effect of the kind we find in nature. Instead of that, we attempt to develop a philosophy of history by which we seek to grasp the points of view on the basis of which mankind designs its economic, political, and cultural activities. Here we speak of paradigms, meaning hypotheses, assumptions according to which we think we are constructing a model and determining the decisive exigencies and the ways that men perceive, and thus reach a picture of why men act as they do and what goals they have in mind. That there have been huge differences in these factors is shown by the history of art: a gothic cathedral looks different from the church in Stefansplatz and different from the Karlskirche; and the church in Radezkyplatz exhibits a building concept different from the Romanesque Heiligenkreuz Abbey.

From such a history of art we learn that over the centuries there have been people who had very different concepts of what art could be. In choosing this example I have already reached an understanding, namely, that a great variety of things have been taken to be beautiful and useful. Nevertheless, and this is my point, this understanding is essentially different and separate from the understanding that operates in the natural sciences. I believe that here you have a learned a little something, and I conclude here, since otherwise your concentration might be overtaxed.

Thinking of you, your R.

4.

Fruitful Doubt

Dear Nina,

In my previous letter I mentioned the role of being skeptical in reaching understanding. This has been a theme in philosophy for about 350 years. One can say that it was "discovered" by Descartes, namely the idea of putting a variety of hypotheses and the theories they each entail to the test. But now I have mentioned a specific mathematician and philosopher, which I did not really want to do since I am not trying to give you a lesson: rather it is a thought-process we are trying to conceive of, together. Descartes applied doubt to many assertions of science and also to his own understanding, and even came to see doubting as a productive force. As long as we doubt we remain rooted in the basis of thinking. In mathematics it is a relatively simple matter: if I say 9 x 9 is 82, you will of course express your doubt. I would answer by saying that I did not know any better. But because you corrected me, I come to know that it must make 81. Yet what is the problem here? I already mentioned, in Letter 2, that this method of doubting is entirely appropriate in the natural sciences, but when we turn to the humanities there is never an area in which we get answers as clear as those to the question about 9 x 9. And yet, from the 17th century on, one was of the opinion that the foundations of *every* area of knowledge could be made more and more secure through doubt, on the grounds that doubting enables one to distinguish "true" from "false."

I can offer you a simple example. In mathematics it is clear that we must distinguish the true from the false: just so, we make a calculation to find out what the truth is. In the case of every homework problem the teacher knows the "right answer." But let is consider an essay written for a German class. The teacher corrects it, telling me that for some years now one must write *dass* with two s's, even though I learned to write it with an ß. Why should it be counted an error that I still write it *daß*? And it's even worse, in a manuscript of Goethe: today it would be a sea of red ink! In fact a novel by Goethe would get a "Fail" because of its many spelling errors. But Goethe was quite good at German, wasn't he?

Indeed we find out that Grammar and also Spelling are always changing. What was right before is wrong today. Why? Because language and writing, and 9 x 9, are different "things." I cannot therefore say that something in Goethe is wrong in the same sense I can say a calculation is wrong.

Doubt is itself a perfectly appropriate thing, but not in the same way in the different fields. Unfortunately one has acted as though it were. This has made a lot of trouble for us in philosophy, once we began judging anything people say as if they were calculations, true or false. In the 18th century this became common and many people conceived of themselves as able to sit in judgment over philosophical assertions, and say what was wrong and what was right in them. This led to a further step in philosophy: we replaced the method of doubt with "criticism." You must realize that "criticism" has nothing at all to do with our usual understanding of the term – as when I might "criticize" you. "Criticism" comes from the Greeks, and it means *to decide*. Criticism forces me to decide. In the humanities I have many questions before me, many objects and many ideas, about which I must decide. Criticism introduces the requirement to make a decision that will enable me to do the right thing. It is no longer a matter of doubting – at this point that seems an awfully unclear and uncertain way of proceeding. On the contrary, I need positive instruction about which way I am to go, which way I should live, that will stand by my side and give me counsels that I can follow. This is what "criticism" meant, once before.

To go back, what I wanted to tell you about before is much easier to understand than what is involved here. As I said, a problem arises when one starts applying doubt to anything and everything. It soon becomes obvious that doubt does not take me very far. Think again about how we entertain the belief that the earth orbits the sun. The first people to doubt the previous assumptions were on the right track, but they took a great risk in asserting that the earth is not the center of the universe. And there we saw that in all such natural sciences doubt can be of very great use. And yet, is it so everywhere and anywhere? According to our experience, it is not so true in other fields of knowledge. What are we to do when as humans we are not thinking all the time about the nature of the universe but instead must act in the here and now, and must recognize what is going on around us in order to manage our lives? In other times it was religion that played the role as counsellor at our side, and yet with skepticism religions lost much of their appeal and authority. And so we come to think we must erect a system that will likewise reliably provide answers to our questions. This is what brought about our current reliance on science, and this is why we only believe things that have been scientifically proven.

If you remember, I pointed out early on that this puts too great a burden on the sciences, for they are alive as it were, ever evolving and getting their orientation from the latest new discoveries. Because of our reliance on science we become unable to find answers how to live our lives and what is the goal of life: science can't tell us! The religions "know" it, but under the influence of skepticism and a suspicion that perhaps our credulity is being manipulated by religion, we have put it into a position where it can no longer serve as counsellor by our side. One has even come to take pride in no longer relying upon religion for his outlook on human existence.

But I must again go back to the beginning. The significance of the "critiques" of reason and of judgment is that on the one hand they show that we are often on the wrong path or even lost in error, but on the other hand they say that if we just make a practice of applying them to our thought we will at least achieve a purification of the judgments and "conceptions" we have carried along in us so far. But what is reasonable about that if we already think we have been following our reason all along? Have there not been many atrocities committed in the wake of criticism? Thus, we must find a new and different grounding for our reason, far more humane and always considerate of our neighbor. That would be a great step!

All the best, your R.

5.
Politics and Philosophy

Dear Nina,

The last paragraphs of my previous letter indicate the problems that philosophy faces. Originally, European philosophy was occupied with reviving the heritage of Greek antiquity on the one hand, and becoming harmonized with

Christian theology on the other, but after the crisis of faith the program of philosophy changed. Philosophy became the pathmaker for modern science through criticism. I mentioned that already. With this development and the emancipation from theology, one saw a need to redefine. The natural sciences had left it in the dust: any mathematician or physicist would now smile at how imprecise philosophy's way of thinking was. And so in philosophy one focused on the problem of foundations, which means on reasoning, for example, and on ethics, and social morality. Contributing to the need to do this was the fact that alongside the monarchic absolutism a new bourgeoisie was emerging, and soon a bourgeois society, initially concentrated in cities. For this, the new kind of philosophy took an authoritative position. It moreover played a role in the more and more pointed conflict between the King of France and the "people": indeed the goal of the French Revolution of 1789 was a new and independent kind of thinking. In the course of this great change, the questions of political philosophy became more important than ever. Any important philosopher had to deal with this new reality.

You will now be thinking that things are getting more and more complicated – and this is partly true, but on the other hand things were always complicated: what was new was that now, in contrast with the Middle Ages or Late Antiquity, we were directly affected by basic and general philosophical positions. Suddenly we have a philosophy of economic affairs, or at least a new theory of society; suddenly we are searching for a philosophy of history that goes deeper than a chronicle of successive emperors, kings, and popes. Indeed, philosophy was called upon to legitimate a system of laws. This really sounds complicated but it isn't. When today we say that everyone is equal before the law, this juridical formulation was born out of the spirit of philosophy, which was cognizant of the basic principles of social equality. Though today we accept this idea without difficulty, at the time of the French Revolution it was emblazoned on their banners as a principle, even if the Revolution soon betrayed it. The betrayal went unnoticed because, with the horrible Napoleonic War that followed the Revolution one came to believe that such equality had to be opposed. Likewise the other criteria introduced by the philosophy of the enlightenment – i.e., Freedom and Brotherhood – had indeed become watchwords of the Revolution, but were soon deprived of their inspiring authority and valorization. In the Napoleonic wars, not only was the old order of the Habsburg emperors broken up, but also that of the kings and dukes. The old empire, which had been in place since the Ninth Century, comes to an end, and in its place the erstwhile emperor, in 1806, declares himself the Emperor of Austria. Many European lands are in political upheaval. Thus, the question arises: What did political philosophy lead to? On the one hand it supported the idea of a republic, which however in Paris had failed; and on the other hand many philosophers feared that this new order would harm the "nature" of man. Many romantics shared this fear, and so also a romantic philosophy called for a political system modelled on the old idea of empire. The so-called Biedermeier style of this period was hardly attractive: given the anxiety in the face of the Revolution it had installed a rigid and authoritarian system, which lasted up until 1848. A philosophy that we would today count as conservative had basically the goal of providing enlightenment about the Enlightenment. Thereupon a reconstruction of the past became a matter of systematic historical research, art and culture became sciences, and philosophy once again took on the role of queen. Even today the philosophers involved have maintained their stature – I need only list their names since they are spoken of in other books: Kant, Hegel, Friedrich Schlegel, Fichte, Schelling, and a few others....

You must forgive me for tarrying so long with historical examples, but they ought to show you that the basic questions of life returned to the center of philosophical interest, and that one generally hoped that philosophy would be able to answer them.

It cannot be said that philosophy failed to provide an answer, but one must point out first that subsequently the orientation and schools and positions were faced with the new challenge of interpreting the actual state of society with the new science, and that on the other hand more and more often they interpreted society according to either utopian or ideological criteria. Among the utopian ones were the many policies and plans encouraged by the Revolution's thought about an ideal state, in which fraternity and solidarity are cultivated. In the end these finally received their implementation in the Russian Revolution of October, 1917, but soon collapsed into the horror of an evil dictatorship. The ideological ones consisted in philosophical schemes in which an historical interpretation of man or of man as a social animal were formulated, in which the interpretation took precedence over the actuality of the world in which men are living. Terms were developed that could serve either as battle-cries or as justifications for the role individuals were to have in these schemes. Some of the ideologists were called materialists and others idealists: the one wanted to bring healing to the world with their analysis, while the others thought that only in anarchy could man attain his freedom. Still others were convinced that only in recognizing the real facts could one make declarations about man and world, and therewith called themselves positivists.

At this point you will be somewhat confused, for at the beginning you anticipated that you would come to have some clear understanding of what the objects of thought are, though by now we are further from an answer than ever! Philosophers were teaching at almost every university, nearly all of them were writing their studies, and one expected not agreement among them so much as controversy. By the end of the 19th century it was really incredible how many "philosophies" had come about, how many orientations and doctrines. And still this was not enough. Other philosophers established themselves as completely separate from and deliberately outside the universities. The private intellectual became a new type who widened the colorful spectrum of philosophy even further, at the beginning of the 20th century.

And now we have begun to take the next step, and we shall see where it will take us from here.

All the best, your R.

6.
Between Marxism and Phenomenology

Dear Nina, Dear Julian,

If I may give a gross characterization of philosophy, overall in the 20th century I see two positions of importance. The first one I would call the ideological tradition, in which the social philosophy of Marx is to be classed along with other scientific studies, namely the psychoanalysis of Freud, social analysis after the First and Second World Wars, and the history and theory of economics. This shows that philosophy which centuries ago had been the basis for the "special sciences" and the queen of physical and mathematical theory, the theory of man (anthropology and ethnology) and psychology, now had conversely to get new knowledge and theories from them, instead. On the one hand one wanted to keep up with the present but on the other one felt he was still required to interpret the new realities of the 19th century.

The mark of an ideological position in philosophy is that it adopts a fundamentally critical position in its analysis that is based on a fixed concept of a theory of society that relates society to economic events. It is thought that the money economy and industrialization have shaped a new kind of man, who makes his way through life unfree and even "alienated," a state of living always determined by capital and his wages. The individual's wages and income are determined by forces beyond his control. This is a brief characterization of Marxism, which surely identified one important factor, at least: the relation between capital and labor. The implication is that in politics it is always necessary to manage things by balancing "fair prices" and "fair wages."

Many elements in the critical apparatus of Marxism correctly interpreted the new relations that characterize modern society, but it soon placed these relations into the hands of a political program which, in the extreme of communism, spelled a fearsome catastrophe for people. The "moderate" form of this, social democracy, wants to achieve relative harmony between capital and labor, but by means of achieving a democratic consensus. We can say in general that this is a political philosophy that goes so far as to condemn all previous philosophizing for having been blind to the life-problems of the people.

The second position, running counter to the first but difficult to characterize in a unified way, gives central place to the people's actual life-world. I would like to call this position the philosophy of the life-world (*Lebenswelt*). The first person to think of the life-world in philosophy was Franz Brentano, after the middle of the 19th century. Subsequently many schools were founded which only came into prominence in the 20th century. These currents of thought were counted conservative, and though formulated as a reaction against the French Revolution they advanced to become a political force of themselves.

I have forgone to mention a third school. This is positivism, which also was established in Austria, as was the life-world school. Indeed, in Austria modern philosophy was very advanced.

Now I will illustrate these three schools with a parable. A wanderer comes into a town. He sees many people and among them very poor men, begging for bread or spare change in the marketplace. Immediately the wanderer, who is a dyed-in-the-wool Marxist, cries out that men are being treated as commodities, like potatoes or spinach sold at market; it is sheer exploitation and this is why poverty exists. How shameful that poverty exists! Another wanderer comes into the market and notices the hustle and bustle of activity, and how important the marketplace is for people: they just want to cook a good meal and to make up their own minds whether it will be wiener schnitzel today and perhaps spinach pancakes tomorrow. He notices that eating habits have a lot to do with rituals, with informal rules about how and when to eat. He notes that as a matter of fact the electric stove changed the practice of cooking. Of course he notices the poverty, but he is more interested in the general attitude toward everyday behavior, what are the criteria by which things are being managed, the kind of mentality that is present in the city. In fact there is a different "mentality" in each town: in the one, people are thinking only about money; in the other they are busy thinking about whether they need a second concert hall. In a third town, everybody is upset because a highway is being put right through the center. And thus, mentalities develop: the musical town wants more peace, the other less traffic, and the first think above all about how they can motivate people to invest in their town.

I have probably chosen a poor example, but now let's have the positivist come into the town. He will determine through factual assessment that 20% are employed, that it turns out 55% are women, and 20% are younger than 20 years old. The positivist will then try to determine which predispositions for taking action prevail in this town. Does one want more inhabitants? Does one want more facilities for learning or vocational training? It is this factual assessment of the town that the positivist counts as its basic structure. It is not his job to become the mayor in order to remedy the deficiencies, to fight poverty, but he can determine the political status quo, what brought it about, and he will begin searching for the factors that have such measurable effects in the town.

I don't know if I have succeeded to evoke a vivid picture of philosophizing. And I am aware that my hasty sketch might create a false picture. Still, I have tried. What is most important to me is that you now become acquainted at least a little with philosophy. Today it lives a shadowy existence in the back of people's minds, and also of those in power. Nobody takes it seriously or busies himself with it. I would say it will soon suffer the fate the Church suffers today. The current sense of theology is that it has become an applied mysticism, or according to the "ideological" view, merely a means by which the Church wants to assert its power. This is of course nonsense because it is only a half-truth.

Here is how I want to make this clear for you: It is abusive that some "theology" should today try to formulate an interpretation of the Lord. This is a violation of the sacred. The Church – whatever form it takes on – is not only an attempt to guarantee the relation between man and the sacred but also to revitalize this relationship between man and the sacred over and over again, throughout history. In the Catholic form the Church is also the Body of the Lord – the *corpus mysticum* of Christ. This is for me also the basis for viewing every assault as an act of violence against Christ. One can go further in this thought, with theology. In philosophy it is perfectly analogous. Philosophy is the guarantee that thinking, on the one hand, must be possible, but on the other hand, only it is able to reflect on how well innovations and the masterworks of technology and huge discoveries, as well as wealth, are to be understood. It is said that due to the media the human element is lost, but in fact the very notion of humanity as the "user" must be relocated in the technical apparatus! – an entirely different "life-world!" This is a clearly a threat to the *condicio humana* – the conditions of human life – and we are called upon to manage these conditions of our lives with dignity and responsibility. Are we doing this? I believe you have already seen that many things are out of joint. Think about this, and if you do, you are already doing what philosophy is for!

Thinking of you often, my warmest greetings to you – R.

7.
Consciousness a Creature of Technology

Dear Nina, Dear Julian,

First off, I must make it clear that all that I am writing will also be going out to Marie and Vicky at the appropriate time. They must not be left out – it is only because they are so young that they are not yet reading these writings.

By now you have noticed that one can no longer speak of the special topics of philosophy without further ado. I have already written that philosophy has not only lost its importance for determining and defining the separate areas of knowledge, but that the special areas themselves have come to develop their own "philosophy," specific only to their field. and therefore they no longer rely upon progress in philosophy itself as they had 200 years ago. Indeed in the name of "practical relevance," so called – that is, the successes brought about by the sciences for our daily lives – so many sciences such as physics, chemistry, and electrical engineering and the more recent field of informatics think they are ahead of philosophy by more than a nose. This means that the way philosophy is presented in the universities and schools is little more than a looking back into history, and a regurgitation of old topics. But philosophy always has the ability to re-think the old topics, since innovations from the special sciences are introduced now and then that irreversibly alter the basic setting of human consciousness. You only need to imagine how it is a completely different experience to travel to

Salzburg by horse-drawn carriage rather than by train. Because of the distance to Salzburg the emperor outfitted the cloisters on the way magnificently, and one could spend the night in fine fashion. These days it's about 170 minutes to Salzburg. And so not only technology but philosophy also thinks carefully about "acceleration" – Do we under the influence of technology now live in a life-world that is more "fleeting" and more "superficial"? To answer this we will start by looking into the old sources to determine whether people really were so contemplative as we now wish we were and yearn to be? Has the feeling of being on a trip become different? These descriptions give the philosopher occasion to think about whether our "life-world" might be breaking up into pieces that no longer fit together. We can perhaps present the problem the other way around: When Joseph Haydn as he was moving to London said good-bye to Mozart in Vienna, he thought because of his advanced age that he would never see Mozart again. In fact they did not see each other again, but for exactly the opposite reason: Mozart died much earlier than Haydn thought he would.

When we say good-bye today, we never have the feeling we will never see the person again: our technology has enabled continuous connection with each other, with the telephone, electronic mail, and connection by video. In the past it was at best by a letter one might send from London to Vienna. And one had to wait three weeks for an answer – if things went smoothly. The philosopher asks what this does to people. This appearance of nearness between the continents, created by technology, hardly fosters the intimacy and sincerity that a letter would contain some 300 years ago. Indeed if we put modern communication to the test, it shows an enormous superficiality and carelessness. Have you seen the unbelievably stupid questions or statements in emails? On the cellphone one asks "Where are you?" or "How's the weather" having nothing else to say. I could give a whole series of examples of things that are never said in letters. It is not that things must be "more essential" in letters, but rather that one will likely take more care to ask better questions or provide more interesting messages. The philosopher will have to take these changes into account, for the world we actually live in is different from the way it was 100 years ago.

We must notice things like this because our consciousness – as well as our position in time and existence and our values about reality – develop out of them.

Consciousness ranks among the truly more "complex" areas in philosophy. If I may take my lead from the Greeks, *syneidesis* means a co-knowing, or better a co-seeing. And this is not such a bad metaphor for consciousness, since it has the property of producing a synthesis of the given impressions of the social and natural background with one's own experiences and knowledge. As you surely know, what you have lived through leaves permanent impressions deep in your consciousness, impressions that always come back to the surface when a similar thing happens again. From consciousness we then receive advice about how to act: it moves us to act, though we are only half aware of this. There have been interpretations of this for some time: the first "modern" ones come from the 17th century. Consciousness is always bringing awareness of our past actions back to us, through our memory – for instance in the way we judge things. These judgments are literally "complex" in the sense of being interwoven. They weave together mediated and traditional experience on the one hand with the personal experience of one's own, and out of this comes an assessment and a judgment. Prejudices come to the surface when we simply adopt value judgments without testing them by own's own lights. There can be sweeping judgments in consciousness also, or sweeping thoughts. I remember having heard descriptions that "gypsies steal." From an interdisciplinary study in Hungary I learned about an entire Roma village, and I hardly got the impression that its inhabitants lived off of theft. Quite to the contrary. Surely their way of living was very different from mine, and I could not imagine taking part in that way of life, but in itself that does not warrant accusing them of criminal behavior. And so one had to abandon this prejudice and make new one.

Indeed there are "patterns" in our consciousness that we apply without much thinking, when the situation allows it. So when you visit some neighborhood in the city you have been warned about it is certainly not a prejudice that makes you remain cautious. It would be criminal recklessness to stroll through the streets without paying attention. Also, in consciousness psychological reactions are at work that sometimes play a proper role but sometimes play an improper one. Very shortly before the end of the armistice of 1945, the air-raid alarms were still being set off: sirens were sounded and we were to make our way to the basement to protect ourselves from the bombs. And when I hear those alarms in the country-side always on Saturday at 12:00 noon, a shiver shoots down my spine, since I always remember those air-raid warnings. It is deeply etched in my consciousness. Reason instructs me that this signal on Saturday is only a test, to ensure the siren will function properly in an emergency. Therefore my shock of terror is brief, a sudden intrusion into the present moment of a terrible time of fear and distress. What is important here is the observation that I can correct a deeply entrenched fear and in a second or two can tell myself that there is no imminent danger.

We read in the philosophers that they prize critical consciousness, and indeed recommend that one must make critical consciousness his own in order not to become a victim of manipulation. We are often manipulated; often it is pleasing, as when we make our pilgrimage to the "mall" where all our wishes come true. Money of course is necessary, but I am talking about something else. And these same philosophers are saddened to see a "false consciousness" in people. This becomes a reproach directed against bourgeois society in particular, because lies and deception prevail in it, as well as desire and envy and avarice, and these go unnoticed since the advertisers dress them up with politeness and courtesy, with sweet-sounding slogans and false promises. This is why bourgeois society fell prey to false consciousness in the 19th century. But surely this was present earlier. We know indeed descriptions of dissimulations and lies from late antiquity – as when one wants to project a higher worth outwardly than the true one.

If you want to find out how much such behaviors determine the social life of a small town, then I suggest you read Gottfried Keller's *Clothes Make the Man*. Or – if you want to read a delicious comedy, Nikolai Gogol's *Government Inspector*.

And now I have written a long letter to you! I hope you have the patience to read and to absorb these observations.

All the best, Your R.

8.
What is an Hypothesis?

Dear Nina, Dear Julian,

I will try again to describe something that turns out to be more difficult than I thought at first. You have by now read about cognition, consciousness, doubt, and skepsis, and you have understood what I have said more or less. That doesn't matter since my letters, if you save and keep them, will be of help to you later, to clear up some matter that I once upon a time I might have presented to you.

I notice that the statements I have made so far in my writings depend upon assumptions that themselves must be examined. This basic thought – that what has been said so far has relied upon an assumption – plays a distinct role in philosophy. Already in Greek antiquity a word was created for such assumptions which you surely know already: "hypothesis," a term often used by Plato. And as you can see the word has retained its Greek form.

I must say in advance that in our usage there is a certain carelessness to be observed, in particular that on the one hand an hypothesis is too soon called a theory, which is horrible nonsense, and on the other hand that the term hypothesis is sometimes given a derogatory meaning, as if it were the word for ignorance or a lack of knowledge.

Thus, I will take it on myself to vindicate both these concepts especially that of hypothesis. For it is an essential prerequisite for achieving results, not only for science but also for philosophy. The operation of hypotheses is especially visible in the natural sciences, for there, most questions of research are built on hypotheses. Before we had technical apparatus as accurate as what we now have, astronomy was dependent upon hypotheses. For example, one could see the heavenly bodies with the naked eye – sun, moon, stars –; one could observe their motions and one sought an explanation. And here it was no surprise that we thought, at the beginning, that they all orbited our earth. Moreover it appeared not to be wrong, for just as the sun rose every morning, one saw stars that disappeared for half the year but then came back into view. Thus there must be a "celestial mechanics" that keeps everything going and in the manner of a giant clock governs it all to make it go in a fixed cycle. Obviously one observed that the sun rose earlier in the summer, and later in winter, and in a "different" place, and reliably so. Since it was conceived in this way one could fabricate a sundial that told the approximate time by the place the shadow of the gnomon fell on the dial.

On a south buttress of the Stephanskirche you can see a sundial that a famous mathematician fabricated so that one could easily tell the time. Regiomontanus began studying mathematics in Vienna in 1450 and soon became famous for his mathematical investigations. And anyone who worked in astronomy at that time also studied astrology, conceived on a mathematical basis. This will seem strange to you, for we have long since separated the previously united studies of astronomy and astrology because of astrology's often reckless predictions about our lives. Regiomontanus in fact cast an astrological chart for Emperor Friedrich III. One was proceeding from an hypothesis: that the course of the stars bore an analogy to the course of people's lives.

Here we have a good example of hypotheses. The hypothesis of astronomy rested on the notion that the calculation of the movements of the heavenly bodies was to be based on the assumption that everything rotated around the earth. Of course, this was believed to be true for a very long time, since countless calculations showed that many things could successfully be explained in this way. We understood the reason for the seasons, we could predict where and when the sun would "rise" or would "set" this coming spring. Whereas the assumption of the Greeks that the earth was a disk could not explain the cycle of the year at all – why it became dark earlier at one time and later at another time – the Egyptians hypothesized that the interplay between the sun and the moon was responsible for the tides of the sea, and in particular caused the flooding of the Nile, which was very important for agriculture. The Egyptians accordingly surveyed the banks of the Nile in order to have a way to determine permanently which plots of cultivated land belonged to whom. This was actually the origin of geo-metry.

You have since been told not only that the earth is "spherical" but that it orbits the sun and not the other way around. And you will also have heard that this insight, during the Renaissance – around 1480 – initiated a "revolution," because now man no longer saw himself as the center of creation.

Now I must cause you a little confusion. As good students you have accepted these insights and probably you have come to be convinced by your teachers that this relation between earth and sun is a fact, and that the hypothesis is from now on secure and correct, and indeed is no longer a hypothesis, but rather that it is really the truth that the earth has this position, analogous to the positions of Mars or Venus. And in the 17th century we learned quite a lot about the regularity of these courses of movement, that the paths of the orbits were elliptical, and many other things. Also, there are rules of gravity and momentum. I have too little knowledge to give you a complete picture of this, which is of such great importance for our life on earth. Still, in the tradition of skepsis I want to make an objection: you are surely getting a correct rendition of our current knowledge, but hypotheses lie behind this knowledge. Who can say that in 100 years we might not be using a different assumption? Who says that the hypothesis that the earth orbits the sun will be true for all eternity? Indeed, it can be the case that the sun also "moves," and it can be that the so-called fixed stars move as well from another vantage point, and seem unmoving only from our vantage point. What I am saying is that every hypothesis is useful only so long as it supplies us with explanations or answers to our current questions. And as you know, not only will we always have new questions, but we will also want to have an explanation why things are the way we think they are.

I really hope I have explained to you something of the meaning of hypothesis.

We must also know that hypotheses can be like prejudices. A weatherman announces in his report a prediction of the weather, that tomorrow it will be cold and foggy. He points to storms on a weather map, showing that over here, rain clouds are gathering. Thanks to our technology these are assumptions that have some truth in them. Satellite photos have been taken, as well as measurements of temperature taken in little meteorological stations up in the mountains that transmit their data. And thus, the weatherman gathers the data, and interprets it, and announces what the weather might be tomorrow. This is of great importance for agriculture and for traffic, as well as for hikers in the mountains and for planning school excursions. What the weatherman has made in his daily assembling of data is not a theory he derived from the data: rather, it is an hypothesis. Thanks to the hypothesis he can do a good job of predicting the weather, but we have often experienced that it is raining hard a couple of kilometers away but not right where we are. And we become annoyed because we could have made our excursion without getting wet: it turned out to be true for many regions, but not for ours: it was only an hypothesis.

Hence a famous philosopher came up with the idea that part of the nature of an hypothesis is that it is not the sort of thing that has to be "correct" in general. Hypothesis is very close to probability – so that there can be a high probability that it will rain, but whether it will rain in Radetzkystrasse in Vienna or in Markgrafenstrasse in Berlin is not being asserted as a certainty. Karl Popper – that is the philosopher's name – took the position that any hypothesis only becomes meaningful if its contradictory can be formulated. If that is not the case, then we are not dealing with a hypothesis but rather with an assertion, if it is alleging it is factually true, or with an ideological statement which means to assert a certainty or tell us what the truth is.

Now we have come to a point of extraordinary significance. If an hypothesis cannot be "falsified" (this is Popper's term) and is incapable of being contradicted, then what we are dealing with is either an ideology or an untruth or a truth. And we notice immediately that so far in these letters we have not yet talked about truth. This does not mean that philosophy does not care about truth, but that in the course of the 19th century it gave up the attempt to reach an insight into truth. Earlier on we said that so-and-so was true or false, but since 1900 we say it is "right" or "wrong." With this, thinking has an entirely different relation to our everyday reality. One can calculate correctly, but this does not bring one a bit closer to truth. One can, through research, conclude something correct or incorrect and yet we no longer connect that process with a desire to have learned a truth. I will return to this problem in another context.

I have written that with this realistic estimate of our current reality we can develop a lot of hypotheses which, I claimed, operate like prejudices in our consciousness or have a similar function. Thus, an hypothesis aims at establishing what we already anticipate, an "imagined actuality," which as a result of an analysis will be "verified" or "falsified," so that hypotheses are proven to be true or not true. In "standard" science what happens is that a "false" hypothesis is soon dropped. I would even claim that a false hypothesis contributes more to our knowledge than a series of correct ones. Thus, I must write that this method of distinguishing "wrong" and "right" is often mentioned and recommended, but I have never read about a scientist beginning from a "wrong" hypothesis. Only in the aftermath do they criticize that, and in other scholars. This has always made me wonder; and thus I would say that this "model" of Popper's requires one to be terribly optimistic about research, and even more, to be blessed with very good luck, if he has never to go down the wrong path.

So, we should once again repeat that hypotheses include a certain knowledge that results from "premises," so-called. A "premise" – something you cannot yet know – is always formulated in propositions, which can be presented in the form of "if … then" inferences. We are less happy with the premises for an hypothesis that is predominantly a so-called "inductive inference," which those who do philosophy do not like at all. In that case an inductive inference moves from a content that is unclear to an explanation that is only possible. You must realize that for many hundreds of years it was the fate of navigation at sea to hold to the right course on the basis of "unclear data" – such as fog. We owe the discovery of the "Americas" to a daring inductive inference, but at least the skills of the seaman were well enough developed to pull through this adventure. Only with the discovery of the clock could one determine the position of his ship in fog, and thereby hundreds of deaths at sea were avoided, for they could avoid the cliffs at Cornwall before it was too late. Challenging the logic of inferences should not be allowed to vitiate our longstanding perceptions of facts. We are thus in the situation of gradually reaching modest areas of knowledge from the implications of things that are uncertain, but these have their own inner shortcomings in case our "interests" in the nature of these clarifications have changed. But I have already pointed this out.

Now I must again return to the beginning. I have claimed that in the loss of linguistic knowledge, familiarity with important terms was lost. Not only do we call something a theory too readily, but in our eyes hypotheses are generally viewed as uncertainties. And nothing is worse in scientific work than having to deal with uncertainties. This is probably the reason that we think we can eliminate uncertainty with empiricism. Empiricism ought to mean that we begin to investigate facts. However the method of investigation has changed. Whereas for a long time we investigated the properties of a given thing, today we are more interested in that thing's use and applicability. Empirical social research provides an example of this, where in conscious disregard for premises one can, turn a single event into a plausible assertion in the blink of an eye. In this distorted form of empiricism the premises are assigned to hypotheses according to whatever interpretation seems opportune.

But now I have polemicized about a kind of social research that has the notion that of all things we must approach the most solid hypotheses with distrust, but must trust the most speculative ones with minimal hesitancy. Thus, important factors in our life-world, such as space, time, movement, law, causality – receive less attention, while the more complex and abstract inter-relationships such as economics or society seem to be the most obvious things in the world. Our understanding of the world always depends to such an extent on the words we use that we are only given a choice between more and less probable hypotheses.

I admit this has not only become a longer letter: there is even a danger that "it seems all Greek to you," strange and difficult to read, and so you might feel like putting the letter aside or even putting it out of your mind.

That would be a shame. I know a little about science. And probably I have made the mistake of connecting a factual problem – that of the hypothesis – with my own experiences. And so you are left with the question whether one can keep such experiences completely separate from one's description of an hypothesis.

All the best, your R.

9.
What is a Theory?

Dear Nina, Dear Julian,

I am conscious of the fact that it is really hard work for you to read such difficult things – so, read the same passage two or three times, or wait a few years until you have a problem of the sort I am facing. At that point you should consult these letters, since they present an attempt to clarify some real issues.

We must now deal with the question of what a theory is. Of course it is always a good idea to look at the Greek derivation of a term. Originally, theory means God's view, the view of *theos*. The second part, "-ory," comes from *horao*, to see, the root contained in our word "panorama," which is an overall view of the surroundings as seen from a mountain top. It is not easy to determine whether what is here meant is that God sees the world, or that one, as a man, wishes to see God.

We can already see assumptions operating in this philological derivation. With "theory" a reality comes into view that has broader and greater dimensions than previously taken in – than previous views from the mountain top. Immediately theories come to mind, all of which come from the natural sciences. From the theory of gravity according to Isaac Newton to Einstein's theory of relativity or the quantum theory of physics, it is indeed amusing that very advanced natural science needs theoretical assumptions, whereas in the humanities and social sciences we think we can do without them as being inappropriate for us.

In the field of medicine it is very easy to track at what point a change in the interpretation of a tumor or a cancer was introduced, and when the treatment for it was revised. If the issue were not so serious one could almost speak of it as a matter of fashion. Up until the 1950's one trusted in surgical intervention. One thought that cutting out a foreign growth would be enough to defeat the cancer. This turns out obviously not to be the case. Courageous scientists went further, and attempted radioactive irradiation. It was believed that healing could be achieved by destroying the cancer cells. Of course it is not as simple as that, for there is a variety of oncological manifestations, but one thought one had learned that radioactive waves did, in general, destroy cells, and so one focused the waves on the diseased cells and destroyed these. After that one became convinced that cancer was the result of a "failure in immune response" in which the immune system for some unknown reason does not get rid of diseased cells. The system probably has this ability, given the fact that we produce such diseased cells every half hour, but as long as the control mechanisms work properly they will be eliminated before they become problems.

I do not want to overly burden you with this description, and in all likelihood even by the time I have written it down my description will no longer be up to date. But even this is enough to show that a theory must have a connection with real states of affairs in order to set forth an interpretation of abnormal developments or diseases.

And yet this is only one facet of the problem and there are many others. A theory must not only bring hypotheses together, must test not only what they say, but also to what areas of reality the theory itself brings a new view of "things;" and therewith it must carry out a systematic revision of many assumptions. The outcome is not just knowing more but also knowing differently than before. One can therefore observe that a theory must not only be related to reality, but must significantly broaden the scope of its subject matter, as well as to specialize or even revise insights previously attained.

In many TV news broadcasts you have probably seen pollsters, political scientists, sociologists, and psychologists who give accounts of the insights that they have reached through an empirical treatment of a given question. One will wait in vain for them to talk concretely about a theory. But as we know – I have already mentioned this in my treatment of hypotheses – their hypothesis is called a theory and is immediately justified by reference to the phenomena of change, or modernization, or to general dysfunctionalities such as the shortcomings of the political or social system. The justification is secured by data they have collected, empirically. At this point one may well ask not only whether it is anything more than people's states of mind that are being reproduced in these reports: what is missing above all is representing how things change, for if a change appears to constitute a new social form, a theory would need to be formulated about what led to this newly salient state of affairs. At best, hypotheses can assert that immigration, unemployment, failure of integration, and the processes of political transformation are causes of social change. One can very well ask whether a cultural change might not have exerted an even greater influence, whether the media have not produced a state of mind, have presented a different reality, and have brought about a new eclipse of the understanding. Because of their truncating, many contributing phenomena are ignored that go beyond a simple survey of "attitudes."

It is exactly the lack of theory that hobbles ascertaining possible alternatives. Of course one latches onto the solid data, brought together by mental drives, and treats the picture one gets as reality. This kind of critique reveals that we are coming to be increasingly. Whereas for example in a theory of capital and labor and their reciprocal relation, a grounding in sociopolitics was a prerequisite in order to eliminate misery in society, today in all likelihood we would not even begin to design a new way to solve the problem, since "theories" are implacably opposed to one another: the one speaking for the pursuit of profit being enough to pay for welfare, and the other of the abolition of social classes so as to maximize profit overall. To mediate this disagreement, which the doctrine and theory of Austrian Marxism once was able to do, is no longer possible.

One can easily see, even from a few simple examples, that in distinction from a hypothesis a theory is always interdependent with actual reality. Even if I should present a theory of social cohesion in the hierarchy of ants, it will likely be understood as advocating some political position. This would be nonsensical, but I am sure that not a few are inspired by the notion of an Ant-State, since here one is spared the complications of independent action and thinking.

I would like to note, in conclusion, that there is a wealth of theories in the natural sciences which we know by name though we hardly know what they say, whereas in the human and social sciences a distortion has occurred because the automated analysis of databases yields certain correlations that have no meaning and yet such results are taken to constitute a theoretical investigation of a subject matter.

I will now detain you no longer, and wish you beautiful autumn days.

Your R.

10.
A Plea for Humor

Dear Nina, Dear Julian,

In this "interlude" I want to make it clear to you that all thinking ought to be accompanied with humor. This is easier to write than to come to know, and to practice. Humor – by which I mean free and open laughter – is a very rare virtue.

By philology we are taught that humor clearly existed in ancient Greece, or else comedy would not have arisen as a genre of its own. Gradually it achieved a rank equal to that of tragedy in the public consciousness of Athens, since humor is not about the grotesque, or clumsy jokes, or even about disrespect for a person, all of which do arouse the laughter of the public. Rather, humor's task is to reveal subtle but surprising connections that if one is too serious he will not notice. To put it more clearly: whereas a person might brood over and be unable to explain a given thing, humor can a suddenly shed light onto the situation, and with laughter this surprising solution of the problem is acknowledged – as if "the scales had fallen from my eyes."

I grant you that my writing about this is humorless. Don't be surprised, it's only because I have not come up with a joke by which I might have conveyed the same lesson!

To get back to business, the "Greeks" knew about humor. They had a good belly laugh when they heard that the great mathematician and astronomer, Thales of Miletus, around 590 BC, fell into a well while looking skyward to observe the stars. A Thracian maid had to pull him out and berated him for knowing something about the stars, alright, but nothing about the world down here. He would not have fallen into the well if he had been paying attention to the path he was on instead of the stars. At the same time it was a fable to illustrate that philosophers run the risk of losing sight of the reality that is right in front of them.

If we follow this further we can quickly see that it is not so easy to distinguish humor from an ironic commentary that is entirely malicious. It was in Roman antiquity that the first satires were written. The philosopher Seneca wrote the famous *Pumpkinification of Claudius Caesar* – in which the emperor turns into a pumpkin – this was the way Seneca with his poetry got his revenge on the lunatic emperor.

I know of only one culture in which even death is apparently met with humor. The Etruscans were a very secretive people who were completely supplanted by the "Romans." Only in the last hundred years have they returned to the center of archaeological interest, and from their relics we can see that they made everything into a joke. Whether it is a candlestick or an oil-lamp or a doorknob, everything provided an occasion for humorous play. Actually, the Etruscans should be designated as the discovers of humor.

One can find many examples in the history of literature, but they take us no further. Remember: we are pursuing the question why humor ought to accompany our thinking.

This is not easy! Probably the word we must use in German is *Witz* (English "wit"). Wit denotes a sharp mind, quick to grasp what is going on, especially like a flash of insight that suddenly enables one to see through things that one before had thought were impenetrable. If "wit" possessed this noteworthy meaning in the 18th century, then one can be sure that it is to be associated with the ability to judge (criticism, again). Wit breaks through all previous barriers and reservations, and identifies an actuality that we up til then did not dare to acknowledge. It is like a shortcut on a long path.

A dog tells his fellow, "My master is unspeakably dumb. When I bring him the ball, he takes the slobbery thing and throws it away – over and over again."

From the dog's point of view "retrieving," as it is called, which is thought to be part of dog-training, is just an idiotic thing to do. This altering of perspective is the essence of humor.

A witty thing coming from a sharp mind helps us adopt a different point of view, and with this the facts change. Unbelievable as it may sound, Germans were thought to be funny in the 18th century, and even the English. But they had gotten their knack for humor from France, and they in turn had gotten this double way of viewing things from Italy, starting with the mannerism of the 16th century. The manneristic painting of Pieter Brueghel is a document of the satirical side of humor. In fact Dutch painting in this period groomed a fine irony and admonition to see things with different eyes. What was depicted in the paintings were festivals, boisterous dinners in which drinking was always involved. The central idea is cheerfulness, which clearly fostered free thinking. Even little children are there, licking the bowls with relish and enjoying the creams and sauces; and the leftovers are given to the dogs stationed in wait beneath the tables.

For a philosopher, preoccupied by theorizing, humor can provide an empirical insight, revealing the other side of the matter – though not the couch potato, the grumpy broody person, or the humorless loner. If the charge of "unworldliness" has been brought against the philosophers ever since the laughter of the Thracian maid, let them finally defend themselves against it with a humor of their own. This is what distinguishes the real philosopher: that he, too, can laugh.

We are now on a track that leads directly to Freud's interpretation of jokes. He thought that in jokes the hidden or repressed inside a person is expressed outwardly, indeed that in a joke oppressive circumstances are not only compensated for, but even overcome. His book on jokes might even be more important for the understanding of psychoanalysis than his *Interpretation of Dreams*. Jokes bring about a "Reduction of Complexity" – that is, they bring complicated things back down to earth. Some philosophical treatises might have benefitted from having some humor in them. In that case philosophy probably would never have come up with the representation of man as a "deficient being!" The conscious insinuation that man is virtually a Hobbesian "ravenous wolf" (a common remark in the 16th century, later fated to be linked with the beginning of the socialization process ... !) and many more such remarks, not only express clear contempt for humanity but also, even though they often seem justified, can lead finally to attempt to manipulate this "monster" as if nothing better can be expected of him. Indeed the unbelievable achievements of human beings from the beginning up to today will never be enough to discredit this view since the essence of being human is seen only in men's defects. From time to time it is used as an argument that a political "domestication" of men is justified, namely a restriction of freedom.

The definitive refutation that man is not an exceptional being is to be found not in descriptions and investigations of humor, but in human laughter – in Homeric laughter as it has been called. Only by laughing is the world overcome: its countervailing power is not to be understood merely as a compensation, nor merely as a release from complex problems. Spontaneous happy-go-lucky and undaunted laughter expresses in its noisiness its superiority over all that. It is a quality beyond the reach of irony for irony, invented by the Romantics, confuses form and content. The writing might make you laugh but in content it is biting irony. Humor never had this sort of thing in mind, for here we find the surprising irrepressibility of a thinking that resists thinking, here lies the best protest against that dreary scientificity that degenerates into the cattle drive of schools and students.

I welcome each communication between us, and I am curious to hear your thoughts!

Yours, R.

11.
Politics and Philosophy Again

Dear Nina, Dear Julian,

We must now turn to a theme that has caused many conflicts in philosophy, both strife and heavy controversy. The theme is the relation between philosophy and politics. Since antiquity philosophy has seen as one of its duties to think carefully about the rules for being in communities. You will certainly have experienced how your parents' behavior changes when a number of guests arrive at your home. For instance, one particularly domineering aunt or uncle, takes over the conversation at the table, even if your parents would not approve of this. And not only does the showy behavior of the guest come across as rather negative: in addition, as you watch you make the observation that it is not proper for a guest to dominate the whole company. And secretly you wonder at the fact that your parents, though they are in charge of everything in the daily life at home, express no criticism; that they do not reprimand the guest. This observation indicates that you already know the rules of etiquette which, you believe, govern one's behavior at tea or at a dinner.

So if you conceive that a similar convention or rule is at work and must be respected in the shared life of many people, then it becomes easy to recognize that communities possess general norms, prescriptions, and settled agreements that keep peace in a community. In fact politics circumscribes conventions for the member of a community as to which tasks, duties, intentions, and goals are to be fulfilled. Soon enough, informally established rules and rituals become laws and binding prescriptions that integrate the action of individuals into the action of the community. You can easily observe community action in any village where a volunteer fire brigade is made up out of all the inhabitants, and puts in place a mechanism for protection and aid in times of emergency. Structurally similar is the goal of an association for beautification or for aiding seniors or for providing childcare.

These simple facts show, about politics, that it concerns the human being: that it starts with him, that it works for him and also works against him. Ever since Plato it was believed that politics should always be pursued in connection with a conception of man. So if the starting point of politics is man, then one must first take a look at man himself. If this is to happen in the context of politics we will bring to light a political consciousness that is *sui generis*. (You must add this to my letter on consciousness). In this political consciousness you will see that some things are alienating. Of all things, in this area men assert an irreversible position: they see their political consciousness as authoritative, and they claim a competence in this area that they deny to politicians.

In a philosophical approach we must analyze exactly these matters and we will probably have to acknowledge that the conception of human action simply cannot be derived from a "self-consciousness of the absolute." This conception does not include some ideal of a paradise or a golden age, nor does it operate under some regime of moral guidance – to the contrary, it is only in contradicting inclinations and excessive desires that morality can be achieved, which in the real process of human life expresses itself with negative assertions: "Thou shalt not kill." If we consider this set of facts, hardly foreign to us (we have had it since the Decalogue), politics appears to arise out of this negative determination, and bases its justification on being a war against evil. Marx is the unambiguous example of one who not only wanted to reduce injustice but also wanted to foster hope for a return to a primitive social paradise and thereby to achieve a final elimination of evil from the world. This comes to be described as a political agenda based on unrealistic and wishful thinking, and yet a realistic view easily collapses into resignation, or else an endless attempt to teach a man to be a man – which soon enough turns into the thought control of a dictatorship.

If you have followed me this far, then I want to mention an important novel that you surely know and have read. Daniel Defoe tells about a certain Robinson Crusoe, the sole survivor of a shipwreck. He reaches land on a deserted island and sets up a new everyday life. What is important for us is that what he describes is not a return to "nature." Rather, he seeks to institute and maintain the achievements of civilization – under very adverse conditions. It therefore comes to a grotesque reversal. Whereas an animal will revert to its relationship with nature, instinctually bent on what is escape, we on the other hand will abandon civilization at no price, even though being civilized takes on so many forms. It is thus the declared intention of politics to secure for us this state of being civilized, and even to expand it, and it is from this that we derive the right to configure our world according to this criterion. At least this has been the case so far.

We cannot stop with this observation. Our connection with being civilized at the same time means that we formulate the idea of our personal freedom in rebellion against social constraints. This sounds like anarchy, but in the case in point we are actually like an animal that has broken out of a zoo and escapes into "freedom," which in the case of an animal is nature. This is not possible for us, although since the 18th century there have always been movements that wanted to break free of culture and civilization. There were similar movements in the Middle Ages also, that wanted to abandon the narrow life of the town, with its tidy timbered houses and bullseye windows and opposed at the same time to those stone churches, and responded by establishing mendicant orders as a counterpoint to the order of the medieval feudal town. And yet this did not fulfill the original impulse to return to nature, but instead was the founding of a new sort of civilization. Politics is always situated within such a field of tensions, even when current themes do not seem to corroborate this.

You will correctly remember at this point that the goal of political action is always freedom, but the criteria of this freedom must be determined. In history we find the unwelcome fact that only the developed types of community have longed for freedom. On the other hand, ethnology teaches us that life outside the tribe meant certain death, so that the primitive life-forms readily see themselves living in bonds, while civilized man considers himself free only in his emancipations – that is, in the possibility of canceling such bonds. One must say that only with the destruction of the tribal structure, after the death of "savage man" – of the noble savage as Rousseau would call him – freedom compensated for this loss, though of course this independence and freedom also brought on a new sense of aloneness. If we again remember Robinson Crusoe, his rescue of the two members from the tribe was a noble deed, according to our civilization, and yet their rescue soon turned "Thursday" and "Friday" into servants of a patron, if not slaves.

This sort of outcome, which we perfected in colonialism, takes us down the wrong road. It has become today a matter of common usage to treat history only in terms of these antinomies and opposites, by which one forgets that with the idea that we are able to attain freedom, we ourselves consciously believe we have the ability to rise above order and nature. Prometheus was able to steal the fire from Olympus and bring this source of a new lifeworld to mankind, and the consequences of the history of creation are quite comparable, even if the foundations, from the dialogue of Moses on Mount Sinai to up Bethlehem, have a different reality content. From there on we know we are made in the image of God, and know what has become of us after our expulsion from paradise.

At this point you can appreciate how philosophy and our theological tradition share points in common. I will come back to one of these when we come to deal with human rights. For now, we must return to juxtaposing politics and philosophy. At least since Machiavelli politics seems to be reconstructing a new "nature." Freedom from coercion – from feudal paternalism – was only the outer indication of a human drive to oppose any confinement or any deprivation of freedom. Thus we see that not only are constraints in our community repugnant to us: even our neighbor can seem a factor that limits and burdens us. The commandment to love your neighbor in fact tells us that we so far have not been successful at accepting our neighbor in all his dimensions. This constant burden has after all become a theme in politics, namely, to protect and foster these "basic cells" of community feeling, which was seen as the basic prerequisite of politics.

It is the conscious distortion of reality for the purpose of being able to cling to the illusion of an enlightened sort of freedom. Thus we are able, right alongside all sympathy for our social talents, to declare our anarchic individuality, which nurtures its sociality merely as an animal seems forced to do so for the sake of reproduction.

In philosophy the image was commonly used that politics is the overcoming of the "anarchic." Of course, sociology has tried to prove, in due course, that through the founding of institutions and the taming of violence in communities or in the "state," politics has brought about an inner peace in society that emerged from the tensions between domination and individual action. One could interpret the goal of politics with Augustine, that in the best case it wants to copy the *civitas Dei*, peace and good will, and sees itself called to this end. For how often politics has failed, how often has it become a distortion, as if cruelties had become virtues!

Politics wants to present itself as an act that coordinates interests for some purpose, and through the inception of political reason we seem to possess a rational principle for the political realm. And yet politics could never entirely stay out of individual tribal structures, which is why it remained all too human. In a philosophical treatment we can even add the analysis that political reason is possible as long as it sticks to reconciling interests. As politics itself emerged out of historical conflicts, it will never entirely forget this theme and this recipe for success. So in its endeavor to reconcile interests in society it takes on the traits of enforcing such interests: it loses the authority of being disinterested and becomes partisan.

It is quite an accomplishment when philosophy brings these lineaments of politics into the light of day, and says about them that they are in all likelihood the indispensable signs of civilization, which has for so long only promised its lofty goals and never yet made good on them, except for a few happy moments, which awakened a vision of paradise.

This was a long story, and I assume I have overloaded you. In any case I wanted to give you this sketch at least once. It lies in your future to pass judgment on it.

With love, your R.

12.
What is Luck?

Dear Nina, Dear Julian – and later on Dear Marie and Vicky also,

Exactly because of the coming 13th letter I must write about luck. I know very well that there is a longstanding superstition that the number 13 is taken either as a messenger of bad luck, or in this case the opposite: good luck.

I can still remember my young son once was playing with a ball and kept pressing his luck and over and over again with the comment, "just barely." He was savoring a "close call," namely, that he had just caught the ball and knew in his heart that he was going to catch it. He was pressing his luck in the thrill that he must either catch the ball or drop it. And so the ball would elude his hands but then he would recover and catch it in a second effort, "just barely."

This memory teaches us that there are two kinds of luck. Luck can refer to the individual situation of a person, and luck can also refer to a particular set of circumstances. The second meaning has a lot to do with chance. And we by now know that there have been many philosophers and mathematicians who have done some careful thinking about chance. The most vulgar version of this belief in luck is found among those who use a system in playing roulette, who are actually of the opinion that there are sequences of numbers that can be ascertained, that there is a regular pattern, according to which a given number between 0 and 36 will re-occur at a certain time. In this case luck means what *hasard* means in French. In German, we *hasardieren* – and we "hazard" in English – when we put all our chips on a single card and hope that everything will come out the way we wish it will. Students often "hazard" at school, when they skip some chapters of the assignment in hopes that only the part they did study will be on the test. And the luck of not being questioned is given the ancient mythical version of an explanation, that the outcome was influenced by certain special objects – such as a mandrake or a chimney sweep they saw on the way to school. The opposite would have happened had a black cat crossed one's path on the way to school.

Now you will be asking what these strange stories have to do with philosophy. I can only say that people have always desired to be able to see a bit into the future, in order to control it or at least to get a hint about what action they ought to take. This began as far back as the various *Books of Dreams* in Babylonia and in Egypt; the Greeks set up an all-knowing woman in Delphi named Pythia. But behind the scenes there was a news gathering operation, so that her answers were not always mere speculation or things she just made up. And I have mentioned already the close connection between astronomy and astrology, which lasted up to the 17th century.

We must recognize the remarkable relationship we have with events that have not yet happened: we are observing them in our imagination all the time, over and over. In fact we are a life-form that is designed for a future: we refer to a future in our thinking, we think about our future action, hoping we will have made the right assumptions. One can refer to this as personal subjective luck upon which all our happiness depends if only our will should succeed. With this we have brought up an area that is not subject to reason only, nor does it entirely correspond to our feelings and emotions: rather, a truly dark field of mystification enters the picture, such that we anticipate – or even want to force – a lucky outcome for our daredevil projects.

Philosophy is involved in this: it is not entirely innocent of such personal illusions – for how often has it taught us that it recommends happiness (*Gluck*) for us and a happy (*glucklich*) life! Naturally it narrowed down this promise quite soon to a promise that a modest and frugal way of living would be the prerequisite for a happy life. Thus it came to be that already in antiquity modesty and self-denial were taken to be a condition for happiness, or at least that an increase of enjoyment would create a momentary happiness – for what lies in wait for us in the end is the negation of all happiness – i.e., death.

We see that in our present times we mostly swing back and forth like a pendulum between these poles, depending upon our current situation, and we probably decide only very late whether our desires are more spiritual or more sensual. We do know fairly well that we will share the fate of King Midas if we have too much luck; or that it is hardly enjoyable – as we think – always to be a lucky devil. The height of personal and political happiness was shown by Franz Grillparzer in the first act of *King Ottokar's Happiness and End*, in which the Bohemian king succeeds in everything – earlier one had called it "fortune" – and yet then his fall and catastrophe could not be avoided.

It is possible to think that these "depictions" of happiness were a popular theme in literature. The sum of all happiness is described and in the end – and this is the metaphor that keeps coming up – happiness is *already* present to one's grasp, namely by preferring modesty over the adventure of some lofty plan or other. Johann Nestroy often presented this theme, and in fact during the Biedermeier period this modest sort of "private" happiness was always preferred to everything else. Even in Adalbert Stifter's *Indian Summer* (1857), private happiness was worth more than all the success of big-time politics – though of course one will need art, the contemplative life of the country, self-discipline, and conscious asceticism to achieve it.

Before we lose ourselves in these lovely conceptions from literature of a life that turns out happy, we must point out that in our civilization we have a highly ambivalent relation to happiness, and yet at bottom we have tried to institutionalize it. The luck of skilled management plays a secure role in the stock exchanges, in stock prices and speculation, and indeed it is able to determine the course of the world; on the other hand we have mechanized and perfected old Pythia. Opinion studies and social research and the predictions that come along with them, which are part of the inventory of our political self-understanding, want to fulfill both our wishes: the future becomes manageable, and at the same time – if politics allows – political policies for the welfare of society can be determined. However, this is where political luck is divorced from power interests. And no matter how lucky a man might be, as a man he needs spirit, joy, cheerfulness, and freedom.

Political happiness will never attain this satisfactory state, for in our awareness of historical vicissitudes we know that "follies" have contributed far more to social happiness, to welfare, and to peace, than have all the social and political sciences taken together. Jonathan Swift wrote this note regarding happiness: "If we carry out an accurate investigation as to what is generally meant by happiness, as it pertains to the mind and to the senses, we will find that all its qualities and vicissitudes are contained in this short description: Happiness is that situation wherein one is uninterruptedly, carefully, and cleverly deceived." This is the dark side of the baroque period, which was hard to beat for pleasure and *joie de vivre…*

This view of Swift is surprisingly pessimistic, which however did not keep us from continuing to seek happiness, and perhaps to find it, too. It is probably a curious turn of speech, if when looking back we say that "each person made his own luck." It is like an obituary that wants to claim something that is pretty improbable.

With greetings of love to you. Enjoy the good luck of leading a well-cared for life in childhood (… or having led one) – RK.

13.
Are We Still of Any Use?

Dear Nina, Dear Julian, and then of course Marie and Vicky,

In my most recent I have challenged you a lot and of course I cannot know whether they are still readable and still interest you. So you have to make the best of these texts for these are my signs to you that I am alive – and I can offer you nothing better nor more exciting.

Today I want to deal with a question that once was posed by a theologian. He sat condemned in prison and was awaiting only his death. Dietrich Bonhoeffer wrote *Resistance and Surrender* in captivity, and I heartily recommend this book to you. It is a special testament of a martyr, who took on death precisely to bear witness to our faith. At one point he asks the question. "Are we still of any use?" He meant this in two respects. First he was of course raising the issue whether we have remained in our discipleship in Christ – as baptized individuals and members of the church; but the question was also asking whether we are living our lives with responsibility to others. As you know, at the present time (2020 in Europe) we have no enemies in the area, and since we are not at present in a state of war we have no defined enemy, as there was 70 or 80 years ago. And yet we do have enemies, in a way. There are countless seductions that are soliciting our attention, daily and hourly, served up to us by technology; we have enemies whispering relativism in our ears. Both of these look quite harmless, even close up. And if Bonhoeffer asks us today about our usefulness we cannot point to our ability to use our technological apparatus, our primary source of entertainment: that would misunderstand the question. We'd still be useful if we cared for the sick and gave aid and donations to the Third World.

So we are dodging his question. How are we to work ourselves free from this apparatus, both in our work environment and in our leisure time, equipment that threatens to strangle us like an octopus? I find this difficult to answer. It is not a matter simply of switching the devices off, or not acquiring them in the first place.

Rather, we must learn to be "alone" and by ourselves for once, to stroll through a forest slowly, very slowly, without using a phone. I have no advice for you about how to do this. I can only write you not do what nearly everyone is already doing at every opportunity, whether in the bus or on the subway – do not devote yourself, subordinate yourself, to these electronic devices. If I tell you for example that there are people who pray the rosary in silence, or that Buddhists make a conscious decision to retreat from the world around them and immerse themselves in meditation, you will be surprised that there is, or ever was, such a thing as this. If I say to you that the "users'" behavior may look like these, but say that their behavior is relying on external stimuli, and they are always intent upon distraction, and never find concentration in the manner of an inner dialogue, then you might perceive the difference. We are utterly useless if we experience our world predominantly through these media of communication, which in fact is the case, and if I am always being "on line," whereas in truth I no longer have an I, but rather I disperse it by chattering. We are useless if we keep to this lassitude, where we might use a lot of words but never keep our word.

Maybe I was too moralistic just now, which might put you off. But we must take this question of our usefulness even more seriously! Bonhoeffer thought that we must take a stand in our attitudes and by clarifying our thinking. He was acting in opposition to National Socialism and willingly sacrificed his life for the truth. If Christianity still exists today it is because of this unambiguous devotion, which was also meant as a message to his friends and his family to encourage them to resist evil unconditionally.

And here I will tell you another story. In Austria we honor a pious young father of a family who in that hellish time refused military service. And besides Franz Jägerstätter there was also Ernst Volkmann, a guitar manufacturer and a sacristan, who also refused to serve. Both were executed. And I know some who think, on the contrary that, both because of their family and the uncertain future, they should have taken on military service. What was needed was a compromise.

Now I ask you: can one enter into a compromise with the devil?

After all I had a father who as luck would have it did not face this dilemma – instead he lost everything in 1938, even his position at the University. Somehow he got a job as librarian for Count Wilczek and was able to support the family thanks to secret gifts of money from Cardinal Innitzer of Vienna. On the second day after the Anschluss the Gestapo arrived at our house but they couldn't find anything incriminating. He was drafted into military service around 1941 but friends helped him get a very comfortable assignment in Amstetten. His commanding officer was Major Karl Biedermann, who even as late as 1945 was hanged in Floridsdorf am Spitz as a collaborator, along with Alfred Huth and Rudolf Raschke. My father, released from the military early thanks to the help of many friends, served as a messenger to forward the appropriate papers of his friends, and others as well, to certain offices in order to certify (their) unfitness for military service. Thus he came once again under the purview of the Gestapo, but by then the Soviet army was standing at the gates of Vienna.

I tell you this family history since in the case of Jägerstätter it is sometimes said, as I just wrote, that he should have made a compromise. Even the bishop in charge tried to change Jägersätter's mind so that he could avoid death. He was unsuccessful. You must understand that both attitudes, that of the bishop and that of Jägerstätter, were justified. As bishop I must not send anyone to death – indeed, I must apprise him of all the problems that would ensue for his family!

In a such situation the famous social philosopher Eric Voegelin used to say, "I am not obliged to let myself be hanged" – and he escaped into Switzerland at the last minute. The bishop had the duty to act as he did, even if in our "standard" history of the period he is accused of being an opportunist for the National Socialist regime. This is of course nonsense. As the "shepherd of his flock" he must take care for their welfare. Jägerstätter must decide for himself, and he chose in favor of his faith and against an unjust war.

Because of these men and because of women like Sister Maria Restituta Kafka and Edith Stein, the continuity of faith and of Christianity was preserved! As Father Alfred Delp was being led to the gallows, the hangman asked him whether he knew what lay before him. Delp answered, "In ten minutes I will know better than you... ."

And so, when I repeat the question, Are we still of any use? we must always keep the courage of these people in mind. Of course I hope that you never meet with these circumstances, that you never know the gruesome face of war and dictatorship! And yet there are dangers in which you must take a stand – and I hope you will be able to resist! For this we need to take a resolute stand – always.

You notice that at this point one of the most important questions of ethics has been broached. When I read ethics – and this is always the main topic of many books – I am regularly surprised how undramatically ethics is treated. Yet ethics became a real topic early on, with Sophocles: his *Antigone*! What is involved in this drama is "merely" the right to bury one's brother, which the king of Thebes has forbidden. As relativists, nowadays, we would say that the brother is already dead: why does Antigone provoke the king when she surely was aware what the consequences would be? Here you can see for the first time the distinction between the divine law and the law of the world, as the Greeks understood it. Today we believe that there is only the law of the world. This is why our human rights lose their true force, if their grounding is seen "only" in the "material" or physical appearance of man. In the image and likeness of God, and therefore in divine law, the rights of man are an irreversible commandment, whether viewed in the manner of the Enlightenment or that of Christianity.

His question was probably not directed to our usefulness in our working life, whether one is a good engineer or a devoted teacher, though that provides the necessary foundation. Rather, usefulness in our time would be resisting the spread of the engineer's technology that is conditioning us, which obviously intends to manipulate man. Evidence we are useful comes when the schoolteacher takes the chance of calling out the blatant flaws in the required curriculum. In both cases the conditions of the human are being violated. And we know that in both these areas, a depressing silence is the norm.

I know quite well that when even as a child one possesses a strong sense of what is right, one is quite ready to raise a protest, to make vehement criticisms and to feel indignation. I myself lived through it, and I call upon your wisdom to prevent you from allowing the institutions to impale you headlong. Their power and competency of discrimination is perfectly suited either to maintain an unjust state of affairs or even to enact one. Unfortunately redresses through constitutional means are too weak and too complicated to attempt, to improve one's chances of success. Even this is only a mild objection against the weakness of constitutional means. I am afraid that these "legal remedies" are dwindling more and more, not out of political policy but because of the incredible lack of concern and indifference among the personnel running legal institutions. I do not want to continue complaining, nor do I want to represent protest as entirely ineffective, but I will remark that one needs a very great amount of courage, self-awareness, and endurance to continue with such procedures in the face of likely defeat in most cases.

In retrospect, I am not quite sure my youthful actions at the time were correct. It was German class, in the third form. Presentations were assigned to the students – more exactly, debating exercises on topics of our choice. The first time I chose the then-current subject, "The Language of Bees," thinking of the Nobel prize winner, Karl von Frisch. And another student spoke, to everyone's surprise, about the defense of Vienna against the Russian army. It was known that the Austrian master-sergeant, Ferdinand Käs, whom I later came to know well, divulged the plans for the defense of Vienna to the Soviet command, just in time and at the risk of his life. Because of this the Soviets altered their plan of attack and unexpectedly drove into the city from the south. In the exercise the student called Käs, who later became the head of the gendarmerie, a traitor, above all because he thwarted the defense of Vienna, with all its consequences. Just before the next school exercise I declared to my father that, in protest against the content of that exercise, which even the teacher did not contradict, I would not do my in-class exercises. I was twelve at the time, and I found it outrageous that such a thing could be said in 1953. So my father called up the director and informed him about it, and the teacher was admonished and then was visibly relieved because I had begun writing my homework again. However, the theme he assigned me was, "I will have to think about that for a long time." I couldn't let the opportunity pass, and so in my exercise I described that exercise, criticized the speaker and the teacher, and criticized the teacher for violating his duty as corrector of its contents. It did not take long to write and so I had time to make a copy of the essay. I had an inkling that this in-class exercise would have repercussions. And yes, in the next hour after the classwork, I was forced to leave the school, after having to listen of course to the roaring reproaches of the school director. Against all rules and regulations I was summarily banned from attending the school, one hour after the classwork. Of course my father stepped in and within two days the teacher was transferred and the director had to let me back into the school. In gross violation of my exercise's legitimacy as a "document in evidence" the school was accused of ripping my work out of my workbook! On the basis of his misappropriation of the evidence the teacher's removal was justified. In presenting my side of the story, the copy I had made of course served me very well!

At the start my victory was a memorable event. It was clearly a mistake that I decided to stay in the school although the superintendent of schools offered that I might change schools and classes. I was too self-confident and so I chose to return to the parallel class; and this meant that all the way up to the Matura I had to run the gauntlet, since the "incriminated" teachers certainly let their disapproval of me be felt. One of them, needless to say the history teacher, declared to the class that he could very easily talk about the forementioned period in our history, except that there was a student in the class who would turn him in for commemorating National Socialism's role in building highways and helping with the fight against unemployment. The geography and chemistry teacher was far more insidious: he never missed an opportunity to make antisemitic remarks, he even deemed it appropriate to praise Rommel's success in Northern Africa, and he blamed the defeat of the National Socialist regime on the many traitors and "the Jews" from the American east coast. In chemistry he was a perfect numbskull, since he knew neither the valences of the components in a compound, nor was he familiar with the chains of acids and bases. The formulas he wrote on the blackboard were most of the time incorrect, and often he would have a glance at the book and then tell us that "of course" hydrogen has a valence of one and "as we know" sulfur has different valences. And then, before the geography lesson the "characteristics" of the Jews had been drawn on the blackboard – a crooked nose or temple-curls (*beikeles*). This "tone" in the classroom corresponded with that of the entire school, also probably with the teaching personnel as well. It cost me my health – stomach ulcer and chronic nausea – and I lost a year. I would probably never have passed my Matura in geography, the subject I stubbornly chose, if it had not been for Professor Franz Klasek, my art teacher, who traced out the roads of the Sahara for me on a blotter. He was my mentor throughout school, and introduced me to painting.

So I have written at length about my life, but all along in connection with the question, Are we still useful? At the time I would have felt I was very useful because I had taken an unmistakable position in opposition to dictatorship and war. And in Austria such historical garbage as this is always washed up on the shore at the time of intellectual high waters, and for almost inconceivable reasons is portrayed as political discussion or even dialogue. During my time of study the subject of history was hardly exempt from these criminal intentions, only shifted into the sentimental and weepy in the interpretation of 1848 – my interests had been influenced far more by the phenomenological interpretation of history than by history as a series of events, which was hardly more than a chronology. So I was soon off to other shores.

I believed that out of a love for general knowledge and for a fundamental respect for the very highly diverse forms of science – from the tragedies of the Greeks to the lessons on logic or philosophy, and short visits to lectures on the natural sciences, and then of course the history of art – that I could pull off a "specialization in unspecialization," which later I needed so much when I became a teacher.

I will not here follow out a narrative of my entire life history, but I will encourage Julian in particular to endure the bullying in his school classes in Berlin with equanimity and inner strength. I know how bad such a situation is, how difficult it is to endure it, and you must know that I will step in for you any time – all you have to do is call. It's not something to let go by. I experienced it with my father, how he would always rush to school like a roaring lion. I can only hope that schools today are somehow more sensible than before...

Are we still of any use? I want in your case to answer Yes, for I see in you a set of beautiful qualities, even virtues. Nina's warmth, coupled with her inquisitiveness, is striking. Julian's peacefulness and his love of music is rewarding; Marie's steadfastness and self-sufficiency are virtuous, and the way Vicky is shaping her self-confident way of being bodes a stable mind in the future.

All the best, Your R.

14.
Non schola sed vita discimus...

Dear Nina, Dear Julian,

Those memories from the time I was in school are probably a good reflection of the general state of consciousness that was especially represented in the "bourgeois" districts of the city. This makes the backlash that triggered a "cultural revolution" in the mid-60's more understandable. From the USA the protest against the Vietnam War had spread to Europe, first to Paris and then to Berlin. The part taken by Austria was to be assessed very differently: here, any participation in the widespread protest movement of western Europe was at first quite restrained. Because of the celebrations of "600 Years of the University of Vienna" a series of events had of all things been organized by "conservative" students, who bewailed the "spiritual backwardness" of Vienna, and combined their criticism with a demand that a chair should finally be established for Marxism. From 1965 on, this lack of Marxism in the curriculum was regularly brought up and the "holy pillars" of this point of view were Ernst Bloch, Theodor Adorno, Herbert Marcuse, Jürgen Habermas – i.e., embodiments of very different positions within the spectrum of the "left." Ernst Bloch impressed me but then again disappointed me: on the one hand the "cold war" between East and West was a reality the endurance and inexorability of which one could not overlook, but on the other, Bloch resigned himself to the outcome of a modest prosperity because the working class had lost its political élan. In Berlin and Paris, student protests were the order of the day, whereas in Vienna the most impressive revolutionary act was the defacement of a lecture hall by Otto Mühl or Peter Jirak and others. This robbed me of any sympathy with the widely bruited social criticism of the Frankfurt School and Herbert Marcuse. The learning activities at the University came to a virtual halt. At the same time, Sudeten protests took place against a professor of world trade, Taras Borodajkewycz. This man did not hesitate to characterize different scientists in terms of their racial heritage, among them Hans Kelsen, and thus was celebrating, as it were, a continuation of a "history" that had ended in death and hardship, in 1945. At a street fight between socialist students and German national fraternities a man was killed, Ernst Kirchweger, in April, 1965. Along with other students I was invited to the memorial service in Heldenplatz, in order to dampen the "left wing bias" of the event. I quite willingly did this, since I hated nothing more than these haughty bands of students that would go out marching every Wednesday continuing to represent their embodiment of "false consciousness." That was when the sculpture of Josef Müllner in the lecture hall of the University, a bust of Siegfried from 1923 for the memory of the students that died in the First World War, became for the first time a focus of attention.

Much later, in the middle of the 80's, a protest arose against this sculpture as if it were the nefarious embodiment of this disgusting cult. I myself saw totally ignorant female students spitting on the bust. Its nose was broken off, as the Turks had once done to the tombs of the Babenburgers in Heiligenkreuz. Nobody knew by whom the sculpture had been made. Since then the sculpture can be seen, soiled under plexiglass, in the arcade courtyard of the University, condemned to insignificance.

It was high time for me to return to philosophy. Because of my cordial relationship with Ernst Topitsch, who had in the meanwhile become a professor in Heidelberg, positivism was not foreign to me: indeed I was sympathetic to it because of its drive against all forms of ideology. This was the time when one got from positivism a matter-of-factness that could be used to confront most philosophical positions. Most importantly it directed its suspicion of ideology against neo-Marxism, of course because of the turbulence and radicalization that led to such horrific consequences. In contrast, positivism looked like a stronghold of reason, as it were the antidote to overheated political illusions; and Topitsch, who while still in Vienna had directed his suspicion of ideology against natural law, Scholasticism, and Dogmatics, turned his attention in Heidelberg toward a political radicalism that organized assassinations in the 70's and didn't even refrain from murder.

This attitude of a generalized suspicion of ideology was for me too weak an argument. On top of that, what was proclaimed as matter-of-factness morphed into political propaganda and lost its purificatory power, because of which a search for a new perspective became ever more urgent. In my encounter with Michael Benedikt it became clear to me that the empiricism of this philosopher – something that had become a genuine tradition in Austria – might make it possible to formulate once again an unbiased philosophy. Suddenly philosophical treasures could be brought forth that had since become suppressed in the official work of the University, from Alois Dempf to Paul Feyerabend. This then led to a project to reconstruct Austrian philosophy from 1450 to 2000. The name adopted for the project, "Repressed Humanism – Delayed Enlightenment," became the program for the work.

I do not want to go any further into this – if you find it interesting the thick volumes of the study are there to be consulted. In each of them I made contributions, essentially to fill in the "gaps." And here my generalism became an advantage. I had to make the bridge to philosophy in music, in painting, and in literature, and on top of that in the philosophical themes in sociology.

The collaboration with Michael Benedikt was extraordinarily fruitful and instructive. Before we concentrated on the work of editing, we held long and exciting discussions for which I can thank becoming intimately involved in philosophy. We did not try to ingratiate each other; rather, we had heated debates on the conceptions of philosophy from Leibniz to Eric Voegelin, from the 17th century to the 20th.

One must be aware that as late as the 60's something of a wall was built at the Institute of Philosophy, which at the time was housed in the new building of the Institute, to separate the two chairs. The assistants were divided up as if into two discipleships; the one did not greet the other, and resentment and distaste for each other was expressed at every opportunity, even in administrative matters. At the same time as the Berlin Wall, the wall within Viennese philosophy was a conscious indication of intransigence. At that time Benedikt had somehow managed to find his way between the two fronts; Feyerabend and Topitsch had emigrated abroad, and so the way became clear for a philosophy that staged itself as virtually totalitarian and sought to advance a systematic philosophy that hearkened back to Hegel. It would be false to assume that the "left" track followed after Hegel: rather it was a "rightist Hegelianism," whose political outlook had already been embodied in Bismarck. No more needs to be written about it. Leanings toward the "Third Reich" were partly covered up and partly glossed over.

I must revert to representing the state of mind that I wanted to present to you. It is always important to recapitulate the background of events, in order to get an idea of the manner of the representation and the relative importance of agreements and disagreements.

For philosophic reflection it is important to disclose accurately this common thread to remain as close as possible to the facts that are essential ingredients of our intellectual history. You will by now understand why I am narrating this history in such detail, since I want you to be able to see that National Socialism brought about a lasting cultural rupture in our country. A famous author, Thomas Bernhard, placed this issue into the center of his work, with irony and rage, but was soon taken to be a mere humorist: his stage plays were met with glad laughter while they should have sent a chill down the spine. This shows how we are nearly incapable of reflection, a reflection that would start with an acknowledgment of the many crimes and evildoings, and only then slowly recover the Austrian spirit that is present throughout Austrian literature, from Franz Grillparzer to Adalbert Stifter, and from Robert Musil to Hermann Broch.

I now view the discovery of these forgotten treasures in blacker terms than ever. In a complete misunderstanding of the guardianship of our "national culture," as it is styled by our politicians at the openings of festivals, the universities have increasingly stopped taking responsibility for it. As an example I can merely cite the recent case of a Germanist from Germany, recruited to teach in Vienna, who rejected a student's dissertation on Heimito von Doderer because Doderer does not qualify for inclusion in the body of German literature. A similar suggestion can be made in music history: Franz Schubert has now been classified as a German Romantic; and in art history, courses on Austrian painting – Klimt, Schiele, Kokoschka, Gerstl – are no longer offered.

I describe this in so much detail, because in its intellectual history up to now, despite a certain backwardness, the Austrian identity had somehow been maintained, and yet now a Zeitgeist imported from Germany began to define the fields of knowledge. It is not nationalism to lament that for those who are studying today, the "bodies of knowledge" indigenous to this country are being lost forever. If the identity of this country is perceived only in the kitsch of Empress Sisi in a historicized way, and in the ghastly Strauss waltzes and its drinking of wine, great contributions to European history are erased from consciousness.

Lament is my way of rendering my reflection, in which I wonder within myself how in the future one will be able to learn the unique qualities of this land, and to what extend the former "cosmopolitan" outlook will be preserved? A significant indication is the non-appearance of a new edition of Grillparzer's diaries, which appeared in an edition of 42 volumes, only in 1909 and then in 1948. In these is the most essential documentation of our self-understanding, whether in his relentless criticism of Hegel, or in his reconstruction of our independent way of thinking.

And if I may indulge in lamentation once again, I will sum up my overall impressions. Here I would point out not only this suicidal tendency to identify Austria with the Habsburgs but also the inability to free ourselves from a nostalgic self-pity that has always been misplaced, and which accounts for a hatred of history that destroys our heritage. Salient examples are the building boom in the Heldenplatz, or the partial demolition of the Steinhof, where Otto Wagner had planned to build a truly magnificent hospital, or the vulgar commercialization of the old collections in the museums.

Before we wander all over the board, these are the results that accompany any reflection here in Vienna. It may well be that this discrepancy between the old and the new has always been a source of stimulation, and yet that is only an hypothesis from the history of literature. It can be that in Vienna the "most progressive" situation has been created, in which a self-righteous vanity and a flipside of hatred are present at the same time.

In the next letter I must finally regather myself so as not to push the representation of this pathology too far. It could well be that by the time you read this, a "change in the times" will have set in. With this I want now to close.

All the best, your R.

15.
Who Teaches Us Human Rights?

Dear Nina, Dear Julian,

It was a beautiful surprise, Nina, to run into you by chance at Schwedenplatz. You had just come from school and were waiting for the streetcar which come way too quick. I would have enjoyed running into Julian also, but unfortunately he is too far away, in Berlin....

In both the last letters I told you about my experiences while in school, and then about my years at university. In this the problem comes into view that once upon a time prompted the exclamation, "You don't understand the children!" Even earlier the father of Montaigne was wise enough to enable his famous son to have a completely open education in lessons without formal curriculum. Later, Montaigne wrote, about education, "Most educational institutions are a dungeon full of incarcerated youths ... it would be far more appropriate if the schoolrooms were strewn with flowers and leaves rather than with bloodied birch-rods."

I am not sure whether schools by now have become better, but at least in "my time" I can say the learning institutions often caused unpleasant distress. True learning was not going on: one welcomed class hours being cancelled and lectures being delayed for any reason, and because of the tedious details any desire for knowledge was lulled to sleep. And yet it would have been great if a teacher of chemistry had asked himself why this or that matter was not understood. I had two teachers who not only aroused our interest out of enthusiasm for their field, but also instilled in us a penchant, a desire, to know more. In one school it was the biologist, Camillo Giefing, for whom a student would willingly tidy up his "cabinet" – his modest collection of taxidermed animals, and bones, and old display cards, and countless rocks – and in the course of doing so would learn a lot about the current state of knowledge. This nudged me into an interest in bees, in the social organization of the bee "citizens" and in the way they communicate. In the other school it was the art teacher who awakened an enthusiasm for paintings in me, and also encouraged me myself to paint. Franz Klasek at that time became my mentor in that school. We were both clearly outsiders, for Klasek spoke a broad Viennese dialect which I had not heard before, and he read out to us in his dialect from the most famous art historians which impressed only me in the class. It was the time when the class was divided into music and art education as alternatives – one of the biggest stupidities of school administration. So I had to learn the basics of music on my own, and was a fanatical listener to the records, from Johann Sebastian Bach to Richard Strauss. During my military service I discovered in the barracks an abandoned library left behind by the US Army, and to my delight the important work of Alfred Einstein, who was the pioneer of music history, fell into my hands. His analyses of the Romantics and of Mozart finally provided me the foundations in music that I had so sorely missed. Later there were the clever interpretations of Ernest Ansermet, who had done a phenomenology of music, or the very sensible comments by Glenn Gould on Joseph Haydn. And of course the musical writings of Adorno on Schubert and Berg also played a role.

The meaning of this history is that I am living proof that despite little background and a really limited talent, a passion can nevertheless be kindled – a curiosity and thirst for knowledge – which all on its own leads to a journey of discovery. Finally, but quite late, this was also the case in literature, i.e., in the reappraisal of great works that had received too little attention since one thought that a study in school had been enough. I learned, in time, from Friedrich Nietzsche, that all literature mentioned in school loses its meaning when spoken of in school – and so I was finally surprised, much later, by reading the *Sorrows of Werther* and Stifter's *Indian Sommer* and many other works. In German class, Stifter was literally dead and gone, since *My Great-grandfather's Portfolio* is entirely unsuitable for 13-year-olds. But then, what should 13-year-olds read? I don't know – how is it for you? Likely, reading *Harry Potter* is already a stunning achievement – to move into this world of fable, into this mysticism of the moderns – but this subject would not have appealed to me. What interests me in literature is an authentic depiction of a period, and how at the same time the author's present is being interpreted, perceived, and dealt with in a plot in which the drama of man unfolds. This is what impresses me about Goethe's *Werther*, since the story of his sorrows is blended with an intimate depiction of German history in 1780, with its strange "political theology." In this sense Grillparzer's *Poor Minstrel* is a great narration that reflects the depressed and depressing life in Vienna's Second District and draws a contrast with the mentality of the Biedermeier period. I have already mentioned the diaries of Grillparzer, which unfortunately seem no longer available. They are a treasure house of sensitive analyses and an historical source of the highest importance, to which now even Germanists seem to pay no attention. As to the 20th century authors who captivated me I can hardly even start listing them – from Thomas Mann to Robert Musil and Hermann Broch.

If courses in school do not succeed to lead these works to be brought up again much later, to be studied anew and to taking up reading their precise descriptions anew, the whole treatment of literature at school has "gone to the dogs."

What I actually wanted to write about in this letter is something else. As it is, I wanted to add a couple of sentences to the previous letters, but once again I have gotten into a lot of detail, though I did not have it in mind to do so.

The fact was, I wanted to write about the meaning of human rights. I believe that bringing them up now is more appropriate than ever. We live in a time in which their importance is uncontested, and yet notorious violations of them are more irritating than ever. We pay lip service to these indivisible rights but in the next breath we violate them. About this disconnect we are not even horrified. Rather, for the holidays we adopt a humane vocabulary and make elegant speeches, and then once we return to work we acknowledge the violations with gestures of helplessness. And a still more evil variant has now been introduced, in which human rights have become misused in slogans for political parties, some of them seeing in human rights an absurd exaggeration, an exaggeration of humane concerns, and others, on the other hand, exploiting them as an effective provocation by which they continually seek to embarrass political regimes. Proper actions are taken here and there though not with the intention of obeying the imperative but for specious political show.

It is clear that in the interpretation of human rights, we possess an historical documentation whose origin is already fraught with a never-ending dispute. Human rights are sometimes mentioned by the reformed churches as its most significant victory over the papal church, above all since it was through them that the "freedom of the Christian man" came into being. All subsequent theories of natural rights were based on this new principle, until the liberal interpretation of natural rights in the 18th century abandoned their Christian framework. This was also the basis for a new formulation of human rights, coming with the Enlightenment, which now offered a distinct, "European" variant. In the Declaration of Independence of 1776, human rights were the godfather of the early history of the USA and were introduced again in the time of the French Revolution. Since then human rights have been the centerpoint for the constitutions of modern democracy, and found their universal articulation in the "Declaration" of 1948, as if to commemorate a condemnation of all future cruelty. A political consensus brought 48 countries together to redress the shock of the Second World War with a special protection for the individual person.

History here teaches us many lessons. On the one hand the binding nature of human rights came into question, for they point toward a conception of man that has strongly European elements; on the other hand, entirely different factors seem to legitimate the protections or even to delegitimate them, which were allowed to be based on and derived from a decision having to do with political expediency. Already in the "Declaration of Independence," which consciously set down the integrity of the individual as the most enduring principle, the protection was withheld from the indigenous cultures and tribes, and "did not count for the indians," just as the "Declaration" of 1948 does not apply to the Kurds and certain ethnic groups – for instance the Ugarits – because they cannot produce the prerequisite political form or identity. Nomadic cultures are not included in the catalog of measures for human rights, as is also the case under the statist omnipotence of China, where the minority has no voice at all. In the "People's Congress," about 5000 delegates are seated, and yet for a "Tibetan" or a muslim minority there is no representation. Whatever efforts are made to recognize such "ethnic islands," the "protecting powers" disown their responsibility as having to do merely with a "special case" and a "peculiarity," even if such peoples possess language and writing, history, and cultural articulation that together constitute an established identity.

I don't want to delve more deeply into this difficult matter of international rights since I am a layman, but I can see very clearly how human rights which we need more urgently than ever, are becoming a plaything of disgraceful interests and of insinuations, lies and historical distortions. These rights are almost guaranteed to be secured in liberal constitutional states but if you look into their laws and rules of asylum this assumption is immediately seen to be only partly true.

In the historical context we can see that human rights are validated only with certain qualifications. Thus the first effort is to withhold them from people seeking protection, and largely to deny this right to those who are fleeing, to minorities, and to the victims of persecution. Emergencies like these, which are always re-occurring in history, are today becoming more acute because of circumstances that obviously affect all of humanity: overpopulation and climate change are changing the "biosphere," constricting the habitat in such an irreversible way that human rights appear to be unenforceable to the necessary extent. The old statement of Rousseau that men were born free is undergoing certain curtailments that obviously do violence to this principle of equality because of the destruction of its natural foundations. As already in the 19th century, the urban population divided itself into eastern and western districts, the one having to deal with air pollution, poorly equipped municipal facilities, while the west side of the city developed itself into exclusive residential districts and privileged zones. This phenomenon is today the rule worldwide, and already many well-off persons have decided to leave the old world behind in time to spend the rest of their lives on islands, peninsulas, and favored coastal areas along the Pacific Ocean. Since quality of life must be seen as included in human rights, it's a depressing state of affairs that more and more people are finding no healthy place to live.

We are now faced with the fact that human rights have been expanded, so that they are no longer seen so much as a protection of peoples, societies, and groups, but are far more specialized as pertaining to individual persons. The "individual" should after all potentially have access to justice, he ought to be able to sue his state and make legitimate demands. To our surprise we are dealing with a kind of cosmopolitanism: through human rights individuals turn into citizens of the world who hypothetically stand on the same level as political bodies and state institutions.

Here we must pause. With the widening of human rights the circumstances of life in society will have to be taken into account. On special days of the year designated specialness ought to be remembered, whether it is the children, or the elders, or disabled persons, with a special disease or gender. We know well that the awarding of rights "from" someone always entails rights "to" someone.

Human rights are achieved by a narrowing of freedom and equality, and according to this, the "needs" of human beings must be measured. At first, "general" freedoms counted as part of human rights, in the demands of the 1848 Revolution – freedom of the press, of assembly, of religion, freedom of expression and of association – and the state was obliged to realize them. In the second "wave" the rights of the person were expanded to subjects other than persons. Thus the family is also included among human rights, and religious or ethnic minorities, and finally "non-human" subjects. Much later this widening inclusion became the basis for the ecological movement, and demanded respect for animals also, as well as a prohibition against exploiting them. In the end all forms of life were included in this order.

In the third wave, in the general understanding it ceased to be man that was understood as the object to protect: rather, a protection of his "specificity" was demanded. With equal treatment all individuals must be conceded integrity in whatever respect, whether in terms of their gender, their age, their disabilities, or even their self-assumed idiosyncrasies. This led to a specialization of human rights, which brought about a remarkable twist in what was counted to be worth protecting. In 1952 the Convention on the Political Rights of Women was adopted, in 1959 the Declaration of the Rights of Children, in 1971 the Declaration of the Rights of the Mentally Disabled, in 1975 the Declaration of the Rights of Physically Disabled, and in 1982 the UN World Congress on the Rights of the Elderly was held in Vienna.

Along with the criterion of this more personal focus, human rights proliferated more and more in the wider domain of social politics, and formulated a significant extension of social law, in contrast with the formulation of the "old" human rights which seemed to have had in mind a more "abstract" man. And at the same time that in the extending of the scope we are recognizing more and more the application of the honorable principle of humaneness, not only do solutions for present problems or violations of rights become more difficult, but soon enough we face the irreconcilable opposition of similarity and difference. In the end it becomes clear that the "human," or whatever term we are now to use for mankind, is less and less suited to the definition that we have used since John Locke's rationalism. To the contrary, the criterion for the demands of human rights is understood more and more in the differentiating feature, in the consideration and valorization of the extraordinary, which is now to be thought of as constituting a new kind of moral sanction.

The recent history of art can serve as an example of this, according to which making judgments appears no longer to be allowed: we are expected simply to accept surprising irritations. In light of such a comparison it may happen that human rights finally take on the appearance of excessive demands, their intention and application formulated more and more as a wish, so that the time-honored goal of securing freedom and equality is undermined. This tendency has strong support in the difficulty we have agreeing about what makes man unique, who according to the Declarations or Statements must be classed more and more as a deficient being than as the creature drawn by Leonardo, in whom the physical uniqueness and spiritual particularity of man was represented. With the change from the legal-philosophical justification of man to his characterization in positive law, man is overall viewed within the "Evolution of the Species" and no longer seen in the light of natural rights, in which he or she had been the "pattern of the ideal type."

All the best, I remain, your R.

16.
A Sketch of Industrial Culture

Dear Nina, Dear Julian,

In the last letter I wrestled with the issue of human rights, which I wanted to tell you about since whatever form they take on they then become part of the new stock of our world. Every thought here leads us to the concept of "humanity," which, because of all the possible developments and discoveries, has become a reality, since nobody lives completely separated from other cultures. One can reach them in about 12 hours or a bit more and move among them. A plane flight makes it possible for us to have breakfast in Vienna and, thanks to the time-change, lunch in New York. If one flies in the opposite direction he will take his next breakfast in Tokyo. To admire such accelerations is one side of the coin, the other is the mental mastering of these "other worlds," if we have not yet standardized and reduced them into a "worldwide industrial culture" and made them interchangeable. It is partly amusing and partly alarming that with this "mixing together" and overlapping, dissension grows and areas of conflict increase in number: one can even say that with the enlarged concept of a common life-world on this earth, racism and enmities arise out of nowhere – and antisemitism is not the only index of this.

While world travels are a constant topic in every café, because of so much travelling and thanks to transcontinental flights one thinks he has become a citizen of the world, and thus the talk will be about a view of the world that produces more and more absurdities the longer it goes on. The "man of the world" starts off by pretending that he ought to eat sushi with chopsticks, that he has latched on to Japanese culture from the first moment, that sometimes he is more Japanese than a Japanese, since he prefers Red Bull, the drink made of rice. A "world traveler" will interrupt a "citizen of the world" and loudly proclaim that the poverty of the developing countries is largely a fiction, for in the hotel near the pyramids there were Arabian families that consistently flaunted the most expensive wardrobes from Paris or Rome. And then the "globetrotter" will humbly recall that on his motorcycle trip across the Gobi Desert he had the impression that Americanism is destroying everything. To the right and left of the footpath up to the top of Fujiyama there are more empty Coca Cola cans than in an Italian landfill. In this world the only thing left in its natural state – for this is the current term for it – is abandoned factory buildings. Ailanthus and balsam grow on the crumbling walls of what was once a machinery building, and in the cracks between the slabs grow undesired dandelions. There one still can encounter the hardiness of nature, which one seeks in vain visiting the natural reserves. And the globetrotter would have offered a still grimmer vignette if a world champion had not yet interrupted him, who owes his success to an unbelievable advantage in anatomical endowment. The champion has to inform the group that it is due to changing times that there is no place for an iceberg or a polar bear in this world, which of course were not always there in the first place. This is all a normal evolution that has no sympathy for rhinoceroses or tigers, which owe their future existence to their "musealization" in the zoos. These pristine regions and reserves urgently need to be developed so as to optimize their yield. Didn't we begin developing lands four hundred years ago? Now we are near completing this gigantic project, and realizing a new kind of nature that accords with the demands of civilization.

These words aroused a tumult in the coffee house. Of all things, our world champion at shooting clay pigeons had described what the previous speakers were destroying and continue to destroy by their world travels. And because they paid for the trips by spartan sacrifices and a modest lifestyle, those he was criticizing were outraged and would like to have torn the champ's head off. In confirmation of the generous demands on behalf of foreign cultures it was repeated over and over again that the people in Djibouti would have starved if certain ones of us had not bought these trinkets in their market. And that in New Delhi or Mumbai an order for five suits fed an entire family. And that in Sub-Saharan Africa candies had been thrown into the crowds of children in the villages. Any trip to these lands would be a real aid to development and would promote needful modernization. However righteous this group might be in their city life, in the heat of the war of words almost all of them would have rejected the accusations of this critic with indignation – but he had already left for home.

I have told this story here to loosen things up, since in the wake of human rights this became necessary. On the other hand, you can see from the story that most people downplay the preservation of nature as fundamental to our existence. One still feels it is necessary to conquer nature in its vastness, to make it serve us in the use we make of it. And what has succeeded most effectively to destroy the world is not wars but tourism. No artillery unit in an army moving through on an expedition has as great a destructive effect as tourists, who like a swarm of locusts mercilessly lay cultures to waste. Ironically, tourism has led to our view of the world. And not a few think they have reached an understanding of the world since with their far-flung travels they have visited some places or other, and have invaded temples and churches in their leisure clothes so that they may then render their judgment. Their worldview is thus drawn from the language they already have on hand, and from their talking with each other. And thus everyone has his own view of the world, which reflects his own ignorance and prejudices in a really pathetic way.

The question really is whether we can continue to plunder our planet in this way. Every museum reports to us what we have lost. Over and over I think of a large wall in Vienna's Museum of Natural History on which a most complete variety of protected birds is on display, and one can read at the bottom of the display that two thirds of these no longer exist in Central Europe. And then the nightmarish thought creeps into my mind that the overwhelming majority of people view this situation as normal. Many probably think they cannot give up long distance travel, the pleasure of hunting, or the little cottage on the green just for the sake of these animals. I could never understand how an emperor, alone in the large area of Bad Ischl, would wish to shoot over ten thousand chamois. It seems to me infinitely boring to lie in ambush for these animals and then shoot them – and do this a thousand times over! Although the universities in the Danube Monarchy made incredible progress, the emperor had the least interest in them, and instead of having a chat with one of their professors he climbed up to a high vantage point so he could kill a rare heather cock.

One could say it belongs to the feudal mindset to go hunting, and yet today we have a thousand "emperors" that act that same way. Completely thoughtless, the branch manager of a bank, the department head of a large company, high officials and speculating investors, their rifles equipped with sighting scopes, go off into the forests in order to experience this bloody work as a form of pleasure-hunting. Because of this bad behavior it is understandable that the more recent formulations of human rights have been extended to animals as well, and have adopted the goal of preserving the entire biosphere.

I have briefly touched upon some topics regarding our civilization by which I want gently to make it clear that we are responsible for the condition of this world. When "we" hand this world over to you – we who over the last decades have carried out an unprecedented depredation – then I hope that your efforts will be directed more to repair this world than to continue the exploitation. It is a grotesque thing to observe that in the brief period of the pandemic, in spring 2020, it was again possible to see a blue sky with no con-air trails from airplanes and that the city itself could be experienced in its finer detail. It is a bitter thing that it took a plague to return us to the "normality" of our life-relationships, whereas we would not on our own initiative have been willing to live more ascetically and with conscientious reserve.

In this letter I have offered nothing new but rather have brought up what is already being talked about. But what is missing in these stories is reflection on a certain new topic that has become an "anthropological constant." Acceleration has been transferred into our bodies, and we now have become virtual projectiles. In the accounts of our civilization we are glossing over the fact that our technical apparatuses, to a considerable extent, were borrowed from military technology. And if war was not able to bring about "total mobilization" – since even under a dictatorship it was not possible to make everyone into a soldier – such a mobilization does take place at the beginning of every holiday. On highways, airports, and city-exits the "troops" are set into motion against nature. The battles are found no longer on a battlefield (although after auto accidents the highway does come to resemble one); instead, victory beckons any tourist who can occupy a remote mountain village or a sleepy seaside town, or can invade the historical sites and sanctuaries, it matters not which. Tourism has long since implemented a general strategic plan, for these dreamy settlements have come to be surrounded by high-rise buildings that house the expeditionary corps of the leisure companies as if in barracks. They mercilessly pounce on the region in season, or high season, like a Mongol horde. As important as timetables are for traveling, which for starters report the speed, the change in one's location conceals the general "placelessness" that acceleration brings about. Just as one says along the way that he has left many places behind, to arrive at a place is not the goal of the traveling: rather, traveling itself is the goal. This changes our way of looking and of seeing. Whereas old still-life paintings force us into a peaceful and static state of viewing, and into leisure and tranquility, even to determine where we are can hardly be done, while we are speeding along. At a hundred kilometers an hour the physical accoutrements of place are lost. There is only a fictional "here" – within the automobile, or within a train car or the narrow seat of an airplane – but there is no longer a reference to where in the world one actually is. A direct and compelling experience of the "here" while in motion is possible in a sailboat, for the sea is in control of the here and now, and the boat is within it from moment to moment. From the car we cast only fleeting glances, as if we were like Faust, who never wanted to tell a moment, "Stay a while! You are so beautiful!" The space in which we are living loses its actuality – or at least it has a different actuality in which the details of the world are blurred in the flickering of the speed. In 1843 Heinrich Heine complained, "The trains kill space; all that's left is time. If only we had the wherewithal to kill that, too!" And time is domesticated in the timetables, in the signals for the time of take-off and landing. Time turns into a function, and its fate is that it loses its astronomical dimension: The train comes first, the sun second.

With best wishes, I remain, your R.

17.
Enlightenment in a Good Sense

Dear Nina, Dear Julian,

In the last two letters I have ventured far into topics by which many of us think we are not only affected, but about which we also have own strong opinions. From human rights to climate change, broad and current themes on which we have been thinking for over three decades, we have been and will be directly affected. We do not know whether we can make our way through this huge amount of migration, unprecedented in world history, without succumbing to hate and prejudice; and we basically want to avoid following out the consequences of our effects on the environment. Unfortunately both these factors are being under-represented. Many think the effect of migration in particular is affecting only individual and social aspects of our environment, and on the other hand one can interpret climate change as entirely natural manifestations of natural fluctuations in the history of the earth. Contradictory attitudes result that seem nearly irreconcilable and are being brought to a head by the media.

In these disputes we are experiencing very clearly how one side criticizes the other, namely by ripping the contrary position to shreds. It is a similar situation these days when the measures taken against the pandemic of 2020 and 2021 are held to be senseless, or even that hidden forces are controlling them, forces that willfully tipped mankind into this crisis. And the more such irrationality influences the formulation of our ideas, the more often one hears criticism that is not directed against one's own position and might just lead one to reflect: instead other opinions than one's own are castigated and depicted as attempts to manipulate us.

In the analysis of these irreconcilable differences we are sadly forced to discover that criticism has nearly lost its proper function as an unconditional testing of statements. Let us recall that the flowering of criticism took place in the 18th century, above all in the appearance of the three critiques of Immanuel Kant (the Critiques of Judgment and of Pure and Practical Reason), a momentous step for philosophy and science. That was the last time philosophy was able to claim an authoritative role in science and in thinking. Criticism had already become a theme in the 15th and 16th centuries and therewith had taken up a new role in the self-interpretation of society, culture, and history (you must always keep in mind that these enormous steps into new frontiers of thinking had little or no precedent, and had an effect as far-reaching as the change from the geocentric to the heliocentric conception of the world).

From Kant's very titles it is immediately visible that criticism can only be articulated as a critique "of something." And that takes us back to a situation that has long remained unclear. Christianity shares with Judaism the obligation to reflect upon one's own way of life. Two "moments" issue from this: one is the recognition that throughout life one is walking on a tightrope between self-control and an awareness of one's sinfulness. The other "moment" defines the rules, "laws," and codifies permissible and impermissible behavior, starting with receiving the Commandments on Mount Sinai. Out of this juxtaposition of "moments" there results – sociologically speaking – a regulation of behavior exercised either by the recognition just mentioned, or by a power that that recognition seems to legitimate. Perhaps I am now making a terrible oversimplification, but this juxtaposition continues throughout the Middle Ages inherent in the relation between the political and spiritual institutions that directly affected people. One possible way out of it was to enter a cloister, which accommodated the idea of inner freedom with a stricter rule. And in the tension of this juxtaposition of "moments," criticism was born, and it began to question their legitimacy. It became a characteristic of the Reformation to question the legitimacy of judging and condemning persons.

In the phase of "secularization," which can though only inadequately be formulated as reducing the life-world to worldliness, completely new factors for the political zones of Europe and the representation of the individual were introduced, which focused on the new consciousness of the Enlightenment. A lot of excitement was aroused by the view of Kant which he set forth in 1784 by asking and answering, "What is Enlightenment?" The critique was directed against people who are stuck in a benighted state or worse are held there by the authorities. It is basically a sermon in which he tried to foment courage and determination to bring this situation to an end. The alternative does not stop at reaching full enlightenment but increases also the demand to adopt a critical distance from "things." This result however does not constitute the full significance of the new function of criticism. For Immanuel Kant it should surely accompany the ways of acquiring knowledge; criticism should advocate continual repetition of controls and tests in science in order to achieve certainty, and yet this achieved knowledge soon runs up against limits.

To take this writing on the Enlightenment as a document that advocated freedom, by arguing that with enlightenment a certain personal sovereignty is achieved, was a mistake. Enlightenment in its wider implication is an idea of how knowledge is to be seen and where the limits are finally to be recognized. For this one no longer needs to rely upon authorities and their prescriptions, nor upon obedience: rather this idea itself is what must impose these limits on knowledge, and in this way knowledge won its autonomy.

If you have followed the thought this far you can breathe a sigh of relief, for you now grasp an essential point about the Enlightenment. You are still in the 18th century, and if the gruesome events of the French Revolution have not yet taken place, nor the wars in its aftermath, you would have before you the best period of European history. Thinking critically while strolling among flowerbeds in the midst of the enchanting baroque gardens, and then entering a dignified reference library in which all the important works from Montaigne to Rousseau are within ready reach, and then in the late afternoon hearing a quartet by Joseph Haydn – Yes, it must have been a wonderful time, merely a few seconds in the history of the world. Criticism pulled aside a thick curtain and we thought we could now see the world as it is, secure in our presumption of freedom and equality. Just so, I add here a spirited paragraph from the Austrian Civil Code of 1811 (I thank my friend Karl Preslmayr for bringing it to my attention):

> On the Character of the Human Being: §16 Inborn Rights. Every human being has inborn rights, as is already evident to reason, and therefore is to be treated as a person. Slavery or indentured servitude, and the use of any power in practicing of it, is not allowed in these lands.

With this, human rights and the Enlightenment obtain their foundation.

It is likely that only literary sources are suitable to recall this paradisiacal state of affairs. Since then many earthquakes have shaken Europe. The position of Kant led in its aftermath to very different patterns of thought. Out of the turmoil of the Revolution many states were formed, so it became urgent to ask whether they now would exercise authority over their inhabitants and would find a legitimation for this in the use of reason or in a political rationality. Legitimacy no longer came from throne and altar, as historiography puts it, but from an administration based on law, a universally valid order of law, which constituted the beginning of a political way of forming opinion and reaching consensus among the bourgeoisie.

An opposite tendency exploited political reason to legitimate a power-state, which now usurped the agenda of society, economy, and law, and sanctioned only "enlightened" history as embodied in the political reality from Napoleon III to Otto von Bismarck.

A third line was derived strictly as a scientific outlook, and thought it had not misunderstood Kant when it saw in criticism a method with the help of which correct advances in knowledge became possible, though still accompanied by criticism. Thus a positivist concept of science was established. The advantage was that in accordance with painstaking advances in knowledge, all future scientific assertions would deserve to be trusted.

We know that criticism was used in very different ways, among which maintaining the criteria of knowledge was always the most important. But it did not stop with such merely theoretical implications. It was not until the 20th century that "people" appropriated criticism to themselves and adopted a "critical consciousness," and criticism was no longer understood as a discipline of betterment, as for example through the ruthless testing of scientific findings. Instead, criticism mutated into an internalized "attitude" which could no longer give criticism any such justification. Too often an analysis carried out on the empirical level was passed off as having reached a critical position, whereby the "critical" element could only refer to the manner of presentation as its ground for the claim of being critical. There were further issues that prevented criticism from being the fashion but rather often the term was misused, without any recognizable frame of reference, as if certain "relations" in society or state or economy had been tested critically. With the adjective "critical," Kant's instrument degenerated into a generic notion. Furthermore, the attitude about historiography changed considerably, for history was no longer understood as an analysis of actual conditions and phenomena: rather, "criticism" sought to establish its position in generalizations, whereas historical facts were merely information about singular and individual things. It may well be that the process of civilization is universal throughout the world, and yet can a universal method of criticism to be applied across the board to evaluate all its varieties?

We can stop with this question. The picture I wanted to offer was not only to present the meaning of criticism but at the same time to recognize how criticism underwent a functional change, partly that it loosened up historical conditions and constraints, but partly, in its alienation from them, that it could take on an authoritarian flavor. During the 20th century the particular qualities of criticism appeared in an essentialist characterization of all possible areas – from critical medicine, critical psychiatry, critical economics, up to critical theory…

Wishing you all the best, I remain your R.

18.
Remembrance and Memory

Dear Nina, Dear Julian,

I am often confronted with the question, "But will the grandchildren actually read this?" It is often the fate of a correspondence, especially when it is carried out so one-sidedly, simply to be forgotten. We are now living in a time that has problems with forgetting. On the one hand something is intentionally forgotten, especially something about the Second World War; on the other hand it is a given that of course one is not able to remember everything. Horrible and gruesome things cannot be remembered often enough, because the organized disregard for humanity and the infamy of a criminal ideology that acted as though it were the culmination of history, organized a governmental terrorization that succeeded to drive millions to their doom – all of that is a fixed part of our "culture of memory" which is inscribed in our remembrance.

It is difficult to write dispassionately about the difference between remembrance and memory. In order to illustrate remembrance, I know the rather coarse story that at the time of establishing boundaries, the mayor and witnesses always took a boy along and gave him a sharp slap at the place where a boundary stone was to be put. Perhaps it did not stop at one slap. One was convinced that the boy would thereby hold the place in his remembrance. Even the moving of the boundary stone would change nothing. Similar things are said about the customs of an illiterate culture, which kept perceptions, experiences, or even constellations of them in their remembrance. Thus it was not surprising that the long narrations of Homer persisted in remembrance and could be recited over and over, for which the verse-form and the rhythm of the speech was helpful and even a support for remembrance. At this point it should be added that once literacy came there was no longer a need for performances from memory, and soon such long performances were no longer done.

I want to make a quick note that for questions about such important concepts as memory and remembrance, looking into *Grimm's Dictionary* is fundamental for getting all that a given word can mean and for tracing its history. (I am curious to know which of you will someday own the *Grimm's Dictionary*. I have spent many enjoyable hours with these 32 volumes and have always been pleasantly enriched).

I have to confess that at first I thought I would be able to clarify these two terms quickly and without difficulty, but soon I had to give up hope. I found it extraordinarily difficult to distinguish the two concepts, especially after going through a course on Hegel's *Encyclopedia of the Philosophical Sciences*. To sum it up one can say that Hegel understood a "name-related" remembrance over against two other categories. So for a quick example, I have in my remembrance the great Maria Theresa as the regent of the Austrian territories. I cannot have her in my memory, however, since I never met her. I have in remembrance that she was not only the mother of sixteen children, but had to carry out three grim wars against Prussia, was able to win Hungary over with great difficulty, and at the same time began an orderly reform of the state administration. Committed more or less to the Enlightenment, and tied down by a popular piety that pushed her into anti-Judaism, she formed this "heritage of Austria" into a stable political force, which her two sons, Joseph and Leopold, then continued. In remembrance I have it that after seizing the High Castle from the inheritance of Prince Eugene of Savoy, she set up her widow's residence there so that she could look across and see what was then the main Hungarian city, Pressburg/Poson – today Bratislava – in thankful memory. Again, it is only books about Maria Theresa that I have in my memory, for example Oswald Redlich's, and then a document in the state archives on which Maria Theresa had carelessly poured a cup of cocoa. Guiltily, she noted in handwriting on the document: "Shame on me....."

I thought of this story for the explanation of remembrance, and on top of that according to Hegel's dictum, admittedly with the help of the *Grimm's* which helped me very much, namely to derive remembrance from the verb to "think of" (*gedenken*). Allegedly, Martin Luther had already had this in mind, as did the subsequent language use of the 17th century, of course. And at the same time I want to point out that in my "thinking of" the great Maria Theresa, I remember books about her. With that we have a first hint.

Now I must tell you about a search I made that was quite unsuccessful. At the beginning I thought I would find both these concepts among "the psychologists." Far from it! At the first try, hoping some brainstorm would present me an illustration and their difference, I encountered only confusing materials freighted with the current humbug of psychological statistics. All along, however, a toy train-set kept coming to mind. It goes along tracks already laid out, and the movement of the little trains has nothing to do with my childhood enjoyment in the fact of having a miniature reality inside my room, that hearkens to me, that I command and rule over. And besides one can stage a quiet and creepy collision by setting up the tracks to intersect. I have a perfect memory of such experiences. Little figurines with suicidal tendencies were set onto the rails and the big old locomotive would cut off their heads; or on board the baggage car there would be a parrot who avenged this torture with strong pecks, which he was otherwise not wont to do. I have it in my memory as if it happened yesterday that once there was a parakeet on board, and going around a pond that we made out of a bowl, the baggage car derailed and everything ended up in the water. At the station a relief train with a crane was assembled as fast as we could, but it arrived too late for the parakeet: it had drowned in the meanwhile. These are all memories that have survived since childhood – islands that in retrospect look like a lost land of happiness, and make me quite wistful.

So, while science, which I thought would be able to "enlighten" me, had none of the vividness that can be relied upon always to bring back my memories, an historical science can at the very least keep a remembrance alive. And thus I have brought the two different concepts together in a single sentence. And I must immediately warn you that here the root of an ambiguity can be fostered. It is again *Grimm's* that made me notice that remembrance is something special, for it is not only a visualization, as a picture in my mind, of an experience I never had, but it produces a "mindfulness" in the future. And here I can give you a string of examples.

In any city we have monuments, memorial structures, and inscriptions, that are meant to remember people. Do they do so? Rather, the monuments want one to keep a person in remembrance, that the intention of that person is recognized as a model and affects thereby what one will do in the future. Let's assume we were walking through the arcade at the University. Many sculptures were put on display there with the purpose of remembrance, for instance to keep before ourselves a model of physics in the person of Christian Doppler – forever, as long as there is physics. A shift in my feeling always comes upon me when I remember again a famous person in science. The famous professor of public law, Adolf Merkl, is a bit weaker in my remembrance but I have a good memory of him because of his very noticeable behavior. Since I am not a jurist I can give a scientific assessment with only partial understanding, but I can full well judge that he was an eccentric. On the one hand he turned Hans Kelsen's pure theory of law into a suitable constitutional instrument: in fact the idea of a graduated structure in a constitution in the organization of political representation, came from Merkl (if I have reproduced this correctly). But on the other hand as the neighbor of a well-known wine-bar he was militantly anti-alcohol and never failed to argue with inebriated people as they walked by his house. Once, in the hospital, a nurse wanted to give him a rubdown with alcohol, which he firmly refused: "I will never come into contact with alcohol, neither externally nor internally."

The great Adolf Merkl, whom I got to know when I was a child, was nevertheless in my eyes a model for righteousness and implacability in advocating legal positivism – so he exists in my remembrance as well as in my memory.

Perhaps you will object that I am making it too easy for myself. I believe that I have at least made an effort toward clarifying two very important concepts. You know as I have already said that we live in a very ambivalent time. On the one hand everything is always retrievable into the present; on the other hand we appear to be forgetting, to have forgotten. With this we can remark that we are subject to an unbelievable amount of manipulation. Since the time when the *acta* (records) were invented – it was in the 17th century – everything is recorded, nothing is forgotten. There is a depressing proverb in Latin: *quod non est in actis non est in mundo* ("What doesn't make it into the records is gone from the world"). And one can hear murmuring in the archives, accusations, that seem still to lie dormant. It is not the Last Judgment yet, but nothing is erased, neither an administrative penalty nor an imprisonment. And we can say a hundred times that a penalty after so-and-so many years was served out, and yet the crime is still there in the archives, unexpunged. Thus, we live in a present in which there is no pardon or release from guilt. Yet there is the old prayer, though we say it to ourselves thoughtlessly, "Forgive us our sins as we forgive those who sin against us."

In the middle of the Enlightenment we find that we are not able to exonerate ourselves from a guilty act; instead we are always reminded of it. It is the flipside of the so-called general forgiveness from guilt, which I recognize in its metaphysical context. And we ought to think that we are not weighed down with guilt, but if we take a glance at the archives we learn better. In old cultures, guilt or criminal injury of our neighbor was expunged by means of ritual, with an acknowledgment of guilt, and then remorse, and then apology; but in our civilization guilt now permanently remains. In Egyptian antiquity one had celebrated the festival of the fake Pharaoh, who had to take all guilt upon himself on that day, which is why at sunset he had to be killed to pay off the debts. Today, before elections, every newspaper dwells on insinuations and slanders shockingly brought to light, and in the cheapest way a general amnesty is granted by the majority, the "moral judges": nobody is free of guilt! This has, on the one hand, formed our "culture of memory" but on the other hand has destroyed remembrance. Out of history one will no longer be able to "draw upon" any model, for nobody is fit to be a model once I learn a little more about his life. And so remembering and remembrance rotate about their own axis, will be dictated partly by what one will be allowed to remember, and are even able to erase remembrance. This is the place where media play a primary role. On the one hand they suggest bringing everything into the light of day, so to render what is the reality of it; on the other they pervert their "democratizing" role and become institutions that mercilessly knock every hero off his pedestal.

A harrowing case of such manipulation came to light in Steven Spielberg's movie, "Schindler's List." With the founding of the Munich Institute for Current History in 1952, a hundred historians began to probe and study the archives. Witnesses and survivors were interviewed, in order to reach a competent representation of the horror. No historian noticed that there were also people who saved lives, with incredible sophistication and cold-bloodedness. It was a movie producer who of course did not directly represent the department of history, that discovered Oskar Schindler, whose huge imposture was to save inmates from concentration camps.

This opens up a further debate for us. How should remembrance be dealt with, if a positive identification is not allowed? What would memory look like, if one can remember no men or women who were heroes? Did contemporary historiography have the urgent task of spreading the totality of the horror over all those years? Should history be deprived of the diversity that has characterized the world we live in, up to now? Are we to interpret this "unexpurgating maximization" of the gruesome disaster through the publishing of records to mean that there was no recourse to take against all this devilry? Haven't we also, because of the power of evil, become victims? Isn't this the basis of our debate over collective guilt? And if we think only of the victims of genocide, who moreover were victims only at the end, shouldn't one now have more thoughts in one's mind?

I have only one more thing to say here, which will astound you. In the development of philosophy we read two terrifying statements, in which, unfortunately, an historical fact is fulfilled with anti-Judaism turning into anti-Semitism. The former has a basis in religion, as bitter as it is to admit – and in the midst of the Enlightenment and the industrial revolution, it turned into anti-Semitism. In philosophy people thought – Hegel already formulated it clearly – that the continued existence of the Jewish communities is a scandal (!), for in the progress of world history the world spirit has cancelled the old biblical history. And second, around the same time, philosophers declared, "God is dead!" Interpreting these statements, the Jews are taken to be the trace of the ancient God of Israel. If God still exists, it is because of these witnesses. Perhaps this implication explains the murderous and obsessive frenzy to kill all Jews, since, with the last of these persons murdered, the death of God is made final. If one looks back over what happened in the war it was an enormous waste of military strength to organize an expenditure of that size just because of these poor people. So, did the murder of the Jews have the goal of carrying out the death of God? Is this not a better explanation than interpreting the holocaust as a result of anti-Semitism? In philosophy we find these horrible statements. From Hegel to Nietzsche (or even Heidegger?) this path of thought can be followed, as it is laid out in Karl Löwith's *World History and Salvation History*.

And so in view of these memories I have a wish for you that above all else you will be spared such changes in the times – and that you may lead a sheltered life in joy and freedom!

With love, Your R.

19.
Does a Theory of History Exist?

Dear Nina, Dear Julian,

My last letter calls for an epilogue, to be formulated under the conditions of forgetting/repressing or remembering/commemorating. It is immediately easy to guess why, after the suicide of Europe in the 20th century, any interpretation of History, any description has broken off from the continuity of historiography. The famous historian Jan Palacky had already prophesied 150 years ago that Russia and the USA would become the world powers and would take over the position of Europe. In fact, in Europe, with two world wars and through the abuse of power, such suffering was brought about that historiography could no longer proceed in the traditional way. It had already been shown in the historicism of 1800 that the history of rule based on a series of successive kings, princes, and popes was no longer sustainable. There must be other factors of historical importance worth investigating. And so for more than 200 years one has had recourse to archives, in order to pick out new phenomena that might reveal equally important and relevant facts of history. Of course these archives had always existed. In them everything had been kept for the sake of proving, in legal or land disputes, when and how a stretch of land or a city came to be under the rule of a principality or under which conditions a peaceful settlement could be reached. Since disputes between inhabitants to be judged such intramural land conflicts were also recorded and there to be found in the archives.

In historicism a genuinely new sort of history of rule was sketched out in order to reconstruct a structure of meaning of a different sort. Since then, after the French Revolution one became aware that the traditional notion that political stability is rooted in power was no longer tenable. By the time of the Enlightenment the aura of the holy crown was no longer believed in. Joseph II himself struck out the conventional phrase, "Emperor by the Grace of God," from the *arenga* of his imperial charter with his own hand. Another "power-model" provided in the *History of the Papacy* by Leopold von Ranke became an important example of this. And at the same time the history of law, which was treated as an independent field of study in the work of Friedrich von Savigny, became a theme. Here, the role of Roman law in the Middle Ages was investigated and its institutional character within the political system was comprehensively presented. Actually, one had been able to refer to the project of historicism as an enlightening of the Enlightenment. Thus generalizations became the goal for research; the "coming to be" of states, the continuity of a people, and the special function of institutions such as the administration or the courts. The Brothers Grimm as we know sat in on the lectures of Savigny, and here learned about the bond between law and language. Quickly one connected the development of a specific language with a certain people which then, at least since Johann Gottfried Herder, became the criterion for national identity. Despite enormous conflicts the Thirty Years War came to an end with a million dead, in 1648; the wars of succession in Spain and Bavaria followed, and at the same time the Ottoman war of conquest, which greatly endangered Central Europe, was taking place; out of that followed the three Silesian wars: in a word the times were far from peaceful – and yet the historians were asking themselves what motives history was made of, what were the institutions, and what role did the reformed church and the papal church play? What role had the universities played? Which phenomena or institutions had a stabilizing effect on society in these tumultuous times and what could have caused the tumult? So we were only one step away from an intellectual history, which then became important in the 19th and 20th centuries. Both my teachers, Friedrich Engel-Janosi and Friedrich Heer were internationally recognized names in this field. In this discipline one had brought together all conceivable factors that Hegel had succinctly included under the concept of "Zeitgeist," which itself became a tangible reality within the "History of the Spirit."

I justify my long-winded introduction with the fact that we can no longer write this kind of a representation of history. Because of the dictatorships that in an incomparable way disregarded human rights, and because of rulers who can be classified as successors of insane Roman tyrants, the criteria for historiography in place up to that time had become obsolete. The venerable criteria for historiography, which had been oriented toward humanity, toward the struggle for freedom and equality and rehabilitating the dignity of man and the conditions for erecting a constitutional state, seemed to be obliterated. At best a historiography can free itself from the pull of the totalitarian element, if it reflects a different evaluation and ordering of the historical phenomena. Directly because of the occurrences between 1930 and 1945, historiography was needed for a rehabilitation of political morality and a rebirth of social ethics. Of course all this had begun earlier: World War I was in not only a prelude to the greater horror, but as Karl Kraus wrote it was an acclimatization of nearly everybody to cruelty as routine. With bitterness one must add that a world war was only possible after the adoption of universal conscription. During the war of the coalition against France, revolutionary politics had seized upon this as a method for defense. Before that, only a couple thousand men on average stood off against each other on the battlefield; but with the recruitment of the entire male population up to the age of 40, with a simultaneous modernization of the means of transport, some hundred thousand were ordered to the front lines. In the First World War a million were sent to Verdun, to Tannenberg, and to Isonzo and perished. A "private undertaking" to "wage war" gave way to nationalized warfare (a point that first became clear to me in the course of correcting the dissertation of Christian Beaufort-Spontin on the 17th century Orange Army Reform of the Netherlands).

This direct line of progress in history was almost wantonly broken in the 20th century, and it will probably be a purely arbitrary act to want to take it back up, at some random point in history. It is part of the concept of the post-modern, after 1980, to fix this point according to one's own arbitrary measure. It is the same in architecture, in the way one finds it appropriate to be able to juxtapose historical styles with contemporary designs. One can see this in the designs of Hans Hollein, who counts among the Viennese pioneers of postmodern architecture.

Fernand Braudel was the trailblazer of this path in historical research, who in his comprehensive representation of France in two volumes (*The Identity of France*, 1988-90) does not mention the central experience of the French Revolution. A post-modern viewpoint – I would say – was offered by Jürgen Osterhammel in his study, *The Transformation of the World* (2010). Therein the new phenomena of the 19th century – such as media, photography, statistics, and many others – get their own interpretation in terms of the parameters of space and time. In my estimation one finds there the attitude that the supposed endpoint of history which, with Auschwitz and Hiroshima, drove mankind into what Paul Celan called a "death-fugue," is being overplayed. With Auschwitz and Hiroshima there was to be no place for future history. Around 1965 there was a vigorous debate whether, after Auschwitz, a poem could be composed. At that time, only the lyric poems of Nelly Sachs, Paul Celan, and Else Lasker-Schüler were exempt from this verdict.

Any historiography that sought to bridge a continuity across these turning points of horror was soon suspected of suppressing the "actual" history of horror. The argument was voiced that memories of suffering and violence would become lifeless archival material, thereby actually aiding and abetting the suppression or the forgetting. Of course the opposite position moved, in nearly religious terms, toward the totality of the holocaust, which entailed not only the complete obliteration of Jewry but also the implication that Judaism no longer exists. It is another obstacle for history, which after all thrives on tying things together across the centuries with invisible bonds. Because of the horribleness of death and murder one can no longer assert that there is continuity in history. First off, the hypothesis was taken up that we might now be living during the end of history or even have reached an end of history. It is a noteworthy reappearance of an attitude from the Judeo-Christian salvation history, according to which the End arrives with the appearance of the Messiah. The holocaust was referred to as an end of this kind. This theological dimension must deliberately be kept in mind so as to understand how Auschwitz can be seen as a "merging" of world history and salvation history.

If we follow the path that the herd of historical sciences have established, a drama of this sort was not understood. In the consideration of the violation of humanity one could often track down the various ways of evaluation. One either formulated an attempt to make the crimes equivalent, as an apology: for example with respect to the operation of the concentration camps, it will be said the British were the founders of it, when they imprisoned the Boers, and that it is the national socialist variant of the "trivialization" of their own crime; likewise, the murder of five million Kulaks was a result of progress in the Soviet Union at that time, for there was no alternative for dealing with the reactionary farmers, the Leninist variant of a "trivialization." One can stretch and twist things as one wants: in an ideological context, history takes a detour from the path of its rightful calling with opportunism ever ready to guide the way. What opportunism here means is to seize onto mere facts of history at any price and to interpret the phenomena of the time without a "philosophy of history." This we may count an exceptionally paradoxical kind of suppression.

Another form of suppression was to approve of the horrible experiences in China. As the "Cultural Revolution" began to rage in 1966, for the sake of which some 50 million men fell as victims, Mao's *Little Red Book* became a bestseller in Europe and became the *vademecum* of the "extra-parliamentary opposition." Particularly grotesque were the protest marches near the Berlin Wall, since the marchers were all deeply entranced with the coming socialism, whether that of Mao or that of Ho Chi Minh, and were therefore not disposed to take a glance at the socialism of the GDR visible over the wall. This myopia was widespread, indeed an infectious disease, and it primarily affected the universities, and thus the intellectual elite. That was grotesque. Opportunism refuses to see the gruesome consequence of an ideology, and even denies it; "text blocks" of the ideology are taken in mechanically, word for word, and brainwashing distorts any view of actual reality. (It reminds me of the asseverations of people who lived in the neighborhood of the concentration camps that they had not been aware of anything…).

Contemporary history has itself paradoxically narrowed the analysis of the period from 1900 to 1950. Indeed very often it seemed to take on the role of the accuser and defined not only the essence of dictatorship but allowed itself at the same time to complain that these political perversions were difficult to escape. It was contemporary history, founded in Munich in 1952, that was called upon to reconstruct the German consciousness, and also achieved clarity about the time of this regime. The more light that was shed on this darkness, one was able not only to measure the organizing power of an ideology, but also very soon met with the question how this catastrophe with racial hatred and anti-intellectualism, in Germany of all places, indeed throughout Central Europe, could take place. In the "quarrel of the historians" in 1986/1987, which has almost completely been forgotten, it was clearly visible that it had to do with the whole of German history, and whereas sociologists, political commentators, Germanists and jurists, theologians and educationists, took part in it, the historians were virtually thrust aside. Suddenly the appearance of National Socialism had been subjected to a "more general" analysis, in which the body of historical findings would no longer be accorded the primary role. Right away, moral questions were added to the facts – however, facts had not often been treated satisfactorily. If one wants to summarize the results of the quarrel, this gruesomeness was the result of an inconceivable doom that of course had its roots in Germany and yet such things are there to be found in the modern era in all political and social systems. (We must at some point shed some more light on this, since we now read we are in a crisis of democracy…). With this, fascism had become the common name for all kinds of authoritarian structures and perverse reminiscences – all the way to South America. In the comprehensive identification of political phenomena the question was raised as to the collective guilt of the Germans, which was not articulated according to facts. Instead, more and more often the question was treated on its face, according to political morality. The basis for this hypothesis was the publication *The Authoritarian Personality*, which Max Horkheimer and Theodor Adorno had composed much earlier.

Put in gross terms, in the end this "quarrel of the historians" was faced with the dilemma whether this dictatorship was so perfectly staged that almost nobody was in a position to escape its power, in which case the hypothesis of collective guilt is no longer valid. It is truly a mark of evil not only to appear to be good: it also includes an enormous power of seduction, a cleverness, to which we are subject. Simone Weil formulated it in this way, and I have always followed her idea. However, at just this point, contemporary history turned this powerful dimension of evil into a moral-political duty and declared, *grosso modo* in retrospect, that one should have risen to the challenge of heroism.

I have heard this accusation so often in lectures – that too few decided to rise in heroic opposition. True, this staying-out variant of political behavior would have been desirable, and yet to hear of a lack of courage and resistance in lectures pricked up my ears. In most cases the lecturers were professors who during the tumultuous situation in universities after 1970, neither in academic committees nor in the sessions at the institute, advocated unregulated freedom of teaching – until this began to be defined ideologically and to be demanded through brute force.

I have deliberately shortened this account. However, under this point of view the "small" heroic deeds in everyday life during the Nazi regime were not adequately appreciated – or else they were racked up to a certain senselessness. Only now, 70 years after that regime, is the everyday courage and resistance being acknowledged, which is likely the result of *Schindler's List*, the successful film of Steven Spielberg.

You will by now have the impression that I have completely lost the topic that I had placed before myself at the beginning. I, too, have this impression from looking through what I have written. At the same time however I have given some underpinning to my assertion that the historiography of Central Europe at least, and even of Europe, can hardly disassociate itself from this *mene tekal* in the 20th century. So the grotesque situation come about that contemporary history was not only "outdated," which would correspond with the content of the postmoderns, but for its "temperament" it needed this horrific scenario of dictatorships in order to say what it says. All that happens later is either merely a consequence, or hardly worth mentioning or studying.

Meanwhile, "contemporary history" has come to be written on an entirely different level – i.e., in the studies and empirical analyses of social research. Here, society is either represented in its state of constant agitation, or in the state of increasing infantilism, or in the no longer reversible danger of total manipulation, if one believes Shoshana Zuboff's *Surveillance Capitalism*, or instead the *Disaster Capitalism* of Naomi Klein. In these analyses natural and environmental catastrophes are seen as a stabilization of capitalism, more recently, allowing the repertoire of policies of exploitation and relocation, as if the victims of freak weather events had become slaves. In Zuboff, consternation is peaked in regard to the lack of a scientific ethics, for the powerful electronic communication technologies are being upgraded to the end of manipulative purposes, with the help of the best universities. (Utterly forgotten is the old debate when Robert Oppenheimer or Edward Teller were accused of collaboration in developing the atom bomb.)

These bitter perspectives have not found their way into contemporary history. I consider it a gross and even scandalous shortcoming in what had before been an empirical and historical science, which had designed for itself such a method exactly 300 years ago. Historical facts presented in documents provided the foundation for historical analysis, and the methods of hermeneutics in the treatment of individual phenomena had not yet come into contradiction. "How it actually happened" was what Leopold von Ranke wanted to know, and yet today I ask myself, "Who wants to answer this question regarding the dramatic situation we presently find around us?"

So, are we standing at the end of history? Perhaps I can add something to this question, once I finally have read through the posthumous publication of Agnes Heller on this topic.

I hope you will check my thoughts someday against what you yourselves know – and I hope the result will be different one from what mine now is.

All my best, your R.

20.
On Responsibility

Dear Nina, Dear Julian,

First I must tell you about my misfortune. I had written a good many pages about our responsibility and indeed quite comprehensively about it, since for the first time in history we face the question whether we are allowed to do anything we can do. And I had given many examples that showed that we are not strong enough to carry out a responsibility. But all of this was swallowed by the computer!

Many times I have thought of the question addressed to Cain: "Where is your brother?" I fear we will give no different answer than the one Cain gave: "I am not my brother's keeper!" We have developed the shifting of responsibility into a successful skill and learned to use it well. And yet I think that in its historical context it is relatively easy to conclude that we have violated our responsibility. It comes immediately to mind that, in a way similar to Cain, the pretext of the high-ranking supervisors of the concentration camps was always eagerly repeated that they were only carrying out orders. It has always been the same phrase for denying that a criticism or even an accusation is not really legitimate, for if obedience is among the duties of officers then one has fulfilled his duty. This outrageous excuse is not only a symptom of a totalitarian social structure: it is the greatest act of cowardice a man is capable of, to renounce his own role in judging and making decisions. Often the doer of the deed is all too ready to forfeit authority over his own work. This sounds grotesque: the individuals who were involved were in their own estimation masters over life and death. Perhaps the basis for evil in the modern world came into our experience with the drama Faust, for the "philosopher and alchemist" saw himself neither responsible for his student – his *famulus*, Wagner – nor for the bitter fate of "Gretchen" whom he seduced. That this drama became the virtual credo of the Germanists and high school teachers in the 19th and early 20th centuries makes repeating the kernel of Goethe's message a hard saying: that presumption and pride bring about a dialectical inversion of ethics. Thomas Mann saw in this the reflection of the German hero, and in his novel *Doctor Faustus* he thematized the scary ambivalence that Goethe had put into the mouth of his character, Mephistopheles: "a part of that power that always wants evil and always creates good." One cannot immediately grasp the outrageousness of this diabolical formulation! By what I make of it, Goethe pressed his irony too far, for as a poet he must have known about its demoralizing effect.

In the way I have described it, responsibility always appears to have an historical significance and meaning. But meanwhile an entirely different constellation has arrived, that not only makes responsibility harder to recognize, but also seems to have pushed it far out of our reach What kind of responsibility do the psychologists have, and the system-theorists, and the linguists and system-analysts who devote themselves all too gladly to the subject of how people can be influenced, indeed how influence can even determine the repertoire of actions available to a man. Again I would mention Shoshana Zuboff, who describes exactly this outlook in the various efforts of the scientific departments of communications companies. She argues that Google brought the computer into the field of human behavior. And the growing number of "Google services" increases interactions on the "web." The number of search-terms entered, the length of stay at a website, and "clicking patterns" lead to a "wake of collateral data."

You will be reading this information for the first time in some years, I really hope, and in the meanwhile progress will have been extended so far that you will only laugh to hear about these old processes. I fear that communication technology has placed you so broadly under its surveillance that you probably will maintain free space for yourself only by means of renouncing it and doing without it.

With this, the problem of responsibility becomes ever more obscure, for on the one hand people see themselves as so-called "small cogs" in their workplace; the complex processes of work show on the one hand a huge division of tasks sliding into anonymity, and on the other hand there is the sense of one's personal self-interpretation shifting over more and more to leisure activities, which is why the themes of getting relief and emancipation have become so salient in our social and cultural context. This is the pre-history indicating an insidious disappearance of responsibility. In the very midst of a mechanization of the daily actions of our lives, we playfully enter the paradise of technology. And the more this accompanies our daily actions, the more satisfying it becomes, to the point that we hardly notice how subtly our decisions have been taken out of our hands. This begins with the questionnaire and the alternatives it presents to us "Do you agree? Do you disagree? Do you agree more than you disagree?" Indeed the questionnaire was at first a method used by the police – so that by now, in its use in empirical social science to explore human behavior, it has come back to its roots in "police science."

With the technological intensification we take on the thought-paths of our electronic devices. In the double sense of the verb *fesseln*, they both capture and enchant us; and in the midst of our belief in progress and in the omnipotence of science, which is already being generated outside us, we see ever more emphatically that there is no longer a path back to freedom, for we have failed to bring this "death-fugue" to a halt in time. As if with an atom bomb lacking form and measure, a gruesome chimaera looms toward us, dissolving our bond with humanity. In this vortex, responsibility is suspended.

Winston Churchill once wrote that the 19th and 20th centuries differed in that in the first great men faced small problems, and in the second small men faced great problems. Just so, I ask myself what men and women must be like in the 21st century so as to master the millstone of problems that Sisyphus over and over again failed to master.

In the early literature of the 20th century, out of an impenetrable fog of various developments in art, science, technology, and politics, a living being emerges that will be referred to as "collective man." Thus the question to Cain again becomes real and the answer will be repeated, with variations. The "collective man" – who following Friedrich Nietzsche is cited (whatever the sense…) in Joseph Schumpeter as well as in Robert Musil, Hermann Broch and then by sociologists like Werner Sombart, Arnold Gehlen and in Futurism – sees himself as free from responsibility, and yet has no clue that such a person can also be a criminal and a fool. And the better this new anthropological emanation gets analyzed, the more emphatically does one observe that he has detached himself from any historical contextuality.

Now I can add various things. These innovations increased more and more in the very externally successful contexts of action and exploitation, even seeming to outstrip man himself, but therewith drove an historical "process" to a decisive point. It may certainly not be an endpoint, which is beyond human ability to measure, but it is at least a caesura, the beginning of an "axis time" of the kind Karl Jaspers described. It is part of the essence of our time that great ideas, which we should have promoted, have not only been swallowed up in technology but are no longer openly available to us. This can be one of those views, as there have always been, that were once catastrophically wrong but at another time could function as an enlightened idea that could explain things to us – but that says nothing at all. An opinion has nothing to do with an idea that we currently lack. I think that at the beginning of the 20th century one was diverted from ideas, and we have positivism to thank for it, for the primacy of ideas was no longer defendable. One felt he was heavily overtaxed as an heir to a treasure-chest of ideas since Hegel. Hegel with his idea of history brought to an end the irksome self-flagellation of Kantian criticism, and thereby opened up great new perspectives for the 19th century. However, that great success, to which Marx was a contributor, was accompanied by an ongoing triumph of history, so that through the talent of Otto von Bismarck it was to become thinkable that a thousand-year regime of reason and freedom would come to pass. But it was also part of Hegel's intention that these plans of science, culture, and politics would never go beyond phantasies. And yet in fact the very opposite took place! From historicism to grand opera, from modern imperialism to the powerful expansion of industrial and productive forces, man in a way already perceptible in Romanticism had become a hero – a Theseus, according to the sculpture of Antonio Canova. The predecessor of the "collective man" had been the "heroic man" who, at first unruly and still "natural" like Caspar Hauser, formulated his choices quickly – but what was the goal? It was the will for life, for power, for belief, for death. This disturbance of equilibrium is what the "collective man" inherited, which is why Sigmund Freud ascribed to him an "oceanic world of feelings."

In reading these lines you will ask whether I have lost the thread. We started off with responsibility, no? I may here answer that I had wanted to write how responsibility disappeared. With the loss of responsibility it is the "upwardly driven," the upstart, or the master of suppression who becomes the ruler. A formlessness sets in, which I first observed in the action of the law-courts, from listening to dozens of cases, which brought to my mind also the loss of righteousness in law. The political species of formlessness are anarchy, dictatorship, nihilism. All three can be experienced as a single cozy household, as long as there are slaves or persons unfree. Maybe I made the mistake of going through the sequence of events too quickly. Under the precondition that everything depends on everything, you must forgive me my jumps to the side and my cross-references. And if I come to the conclusion that responsibility barely exists, I will give you two reasons. As one reason I cite the rather laughable action of the local government of Vienna. When or where a mistake or a scandal breaks out, it is the habitual response of the current city council to "assume political responsibility" for it. In truth this means nothing – the council continues in its duties and the everyday life of the governmental departments goes on unaffected and unaltered. The other reason for the loss of responsibility lies in the fact that responsibility presupposes a sort of anthropocentrism. With technology this also has been lost, no less than astronomy shattered the geocentric view of the world.

Looking over these last lines now, I am no longer unhappy to have lost the first version in the "orcus" – the underworld – of the computer. In my first version, I basically expressed something dealt with in the Tao Te Ching. To the question why he wanted no irrigation system for his garden requiring his slaves to carry in water-pail after water-pail for the plants with great labor, the master replied (according to an English translation), "Give men a device and they become wise in their own devices." It is exactly the sort of "appropriation" I had already experienced in the development of empirical social research at the Institute for Sociology in the 50's. The subservience and at the same time "technification" in their faces left me very disturbed. Not only did they have devices, but probably were also wise in their devices, and cunning. And the so-called new science legitimated this depraved state. In the first version of this letter I had begun with this example. It would probably have been far too obscure.

All the best, your R.

21.
Conceptions of Humanity

Dear Nina, Dear Julian,

Some of my "associates" have looked at my letters to you, and I must say I have not found much approval from them. As to their excuses they say first of all that the topics are too difficult for young readers. Behind that excuse, in my opinion, is a rejection of my presentation: that it is not only hard to read but also that I am taking aim at matters that are probably considered by many to be irrelevant. Philosophical discussions have no place in our present time. Even if I concede to them that I have treated a subject too imprecisely, too partially, too long-windedly, an improvement or a shortening would help not at all, for the subject itself is no longer significant. Philosophical talent would today do better to argue scientifically, and would be able to do more by having recourse to the nature-philosophy of Ionia, as Erwin Schrödinger had, than by overcoming the Kantian criticism with the Hegelian world of ideas.

Whereas the former, committed to the Enlightenment, called for a self-reflection and self-determination by means of criticism, Hegel with his version of phenomenology quickly captured people's hearts by identifying Idea and Spirit, which influenced the entire range of political-philosophical options all the way from Marx to Bismarck. The philosopher of history Alois Dempf referred in a lecture to Hegel's philosophy as a storm of Mongols that overran everything up until then, and the advance of right wing and left wing Hegelianisms could only be brought to a halt by positivism, in particular that of Ernst Mach and Ludwig Boltzmann, both in Vienna. Then there was the Vienna Circle which tried to grasp reality in a pragmatic way, until the "physicalism" of Otto Neurath cultivated a dogmatism tenacious but dull.

Of course, what I remember from the history of philosophy always gets in the way of my presentations, and with this nobody today can even begin to deal, unless he should replace philosophizing with excursions into the history of philosophy. This calls to mind the bet that a sparrow can fly higher than an eagle because the eagle could carry the sparrow on his back. One can look brilliant when dealing in the history of philosophy.

Even to this side-remark a comment must be added. For it is an indication of the loss of meaning in an area of study when that study enters the phase of giving an historical account of itself. While this represents an ongoing self-assurance about its area and the meaning of knowledge it has accrued so far, it reveals at the same time a lack of innovation.

I want to carry my complaining no further, for every reader thinks that what was written could have been written better, or else that it does not correspond with the expectation that one has about how things will be said. And so I can quickly go on with a subject that one does not expect, nor would anyone associate anything in particular with it. If I may recall a small political reference once again, politics since the Enlightenment was more and more widely and strongly bound up with and oriented toward ethics. This being bound up is exactly the compromise it makes for mediating between the societal and individual. The ethical man is not of a great design – of the sort one contemplates in the David of Michelangelo as the model of the fully realized human in the Renaissance. The ethical man as he was often described in an ideal way in the lodges of the Freemasons of the 19th century from Baron von Knigge to Joseph von Sonnenfels, sees himself neither as a unique individual nor as a product of his environment and conditions. Immediately this ethical and enlightened man was the counterpart of the aesthete. Since Romanticism the problem of aesthetics lay in the assertion that in Romanticism the uniqueness of art and of the artist was consummated, that with the "freedom" of art, the artist is finally released from all ethical considerations. If we think of the advent of the great performers of music, we see before us the "aesthete" who as it were appears to invent the composition spontaneously, though of course he was not the composer. This is how the aesthetical man invokes a false kind of uniqueness when he presents himself as a "prodigy," whereas the religious man in his piety is the true exception.

Everything we are talking about here is based on the ideas of the 19th century. As a "middle way," binding ethics remained the basis for the bourgeois legal codes, which sought to secure freedom through equality. That was the triumph of the "ethical man," who could look back upon history imbued with ethics and make his judgments about history according to ethical criteria.

If we may again look back to antiquity, the "ethical man" for the "Greeks" is represented in classical tragedy and is present in every political deliberation. The perfection of the hero is unthinkable without exemplary ethical behavior; in fact he was the very model of the virtues. The virtues were real and became visible in his relations and dealings in exceptional situations. A violation of virtue draws the chain of doom onto the scene, in the course of which the blind seer reveals the truth and communicates it to the people. It is information-politics and the persons who committed the act do not want to understand, and thereby they complete the tragic action.

In Athens politics still encompassed the whole person. In the political institutions there was a lot of talk about political perspectives aiming at a system of alliances, which had in mind protection against the "Persians" among other things. In the *Republic*, Plato designed a political philosophy that could not have been sustained without ethics.

Of course, all this is again too long. My precious critics will be thinking, "Who is interested in the concept of ethics in Greek antiquity?" Admittedly, the dedication my father wrote into one of my books reads: "Keep in mind: Jerusalem, Athens, and Rome are the bases for your thinking." Out of them, European history was born. That has always stuck in my memory and this admonition of my father has been proved true more than ever, since after the 20th century, despite high-hearted efforts, we can no longer unify Europe. Jerusalem we have embezzled and have favored political religions rather than the core of its message about the binding covenant between the Lord and the people of Israel; Athens has entirely fallen out our horizon except as a tourist destination; and Rome? Eugen Rosenstock-Huessy once designated which institutions make up what is specifically European: The English parliament, the French Academy, the Roman Church, and the Prussian General Staff. To the extent we can take this seriously, we see in it what the losses are in which we must now acquiesce: none of these institutions has retained its validity.

At this point one can clearly recognize that at the beginning of the 19th century these institutions still existed. But since the French Revolution they had lost their classical form: the revolution brought about a paradox of the individual "turning inward" to the inner life in the privacy of the bourgeois ethic, and this can amount to a blatant rejection of the "political man" of Greek antiquity.

Once again I must clarify the meaning of this change with a political comparison. The institutions in question, both the ancient ones and those of the Middle Ages, entered into a state of crisis because of the Reformation, which could only be brought to an end in the 17th century by finding substitutes. Christianity, now broken up, substituted for the unity of the Church by means of "imitating" it, with the empowerment of the state, with art, with science, and with law. In the decor of the baroque or in the powerful music of Johann Sebastian Bach the old unity was evoked once again, through culture; but this was to be brought to end in 1789, and this time forever. The consequent political "unifications" following the Congress of Vienna then achieved some stability in "negative forms," predominantly in the aestheticization of politics and art. Hegel called this "Art-religion," which was able to envision the erstwhile unity in "beautiful appearance," in the carrying out of political liturgies, and in military glorification and exuberance. There is now the "aesthetic man" – of which there were many, from Richard Wagner and Giuseppe Verdi to Franz von Stuck and Hans Makart – and his counterpart, the "demonic man."

In the photograph of Friedrich Nietzsche we can get an estimate of this "demonism," which of course was explicitly named as such in the novel of Fyodor Dostoevsky. The central figure of the novel was the anarchist Sergei Necaev, who was involved in a murder in St. Petersburg. Necaev fled to Belgium through Switzerland and joined up with the group associated with the "First Socialist International." He succeeded in stoking up the quarrel between Marx and Bakunin. Dostoevsky was present as an observer at the trial of Necaev, in 1873 at St. Petersburg.

At the same time, "genius" emancipates itself from the ethic of the bourgeois. A political anthropomorphism has become the subject of the human sciences. Whereas in the 18th century the "noble savage" was felt to be charming and unspoiled by decadence and moral mendacity, the "great men" were now raised up and appeared in monumental statues in every city. In this notion of "greatness," the prevalent ethical criteria of bourgeois society were interrupted. From this point forward we come to know the difference between Macbeth and an ordinary murderer. And the similarity is a foreshadowing of a second lieutenant who could become the emperor and could want to hold the world within his imperial regime.

At this point I have wandered far off in my imaginings. I wanted to offer this scenario in a nutshell, as if it were a stage play. And now the reference back to the Greeks finds its significance, for there the clues were present. We have altered them and thereby revealed them again, as for instance in the vocabulary of our democracies. At least they have remained unscathed in the political lexicon, though at present we fear the demise of this system. I can easily fill a bookshelf with publications hot off the press, in which the downfall of democracy is bewailed. Even the loss of ethics has just now occurred, ethics which once preoccupied the "world of yesteryear" – 1918 – and now it lights upon our world once again in the current political caricatures of Russia and the United States. They were taken, 100 years ago, to embody the promising perspectives after the collapse of "Europe."

Once again I have supplied you with quite enough for a while.
All my best – may you not be too discouraged by what you are reading! Your R.

22.
History as a Fantasy

Dear Nina, Dear Julian,

Perhaps my last three letters were rather heavy fare. The flight of thought over hundreds of years is not easy to comprehend, for men are surely not migratory birds, even though they sit in airplanes. Unnoticed, the landscape below slides by beneath the portholes of the space-ship, which one does not look down at until landing. Whereas the migrating bird completes its long journey consciously and in a timely manner, in accordance with its "inner compass," the guest on an airplane only knows the destination and waits impatiently for the end, bored by the journey. And so, today I treat you to a surreal story.

The journey through history is always partly exhausting and partly overwhelming. The landing in the present is somewhat bumpy. Hermann Lübbe has said about this that because of the fleetingness of modernity we have, in our present, only an abbreviated stay. So we live basically in a transit lounge. The state has taken on this quality. We notice the transformations when we remember former times, when the state still dominated all areas of life. Now we wonder about at the dissolution of statehood, due to claims that we must be sparing of public spending, perhaps a deformation of the state leading to its disappearance. One can then say the state exists only in our minds. Even governmental organs are no ample proof that the state exists, even if they do patrol the streets. Perhaps they do this only on their own initiative? Who are these agents of order that control our baggage at the airports, before whom we take off our belts and our shoes? We assume there must still be a state, for we have a passport in which one's citizenship in a state is indicated. Are the many security personnel perhaps the result of a private state? With our own strength we would not be able to maintain order properly, to which the state still pays attention; but are the ordering powers still in service to a state?

The state has its meaning through a modernization that in its essentials was brought about by the old social democracy more than a hundred years ago. In particular, you can study this new perspective in Vienna between 1920 and 1930, and despite heavy controversy the conservatives were well advised to take part, half-heartedly, in the development of the social welfare state. The quarrel, strengthened by mistrust, was stronger; the civil war in 1934 was the result, and therewith Austria was no longer in a position to assert its independence in 1938.

I am narrating this "interlude" of Austrian history because after 1945 a republic was again established, which was built on a political consensus whose special difference was the close relationship between the organs of the state and the economic interest groups. In plain speech that meant that management, labor and the industrial organizations, building trades and workers' unions developed a partnership and all social and economic questions were managed collaboratively. Basically, a "strong" state came to be, which was therefore not noticed, since the emergencies after the World War did not at the time allow for any prosperity, which was reached later. Moreover, Austria was divided into four occupation zones – like Germany. Only after 1955, after the departure of the occupying forces, did independently responsible political management become possible. Lower Austria, Burgenland, and the Mühl quarter of Upper Austria belonged to the soviet occupied zone, Upper Austria and Salzburg to the American, Tirol and Vorarlburg to the French, and Styria with Carinthia to the British zone. Vienna was governed as a unit by the four powers on a rotating basis. It redounds to the talent of the Austrian federal government to have maintained the unity of the country.

One can get the impression that the one party broke away from its own continuity, with the change of the conservative self-understanding into a liberal-economic interest group, while the social democrats were no longer to be identified with their previous conception of society. They might have formed a government in 1970, but it was a self-alignment with an unspecified socialism embodied in the party elite. Could one anticipate a resuscitation of politics in this "socialism?" Instead this "revitalization" of the political was achieved by the growing importance of the right-wing Freedom Party, which was euphemistically categorized as national-liberal, but remained rooted in the dregs of a mentality that was able to swindle its way through 1945. The alternative to "revitalization" was offered by the "green" movement in protest against the building of a Danube power plant and against the activation of an atomic power plant in Zwentendorf. These developments could be taken to constitute a trans-political process by which the present, and history, were being dissolved. Thus one cannot recognize a state-political ordering of the social powers in an allocation of seats in parliament, nor in the model ministries, but in the interest of belonging to one of the sectors of the European economic order. There were three of these: the soviet-dominated COMECON, the EFTA dominated by England, and the EWG, which was established by the Paris-Berlin axis after the Montan Union (the European Coal and Steel Community).

You could now easily read about the details of this history from a history book, so I will spare myself a detailed description. When I wrote just now that political management after 1970 was not to be "revitalized," where it might have been expected, this is a harsh criticism of the impressive Federal Chancellor, Bruno Kreisky. He had in fact done everything to entrust political management back to the government, to dominate it himself, and thus a "wave of modernization" spread through the country, which two or three years earlier was thought to be impossible. Programs of reform in unusual numbers wakened the impression that no stone would still rest upon another, but everything would change. And yet looking back on this modernization I want to put things into perspective, since on the one hand the Freedom Party under Kreisky was criticized as to its political competence, which then proved to be unfortunate, and on the other hand the "green movement" had become a political force that succeeded to make alternative economic and energy policies the topic of all future political debate.

And in conversation with the Federal Chancellor, he wanted to make me believe that the "conservative" party harbored far more former Nazis than the Freedom Party. He "baptized" the members of this party, which had always been disloyal to Austria, in order to use them to form a stable government in the future. He never needed to do that and yet, for reasons I could not understand, he wanted to make a strong case that this FPÖ was not so very different from the liberal party in Sweden. And so I got the impression of an extraordinary psycho-profile.

This was a materialization of the conceptual value system of politics, which had been dragged around for some time without one's really being aware of its consequences. Progress, historical morality, and fact-based politics proclaimed as a new "objectivity," including a political intelligence only feigned and a pragmatism from a supposedly Scandinavian brand of socialism were the repertoire; and it seemed to bring to "political power" a fantasy that Kreisky himself had inaugurated. This politics however went off into the imaginary realm far more than was then recognized, and flirted more with past things than future, which in Austria is always the sign of success. In the conflict with his minister of finance and with the larger conflict with Simon Wiesenthal, Bruno Kreisky had almost squandered his reputation in the eyes of his own party. So the vote on "Zwentendorf" went sideways and many programs of reform were thereby undermined – such as the reform of the military, the politics of health, and the politics of science. Of course this could not be blamed on the Chancellor alone, but he was no longer able to maintain his appeal as a political reformer after 1975. The appeal had come to be only superficial. The imaginary element of politics was better aroused in the concert hall, on the occasion of the party's celebration with a new rendition of the symphonies of Gustav Mahler under Leonard Bernstein – otherwise it was buried in the drawers of the ministries and soon forgotten.

The great chancellor had had to experience that his early pledge to reconcile idea and actuality, word and deed, and the legalization of realistic illusions of the social element, were simply forgotten. It was likely that he was impressed, in the end, by my comparison of him with King Ottokar the Second Permysl, which I had sent him, for unlike many others he immediately understood this allusion, thanks to his education in history. Ottokar, in Austrian historiography with its Habsburg way of seeing things, was portrayed as an enemy, though conversely he became a grandiose political reformer for Lower Austria and Styria – and had failed. One can still join Bernard Mandeville in asserting that political goals remain real as long as their deceptive promises can be made to pay off politically.

Just as I started today from the sense that the state seems only imaginary, the period after 1980 is the vanishing point. To the extent that political theory according to the criteria of socialism was able to analyze the equipment of the state under a problematic coalition, a sustainable destruction of the political consensus after 1945 was made permanent. The corruption scandals were an additional challenge for the "actual" actuality and they exposed the political "class." The reciprocal relation of political and deceptive promises had solidified in a political ennui, which was to be interrupted only with the efforts of joining the European Union.

Thus the wish to incorporate values on a European scale became an Austrian one, as for example by pooling the economic powers of the continent and by normalizing quality control. Thus the evil insinuation that politics was a cynical exercise of power was set aside.

That sort of thing was not allowed, in the judgment of the EU of Brussels. Here, from now on, would the reconciliation of the actual with the rational lie; here the concord among the peoples of Europe was the fulfillment of a "primal wish," to secure peace forever, to make Europe into a political body forever. Those were lofty goals. Perhaps one at that time was actually able to believe that in the European Union the members would become equipped with a kind of power that no longer could be expected on the national level.

This dream was soon rudely awakened by the "Yugoslavia Conflict." The "complicity" with former "constituent republics" showed the European Union to be tangled up in interests both old and senseless, whose origin reached almost as far back as the time before the First World War. Thus guardians of virtue no longer constituted a majority in the European Parliament; rather, an unexpected cynical practice could be detected. And it was not only the disappointments about this that weakened the EU: the member states themselves lost sight of the goal of membership. At this point the committees of Brussels associated with its General Secretary offered themselves as impartial administrators – but impartial from what? This moral, historical, and political artifact had neither pathos nor power. Perhaps this shortcoming comes to its best expression in the way that the universal banknotes of the EU display no universal political symbol for Europe, nor can you read (what you can on every Dollar) a guarantee from a central European bank. Instead there is depicted an imaginary tower and a bridge, as though the Pont Neuf in Paris or the Ponte Vecchio in Florence were not already common symbols for Europeans. However, knowledgeable observers will notice a nearly anonymous signature of a central bank president.

This admittedly superficial observation shows that one has begun to exchange the frog's perspective in his own country for the perspective of Europe.

Of all things, the political transformation of the state in Austria took place in 2000. Even though the incumbent chancellor, Schüssel, was able to design a coalition with surprising skill, even though his party in the election came out only in third place, one was able to recognize no other goals than to rule at any price. The very phenomena I have recounted above emphatically come to the surface. There was talk of privatizing sovereign administrations previously belonging to the state, the "de-pragmatization" of the civil servants, the drastic cutting back of the budget deficit. As little as the opposition was entitled to criticize this coalition with the FPÖ, with which it was at first allied, so dangerous was the intended starvation diet for the "lean state" to the "denationalization" of the state. This was not only a conscious contradiction against the history of the country, which always had correctly carried out the bureaucratic execution of the political will, but soon new "malversations" occurred, that even suggested a diminished loyalty to the state, when the finance minister himself appeared to be involved in the sale of formerly state-owned real estate. His own good fortune was that the supply of judges had by then also been slimmed down.

The structural ambivalence there to be observed in political representations opened up the insight that politics is a game by which society squanders its own sociability. If one now sets out what sociology has always asserted, that a society is generally considered to be sociable, the loss of this can have important consequences. The wave of migration has put this assertion to a hard test, as it has also raised the fearful question whether because of the weakness of these state institutions a situation arises that Thomas Hobbes had grimly identified as the core of future bourgeois society – *homo homini lupus* ("Man is wolf to man").

You will surely read this sketch with the strong impression of reading memories from my own life, and yet it remains for you to decide whether some point – or several points – were here touched upon that allow you to understand your own times better. The significance then of what I have written is as a source because by transcribing them the initial actuality of phenomena obviously takes on the status of an object.

I must apologize that many parts of this letter are likely difficult reading, laborious to the point of difficulty – and I think that my "shorthand" does touch upon the flow of the experiences but does not render the fullness of how things took place. It might suffice as an apology that I am writing a letter, not a book...

I have here peppered the letter with Austrian examples, with my grandchildren in Berlin in mind: for they probably never hear any details about Austrian history, nor in all likelihood can participate in the lifeworld that was my own...

All the best, your R.

23.
What Can Empiricism Resolve?

Dear Nina, Dear Julian – and of course also Marie and Vicky,

Just now I have received a photo from Berlin of Julian and Marie. With visible concentration they are playing chess in a cafe. This is a game I could never get into, probably because I lost the first games I played, a "hundred" years ago. But also I chose a different procedure of thinking, and this explains why I studied history and not astrology or statistics. I was hardly curious about the future, for in my outlook it seldom boded well, whereas looking back is sometimes satisfying since one can choose, out of curiosity, a time when it appears history went along exceptionally pleasantly. Thanks to a knowledge of history one sees oneself as a "world spirit," if it is not too presumptuous to put it this way, for with a higher degree of certainty one can predict a great future for one development, and quite the opposite for another. Even a lucky devil like Pericles could not overturn my judgment that after him the luster of Athens would quickly fade. For the historian it is of course no feat to prophesy this, since not only do numerous findings confirm the impending political catastrophe, but that was the first time that a political theory had more meaning than a politics that tends toward an authoritarian system. And yet the uncle of Plato was one of the "Thirty Tyrants" of 403/402BC, so the philosopher knew not only the terrible consequences of the Periclean policy but also the burden his uncle bore in managing a bankrupt Athens. I've always been irritated that the extremely influential philosopher Karl Popper declared Plato to be the author of all politico-philosophical evils, and in *The Poverty of Historicism* and also in his *Open Society* saw Plato as a proto-fascist. This is pure nonsense, above all if one knows that the positivism, though much celebrated, was not quite immune to the danger of totalitarianism.

I did not at all want to describe this, as of yet.

I arrived at these thoughts because I saw the picture of Marie and Julian at chess. Thus I must again bring this to a close at the earliest opportunity, since otherwise the criticisms will mount up that there are still many other topics I must cover. In our times it has actually occurred that one expects, in the first sentence, a full rendition of any of topic in the world, and any writer that needs a second sentence immediately loses prestige. Basically this is "Google behavior," since one there learns directly, without beating around the bush, in a tenth of a second, what he wants to know. One then expects the same thing from the person he is talking with. And so, one is never disappointed by the electronic system for the answer is immediately there, whereas even for a question about a street he seldom gets an exactly correct answer. With bitter irony one can now be sure that with Google and positivism, nothing will ever go wrong.

So I now begin with the topic that I had in mind, and once again I take you back to Greek antiquity. We often hear the word "metaphysics" and really do not know what to make of it. We are seriously of the opinion that metaphysics belongs to the field of religion, since it is indeed religion that wants to set forth the belief, uncontradicted, that there exists a metaphysical being, and other such things. This representation of its content is already a sufficient indication of the lamentable level of philosophizing these days. By this term Andronicus of Rhodes had nothing more in mind than, in the ordering of the works of Aristotle, to bring together into a group of their own all the writings that did not deal with physics. But soon, metaphysics was seen as something more than a field "after physics."

Only in the 18th century did the word become current, and soon became a fighting word. The positivistic propaganda immediately saw in it a penchant for theology, in which the power of imagination rules whereas controlled rational argumentation counts for nothing.

But this is not the complete story about metaphysics, since metaphysics is, much more, the study of our being and existence. Obviously in the procedure of metaphysics a rational analysis of the objects that exist will be called for, which then will also go beyond the realm of the natural sciences. While the positivists then refer themselves to the learning of the natural sciences and they switch off all emotion and imagination, the "philosophers of being" allow these "immaterial" elements into their field of research. As we know, in our use of language every word has an "aura" about it, a dimension that brings together all its past, present, and future meanings. There is as it were, a "spatial reality" added to the word, that we always also "mean at the same time." This "spatiality" of the word is especially visible in a word-play, in a consciously intended allusion to an "ambiguity" in the expression.

Designated in this way, it strikes us immediately that metaphysics and ontology must basically research the same area. This is correct, with a restriction: ontology refers to the structure of being, to the being of "what is being," whereas metaphysics sees its contribution as having to do with the formulation of valid statements on the "existence of what is being." But one will be unable to suppress his skepticism when he feels a lack of empirical clarity in these generalized and redundant sounding formulations. Exactly this tendency in philosophy – to juggle words – has not only taken me farther from such formulations, but makes any dialogue terribly laborious and consequently boring: the sequence of present tense participles and nominal infinitives makes no attempt to connect the concepts involved. If metaphysics declares that it works on the cognition of an "existence of the being-in-itself" one needs patience and a big dose of sympathy to enable oneself to follow these turns of phrase and to act as if he understands.

With this I am not retreating back to a positivistic position, with the purpose of being able to achieve exactitude about actual reality (even in positivism this is not at all "automatically" the case), but rather I am complaining about the loss of "intersubjectivity" that philosophy risked, especially German philosophy since Hegel, and that it saw no longer a need to be understandable. In the realm of ontology Heidegger is well known to have succeeded to oust everyone else from the field, even Edmund Husserl, in order then to make all metaphysics esoteric. Likewise, later, in our contemporary art, it became standard that to fail to understand the content redounds to the shame of the listener or the reader. Basically, the author was forgiven if one could not follow him in his airy flights. And a person finds himself thrown off the path of the discourse as if from the car of a roller coaster if he feels any doubt about a neologism or an arbitrary linguistic formation. And mostly these powerful speech-eruptions were delivered to a nodding group of listeners, who not only had understood it all anyway, but also honored the master with devotion.

This rant of mine is for the purpose of remembering that of course empiricism does have its place in metaphysics. This empiricism of course has an entirely broader methodological orientation than it has in the natural sciences, and yet one is basically bound to a philosophical empiricism that goes beyond the ontological determination of our existence as so far understood. Although I do not want to lead you into these labyrinths – from which even if there is an exit, an exit is still uncertain – there is in metaphysics an agreement to investigate our existence, the determinants of our life, the place of the world in the cosmos. Obviously metaphysics must in general be won from our experience, for which nothing in any case can serve as a substitute. Furthermore, it is important to separate this empiricism from materialism, since experience includes also an ability to perceive in an intellectual way, and does not rely solely on experiments. It is indeed clear that our knowledge does not stem from sense-experience alone. Conversely, however, this also means that an *a priori* cognition, which even Kant had conceded, appears to our surprise not to be possible.

The "metaphysicians," who began to orient themselves more and more to the works of Aristotle, reject "intuitive" methods, and as such they probably take a critical stance toward hermeneutics also, unless reality contains intelligible entities that are just as clear-cut as sensible entities.

But now I must strongly chastise myself, for I have to ask myself whether one can make sense of all this abstract talk. I must take on the question whether these thoughts have any meaning at all. If we at this moment direct our attention back to metaphysics then we will already know that in its investigations, it not only considers very closely the existence of mankind and not only being in general, but rather that under the regime of a philosophical empiricism it comes to be able to exhibit the dignity of man. And in this cognition is grounded the foundation of human rights, of the meanings of freedom, and the securing of the integrity of man. One may say that these crucial aspects of what it is to be human have received too little consideration, but nevertheless we have become cognizant of them! A murder that in a dictatorship might appear to be permissible and bring on no punishment, remains a murder. I hear loud and clear the warning of Sophocles, who in his *Antigone*, as a "metaphysician" brings a "metaphysics" of law onto the stage, against the rule of law in Thebes, which in this case is a human right. We would not be able to formulate a consistent statement about law if we had not through metaphysics opened up an idea of righteousness. It is likely the flaw of positive law, in its essentially pessimistic character, that in addition to recognizing the casual arbitrariness of justice about which it says a great deal, it therewith opens the doors to a despotic arbitrariness of laws as well. Did Creon have right on his side when he condemned Antigone to death?

Warmest of greetings, Your R.

24.
Were the "Good Old Days" Good?

Dear Nina, Dear Julian and Siblings,

I have plagued you with these many letters, and as you have read them, at least here and there you will be asking yourselves, "Do they add up to anything?" Perhaps you will take them up again after many years and will above all wonder at being confronted with a period that might just seem peculiar to you.

To that I can reply that you will be in a situation similar to one that I was in, during those days when our grandmother, Augustine Kykowski Eisert, told us about *her* times. Her own conception was that up until the First World War she lived in a golden era. Her stepfather, Heinrich Stagl, owned a large villa on the Hohe Warte, which accommodated the whole family, as she said. There were six "children," after all, of which at least four were married before 1914. How this household worked I cannot report to you. In any case I found these great-aunts, whom I still knew, quite complicated, quick to indignation or "*verschnupft*" as they say in Viennese ("getting their nose out of joint" in English!), which is why the grandmother would try to resolve the "*faschés*," as she called the family squabbles, by telephone.

So this villa, which still stands today and is the seat of the Saudi-Arabian Embassy, reverted to my grandmother after the very early death of my grandfather around 1909, as her residence. My mother and her brother spent their childhood for the time being in this villa. I remember the report that on Sunday they would go to Stephansdom by *fiaker* (the horse-drawn hackney-coaches still to be seen there) – never on time – so that one would arrive at the cathedral after the sermon. In any case there was a high mass with chorus and orchestra and I always had the impression that our noble family had been driven to the cathedral for the music. Afterwards it was "to the Sacher" for lunch. And without missing a stroke my grandmother would rave about Emperor Franz Joseph. His picture also hung in her closet. One was mighty proud if he saw his coach on the Wienzeile at the Naschmarkt on its way to Schönbrunn, with the tired figure of the monarch within. In any case the head of our family was a developer who had had countless tenements built, one just as anti-social as the next, but even my father was not allowed to criticize this kind of dwelling: immediately the grandmother would shush him and play the trump card of the "Good Old Days" – which after 1945 was of course hard to gainsay.

In any case the First World War entirely destabilized this family. Though the great-grandfather, the developer, would still spend his vacations with Mayor Karl Lueger in the South Tirol, everything was lost in 1918-19 – the company, the villa, the "servants." As for money, one had of course invested it in war bonds in 1914. The motto of the bonds was, "I gave gold for iron" – and far more than one would guess these days people readily invested in these bonds. By 1918 one could use them for wallpaper. That was the picture commonly drawn at that time of what these bonds were good for in the end.

As a widow the grandmother was barely in a position to feed the children. She moved in with the Stagl side of her family in St. Florian, near Linz. She had spent her childhood there and now reconnected with that time, which was then a happy time once again. On the one hand all the children had escaped the hunger and wave of influenza that swept through Vienna; on the other, the family there belonged to a "country bourgeoisie" that played a highly esteemed role in the monastery of the Augustinian canons: church music. The uncle was the organist of the monastery organ and thus was close to Anton Bruckner. The aunt, supposedly the apple of the composer's eye, organized the amateur theatre and as a strict teacher provided for education and culture in the village. The grandmother reported with conviction that as a child she had received letters from Bruckner and passed them on to her aunt. Thus, piano reductions for four hands of Bruckner's symphonies became the favorite pastime. The uncle and his niece – my grandmother, that is – loved to play the *Fourth Symphony* on the piano, which is said to be a rendition of the landscape of Upper Austria. And during those days in Sankt Florian they regretted not having piano reductions of the symphonies of Gustav Mahler. So she reported. Over and over she recalled that in 1905 she had heard the first performance of the *Kindertotenlieder* in the Small Hall at the Vienna Musikverein. She would probably have counted it one of the high points of her life.

One can imagine that in the upper-middle-class milieu of Vienna there was a lot of complaining about Karl Kraus. Even in the 1950's my grandmother referred to him as "Fackel-Kraus," as the person said to be behind all the bad gossip. And with the loss of their social position the brothers moved closer and closer to German Nationalism. Although two of them, Heinrich and Alfred, were unable to gain a footing in the First Republic, Heinrich had in fact built two churches in Vienna with his father; and both the others had been proud cavalry officers in the World War, and had law degrees. So Friedrich and Hans still held their own, with Friedrich becoming a renowned jurist and the editor of many law reviews; and during his tenure as a judge, he was moving closer to National Socialism. Thus, immediately after the Anschluss of 1938 he became a local ministerial director for the Berlin Ministry of Justice. Because of my father, who during the same time lost his position as Dozent at the University of Vienna, my grandmother was in a "quandary," namely, having a successful brother and an unemployed son-in-law. So the daughter-in-law of the grandmother wrote encouraging letters from Berlin, reassuring her that my father, in the future expansion of the "Reich" would again find employment. In the jubilation of the Nazi advance both eastward and westward, thoughts of that sort were common. In Berlin there was a strong conviction that "Germany is ours today, but tomorrow the whole world...."

I want to stop here and report no further on my grandmother, for in looking back the number of happy years in her life could probably be counted on one hand. And yet even today I wonder at how she was always able to make a meal out of "nothing." I see clearly before me that during the morning in the room without heat she would serve us hot pea soup, and that again in the evening there would always be something in our dish – probably something one would not eat today.

Her youngest sister had fared much better – until 1943-44 at least. Aunt Harry had married into money, was her father's "little princess," and was able to continue in the noble life that for her sisters had abruptly come to an end in 1918-19. Her husband was a building engineer, the family owned a factory for silverware, and so the amenities of her life even after the World War remained "commensurate with her status." Lunch "at the Sacher" was obligatory. After all her brother-in-law Richard was obviously a capable man. Among other things he had worked on the building of the Rax railway and profited from it. Despite the hardships in Vienna my youngest great-aunt had noble tastes and was temporarily engaged in equipping the hunting lodge in Ennstal. Her happiness came to an end abruptly: her husband fell terribly ill and their son was killed in Russia. Within two weeks both husband Richard and son Heinz were dead. And as a consequence economic support was no longer available to her. She spent her dotage in the Ennstal hunting lodge without electric lights, with little heat, and water out of a nearby well. There is a portrait that recounts her happy times, a laughing and delightful young lady looking out with anticipation.

I can end here. It is likely that I will turn again and again to such "family stories." It is important to say "into what one is born," how life proceeds full of changes; and over and over one remembers the remark of Goethe that in a life there are really very few happy hours. Of course one must object that my life was happier, continuously, than that of my grandparents and great-grandparents. My life was not interrupted by two insane wars. I was permitted to grow up with my two brothers without anxiety, and we no longer had to fear a dictatorship. I loathe how some people – perhaps still "Nazi's" – complain about how terrible the times were after 1945: the occupation of the country, the hardships, the poor supplies. Only a person who was spared the terror before 1945 can say that – or else was one of those who orchestrated it.

If I might briefly bring the focus back to my grandmother, in order to call her back to memory, she found in music "the other life." I still see her before me, laying down her cards in a game of solitaire and listening pensively to the music of Richard Strauss – or whichever composer it might be.

For Julian, Marie, and Vicky, my grandmother is always present: right by the front door of your house in Berlin there hang two life-sized photographs, rare as well as expensive, the one of your great-grandmother, and the other of your great-grandfather, not long after their wedding. There you see no sign of the turns of fortune that were to befall them, no sign of anxiety, need, misery, and death – which would in the end determine the larger contours of my grandmother's life.

All the best, Your R.

25.
Signs of an End Time?

Dear Nina, Dear Julian, and Dear Marie and Vicky,

I suppose my last letter served as a bit of relaxation. Since then I began reading Agnes Heller's book, which I already mentioned to you, and I have the book right in front of me. As much as I can say so far is that it is a "compare-and-contrast" between philosophy and tragic drama. That a consciousness of their relationship goes back to antiquity is the consensus judgment of this history. Of course it is emphasized by the title *The End of History*, that it is about a change in the meanings of the two cultural phenomena. When philosophy suffers from consumption tragedy takes its place, and vice-versa. This observation has of course been analyzed from many sides and is not black and white, as one can guess. So it is pleasant to learn that the "end" that is being invoked by Agnes Heller does not occur according to the dramaturgical conceptualizations it has received from Oswald Spengler or Francis Fukuyama – she thinks much more that in each case "theater" or philosophy come to an end in their own times.

This reminds me of my article about the end of music, which I can no longer locate. I had written at the time, if I remember correctly, that some composers around 1900 were of the opinion that music, primarily European music, had come to its end. Ottorino Respighi or Ermanno Wolf-Ferrari, and even Johannes Brahms, spoke very pessimistically about the future development of music. That somewhat later, around 1930, Wilhelm Furtwängler was of the same opinion is not surprising, for by then strong cultural-political programs had come to the fore. Some derived this diagnosis from the circumstance that basically there were no new musical instruments, even though a few decades before the idea of special sounds and tones demanded new instruments. Richard Wagner had worked on this in detail, and modified wind instruments according to his own designs. If we take a look at the development of the piano, one notices immediately that this instrument after Ludwig van Beethoven got an extremely different way of making its sound and a different mechanical apparatus. By comparison a cembalo or a clavichord had the sound of a dulcimer. And if we listen to the *Well-tempered Clavier* by Johann Sebastian Bach today, we would shudder to hear it played on such an instrument. On the other hand the clavichord was the sort of sound Bach had in mind for the expression of tonal moods. After all, there were directors – Christopher Hogwood, who died around 2014, and Nicholas Harnencourt (died 2016) – who set about playing Bach's orchestral works in their "original" orchestration, and with historical instruments. The raw sound that "brushed against the grain" and the "shrill sounding tutti's" in the orchestra took a while to get used to. I thought that a kind of historicism had arrived in the interpretation and reproduction of music. Thereby I had nothing against other or new listening experiences, which are indeed very much limited by the electro-acoustical reproduction of music. Surely, the "silky" sound of the violins was consciously avoided in the "original" version. This cannot hide the fact that only one instrument was invented for "modern" music: the saxophone. In the *Pictures at an Exhibition* by Modeste Moussorgsky the saxophone became the "voice" of a wailing beggar. This sort of naturalism, in the saxophone and the trumpet, eventually came over into jazz and continued to be used as a "human voice" as opposed to the natural voice of an Afro-American. Thus New Orleans entered the continuity of musical creations, a topic to which we will return. And of course we encounter the saxophone in the impressionism of Maurice Ravel and Claude Debussy.

My digression has again become quite detailed, but often we must take a detour in order to grasp the true dimensions of a given subject. In any case, it did appear to some for a while that the prognosis had come true, that music was "at its end," especially with the way musical thoughts were strictly bound to the rigid scheme of the twelve-tone music, which only Anton Webern was able to creatively resist.

If I might now return to literature, Heller's question is important – how is the relation between philosophy and "dramatic literature" seen in modern times – after Hegel. I will tell you more about this in detail. As far as I can see so far, this work of Heller's is also as meaningful as other studies of hers, which I have used in my lectures – for example "Is Modernity Livable?" and "Biopolitics." I can recommend both these books to you, not too long, since one will not so often read such insights about the political and the "trans-political." I am convinced that even years after the publication, both these great essays involve clearsighted diagnoses, in which the process by which our civilization is transforming were already being described.

If I may now come to a topic that I should have written about to you before, I want here to report on the difficulty in our present times of speaking about things that are extraordinary. If we have learned from Franz Grillparzer that measure and the middle way have nothing to do with middling but are far closer to being connected with nature and with traditions, then I can well present it to you that there remains little place for the talent of graceful modesty. We were of the view that the unusual and the gifted are the essential criteria, not modesty. So we encounter in the 19th century, to our amazement, that being extraordinary and being gifted are the criteria by which to evaluate culture and the times. It has become a criterion of value that also today has high importance, especially during one's youth. From our youth one hopes to see special achievements, impressive talents, a suitability to acquire knowledge of diverse kinds. Now, in the context of our civilization, this exceptionalness is always oriented toward ascending in social importance in the future. Thus, in the past, if these talents were formulated as divine, before Calvin materialized the divine grace in the sacrament, so then both of these – being extraordinary and being graced – despite their differences were applied to describing ways of life. The "extraordinary" is the distinctive mark of the child prodigy since the 18th century. Later it is "genius," which we often encounter in the 19th century (and bandied about in every Viennese café). This is a freak of nature, a genetically exceptional uniqueness, like an albino among animals. And even in ordinary life, in family among friends or in one's profession, there can be an exceptional luck, a grace for which one must be thankful as much as for one's his health.

In this bifurcation one thought he could describe what is unique about life – in contrast with all earlier discoveries. Countless biographies were composed on this principle. And with the reference to the child prodigy, in the 18th century we find not only Mozart: also a reversal was there to be observed. Life was no longer enveloped in the holy, in the mystery, in the wonderful, nor experienced that way: rather the worship of life took on a form that one recognizes from antiquity as Epicureanism. Now, it is taken to be the real life, which the natural sciences began to explain quite well enough, as they also explained the origin of the world in the sense of Ernst Haeckel. From now on life has a value in itself that lies in human hands. Even with the negative side, based on an ability to suffer, "stemming" from Russia, which affirms life and experiences in suffering an enhancement of that ability – even this becomes a secular cult in literature. Russian literature even outside of Russia proper was the basis for a new justification of this mentality connecting life and suffering.

Amoralism, which Nietzsche posed counter to traditional ethics in order to prove its hypocrisy and its advocacy of "slave morality," pursued the goal of creating the heroic man, an "Übermensch." With God-lessness man himself had become a mortal god. Thinking here of Agnes Heller, the answer for such a perspective, in every direction or even "movement," was enthusiasm which soon became a ferment of the political realm. Whether it be the opera with its hysterical sopranos and the shills of art-religion, or it be philosophy with its adepts, both asserted they had knowledge of a reality that was no longer the reality of bourgeois-industrial society.

One must always recognize the sequence. It starts entirely harmlessly, even with the magic of Mozart's compositions, with the dalliance in the rococo, and yet behind this already stands secularism, in Rousseau, which is more than a critique of Church and religion. With the enormous liberations of the Enlightenment, the self-determination of men was in no way realized. Not even the revolution brought this about, but rather the contrary. The complaints about the Middle Ages being cruel were justified, but the revolution deserved a stronger complaint, that it had been even more cruel against its own spirit.

I have always wondered at the fact that the Enlightenment ended in the horrors of the guillotine, of all things, although one knew very well our *condition humaine* and also despite the fact that the project of humanity was taken up in that knowledge, from questions of hygiene to the development of schools. This found its definitive expression in the desolate phantasies of Donatien de Sade. New, in the infamous writings, is the "assessment" of human relationships, which was not much more than a relation between sexuality and cruelty. New in these cerebral fantasies is the surrender of human intimacy to perverse imagination. It was the prelude for the list of tortures and torments for which the 20th century supplied the personnel. Before we reached those shallows, however, the disdain for mankind of de Sade stands in contrast with the *Ring of the Niebelung* by Richard Wagner.

If one had thought that the uncovering of the grim world of "Ossian," a forgery by Macpherson from 1760, was nevertheless not the reality, still the grim sounds of Wagner's overture repeat this characterization of the world as a "Götterdämmerung." Poorly contrived gods, who were as oppressive as the bygone and defeated Greek Titans, have nothing else in mind than to annihilate their own "world." In the paintings of William Blake and Wilhelm Füssli one can see this horrible world of spirits brought out once again, if the operas of Wagner had not been enough to satisfy the longing for gruesomeness.

One must keep in mind that under such desolated "thought-worlds" individualism was promoted and understood itself moreover as being advantaged by its emancipation. It is unbelievable how this madness could get its hold on the special sciences – in biology, anthropology, ethnology, and history. It was in race, then, that the highest stuff of being human was erected. Kindredness and difference among men were reduced to being a member of a race. It was the "old" positivists, especially Ludwig Gumplowicz, that saw through this madness. At the same time came the advent of sociological analysis.

The problem entailed by what we have identified here as the criterion for the gifted and the extraordinary, was the creation of the demonic. The demonic had a special career particularly in Central Europe. In Russia it counted virtually as a "culture model," not in Rasputin, not in these celebrities who show up again in novels, but rather in a unique mysticism found in Fyodor Dostoevsky or in the priesthood of the poet in Leo Tolstoy. In Central Europe the demonic element conquers nationalism. Obviously a space within the mental structure had remained empty, and into this space settled the "spirit powers," of the sort we today suspect to be at work again in conspiracies. The entire vocabulary, which only disturbs us, raises up the demonic. A people is no longer just a people, a culture not a simple way of life: history is the imitation on a collective scale of the fate of Siegfried. The fact that the adjective "German" especially awakened this demonic power counts among the most enduring harms to "Germany" since Bismarck. The memory of the Paulskirche is forgotten – as if this symbol for democracy and the rule of law were a captive of the German "Michael." For now on, a sense of historico-political causality became a motive for political policy. "Because Germany … therefore Germany" – up to 1914.

I am afraid I have rushed through this history at a gallop. However much you could keep up with me, I was already off and gone. But if you calmly trace these outlines you will come to grasp this madness. It would be as easy as connecting the dots. If you do this then you will reach a very rational grasp on reality. I have here only named the ciphers, form 1 to 100, and if you follow these then you will see clearly how the extraordinary moved through the genius to the demonic, and the blessed moved over from those God chose, to the Führer. I have made out nothing more than what Franz Grillparzer noted down in his diary: From humanity through nationality there is but a short step to bestiality.

There will be many who mistrust this interpretation of intellectual history. On that I do not want to comment here. I do however remember that in his obituary for Max Weber, Eric Voegelin wrote that he was impressive for science – because of his demonic character he was able to grasp a social state of affairs. Around 1920, Voegelin, whose political philosophy I always admired, had identified a motif for which historians found no use, and yet out of the philosophy of history the quality of demonism was there to be noticed, for this is always ascribed to Adolf H.

Here I want to stop, for the time being.

I will reconstruct this pre-history of your present times later. I very much hope you will consider the information I will give you then. You must know that in modern times all these factors that have so long had their place as parts of history, suddenly expand. That is exactly the purpose of my representation. These delineations become the characteristics of modernity. I have not described much else than this, to you, here.

With love, Your R.

26.
Shadows of Modernity

Dear Nina, Dear Julian, also Dear Marie and Vicky

Yesterday evening – 2 November 2020 – a little while ago, not far from our house, a terrorist attack took place. According to the reports four men were murdered. The police shot one terrorist, but it is not certain whether there was one or two, or more. In any case a curfew was imposed and so I am staying home. Whatever the motives of the terrorists, it is a telling sign of an increasing aggressiveness in the societies of Europe. Unfortunately, one must take note of the fact that even after many years immigrants find less and less satisfactory cultural (!) opportunities. Over recent years a huge wave of migration has spread through Europe and the European institutions did not do enough in response. Once other immigrants have spent as much time here as the terrorist had, and once children are born in the same milieu, the security risk could rise exponentially.

It is not the case that tensions usual to a suburb lead to such dangers as terrorism and sabotage. Even if one can say that "native" persons disenfranchised by modernization face off with immigrants similarly left behind, and that each side sees itself forced to unite as an interest group against the other, so that the one group become racists, it is not the case that the opposite side is necessarily dominated by Islamists. Certainly the Islamic religious communities have no good influence on their clientele; they seem to radicalize them and motivate such acts in an abuse of their creed. We have experienced such crimes in several cities in Europe, and frankly the majority of us are at a loss how we might be able to achieve integration.

Because of the strong minorities in the cities there has been an increasing rejection of the customs of the host countries, especially in the third generation after the immigration. To put it even more harshly the host society is depicted by parts of the minority as the enemy. Thirty years ago Shmuel Eisenstadt, in the *Antinomy of Modernity*, precisely identified the phenomenon that is afflicting us today in Europe: a decreasing willingness to integrate and the notion of a long-obsolete "religion" that would legitimate extremism. Yet it is even more frightening that even then it was recognized that an economic upswing in the families that had immigrated did not mitigate the hatred. In contrast with the United States, in which there have been several widely agreed upon factors during immigration such as deeply similar formulations of religious belief and an aesthetic amalgamation of music and musical culture, we for our part are not managing the emotional hardships of these people at all, even after they have lived here for three generations.

In the US there were relatively favorable conditions for multiculturalism, even if it took considerable effort and sacrifice, too, to stabilize it within society. In Europe these conditions are absent, since immigration not only has a different "character" but the essential factors for integration which were already halfway present in the US, are entirely absent here.

In the case of European societies, as we know from history, a common creed, school attendance, military service, and assimilation in language-use have been important factors for integration. In these the "basic cultural techniques" had come to be learned. We must acknowledge that today these same stabilizing factors seem to be considerably weakened. And they are even weaker than we fear, if one considers that no agreement at all can be found in the basic ways of thinking about the problem. The economic incentives and successes and the dominance of a picturesque "open market," which one likes to describe as the result of successful integration, have a much more restricted importance for living together in society than we would like to think.

If I may here present an example, the great peace treaty of Münster and Osnabrück in 1648, the Peace of Westphalia, functioned in the development of Europe as a model for achieving peace all across the war-torn continent. Its success, which was also politically enforced at the cost of many hardships, brought about a stabilization of political and religious structures. This was possible despite the disruption of cultural, social, and political homogeneity.

What will always be overlooked is the fact that terrorists, coming from what they imagine to be their Islamic world, understand themselves to be revolutionaries. They are ultimately like "step-children" of the French Revolution and see violence as integral to their "political theology." This transformation just now became visible in Vienna in a very exemplary case, as it did a few weeks ago in Paris.

After the murder of two teachers in France, I repeatedly remarked in debates that we are coming up against the limits of tolerance in our civilization. And these limits are transgressed in an "inverse proportion." Tolerance of the old kind is transformed, on the one hand, into a justification for permissiveness – liberality is supposed to include license; and on the other hand personal moral conscience now has less legitimacy. Individual "self-control" is taken to be an unsupportable giving-in. Manès Sperber called this phenomenon the absence of "private righteousness." The development of art has tested the boundaries of tolerable freedom and has castigated any restriction of itself as illiberality. It sees itself bound by no "private righteousness," just as it no longer needs to display the professionalism of the craftsman. One can say that the freedom of art can even call into question the politically protected integrity of the person. This mismatch cost the lives of two teachers in France. Thus, the problem of the magazine *Charlie Hebdo – Journal satirique & laïque*, remains significant for us, because this magazine also trades under the title of "art," though the socio-cultural "boundary conditions" of our old Basic Law of 1867 no longer apply to it.

Looking through the magazine's rather clumsy caricatures one could call them tasteless and vulgar were it not for the fact that these productions claim the rights protected by the freedom art. In Stuttgart, just now in September 2020, the display "spaces" of the Kunsthaus offered less than poorly done drawings with pornographic content. In this case also the designation "Art" warded off any objections to such a nuisance.

So we have to deal with still more terror, aesthetic (!) as well as political. After all "religious dogma" will remain connected with the social organization of Islam. We will have to observe how "ontological concepts" make use of terrorist intentions and deliberately destabilize the parameters of political order and its legitimacy as well as governmental responsibility. It is also, regrettably, a sign of modernity that on the one hand the autonomy of political, cultural, and economic areas has widened, while on the other the penetration of the "political center" by the political "periphery" has increased. This means populism on the one hand but fundamentalism on the other. And the stratum or minority that is receptive to the message of fundamentalism is by no means the lowest economic stratum. The middle classes, which of course appear to be integrated, have come to see themselves as disenfranchised of their traditional professions and social rank. It was from these that they derived their virtues, which they now more and more must derive from their memories of the past.

Over and over, one is horrified by the frenzy of terrorism. And if it were said that in this the aftermath of the French Revolution lingers, and seduces terrorists to this "Jacobism," then one would begin to understand the ambivalence of the modern age. On the level of culture, in modernity there is no longer a social consensus; instead, in the midst of a disorderly world, an extremism steps forth, which interprets the social environment along with its dissonances and then demands that a state of affairs be achieved that will bring about the Jacobin fiction. With this dissolution of the social system, all variants can enter as equal in rank. The Enlightenment can be presented with just as much fervor as the violent implementation of authoritarian goals. Thus, in modernity, the dimension of the utopian and of the bourgeois draw images of themselves that are on a par: the revolutionary is on a par with the "normal." Basically, socio-economic conditions are the only basis for socialization and sociability. If industrialization went hand in hand with modernity, so also basic institutional patterns emerged that provoke institutional reactions.

One can now read and see on TV that this attack, which took place in the side-streets I often pass through, will have a lasting effect on this city. Because it happened nearby it was additionally incumbent upon me to report on it. The attack was reason enough to address, for once, these pressing questions.

So I send you my best greetings: Your R.

27.
A Crisis of Credibility

Dear Nina, Dear Julian, Vicky, and Marie,

As my letters go on I should perhaps turn to topics that promise to have a longer "shelf-life" within the horizon of problems. It is clear to me that in the course of my writing, themes, problematics, and questions will be touched upon that will not be understood right away, since you are of "another" generation and thus have different background knowledge. Often enough I must put up with the critique as to what I can or cannot assume my readers know – in this case, you. If because of my age I am not impressed with digital dexterity in the use of electronic gadgets, nor break out in amazement in the case of a nimble handling and masterful exploration of the internet labyrinth of imaginary knowledge, at the same time I must confess that I know too little about this "track" of acquiring and dealing with knowledge. And yet I think my objections and doubts are justified. I would be more amazed by a piano performance of one of Franz Schubert's *German Dances*. I would even say that the "logic" of its composition is entirely accessible; conversely, access to the electronic labyrinth seems to me to be not so easily communicated. Perhaps our difference in age plays a role, yet I often have the experience of being more quickly and better informed by the *Encyclopedia Britannica*. I would not want to advise anybody to enter the mathematical term "integral" into a search engine. If you do this you will sit for a while before your PC and be riddled by which representation you get back is believable. You will not get an answer that also gives you a reference to its source. And the time will come that in a search engine under "Mozart" you will sooner get a reference to a nougat confection with pistachio filling than a reference to the composer. Of course my sardonic remarks come from the concern that the good old books, the reliable lexicons, the bulky handbooks, will disappear from the horizon. I want to recommend them to you over and over, exactly because they constitute the collected documentation of the state of knowledge. I am happy to look into the *Rotteck-Welckersches Staatslexicon* of 1930, since on the one hand it turned out to be a rich historical source and on the other I can see very well the social, political, and historical shift since then. I get additional information exactly because of its being "obsolescent." It is just this dimension that is missing in the search engine. And I use it, like right now while writing, only when I am uncertain of a spelling. In the course of my writing you perhaps remember I told you about the unfortunate King of Corinth, Sisyphus, but I was uncertain just then about the spelling. For this the electronic system is excellent: I get information immediately. And I can stay at my desk. Just imagine, if I wanted to look it up in the dictionary I would have to go over to the books, and I am not sure what would happen to me over there: maybe I would "lose" myself in front of the wall of books.

…

I had to interrupt the letter, since I needed to prepare for my lecture. Looking back over what I had written, I must temper my aversion to the electronic data management and data collection. Of course we have in our hands some excellent equipment here; of course we admire that with a small device we can call up Kamtschatka on the spur of the moment. (I remember the time the late Section Leader Kurt Haslinger called me on his cellphone to arrange a meeting but he was completely surprised to find me in San Francisco on Belvedere Street. He counted as one of the most important officials in our Treasury Department and as an "old" style social democrat was a representative of that particular kind of secular culture. It was on his initiative that the "old" Josephine General Hospital became a part of the University).

The flipside, however, shows a different picture. Dependence on the cellphone is plain to see. In a sort of reversal, the telephone creates as it were a "service personnel" who cannot leave the device, playing, listening to music, exchanging banalities, chatting, tied up by constantly being in contact – which can well count as a symptom of the change in our ways of being in contact with one another. From this point of view the weakening of our ways of being in contact becomes a problem in the relation with one's neighbor. To communicate with him through the device is not so much a matter of being in contact with him – however much we may be fibbing to ourselves – as it is a pretext for returning to intimacy with the device.

You will hardly come to share this view, since there will be no slowing in technology's pervasive "growth" into our lifeworld. Technology has already become a part of our equipment as humans. I allude to the telephone only to point out the drying up of our language. Perhaps this will turn out differently in your time, as I hope, but a dialogical analysis of this general chattiness, this incessant blib-blab, reveals a deterioration of language. It is the expression of a profound weariness in Europe. By knowing how in National Socialism our speech was violated, how our language was even taken away from us, we can at least know how to measure how much the broadcasting of this incessant chatter through the mundane media drives us into silence. From totalitarianism came the "prayer wheel speech" in Soviet Russia or the blabbering of the film industry in the USA. One could say that the languages that came from that have become virtual machines: in "slang" we notice the "tools" made of screws, bolts, wires, and studs.

Speaking machines leave no space for the natural development of language. The computer has considerably reinforced this, and language is being ossified into formulas. I think of the great Gospel of John: "In the beginning was the word, and the word was with God... ." In truth, language is the most alive part of life.

Language becomes something else when it becomes a tool. We already notice this in the case of the fierce battles that were brought against oratory in Greek antiquity. As soon as one noticed that the language being used had lost its connection with truthfulness – that oratory had become an instrument of propaganda – a wild uproar and most virulent criticism followed.

Imagine a speaking that is no longer an imitation of the way a stage actor speaks, whether a movie hero or a cartoon figure such as are often used as a model in school – but has become the speech that comes out of a computer, out of the speech apparatus and robots equipped with artificial intelligence. The actors were still authentic witnesses of a kind of speech that poets designed for the theater; but these machines become our interlocutors, and are doing so ever more often and more extensively, and in the information they provide they are more reliable than people.

Once again I want to tell you how I came to this point. Quite simply, I showed how these writing and speaking devices have settled into our lives, skillfully robbing us of the "You," since the reciprocity between the I and the communication machine is always more stimulating than a quiet interlocutor in the evening. Indeed we know that children are already tapping SMS messages under the dinner table. In Eugen Rosenstock-Huessy we still find the different activities of speaking distinguished: The soul *speaks*. The school-word *defines*. The catchword *hammers*. We are hardly aware of the differences any more.

Here I want to stop. Perhaps you will think about when and for what purpose you use these three kinds of speaking, and how often.

With my best greetings, I remain, Your R.

28.
On Language and Speaking

Dear Nina, Dear Julian and Your Sisters,

In my last writing I gradually approached the nature of language. In any case the result was disenchanting. I described rather longwindedly by way of a contrast how technological devices dominate our communication and how with them we are losing our formerly comprehensive ability to express ourselves. Every instruction sheet that comes with a device teaches us that people can no longer describe in writing how one is to use this new thing we have acquired. They are no longer people! Regularly I am reassured that these instructions for use are also already produced by writing robots, so you can no longer expect a description that makes sense. Finally, that unbelievable grammatical errors come along with it is no longer surprising. One can ask the question, Are we passing along any ideas, advice, warnings, or instructions to the machines?

If human speech still exists, we have separated our realm of speech from that of natural sounds, and from the shrieks and yelping of animals. It was an effect of idealism to distinguish between sense and nonsense, and the bodily world as opposed to the world of thought. We learned to use a speech with articulations and accents, that is not mindless even if it has a very strongly sensory expression. Speech sometimes seems like a thought which in itself lacks the quality of embodiedness. Speech has a unique make-up of voiced pitches or tones, which leads us to think we cannot assign a material to speech. This is certainly false, and yet we believe emotionally that speech is something other than the rushing sound of a waterfall or the humming of a motor.

Since I am not at all at home with the physiology of our ability to speak, I will turn immediately to the problem how we can live in a world, or think we do, that is now seen as either a physical or a scientific world. It was Edmund Husserl who put forward the observation that we seem to live in both these worlds – based on our orientation – and that these worlds are fairly much separate and independent of each other. The one claims to be an objectively observable world, the other is designated as subjective, which means nothing but that we possess a stand-alone "lifeworld." It has nothing to do with the other world. Immediately we realize that we can only find our way around in these two separate worlds to a limited extent. For this division we have René Descartes to thank. He drew the distinction scrupulously. For the natural scientist this simplified considerably the scope of his investigations. Since him, we happily take a walk with our backpack through nature, we find pleasure in it – which is however only an aesthetic perception of nature. As an object of research we have the "true" nature in the laboratory, on the dissecting table, or even in the drum in which we collect plants. The colorful autumn leaf we see on our hike is seen differently from the same leaf pressed and archived in our natural history booklet.

We must remember that in antiquity nature was a living thing. In that nature, there were gods, all sorts of mysterious forces, about which we laugh today. But do we know reality better in every way? It may be that these extraordinary natural forces were often deduced from an esoteric interpretation. But we can leave that aside, for we will not here evaluate whether it is true or false. I do lean more toward doubting it, I do not think much about Bach's flower-remedies, but I am very tolerant about enthusiastically presented successes of the healing powers of nature. More important is that we did not insist upon the conversions and revelations in such a way as to drive out men's belief in gods. We are sooner unsettled by the thought that nature possesses tremendous power, which is why our acts can be held to be laughable. We thought that way in the 19th century. And in every report about a natural catastrophe we now hear that the powers of nature overwhelmed us. Probably we have this broken relationship with nature because of the way it possesses a permanence of life that we can only dream of for ourselves. Hence we made nature bodily and broadened our own outlook with a new understanding, that nature consists only of physical and chemical matter. Suddenly nature seems controllable, almost puny. This seemed a successful way to take revenge. Indeed there no longer are any gods. We have even been able to put our sense of the passing of the seasons into perspective. We began to manage our time in terms of clocks, and with our machines for measuring time we lost our sense of time, a sense constantly present in nature. In nature we had, earlier, even observed rhythms. There were sequences, the opening up of flowers and their closing in the evening. And yet we think, under the influence of Descartes, that we are dealing with a dead nature. And we were totally convinced of that. Philosophy supported us in this for it got us to believe our hunch that nature has no consciousness of itself. Quite proudly we inferred that nature is basically a "dead" thing.

Already in antiquity we separated time from nature, in order to provide ourselves an independent measurement of time, with which to measure the duration of work, to agree on times to start and stop, and to discuss our schedules. From the sundial or hourglass to the mechanical clock a long time passed, and yet these were all successful efforts to come into possession of time. Strange however is the boastful idea of mastering death, that one was preparing a kingdom of the dead in order to go on living and ruling there through eternity. Whether it was in Egypt or China, in any case the time of the world and the time of a life broke apart, and the more we recognized our notion of life-time as limited, the more we claimed the world-time to be ours.

In any case we had a lot of trouble starting from life and not from the dead things of the physical world. More and more we needed speech as a companion along the way, so as to penetrate the darkness of the burial chambers and caves and, bringing back a narrative from the world of the dead, to win life again in their shadow. This shuddering Kingdom of the Dead of the Egyptians underwent an astonishing repetition in the death cult of the National Socialists. Eric Voegelin published this political reflection already in 1938, and with great luck escaped the National Socialist angels of death wearing the uniform of the Gestapo.

Perhaps you are thinking of the many features of cultural history where these Kingdoms of the Dead were erected with gigantic effort; perhaps you also think of the ancient poems in which demi-goddesses visited the underworld and the "lifeworld" one after the other, or though damned were released from the underworld to return to life, or others again who were thrown from Olympus whereby we began to take advantage of the fire brought to us.

Because of these disturbing stories speech moves more and more into the central position and its written form is preserved in the sacred books. Over and over again a psalm begins with "Hear, O Israel!" Obviously speech against death is located within the world. Thus it can never be nonsensical, as the records reliably show – in rich metaphor and in the form of lyrical description. They must always bear witness to life! Through speech, life takes on a bodily form. This teaches us that with language, phenomena of our existence that are reducible to physics cannot be what existence is about.

Even at the risk that you will only be shaking your head when you read these lines, we cannot avoid the problem that language was neither a development derivable from evolution, nor was an gradually improving arrangement of what had been animal sounds. It is not just an audible causal connection between the properties of the throat and an acoustical specialization according to exact rules of sound formation, but rather it seems to be a singularity unto itself and yet understood by all. It does not go along with the progress from physics through chemistry to biology, psychology, and sociology; rather it is, all along, a "thing for itself." Although it establishes these fields in their manifold articulations, in the form of publications, it does not allow itself to be confined to them, even if we think of a meta-language, of things to replace it with, and linguistic rules. Language stems from no isotope, no molecule, nor a wave or a proton.

If we open up the *Grimms' Dictionary* we encounter the living organism of "speech," and it is nothing but the collection of all words. Any yet they refer to origin, relationship, and include even the "aura" of the wide denotation of words. Of course, language is not there mere etymology, nor is it represented in terms of linguistics, nor does it allow itself to be represented sufficiently in philological comparisons. Rather, the life of language is always proof that it was brought into the world the way fire was by Prometheus. Life and language are bound together most intimately.

I must briefly mention that I have over and over circled around these thoughts in long conversations with Philip Roessler. Although his insistent manner irritated and even annoyed me – and I very well know how to distinguish between the person and the subject matter – he always used the expression, "to come into language." He meant by it that our speaking is not authentic "speaking." Instead, as Eugen Rosenstock-Huessy said, speech as a catchword or as a definition in the authoritarian form from school, denies us the speech of the soul. Roessler had over and over repeated this in his objections – indeed voiced it as a reproach – whereby in these unpleasant situations I was at a loss what to answer. Later it became clear to me that we must struggle more and more to reach the speech of the soul.

Crucial in my recollection is the insight that contrary to our usual practices we appear to forget the thing that first endowed us with soul and spirit, and that both would remain mute if speech did not take pity on them both. Thus, through language it becomes clear that we are only able to bring our uniqueness, and even our talent, to expression if speech understands how to bring the real indications of our "vitality" into sound, and thus make to them audible in language. Transformation and turning.

Probably the crying of a baby is not to be thought of as on a par with the wailing of an animal, as obvious as this interpretation might be to a psychologist, but rather is the first authentic sound between complaint and joy in the form of speech. As we know, we escape death through transformation. We know we are living beings, when we understand ourselves as turning.

I cannot judge how far these virtually poetical images I have chosen are comprehensible. Perhaps I can clarify things with a simple example. Certainly you have heard that Austria until 1945 was occupied by a dictatorship, the reality of which will probably yet be a subject for these writings. In the first place it was just a completely perverse "political theology," which was "applied" here and completely "freed" itself from all former respect for the person. Consequently, the ideological design for this is called the "Myth of the 20th Century," by Alfred Rosenberg. And its supporters made the representation that one could not know what these rulers were up to. All this was a sort of "protective assertion." The restoration of Austria was not only through and through a remarkable step toward a consensus democracy, in order to restore unity, but in the really impressive "Heimatfilm" the people recovered their identity, in pictures and in speech. Actors with Austrian accents and the landscape of the Wachau depicted a simulacrum that could immediately be recognized. It was unbelievably important to show Austria through a shallow screenplay. One of course knew that being the scene of action for the *Nibelungenlied* was inscribed in the history of the area, but also that it was the hardy cradle of all that was to happen. A renegade from Braunau was trying to annihilate just that. And the viewers were able to push away the years gone by – at least for the duration of the film, especially when Hans Moser sang his couplet with the zither.

Very different was what went on in the Burgtheater. In the wake of general reforms and "modernizations" some thought was given also to the theater – in 1986! And it is typical of this country to bring in a German director for such a task. In complete ignorance of the traditional language of the theater, in ignorance of the special idioms, this director expelled our "mother tongue," and thereby set aside our identity; and from then on a mediocre German, more suitable for TV reruns, became the language of the theater, unsuitable in its declamation to fill the large hall of the audience. In an artful way Herr Direktor hid himself behind Thomas Bernhard and exploited the poet's intimate discussion of the "country" to set forth his extravagant production concept. For the sweeping blow of the poet in his *Heldenplatz*, Claus Peymann brought in as his production concept the general bringing to light of the Nazi period, his achievement as a pompous German (a *"Piefke"*) over against the *"östreichschen Hammelbeine"* (Austrians with mutton legs) who long since had to be carried. This same director was also of the opinion that the uniform used in the ticket office, the old dress uniform of brown cloth, stemmed from the Nazi era and he got rid of that too – a series of stupidities by an ignoramus. It was the first step in an expanding obliteration of what Austria is, and it went unnoticed. This obliteration continued in the planning policies regarding spaces, locations, and the city. Since then we speak a TV-language, and already the children are using the icon-language of the advertisements for German products on television to express something that seems special to them.

With this "interlude" I want to commemorate how much the particular idiomatics of a language over and over bring to mind historical continuity. There can always be political disruptions; language becomes one's homeland. Among the Jews one gets a rough idea how language can become one's homeland. In Austria this was the case now and then, whether it was in the language in the university against the "German" professors in the 19th century, or the imitation of pompous Germans (*Piefkenesischen*) in movies and radio. In old movies one can get a rough idea of how we once spoke – for instance, in "1 April 2000." Still I can hear the voices of Raoul Aslan or Attila Hörbiger, and Albin Skoda, Josef Meinrad, Oskar Werner, Helmut Lohner or Peter Matic. The great actresses were Paula Wessely, Judith Holzmeister, Elizabeth Ort, Inge Konradi, Adrienne Gessner, who through their speech remind one of what is Austrian though its name is obliterated. I remember also the narration by Grete Wiesenthal, who right on the day of the Anschluss in March of 1938 went for a walk in Belvedere Park – in sadness – and came across Franz Theodor Csokor. To him she said, "Please come to me this evening, there will always be a bit of Austria on hand." And I was sitting in their salon in Modenapark, and soon it became clear to me, in 1963, during the narration, because of the language of Grete Wiesenthal, that in her intonation and voice there was an Austria in which I would never again live. The great old lady once upon a time at the beginning of the Salzburg Festival was the first expressionist dancer under Max Reinhardt, and in her salon were Alois Dempf and Friedrich Heer, and my father – and even Monseigneur Otto Mauer, about whom I will surely report later.

These recountings are important little stones for a mosaic in which one can reconstruct the country robbed of its language. It was a robbery-murder! That took place much later! What National Socialism was unable to do was pulled off by the culture industry, thanks to its racketeers and crooks – probably after 1970 and then in the provocative tackiness of a city council who thought that the vulgar was the real thing. Even this proves, though it is only a small indication of the significance, that there is a much larger dimension at stake.

We have the allowed the salt of our language of belief to lose its savor. I connect this intentionally to the question of Dietrich Bonhoeffer: Are we still useful? And I am unable to answer it. I lack the voice for it, which language has to make audible. Useful?

Our language tells us – indeed it reflects – that we have betrayed it. And this was not so in 1938. The enemies of our language did not rob us of our language! To do that they were not able. It was we, who surrendered everything out of our lack of character and for the sake of cheap marketing, which seemed so sacred to us. We were not annexed, we sold ourselves out. Or out of hatred, everything that appeared to be sacred we consciously immediately and fervently destroyed. Only after National Socialism did we begin this relentless "purification" of our language and speech, so that no one any longer can hear the word – that old Word. It is a bitter story.

I very much hope that you will forgive me for this "excursion" into the catacombs of our sins!

After the loss of speech, we have, with the help of psychology, blithely done away with the person. He is somewhere between a neurotically deficient being, competent to do nothing and responsible for nothing – maybe a Viennese! We would have gotten our idea of man, through our history, out of our message of faith, in which the Jewish is incorporated in Christ. This nobody wants to still hear. And yet who will still want to know it?

For the time I will end with a sentence that Eugen Rosenstock-Huessy wrote down in 1912: "Language is wiser than the thinker, who himself opines that he is thinking where however he is only 'speaking,' and so he faithfully trusts the authority of the stuff of speech; it guides his conceptions, unawares and forward into an unknown future." And, "Poetry is often the form of scientific truth a century ahead of time."

With hugs, Your R.

29.
De amicitia

Dear Nina, Dear Julian and your sisters, Marie and Vicky,

Now I have to pause for a moment. A serious mistake has crept into the sequence of the letters, which was noticed and reported by my friend Kenneth Quandt during the translation work. He asked me to complete three missing letters with three topics, which he suggested should treat on the one hand my close circle of friends on Sunday in the Café-Konditorei "Heiner" in the Wollzeile, and about my "activity" for many years in the gymnastic club "Holmes Place," and finally about the visit Kenneth and I made together to the Benedictine monastery, Kremsmünster, around 2013.

I cannot yet come to terms with this suggestion of Ken's, since our time together in Kremsmünster on the one hand and the ominous prospect of morning gymnastics at Holmes Place over the years, present two pictures hard to reconcile!

When I write about the friendship that has united me with Ken for more than twenty years now, I attach to it such beautiful memories and suggestions that show me to be in a perpetual debt of gratitude. It is one of Ken's peculiarities always to ask questions, always to revisit a subject, and it is not easy always to find the appropriate answer. To my mind, two relationships were of great importance: besides Ken I am thinking of Helmut Kohlenberger, whom I had met in Vienna around 1977. The difference with Ken was that Kohlenberger not only was leading an intellectual wandering life like a medieval monk, but that his points of reference ranged from philosophy to extraordinary people. He was in a very intimate relationship with Manès Sperber or Leszek Kolakowski, with Friedrich Tenbruck or E. M. Cioran, with Andre Glucksmann and Michael Benedikt. It was not easy to "settle down" in the rather overwhelming spatial diversity of his thought world, because he was always hurrying from place to place, was always intellectually in motion, so that even in conversations it was not easy to follow what he was saying. He was interested in "revitalizing" the philosophy that had been largely destroyed by totalitarianism, and he had basically not been infected by the mentality that characterized neo-Marxism during the 1970s. Very well camouflaged under the catchword "Frankfurt School," this revival of Marxism with the addition of psychoanalysis and sociology had become a recipe for success, "colonizing" most of the full professorships of the universities. Kohlenberger clearly recognized the resulting standstill at the universities, fought against it, and argued against it. Therefore, he was fundamentally at war with the respective institutes of philosophy and sociology, and this determined his existence, his way of life, which I previously compared to a monk's. Thus he was driven to hurry without rest through the world of thought. Nowhere could he find a long-term home. Probably Hilde Domin's characterization of Kohlenberger was accurate when she said to me that he has a finger in many pies.

In the same way, the aforementioned friendship with Ken was important for me. It was a very different relationship compared to Kohlenberger. When I wrote that it was difficult to escape Ken's questions, they were meaningful for me in two ways. On the one hand, he forced me to sharpen my thoughts, to be exact and precise; on the other hand, he broadened the horizon with his questions: indeed, one was forced to go far out, to change coordinates, to extend the evidence into distant fields of knowledge in order to clarify a fact. In particular, during the writing of the sketches regarding Art Religion, which was realized as a book through the translation by Ken (*The Revelation of Art Religion*), he immediately established a control mechanism during the translation for keeping track of details, under which one was literally at his mercy. This at times strained the friendship. The debates that Ken's questions unleashed also sometimes became unpleasant, for Ken never let up, demanding a clearer clarification of the facts. At times I was annoyed by the wave of the hand with which he demanded that one proceed more and more precisely and with proof of the quoted positions. It was an incredible achievement that with the translation Ken retrieved the English version of every reference the book made to the literature, and it was not uncommon to find that the two language habits – German and English – constitute distinct worlds.

All these inconveniences of working with Ken were quickly forgotten, because Ken liked to "drill" and be annoying like a dentist, but quickly his refreshing laugh relieved any tension.

This laughter of Ken always came, at the end of an exhaustive debate. The situation never arose that highly opposing points of view could have damaged the friendship. If the laughter with Kohlenberger was always borne by irony, the tip of an unforgiving criticism of philosophy when it had lost itself either in flat empiricism or even in an ideology, the laughter with Ken was the return to the reality of life.

These two friendships deserve a closer look. We are familiar with Friedrich Schiller's *Ode to Joy*, which Beethoven set to music in the 9th Symphony. There it says, among other things: "...whoever has succeeded in the great attempt to be a friend of a friend, whoever has won a lovely wife, let him add his jubilation." A complement to this is found in Schiller's "Bürgschaft," in which the assassination attempt by Mörus against the tyrant fails and the tyrant demands that a friend be the bond for the assassin with his life. The "happy ending" converts the tyrant to humanness and to request that he be included in this bond of friendship. From this we learn that friendship became a distinct social category in the early days of bourgeois society. Until the 19th century, friendship was considered a special virtue because one enters into it without coercion or ulterior motives, or even a thought for advantage. On the one hand, this "affective act," as Max Weber would have called it, evinces a special social category in bourgeois society; on the other hand, friendship had become a social-constitutive principle in the 18th century, comparable to genealogy among the nobility. A special case was Hegel, Hölderlin, and Schelling dancing around the newly erected tree of liberty in Tübingen in 1793, which was meant to celebrate the "blessings" of the French Revolution.

The further characteristic of friendship in the historical development between 1750 and 1850 was the openness of conversation, confidentiality, and the free exchange of opinions. After all, friendships were the foundation for the early democratic parties, for the pursuit of common political goals, and thus also for the secrecy which had to withstand the pressure of the police authorities before the constitutional reform of 1867, in the Danube Monarchy.

I myself learned of this kind of friendship from the friendship my father had all his life with Friedrich Heer and Wilfried Daim. From this friendship came joint work during the 1950s about what was then the constitution of the Roman Church, which had shown little reflection on the events of World War II and had failed to reformulate the church constitution with a greater appreciation of the "laity," and to further dampen the feudal remnants in the church, which had long since ceased to be able to hold their own in a democracy. I still remember very clearly the insinuations launched against this "gang of three" – the ban on my father speaking ordained by Cardinal König within the diocese, the countless disputes with the "milieu Catholics" in Austria, who were still powerful at that time. The criticisms were clearly laid out, but the Catholic Church did not understand them or at least mistook these exhortations to reform and steered steadfastly into this crisis, which has now almost taken the Church "hostage." Increasing secularism and a lack of interest in fundamental theological questions have become so strong that the Church, including the Reformed Church in Europe, have become "cultural by-products" and, after the cases of child abuse in almost all dioceses, are held less important than the immigration from the Islamic states.

The friendship with Kohlenberger and Quandt have a quality comparable to what I remember from my father's friendships. Granted, there was no similar test to pass as my father had to pass in the time of National Socialism. Though in the time of totalitarianism friendship again became an existential necessity through which a subversive activity against the regime could be carried out, in our own friendships this burden was not present. However, I lived through the way that because of Kohlenberger's trenchant position in philosophy at a few institutes, he was continually under the arrest of the prevailing outlook – so that his advancement in scientific work was hindered rather than tolerated. This always led Kohlenberger to the lifestyle of a *vagans clericus*, which made it difficult for him to work.

A completely different kind of friendship had connected me with Hans Preiner. I got to know him during the 1960s. Officially, he had studied law in Graz; in fact, he had been active in cultural politics in Graz to a remarkable degree. Among other things, he was responsible for the "entry" of Elias Canetti into Austria, he promoted a position more distanced from Marxist mentalities, and he promoted and publicized William Johnston's work, *The Austrian Mind*, on the history of Austrian intellectual life between 1880 and 1930. In his Viennese activity he had tried to influence the cultural policy of the Ministry of Education, which tended to end in disagreements. He was instrumental in drafting the libretto for the "State Operetta," which was set to music by Otto Zykan during the "golden" reign of Bruno Kreisky. The rendition on television stimulated some outrage.

Preiner visited me in Vienna around 1960 to initiate a political alternative in the student milieu. I had achieved some notoriety because I had held the funeral oration at Heldenplatz for Ernst Kirchweger, who had been slain during a demonstration against neo-Nazis. Contrary to Hans Preiner's imagination the initiative did not succeed since at that time a "bourgeois" alternative to the conservative Student Union had no chance. In any case, these modest political attempts were enough to be punished at the Institute of History. At the Institute of History, a National Socialist tendency was still present in the academic administrative staff, and my decisive position against this Hitlerism earned fierce and vociferous criticism from some professors. The great exception was Erich Zöllner and, of course, Friedrich Heer. Any change at the Institute was only gradual and due more due to "biological" causes, and less because of new convictions. This put the university in a rather dubious light and called for reform, which in fact was initiated at the beginning of the 1970s. So it was part of a typical manifestation among Austrian students, more than 50 years ago, that a third of them would prefer political representation that could be described as right-wing extremist. Only much later did a "normalization" occur, basically with the founding of the "green movement," which arose in Austria out of the protest against nuclear energy and against the development of the Danube floodplains east of Vienna.

If I remember correctly, before 1970 traditional "friendship alliances" had also been politically relevant. First and foremost, it was the student clubs that operated under the banner of friendship. A community of interests developed among them very quickly, a "friendship economy" that made it much easier to get ahead in business and politics. Although especially after 1918 this was a rallying point for those young intellectuals who rebelled against the dominance of political-liberal forces at university and in academia, after 1945 this ideological position was far overshadowed by obvious favors and privileges. All the way up to the federal ministries, the staffing had been arranged according to "red," meaning Social Democratic, or "black," meaning conservative. For the Social Democrats, after all, the greeting since their founding had been "friendship," just as for their opponents, "friendship for life" had repeatedly been spoken of as a special social value. All this had nothing to do with my previous remarks on friendship. The meaning of friendship, which had been so important in Romanticism, of which the relationship between Goethe and Schiller had been the paradigm, had long since been lost and came to have a rather negative connotation.

All the things I am recalling are shaped by my own life and by the recognition that such friendship associations as these, at least after 1990, are no longer so important. The lodges of the Freemasons which once determined the political climate in Austria, had to recognize this the same way the student corporations had to. From this, mentalities had developed that only after 1970 underwent a significant change, under Bruno Kreisky. Of course, the question remains unanswerable whether and to what extent the "instrumentalization" of friendships, which had almost become a characteristic of Austrian society, led to surrendering to the unfortunate automatism between complicity and coercion on the one hand, and whether on the other hand a sort of solidarity had been handed down by it, which is more than just a helpfulness, which remains more than just "neighborly help," but realizes the high social value of ties and obligations. It shows itself in a giving of help that does not expect thanks, it shows itself in devotion that is almost the Christian virtue of charity. In sociology, it would have been easy to study this kind of social cohesion through friendship, but the cause of this social "stability" did not interest anyone since Max Weber. The network of relationships through friendship was soon suspected as an instrument of corruption, soon was portrayed as a perverted means for professional advancement, and had forfeited any old valorizations of friendship from before 1850.

Thus it has always been important to me to keep the contact with Helmut Kohlenberger and Ken Quandt, and I have profited from the generosity in the passing on of thoughts, and hope that my friends have drawn a comparable "benefit" from the friendship with me. Therefore I have told you about it to encourage you here to realize exactly that part of Schiller's sentence in your own life: "...to be a friend of a friend...."

Best regards I remain your R.

30.
The Encounter with Painting

Dear Nina, Dear Julian and Marie and Vicky,

First I must vent my anger. Some clumsy error, and the last two pages disappeared from my computer. I can of course reconstruct them but it is terribly annoying.

In the original beginning of this letter I was returning to the topic of two letters back. In support of my assertion that we will be communicating with machines or speaking devices I had mentioned Thomas Friedman, who a few pages into his book *The World is Flat* shares his feeling that our interlocutors for everyday questions are speaking machines. They know where we have left things, when and how we forgot the password, or what we should be thinking about when we search for our documents. Somebody who sits somewhere in New Delhi is entrusted with my problem. Generally it is an unemployed computer scientist. Once he becomes too expensive even he will be replaced with a machine. I can only repeat that I wish for you that you will be communicating with flesh and blood people and not with an automaton.

Now I want to go into a question I often encounter. People sometimes express incredulity that I have knowledge in several fields. These days people become a bit skeptical if one acts as if he has a somewhat broader knowledge. I have an answer to this question that some will find unsatisfactory, while for others it will strain their credulity even further. My way through school was something of a gauntlet. First there were health problems that today would be deemed psychosomatic. Migraines and appendicitis were my most protracted impairments. Even the removal of the appendix brought little relief. After that there was a terrible inflammation of the joints that lasted even longer, and then gastritis. Looking back it is hard to say which was the greatest impairment of my health. Already in the elementary school I suffered from the noise of the screaming, the trampling racket of a hundred children, the smell that emanated from the lunch being served – a lunch that was mandatory in 1947. And I have already described how this misery of attending school was continued in the Piarist Gymnasium. I already reported how I was beset with many difficulties because I would unequivocally refuse to tolerate any whiff of National Socialism. In that school this was not easy. On the one hand there were confessed Nazis in the teaching staff, and on the other hand the principal, a puny man, was perfectly ready to compromise for the sake of maintaining peace in the teachers' conference room, even though he came from a Jewish family. When he in his unique role of both counsellor and director expelled me from the school, I wondered what shadow it was that he was dodging, the day he planted himself six inches before me, yelled at me, and sent me home. After all he had put a known Nazi, the teacher of geography and chemistry, in charge of the curriculum of the school.

Later I got to know this character, who apparently hoped to block my Matura by any means possible. In geography he loved to teach about the expedition of Rommel in North Africa, in which he apparently had taken part. He peppered his commentary on Rommel's expedition now and then with references to the present – that for instance the *Yiddelach* now rule our country, and that the fate of the republic would now be decided in Judengasse. It was almost unbearable to hear this nonsense, with which nevertheless a third of the class agreed. In chemistry he was even more miserable, because brainless. Of course a whole series of advances in the history of the field were the work of Jewish scholars, but Herr Professor had completed his Aryan education in the Nazi period, so he was not up to date on the current knowledge of the field. Nor was he equipped to explain the structure of a chemical formula. He always copied them from the textbook, often erroneously; and always accompanied the corrections he had to make with a confusing aside, "Uh huh, clear as daylight." He would lick his finger to erase the wrong valences he had written on the blackboard, the basics of which he did not understand. Thus he never was able to write the formula for alcohol on the board without correcting it. The basic rules of set theory were likewise unfamiliar to him. This teacher was tricky, insidious, and nasty, underhanded, and a malicious anti-Semite – and of course a typical Austrian victim of misunderstood Germanness. At the time I wished he would get scabies all over his body. And I am afraid I have never relinquished this wish.

The teacher of gymnastics and history was the alternative to a Nazi. He was insecure, and sentimentally attached the Reich, which contrary to his historical knowledge had been the Nazi one. His tearful complaints about the condemnation of that period, and about how it was reached in error, were striking. Once he got carried away pointing out that he could tell the truth (!) about that special time, but that in the class there was a certain student who would report him for doing so – looking over at me, reproachfully, as if the historical truth could not be brought to light because of me.

These circumstances were hardly good for my migraines nor helped to abate my gastritis. I can thank my parents for accompanying me on this path of woe and sharing it with me. I thank my dear Mother, who had to sign the notes needed to excuse me from attending these lessons although she herself had once been a teacher. These enabled me to spend something more than a third of the time outside of school. When I came near the school in the morning and went down the Piaristengasse, my stomach would already be cramping, I would be struck with a wave of nausea, and then I would be met with the senseless noise of a hundred people raging around on the ground floor. It was a purgatory. Always I was trying to figure out who among the teachers was still a Nazi. And there must have been some. When a poster for the exhibition of Josef Mikl was posted on the bulletin board, which itself was quite a surprise, there ensued a disgusting orgy of insults brought by teachers and students alike. And pity upon the poor classmate whose name also happened to be Mikl. He was subjected to scorn and derision for days.

I owe my graduation from school in large part to my art teacher, Franz Klasek. I cannot overestimate his importance for what I was to become. Of course what tied us together was our similar status as "underdogs" in the school. His Viennese dialect, his manner of speaking and expressing himself, had brought him securely to a less than high estimation among his professional colleagues. His lessons were formal, but the content was what mattered so much. Since only a small portion of my group had chosen to take "art," we were only seven students in the drawing studio. The other part of the group selected the "music" option, but the lessons there did not have much to do with the title. Mostly it was a matter of listening to records – operas and classical symphonies – and having an uncritical enthusiasm aroused.

Still I remember the disputes during the breaks in the lectures, for the predominant part of the group was devoted to the clearly important conductor, Herbert von Karajan, and also of course to Richard Wagner, whereas my preference, thanks to Klasek, was for the moderns and so I would vouch for Carl Orff's opera *Die Kluge*, for Ernst Krenek's *Jonny spielt auf*, or for the *Classical Symphony* of Sergei Prokofiev. I had seen the television production of Orff's opera and was deeply impressed. Today this opera has become a standard and would cause no controversy.

Looking back I can see that the majority of my fellow students came from educated homes. The parents were physicians, pharmacists, lawyers, or owners of large companies, so that at that time this bourgeois milieu kept to the usual prejudice against the moderns. The visible indication of success was now a car, in which the "better" students would either be brought to the school or picked up. And there was a lot more behind that. During the 50's this group could regain a foothold, and could again display that they belonged to the privileged social class with their status symbols, having become adept at forgetting and repressing. The after-effects of National Socialism were truly palpable, and yet in the eyes of the "survivors" those times were seen only as a period like whooping cough and measles. And indeed it was quite common that one had "had" measles or scarlet fever once, as a child. So the past was always both things: great and terrible.

Helmut Qualtinger's *Herr Karl* was a brilliant document for the social history of the period, albeit dealing with the social underclass. In the upper and middle classes the coming to terms was similar: surely with more snobbism and sometimes also the open and visible approval of the "achievements" of the Third Reich such as relieving unemployment and developing the highways.

From these remarks one can get a good sense of the "climate" that prevailed in the bourgeois districts of Vienna, and not often did one encounter a renunciation of the "worldview" that had led to these devastating catastrophes. One always accounted for the crimes as the sort of phenomena that usually accompany war, and so confiscations, robbery, murder, and terror were not reckoned to have been due to the "excess diligence" of those involved in the dictatorship, but counted only as the normal horrors of war which were forced on us by the Third Reich – so one said.

It is obvious that exactly because of the common attitude about the time between 1938 and 1945, the relationship between the teacher and the student – between Franz Klasek and me, that is – would become closer. In his lectures, he was able to pursue a double goal since he had a double period. Of course there were the drawing exercises, the suggestions about the formation of a picture with various materials; but in the second half he turned to a profound meditation on art history. Even during the study of art history at the university, the names of Heinrich Wölfflin and Jacob Burckhardt were not mentioned, nor the Viennese School of art history according to Alois Riegl. In the university, very early, the teaching dealt with a "theory-less history," as Peter Burke was later to describe it.

The teaching of Klasek was based on criteria for evaluation that he got from Wölfflin, which enabled one to classify the stylistic and historical characteristics of the painting. Still today I use this scheme when I have to explain a painting. When I visited the Villa Borghese in February 2020 with a group of students, I had to lead the group *ex tempore*. The Wölfflin-Klasek schema I had learned came in handy.

As for the study of painting, Klasek encouraged me to take it up painting more methodically and seriously. He recognized I had an inclination toward painting and drawing, and he criticized my first attempts in a way that was clear and objective. Some he found bad, others on the other hand were good. It was also a prerequisite to get to know his own paintings. As best as I can remember he was partly devoted to the so-called abstract art, and partly to objective representation. What stood out was that his top priority was a cool expression, a clear form. It was often done with darkened shades of blue. That showed he was close to the Czech synthetic abstract painters, following Frantisek Kupka. The "objective" character in his painting followed Emil Orlik. I was once in Orlik's studio and was impressed by his work, although the way he managed representation was not so accessible.

I am afraid I am now going too much into detail. I hope you can understand what I am basically saying. The time that I was liberated from being at school I spent in the museums. Around 9AM I was already at the Kunsthistorisches Museum, and the only visitor. At first I drew suspicious looks from the guards but then they got used to me. I spent the morning with "my" painting collection, and probably got to know the paintings more deeply and more extensively than the archdukes or even the emperor. My focus was not only on the paintings, hanging there in mystical silence; I also brought my other things with me, the things that seemed important. Novels and plays, books on modern history, expositions of the history of natural science. So I would spread out my little library on a comfortable bench, and if things got to be too much I would wander through the collection as if I owned it, gazing in admiration now at a van Dyck, and then at the *Cardinal Albergati* of Jan van Eyck. This kind of intimate encounter the horrible tourism of the city has forever destroyed. And when I had had enough of it all, I would wander off to the Upper Belvedere and would eye Egon Schiele with similar interest or Richard Gerstl and Oskar Kokoschka. I familiarized myself with Herbert Boeckl and found engaging my cautious willingness to gaze on Gustav Klimt. Now and then I would linger at the marble bust of Beethoven, a work by Max Klinger, which I was astonished later to encounter in the residence of Philip Roessler.

At this point I must say in advance that in 1951, alone and without the recommendation of "adults," I went to the exhibition of Oskar Kokoschka in the Vienna Succession. I was much taken with the late expressionist works: they touched me deeply. The late works, which were taken to be representative, as for example in their depiction of the renovated Staatsoper, appealed to me not at all. The works of the Salzburg period of this painter I found repugnant. And yet I would have immediately taken sides with the painter the time I overheard a German visitor arguing with a guard. It had to do with a portrait of Ludwig Erhart, who later became the German chancellor. The German's outrage was amusing to me. When I got home Grete Wiesenthal was visiting. She was astonished that I had wandered into the Succession exhibition all by myself at age ten, to encounter Kokoschka. Of course, she had known him personally.

So, one can imagine that on the next day the path to the schoolhouse was hardly attractive; and so, with my mother's note to excuse me, I wandered now through the galleries of Vienna. My itinerary went first "to the Griechenbeisl" and was then continued in the Galerie Würthle and the whole round led me to the gallery next to St. Stephen's. These were all familiar addresses, and here I encountered those who had real rank and fame in painting. I observed Josef Mikl framing his paintings, and Ioannis Avramidis setting up a sculpture, and Clemens Hutter in the midst of deciding how to hang his paintings. I had become a silent onlooker, at age 12 or 13. Some of what I saw seemed overstated, even childish. And the grand master Friedensreich Hundertwasser left me with the impression that his works were utterly infantile. The "boastful swagger" in his wordy speeches got on my nerves. In all likelihood I am doing him a disservice, but in any case I later had a detailed correspondence with him, in which he was trying to justify his pathetic architecture.

Here I want to break off, again. I just wanted to describe for you how I was able to observe the culture business as a "child." Again and again, unnoticed and quiet, I stood in some corner or window niche while the masters spoke about their projects, presented their pictures, and surprised me with their vanity. One day I came from the Kunsthistorisches Museum to the gallery next to St. Stephen's and heard the "harangue" of the Monseigneur on art and faith. Monseigneur Mauer seemed to me at the time a very suspect character, like the "Grand Inquisitor" in Dostoevsky's novel. Indeed he was able to play the part and make it "real." It was all terribly disgusting, above all his presumption of authority and his self-glorification.

Had there not been a cycle of exhibitions in the Upper Belvedere, of van Gogh, Paul Gauguin and Paul Cezanne, I might have been left in the dark. The great masters in the gallery at St. Stephen's offered something more on the order of decorations – until Peter Pongratz. I need not mention that in the paintings of Vincent van Gogh you could see his heart's blood, in those of Cezanne the highest discipline. Perhaps I can write later about what these great painters were about, which would affect the way we see ever since.

In any case, Franz Klasek knew about these trips of mine, half excused and half not-excused, and he did not report them to the school authorities. He knew about the unexcused hour when I saw Fritz Wotruba personally supervise the installation of his sculpture at the edge of the Marzpark in front of the Stadtshalle. I stood by, at a distance, and I was immediately taken with the work. Surely I thought it better than the sculpture of Wander Bertoni in the "courtyard" of the Stadtshalle. To me that looked like a stunt plane that had crashed.

There are so many impressions from my youth I could tell you about! It was always about these masterpieces. The upper floor of the Academy of Fine Art at Schillerplatz, the Museum of Applied Arts at Stubenring, all of which have a place in the inventory of my consciousness – and probably by then I had become 15.

During that time I developed an unerring ability to judge, which is why I am so opposed to the developments in our art over the last three decades, whatever their official dignity and appreciation. When I see these consumptive regurgitations of old "ideas," which once were revolutionary acts, I can only politely nod, for all the effort of painting large canvases is only an excuse for artistic incompetence. This is why these longwinded stories have to be invented in the catalogues, to explain in writing what is not there to be seen on the canvas.

Again I must commemorate Franz Klasek and the correctness of his careful interpretation of paintings. It would have been easy to discredit Wilhelm Leibl's *Praying* as naturalism, and Georg Waldmüller even easier, which however was never the case, since he projected the *Bauernstube* by Albin Egger-Lienz next to the Liebl onto the screen, and then the *Insassen eines Altenheims* by Max Liebermann. It brings me to tears no longer to be able to reproduce his comments, his gradual approach to these very different paintings and his evaluation of each of the three. While my fellow students were coming out of the music lecture raving that Karajan had conducted everything in the best way, we came out of the hours with Klasek speechless – for that kind of self-satisfied enthusiasm had been utterly beaten out of us.

I have written you a long letter this time. The special circumstance was that I wanted to make my own person more clearly understandable to you by describing an "other." Let my teacher forgive me for this – and yet wasn't this his job? Was it because of this that he made my life possible, when at my Matura he slipped that piece of blotting paper between my papers, on which the answers to the geography questions were written? That was Franz Klasek!

I hope such a man will show up at a critical moment in your lives! I really wanted to share this with you!

With love, Your R.

31.
Who Determines our Social Abilities?

Dear Nina, Dear Julian,

In Letter 30 I said a lot about myself, which shows how easily writing can flow on and on. In all likelihood the two corner-stones of my presentation were the very "intimate" experience of art which began with my early visits to the museum, and as a counterpoint my experience at school. The net result should be the message that school must not at any price be the place that book title was talking about, which asked: *Do You Hear the Children Crying? A Psychogenetic History of Childhood.* Lloyd de Mause was referring not only to the psychogenetic development of children but also presenting an admonition to schools as an institution, that they must recognize that not every child is equally able to deal with the way a school is organized. These days schools in all European states are overtaxed, since on the one hand they are making up for the absence of the traditional family, and on the other the students in a given classroom do not share a homogeneous social or cultural milieu so that the job of teaching faces an almost insurmountable hurdle in seeing to it that what is said in the lessons is being understood. Only rarely are measures being adopted to deal with this, which should begin with drastically reducing the number of students in a class. In Austria the situation is extreme. I suspect that the learning goals have become more modest, just as one can no longer rely on presuming background knowledge. The new "Central Matura" will not alter this, nor will the crippling debates about various regroupings of students and methods of tracking. The whole debate, which has gone on for forty years (!), is clearly missing the point and thus becomes an ideal sandbox for education politicians. To respond to the needs of an educational curriculum by fighting over the organization of the school routine represents the very bankruptcy of the system of education.

I won't express my shock about this any longer. Perhaps children are lucky enough to acquire in some other way the knowledge that is now being presented only with difficulty in school lessons. Any teacher, whether a woman or a man, will not be supported by their departments, faces the daily demands alone, and must discover innovative ways to deal with the difficulty. So the children will go on crying.

I must turn to what is a very current problem, the more than difficult election of a US President. This election, in 2020, presents in many ways a depressing picture of the situation in the USA. As you know Donald Trump has been in power for four years and he has taken every opportunity to show himself a vulgar person, to make arbitrary decisions, and to make foolhardy pronouncements. This in itself should be seen as a change in the structure of democracy. And the media – television and the so-called social media – pushed the extravagance of this President even further. This reciprocal conflict increased political desultoriness, arbitrariness, and obscenity. And since the image of the President is drawn by the media, the media became more and more powerful at defining the political landscape: they could "de-select" topics or highlight them, they could heighten sympathy or antipathy for political programs and initiatives; and the more one thinks that the social media foster democracy, the lower the level of political discourse sinks. Politics, the political, had increasingly lost its place during the 20th century, in particular as to where political intentions come from and how they determine the way things are managed. In the grossest terms, politics has lost its credibility during a period marked at the same time by the destruction of the biosphere, and it defends its questionable status through zealous investigations that lead nowhere. These are unavoidable, since the "media," which previously consisted in daily newspapers and then also radio, forced upon us a dichotomy in the presentation of problems: Either – Or, For – Against. Thus, politics was caught in a lopsided vortex of one-sidednesses.

I can introduce a good example: When I discussed the question of atomic energy with my friends on the occasion of Zwentendorf, Bruno Kreisky was only willing to discuss the question because he was running for election in the national parliamentary election of 1975. "We," as the "Re-election Committee," could play no more than the role of his "court jester," so we were unable to move him toward a more cautiously couched evaluation of the question. We were in fact "allowed" to organize a conference in which physicists and Nobel Prize winners in physics took part, but this moved the position of the union and the party not a single millimeter.

This example teaches how these self-justifying dichotomies eventually become decisive and, in the force-field of politics, can never seem to budge. If one wants to analyze it philosophically, which is something we hardly witness any more, one must ground contemporary politics' loss of its way on the fact that the universal terms "politics," "culture," and "society" have undergone a relentless "de-ontologization." This had been done in the name of "factuality" and was furthered by "de-essentialization," which even affected social philosophy. At the risk of not being understood at all, I will claim that this hearkens back to the fundamental question whether the old distinction between social and natural ontology is still accepted. Unfortunately, positivist positions, of all things, have made the mistake of explaining particular social phenomena in the manner of "natural science" and thereby a new ideology was established. What followed in its wake was successful and well-endowed think-tanks that constantly focused on the investigation of "attitudes," but the results were undatable snapshots or a misuse of history in its being used merely to corroborate pre-determined assertions. Answers given in interviews become the basis for empirical findings and history becomes a picture book in which one cites whichever page he wants to support his own position.

In the example about Bruno Kreisky, the takeaway, which in no way diminishes his importance, is that the problem arises from the "anti-metaphysical" core of politics, especially in the legacy of Karl Marx or later Karl Kautsky. More and more the horizon of possibilities is determined by opportunism. This is touted as "realism," and also as freeing one from a distorted perception of reality. In other words, party discipline becomes the stand-in for reason! We must thus acquiesce in the fact that through the media with its emphasis on the "dichotomizing" of politics, new "time perspectives" came into being, which influence our consciousness and the way we view history or culture, as for instance a concern about climate change, the disturbing prospect of increased unemployment, a fundamental debate over the procurement of energy, or a disagreement about the future of the automobile. In an historical perspective, our disagreements on these matters seem to be stripped of any connection with traditions, and hasten us toward what seems to be the brink of a "democratic revolution." This sort of revolution was ushered in by the "flower children" and the "be-ins" in New York's Central Park around 1965. It was the motive also for the Paris demonstrations which along with New York put forth demands that were more suited to the Bronx than to the Latin Quarter of Paris. This began also with a "student revolution" in 1968 and continued when terrorists came onto the scene, with their illegitimate designation as an "extra-parliamentarian opposition party." The green movement often toyed with this idea, in the sense of speculating on circumventing elections, the traditional means of political decision-making. Nature was a sufficient and serious enough justification for trumping everything and everyone. It was a new metaphysics that was not insignificant. Formerly, the people received their political legitimation as having themselves emerged from "nature."

Politics has been done a disservice, but this development would have come about in any case. The sociologist Niklas Luhmann described the situation wherein politics gets an equal rank in the hierarchy of social and political valorization as leisure time or health. Politics is, after all, but a single aspect of the social world, as is sports or membership in the Friends of Nature – no more and no less. From then on its role becomes limited. Politics is – it is grotesque to notice?? – barely capable of "steering the ship of state": without a perspective, a goal, or even an illusion, the steering is hardly a real activity, and all that remains is an obsolete image of a "statesman" in charge. When a civilization becomes extremist the rationalism of democracy can be forced into contradictions. Another way of putting it is that democracy no longer corresponds "culturally" to political-aesthetic expectations, something every dictatorship up to now has seemed easily able to pull off. Thus the mantle of multiculturism is extended over everything, through which the whole underpinning of the democracy is shaken. Political stability will now be reached by a detour to a very extreme form of equality, as for instance in the equal status of women in all political areas, in weakening discrimination against same-sex relationships, in recognizing factors of sexual categorization that were not definable before, and in an assault on other distinctions, as yet undetermined, the validity of which is no longer to have any meaning. Of all things, in the very advancement of democracy, thanks to the participation of the media in fomenting indignation and disparagement, forms of culture that are mere states of mind or fashion are now taking the place previously held by democratic institutions, which operated under a self-understanding consisting entirely in a "community of values." The fatal consequence is an intensification of the refusal to look and see and a denial of what is actually happening, a blindness that comes in through the media of all things, although they assert that only through them is one able to see what is going on. This blindness gives place for an indefinite flow of events, replacing in this way the realm defined by politics. Political action accordingly becomes a matter of putting out fires and dealing with dire emergencies that dictate the day to day events. (In art this is going on in the creation of alternative realities precisely through inevitable and ready-made references to current events).

This representation must be examined repeatedly. Always we are anticipating a state of affairs and an interpretation based on our knowledge of history. Our problem is that the framework of world politics at present is set by the economic state of things, so that politics resigns itself to this as its "reality principle." At present it is world trade that governs the relations of states, of continents, and of cultures. With that the social space is "divided," and therefore consists in consumer's attitudes and the economic constraints that determine them. If we hope for a continuation of democratic politics as a way out of these difficulties, we have to accept the breaks in the framework prerequisite to democracy, at least with the "disembodiments": the disembodiment of power through the media, the disembodiment of law that cannot assert its legitimacy since there are at least two orders of law (in Europe, the general public law and an informal Islamic law), the disembodiment of thought in its rigid narrowing of a reality that is not real enough, and the disembodiment of the social, for as sociology points out, society can no longer be made out…

At a gallop I have quickly rendered the current state of things. Does it stand up to closer scrutiny? I imagine that even these splinters of thought correspond more closely to our situation than the soothing yearly reports of corporations in which we read about the stable state of things.

With many greetings I remain, Yours, R.

32.
The Problem of Comprehensibility

Dear Nina, Dear Julian and Your sisters,

Often I get no great approval for my letters nor even an acknowledgement. So I am curious how the reading of them will someday go for you…

After considering them only briefly, the readers to whom I send copies out of curiosity, object both that the content is hard to understand and that the manner of presentation is hard to follow. To this I must reply that one ought to try repairing a simple watch some time. Since few are familiar with how to do this, they will avoid even opening up the watch case. This means not at all that one will set the watch aside and will no longer use it to tell time. The knowledge for "reading" a watch is widespread, but not for repairing one. This example serves to clarify that in the human studies a language similar to everyday is used, a similar grammar, a similar orthography and similar meanings in the use of words are in place, and yet the sentences are understood only with difficulty. This is due to the high complexity of the thinking; and I make this assertion as applying to myself.

In one of the first letters I already raised this problem, and told you that the problem in the human and social sciences is that we think we should use the "same" language as we use in our everyday talk, but unfortunately this is not true. Given the formalistic language of mathematics or physics such objections are seldom raised, since if a statement is not understood one is politely told to learn the prerequisites – including the technical terminology – if he wants to understand. So it is a pity for philosophy that it cannot anticipate a similar kind of deference.

I say this to my contemporaries, but all the more do I want to say it to you: one must take in what one reads, indeed one ought to think hard about what is being said or what is being talked about. It may well be that a sentence be as complex as Newton's theory of gravity.

Is it only because the mathematical model on which it is based is hard to understand, that Newton's theory should not be thought through closely or should even be considered to be false? Are the assertions of genetics perhaps also incorrect since we barely know the enormous, complex, and reciprocal relations between biology and biochemistry? And are the broad areas of the politics less complex than biology? Are social phenomena fundamentally simpler than a theorem in mathematics? Even when an American president does not leave the impression of having the mind of a philosopher, and creates the impression of being incredibly vulgar, the complexity of politics is not reduced – it is only greatly wounded.

That is one side of the coin. Granted, because you are my grandchildren you can insist upon my being understandable, yet as proper as that may be it is also true that a carefully formulated listing of the critical issues is not as easy as pointing something out in a picture book. So if I am lucky one of my grandchildren will understand my claim. That in itself would already be fantastic. On the other side of the coin there is the fearsome possibility that all these letters will simply be forgotten, as are so many other historical things....

The reason I am focusing on this is that the letters often refer to the realm of politics. Thus the letters are likely to be an interesting source for history, suitable one day to help you understand better the present you will be finding yourselves in forty years from now. Thus, if volcanic eruptions have an aftereffect that lasts decades or even centuries on cultures or on the history of human settlements, and if atomic accidents as at Fukushima in 2011 raise concerns for at least a couple of years about re-thinking atomic energy as a source, so also will certain similar events have a comparable effect whether they be wars, plagues, famines, or climate change. The Second World War is a lesson that encourages people to become more concerned about peace, and so have we done a lot to bring the wish for peace to fulfillment. The question of course remains whether the things we have brought about will be strong enough to pre-empt future conflicts. Our wishes today can tomorrow come to be realized, our anxieties today can tomorrow develop into prejudices, and our pride in progress today can tomorrow become the cause of astounding failures.

Probably the difficult thing about the science of history is that one must relate the sequence of events one discovers there to oneself, in order to be able to begin to reflect on them philosophically. Already Friedrich Schiller asked the question: What do we mean and what is our goal in studying universal history? I am not at all making a plea for some boundless subjectivity, but each of us nevertheless counts as products of history. This can express itself in the endorsement of a period that was experienced as positive and remains anchored in our remembrance as the "good old days;" or in the condemnation of a period of time in which murders, gassings, and conflagration appeared to be permissible and still horrify us today – or conversely can find a strengthened recrudescence bordering on insanity. And however that may be, every reader is being confronted with these epistolary relics and must deal with them as an archivist deals with the objects in his collection. It is the virtue of an archivist to track down a name mentioned in a document. If the name Bruno Kreisky draws in you a blank, and if you cannot rely upon some bit of historical writing to give you any clue who he was or what he was, you must reconstruct the person from references to him by name, which will lead at times to a very vivid picture but at other times a very pale one, depending on the state of the sources.

Don't let this get you down!

At the beginning of my studies nobody told me what simony is, or allodial title, or a feifdom as opposed to an after-feifdom, or a bann, or a transfer to a commend, or a gubernial administration, or the main conclusion of the Imperial Deputation of 1803. But it was exactly within the context of these terms that one needed to ascertain what was concretely going on, what it meant, and what was then the result when such institutions were abolished. For this, patience is needed as a prerequisite. Repairing a watch requires patience, and accuracy and knowledge – and a watch surely has great historical importance – and it's similar with written documents. My manner of presentation is quite different from a bad habit strangely cultivated in the lectures at the Institute of Art History. Understandability and accuracy were central as positivistic axioms, and yet these lectures are fraught with spurious complications, and when you tracked them down you saw how childish were their obfuscations. When a painting was to be dated, several of the lecturers said it was created before the first half of the second third of the third fourth of the 15th century (i.e., 1457). Let *them* to perform the calculation!

Now I must come to the purpose of this letter.

The manner of dealing with politics has the same basis as the manner of dealing with physics. Behind both one will be able recognize a religion. What I here mean by "religion" is what the term meant in the Treaty of Westphalia, at the "beginning of the second third of the second half of the last fifth of the first half of the 17th century." It denotes a confessional attachment (from the Latin *ligare*) to a congregation, to a community of like-minded fellow believers. Anybody can decide which of these he belongs to. Thus, religion is not the same thing as faith. In the 17th century religion was a political and legal concept used in connection with religious freedom – a freedom of attachment. It is this kind of religion that made it possible for all the sciences, especially the natural sciences, to claim to be of equal value and to apply across all national borders, and gave the impression of leaving behind all the narrow and confining old confessions. Universality was provided for by maintaining Latin as the common written language. Only when a country's own language became the language of science, in the wake of the Enlightenment, did translations of the old books distort the knowledge that had been held in common. "Natural laws" were never referred to as "laws" in Latin but were *proportiones* – relations. In this case the language of the jurists penetrated the language of the natural sciences. This usage is basically where the high-handedness of the natural sciences comes from. However, this "freedom of religion" in the natural sciences finally was brought under the jurisdiction of states, from 1946 on. The discoveries of physics may now no longer be shared across national borders. After the dropping of the atomic bomb they became secret and were guarded by state interests. And the thief of this secret came to be celebrated as a Prometheus. Because of the subsidies provided by the states the notion that the natural sciences were an international affair became a thorn in the side of national sovereignty. From there on the joint undertakings within a university soon got a national designation, in the manner of the Prussian Academy of Sciences, and the French Academy, and the British Museum.

We are continually confronted by the question whether the creeds of the natural sciences still have anything to do with us. Should we undergo a conversion with respect to the Big Nebula or the Big Bang or the explosions on the Sun? Overall, the stock of positivism is always going up, and so is that of the natural sciences, whereas theology and human sciences have taken a hit – and have fallen far below par value. Thus, many investors are anxiously switching sides and are selling their souls at a loss, though in any case they already were of the opinion that the soul is an asset of zero worth. And all are taking refuge in the stanchions of the positive sciences as if they had always known that there is no God. He is a fiction, as will be reported in the analysis and evaluation of the ontological currencies, and even when the smart advice is to diversify, there is no reason to hold any paper assets in your portfolio that are certain never to go up in value nor to pay a dividend – and yet, who knows?

The complete shift of tone in what I have here written is partly due to fatigue, but in part because I wanted to sneak up on this depressing situation, which we must overcome. It will not be overcome with "killer arguments," with long proofs that shy not at all from blasphemy, but with the humility of making our contributions keeping in mind one's neighbor. Our difficulty has mostly been managed by separating out the worlds in which we exist. This has been seductive. We hear that this separation has only an upside, and that what we once spoke of as faith is still allowable for us, as a private matter. The compartmentalization of the world was a recipe for success but at the same time a loss of that other world that history reminds us of, that a church in every town reminds us of, or a temple or a mosque, which are not to be passed off as mere relics of false consciousness. This much is already rather glib. In all likelihood we will only look to the compelling logic of the natural sciences to overcome the problem of the way we are. And yet the successes of transplant medicine will not do it, nor some future solution of our difficulties in managing energy. What we see these sciences providing our world with is nothing but a notice of divorce – that is, a banishing of the spiritual part from our minds as being mere appearance and nonsense. Instead of the unity of faith, divisions multiply in the establishing of countless fields and subfields that produce knowledge that cannot be brought together and comprehended, and that advise us to aquiesce to live in the insecurity of this physical world. There is no need for an argument that only the physical world exists. Despite positivism we acquiesce in our empirical investigations: this physical world will become the object of our metaphysics, or has already become so and will remain so. And even with such metaphysics the spiritual question comes back into play. That is the darned thing about metaphysics, that it's always positing other dimensions whose reality we continually must acknowledge, though there is nothing there to latch onto with your hands. Thus we will be reminded of the spiritual world: it is the other, repressed part. Of all things this world that was deemed imaginary only up to now, becomes the very object upon which physics focusses, if we follow the outlook of Kant. And this other world got its strange justification when Albert Einstein couched it within its cosmic conditionality, and described it in the simple formula, $e=mc^2$. And yet this ideal and aesthetic formulation becomes practical only if we adopt the antique hypothesis that the world is a disk.

These are all incredible riddles. Thus I do not trust the physicists I mentioned to guide me on my way, for the physical nature we putatively have decoded depends on the paradox that contradicts the first sentence of the creed. It is, however, a sentence that is peculiar to all magic religions.

After this perplexing conclusion, I will promise to do better in the following letters.

In unswerving affection for you, your R.

33.
Understanding History through Music

Dear Nina, Dear Julian,

Whenever we had to take excursions into the past, the map we used was philosophy. Without this map we would not have been able to decode the meaning of history. If we now call the 20th century to mind, a time completely prior to your time of life, that century began with sound and fury. We remember clearly the tremendous artistic development. Of course Vienna played a large part in it, even if not as large as many Viennese assume. Still, one must not put his light under a bushel. Music, architecture, poetry, and painting had created a world that consciously kept a critical distance from politics. And the answer, which one takes as a part of the theory of culture, was that in the midst of this tremendous aesthetization of our world in the direction of beautiful appearance, the other world sent a reactive message. This other world was consciously risking its survival if it hoped to maintain the old delineations of politics. Against the disturbing aesthetic of the moderns and against the various popular movements and mass parties, help could be gotten only from war. For the one side, in accordance with the enormous changes, only a victory could save the old situation – if there *was* anything to save. This hit the countries of Central Europe like a blow from a club. The First World War brought forth many interpretations trying to understand this scandalous experience as well as its consequences. It appeared, at least, that some of these succeeded. They regretted that the peace agreements in the Paris suburbs did not lead to peace. The "stations" of the suffering were St. Germain, Versailles, Trianon, Sevres. The insecure representatives of the new states were paraded in these places, although they did not represent what they were summoned to Paris for. And yet the historians developed categories that somehow were meant to bring order into these confused affairs. Essentially, they applied the fundamental ideas of the 19th century supplemented with ideas from early US history.

The Second World War was not at all comparable. There is no need to make a judgment about this event in the history of war. What was new was that two powers formed an alliance, despite their opposing worldviews – the Soviet Union and the USA both pretended they were able to solve the riddles of the world through political and economic policies. It was also new was that the civilian population was targeted to be used as combatants, which up until then would never been allowed by international law; and the visible aftereffects of this were also new, and in subsequent years became more and more obvious, more tangible, telling a disgusting story. And new also was that a Marxist interpretation of this time of war was absent – or proved unsatisfactory.

In any case both wars expressed every pair of opposites, behind which people gathered ideologically, and thought that in these oppositions they were seeing the underlying movement that led to the war. Thus, Germanism was fighting against Slavicism, and ultimately it was a choice between democracy and monarchy/ theocracy. That imperialism and capitalism *versus* revolutionary socialism or communism was also at play was only a way of generalizing the conflict in economic terms. In the shadow of such tensions a new sort of excessive subjectivism was thriving, which in fact had been foreshadowed in the world of painting.

All these basic programs or developments, which received clear attribution to their authors, had a common perspective. They treated the war from the perspective of peace and of life, and were not willing to admit that the events of war stemmed from fundamentally dark motives and always had a dark side, and interrupted life all the more violently. Both wars were fought with "fury," since for the first time people were convinced that after the "storm of steel" one would rise up cleansed, renewed, and vindicated. Finally there would be clear losers whom one had felt all along he was better than: the "West" above the Reich, the Wilhelmine "Reich" above the "Russians." The problem was, if one views war from the perspective of life, that these wars cost so many million men their lives and compromised the history of the previous centuries. A bit earlier, in painting, poetry, and music, life was invoked, nymphs celebrated eternal youth in Stravinsky's *Rite of Spring*. Was heroic death now to interrupt this and bring to light a special new ideal, an exception to the continuity of life? By philosophy – in particular, Hegel – war was indeed already celebrated as a healing shock, and the most zealous "Hegel reader" that voiced this evaluation was Dostoevsky. The decadent bourgeoisie deserved this shock: after all, the market crash and "Black

Friday," first in Vienna on 9 May 1873 and in Paris on 9 August 1882, had achieved nothing.

However, one had come very far from the statement of Heraclitus, "War is the father of all things." One had rejected in principle to accept a "dynamics of catastrophe" – until 1914. The interpretation of conflict during the 19th century was always articulated as a disturbance of the ongoing need for peace, and European peace movements were quite at home in all the major cities of Europe. In Berta von Suttner's call to "lay down your arms," a voice was raised once again, as if it were a futile witness from the 19th century now arriving too late. And the social democrats in Europe swore all the sacred oaths to each other never to take up arms against each other. It was then that this slogan of passive resistance was first formulated: "Imagine there was a war and nobody came." Conversely, Robert Musil, even before the outbreak of the First World War, noted: "Everyone speaks of freedom and so war is at the door."

So this belligerent frenzy of the 20th century cannot be explained out of the previous conditions of the 19th. The enmities were all formulated *a posteriori* and were fueled by hatred after 1918. What comes from the 19th century is, rather, this indomitable will striving for whatever goal it might adopt. Programs, ideas, and goals were carried out with this stubborn will, with Friedrich Nietzsche no longer a foreign word in philosophy who obviously could be responsible for chasing down millions to their death. One can hardly measure that from now on peoples fell upon each other as if in the Battle of the Cyclops and killed each other with bitterness. It would take no more than a week to recognize that this murder and suicide hardly promised a flourishing life to come, and yet one continued in this bloody handiwork for years – and even that was not enough.

All factors were pushing toward this war, about which people thought it would be the long awaited final war of liberation for each and all of the belligerents. Liberation from what? In particular one actually thought that after the war all ocean navigation along with the projects of colonization could proceed without competition, that the seizure of lands in the east would be justified as convenient for our livelihood, that the threats of the mass political parties would easily be warded off, and that parliament would address grievances. However one wants to interpret it, one saw oneself overall as living in the aftermath of the Napoleonic Wars, which were ultimately "a blessing," since on the one hand Napoleon had brought the Code Civil across the Rhine, the victorious powers were stabilized in Central Europe as Prussia and the Imperial State of Austria, and Russia had finally rejoined the history of Central Europe for good – while on the other hand the socio-cultural changes were a clear indication of modernization, inspired by the slogans of the French Revolution.

And in the World War all the great wars were suddenly brought together, the meaning of which obviously lay in conducting this decisive battle for ever and for all times. The Thirty Years War was guided by the fiction that it would re-establish the unity of Western Christianity. The crusades were likewise an indication that Western Christianity was entitled to supremacy, and thus must repudiate the legitimate exercise of power by the Sultan, in the Middle East.

On the eve of this World War, in 1914, the idea was advocated with eloquence that there is no positive and objective meaning to the world, that it cannot be given a foundation, that only man has the power of defining the question and that it lies with him to determine the meaning. Upon the status of this man now depends what he is able to determine, and it belongs to the powerful one to carry out this meaning, so that it lies in his power to impose his will on the world. The mood before this war was like an objectification of social Darwinism, as if the world lies open not only to the capable but also to the stronger, and also that it is rightly theirs. Two giants faced off, of which the one was more interested in the continuation of the status quo while the other sought to change exactly this by radical means.

If one wants at this point to believe the sociologist of elite-theory, Vilfredo Pareto, with the war we set into motion a chaotic riot of elites. Nobody was in a position to bring it to a halt without the madness being even further intensified. The cycle flooded the high offices of state with very different sorts of persons whose righteousness was dubious, though this is not at all a statement easy to defend. One can think that, basically, contradictory motives were amalgamated into "ideas." I can give you as an example the way thoughts derived from Christianity came to be perverted. In Karl Kraus's *Last Days of Mankind*, one will find citations that are simply shocking. It is the thoroughgoing betrayal by Christians of Christ. Another example is the high praise given democracy in the West at the same time that European imperialism is being fostered. What are the states fighting for? And thus the miserable end was again a paradox. The poorest country, shaken by the October Revolution and with the Peace of Brest-Litovsk, waving the white flag, as it were, against the ideas of the old revolution of the "West," promised to become a bearer of hope for the future of socialism. The USA, against its will, got involved in European politics to decide the war, and then left Paris during the peace negotiations.

Of course men are not drawn into war because of ideas and did not continue the murderous slaughter at Uschok Pass, at Verdun, or at Isonzo "of their own accord," but their endurance did bring about the gruesome continuation of the war in thought, even after 1918. This was the first time that such a tremendous war came to an end with neither emotional nor rational closure.

In all likelihood the defeat of the Central Powers was not only the hoped for initiation of a New European Order, which basically failed, but more: in Germany a "culture of defeat" developed. It can be explained with the most highly contradictory factors, for on the one hand the ossified structures were still supported, but on the other hand they had been immersed in an incomparable modernity through the "conservative revolution" of Bismarck. One must always try to imagine how a Prussian military caste, a narrow bureaucracy, and a bigoted Lutheran Church along with anti-Semitism built the foundation for the technological modernization and organization of factories, and at the same time, just after the systematic increase of power in Central Europe, they attained for the first time a unified voice of their own, as a new German imperial empire. The high-minded euphoria was unquenchable, the echo of which can be read about later in Thomas Mann; and yet at the same time it was a variant of revolution. It is the "technician-man" in the form of the German engineer and master craftsman, who in this phase was the embodiment of the doctrine based on discipline. It is this "bone-crusher" with its power, organization, and social management that shapes Germany, and which in the work of Max Weber took the stage as good old Germany. Max Weber described this social-mechanical German world, which in subsequent years made the German into a "worker" in the sense of Ernst Jünger. In this type lies the other revolutionary aspect, which a society of a mechanical form needs. And in him, finally, is the will to run everything as if it were a business. Meanwhile both of Germany's competitors had collapsed: France had squandered its "Carolingian heritage" in the rule of Napoleon III; and Austro-Hungary had become a "European China," as Marx wrote.

Now we should recall Friedrich Meinecke, who in *Cosmopolitanism and the Nationstate* sets out the different political arrangements from Ranke to Bismarck. In distinction from political romanticism, Bismarck wanted to take over the rule and productivity of the planet, speaking of this in perfectly concrete terms in the speech to the Congress of Berlin in 1872, albeit with the exaggerated discipline of an obedient servitude. Probably Benjamin Disraeli was correct in thinking that Bismarck made Germany great but made the Germans small.

Conservative structures, of all things, made the reconstruction possible, in the midst of the first defeat in 1918. One can perhaps represent this with the ideas of Edmund Husserl, by following out the transformation of science into technology. And nobody can doubt that this enormous outbreak of sciences can also be called a revolution of its own. The "German mandarins," as Fritz Ringer called them, allowed all the damage and destruction to be forgotten, for at the technical training institutions and in the faculties of the natural sciences, zeal and ambition continued unabated. The philosophical tradition could be associated with this, as carried forward by the figures of Werner Sombart, Othmar Spann, Max Scheler, Martin Heidegger, and Arnold Gehlen.

Is all this too "abstract?" The 20th century looks so simple because of the wars, and it seems that through the wars it had brought about a tremendous realignment of the world powers, but at the same time there came to be a technological "universality" in world-industrial culture, in "globalization," and in the advent of a "post-industrial" society.

In a good many representations you will surely become familiar with the history of the second half of the 20th century. Of course even the constitutional government of Bonn took part at least, in the denial of Germany through its division into four occupation zones. But the question remains mostly unanswered how this could be the case. Surely this was not due to clever politicians, the flow of trade in society, or bright professors! Probably even then the operation of Max Weber's mechanisms of domination were no longer present. The corset was the frame of the Cold War, the conflict between East and West, and yet this was all the consequence of war.

If then I may give a sketch in this letter, I would not avoid saying that this enormous change in the world was provoked by both these wars. Was Heraclitus right? Will all the pent-up forces be released in war? This means also however that if war is a monster, as Francisco Goya had painted it to be, driving men to an animal frenzy, then man is merely a switch in the tracks of history, actuated perhaps magnetically and setting things off in that fateful direction. Ernst Jünger raved about a total mobilization in which he meant to include the military as well as factory workers and people in workshops and companies. In the meantime, after the mobilization of economic forces, a gigantic body has emerged, that works "like a man," and fights and sees in this the task of creating a future. In its far-reaching effects Bismarck's concept has taken the state of the world out of the "status quo," and has altered it, and at the same time has conjured conflict on a planetary scale. Of course one must not explain this in a linear way as a mere sequela of war. In fact, we now are warring against war. A bit of dialectic must be brought in. If you will, for the first time the Russian revolutionaries in 1917 started a war against war – and won. The results can characterized in terms of international law only with difficulty. Are irregular troops fighters for peace? Do guerillas constitute the voice of a repressed people? Overall, the exhaustion after both World Wars had the consequence of greatly re-enforcing interests in the form of civil wars or paramilitary formations. Of course, there still are remnants of genuine war, but for the most part their success is greatly limited.

I have described many times in previous letters how in the 19th century some people expressed the fear that Europe was planning a collective suicide. At the very time of the First World War, Igor Stravinsky composed *Le Sacre de Printemps – The Sacrifice of Spring*. It encapsulated the European suicide in a ritual of a bizarre ethnology. Later, of all things, warnings appeared in music very difficult to understand, but they were no longer heard in Europe: Bela Bartok, in *The Miraculous Mandarin*, describes the ugliness and repulsiveness of the world in 1927. This obscene world sank to the bottom in the Second World War, and to accompany its media-politics, its brainwashing with its announcements and proclamations, the *Preludes* of Franz Liszt (1854) were chosen or in the case of serious reports, the overture of Wagner's *Götterdämmerung*. There was no longer a path into freedom. Now only a disturbing voice remained, expressing at once a requiem and a ray of hope: Arnold Schoenberg's *A Survivor of Warsaw* (1947).

Europe apparently mobilized all its powers during its wars out of a misunderstanding of Heraclitus. In his way of thinking, the power of confirmation was achieved through war, as the prerequisite to create a new world. Thus the wars in the 20th century were a terrible failure since the one unanimous goal was not reached: Freedom. It had been preserved by emigrants who left Europe, and was established and nourished in a constitution. The idea of freedom had come to "America" with the "Mayflower," and had to be exported back to Europe. Freedom had not been a predominant concern in Europe.

I do not know whether I can be satisfied by this picture. I have only put on paper an excursus that might give you the "color" and quality of a period. And if you should want to hear what destroyed this Europe of the 20th century, I would recommend that you can relatively quickly experience it in its music.

I recommend to you the *First Symphony* of Gustav Mahler, the "Titan" (1898). Or as a contrasting program, *Ein Heldenleben* by Richard Strauss, an orchestral suite, Op.40 (1898). After that, Igor Stravinsky, *Le Sacre de Printemps* (pictures from the heathen part of Russia: 1913); Dmitri Shostakovich, *Waltz #2* (1958?); the adaptations of the waltzes of Johann Strauss by Arnold Schoenberg, Alban Berg, and Anton Webern (1921). Sergei Prokofiev, *The Classical Symphony* (1918); Alban Berg, *Lyric Suite* (1926); Maurice Ravel, *Bolero* (1928); George Gershwin, *Rhapsody in Blue* (1928).

I think that these recommendations ought to provide you an acoustical impression of that time.

All the best, I remain Yours R.

34.
Portrait of an Aunt

Dear Nina, Dear Julian Dear Marie and Vicky,

The last letters I sent you were altogether difficult: my main purpose was to produce a summary of facts rather than thinking of you during the writing of them. They are a report that inventoried everything that went on in my time of life – a presentation of what I have tried to do with the many inheritances, or what I have retained from that inheritance. What I mean by this is relatively easy to explain and then perhaps you can better order my memories. If I remember correctly my childhood actually began right at the end of the war. From the time before the end I have two or three impressions that are extremely vivid in my mind. It was a time completely free of trouble, unaffected by any dangers of war, there at the hunting lodge of my aunt Henrietta. I have already mentioned her to you. Until the death of her son and husband she was in all likelihood a happy person. She must have been, since up to the end it was in her hands to make whatever she wanted of her life. If you should even have a chance to see the portrait of her you will encounter a very sweet and laughing young lady looking out at you, though probably older than the expression on her face and her posture testify. As her father's "little princess" she was spoiled and loved and so at age 18 – at the age when she must have been painted – she was naïve, well taken care of, and carefree. I could today point to no portrait that documents so well a human being free from harm. This was what the photographer's customer hoped for after all, and nothing was to becloud her bright visage. I can remember this glowing face since she never lost it with age. She would come to Vienna regularly to visit the cemetery, and would stay with us.

I give such a detailed description since nobody after me will remember her. After me she will be completely forgotten. This shouldn't happen to anybody! I remember her because of the portrait, since this unpretentiousness of hers was the "natural" bearing of people in the upper bourgeoisie who had no clue that a few years later a war would begin and everything would be destroyed. Every time I see the portrait it reminds me right away of the sad story of the soldier in Igor Stravinsky's *Histoire du soldat*, based on the text of Charles Ferdinand Ramuz, and composed in 1917. This music is the perfect record of the dissonance that accompanied the beginning of that century.

And when in the Second World War Vienna was bombed, we moved for some time to the hunting lodge in Ennstal, near Anzenbach. I now remember the lodge by its "Christ-Child," a sculpture from about 1820, which our uncle had placed on the altar in the chapel of the lodge. It later came to my mother as an heirloom. And because my great-aunt's son, who died young, was my godfather, so I later inherited this sculpture, and it has become very close to my heart.

There was a bit of trouble at that time in Anzenbach. My father told me about a farmer and hunter living nearby who would always announce with rash anger that if a parachutist should land in the area he would shoot him right away. It was a story often reported since everyone was astonished that such a man despite the defeat we anticipated continued to possess a lust for murder – doubly gruesome since the outcome was already decided. What a temper this man must have had, who had the semblance of living in harmony with nature but would persistently express such hotheaded thoughts of killing. It must have been doubly uncomfortable since nobody dared contradict him: one could count on an immediate report to the Gestapo or who knows who. And he was something of a pasha in his small town always threatening that a wrong word might have consequences. All I remember about it was that when this no good man would show up, the talk of the grown-ups would fall silent while he would check the table to see if any smuggled goods were being eaten, or even if a deserter was being hidden. To mention this monster at all, here, is already too much.

At that time of my childhood on I learned that any appearance of a closeness with nature leads to false conclusions. Goatskin hats and Tyrolean loden coats do not at all indicate a good man. Most often, hidden under these clothes, there lies implacable hatred. If we could know why these men are so full of hate we could help, but these men-of-the-land hate for the sake of hate. Hermann Bahr, who was born in Wels, wrote that though he would always hear that a man takes a walk in nature on Sunday because only there will he encounter God, he never saw anybody praying there. So these were not only excuses but also a lie. This is just a comment about that connection with nature one is always looking for in farmers and never encounters. For any farmer, nature is drudgery, and a dreaded cross to bear. Therefore he hates nature with his entire soul. Because of the late Romantics by which they were promised to be exonerated of the tithe and promised military exemption on top of it, the rural population parrots the nonsense that the vacationers from cities are always singing after a mountain climb. Hardly a single farmer ever scaled a mountain, and no mountain farmer dared to attempt scaling Dachstein or Montblanc – not at all because he was afraid to, but because the phenomena of nature for people of his profession are completely uninteresting.

The greatest insult to a farmer would be to envy him because of the beauty of nature that he is imagined daily to enjoy. Nature is his workshop, an unhappy one on top of it. Snow and rain are his lot, as for the wild animals, and his work is for the most part needing to feed dumb cattle – summer and winter, year in and year out. And this is how I had explained to myself the gruesome shiftiness of a man who kept his hunting rifle with him like a bride, and guaranteed he could ambush anybody he might suspect of infringing upon his rules and those of the regime.

Another thing I remember is staying in the basement of our apartment house during the air-raids. I cannot say much about it since I felt none of the anxiety the adults felt. Usually I sat on my grandmother's lap, and usually I would fall fast asleep when the first bombs would strike our neighborhood. Then I would immediately feel the shaking of the building, see the burst of light; sometimes darkness, which led to lighting up the candles. Soviet soldiers once made their way into the cellar and shone their flashlights into our faces. The rumor was that Russians supposedly steal like ravens, which is why I had all the jewelry around my neck, since there was another rumor that the Russians love children and are kind to them.

I have a clear memory that during the war our building was shelled and the walls of the room were broken down. When we returned to our apartment I marveled at the fallen walls: the width of the room was wonderful. After the work of clearing the rubble away, it was like paradise for me, to be able to ride my bicycle through the room which was now quite wide. It was far less dangerous than the street. There one ran into these soldiers and those soldiers, and I couldn't tell which. Below ground one found Soviet soldiers, overall friendly, and they saved us from starving to death. When we had to spend days in the cellar we got very hungry. It was these soldiers who plundered a sweet shop located in the neighborhood and brought us a huge jar of marmalade and another one of artisan honey. These for some time were a helpful stopgap against our hunger.

One event showed us how people are changed in the time of a dictatorship. The father-in-law of my mother's brother lived out beyond the Westbahnhof. Hungry and desperate, during a pause in the battles, he was trying to get something to eat and arrived at our place. My grandmother gave him some of the marmalade the Russians had "arranged" for us. While Mr. High-School Principal was packing up the marmalade he let us know that we could now thank him for not reporting us. This is just one "incidental story" that shows you that a devilish regime destroys families, and drives everyone toward hatred and underhandedness. I remembered this story especially when I was browsing through a little book of Michel Foucault on the *Infamy of Men*, about the archives of the 17th century. I hope you will not need to undergo these experiences – here using these words I cling to against all such experiences.

With the end of the war, a burnt out panzer tank had become the scene for many adventures, on the one hand, and on the other I can still see today the time the Soviet-Russian soldiers drove a herd of cattle along the Gürtel, and then a herd of horses and then of sheep. Everywhere from the balcony window the herds were impossible to miss. Here and there cows would charge toward the lilac bushes and feed on them as long as they could before being driven further along.

My childhood was above all dominated by an image about which I can't say whether it might only my own personal impression, since I have it in front of me like a color photograph. It is morning time, two hours before school. A single light bulb in a chandelier was the only light in the room. The windows were covered over with cardboard. There at the big table my grandmother was in charge and was ladling hot pea soup out of a large pot. Around the table sat my parents and my brothers. Since I did not yet attend school I was sitting on a pile of newspapers in the corner of the room. In all likelihood the impression I have of this scene is so clear because I was positioned like a photographer. All around everything was dark. The war had ended some time before.

When I think of the works of Gertrude Stein, an American who came to live in Paris, France, and there, in 1944, composed an important novel – *Wars I Have Seen*, published in 1945 – I remember having felt a similar phenomenon she described, of time stopping. It is really a kind of still photography. And if time should continue, then there is a sequence of photographs, one coming after the other. One can rather easily give the cause, since we already have been living in the era of photography and have learned to look in the way the photographic apparatus does. In contrast with the running images or a film, with a still photo a close examination became thinkable, and with this an interpretation of a fixed image. Television no longer allows such an "immersion" in the image. A "snapshot" – and our remembrance offers us an uninterrupted sequence of snapshots – is of a different quality than a filmed documentary.

I can remember accompanying my father to the university. I was not at all bothered by ruins and debris. The "Staircase of the Jurists" had been partly destroyed and there above it stood, majestically, an emperor without a head. Still today I hear my father's voice in my ear, saying they would put a "head too large" back on the emperor although it was still possible to choose a better proportion. Then we clattered our way up the half destroyed staircase into the dean's office. The upshot of the visit was that my father was allowed to offer his lectures at home. The university building had been partly destroyed. And Gertrude Stein reported, in the first sentence of her book what I am telling here in a roundabout way: "I do not know whether I should report the things I don't remember as also the things I do remember…" And "before me" as it were, I see the large portrait of Gertrude Stein done by Picasso around 1902.

People had been saying for months that the war was coming to an end, and it now it had, but left no effect upon me. An arena for adventure had been created and opened up. The children were fascinated by the ruins. I myself wondered at the half broken down statues at the old Westbahnhof. They lay on the ground like fallen heroes of antiquity. Later I remembered these "images" when I studied the paintings of Giorgio de Chirico. With the remembrance of this "building sculpture," Futurism seemed to me problematic from the beginning, for it holds out a wish for an aesthetic of totalitarianism. Mussolini's buildings have this character – around the Mausoleum of Augustus in Rome, of all places.

But now you must forgive me. The memories force upon me associations and from these comes forth the material for making a diagnosis. It is a process in art history that the art historians too seldom notice. Our Greek athlete, if he is still present in the Ephesus collection and has not been sent on a journey elsewhere traveling from one exhibit to the next, reappears a dozen times, be it as a conscious homage in the Renaissance to antiquity, or as the image of the beautiful young man as in Classicism, in any case he is no longer a hero and hardly an athlete. The huge Theseus by Antonio Canova in the Kunsthistorisches Museum is far too beautiful to risk his looks pursing the life of a hero. And in fact Canova always designed most beautiful legs for men – always: even for the angel on the tomb of Archduchess Maria Christina, around 1800, in the Augustinian Church in Vienna.

But now I really must return. If a memory is pulled out of remembrance like a photo out of an album, one understands that countless thoughts are immediately attached to it, indeed that they show the path through an entire biography so as to find a place in a new order and in doing so bring up a new structure of meaning. This can serve as an explanation for you. You can immediately come along with me, and follow as starting points the references I make to paintings, sculptures, novels, or architecture, I mention now as having seen before, whether the Theseus or the portrait of Gertrude Stein by Picasso. This is not a parade of personal vanity to impress you but rather I provide you source-clues so that in this our thoughts might meet. And it is truly touching when your eyes see the same thing that I have also seen fifty years ago. Likewise it is touching if you compare your thoughts with mine: in the difference of the thoughts your present receives its uniqueness and immediately it constitutes history and a history of lastingness: the *longue durée* of Fernand Braudel.

Is that so complicated?

These edgeless thoughts seem to have a life of their own, a life as individual as my own life. And yet I have not written this out of my personal motive, for still today my thoughts are of interest to nobody. My thoughts have never interested anybody; even in the immediate family they have hardly been noticed. I understand this, for I have never been able to tell my whole story from turning point to turning point, even though some of these pictures I have were in all likelihood inaccurate. It will affect everyone about equally whether he has been able to tell his story, or has not been able to. It is like the scattered treatment one finds in television reportage. One must be allowed to say "his piece" as to what he has come to know, all the cases brought together as in a school report. It is not so simple as to say that "eyewitnesses" determine the "times." In my own case I have understood, now and then, the "times" – my time in time. This brought me, entirely against my usual habit of self-sufficiency, into the world of high politics embodied by Bruno Kreisky, which brought me to dissenting against a party whose coherence consisted only in its embrace of a laicism held over since the 19th century, a dissent that seemed to me further justified when Kreisky unleashed a senseless conflict with Simon Wiesenthal. Perhaps I will describe this, later.

Though the letter began in such a leisurely way we've now gotten into the years 1975-6. The lesson of those years soured me on "politics" or from any participation in it. On the one hand I would be beginning an uncertain career at the cost of my children and at the cost of family and of the blessings of evening hours at home with flute and song. Ought I get involved in these shallow intrigues and foul slanders? This I had in fact seen, from very close up. If anything noteworthy ever happened it usually achieved only the minimum of what was possible. And is there any point in arguing for a minimalism that is pubescently retarded? About this I will write you later. It is the beauty of democracy that one can choose and ought not let himself be led astray if political people deceive him saying everything is due not only to their performance but to their persistence at working on the issue. I think if their persistence led to anything it was toward consolidating their mandate in the parliament. If there had been any opposition in the so-called "committees" such talk was always brought up like a magic word, and all would fall silent in their meetings even if somebody had proposed that 2+2 makes 5.

This remarkable culture, whose "inner logic" only an ethnologist in African Studies would have been able to explain, was at the time – for fifty years and more – a variant of the democratic, but it had become clear that this "reservoir" of "political numinousness," itself a sort of laicist "mystique of the republic," will come to an end one day. I ask myself, will you be there for that ending, and be able to take part at the beginning of the next variant of the political – without yourselves having become opportunists?

Yes, I suspect that we now have before us completely new political questions. It is not certain whether these questions will still be raised within a republic, within a government of laws, within the maintenance of rights of freedom for corporations and individuals, or whether that will be swept away by a populism like Austrian flags strewn on the ground after a soccer match. (Even this had been sold out, for in the white band of the flag the logo of a Salzburg brewery was emblazoned!).

Has the Austrian Republic lost all shame in this last decade?

You will be able to judge this some day…

Now however, I actually close! It went too far. If you should be confused browse the previous letters. These show the way to Letter #33.

All my love, Your R.

35.
Stories about Little Rascals

Dear Nina, Dear Julian,

Perhaps Julian can read this letter to his sisters. One could even make it a "bedtime story," to the advantage of all: Julian could practice reading fluently and most important aloud, while Marie and Vicky could listen and hear some vocabulary words for the first time.

With this in mind I want to tell you some rather funny stories. They are about school. I remember that there was once a basketball "championship" between two classes. During one of the lecture hours the game had begun, which obviously the teacher who was in charge of the hour allowed. So there were 6 or 7 students missing from the lecture. We absolutely wanted to watch the game. The overwhelming majority of the students watched through the windows in the hallway. The teacher admonished and told us in unambiguous terms to return to the classrooms, but nobody obeyed. A single student was left in the class, one who was always very well-behaved.

The teacher – in Austria the teachers in gymnasium are "professors" – tried to grab some students by the arm and pull them into the classroom. Once he had done this he wanted to herd the next students into the classroom but in the meantime those who had been forcibly "captured" creeped back to the door and out, to watch more of the game. The professor had to recognize that his stratagem was a complete failure. He became more and more angry, and began to scold us loudly and threaten us but he had used up any respect he had. Even to report them to the school director would be fruitless. To the contrary among the students very happy voices prevailed, since our class's team was far in the lead. So since his threats did not work the teacher ran furiously back into the classroom to write the names of those who were absent into his marking book. This would constitute a severe sanction and usually resulted in lowering the grade for behavior. Before he began the entries he became aware that he would not be able to enter all the names of the students in the space provided in the book. Then he saw the well-behaved student at his seat. Of all things he put that student's name into the book. Since the poor student now noticed he had become the victim of an absurd mistake he protested out loud. Meanwhile the game had come to an end. Slowly the students returned to the class. But in the room the wronged one continued to complain, loud and indignant. So the lessons could not be started. And because of the loud protest the professor noted the good student down a second time in the book, because now he was ruining the lesson. The result hardly brought about the observance of class discipline … The remainder of the hour was devoted to laughter and the loud shouts of protest from the twice-punished.

One day it was time for chemistry. This had its own room. Apparently the plan for the class was to demonstrate phosphorus. The teacher explained in detail that it is to be observed in the case of phosphorus that on the one hand it was necessary for life, but on the other it was dangerously flammable. Because of this, phosphorus was kept in its own container immersed in oil since it would immediately ignite if exposed to the air. Herr Professor carefully held a little piece of phosphorus in a pair of tongs and laid it onto a dish. At first all was still, so that we had to kill some time while waiting for the phosphorus finally to ignite. Time went on and the phosphorus neither smoked nor flamed. All of us awaited the horrible stench but nothing happened. Even the professor became impatient. He conceded that its long immersion in oil was hindering rapid ignition. When that still didn't happen he took up a Bunsen burner to light the phosphorus. Even this action had no success. The professor took the phosphorus in his fingers in order to show it to the class and explain its nature and how it is mined. Then he laid the phosphorus back down. Very soon his fingers began to smoke. The burning must have hurt a lot, since he quickly tried putting his fingers under the water faucet. And that did little good.

Earlier on, the subject of biology was called "natural history." It was probably the most far-reaching subject in the curriculum. Biology even today is the longest course of study in the university, longer than medicine or ancient numismatics. But in my school's curriculum the subject had a much reduced importance. It had its own school room and its own cabinet of natural history, which however was never used. The professor himself had a liking for minerology. In his lectures he showed from his "cathedra" various stones, which one was to to recognize after looking at them briefly. In the test these stones would be laid out and one had to identify them. The rock-crystal, sandstone, limestone, coal, or salt were not difficult, but how could one recognize feldspar, olivine, and the thousands of various ore-bearing stones? The first tests ended in disaster. One would eye a given stone in perplexity, and did not even know how to make a start. So I volunteered to clean up the natural history cabinet. In the afternoon the exhibits were to be placed into their glass cases, the stuffed fox among the canine carnivores, the wildcat into its corresponding group. It was a creepy job. My goal was to get a close look at the mineral collection: every stone lay in its correct place, and in front of it was a card referring to its chemical composition and where it had been found. Onto the stones themselves numbers had been glued. So I noted that in fact a number had something to do with the description of the stone. In the end one by one I had made a list of something like 50 minerals. If one could master these numbered descriptions by heart, one would be able to guess the name of the stone that was set before him. And that is how it went. The list was copied and the students learned it by heart. Thus all one needed for the test was to take a quick glance at the stone, and then to shoot back an answer like a pistol shot. The professor was more and more impressed, since not even the classical methods were needed for identifying bauxite and not confusing it with pitchblende. To recognize amethyst was easy; conversely the answer that pyrite was sulphur was a surprise. From then on all that was needed was a quick look – at the number! – and one named the stone. The professor was of the opinion that he had never taught a class that had such mineralogical knowledge. All of us came proudly out of the lesson, but hardly got around the corner before we acknowledged the praise with loud laughter.

There was also a teacher of Latin. As a "classical philologist" he was not entirely "solid" in his subject. Students immediately recognize any weakness in their teachers. Even in the reading of Cicero's infamous complaints against Verres or Catiline, the man showed shortcomings of several kinds. Still worse shortcomings showed up in Sallust or Horace or Vergil. Given the way he was translating we soon saw that he was relying upon help. At that time there were these little booklets called "greasers" that one would happily use to cheat at schoolwork. We noticed that the said "greasers" were regularly folded into the professor's school books. If a student stuttered in his attempt to translate, he would become impatient and give a correction that was word for word from the "greaser." We figured this out very soon. At the beginning of one Latin class he had laid his book on the table but had to leave the classroom suddenly to take care of something. One just had to seize the opportunity! We switched the greaser for another one. Unaware, the teacher returned to the room. He took up his book and chose a student to begin the translating. In truth an oration of Cicero's is not easy, but now the teacher stuttered even more than the student. While it is the case that texts of Cicero are hard to understand, we now heard a sentence that was completely incomprehensible. Whether his translation even *had* a meaning I am still not sure. Perhaps one would not have pulled these strings against this teacher if he had not treated the halting attempts of the students as if the matter were all quite easy. He would read such passages smoothly and quickly, without explaining the sentence structure or the turns of speech.

I have already described general matters about the school in an earlier letter and so I do not want to go on. Perhaps it is thanks to my particular aversion to the school I attended, that I recognized that one must not dislike the facilities of the educational system in general: needless to say there were other, better schools. In all likelihood there are today fewer Nazis and extremists in schools, and hopefully so into the future. Looking back I have learned on the basis of negative experiences to acquire knowledge by other perhaps more successful avenues. I have already given you a hint: there were the museums, the collections, the quiet art cabinets. Today, in the Kunsthistorisches Museum there is still a single room that has the atmosphere that the painting galleries used to have: the coin collection. This interests me only moderately; unfortunately, the medals get the better display, and I miss an attractive display of Greek and Roman coins. I had learned the sequence of the soldier-emperors and the adoptive emperors through the coins, and learned through the "coin-images" about the division between the Eastern and Western Roman Empire.

If I add another story, you will have to make a mighty jump with me. I was already about forty years old. My penchant or preference for museums had not changed. It was advanced through my friendship with Christian Beaufort-Spontin, who meanwhile had become Director of the Collection of Arms and Armor in the Neue Burg. I remember with pleasure my visits to the office of the Director. The dimensions of the room were enormous – as I remember, the ceiling was 20 or 30 feet high and the room itself, though small on the scale of the Neue Burg, was more than spacious. The one window gave on a view of the Heldenplatz and, the other the Ringstrasse and the Kunsthistorisches Museum. I could not get enough of the view. At that time, at least, there was still to be seen a panorama of the city that one could cite as a jewel of urban planning. In a graceful line-up one could see the outer castle gate, next to it the Parliament, the City Hall, the towers of the Votive Church, the Burgtheater, the Federal Chancellery and finally the Palace of Leopold. It was a majestic vision framed in the far background by the Wienerwald. In the room itself there lay folios, and archives on an elegant writing table in the Josephinian style. My curiosity was rewarded, since he told me it was the writing table of Emperor Franz the First. In my imagination I painted a picture of the emperor bent over in study of Lavater's books on physiognomy. It is reported that he would consult these portraits over and over, in order to learn more about the character of a man he thought he should hire. His Majesty was a suspicious man and hoped to get help from physiognomy for making his decisions.

We had coffee on a pietra-dura table that displayed all the kinds of marble from the monarchy of the 18th century and taught the imperial user how various were the marbles he might encounter. It is thinkable that Maria Theresa had once on this breakfast table drunk her hot chocolate – or something else.

Here I will break off this narrative: it hurts. This beautiful square was destroyed. Pre-fabricated houses were erected, serving as temporary quarters for the Parliament. Because of the ponderous installations in heavy concrete, all the buildings in contrast showed them to be a clumsy lie. Allegedly everything will be returned to its former state – who believes that? Meanwhile companies are applying to build a package distribution center underneath the Heldenplatz, to manage 72 million parcels. Even optimists who mouth "protecting the monuments" will be surprised if after years people get used to the sight, and trucks will be carrying out the distribution of parcels for Vienna. The function of Neue Burg has long been a thorn in the side of the city administrators. Since only money counts and with money any vulgar baseness can be financed, the old documents will be removed from Neue Burg piece by piece, and bit by bit, contemporary documentation on civil war, and fascism will be brought in for storage. And next to this of course a "World Museum" – a huge imposture. The work of demolition will be crowned when a "Hitler Café" is built on the balcony of the Neue Burg, which is already called the Hitler Balcony – perhaps also with a paper-maché Hitler, with which one can be photographed: a photo with Hitler on the Neue Burg balcony will cost you 15 euros.

So at that time, when one had no idea this square would ever become the victim of planned demolitions and eradications, I visited Christian Beaufort in the museum on New Year's Day, in order to bring in the New Year with a bottle of Zwetschken Schnapps. From the heated office of the Director one could see the somewhat snowy square, like a fairy tale of history that had not yet happened. After the usual coffee we wanted to start the New Year in a festive way. But the bottle was corked and in the office there was no corkscrew. We searched everywhere and found nothing. Then the Director came up with the brilliant idea that among the collections the hunting cutlery of Ferdinand II was on display in a glass case, and any hunting cutlery would of course have a corkscrew. With an air of official duty and the assiduousness of highest interest in art history, we marched through the halls of the collections; Christian opened the display case, put on his cotton gloves, and took the sought after instrument out of the hunter's parcel. With the corkscrew, smithed by hand in the 17th century, we then opened the bottle, wished each other "Prosit Neujahr," and drank the old schnapps with the greatest of pleasure.

This story is witness of my own "good old times." Guidelines, definitions, decrees, ordinances, and laws were still enforced. After forty years, in my view, this has changed considerably. I fear that the jurisdiction of law and right has dwindled. And it is not only political pressure that seeks to strain the administrative law to the breaking point: the administration itself sees itself as bound no longer by administrative law as once was expected. On this I will report to you later…

Best of wishes, I remain Your R.

36.
How History Influences Political Philosophy

Dear Nina, Dear Julian,

Though in the last letter I promised to write more lighthearted things, I still have to add some thoughts to what I had recalled, thoughts having to do with a reaction to the increasing destruction of city structures from times before, and to expose, with the example of the Heldenplatz, the disharmony within the Austrian self-understanding. Of course a few "less sympathetic souls" will think that I am being oversensitive in this matter, and perhaps also that I see dangers that are not real – but the architecture theorist Sybil Moholy-Nagy once wrote, in her *City as Destiny*, that 130 years before my "time," there was, according to the school of Lewis Mumford, a fundamental hatred of the city which, in a conscious rejection of the city center, led not only to an extreme urban sprawl into the green areas around the capitals, but fundamentally dismissed city centers as "cesspools of vice" and the root of all disease and epidemics. In Vienna the change of city functions had not been carried out according to the template of Mumford, but at least in a sustainable way though unfortunately with no aesthetic ambition of the sort one still always expected in Vienna because of the tradition in architecture since Otto Wagner. These obvious disruptions of our civil framework only depict what was already going on in the development of the state at large. If for instance a department store were built in the city center in 2010, one might be allowed to propose that the façade should resemble a man-hole cover. And if the English architect in question emphasized that he had thoroughly consulted with the city personnel in the project, and had negotiated with them all the fundamentals of the project, and that he wanted to capture the atmosphere and impress it upon his design, so one must acknowledge that exactly this point of view had won the day. The big-name architect's justification is a perfect irony in the case of Vienna, for clearly the new building does in fact reflect the outcome of an analysis of Vienna. And that is, that it is a man-hole cover. Of course the name given to the building is now typical in Vienna: World City House.

I do not want to write in such a way about architecture as would suggest there is some surprising machination going on in Vienna. If I were to say it is just the underlying political situation coming to the surface, it must indeed be due to the erosion of the planning staff, due to neglect and indifference, to a cheapened profiteering, and to a deeper contempt for the people who spend their lives in this city. It begins with the conscious destruction of the city's idyllic places, the small areas that somehow resulted from an unassuming suburban pattern. In Vienna these were the neighborhoods that are now dubbed as Heurige districts, and in the pre-industrial dwellings now on land slated for change. Only Oberlaa is still there, since for a long time it has remained undiscovered by speculators. No longer does it do any good to lament: with the growth of the city the regression of Vienna into the insignificance it suffered in the early Middle Ages can hardly be avoided any longer. But barracks-like residences dominate the scene: an incarnation of hatred for the city.

If it is correct that in the teaching of Hegel religion and history are the focuses of the spiritual life, and even in the blending of them – while of course these go through different political "temperaments" – he saw the concrete incarnation of history in the state. They find exactly this blending in the cityscape with its gothic dome and the palatial area, which not only house the political administration but also in a genealogical sense is the site of the generations – and thus of history.

Religion becomes secularized in the Enlightenment and is institutionalized as membership in a church that is connected with the state. The mythical content is integrated into the state – something for which nationalism is a persistent proof. For the mythification of the state we can look to Prussia. The Prussian state became a church so to speak, starting with Friedrich II. In this secular church after the time of Hegel, the individuals play puppets enacting the puppet show of world history. For Hegel the director of this political play was the "idea" which soon saw itself embodied – in "great men." The ideas became agents operating through the individuals, who are the "actual" leaders.

What I am here sharing with you is the prelude to a history that is hardly understandable if one does not know how the agency of such political ideas is constituted, and in a dialectical way, as parties – thus as a part of the whole taking upon themselves responsibility for the whole, so that the parties become a totality, and totalitarian. This is the final state that had begun so promisingly, so soon before. Some sentences back I pointed out this blending: religion and history hasten toward the decision, and the "kairos," the moment, arrives in the French Revolution. It is both the final state and a promise at the same time. Grandiose ethical criteria push to be realized – equality, liberty, brotherhood – and they hurtle into terror, of red and white kinds. These criteria remained as "idea" and spawned dozens of plans, as well as Hegel's idea of the state, but they lacked as so often a political "personnel." Thus, lofty goals are proclaimed, ideas of freedom, of peace, of social justice, of participation, and of the rule of law. The chances for realizing these arise here and there, especially in the new USA, and one comes to understand the state as fundamentally the power that protects these goals. Little will it have been thought that the political personnel would undergo a change. The former pioneers, the pillars of all democratizations, will be replaced partly by ideologues and partly by anyone who senses a chance for exercising unlimited power in the management of the state. All this is fulfilled in the 20th century.

I can well remember how in elementary school, on the occasion of the 80th birthday of the Federal President, Karl Renner, a touching celebration took place. The war was still deep in our bones, but we sang: "Courageous in new times, free and courageous see us stride…." Thereupon we sang the "Violet" to the melody of Mozart: "Once a boy saw a little rose…." On the podium of the festivity room there stood an armchair, and on the armchair was another armchair, on which the picture of the Federal President was enthroned. Today (2020) we would find it laughable, yet then one was not worried about pulling off a "perfect presentation." We had noticed only that the teachers were not indifferent about it. There was no ironic remark, as one would expect today. Today one would not be able to throw such a party. It would be lambasted with ridicule. Basically this was my "primary experience" of the state: the photo of Karl Renner enthroned on an armchair on an armchair. Since then I know the stanzas of the Federal Anthem by heart, since we practiced it for the celebration: *Hast seit frühen Ahnentagen / hoher Sendung Last getragen* ("You [Austria] have been carrying heavy loads since early ancestral days").

If I ask myself today whether this state is still aware of that historical role, a shadow of doubt comes over me. As far as I can evaluate things, the Social Democratic Party, since Bruno Kreisky and Franz Vranitzky, has dropped any consciousness for the republic. Whatever is left of it is confined in immobility by pressures from our neighbors crowding closely around. The self-assurance that was gained by negating political creative power, had the highly negative effect on the requisite righteousness that today appears to be very nearly unknown to the political elite. The series of scandals, which reached a momentary climax in the scandal of the Austrian Hospital – the renovation of the General Hospital in Vienna, whose completion took about as much time as the construction of the airport in Berlin – was then surpassed by the purchase of the airplanes for the armed forces. Just think: the Airbus company confessed they had accepted about 80 million euros as a bribe. And yet the investigations of the public prosecutor's office were stopped by a high official in the ministry. Just think: with the bankruptcy of a Carinthian bank large-scale public corruption came to light. After the investigation no accusations followed, no trial, and the paper trail was hastily shredded, rendering any future investigation impossible. Just think: before that, the bankruptcy of a Viennese bank with huge industrial investments was quietly "buried." When one of the recipients of a very great amount of money stated that he had used the money to buy paintings, everybody was satisfied. But the result was that the unions in Austria lost their political power. Just think: the "privatization" of the real-estate assets of the republic was accompanied with extraordinary perks, and yet the trial against the former finance minister will clearly drag on so long that no result will be reached.

With these scandals I do not mean to express moral indignation, which would be laughable: I am only describing what has become of Hegel's former state. I note only that the "personnel" has changed. Today the generation that rebuilt the state from its ashes is off and gone: Karl Renner and Theodor Körner, Julius Raab and Leopold Figl. One ought not to cry over it; this is how history goes. No comparison is possible between Emperor Maximillian I and Emperor Franz Joseph. But probably the basic consensus to which Austria owes its resurgence has been lost. Along with this the very vocabulary has changed. When I referred to architecture at the beginning of the letter, I then wanted to say that no effort is seen for building something similar, in the contemporary sense, to the Hospital at Steinhof, which one is now destroying, like the Werkbundsiedlung in the 13th District.

If one must interpret what is now being built in Vienna, it is the echo of National Socialism.

Even at this point I want to reach back to Hegel. It lay in his genius to turn the vocabulary of philosophy upside down. For what did "pure reason" become after Kant? If the mottos of the Revolution were beheaded, why not the pivotal terms in philosophy? It was basically an atrocity to explain history, all its the crimes and intrigues, tricks and vile murders, as constituted by the spirit of the world. And one hardly begins studying Hegel's account before reading that immediately afterwards this is also to be progress in the consciousness of freedom; and all three concepts, over which Kant labored, take on a completely different meaning in Hegel. And in the midst of this exercise in confusion, Marx sought the source of reason in economics. This was hardly a bad decision, but from then on hysteria and wild speculation have only increased. I do not see it differently, since I still am a creature of the 20th century.

I promise you I will continue these unruly thoughts once again. I live in a time of complete insensitivity or also of resentment, but like a steersman I will try to hold to the course. The course? Yes, it has nothing to do with the stock market, nor with the rising and falling of stock prices, but with observations that serve as records of these aberrations... .

I send you hugs, Your R.

37.
What Does Architecture Tell Us?

Dear Nina, Dear Julian, and Marie and Vicky,

In my presentations you will already have figured out that the state of a factual matter comes to be explained by examples from a different area. For the latest matter I wanted, with a short description of a theory of the state summarized from Hegel, to bring to your attention the consequences as well as the ensuing changes. And for the explanation I brought in my perceptions from "public life" in the way I interpret contemporary architecture, which was suitable to illustrate the current management of our country through city planning and what is being built. To what extent I have succeeded, your own evaluation will decide. Now I want to tell you something more about architecture. Probably I should begin with a citation from Leonardo Benevolo, from 1970. He wrote a very comprehensive book on the *History of the City* and, in the present case, on the origins of modern city planning: "What is typical in our culture is shown ... through the example of Jeremy Bentham, who spent the best years of his life and a good deal of his inheritance, to create his 'Panopticon,' a model prison built in such a way that there needs to be only one guard ... with the help of a system of mirrors that allow him to see the prisoners without himself being seen."

If you conceive how the extremely influential doctrines of this philosopher changed the world, it's remarkable that he expended so much thought on a model prison. Doesn't this project go against his basic position of securing the greatest happiness for the greatest number? Doesn't the confined form of life in a prison contradict the basic position of his utilitarianism, namely his fanatical devotion to efficiency of use? One must be careful not to press the comparison too far, but it is surely strange that while the prison is not the place where one really lives, what happiness is achieved by making it efficient? In considering this building we encounter the dichotomy of "structural perfection" and "functional perfection" in the design theory of architecture. I'd guess that as to *structural* perfection, we do wonder at skyscrapers but the Gothic tower serves just as well as a cause of wonder. And we can readily browse through all of history and count up the wonders in which the structure gives buildings their "language" and what they are expressing. Conversely the *function* of a house is the maximal comfort for the user, if the functions in a house, in the design of its rooms, correspond to the possibilities it provides for its use. Indeed with the decision in principle to build houses in accordance with their function, the basis for modern architecture was born. Of course the dichotomy in question is not a new thing: Vitruvius had conceived of both points of view as basic in architecture, calling them *firmitas* and *utilitas*; but by now these two criteria have become radicalized.

It is amusing to view old books about architecture on the display tables and wonder on the one hand over these huge "discoveries" and on the other to recognize that one has always striven toward a certain "rationalism" in architecture, without however recognizing, of all things, that mastering functionality would also need to take this rationalism into account. Very late did it become clear to us that the hypertrophy of constructing larger and larger palaces could not meet this demand, however magnificent their appointments might have been. At the same time we are told, in the history of construction, that the aspect of construction basically called for less attention than bringing construction together with an appropriate concept of the functions. If you look at a baroque castle you will quickly recognize that the owner should have used a bicycle to pass through the rooms, if only such were appropriate to his standing. Today after all we build hospitals that have comparable dimensions, and indeed a motorized gurney is provided for moving from nursing station to operating room.

Structural conceptualizations are to be seen as an inner language of a building: they are like monologues that comment on inanimate phenomena, spin thoughts, and even encourage one to the bold thought of constructing a cupola. Functionalism can achieve this clarity of design only with difficulty. On the one hand it calls for "learning by doing," and on the other, the functions will always be defined in different ways by the users. Thus up until the 20th century we rarely find functional arrangements, unless the function of pure experience and pure enjoyment calls for architecture that has no other purpose– as in Andrea Palladio.

In both approaches, the structural and the functional, the struggle for technical beauty dominates. We of course immediately notice that they both achieve their ideals in magnificent bridges, viaducts, and in railway structures: a kind of perfection had really been achieved, but that cannot be carried over into residential architecture. One can hardly believe it, but soon behind each of the positions an ideological concept was to be found. In the structural version one had in mind, with its conceptual clarity, to set aside the confusions introduced by historicism. It was primarily a battle against the perversity of decadent civilization. One joined in the criticism of Rousseau against the rococo; one allowed himself however not to speculate about what ought to be defined as natural. With constructivism one basically closed himself off from any debate, but thinks instead of the "second nature" which is given to mankind in culture. It is an interpretation of the philosophy of Francis Bacon, from the 17th century, for whom the environment is to be ordered according to the laws of reason. Put another way, one was proceeding from the idea that all forms and qualities in nature follow laws that the human being is equipped to intuit because analogous structures lie within one's self. From this outlook man's position becomes ambivalent: he belongs to nature and yet at the same time rises above it. The best illustration is the famous cupola at Santa Maria del Fiore, the cathedral of Florence, where an example of tremendous construction by Filippo Brunelleschi arches as it were over the whole city, suggesting also the idea of the firmament, or a super-nature.

The "functionalists" never thought in these categories. Their interests focused much more on the individual needs of man. It was important to recognize that one was not dealing with hermits, but with how to create an individual's space surrounded by countless others. David Hume gave a quite precise formulation: "The comfortableness of a house, the strength of a horse, the spaciousness, solidity, and speed of a fast ship make up the distinct beauty belonging to these various objects. An object that will be called beautiful is pleasing only because it has the tendency to bring forth a distinct effect." Jeremy Bentham connected his socio-philosophical elaborations with this viewpoint, extending it to the economy, to aesthetics, daily life, and the wish for happiness. All of this is contained in Bentham's approach to morality and to lawmaking. The standard is fitness for the goal, which is the engine for enriching happiness and well-being.

If I may allow myself to take up these theoretical inferences from the history of the ideas of architecture, I do so with a view first to justify my current criticism, and second to stress in this representation the qualitative difference between the building traditions that have come down to us. One can make dozens of arguments in meetings, from too little money to the cost of land and of construction, from building codes to procurement of permits, but these are only the negative penumbra of an architecture of deliberate dullness. Whereas in the 19th century one still knew the stature of a science of architecture, at present we only rarely experience examples of an aesthetic that is determined by expediency. Already in 1759 William Chambers remarked, in his *Treatise on Civil Architecture*, "Architecture paves the way for commerce: it builds ships and ports and warehouses for receiving and storing goods; it lays out streets ... it levels hills, it fills valleys, it spans bridges over deep and raging rivers ... and thus it eases the trading of wares. Commerce leads to prosperity and prosperity leads to well-being. Pride and pleasures in turn bring forth a thousand refinements, which in very large part could not be achieved without the help of architecture." This prelude of the future function of the cities of millions shows unambiguously the goal that was to be achieved by architecture and city planning. Of course the first great sin was to crowd and fill the large cities during the 19th century with tenement housing; and the architects who did this were the ones who are counted among the great social politicians, who wanted to end these crimes against people who in addition had no wealth – by means of social housing.

Now you can see relatively clearly the purpose of what I am writing here. It was only in the 20th century that the break occurred, which I describe in this way: practicality, which in Vienna was embodied by Adolf Loos, became a straitjacket for housing. This becomes clear in the adoption of new units of measurement. Whereas Adolf Loos had based his designs on the old measures that accommodated the body and corresponded to the "nature" of man, one now switched to the "technical metric measures of Paris," adopted in the French Revolution. The meter was originally intended to be the smallest unit according to the circumference of the earth. Otto Wagner already allowed the staircases to the station stops of the city road to be built only according to the Schönbrunn yard-measurement, but also used units based on body proportions. In Central Europe one had begun to build in the National Socialist manner, since after 1945 the architects who were educated then were doing the reconstruction. Only in the rarest cases was a different accent considered. A commonplace understanding of cost-benefit relations prevailed, which began to colonize the ideas of architecture throughout the world. This tendency of "globalization" was supported by the spread of Stalinist architecture. And thus two totalitarian systems have had a lasting effect on our later aesthetics, and indicate a durability and dominance that casts the schools of architecture in a rather unfavorable light.

Now I have kept you for a long time. It would be a fine reward for this work of writing if you would finally begin to see your life-world with different eyes. Then you would be able to recognize that in opposition to the tradition of humanism a certain quality of life is being withheld from you. Earlier, it was the professional duty of the architect to build exactly what served to better the living environment. A result based on this professional ethic I have not seen for quite a long time …

All the best, your R.

38.
The Old Relation
between Art and Politics

Dear Nina, Dear Julian and Marie along with Vicki,

As I look back at these last letters and go through them, what is becoming clear is that in (my) present time we perhaps find ourselves in a new kind of crisis. If I think of the 18th century, when in the course of those years one felt that he recognized a crisis, it was the Enlightenment in general which, carried along by philosophy, was trying to open a new perspective. It may well ask whether this way was the right one; the facts of history teach us that it led to a multiplication of problems. Though it is somewhat too simple to say that these problems have from then on – from 1789 – marked the political orientations as either "conservative" or "progressive" – originally in Spain – still, these opposing movements became the origin for partisan democracy. In order for that time to arrive, decisive incidents in history had to happen that would "sharpen" the political situation to such an extent that only an either/or remained.

For the most part, both revolutions hold a place in our minds, the American and the French as well, by which the overthrow of Paris became the igniting spark for all Europe if not the whole world. And to draw upon my last letter, it is the rather absurd and also totalitarian architecture – or better, these architectural nightmares – that pay good witness for what direction the revolutionary element was going, though at the same time the characteristics of absolutism were also maintained. There is no way to understand this better than in the planning of the salt-works town, Chaux, in 1778, by Claude Nicolas Ledoux; or in the designs of Étienne-Louis Boullée for a 1784 cenotaph for Isaac Newton. The overheated fantasy of pure form, the dominance of geometry, the style predominantly doctrinaire, and the disturbing ambivalence between the totalitarian and the revolutionary ought to perplex anybody, for these are the first signs of modernity approaching. You have to ask yourself, when you see reproductions of these plans, designs, and sketches, how these strange products of the imagination make you feel – to what extent you feel you are being spoken to, or whether you simply reject these "pictures" and perhaps even find them alarming. As one reflects upon this development in art history, he also may consider the seldom noticed "fetishistic plans" of the baroque, the dismissive and ruthless gesture of a graceless geometrization, as if all the elements of nature could be represented in this formalistic way. Just as in the formal garden of the baroque the intrusion of the human knows no bounds – indeed it is a "rape" of nature that is there on display, and scene-setting appears to be more important than respect for what has "come to be" – so also these sketches and plans are an essential source for understanding political extremes. Very soon after the revolution had sought to abolish social classes and strata, we turn the page and find terror, out of which a new emperor, polished and shiny, was "invented" – Napoleon. From the euphoria of planning sprang an "axis-planning" (in the manner of Albert Speer), a renewal of the "planning grid" of antiquity to be seen in the founding designs of American cities.

A comparable "revolution" took place in the theater. The most important and influential step was the *Marriage of Figaro* by Pierre Augustin Beaumarchais. The incredible circumstances surrounding the banning of its performance in themselves constitute a bit of "political theatre." In the end the King himself (Louis XV) had to impose his prohibition, since neither the censor nor the minister of justice dared to do so. Out of a wanton willfulness or a test of strength, the brother of the King, wanted it to be performed for his birthday, in 1784, but right in the presence of the assembled court nobility the police arrived and forbade the performance. It was princes, counts, and barons who loudly protested the censorship, at the performance. The revolution had already arrived! Three months later a rehearsal was produced, once again at the country castle of the King's brother.

For a sociologist the decisive question is which cultural sector should be seen as the more important. Art and politics were two fully differentiated systems and for the first time art was victorious over the traditional ruling power of Versailles, in its political assertion of equality.

The aftermath was of course more embarrassing for the King. Art, already in its most general sense, had so high a rank in the society of the Estates that the prohibition of the performance came across as an intolerable paternalism being asserted over all the arts. During the excited debates Beaumarchais publicly announced his retirement from public life in protest. This also was felt to be an intolerable turn of events, for in that time an artist represented the cultural self-understanding of the elites. Thus the King himself had to mediate. Money was offered to the poet, then a badge of honor, but Beaumarchais turned them down and continued sulking. One had to ask, how could Beaumarchais be appeased? Rather haughtily he replied that the queen, Marie Antoinette, would have to read aloud from his play during the King's meal. It was an humiliation, but the King acquiesced nevertheless. This was the second step toward dismantling the monarchy. The King's meal had become a showcase for politics.

The "moral" defeat since then pushes any subsequent conservatism into obsolescence, even into the irrational: namely, a refusal to look at the present. Conversely, the consequences of the revolution underwent their own conjugation, into the bourgeois orientations of the liberals or the nationalists. Of course the

French Revolution surpassed all previous upheavals. Whereas the "Glorious Revolution" in England was still carried out by the tension between theological reform and the political attempt to oppose the royal house, the plan of a precocious delimitation of absolutism; whereas the uprisings in France consisted in a conflict between feudal possession of land and farming serfs or the battle of the farmers, as a consequence of the Reformation; the Revolution from 1789 had a definite direction of its own. First, the executor of this idea was Napoleon. He demolished the German principates and confined the Pope within his territories, which an enlightenment thinker would have thought impossible. The "universality" of the French Revolution was succeeded by a capitalist version, and as a revolutionary power capitalism determined what has been happening in politics and economics ever since, up to the 21st century: In 1989, it brought even communism to its knees.

I began this letter with the assertion that just now we are facing a crisis. Of course it was not brought on by the pandemic in 2020, nor was it brought upon us with the failure of the banks, the stock markets, and stocks prices after the successful victory of capitalism over communism and even socialism. It was also not brought upon us by a new realization that climate and environment must be given a different kind of attention and that they force us to be more prudent about our own resources. So then how is it we are in a crisis, really? The cause probably lies in the poverty of our ideas! We can only imagine a future by means of prospects that date back fifty years. And we will be able to point to many areas in which the future seems to offer no alternatives, anyway. In architecture thousands of buildings, worldwide, are being built every year, that are directed vehemently against our needs for aesthetics and tranquility, and which at the same time damage the environment in a way that can hardly be kept under control. We have indeed our doubts about the economic system of this world and yet we continue with it, either because the alternative is authoritarian socialism or because we choose half-heartedly to join in with it since we do after all draw our dividends from it. Our belief in a pending ecological collapse, or even an economic collapse, opens up an excuse to achieve paradise in the interim, a prospect that now shapes all commerce in a new way. It is not likely that the crisis will go away; more realistically it will become our characteristic since the criteria of this latest "modernity" lead the Western World to appear in a new way. Even contemporary art testifies to the crisis, for how long and how often can one pour a bucket of paint on a canvas, how long and how often can cleaning implements with broom and shovel, cement, rubble, bricks, and coarse gravel be presented as a "ready-made" improvisation, which can only be compulsively repeated again and again? How often can one paint over pictures, copper engravings, steel engravings, and representations of the crucifix? It indicates a crisis – a crisis also recognizable since for the large part it will be institutionalized as a theme of cultural politics in almost any museum, recommended for a viewing that leaves every viewer without a clue. When science failed to overcome the crisis, one shifted one's hopes to art. It had been a common practice for art to maintain a vision of the future as a saving shore, and yet art now commemorates only the end of the war, only destruction, only hopelessness. We have not come much farther, as the collections teach us. They are sunk even deeper in this shoreless ocean of saying nothing. They afford us no vision of a world we were once promised.

One ought not jump to conclusions from this. Who after all knows for sure there are not "other worlds" in our world? Until 1492 "we" had not known that there is an "America," just as we do not know whether there is life on some planet or other. Who after all knows whether a new and original way of pictorial art has been embarked upon in Chile, or who knows here in Vienna whether there is not some great music in North America even now, or as indeed there is, in West Africa. Do we perhaps intend only to go back into that cave Plato always suspected was the abode in which we spend our lives? So something is being withheld from us, and the more we think that reality has a perfect representation in the media, as if a view outward from our cave, the more is it withheld from us, and an attempt will be made to strike us blind.

Surely it is not our destiny to leave behind our world and history and society and culture, and our power to innovate, with this risky game. Have we no idea any more what something new would look like?

We pay for the later consequences of the French Revolution with the loneliness of our thought, with our deracination from all traditions and the loss of continuity. I must write you still more about this – and once I do these letters will amount to nothing other than a report on all the things that seem to be lost.

All the best, I remain, Your R.

39.
State of Mind as a Virtue

Dear Nina, Marie, and Vicki; Dear Julian,

In the last letter a certain problem became clear: one must either resign oneself to the ugly picture – that is, to stand stalwart on the brink of the abyss, "civilizational collapse" – or one must take seriously the latest assertions of art as telling indications about our situation and that civilization is to be judged by different criteria. This is not just a matter of speculating about our future. You remember I once asked in these letters, "Are we still useful?" I merely borrowed it: It was the great martyr Dietrich Bonhoeffer who put the question to us once before, in his last diaries before he was murdered. And if we do think we are useful, then this decline so often predicted will not come about. It can only come about if we begin to doubt our own usefulness. And this can happen to us faster than we might like. Generally, one loses his usefulness if he gives in to opportunism. I myself know that this inner battle against opportunism is a difficult one.

In order to make this clearer for you, I can refer to the TV movies that were broadcast on the occasion of the 90th birthday of Karl Merkatz. Because I got to know the actor, and valued his simple manner, and had heard how his learned profession always imposed on him the duty of being clear and sincere, and that he had learned carpentry, I saw that the tantrum he threw against authorities, no matter which party, was to be taken not as a pleasant joke but rather as a warning to take nothing for granted. I am afraid the directors of the film did not get what was being indicated here. They believed that Merkatz's way of speaking was just an amusing and absurd aspect of his own person.

The first step that leads to personal "usefulness" is virtue, adopting a position. Now you will ask which position I recommend – there are so many positions. On the pragmatic level I will lodge the objection that surely when a person in power violates the moral order one has the duty to protest and object. And that no exceptional state of affairs justifies the violation of moral rules. And we know that such rules were not discovered easily, are not just arbitrary like rules in a game, but that they are empirically grounded, and even when violation "becomes the rule," it does not therewith become sanctioned. In these cases we can say that such contradictions always stem from a disproportion between those in power and those who are affected, but they are not only to be observed there. In the family context one encounters a sort of false reciprocity, and we must be candid about this. It is the spirit of puberty to be contrarian, and so we must always keep in mind that for a teenager to express a contrary opinion might not be merely frivolous or self interested but rather arises out of a sense of an ethical imperative: this is why a young person always sees right through what seems to him a "compromise" made by adults.

Now I have gotten into an inhospitable territory. Back in the 17th century, not only did the natural sciences flourish, but also the understanding of politics. The modern "raison d'état" was developed, political obedience was institutionalized, and the free practice of religion was guaranteed, since from now on religion has an importance more and more restricted to the "state." This strongly affected the church, in this case the Roman Church, which maintained its political position more or less with its Counter-Reformation. Thus the battleground shifted to the relation between politics and morality, a topic that had increasingly been abandoned from the self-representation of the church since the Reformation. We know what Niccolò Machiavelli is supposed to have thought about this; we know that the tight connection of church and the power of the regime was managed in a new way; and we also know that Jean Bodin's writing on the state expands the scope of the state's competence and authority in times of need and emergency, implying that the state, despite the claim of absolute power by Louis XIV, it not to become a tyranny. Thus Machiavelli's vindication of honor was back on the table in politics, never to be taken off it again. At the time, one wrote: *Lex specialis derogat legi generali* ("A more specific law trumps a more general one").

Bodin had described tyranny as the opposite of a "state," so that from this the Spanish theorists of natural law had drawn the conclusion that murdering a tyrannicide was justified. But I did not want to go that far. I have only highlighted one possible consequence in the case of opportunism. Therewith the reference to "leaving truth behind despite better insight" unjustifiably accelerates the problematic situation, since the history of law points to a variety of forces that oppose the system of norms, in accordance with a society of classes. The legal order of the nobility looked different from that of the burghers and the farmers. Besides, we are in the 17th century: new systems of norms arose out of activities brought on by the new mercantile economy, which now had to do with the merchant class. So it was extraordinarily important that a professional ethics arose out of the *ius singulare* mentioned above.

In the wake of this development the fact is significant that with the expansion of the various professions and occupations, very different rules of conduct came about. What is special about these rules of conduct is that while they were bound up with generalized moral norms, very different "methods of implementation" came to be recognized. Thus one guild had stricter laws but another less strict. For example, must a physician tell the truth to a sick patient?

Since we have begun writing about the relation between morality and politics, we must first be clear on whether a politician is bound by a professional ethic analogous to that of a physician, or a peasant, or an employee in a bakery. Immediately we must recognize that with democracy a "deprofessionalization" of the political profession is introduced. One is no longer as before automatically part of the political regime by dint of family background or possession; one is no longer guaranteed representation with a seat or a voice in the legislative assembly by virtue of how much tax he pays or how great are his capital assets. One often hears today that a person is unsuited to a political job because he has not acquired the needed knowledge or is not suited from his work experience. This reminds us that there ought to be a professional group of politicians as was the case a long time ago. Only a member of the noble class was thought eligible to be a minister. Democracy came onto the scene with a completely different conception, namely that everyone has a share of political talent and that taking up of political office is determined by elections, and not birth or wealth. And yet even in a democracy one would grant to politicians a certain latitude for exercising their discretion in meeting goals, demands, and necessities. Actually it is quite simple: in any profession there is a certain discretionary allowance without which one could not carry out his job. In specific professions there are even specific and binding rules that establish a professional ethics and are binding upon those who share them.

Now I must offer you a striking quote from Benedetto Croce's *L'onesta politica*, written in 1945: "Although nobody, when it comes to curing his own wounds or to undergoing a surgery, calls for an honest man … and instead everyone seeks and retains physicians and surgeons who whether honest or not must be cunning in medicine and surgery, … in politics one demands not politicians but honest men who are at best gifted in some other competence." This observation by Benedetto Croce, the great historian and philosopher of culture, hints that amateurism along with "natural talent," which again and again are demanded in democracy, do not suffice, and that such a principle is probably tenable only if the politician has at hand a professional political staff. Max Weber had a similar conception in connection with his notion of a "political calling." The question about morality becomes a problem when it degenerates into the small change of so-called political answerability, in which it would never become clear what sort of answerability could here be meant. Benedetto Croce solved this problem a different way since he not only spoke of the spheres or the areas as if separate from each other but as if the political life basically prepares one for moral life. With this reversal he saw in politics a creative and innovative contribution that always subordinates ethics to new, altered, and broadened rules.

Hegel had made this far easier for himself, for in his eyes even an illegal action was justified in politics. After him, important schools developed which then had an influence on politics, and this fundamental idea proved a disservice to political morale and allowed totalitarian power-grabs at one's own discretion or that of the party.

We often read that democracy is undergoing far-reaching transformations especially due to the growing influence of the media. On the one hand the political options, as reflected in the media at least weekly, evince a thoroughgoing democratization and depict thought as being dynamic, and on the other not a few complain that because of this the "deeper meaning" of political policy is being forfeited. Meanwhile mere opinion surveys not only foster populism but influence political decisions.

When in my role as an editor on domestic politics in 1972 I would attend sessions of parliament as a reporter for radio, there was regularly a rise in excitement among the secretaries of the ministries as 5PM approached. Around this time of day the first newspapers would appear and from these one would learn what was being said about a minister on one or another topic. And it happened more than once that an especially negative response would not only cause more attention to be paid to the matter, but also in a considerable number of cases that a proposed policy would be abandoned. Nobody had the courage to persist under the circumstances and clarify for the journalist or the author of the report why a given line was to be followed. It was clear evidence that published opinion has a stronger effect than public opinion.

The transformations are not limited to that, but become broader in the sense once prognosticated by Vilfredo Pareto, namely that democracy turns itself into an authoritarian and then a fascistic system. Even Pareto joined in voicing the complaint about the downfall of civilization, although with more justification, for in fact this transformation had succeeded, in the case of National Socialism and Fascism, which both had been interpreted as revolutionary forces. The statement by Boris Pasternak in his novel, *Doctor Zhivago* can serve as a summary: "The same thing happens over and over in history. An ideal, a sublime idea, becomes coarsened, becomes materialized. Thus did Greece turn into Rome; thus did the Russia of the Enlightenment turn into that of the Revolution."

But where did Cicero go wrong? You must have heard about Marcus Tullius Cicero in your Latin lessons, if they are still offered. He was a relentless opponent of corruption, opposed a putsch against the republic, and was therefore a bitter opponent of Caesar. As an "amateur philosopher" he knew the fate of Athens, he knew political philosophy and stood more on the side of Aristotle, which marked him as a political pragmatist; and yet at the time he had no reliable allies, whether among the optimates or among his own supporters. He understood the repudiation of Caesar to be the last chance for the republic, and sympathized with those around Brutus, but in the meanwhile the republic itself no longer had any advocates. Already the triumvirate under Caesar, with Pompey and Crassus, was far removed from the political goals Cicero wanted to see realized. Thus he was the last vestige of republican Rome and could do nothing to stop the glorious dictatorship of Augustus.

These days of course other rules apply. This does not mean, however, that a liberal government of laws under a constitution guarantees democracy forever. Perhaps we have seen in 2020 the replacement of democracy in the USA, with the advent of a strongly populist party and the disappearance of the classical power struggle between the majority and the opposition party in the US Congress. Overall, politics is being ruled by entirely different regulative forces that have less and less to do with democracy. Rather than a populism, or a reversion to an authoritarian principle, it is the powerlessness of the "no longer visible" populace, robbed of any voice by the media, and a recasting of the political with economical accents that indicate a dramatic loss of competence in politics. The terminology will not change: the instruments of democracy will continue to be understood in their own terms, just as Hitler did not abolish the Reichstag, but the loss of real functioning becomes evident in the waves of privatization, outsourcing, and the reduction of endeavors previously run by politics for the benefit of private interests.

In the flow of writing I almost forgot what the ethical criteria should be in view of the transformations. It can be that the elected representatives are no longer answerable to those who elected them, but instead become representatives for society or even for the state. Thus their mandate detaches from the will of the people in order to have in mind the interests of the state instead. In Central Europe elected officials have lately had to mitigate overwhelming tensions. In the House of Representatives no consensus is in the offing. Just as the Austrian Parliament was once dissolved by a margin of one vote, in 1934, which "levelled the path" to civil war, so today we think we are in a similarly lawless environment.

I very much hope I can have a chat with you about these topics, not about the media or the expansion of technology but about whether we still conceive of ourselves as political actors, thinking about political institutions, and communicating about them person to person.

Of course I could just cry: after reading my overall representation you can still always see my strong belief in the institutions of politics. But now I am not so certain that my concerns will even be understood. Up until the 18th century, Aristotle's *Nicomachean Ethics* dictated our principles of political virtue. These have today disappeared. If we should ask a representative in parliament about this, ethical rules will be far less familiar than an offsides rule in soccer. The former is something from the dim pages of history; the latter is real, concrete, and on any Sunday an object of heated debate. In all these cases the controversy is cast as moral. We may not however take for granted that the beautiful qualities always be there. It is always storms that annihilate everything, storms that force the sea to wash over the coasts, and that get those who are reluctantly looking for higher ground to admit that actually there is no way back.

Somehow I have gotten off the path. I just wanted to provide you an exact basis about how the rules of conduct and democracy can serve as virtues for carrying out the rule of law. And in the course of doing so I notice that this is futile, or can be futile. Any of the representatives, anybody in leadership, anybody in his party must have recognized he was duty-bound by his private sense of right. Many times Manès Sperber repeated his warning that a government of laws cannot stand if the private sense of right is not a "norm of what ought to be," which makes clear to me my relationship with the community. The great jurist Norberto Bobbio closed his treatment of politics and ethics with the admonition, "Meekness is synonymous with the refusal to use force against anyone and everyone. Meekness is therefore hardly a political virtue, or is even – in a world bespattered with blood by the hatred of those in power, whether great or small – the opposite of politics."

I must end the letter here. If one understands what I am trying to say, he ought to find the foundations of political behavior for the future. It is indeed absurd: meekness and politics! Or did the Gospel not say, "Blessed are the meek, for they shall inherit the earth." Politics is not everything! The outlook that politics is everything is truly scary!

So, I end here. Perhaps more, another time?

Hugs, my beloveds, Your R.

40.
Pedagogy Offsides

Dear Nina, Dear Julian, Vicky, and Marie,

This will surely be a shorter letter. I think that's a good thing, since a long letter makes one groan, especially when it deals with a complex topic. And I can also see that in some of my letters the connection between thoughts is not so clear. Sometimes two or three topics are being presented; the thoughts connecting them might be obvious to me but for the reader they might be obscure. This is a general problem, given what the experience of reading is like these days: How does a person read, if he still reads at all? It was remarkable that the latest Matura in mathematics, in 2019, was a failure because the majority of those taking the test were unable to understand the word problem. It has always been my suspicion that the majority of people are functional illiterates and this specific form of a lack of cultural competence is not "redressed" pedagogically in any way.

I have always said that pedagogics is one of the few subjects at university that does not belong to the canon of the sciences. Though Viennese pedagogy volunteers everywhere to tell us in the most proud and haughty terms that it is an empirical science, these pedagogues have from the beginning misunderstood what people are. They wonder not at all that such a wide variety of educational systems since antiquity has produced such a wide variety of results, hardly any worse than today's ever-so-scientifically supported contemporary one! They actually believe that if they have twenty children before them, sitting quiet and docile at their desks, they can now conduct tests and make measurements, and using this as their data can derive the optimal education and the proper school structure. The result of all this is the Austrian "all levels together" form, about which I have always thought that regardless one still needs the rudiments of useful knowledge; and they predict that besides, all we need will be coming from Japan, China, Korea. School education in Austria means, according to the plans of the educators of highest competence, that "We can settle for less." Under these conditions we are resigning the broad field of educational success to the Asiatic subcontinent, and announce with unquestionable pride that we have made social learning the most important part of education at school. Thus if Seppl, Ibrahim, Padme, Kevin, Sarah, and Igor get along with each other nicely, the goal of learning has been achieved. It appears these youngsters have come to be united in heart and soul, that the dreaded inequality in education has been diminished – while the heads of the sweet little things are full of mush, and they are fingering their telephones like gambling addicts, and their conversations sound like strung together advertisement slogans. And one can aver, according to their respective backgrounds, that Igor does not know Dostoevsky, Sarah has never yet heard the word "Talmud," Padme and Sevil will know nothing of the *West-Eastern Divan*, Kevin has no clue about Henry Miller and Hemingway, and Ibrahim has no idea about the *Kalila wa Dimna*. That Seppl knows nothing of the *Nachsommer* proves he is a successful graduate from one of the better schools.

For me the issue is not the pathetic infection of this universal oblivion, but where and how these youngsters are to find their place. Where will they learn their identity? I have already written that Ibrahim, Padme, at least – and perhaps also Muhammed, who was integrated into the class only recently – have heard an imam in some mosque in the suburbs, who took them into a back room and offered them an invitation to the "Islamic State." And soon all three had enough money in their hands to take a flight to the Near East.

I mustn't take this further. I just recall again that I wrote about the haughtiness of those members of the pedagagic institute and then I had the students they produced before me. In the context of a lecture, one of the "natives" gave the answer that Luther lived in the 18th century. He had no trouble shifting the sovereign of Austria, Maria Theresa, over to the 19th century but began to have difficulty when I asked him whether Emperor Franz Joseph ruled jointly with Hitler. I never had problems with such answers. If the student was ready to take some advice and sacrifice a week of his time to bone up on the fundamentals of European history, he could have repaired all these deficits in very short compass.

I remember chatting with a physicist, some 25 years ago in Ravello, who complained that it was taking more and more time in the first semester to purge the students of the nonsense they had gotten from their schools. While the educators had imagined they had designed the best course prerequisite to physics, the students of Hans Thirring needed two years, as it turned out, put basic understanding of the new physics on a meaningful foundation.

We can take no pride at turning up our noses and complaining about the state of the schools, and yet according to my experience the tenor of education is that one no longer needs to know anything. It is common knowledge that classical philology has been almost completely dropped. It bothers nobody that the foundations of the natural sciences were written in Greek, just as nobody is interested that even a Nobel Prize winner in biochemistry – Manfred Eigen – declared that learning Greek is indispensable if one wants to study chemistry with any success. If you ask a chemist about Heraclitus you look into a face completely stumped, and the person you are looking at will immediately think you are talking about a new chemical element. For a young natural scientist heraclitus and masonite are made of the same elements. They then sit in their laboratories, operate machines that perform automated analysis, and thanks to their equipment continue somehow to give us ever more innovations, in biochemistry.

I do not want to be unfair but there was a time when the reason to study was to meet what is new equipped with knowledge of the old. Isaac Newton once said one must try to climb up upon the shoulders of giants. If I transfer this idea to sociology, to sit on the shoulders of giants counts as a negative. The society of today has no history behind it, the present is no longer a way-station between the past and the future; rather, the here and now is a poorly defined interval of impotence and mental derangement. Basically one would have to rename the European movement in sociology "socio-zoology," since it brought about a complete naturalization of humankind, who more and more often are wearing our pre-history on themselves: tattoos on their happy nakedness. Today I discovered at a gallery the photograph of a naked woman, and on her body was tattooed, in English, "NUDE IS FREEDOM." It is worth noting that freedom was here designated not by the word with the Latin root (*libertas*), but rather the concept was taken from the German root *frei*, in which "freedom" bears no connotation of rectitude. "Freedom" is going to the beach for sunbathing, is gathering somewhere to drink together during a pandemic, is the ego unbounded.

I write you about this since I want to bear witness to an other world, which surely does exist, in other cultures and on other continents. If I again recall the institute of pedagogy, one of the much discussed means of intellectual levelling, meant therewith to continue the tradition of the socialistic educational ideal, was to bring everyone together into the classroom at the same time. It is a mindset unclouded by knowledge of any kind; the studious educational ideals of history are of course nearly unknown. In the 17th century one had probably done more for equal opportunity in education than in the 20th. It would have been unthinkable to conceive of modernization of the "state" if there had been no students in the cloister schools, who came from the most varied of backgrounds. If one sees the rolls of the students at Kremsmuenster one quickly realizes that boisterous farm children sat next to the children of the Count. And if the farm boy showed some deficiency it redounded to the pride of the teacher to bring the lad to the level of the noble adolescents. The graduates rose in rank to the high bureaucracy, represented enlightenment and service, loyalty and the effective discharge of high office. The whole phenomenon of Josephinism would not have been possible without these "burghers" and "peasants." In all likelihood this was still the theme of the social democratic educational republic in Vienna, from Otto Glöckel to Alfred Adler, from 1919 to 1934.

Now I have once again gone far afield from the topic. If I want to declare what happened to us and was brought about by the sciences, I can present an amusing example from my own household. Nobody, unfortunately, understands that my principal aversion to a dishwasher comes not from a mere quirk – it's not just spleen – but from a deep conviction that I can quickly support with the help of the Tao te Ching. Given the disastrous way dishwashers work, I have to make my breakfast on cheap dinnerware from a supermarket. I have to eat off dishes that are basically the equipment of an emergency shelter. In the cupboard there are sets of dishes, indeed one from 1830 Bohemia, and an English one from 1860, and a third one from 1900. My cutlery has been serviceable since 1790, and the last thing I have added was a gilded tea service from Paris, 1840. All this equipment is not being used regularly since it is not "dishwasher-ready." So as I cook, wash, and dry, I take pleasure in the time spent washing and drying the old plates, which sit so lightly in one's hand as if they wanted to nestle there. At least on the biggest holidays I am allowed to set the table with all the treasures of my forefathers. I don't want to prattle on; it is just that every day I experience that more and more my present fails to meet my aesthetic needs. It would certainly be an imposition were I to expect others to provide such services: actually it is a bitter thing that despite the prevailing promise and concern to bring back order, the use of the old bowls and plates is ruled out. As if savages had been invited for dinner – one would once call them Hottentots – so the aesthetical appeal of the dishwasher becomes the norm in daily life.

With this example I only want to show you that no effort is too great, if it means something to you. Any effort, if it matters to you, is justified: neither eating, – not even having caviar and champagne I might say – can give you the pleasure you can have taking such specialties from a caviar dish by Klinkosch and celebrating in such a ceremony the things in our lives that are extraordinary. Instead of teaching the young people about the range of possibilities, and what might only be just beyond the reach of their dreams, they are given "computer lessons" that make available to anybody only what has been prepared for mass consumption.

Yes, I know, I become immediately the object of scorn and mockery, of irony or even annoyance about my play at being aristocratic, since I value a silver spoon more than something from a wholesaler, although I won't soon let go of the pleasure of feeling such an extraordinary handcrafted achievement with my thumb. So, the sense of this letter is this: to find oneself once again in a world in which men for hundreds of years have thought about us selflessly and have left us these good things for our enjoyment. What force is it that has robbed us of this joy?

So ardently do I hope that you will think of me, when one day you undergo such joy!

Your R.

41.
"Culture" as a Political Instrument

Dear Nina, Dear Julian, Marie, and Vicky,

I have now written you 40 letters and these give you quite a good overview of my interests. I want to make this one a Jubilee-Letter, in order to tell you about an extraordinary phenomenon. Cryptically I refer to the general politicization of our culture over the last fifty years. It began with the stage directions at the theatre or at the opera, when for a performance of the *Abduction from the Seraglio* the singers wore al-Fatah costumes and the fez of Yasser Arafat, and had machine guns. At the theater, likewise, brown leather jackets are still preferred – the sort members of the Gestapo would wear – and SS uniforms, and other indications of the time of National Socialism. It could be a play by Friedrich Schiller, *The Robber*, or by William Shakespeare, *Macbeth* – it would be the same trappings, over and over again, pointing toward the disastrous past; and I have mentioned in a previous letter how contemporary historiography in the German speaking world remains fixated on this gruesome era, which thereby is carried forward as a persistent theme and helps to preserve a mindset that ignores all other periods of our past history. These examples lead me to write about the politicization of culture. It will probably not surprise you, since "cultural politics" will probably have continued along the same track it started on around 1990.

We have to deal with such phenomena, phenomena that would beset us with anxiety and horror if we had not already been hardened to insensitivity over them by the mass media. One might well believe the suggestion that certain interest groups have concentrated their attention on cultural politics in order to set political processes into motion by means of this sideshow of theirs.

I recall, in this connection, my description of the events around the *Marriage of Figaro*, in the process of which the revolution of 1789 was heralded. One must anticipate the same sort of thing if the traditional institutions of culture insert themselves into the "culture war" like flamethrowers and act as if they had to put an end to the neo-Biedermeier element of society by any and all means. The current "Regie-Theater" seems to be an act of punishment wreaked on the subscribers. The "right-wing scene" in Europe is calling for a "culture war" of a new coinage, while the answer with "political correctness" is authoritarian to a similar degree and degenerates into dictatorship. That what is involved overall is an attempt to dissolve culture is proven unambiguously by a demonstration in Hamburg, 1993, called "The Post Human."

In this demonstration thirty years ago this "tendency" clearly brought to light its goal in a tangible way. The sculptress Kiki Smith displayed the sculpture "Tale": a woman crawling across the stage, needless to say naked. That during this movement on all fours the woman has to urinate is of course no surprise. The body here bespeaks a loss of control of all kinds. In 2019 one could follow out the progress of Kiki Smith's work in the Lower Belvedere, in Vienna. The focus on feminism and the approach to animalism had been intensified and maintained its obtrusiveness. From the very beginning, her "Tale" wanted to instill disgust and to be repulsive, and it is the dominant assertion of the artist, ever more generally, to present the tortured body in every medium available. And in the commentary Kiki Smith said everybody's body is in this state without exception, and she is now presenting it as a victim on the battlefield of diseases, obsessions, exploitations, and violation. This was at the same time AIDS was at its height. It was to fight against that, as also at the same time against hunger, war, and the oppression of the woman. AIDS and the repression of sexuality was on everybody's mind. From then on people are being held on a leash of bad conscience. The pathography communicated in "Tale" intends to be a judgment against culture in its ultimate form – and irrevocably so. It justifies itself with the assertion that this total dehumanization represents the actual state of affairs. The present is a battlefield for the culture war over the human body.

The organizer of the exhibit, Jeffrey Deitch, frankly explained at the time that one must constantly take control over himself, his body, and the social environment. This would become the lifestyle for anybody who possesses no artistic talent. With this it is completely clear that from now on a new definition of the "body" is to be anticipated: with the "body" man also experiences his functional destiny. The alternatives are experiences with the authentic body. Thus begin certain "self-representations," in which the artists cut their faces, inflict significant damage their bodies and thereby turn their bodies into art-objects. According to their description they are taking the sum of the pains of the world onto themselves. Michael Jackson was on everyone's lips at the time and also the "Multiple-Choice Person," Madonna. One understood them as inviting that anybody can and should make himself be a "wished self." In Vienna Arnulf Rainer had started much earlier with self-flagellation and had himself photographed with a distorted face, which was immediately considered art. One has to imagine that between the first photograph in art history, of Rudolph IV the Duke of Habsburg, and the photo of Arnulf Rainer, the entire range of possibilities was exhausted. But that isn't all. An intensification was introduced in show-business, since much later a pop-singer named Conchita Wurst was able to present her wish-self in a song contest, and the questionable presentation was at the same time a hymn to hermaphrodism. The fact that the victory in the singer's contest was to be expected in any case indicates that an "audience" either had to come to accept it or else remain silent about such provocations. This artist-self of the hermaphrodite was an option that would be elevated to a criterion of contemporary art, and was at the same time a topic for cosmetic surgery, later perhaps genetically manipulated as well. The media turned it into a program to create a person of a new kind. Every talk show followed this subject and oriented itself toward this. In fact this rampant willingness to damage oneself became a cultural paradigm, in which the prerequisite for taking part in art is an artistic self, the painful disavowal of one's physical makeup. The "post-human" was there to be recognized thirty years ago.

That is why I am writing you about this with such frankness: I will not be deterred by the supposedly "artistic" from seeing through to the madness behind it. The artists are experiencing the instrumentalization of themselves and must place themselves second, behind the program of their cultural-political ambitions. With this supporting tailwind an attack on mankind is taking place. Through similar attempts of genetic manipulation and other approaches one can be completely unconcerned since in the meanwhile the boundary lines for protecting the human being have been removed. Art made this destruction of borders possible, and at the same time showed up the discrepancy between the possible provocations by art, and the norms of correctness that have been left behind. The police arrived at the performance of *The Marriage of Figaro*, but now the police would beware of intervening and this holding back shows already how the new aesthetic criteria have achieved the upper hand over both law and politics.

How far this tendency will be continued over the next fifty years is of course an open question. Will one also in the future "create" an enormous fortune? Will one be able to reduce the treasure of our language, like Madonna? Will it be possible in the future to say 80% of what we want to say, if we are restricted to an English vocabulary made up only of "time, baby, love, eyes, heart, word, girl, party, boy, and sex?" Post-humanity has moved quickly into the fields of pornography, power, and gruesomeness, and preferred to abuse visitors of galleries and museums, mocked their political identity, and raised smut to the level of disgust. And that was only the beginning. The turning point was that this enormous collection of smut and gruesome perversion borrowed its legitimacy from a transformation of the political. That is, while art was once attacked for being politically neutral, the generation of 1990 now saw itself as the great-grandchildren of Goya's *Les Maninas*. One is quick to turn up his nose at the rash attempt of that great painter, and believes instead that political assertions are made sharper by a realistic rendition of what is visible. Yet what is one seeing? What does one think he has seen? For the first time telephonic recordings are judged to be testimonies of art. The abused bodies are the witness for our view of our existence. And the artists, who a moment before were cashing in their bank notes, are griping about capitalism, which had so discouraged and alienated them. "Art" makes of itself the permanent political opposition and appropriates the vocabulary of opposition to itself. With this vocabulary, borrowed from reality, it builds its program of "political correctness." The art market reacts to the mentality of the times; the self-appointed elites define and thereby even indeed spread the scandal that human relationships have no other aims than rape and coercion. Props for the disgusting and the abominable are deployed by the artists as a visible commentary – though one may not call it a "perverted naturalism." The artist does not even trouble with a detour through fashioning his expression artfully since he has long since decided to make the statements directly and with the naked object itself. If one should look for the "society" reflected by the "objects," it would consist of embittered rightists, opportunistic dilettantes, craven schmoozers, and single-minded racketeers, who in the meanwhile have served up a redoubtable collection of feral feminist and ethnocentric assertions as if they were art. It all looks like the fairy tale of the Brothers Grimm. The story of the youth who went forth to learn what fear is is being staged.

Never before has one gotten the sense that he is being offered, in galleries, museums, collections and art forums, such cheap attitudes that are only seeking, ever more loudly and with one object and the next, to outdo each other. On the "display panels" that have now ousted the paintings, political consciousness is adequately documented through wild gestures in broad brushstrokes. In case it should not be understood, one can consult the verbal descriptions in which the intention of the piece is given wordy elaboration that cannot be represented in any "picture." A pile of slobs on display in the middle of the exhibition hall is meant to portray the pain of the world; painting on top of painting portrays nihilism, perhaps; a desolate frenzy of colors depicts the withholding of freedom. Perhaps for once the artist himself might see what are his proper objects to be different from all that – it could just happen – and pull himself together and put brush to canvas.

That something succeeds to satisfy what the visitor is hoping for, on the other hand, becomes for the artist a reason to himself abandon the so-called "association of artists." Out of the blue *Der Spiegel*, in issue #15 of 1993, listed the words that express the view of the world according to art. A painter, if he still paints, is accused of "expertism;" a sculptress who still works at rendering the human form is met with the objection of "heterosexism." All this means is that the "David" of Michelangelo represents a repression of homosexuality, while everything traditionally beautiful is denounced as a lie. It is the directors of culture that cause artists to reduce everything in society into pairs of opposites, to bring about a binary codification, by which it would be clear which side a person is on: ugly or beautiful, homosexual or heterosexual, woman versus man, disabled versus hale and emancipated versus dependent are the oppositions. The "balkanization" of consciousness brought on by this is no longer even visible, because of the fog of mental fatigue. It is the basis for the subsequent loss of consensus in politics.

I observed that with every year since 1990 a regulating of speech, coming ever more clearly to light, has found its way into our own way of speaking, to inhibit us. This regulating comes to light in the claim that the plural number has always denoted only the masculine. Thanks to the decline of knowledge, even in the communication of the universities the "impersonal" reference of German "*man*" has been supplemented with "*frau*." Since it was forgotten that "*man*" and the English "one" have the same root, so that they present an unspecified denotation of a person, the university of all things was proud to adopt the gender-specific supplement of *frau*. Now, however, thanks to this "amateurization" in art, this took place anyway, so that even the university's competence and knowledge has been called into question. The frenzy over "gendering" among the "moral police" mattered more than knowledge, and even during the "Yugoslav Crisis," a new academic course given the English title "Lectures in Genderism" was demanded as a high priority by the European Union in the universities, at a time when they were barely able to remain open.

To that story I can add another one: A monument was created to commemorate the death of the university students who fell in World War I. Since the German national corporations held their mid-week meetings at the site of the monument, this "Siegfried Head, out of a perfect confusion fell out of favor. And it didn't help that the monument was made by a Jewish sculptor (Josef Müllner). Since, at the University, though entirely contrary to intellectual history, an exaggerated anguish can go just as unchallenged as a completely disoriented attitude about German nationalism combined with the acceptance of the Nazi era, the politically correct warriors were infuriated. *Sua sponte*, a mass of "the righteous" approached the "Siegfried Head," spat on it and chanted in unison that this scandalous object must be removed. As an eyewitness I was always horrified by their artificial indignation, which they derived such pleasure to express merely as an arbitrary act – and then satisfaction came: the Siegfried Head was removed.

It was no longer such a far cry that in this "art-activism" a distinct "culture" of afflictions would be established – for example, performers would play hunger as if the hunger of the world were manifested in themselves. Women artists saw themselves as suppressed in a general way and came to cherish certain attitudes of their own, so that a distinct mode of representation made its way into the media, namely that these women themselves were the tortured, the hungry, the mistreated, or the people who were broken by the patriarchy. In this fanaticism of righteousness all sense of proportion was lost and it turned into a totalitarian gesture that immediately showed up in the hostile architecture we then experienced. It did not become politically consequential, however, since art in the meantime had more or less lost its standing in society.

In the rituals of affliction everything finally became amassed on a single axis, such that health is seen as evidence of having a robust nature that lacks any compassion for the needs of the world, while conversely paranoid anxieties are taken to be the healthy state par excellence. A tight network of adamant beliefs and exaggerations weighed consciousness down at the same time that it fomented all sorts of hysteria, and discussion could not take place on any level. Sooner or later this will reach political institutions, which will then go through the same course that art had done.

In art a condition of unbounded subjectivity was first introduced, so that the "objects" of art changed. Messages of protest were not meant to be seen in the objects, but rather in the commentaries attached to them. Beuys was the perfect example of this perfect reversal, since he attached to his works some formal schtick that purported to be scientific – unique nonsense formulated in the register of a Nobel Prize winner. In Vienna, Friedensreich Hundertwasser brought about something similar when he published his architectural designs as a first step toward ecological building design, and yet he aspired to blur at all costs any impression that his kind of house could not stand without considerable technological efforts. The rhetoric of the absurd nevertheless dominated the scene – though perhaps to call it absurd is far too programmatic, far too serious, for depicting such an unbounded explosion of expertise, knowledge and work. With "political correctness," as it is called in English, a power seizure has taken place that can spread far beyond the matters of political competence, but can take ideological positions, force a polarized agenda onto every media presentation, and place "politics" in a bad light due to its dependency upon elections. The massive incompetence of needful management indicates the impotence of the political element; conversely the politicized culture has long since taken a stand, was always current with the zeitgeist, and appropriated for itself a power to define the situation from which all access through critical reasoning is barred.

With the insight that natural sciences and social sciences once again are diverging, since the natural sciences foster a value-free culture and the social sciences remain interested only in analyzing social values, these social values can only resort to art, such as it is, for their support. Art could formulate whatever values it wants, but these need to be independent of the dictates of "political correctness," which in the last decades can make use of a legitimation that was never meant in this sense: the totalitarian command wielded by the "politically correct aesthetic" sees itself to be justified in the socio-political promise of artistic freedom – but that promise was already made in 1867.

All the best, Your R.

42.
A Refusal to Look?

Dear Nina, Dear Julian, Marie, and Vicky,

My last writing has plenty of problems. Surely one can raise an objection and shake his head, and see my evaluation of contemporary art as terribly outdated and freighted with traditionalism. It is interesting that an older argument is no longer valued, while the series of contemporary products show no taste. And this I want to investigate a little more closely. The demand for good taste comes from philosophy, and none other than Immanuel Kant dedicated his *Critique of Judgment* to a more focused analysis of the judgment of taste. The overall notion here is that a judgment of taste is subjective. But this judgment is not yet simply a matter of mood or whim, nor a matter of trying to please someone. We are still in the 18th century and free of the points of view of the current trends of aesthetic anarchism, according to which "everything is art."

Kant's idea is that the judgment of taste is a matter of cognition. As such, all cognitions are subjective, and taste in particular. This of course has an emotional interest as a prerequisite. According to Kant it is thereby important that the feeling of enjoyment must be an independent activity carried out by the subject. I believe I remember Kant said: "that is beautiful which is unconcerned with necessity." The path to a psychological concept is thus paved, since Kant does not restrict taste to sensation. The concept of cognition comes into play, for it is out of reason and the faculty of cognition that a judgment is reached, which is related to pleasure and the lack of pleasure. Actually it is quite simple: A painting pleases me, it "appeals" or "speaks" to me, and immediately by my reason and cognitive faculty my perceptions are turned into a positive judgment. And this positive judgment about the painting is moreover free from economical or other interests. My admiration for the painting does not indicate or imply that I intend to buy it. And Kant went even further! The painting, if it pleases me, is "purposively" directed at the relation of my powers of knowing – that is, it was the very purpose of the art of painting to "join together" my powers of cognition.

If we take as an example the famous painting of Delacroix, *Liberté guidant le peuple* (*Liberty Leading the People*), dated 1830, the criterion of beauty is not "automatically" met by the painting itself. Rather, while I am looking at it, a "purposiveness" for the "subjective play of the cognitive faculty" is at work. As I view it longer my eyes move to all the particulars of the painting, they complete their detailed study, and then turn to the view of the whole, and that is the play of the cognitive faculty; and in this consists the "purposiveness" of the painting.

Now a further entailment can be added, that the criterion of beauty is not to be associated with pleasantness: rather, beauty has to do with the subjective state of harmony. It must be in harmony with one's powers of cognition. Still the question remains open whether this subjective judgment of taste also makes a claim of generalizability. This does not have to be given from the outset. Of course the concepts of a later science of art deducible from it teach that there is more than generalized judgments, more than subjective feelings, that do not yet constitute a judgment of taste.

At this point my evaluation of art might start to make sense. If the belief prevails, as it often does, that "tastes" are different, Kant's exposition of the judgment of taste does not go through. And in fact that belief is saying a lot more! It denies my ability to make judgments of taste, it robs me of my competence. And this is exactly the intention of the "culture politics" that I described in my last letter. The independent and unassailable subject is "only" a product of some cultural forces or other, is only an "inner world" within an outer world. Thus a subject would never reach a correct view of the object, for immediately his eye, being a "social organ," has already been "struck blind," unable to see. Thus while even in the modern cartoon the great themes of freedom and beauty are being evoked, institutional guidelines of presentation have already rendered our judgment for us. The subject will now always be vulnerable to the objection of being merely subjective. The solution for the problem is near to hand: The subjective element must adopt distance from itself and follow instead the script of regulative ideas as if they were the "truth." This is the most important step toward a "value-eliminating" culture.

With this simple construction I want wanted to illustrate to you the present state in the "colonization" of our consciousness.

All the best – I remain, Your R.

43.
A View on the Sociology of Religion

Dear Nina, Dear Julian, Vicky, and Marie,

First of all, I am very happy that Julian has sent me his first electronic message. I think this is a big step into this "other" world that at first looks so harmless; and yet the question is whether, given this change, Julian, you will sometime limit how many of the "apps" and programs that are foisted upon you as if they were successful facilitators of communication so as to draw you into this labyrinth. Surrendering yourself to all these systems robs you of your self, at first, and finally of your ego. I would like to know you are protected from this!

This morning I reflected on whether I ought to write a little on the meaning of an institution that is inseparable from European history: the Papacy. It is the last of early-European institutions that is still standing, and has been fighting its way through history since the great migration of peoples. In order to achieve this success there had to be many Popes who with skill, cleverness, knowledge, and even with "grudges" and intrigues guided a church over centuries so that even failures later turned out to be successes – and vice-versa. It is above all the distinguishing feature of a church – and here we are talking about the Roman church, in the first instance – not only with skill to endure historical breaks, which is not always something to view positively, but from event to event to have held the leading role in dramatic crises. Thus Michel Foucault was able to make the profound remark that perhaps the church was central to and was successful through all the revolutions. In terms of its political influence just before the French Revolution "the Church," being the second estate, with its bishops and abbots in the standing parliament was not only the driving force but at the decisive moment turned into the third estate and lifted it into the majority position. Abbot Sieyes wrote the new political program about this subject, "What is the Third Estate?" and with this the fate of the feudal order was sealed.

The position of the "Church" in European history is mostly subject to misinterpretation. Foucault wanted to say that it is difficult to define the Church. If it is to be interpreted as the *papal* church in its historical role, then Martin Luther's complaints and scorn may not be without justification. If one sees it as a *clerical* church one will have far greater difficulty, since under this aspect its often mentioned distance from ecclesiastical power can always be clearly asserted, even though a majority of the clergy stayed in service to Rome and kept their heads low and did not murmur about it. The great reformers all came from "clerical" careers, such as John Wycliffe, Jan Hus, Martin Luther, and Melanchthon. The protest began with the 14th century and sought a "revolution of the church against the pope." Later on, a church characterized by the cloisters in the High Middle Ages became professionalized and restored the two approved ways of life, that of St. Benedict of Nursia and that of Augustine. Without the monastic movement the "colonization" of Europe would have happened much later. And finally, there was an idea that often arose in troubled times of a people's church made up of an alliance between monks, nuns, and the burghers of the towns, hoping to lay claim to the tradition of the Bible. Thus up to the 16th century we were dealing with a plurality of "churches" that had gradually emancipated themselves from the worldly sovereignty of the Frankish king and the autocratic doges. With the advance of civilization, which was originally a very "catholic concept," came a completely altered notion of church and of the care for souls, which is why which the "urban orders" were founded: the Dominican and the Franciscan Orders, the Augustinian Hermits, and the Servites and the Capuchins. In seclusion, and far distant from cities, the Cistercians remained, as did the orders of "strict observance": the Carmelites, the Augustinian Canons, and the Camaldolese.

In all this, however, I have not mentioned a basic distinction, one that most sociologists also do not understand. In one sense Church is of course an organization with a hierarchical structure, but at the same time, in its metaphysical form, it is the mystical body of Christ, the *corpus mysticum Christi*. Thus, I believe that this twofoldness, whose aspects often appear independent of each other, is not only the special nature of the Church, its holiness and its blessed power, but is also something quite alien to any positivistic-empirical treatment. Even Max Weber could make nothing of this church, and thus he focused on the reformed church, which consciously reduced the role of the clergy to a sort of religious "Lutheran" *pater familias*, whence he was able to carry out his pleasant idea that perhaps the graces of the sacraments, in the period of secularization, might likened to the function of capital. This was the overall interpretation of the theory of grace according to Calvin. The question of the reformed churches being "given over" to the respective sovereigns of the lands is a matter for another time – as in the case with Russian Orthodoxy, in which the current president, Vladimir Putin, is also the ecclesiastical head – nominally; in England the queen is so also the head of the "church of her country" – that is, the Anglican confession.

Now I have moved far off my topic. But it is necessary to do so in the case of this very broad subject. The independence of the church was not a topic until the Investiture Controversy, between 1075 and 1122. Up until then the maintenance of the church lay in the hands of Salian, Saxon, and Hohenstaufen emperors. Salvation at that time did not come from Rome: it had to be brought to Rome. What political plans were involved in the emperor's going to Rome are easy to imagine: the legitimation of the empire's territory as well as of its extension to include the Hungarians and the Poles. Thus a coronation in Rome was the visible legitimation but also only because of the fictional genealogy by which one carried soldier-emperors of Rome over to the Frankish ones. That each of these legitimations was necessary is shown in the case of the old imperial crown of Otto I, in the way that the Jewish kings of the Bible are depicted on its enamel plates. The question is, at what point in time did the Roman Church (in Rome) take over the authority of the Saxon emperor? Emperor Henry II had imposed the Aachen liturgy onto the Roman Missal in 1014, and therewith the Aachen credo became binding, and caused the Schism of 1054 with the famous controversy over the "*filioque*" phrase – the break-up between the East and the West, between Orthodoxy and Western Christianity. More than ever the imperial office had become an ecclesiastical one, and the Pope could be happy that the political leadership role was spared him in this confused period. What shows at the same time the strong theological position of the Pope and of the clerical church of the West, is that in all the Councils up until the High Middle Ages the theological position prevailed over political interests in each case. With the Credo of Aachen it became decisive that the Western church is now to be understood as the mystical body of Christ and that the witness of this is the community of the saints.

The only person in the 13th century who understood what had happened in the "West" up until then was Dante Alighieri (1265-1321). In his political writing *de Monarchia* he gave homage to the great emperors and saw in the "empire" a political unification and healing, which the Popes neither understood nor sought to preserve. Dante even thought that the Popes would destroy this Western Christianity. As an adherent to the old "consecrated emperorship" he still recognized the "worldly laymen" – the emperor, and the electors – who were humbled in the Investiture Controversy. In this historical tradition stood the cisalpine "Roman Catholics" who had aligned themselves with the "Ghibellines" in the long war against the "Guelphs." Dante still lives in the time in which the "empire" and the "final judgment" were conceived as a unity, before Petrarch and the poems about nature and landscapes provided a distraction from this sense of political duty. "The Judgment of the world is the History of the world" was the current theme, which immediately reminds us of Hegel, who goes on to make the World Judgment into a "World Spirit."

I have not yet brought up the abuses that brought this "imperial church" into disrepute. Ecclesiastical "offices" were much sought-after perquisites for the nobility, for the up and coming, and they could be easily purchased – for which the name is "simony." And it was a consequential error of Henry III to have applied force to the German Pope, Leo IX. Barely elected, Leo's secret meeting with Hildebrand the monk (later Pope Gregory VII) and the abbot of Cluny took place. Apparently all three were deeply uncomfortable about this imperial theocracy. We have Romanesque churches in Germany and France – in Bamberg, Trier, and Tours – and their very architecture is a document of this "Ghibelline" position.

How shall I make my transition to explain the alteration of the empire? Perhaps it will suffice to point out that the emperor in his office, which is to be considered ecclesiastically, ruled over dominions that were quite unmanageable.

South of the Alps he was like a podesta of the upper Italian cities, and at the same time, as the heir to the Lombardian Iron Crown, was himself a power equal to the Pope; north of the Alps he had nothing comparable since the lands were under the sovereignty of kings. And the unification that was meant finally to bring all these areas "under one crown" was difficult to achieve. Until finally Saxony and Bavaria, Swabia and the Rhineland, and the huge territory of the Teutonic Order up to Konigsberg came to consider themselves to be parts of the "empire," a special political legitimacy had to be devised. In this unification the landscape of "Germany" was established, which however at the same time alienated Upper Italy from the "empire." And what was Italy? All to the south of Rome had become "Byzantine," almost completely. This called for a certain cleverness and diplomacy from every Pope. As the Bishop of Rome he had to respect his Byzantine and Frankish neighbors. So in this connection he was almost nothing but the Bishop of Rome. At the same time he was very intensely involved in the power play going on within the empire. Only the Cluniac Reform brought about the change. The result was the underpinning of the Pope at Rome and a mistrust having to do with the baffling plans of the emperor. On top of all that, the Byzantines were there in South Italy, the Danes were in England, the Moors in Spain. The weakness of Emperor Henry III was already obvious.

Now one must bring up other things, things depressing for a Christian. Not only is the emperor in distress and hardship. With simony, the church also is crucified! And the chickens came home to roost when the emperor now ordained that ecclesiastical offices would be managed by his family. What the Italian *condottiere* would later do had already become the practice during the High Middle Ages. How did it begin? When Emperor Henry III decided at Sutri who, among the three Popes, could really claim the office, the low point of the papacy had been reached – in 1046. In thirty years a completely surprising turnaround had taken place. The Pope retrieved his authority over the church.

The "declaration of war" against the emperor is obvious. In fact, up until the 20th century one can read in the entry for 12 March in the Roman Breviary, that the "people" are freed from their obeyance to the king (Joseph II still ordered this sentence to be pasted over in the Breviary of the Austrian monasteries).

Such releases as these were at the same time a breeding ground for revolution. In the *Dictatus Papae* (1075) the legal grounds were laid, and it was only a matter of interpreting this enormously important document. Not even an emperor would be able to circumvent this edict. Basically, the emperor is "fired" from his holy office as deacon of the empire, taking with him his insignia, which are now kept in the Imperial Treasury in Vienna. These honorable symbols forfeited their halo. With this document the separation from the faithful is perfected. Those who had been monks – brothers – now become clergy. The clerical church begins. If since Otto I the emperor had been deemed "apostolic" and thus a follower of the Lord, so it was the Pope in 1075 who was restored to the succession of the apostles, and therefore "*universalis*" (cf. *Dict.Pap.*§2).

Even if this transition may seem a small step to us it constituted a watershed in European history. The subsequent Popes expanded their supremacy. Innocent

III (1198-1216), Innocent IV (1246), and Boniface VIII (1302) developed and enforced the unity of the Church with their *dictati*. In the *Unam Sanctam* of Pope Boniface one already does without the emperor – i.e., manages without worldly power. This however does not last long: political difficulties multiply but that had no effect on what was to be the first revolution of European history: the Papal Revolution.

We must now see that we are narrating a "political history" that is promoted by the Roman Church. We have completely neglected talking about a church in which countless men and women have biographies worthy of consideration. When I check what a person means by the Church, I always ask him to tell about at least twenty Popes of the Middle Ages, even if only by name, and then twenty saints. The list comes to an end with five or six Popes, but naming the saints is relatively easier: from Peter Damian, one of the "forerunners" of the Papal Revolution, to Francis of Assisi, Thomas Aquinas, Elizabeth of Thüringen or Hildegard von Bingen. Indeed, this discrepancy inspired Karl Renner to write about "The Sociology of Canonizations" in his prospectus for his *Habilitationsschrift*.

At this point the Western Church developed a counterattack against the Islamization of the time with the tracts of Bernard of Clairvaux, which included in the same breath Byzantium. The crusades were a project to tame the European powers. The Pope was to do the taming: he impelled the elites of the West to fetch the relics from Asia Minor. This "raid" on the graves of the earliest Christians in pursuit of the relics of the first martyrs is not easy to interpret. Every city in ancient Christendom built its church on the grave of a saint. Every city saw its own mystical history, its founding dedication, in "its own" martyr, and from there on its future is put into focus in terms of its inner and outer mission. The crusades create the "*miles christianus*" – the Christian soldier – the counterpart of the meek and docile monk. The history of the High Middle Ages is tantamount to the politics of the crusades, under emperors Friedrich I, Henry VI, and Friedrich II. It is the most heated event in European politics and unifies the royal houses. And at the same time one gets involved in the seductive mix-up of confusions. With duplicity the Pope sent the nobility of the empire into this inferno taking place in the Eastern Mediterranean. The militarization of the elites and of their "unfree servants" change the goal of the war – or we may say the original goal was virtually unattainable. This was the pre-history of the entire "service nobility" in Europe, which began with the Griefensteins and the Rabenklaus and ended with the Bismarcks and Bülows. The etiquette of war was articulated in a settlement found among the archives of the empire dating from 1416, which elevated a declaration of war to a "custom of honor."

The legacy of the crusades are the gothic cathedrals, these ships of stone standing as a bulwark against Byzantium and the East. High above stands the vault that looms like heaven over the Christian polis. For the first time the gothic cathedral is not a solid building, in the manner of the Romanesque churches, but a project that is erected by the Christian people, and this constitutes the pre-formation of the city-society of burghers – and the cathedrals reach up to the sky in a memorable way.

I have narrated this episode in such detail for you because out of this come further breaks in history. And the Popes? They needed centuries gradually to see that their "building model" had to fail, basically because of a "failure in planning." They were still able to ignore the outcry of Martin Luther. The Renaissance – a "democratization" of all European and ancient Gods – was so strong that they did not notice that the gigantic project of St. Peter's Basilica was only able to make a theatrical pretense that Christianity was united. Only in the 19th century did one finally realize that a redefinition of the papal church was needed. Since then, the Roman Church has dragged on laboriously, and its uncertain steps point to an uncertainty that each Pope must feel – since Pius XII. This Pope had to realize that no pact is to be made with the devil. Later, one said that John XXIII or John Paul II were able once again to keep up a pace fitting to the present status the Church, but the burdensome history with which it is freighted has not yet been overcome.

Perhaps I will tell you more about the present situation, but for starters I have given you a representation of the history of the church, since on that topic you will may well get no lessons at school.

I wish you are having a good time, and that you come through the pandemic well!

Your R.

44.
Bruno Kreisky – Politics and Emotion

Dear Nina, Dear Julian, Dear Vicky and Marie,

In the last letter I gave you a short history of the Papacy, leaving off at the Middle Ages. Why? Because here were the great opportunities for the papal church to stick to the teachings of the Gospel over other agendas and other motives. There had of course been Popes, like Leo I for instance, and also an Anti-pope who was even canonized – St. Hippolytus (around 230) after whom Saint Pölten was named – who found themselves in accord with the Message, wished to follow it with all their powers, and thus were free from the temptation to pursue a political project. I do not mean to condemn any Popes who believed – I am speculating – that with their political cleverness they would also be serving the legacy of Christ. But where am I to draw the line? Is the next summer palace planned for the Viminal Hill in Rome justified, or the Caelian Hill? A late acquaintance of mine, who was a political scientist, jokingly thought that the Popes in the Renaissance played the *Passion of Christ* "on horseback" (rather than in a manger!). So, there was a quite feudal church. I am repeating myself, since I more than hinted at this in my last letter.

Now I will raise the question whether, in general, historically famous politicians considered what the consequences of their plans for the future would be, and whether they could justify them. It is perhaps a truly surprising question. Since when do we catch ourselves thinking about the consequences of our actions, in order then perhaps to abandon our plan? What are the reasons not to carry out a plan? Historians often make light of this and attempt to explain that if the means for carrying out a plan were lacking a better plan was conceived: that the opposing circumstances were too great. Never have they had the thought that an historical personage refrained from a plan for ethical reasons. We can say without qualification that if a plan is designed and enacted, I am completely responsible for its consequences, even when unforeseen things take place. Even here we encounter the judgment that one must take full responsibility, although the reasons for the judgment might be mitigated by misfortune and bad luck. There is one point, however, in which the politician is particularly responsible for what he does, far into the future: he may never give in to trying to become "his own successor" or to make the conditions for succeeding him more difficult or worse. This brings to mind the bloody joke with which one consoles himself about a dictatorship: the tyrant can get rid of all his competitors except for his heir. The ethical way of expressing this rule is that while one must contribute one link in the chain of generations, for the sake of continuity he must consciously allow the next one the opportunity to join it. More simply said, it is the highest art of statesmanship when after the statesman's regime the state is still standing and is still halfway decent. From a rather near distance I have experienced how an alternative was sought, after Bruno Kreisky. The successor, Fred Sinowatz, had no alternative but to announce at his inauguration as Federal Chancellor that one must get it into their minds that now everything is different.

This anecdote is not saying much. Kreisky was not responsible for the misconceptions about nuclear energy and the referendum against the "Zwentendorf" reactor, for which there were others to blame as being much more responsible, in particular in pushing through a plan whose basis relied upon insufficiently founded hypotheses. Kreisky's responsibility consisted merely in a psychoanalytical interpretation of his relationship with Friedrich Peter, a onetime member of the SS, who apparently declared his support for a minority regime in 1970. And there must have been still further arrangements, not only the change in the right to vote, which favored the FPÖ. Perhaps the talks had become inconclusive, which is why Kreisky might also have been looking toward a coalition with the FPÖ, if the election of 1975 had not come out as an absolute majority. I already reported that Simon Wiesenthal then fought against the decision for that option. And this culminated in two entirely foolish reactions. Kreisky, who was seething with rage, went off on a tangent to initiate an investigative committee in Parliament against Wiesenthal – an impossibility, and therefore outrageous. At the same time this was the beginning of a gradual and continuous gambling away of his reputation with the council of ministries. He complained to me that he no longer had a "majority" in the council of ministers, and his opponent was the then Finance Minister, Hannes Androsch. Of course

Kreisky had squandered his boundless approval, whether in the "Wiesenthal Affair" or the "Zwentendorf Affair"; in either case he had gotten his own "party" to turn against him because of both conflicts. Because of atomic energy, Anton Benya, the president of the Parliament and of the ÖGB got involved in the opposition, as also did moderate members of the Council of Ministers – for instance Christian Broda or Hertha Firnberg, who decidedly rejected Kreisky's showdown with Wiesenthal. Automatically these went over to Androsch, who in the meantime audited the financing of Kreisky's summer home in Mallorca to see whether any "black" money was involved. This undertaking was an immeasurable shock to the Federal Chancellor and affected him deeply. His "counter-blow" was to have the real estate purchases of Androsch in Canada looked into, which he asked me to do.

This deep dissent among those who were making political decisions obviously hobbled the program of reform because they were overwhelmed with emotion. It was grotesque that in 1975 Kreisky had attained an absolute majority but at the same time was condemned to a virtual inability to act. In the sense of political responsibility for a future political arrangement, he had underestimated a possible coalition and did not realize that he was thereby risking to maneuver some successor into just this situation, which would of course be overwhelming. In a personal conversation with the Federal Chancellor I made him aware of this outcome, and warned him that the political constellation in Austria is not like that of the Scandinavian countries. A liberal party in Sweden could not in fact be compared with a Freedom Party. He swept that warning aside and went on and on about how he had not forgotten his incarceration in a detention camp at Wöllersdorf, in 1934, in which he had shared camp life with the illegal National Socialists. This "Nibelung-loyalty" seemed important to him. On the practical level, however, his intention had become clear as to the current division of powers among the parties in Austria: he preferred an alternative to the People's Party, since he did not want under any circumstances to form a government with these "reactionaries." At this time he told me in great detail about a ski vacation when he stayed at the same place as the then-ruling Federal Chancellor Josef Klaus. Being invited for dinner, at the time, encouraged Josef Klaus to tell Kreisky, of all people, "Jewish jokes," and to tell them badly, to boot; and Kreisky was exceptionally piqued by this tasteless behavior. The fact that he disliked Leopold Figl, the Secretary of State in the foreign office, and thought him inappropriate to be a foreign minister since he was deficient in diplomatic relations as well as his knowledge of languages, was only the final straw for him to reject the People's Party forever.

I have gone into great detail. I had by then visited Kreisky only once in his office, along with William Johnston, who had composed an intellectual history of Austria called *The Austrian Mind*. I was really pleased that Kreisky had found time for this. Upon entering his work-room a ritual was always to be expected, of which I was already aware: he would always straighten himself up behind a pile of papers and act as if he had been sitting there behind them in deep study. With a dignified air he came around the desk and told us to have a seat. He chose to decorate the sitting area with the *Adam* of Hausner of all things, something that always bothered me. Then he took Johnston's book into his hands and said, to the American professor, in a tone of heartfelt compassion, that he would have a look at the index of names mentioned and that he would tell a story about each person he knew. It was a detailed afternoon, in which Kreisky many times dismissed his harried secretary who kept trying to remind him of his next appointments, without success.

Now I must go back and pick up the narrative where I left off. For the successor, Fred Sinowatz, one and only one decision was wrested from him, and he had Kreisky to thank for it: namely the decision to form a coalition with the FPÖ. Just as I had reproached Kreisky about what would happen if the ÖVP which he "hated" formed a similar coalition, Sinowatz in fact provided an opportunity for that, which was also introduced in 2000. Franz Vranitzky was not successful in establishing a deep political consensus, which would have prevented such "stunts."

So I have here described a phenomenon that within this form of political responsibility calls for foresight, something that in politics must always have two attributes: far-sightedness must also be met with acquiescence that only in the future may come the achievement of a state of affairs that a society, a people, a political constellation, had always wished for. This is easier said than done. For instance in our present time actions to be taken about the shape of a future are much more difficult to plan, and are far more burdened than a hundred years ago. We indeed sense a deficiency in our politics, that it is hardly if at all "effective" – for where, and in what area, can it still be innovative? In every area it runs into opposition, not because of heightened political sensitivities but because for some time now, demands, imaginary ideas, developments, and shortcomings have been the focus of political policy, but any further measures as they are being hatched seem to be an overreach against already ensconced special interests. Change has become the status quo of our political constitution, and that is perhaps also the reason for exploiting any opportunity to "outsource" the portfolio of political management, to pass off responsibility and competence onto others, and thereby to make an argument that a "pared-down state" would be well advised not to "want to do everything." Certainly, this was immediately celebrated as a success of neo-liberal ideology; progressive critics were already anticipating the return of unvarnished capitalism and yet this was an interpretation that missed the mark. In Europe, with the European Union, a central power was established that – so one understood and believed – would help regulate our economy in the future, and thereby strengthen the conviction that the state, as a superpower, would undermine the integrity of individuals and their personal responsibility if it takes responsibility for everything.

It is now common knowledge that we are formulating a budget for the next year during the Parliament's most important session of the year. The leadership sets their intentions forth, and the legislative representatives make their decisions. Be that as it may, the majority of them speak to a media audience anyway; with debates one attempts to create an instrument in Parliament that is appropriate to allow for a permanent innovation. The funds should be aimed at this and that, and should in general be more focused and more directed for creating a more secure future, full employment, social security, and better health care and schools. The wish-list is endless. This is the moment at which political foresight is called for, and is the moment when one must stick to the decision that has been made. Already the impression has become stronger that the basic ways of political management have changed – indeed, that they had to change – in such a way that a political answerability of a new kind, with new dimensions and contents, measured against unforeseeable future effects in some far-off future, has penetrated into what had been a narrower scope of political action and political ethics, in a way in which at the beginning of the 20th century one had never conceived.

I hope very much that you are having a pleasant time these days, despite the pandemic!

All the best. I remain, your R.

45.
A Glimpse into My Life-World

Dear Nina, dear Julian and dear Marie and Vicky,

A while ago I mentioned that because of an error letter 44 was here repeated as number 45. So Ken Quandt had advised me to use this chance to "catch up" on topics which in his eyes have some importance for my person. It has certainly been an important point for my life to regularly meet three or four friends on Sunday. It was always at the Café-Konditorei "Heiner" in Wollzeile, Sunday after Sunday. There was no need for a special agreement, the participants of the group knew that starting at 10 o'clock in the morning our appointment at Heiner had to be kept. Werner Gihl, Peter Sobolak, later also Wolfgang Hirt, and now and then also Erwin Ungerböck formed with me a group to talk frankly and candidly. Their different professions shaped each of them, each had matured into a personality, and to this day they possess certain unmistakable characteristics. I think I know how to characterize them quite well. In doing so, I must escape the philosophical tradition that sought to emphasize one's own "personality" so that often the individual "coloration" of the person was nearly lost. The notion of "person" had become a guiding concept for jurisprudence; psychology thought it was impossible to do without it, but the notion did not take us far in our analysis. Jurisprudence and psychoanalysis, in their familiarity with theology, knew that with man's expulsion from paradise it became necessary for him to become a person and to take upon himself a certain independence, but this much only betokened one's distance from the Lord. "Behind" that persona, another man was to be seen, a man who had always been addressed by the prophets, who was the central subject for redemption through Christ. The redeemed man had little to do with that personality we so often cite in trying to describe the salient particularity of a human being. In fact what I am here saying shows the lack of understanding involved in treating as the distinguishing feature of an individual the very thing that basically distances him from his "self."

If the question of "self" can be answered at all, then Werner Gihl almost mastered it. For him life seemed to consist only of sunny days. It was part of his talent to assert himself skillfully and with verve in all conceivable situations in life. Luck was certainly not with him from the cradle, but he possessed something that once distinguished Austrians, or rather the Viennese: courage to face life. So often this was the theme in the comedies of Johann Nestroy, just as it was a serious theme in Franz Grillparzer's *Woe to Him Who Lies*. Werner had become a self-confident self-made man, who in his professional life as a barber in a small shop in Liliengasse received insider information from the high officials of the ministries located nearby. And so he freely spread the word about reforms in the tax law, the latest prices of antiques, and which restaurants had the best cuisine. Although he traveled mainly to Bad Ischl or to South Tyrol, and earlier to England for family reasons, he soon became busy with cosmopolitanism, generosity, and general helpfulness. He was equipped with knowledge of what was going on behind the scenes in the nearest alleys, and the flow of information was always being updated, and thus the political sensations taking place in our small state could be learned more quickly from the "Barber" than from radio or television. With his twin brother, Walter, the shop became an agency giving advice on the various situations of life or a place to vent ruthless criticism of any parties that did not fit in with the traditionalist ideology of the Gihls.

For the small group at Heiner on Sunday morning it was probably true that a personality in the Enlightenment sense was not required at the coffee house table. That is, since the 18th century the notion of personality seemed to include a highly problematic characteristic. Even with Kant one could have assumed that a "personality" feels himself superior to the usual ethical basic rules, and can also emancipate himself from them. This independence from the socio-cultural context was still expressed in the Enlightenment with the "creation" of geniuses, of which Mozart was the best known and most famous. With the creation of "great men," the "religion of genius" emerged, which then with Edgar Zilsel began to play a role in sociology for explaining exceptional cultural phenomena.

An equally important member of the "Heiner Group" was Peter Sobolak. He basically joined the group by chance, because for months Werner and I observed that this Peter Sobolak did not have to pay for what he ordered. He always said goodbye with a generous tip, but he did not have to pay the bill. This led to wild speculations on our side. Finally, in order to clear this up we cleverly involved him in a conversation and the persistence of us criminalists finally brought it out that Peter was the owner of a forwarding company, had built it "from the ground up" and also was successful. This success did not come inborn to him either, and later he reported that despite being of a weak constitution, he had chosen freight forwarding as his career. In this way an exemplary family business had been created which by now suffered from the envy of competitors. Peter Sobolak was a definite asset to the duo consisting of Werner and me. As creatures of his incredibly warm and generous manner we were soon enjoying upscale gastronomy, but that was not the main thing. Peter had also developed into a self-made man, had integrated himself into cultural life, and drew from this his independence of thought, which he combined with a high ethos. Responsibility for his employees was never mere talk, with him. Impressive also is his psychological balance, which he lost relatively seldom. And when that rare occasion would come up, he was able to get his point across with a firm slap on the back of the person sitting next to him. Peter is just as willing to help as Werner, perhaps the sector of his assistance is of a somewhat different nature and is predominantly governed by his interests in theater and opera, less to be understood as charity. What is hard to understand is his enthusiasm for soccer, which is also expressed in the fact that he is one of the paying members and sponsors of the soccer club "Rapid." Sometimes I was allowed to accompany him to a game and was surprised that the abundant food being offered before the game and during the break drew more concentrated attention than the excitement of the soccer game. In addition, there is no longer a Viennese club that is still so representative of Austrian soccer the way it was 70 years ago.

In any case, Peter Sobolak was an enrichment and was integrated quite quickly. In his "wake" the former tax consultant of Peter's company joined the group. Erwin Ungerböck shares with Peter an enthusiasm for music. The two of them compete for tickets to symphony concerts or even opera. Erwin pursued art history at the end of his professional life, attended lectures, and since then was always studying. He actually went for exams, even in history, although he set a limit for himself. He did not want to continue the studies through to the thesis, because, as he often repeated, he would want not take a place away from the young students. But presumably Erwin was also uncomfortable with the nature of the art history examinations, for in the early part of his studies the examinations had been more like picture quizzes, a "fact-positivism" oriented toward pseudo-empiricism. Erwin recognized the same style within the Institute of Art History that I had had already experienced some 50 years earlier. Under the long and dominant influence of Renate Wagner-Rieger and Gerhard Schmidt at the Institute, the previous school of art history, created by Riegl and after him Dvorak had been eclipsed. In brief debates with Erwin about art history, this indoctrination into a rather flat positivism showed through very clearly. Erwin studied the given literature extraordinarily closely and it became his habit to interpret the great paintings in their connection with time and place and then with contemporary painters. He had acquired a stupendous knowledge in art history: at times he had to correct his knowledge, but on the whole he was extraordinarily well oriented thanks to the lectures of visiting professors. In him the lack of an intellectual-historical justification of style and method of representation is hard to miss, but the facts that have been added will certainly broaden the picture of art history. Erwin also is a treasured asset during the warm season since his enigmatic humor and a dialect that places him in deepest Lower Austria plays as a colorful backdrop for his cleverness. Even if his inclination to play golf is difficult to understand, following a small white ball all over the place surely satisfies the need for a healthy walk in a pleasant way.

The fourth in the group is Wolfgang Hirt. He joined the group years ago after I met him in the exercise club. He is an extraordinarily helpful person, and makes you forget a great deal, having himself survived the most serious illnesses: two organ transplants. As a builder he had still gotten the old training and therefore has an impressive knowledge of the function of building materials and of the building code and regulations of the municipality that must be observed. Therefore, through Wolfgang, a number of blatant violations against the rules have been made known and he can quite often present a criticism of the sins of builders, so that approving of building measures by the laymen in the coffee house group has become much more rare. Wolfgang surprised us several times with his good-naturedness and to this we owe the fact that for quite a while our celebrations of birthdays and everything else take place in his penthouse, which is also in Wollzeile.

Thus a quite diverse group came into being, which possesses a "right of residence" in the Heiner, Sunday after Sunday. And on occasion when there might have been no topic worth discussing, Werner would step in and report to us in detail about price developments in the most diverse sectors of the economy. Schillings as the medium of exchange still remained his measure, and his detailed commentaries on tax law have since amounted to a history of law. But he was not at all hampered by this and it did not limit his presentations. And if an objection should be raised, it would be Peter trying to interrupt Werner by pointing out it was as if we were being taken to school – a remark that was generally ignored – leading to the infamous slap on the shoulder of the person sitting next to him as proof of the urgency of Peter's request to put in his two cents. It may in itself seem grotesque that such an inhomogeneous group can show so much stability, but it is the proof that the old form of friendship still exists, here and there at least.

I hope you can find something useful in these lines. But they should give you an impression of my "private" life which would not have come about without my mentioning it.

With best regards, I remain your R.

46.
Reconstruction of a Family

Dear Nina, Dear Julek, Marie, and Vicky,

Perhaps you have already asked yourselves why I write nothing about my own specialty, which I have practiced throughout my professional life. The answer is not simple. I will say in advance that my considerations always involve sociological thinking but have always valued themes far off the beaten track as an essential enrichment, seeing the "multi-dimensionality" as advantageous for representing lives in society in their fullness and manifold forms, so as to piece together a picture of "society." My letters do provide an abundance of directions for doing this, and must also be understood within this perspective. Sociology was not foreign to me, given the context of my family. I still remember very exactly how my father had understood this special kind of social science. His own career was not at all simple. Social philosophy led him into sociology. As I saw it, he was, certainly during the First World War, torn between the social criticism that had a partly Marxist background and one that had a deep connection to Catholic social doctrine. As is well known, with the *Rerum Novarum* of 1891 the latter led to huge changes which shook the "churched people," at least. That these initiatives were not only late in coming but also were carried out half-heartedly is not surprising. In the eyes of my father it was clear that the "Church" – here to be understood as a mass term – was not able to resign itself to the signs of the times. Probably the shock of the French Revolution affected the Roman Church all the way down to its members, as did the atrocities it brought on as well as Napoleon's insane "world war," so that the Church felt it had to distance itself from all politics. In addition the members became motivated, for whereas the bishops viewed the involvement of lay persons in politics with suspicion, the lowest echelon of the clergy, close to the members and without support from Rome, got involved in supporting a republic, a social politics, and an alternative cultural politics as the ideal of a "Christian democracy." They were therefore the supporters of the soon to be founded Christian-social parties, that around 1900 rose up to become the strongest force in Central Europe.

This political development, which fought to survive the utter collapse of political traditions in 1918, was the prelude to fundamental political divisions. In a nutshell, the "red" (SPÖ) and the "black" (ÖVP) were caught up in their antagonism and in their worldviews, which in some places became more and more extreme, while in other places half of them were afflicted with a "homesickness" for the time before 1914. Indeed this "nostalgia" was already a sociological phenomenon.

Your great-grandfather was from the time after 1918 far more a "legitimist" – this was the designation for those who supported a "rebirth" of the monarchy – and saw in this a political power that might be able to resolve the horrible confrontation between both of the mass parties. My father's education was flanked by two important persons, on the one side, Hans Kelsen, and on the other Othmar Spann. To characterize both persons here would take us far afield. At the same time he participated in circles that had importance for sociology. There was Ernst Karl Winter, who in many ways became my father's mentor, and also Eric Voegelin. What held their ways of thinking together somehow was the concept of historical sociology and also the history of ideas. Ernst Karl Winter employed historical sociology in a monograph on Rudolph IV and history of ideas in his book on *Socialmetaphysics of the Scholastics*, as well as in his *Plato: The Sociological Element in the Theory of Ideas*. Voegelin later wrote an obituary for

Max Weber in 1921, when he was a student, which already indicated he was an acute philosophical thinker, and thereafter published two impressive theses, *Race and State*, and *The History of the Race Idea*. It was uncannily early that Voegelin recognized the coming danger, and in *Political Religions*, the last book he wrote before his fleeing into Switzerland, he presented an analysis of National Socialism which could still be printed in 1938.

My father's habilitation was entitled *Interest in the Scholastics*, but he remained without a position in the university. Still, he had the opportunity to stay at the university with lecturing assignments. In 1936 he received a special order from the ministry on lectures to offer a course on "Fatherland Education," so-called, before an audience from all the faculties. In this he treated the several worldviews of social philosophy. As far as I can tell from the manuscripts, the orientations of Marxism, positivism, idealism, and materialism were objectively set forth. It goes without saying that after 1938 he was no longer able to be trusted with lecturing. Of course he fell under the observation of the Gestapo, though they withdrew after searching his house without anyone knowing their provocation for doing so.

After 1945 my father took up teaching again and was to be named an Ordinarius for sociology. In these years he devoted himself to the history of sociological theories, to the history of ideas, which appeared in various forms, in longer essays. Given his life history he once again pursued his interest in the church in a sociological aspect. This led also to a book, *The Catholic Church and Scholastic Natural Law*, which caused a considerable sensation. Cardinal Franz König, later taken to be a liberal, imposed a ban against speaking upon my father throughout the entire archdiocese of Vienna. The controversies took on stronger and stronger forms, which were heightened by the fact that Friedrich Heer and Wilfried Daim had taken the same position. If one recapitulates this back-and-forth today, one is bewildered as to what it could be that lay behind such a big uproar in the moderate Catholic "*juste milieu*." It can only be explained by the fact that the Church at the time had more or less ensconced itself within and among the "cultural" Christians (the so-called *Milieu-Christentum*) which in the meanwhile has completely disappeared. The Catholic organizations that preceded the "People's Party" (the ÜFP) melted away and with them so did the majority of the party representation in Parliament, between 1970 to 2000.

Now I have presented you a long story that I began with a different goal in mind. Yet the story helped me to show that very early on – perhaps too early – I knew of the philosophical foundations of social science. Certain authors were familiar to me, for instance Auguste Comte or Saint-Simon, so that at the time I could hardly imagine that there were any sociologists had no interest in these older writings, let alone believing that their own "sociology" would nevertheless be able to make sense of their concrete subject matter, "society." In the "beehive" of the "research center for social sciences" at the university, empirical sociology soon dominated the understanding of the discipline and at the same time devalued the work of the pioneering sociologists. Of all the "founding fathers" of the discipline only Max Weber remained current, and here and there Georg Simmel, and then

Paul Lazersfeld, the first pope of social research as it were, and also Talcott Parsons. Already in my first encounters with the field and its institutionalization it occurred to me that the foundational work of Marx as brought forward by Max Adler was still present in the background for Lazersfeld, but the "research center" saw itself as exempt from considering this foundational science. With wit and diligence the results of research were being churned out like industrial products. One could almost have adopted the slogan, in the manner of a PR man: "We codify everything: just give us more questions!" So an institutional structure was adopted that was likely a prototype, since two or three decades later all the institutes "functioned" in the same way. For a given project a staff of collaborators was hired and paid, and then they were immediately let go once the project was completed. This was the new way of work at the universities. The assistants were also caught up in this process and had no time to advance their own expertise beyond formulating models and empirical methods. It always got on my nerves the way they would so casually talk about society because people immediately disappeared behind such talk. Probably sociology has less and less to say to us today not only because "society" is no longer as homogeneous as it still was some forty years ago, but also because the picture of "society" with which social science now works is a representation from which the "originality" and the uniqueness of people has largely disappeared. With this turning away from history and with a restriction of the hypotheses that one can bring in from social psychology and psychoanalysis, an "abolition of man" has been propagated due to concentration on statistical methods and mathematically formulated social models. That also was the reason that it is impossible for a man to cope with himself. In the mirror of the researches he sees only himself in the mirror and yet at the same time it is an illusion. Insofar as the "subject" of society is still recognized at all sociology sharpens its instruments for accurate analyses, but it can do so only on the condition of making man faceless, his presence barely felt in percentages or as a caricature in an in-depth interview. It is no wonder that the dominant theme today is the struggle for identity. This is the outcome if one treats identity as a product of socialization, so that the endowment of what it means to be human is conferred upon a person from the treasure trove of socializations. Thus he must see himself as exposed to mechanisms of interest that lead him to grasp his existence as an evacuation of meaning. If this was indeed the true meaning of social science, one is on the verge of reaching the goal. Thanks to this inhumanization, man is downgraded from being a "cultural being" to a "social being."

I am referring here not the "old" ordinarius professors, who could still believe the fiction that sociology is an applied science for solving problems in democracies. And sociology still claims this high ranking position, since with a democratic society there are no other fields of science that still possess the significance that historical research once possessed and still earlier theology and heraldry. At present however it is a grave error still to ascribe such power to the social sciences. This assumption stems from one's having decided that social science no longer has anything to do with human life. The opposite was the case since the social sciences have afflicted us in the manner of a natural catastrophe.

Nearly all social areas from now on have been interpreted sociologically, and have moved closer and closer to a completely denatured concept of "understanding," and have not once paid attention to basic and rudimentary phenomenology. We have completely forgotten the special methods of "understanding" laid out by Max Weber, recognizing a wider application for the epistemology of Kant. It would now be a misunderstanding if one were to concede to the social sciences the power to set definitions, which on top of that sits poorly with the general complaint of social scientists that they have lost their influence. Influence relies upon the current state of a general amateurization of social scientific methods, while in more fields of science up to and including medicine, genuine cognition was replaced with questionnaires, and on top of that the adoption of social scientific language. Something like this happened once before with the adoption of the Marxist vocabulary in the language of politics, and now the various alternative sociological theories have joined the same club, as it were, in their use of language. This "sociologization" made the rounds, played the role of knowledge about society, and could be used only as long as men did not intuit its purpose – to turn them into virtual mannequins in a statistical comparative interpretation of the sort Lazersfeld was so fond of carrying out. Institutes for research into opinion, social welfare, and markets are the bearers of applied science up to today. Thus there are groups and movements who come to the fore with their own peculiar understanding of society, and make their way to the high bureaucracy or the secretariats or the ministries, and through party politics enter into a peculiar battle among worldviews, aiming to impose a permanent or sustainable mobilization of the populace according to their peculiar vision. This has now become our history. The concept of sociology indicates – i.e., makes a reference to the fact – that society once existed, but societies' segmentations and fragmentations have now shown that such previous assumptions are false. With bitter irony one can say that social sub-groups have emerged that are placed under permanent observation, while others again do the observing. And who is observing the observers?

All the best to all four of you – Your R.

47.
Cold Feet

Dear Nina, Dear Julian, Dear Marie and Vicky,

Today I was unfortunately not able to write a letter, since I was fully occupied looking for a replacement for our heating system, which went totally kaput. As I have told you already there has been a very distracting chill in our flat for three days now. Today came the heater man, who must make a preliminary survey of the situation to determine what type of heater the new one will be. Since last year there are new regulations, which surprised me somewhat and yet corroborated something I have been noticing. Because of our grandiose new buildings, and the way the windows are done in them, it came to light that traditional heating systems or gas floor heaters are a death trap. Even a bathroom with a window allows no fresh air circulation. Hence the heaters remove so much oxygen that even a person using the bathroom can be asphyxiated. What had for a hundred years been unthinkable – that a room would be built without ventilation – seems in the modern way of building to have become possible. Objectively this must be seen as a step backward. Hence the heater man must test whether a heater will be supplied with enough fresh air given its use of oxygen for the burners. Luckily our flat is within a building from the 14th century, and so there are enough reserves. Had this not been the case, we would have needed to install a second pipe through the chimney up through the roof in order to guarantee the supply of air. A crane would also have been needed, and also a special heater, and all of that would have taken ten days. Ten days of cold, ten days of relying on emergency measures, would have been a difficult challenge. Thus, sitting down to write a letter, brings cold feet along with it, and so I beg your pardon for writing such a brief piece.

My insight that new regulations require additional work for their implementation is worth considering. I have the belief that it is an objective endangerment of persons. A government must take this into account. The endangerment however is especially high in new buildings. That means that a measure becomes necessary because considerable new expenses for the next users of a heating system must be taken into consideration. And I observe that there are more and more measures for guaranteeing our security, which in addition will have to be paid for from now on. If I add the environment and protection of the climate, we are facing an avalanche of expenses in the future, since the cost of improving our ecological situation will fall onto the shoulders of those who are most affected. That is something to think about.

Now however I must unfortunately close. I am cold.

All the best, R.

48.
Schools and Education Policy

Dear Nina, Dear Julian, Dear Marie and Vicky,

I write again, to distract myself from my cold feet. And since you are commuting back and forth between "e-learning" or school at home and normal lessons at school, I will gather my thoughts about school. You will not yet have been told that you come from eleven or twelve generations of teachers who, I believe, practiced this profession in an uninterrupted line. I suppose I can add my brother and myself. And your parents, too, are also close to the teaching profession. And while I am writing you, you will be doing your homework, your arithmetic and your drawing, painting something in your workbooks, or maybe reading some assigned material from school. Meanwhile I am reflecting on school. It may be that for myself, as I have already written, school of course seems important, but is it still appropriate in its present form? Presumably the method for learning to read and write is appropriate, and presumably one not has altered it since the 17th century in any noteworthy way; but I think, on the other hand, that in communicating more advanced scientific matters school has lost its competence – not because knowledge from the sciences can only be represented inadequately, but because there is a tendency to dogmatize scientific work. This implies that an "unschooling of school" ought to take place. If school was earlier able to present the totality of knowledge, which appeared to be possible over and above the specialized departments, these were still fields of knowledge that could be taught traditionally in the sense of Wilhelm von Humboldt, including historicism. What I can remember about the way school became a matter for political discussion was in two respects. There was the controversy about the abolition of the departments of ancient philology, where it was horrible that those who supported this used as their argument the senseless assertion that ancient languages are no longer spoken. And if I should think of everything that is no longer done we would only find only a few things that are practiced by many: should these, for this reason, no longer be taught? As a compensation for this loss an introductory course in "computation" was offered. This would still work, if the justification offered for it were not driven by a taste for modernity and being intellectually "up to date." The other topic of debate was the politics of education in general. The battles raged on about all-day school and about schooling all levels of aptitude together. I think that even at the time of the debates in Parliament this standoff was far removed from the reality of teaching at school. It turned into a battle of worldviews, between the two large political parties, and meanwhile it was hardly noticed that the entire landscape of school classes had hugely changed. There were more and more children "with a migration background" and with a different native language coming to school, and more and more of the "native" children were coming from broken families and failed relationships, and had lost the ground beneath their feet just as the children of the immigrants had. When I once asked, in an interview with Minister of Education Zilk in 1971, whether language teaching would not be provided for students who needed it, he angrily answered that it was their duty to see to it they had mastered the language in which instruction was being done. That was the attitude for a long time and in the meantime the problem has gotten out of hand.

School did not respond to this problem and left it to the individual teacher to deal with it, who had to make her way in this daily battle without support or help from the school administration. If one had then had the idea of an "unschooling" of the schools, one would have been able to redress much earlier and more effectively the problem of learning and development. School itself had become the first place in society in which one only with difficulty could speak about the social reality of everyday school life. I could voice a worse reproach but I hold my tongue, since you are going to school.

If I now play the advocate for a "de-schooling of school," and that this would be a start at solving the problem, I must come up with justifications. The first step, which would require no change in the school building design, would be that no more than ten youngsters be in a class. The group of learners will have a far better exchange of ideas with their teacher, and as to the teachers, they will be very much more able to respond according to the personal difficulties students are having in absorbing the lesson. I surely know that this means an enormous increase in the budget for education – and yet some day politics must be taken seriously, the claim every year, raised for decades in the budget debate in Parliament, that more and more money is needed so that we may succeed as an educational society. One can continue by explaining how school as a whole finds itself in a fundamental crisis. It is basically the victim of a crisis in the sciences we hear about ever since Edmund Husserl, above all because of the crisis in the empirical sciences which, of all things, directly affect the schools in their teaching of the natural sciences. Subjects like physics, chemistry, biology, geography, and also mathematics are deeply involved in education and mental growth, and thus we are serving up to our children fields of knowledge that are not so confident about themselves as they pretend to be.

Now I must refer to publications that led me to this evaluation. We must start from this, that school today is required to do much more than before. It is not only an institution for education and adjustment but more than ever it is called upon to create "free people," or as Rousseau once put it, to form people who are "forced to be free." And Rousseau was deeply convinced that this freedom is reached through education. This is the area for which school must take responsibility in the future. The lofty pedagogical dreams can be reached if, for example, the individual's experience in the classroom holds a higher rank than would be completely appropriated by television and other media. From this a closer and more vital experience of the relationship between knowledge and experience naturally follows. And presumably the most important point is that an "educational society" must not bring about what has been the case up until now: the elimination of being involved, and of serendipity, and of an open and indeterminate situation. Up until today learning means nothing other than the projection of the present into the future, which we then hope will be confirmed by experience at some time later on.

We must specify further the crisis in question. It is a remarkable phenomenon that the greater one's distance from the authentic "production of knowledge" and the activity of research, the more the results of research become dogmatized by teachers, in their reception and then in their dissemination in lessons. It is exactly when hypotheses get turned into warranted assertions that this petrification comes about. And if school claims to stimulate a given student, to advance people's ability, to motivate and to alter attitudes, to solidify identity, and to communicate social roles, there is in the way science is currently viewed a lack of doubt, of uncertainty, and of fostering questions and investigations. School tends to promulgate a prejudice about reality that nothing ought to change and nothing will change – and if it does change, the changes tend toward the fatal direction of infantilization. School ignores to point up the fluidity and mutability of reality. A classic example of this is when pictures by the children are hung on the walls of the staircases, honored as if these were the first steps toward the representation of reality in the "Egyptian manner" – the *Bedeutungsperspective*, according to which more important personages are larger and less important small. And so in Austria we see a rise in consigning children's painting to museality in this posting of "pre-scientific work," as a result of which a child's initial beliefs become irreversible. School must however beware of trying to achieve final knowledge – in the natural sciences in particular – and of falling into a physicalism that almost eclipses new perspectives that come into view almost every day.

If one reviews the old curricula of the universities, the subjects offered fostered development and creativity. One by one these were abolished, aesthetics for instance and finally rhetoric in Vienna around 1820, which is why liberal discourse is no longer to be expected from an academic. Of course I will not saddle school with all problems, nor is it only its graduates all by themselves that bring about the professional narrowing of knowledge. Indeed I ask myself how young people successful in their professions can be proud to say they do not need most of their knowledge. Up until their specialized studies at the university we have served them a knowledge prepared something like "fast food." We have not adequately represented the complexity of the phenomena; we have not emphasized that even every specialization needs a powerful theory in order to be able to specialize at all. What are we getting from a school that on any given day adds information theory and cybernetics, experimental psychology and genetics, and does not notice that the vocabulary of most of these comes from Greek? Doesn't that tell us something? And why should one not get a closer view of the knowledge that serves as our foundation? No – not at all: We notice not at all that in all these subjects, which in whatever form nature does show itself in each case, that nature is only engaged and viewed under a technological or scientific conception with the effect of its being reduced to a "sanitized" reality. One actually ought to notify the school that there are more dimensions of reality which are also and simultaneously present. We can only expect that pedagogics, in its function as a science ancillary to psychology, will on the one hand continue to pursue the project of "secularization" further – i.e., will harden itself to what it sees as an irreversible fact, and does not notice that there is nothing left to secularize after all; we can only expect that the social sciences have devised that school should be an agent of socialization, as the dispensary of the knowledge needed to give the graduates a specialized know-how related to distinct questions, which however seldom shows much use for the world one lives in. Only if one recognizes how this dilemma is playing itself out can one measure the professional burden being borne by an educator, a school teacher, or a professor. What experience of reality can one expect to find in young people? Has any such real experience not long since been absorbed in virtual representations? The elephant is sooner experienced as an image on YouTube than as a member of our world.

At this point we must remark that school must be the place where open as well as real experience takes place! And we remark at the same time that the hoped for reconciliation of nature with society – or vice-versa, in the sense of the ecological projects – has brought on little more than a catastrophic fake fight between special interests, and finally stoked up a catastrophic compromise between a scientific and theoretical recognition of our scientific achievements and the Marxist illusion of a "return to nature" for mankind, finally to shake off the slavery of drudgery, which however will only lead to total enslavement.

What have I written about? About the wish of Rousseau that people be taught to be free. We are doing little, heartily, and I observe in most teachers, both women or men, that at first they came to school with such high goals, but in a short time frustration sets in and the disappearance of any goal, ending in deep resignation. It is the school administrators that kill every outcry, by threatening them with relocation or any other forfeiture whatever. I always tell a joke: everywhere one has heard the boast from many groups, that they have brought about reforms in such a short amount of time. Here is our situation in a nutshell: in the traffic technology we have begun powerful reforms, have redesigned automotive engines, and at the same time are skimping on every source of energy. About school reform we have been talking and talking, for fifty years! The result is hardly noticeable. For the reasons described above, it is virtually immovable and resistant to reform.

So if I advise you take on specialized forms of knowledge and to acquire real knowledge, it is exactly because attending school does not take you very far, nor even mentions them. It would be wrong to assume that I do not recognize what school does contribute, but I am convinced that many hurdles not only hinder an appropriate conveying of knowledge but also thwart an adequate presentation of what knowledge really is.

So now I wish you good times in Vienna, and in Berlin.

Your R.

49.
Thoughts on Music

Dear Nina, Dear Julek and Marie and Vicky,

Many thanks for sending the recording of Julian at the piano. I was taken by his rendition of Chopin's *Études* op.10 n.3. This piece is however well-known in a "sung" version that is a favorite of tenors, called *In Me there Sings a Song*, later favored by pretty sopranos also. It always bothers me when I hear it sung, for then the étude loses its intimacy, its yearning – things so often to be heard in Chopin. And here I must sharply draw myself back since earlier I was not fond of Chopin. I thought of Franz Schubert and sniffed pityingly at Chopin. In one's old age one thinks differently. Chopin was like a master at drawing for the piano. There are extraordinarily sensitive drawings by John Constable, whose precise renditions of nature as it appears always reminded me of music, of Chopin that is, as I just now realize. And when in the *Impromptus* the dramatic element takes hold, or when the dances suggest the futility more than the desire for life as for example in a mazurka, then Frédéric Chopin comes very close to a subtle dramaturgy Caspar David Friedrich puts into his drawings. So you, dear Julian, will be taken into a musical world that is inordinately difficult to understand – indeed it can even be dangerous for you, since basically Chopin's musical language moves on two levels. That is, one could think at the first that his piano music consists of catchy tunes, and can be rendered marvelously like the music of Franz Lehar, and one thinks he must sing along with it – and yet behind this there lurks despair, the shortness of breath of tuberculosis, the anxiety of asphyxiation. With Chopin one always must bring forth the sound of this struggle for life. For a long time I consciously turned my back on Chopin's music since it seemed to me scrawny and often adolescent. Both of the *Revolutionary Études* seemed striking to me, and basically I made the mistake of associating Chopin's music with Franz Liszt's overbearing "show pieces" as well as his intolerable *Les Preludes*; and I thought that in Franz Liszt the consequences of Chopin were revealed, the superficiality and sanctimonious melting away into the musical universe. There was rarely anything real and authentic. By comparison Richard Wagner and his musical picture-painting seemed almost modest. I was not impressed by the pianist's retreat in Mallorca: it surely froze in the rain and fog. Since then the *Raindrop Prelude* no longer seemed to me so warm or clever: indeed in the environment of this former cloister, nestled among the hills of Mallorca, I had to recognize that this beloved German holiday destination was inhospitable and disconcerting. Perhaps it was then that I began to think differently about Chopin. Perhaps it was then that I came to the idea that his "studies" for the piano are a different version of "theme and variations" on the piano – something similar to the *Well-Tempered Clavier* of Johann Sebastian Bach. It that too far-fetched?

I find I am writing lines only for Julian. I once sent him an SMS asking him to name the composers of his piano pieces. I had recommended Haydn to him, the great Joseph Haydn. Although his music for the German hymn is a sturdier example of Haydn's composing, I am aware that no piano teacher in Germany teaches Haydn. The general opinion probably is that it is children's music. German pianists play no Haydn, since – so they say – his piano pieces can be "played with one finger," and they all sound like *Little Hans*, the children's song. There is no edition of Wilhelm Kempf playing Haydn's sonatas. So far only the greatest pianists play him: Glenn Gould, Alfred Brendel, Vladimir Horowitz. Conversely by Sviatoslav Richter there is only a single performance of a single Haydn sonata, so also with Artur Rubenstein. A judgment of taste comes into view, that under the heading of music one has first and foremost in mind an arousing of the emotions that dictates and controls feelings with the purpose of manipulating them. I often "saw" in the concerts of the Philharmonic in Vienna, during in the "stimulating" passages of a symphony with lots of brass and timpani, that the audience would stand up to watch the orchestra as if they were watching a circus stunt. And in the second movement of a traditional symphony the audience broke into two camps: some look at their programs and read about the orchestra's tour to Japan, others relax in a deep sleep. This is the behavior at Viennese concerts. With Haydn's symphonies I do not see this, since his symphonies are too short to fall asleep in. Concerts in Vienna are almost a mere pretext to justify having dinner at the Hotel Imperial.

So I repeat that with Chopin, Julian is confronted with a composition that is not easy to master. I only say this: the étude ought not to turn into a bath of feelings!

Now I must comment on the previous letter, to avoid being misunderstood. I was pleading only for a new representation of knowledge. Up until now the form of communicating about scientific knowledge – especially in the upper grades – is in my view not only obsolete but also continually bound up with a false understanding of science. A physicist once complained to me that it took him some four semesters to drive out a false notion of science his students got from secondary school, and this has not only gotten no better, but one generally lacks the candor to admit that the youth come with the attitude from their education that sciences are overwhelmingly based on "middle-range theories," as Robert K. Merton predicted in 1962. But wait: Haven't I already written you that we no longer have lessons on the nature of theory? And the fatal error is that in our educational institutions we spread the viewpoint that it is too difficult for a school child to understand a theory, so that they never hear what the theories are that "support" everything, and which cognitions apparently legitimate all these countless phenomena. The problem is that of course among the highest administrators of education, the awareness is not so widespread that knowledge is a "living organism." If anything a strong conviction predominates that one has a "solid" knowledge, a tested and controlled knowledge – in fact one would expect to hear the answer that solid and unquestionable knowledge came into the world on the birthday of a committee on education. And according to the field of study, the birthday of the committees and the higher committees on education mark the hours in which reliable knowledge of irreversible laws of nature are born.

I probably formulated the question in too cryptic a way, and that it even has to do with a similar step that we took two hundred years ago with the great reform of education. It has to do not only with a schoolish domination of various disciplinary problems, the healing of a perverted socialization, and so with the setting aside of the known deficiencies of basic cultural abilities (reading, writing, arithmetic, "making sense"), but at the same time with the adaptation of new scientific material to the curriculum. Presumably the latter is far more challenging than is reading these notes of mine. Let me cite a sentence from Carl Friedrich von Weizsäcker's *The Unity of Nature* (1971), the end of which puts us on notice that we are further than ever from reaching such a thing: "It is hardly obvious that a new theory will just pop up to fulfill this condition (i.e., achieving semantic consistency in quantum theory)." Just so, Einstein's famous analysis of contemporaneity was an analysis of the semantic consistency of a theory which was subject to the mathematical challenge of Lorentzian invariance (physical sizes, that do not change under the Lorentz transformation and are therefore invariant); it showed *that space and time had to be interpreted in a new way*, so as to bring daily experience into harmony with the theory.

I want to stop here. I hope that my previous letter has now become more understandable.

All the best, Your R.

50.
Is Social Integration Failing?

Dear Nina, dear Julek, Marie and Vicky,

I do not know who else is reading this! It is only quite discouraging, to hear not a peep from a reader! Nothing! "Breathless silence" would be the stage direction I would put in, if I were writing a play. For me the situation is familiar, even if over and over the hope pushes its way to the forefront that one or another of you might write to me, "Hey you, what's this about Lorentzian invariance?"

Good, it is completely unknown, since we are learning "mathematics" in school for eight years, and no pig says that this relies on a theory, on a daring hypothesis, even if Descartes was called the originator. But no, if I write that they are inadmissible dogmatizations, it is I who am in the wrong, not a recent graduate in some field who barely passed. This makes me angry. It makes me just as angry as when I hear nothing about my references to and about Chopin, as though music were now a soundless art. Today, on the occasion of sharing a snack, I gave the Grand Master of the Teutonic Order *Antinomies of Modernity*, which an adult must know about in order to understand the gruesome acts of murder that will haunt us over and over again in Europe. This was the first time that somebody was interested in understanding the aggression that is affecting us. Or else this problem will be checked off according to a tried and true pattern: foreigners afflicted by racism, terrible errors in immigration policy that has bestowed terrorists on us, and cheap wages in the labor market for these immigrants. All that may be correct – any empirical test could prove it – but are our "presuppositions" correct, a term that already glosses over our chauvinism? At the time I am in despair, which in any event nobody can understand, since more and more these days concepts are getting lost. There was once the optimistic concept of integration, this optimistic judgment that we ought to push for satisfactory integration. This has entirely disappeared. But it was not only our fault: Why should an Arabian integrate? Nobody brought up the comparison that the forcible termination of Moorish culture in Spain was in fact a crime (!), that however all of North Africa was forcibly conquered by Islam, part by part nearly as far as Ethiopia, Asia Minor, and the annexed territories. Does one apparently take this to be the normal course of history? Is history now to be used only for articulating European guilt-feelings?

I am "discouraged" – sullen and even angry. It is as if taking a position against the madness that is driving us is seen as breaking away from all humanity, breaking with a population that no longer sees its task to be giving in, integrating, but lets go of such ways of relating. So this means that the "European" is soon cashed in and will become easy prey for an Islam that in any case asserts it already has been here before – it overran us once before and it surely will wreak upon us this historical failure once again.

I write you this since you here must learn to know about tolerance, a term derived from our language and not from the Muslim one. Of course I know how to make distinctions, but in recent years we have had to recognize that all the laws that we have made for the acceptance of a confessional minority have suddenly proved worthless – indeed they have been overrun. One may say that one thinks differently about this in Austria. Not only do the qualifications, the testimonies, and the cognitions of our mother tongue count for something, but it makes a difference to what extent we can implement our country's language, how long can we try to accede to this gruesome game.

Good night! RK.

51.
Sociology as a Department

Dear Nina, Dear Julian, Marie, and Vicky,

Although I had promised to contact you "tomorrow," two days have now passed in between. This is not because of my dullness, but due to some things I had to take care of. And also it is not because I did not know what I was going to write about. This reminds me of a famous bet. In Vienna there lived, in the middle of the 17th century, a certain Abraham a Santa Clara (Johann Ulrich Megerle), a famous priest at the cathedral, who made a bet with a colleague. Just before the sermon, which at the time was delivered from the famous Pilgrim's Pulpit in St. Stephen's Cathedral, a slip of paper would be handed out with the topic of the sermon written on it. The preacher had to make up his sermon on the spot, speak fluently, and the winner (of the bet) would be the one who succeeded at holding the audience's attention in the mighty nave all the way through to the end. So as Abraham a Santa Clara went to the pulpit he took this slip of paper, looked at it, and could not believe his eyes: there was nothing written on the paper. In a flash he decided to preach on the nothingness of man. And he succeeded in impressing the believers. Abraham was known for his role in the development of our language, for he preached in a baroque German of the sort we can read in Hans Grimmelshausen, Martin Opitz, and Andreas Gryphius. Because of Martin Opitz the German language finally surpassed Latin as the language of literature. One must keep in mind that without the new custom of writing treatises in German, the Enlightenment could not have taken place.

Now: as I am working off my letter-writing debts, I now want for the first time to write something rather detailed about sociology. I passed my entire professional life with this social science, and my entry into the field came about in an unusual way. I had not chosen the path of study prerequisite for sociology, had not learned its "ancillary" sciences, which would have been mathematics and statistics, and had overall not mastered the related empirical methods. If one adds up these deficits, I had at the time (the middle 70's) no qualifications for sociology to present to the department in the university. That I could nevertheless be invested with an assistantship I owe to the happenstance that there was nobody in the department who was "specializing" in social philosophy or in historical sociology – here taken in the sense of Norbert Elias. It was as if a white elephant showed up at the zoo, and was marveled at as a member of a rare species – that's how I felt. Had there been other ulterior motives at the department, I was unaware of them. When I was allowed to offer my first lectures, I dealt with the connection between social history and "social theories" as that term was used at the time, which August Comte famously was first to call "sociology." If one wants to give a common denominator for these theories it would be the social constellation in the 18th century as determined by the two revolutions: the Industrial Revolution and the French Revolution. Given this it was relatively easy to depict socio-economic conditions in flux, and in time this enormous change was given a political conceptual inventory that consisted in the catchwords of the French Revolution.

Today I could not say with certainty whether either revolution would have had the same effect without the other. In any case I noticed at the time that this simple fact astonished the audience, since as "sociologists" they had heard of neither the one nor the other revolution, or else they didn't consider either of them relevant for their field of study. It was doubly interesting that some in the audience, with a clear sympathy for the Frankfurt School along with the student revolution, even claimed some knowledge of sociology without this historical background. Thus the first teaching experience was accompanied by the perception that there was a genuine Viennese tradition of sociological thinking, oriented toward Paul Lazersfeld, who had conducted the first empirical social scientific study around 1932 with his team on the topic, *Unemployment in Marienthal*. The effects of unemployment were investigated with methods taken from statistics and social psychology. Therewith it became possible to apply comparable, even though elaborate, methods to study all topics of society. If one still possessed the social-philosophical tools that were available before 1930, one would have given greater significance to the change in social factors from 1970 on. In Vienna, out of a subjectively chosen horizon of perception, social scientific quantifiables had been declared the object of study, and one approached this field with questionnaires and excerpts from the relevant literature. The big topics came to be youth, family, and elders, which had always "automatically" presented themselves as phenomena in society. This was still possible, since up until the 70's the character of society proved relatively stable. With the student movement, the youth movement, with segmentations and with fragmentations in society, and with birth statistics in huge numbers, society was being destabilized, and this forced sociology to face new demands. And of all things, a science that itself owed its origins to unbelievable phenomena of change was no longer in a position to interpret this break. How can it do so if it is dependent for its project-funding upon third-party research grants, which largely were devoted to studying everyday questions? Soon, an "automatic practice" in the social sciences was subject to an amateurization – that is, survey research, opinion polling, and election projections were given over to sociologists as the scope of their work. And the majority of the department's members scurried off into such laughably subaltern activities as these, merely to attract project funding and get a piece of the cake, which was distributed unfairly anyway. One would have been able to see that all this was going on were it not for the fact that unexpected niches of opportunity were created, because of the reform work at the university – the so-called University Organization Act – which promised a secure livelihood. The "middle level" at the time, the former assistants – appointed as it were to be a one-third faction playing the role of the pointer on a scale between the professors and the students – specialized in a marathon of committee meetings and conferences. That would have been a fun thing, had the "middle level" not in its unrewarded opportunism exploited the service contracts of their colleagues for political advantage. Some time I will tell you how in one of the many elections of the middle level's members the "wrong outcome" took place – so that a colleague took the voting slips out of her hat, tore them up, and boldly declared that the voting had to be done over again. A new understanding of the democratic process became the rule. This new administrator-university had science in mind far less: rather, administrating became the credential, replacing science, along with membership in agencies, commissions, and directorates of the department, which themselves became virtual political instruments in the administration of science. With the ingenious separating out of the facility managers and of the non-academic personnel along with librarians, these became an unassociated institution in the middle of the university. While the department's copying paper, technical equipment, and erasers became goods to fight over and had to be managed according to emergency contingencies, the building facilities administration relocated itself comfortably into the main building on the Ring; the non-academic personnel assigned secretaries according to their whims, which mostly was taken to be an act of revenge since many of these were unable to type at a decent speed; and the high point was the independent libraries, which altered and diminished their service by adopting flexible working hours. The affair was a lesson in wastefulness of every kind.

I write you about this tragic development since only a short time before, sociology – if I may be allowed an all-embracing statement – had claimed that it had its finger on the pulse of the times and of society. The best example came soon before: during the upheaval in the GDR, these same sociologists who had just been claiming that nothing in society is hidden from their view, then declared on television that what developed in the GDR came as a surprise to them and was unforeseeable. And it was apparently an unexpressed agreement among them to disown all awareness in this way, despite questionnaires and opinion surveys.

In my opinion this was a declaration of bankruptcy by a social science whose exponents and members of a most important institute, just a few days before, had demonstrated in Berlin, in what is now Rudi Dutschke-Strasse, against the Springer Verlag and against fascism, and yet did not notice the turbulence in East Berlin only 100 yards away. Already, years before, this "second hand" of the empirical social sciences was not ticking correctly, and was now unable to identify the areas of conflicts within society. One must consider it the fault of the social sciences that they generally did not realize what was behind this enormous surge in migration. That is, a social science that is aware of all the ailments of society – as indeed it claimed – was not equipped to interpret the greatest migration between states in world history, to study it and represent its effect on society with simulation models. Often I spoke with Paul Neurath in my small office at the Institute, who had long since worked on this topic as an emeritus professor. And he would have tussled his hair, if he'd still had any, when he began to talk about the consequences of this immigration with me. Thanks to Paul Neurath I had an early access to this dramatic phenomenon, while in fact people were completely deaf to it. It was for me an indication that sociology had forfeited its competence as an interpreter of social events.

This was the time that my relationship with Michael Benedikt was revived and I became a frequent guest at the department of philosophy. I had gotten to know Benedikt long before, through a reading circle at my home. I remember quite vividly that when he first came into the room he earnestly asked me how my relationship came about with this whore, philosophy. I was so baffled at being asked something like that, by a real life professor, that it took me a while to answer. As yet I had no clue that the sciences partly hang their flag in the wind, and partly tend to conform to political guidelines. The department of philosophy at Vienna was especially infamous for this. Because of Erich Heintel, who had taken his career from Prague to Vienna via Sepp Dietrich's circle for western quartet music – of course an illegal member of the NSDAP before 1938 – it had become clear to me early enough that philosophy is not the vaccine one might have hoped for, given an Eric Voegelin or a Karl Jaspers, but to the contrary that philosophy often played counsellor to the immoral, to the inhumane, and a devotee of perverted irony.

This department of philosophy was unusual overall. Because of irreconcilable differences a wall was erected between the two professorial chairs, around the same time as the Berlin Wall, and any communication between the two fronts was reported and punished. The group around Heintel was always appearing at the seminars in full combat strength yet on one occasion their courage failed them: when Paul Feyerabend was in the lecture hall, Heintel refused to continue his lesson. And Heintel remarked to the last member of the Vienna Circle, Bela Johos, that he may well have thought differently if he had studied with him in Prague. This was the spirit which, of all things during the leadership of Hertha Firnberg, would provide for the foundation of the new universities in Klagenfurt and Salzburg. Thanks to Benedikt I was vaccinated against all viruses, after which our collaboration in the history of philosophy was established.

In the department of sociology the subsequent period was fully occupied with establishing a third professorial chair. The German candidates were always the first chosen. My suggestions to choose Ralf Dahrendorf in private conversations were unfortunately ignored. So other professors were appointed, who immediately gave it to be known that their calling to Vienna was only to be a "part-time" affair. They were ready to be in Vienna for two days a week at best, so that they could get back "home to the *Reich*." Even today one can expect no interest at all for the condition of Austrian problems among the professors hired from Germany. They come to Vienna "with servant, horse and carriage," refuse any integration, and say openly that they will be accepting any next offer they get in Germany. So these teachers have no interest in lecturing, and had no interest in departmental politics. They elaborate their anti-capitalist sociology and then disappear again. The situation got so grotesque that in 2020 the department included over a hundred members, but had completely disappeared from public view. From a distance one might observe that with the overwhelming presence of German professors in Vienna, some internationality of teaching had come about, but the truth is that in the orientations of the special subjects there was, for instance, no more Austrian music and in art history no Austrian painting. In musicology Franz Schubert is listed under German Romantic music and Gustav Klimt is listed not at all.

Now I must go back to my story. At the Institute, the university reform had brought to a halt any interest in traditional science. For example I can mention that if I had left books at my writing table, by the next day they would disappear. Were they stolen? Today I am almost proud that books were still being stolen in the Institute at that time! With the reorganization, along with the comprehensive computerized facilities, books were stolen no more. I believe one could leave a first edition of the Luther-Bible on the table, and it would have aroused nobody's interest. In earlier times, one had to pack everything up at the end of the day and carry it home in a heavy bag, but given the PC and committee meetings, any interest about what an Institute actually consists in, was lost. Am I overstating it? During commission meetings the students present nursed their babies, and knitted and smoked, and yet as soon as an issue would come up for a vote, any suggestion was sure to fail. The breast feeders, the knitters, the smokers and those nodding off, always tipped the scales. The impression would be false, if someone had it, that I objected in every way to these members of the commission. This was not so. Mostly this surprisingly persistent womanly behavior added some legitimacy: at least to introduce a connection with life, with existence and one's profession. The students who voiced their opinions merely out of ideological motives were worse. And thanks to the dean's secretary they got masses of information that harried the commission from reaching a consensus. We now have a Federal President who, as a long-term dean, despite low tides of spirit, guided the faculty through every drought, and yet no one could figure out what this luminary had in mind.

On all these events I could write quite a lot. I could, but that is the past, and the current situation of the university is my witness that the educational goals were no longer being achieved, or else that the goals were reformulated. I can already imagine what one wishes from the graduates: to think "on their own," to know their specialty, to be skeptical in their evaluation of innovations, to be clever at getting along, at teamwork, at hobbies and communal leisure activities.

If I may return to sociology, the challenge to master this discipline in an intellectual way failed in the department. I remember how a colleague who happened a few days later to die, urged me to try hitting him with all my might on his chest since he embodied the power of science even in a physical way. Conversely he sneered that I, a little twerp, utterly lacked the physical prerequisites for science. And all around the coffee table, the colleagues nodded, and gave it to be understood that science is hard bread and brooks only the strongest. And strong indeed was the scholar: strengthened by round after round of beer, he achieved his habilitation, and became a specialist at encoding questionnaires. From that moment I not only bought myself my own coffee maker, but it also became clear to me that interpretation machines would be dominating this science and so it would not be possible to interpret phenomena when they change. I wrote this before and I repeat it, since it points out the problem: surveys are only a result of what happened the day before yesterday. So if today is Monday then the result only gives me knowledge about a state of affairs that occurred on Saturday. Generally speaking, conflicts or social tensions and other social stresses are "multi-dimensional" and I am convinced that a hermeneutic method takes us further, in comparison with a survey that only reflects what one could learn in any bar.

In reviewing what I have said I see I have left out a systematic presentation of the problem in which the social sciences are now involved. I can only apologize, and hold out a promise to consider the matter again. I thought it was essential to begin by describing the lay of the land and sending you that, so as to let the meaning slowly emerge in the analysis.

Now it remains for me to send you my earnest and loving greetings! Your R.

52.
The Fate of Language

Dear Nina, Dear Julian, Vicky, and Marie,

It is truly amazing that over fifty letters have now been sent to you. To what extent they all are readable enough to be enjoyable of course remains an open question. Some writings are easier to read, others more difficult. This brings me to the thought that we are having certain difficulties with our language in the present time. It is plain to see and to hear how difficult it has become to formulate things clearly, to speak in "plain" language, or even to speak in public. What is most remarkable is that we are no longer able to convince each other with words. We know from broadcasts of the Parliament on television that the speeches are basically senseless, at best a formulaic performance, and that the representatives are speaking not at all to each other but are speaking "out the window" when the cameras point at them. To console us we are assured that the representatives do speak to each other in their committees behind closed doors. Similarly, it is completely unclear whether scientific meetings are of any use. Of course the scientists see each other again, they chat about their latest vacations, publications, jobs, honors; but one cannot expect very much of substance, for their most recent research has long since been retrieved from the internet. The problem is not an "absence of real speech" in the midst of chatter: rather it is time to ask the question whether we still can understand each other. It has become common that rather than asking someone we look down to our devices for help. We always knew that there was some difficulty of understanding between the different professions – between disciplines, specialties, and occupations – but now even people in the same field run into difficulties even to chat with each other. Also, a "bad habit" arose some time ago that one does not "keep his word," that one deliberately lies if it is to his advantage, that one does not warn his neighbor of something dangerous, and even that disinformation has become an instrument for intentionally causing confusion. One has to grant that words have become worthless. Misunderstandings arise in a two-fold way: either the sense of the word is no longer understood, or one chooses to speak ambiguously. Shall we say then that our speech is becoming riddled with irony?

This much we know: whoever begins to be insecure about words is becoming insecure in his mind, uncertain of his own humanity. And the ways for ameliorating this are bad off. The "normal register" of language has become extraordinarily vulgar. The coloration of dialects is oriented toward advertisement and television shows. If we compare our speech these days to the "dialect" in the plays of Johann Nestroy, we notice immediately that we have lost any striking use of metaphor, the clever turn of language, and elegance. It may be that Nestroy mastered a special art of formulation, and yet in each case his language was a borrowing from the "speech of the people." In the three main characters of his *Lumpacivagabundus*, Knieriem, Zwirn, and Leim, the speech is indeed of three contemporary types. Most of the turns of phrase or the richly imaginative rendering of a synecdoche are pleasurable in themselves. The accompanying scene-setting is almost unneeded. Conversely, our own expressions have become vague and muffled when they don't resort to scatology. Whereas respect for women had before been an impediment against crass conversation in the society of men, young ladies now show a special penchant for vulgarity. Presumably as a result of a notion of equality one thinks that as a woman she must over-perform in the use of expletives. And finally, thanks to our electronic devices, the new phenomenon is the silencing of communication.

One might just think that with the spread of these devices and their earphones, it would be quieter in the world. This guess is roundly refuted. A cacophony of voices is the normal background noise, supported by so-called music projected everywhere through loudspeakers. Every sound overruns the other, drowns out the other, numbs us and brings on an acoustic exhaustion that surrenders in resignation to these clouds of noise. And then there are the songs of the *castrati* on electric guitar saying something in English. I remind you of one of my letters where I explained that the vocabulary of these songs is limited to about eleven words. Probably these bleating noises are an expression of desperation, or fear, or anxiety about life. At the same time they reveal a most interesting phenomenon: no longer is there any dialogue. The rhetoric of the songs is that of a swansong, continuously saying goodbye with neither emotion nor romance.

It may be the case that I am drawing too many comparisons from music, which is not here my subject. I would have been able to write this as well with a comparison from the career of science. Science is proud that it has separated itself from the wide field of speculation. What one does not think about is the fact that the entirely insecure terrain of the sciences has been lost, but therewith one has also pulled the plug on language. We know this from the case of sociological argumentation, where the power to express is found in tables and percentages and not in the sound of the word as a spur to anamnesis. In the natural sciences, if its language were not formulated innately, a machine language finds a new employment in effecting the exchange of ideas. And this is only the modest beginning, and totally unforeseen.

Let us assume that only cinematic records were being consulted, instead of the countless historical books. Is this the pure description? Is this, then, the objectivity we have long yearned for? Actually, Kant has left us this "Yea," when he set out mathematics as the fundamental criterion for what is scientific, for what in every case must underlie a science. Granted, mathematics does contain countless logical structures, but didn't I say countless letters ago that at the same time all that has been established by this is a giant network of tautological equilibrium? And yet we did not stop there. In philosophy we have appropriated for ourselves a positivism, that has the advantage of honesty: positivists are as respectable as Doubting Thomas, who did not believe what he had not seen with his own eyes – but what then is happening in the untraversable spaces of physics? If we deny a reality which has been proven though we cannot see it, we would quit doing all these experiments immediately. If it is asserted that one could go off into infinite space where more and more galaxies are to be discovered, more and more suns and perhaps even worlds, how then can we treat this statement as actually true? And this representation is meant to bring the entailments near, namely that in view of this infinity, speech is left behind; it is silenced if it now fails to find a place for itself in the surreal and the futuristic, from Hugo Ball or Antonin Artaud up to Stanislaw Lem. Or will language be preserved in the sound-poems of Ernst Jandl? But we no longer understand that language. Language there has lost its communicative function. Long since we have invented metalanguages in order to keep up with what we can no longer express in our language, which merely applies to the world. It was a further step to abjure traditional philosophy, thinking that in the anti-philosophy to come philosophy will stay alive, so we relegate the remnants of philosophy to the realm of mysticism, a realm that philosophy no longer tolerates.

We understand immediately that the anti-philosophical wants to shift the written language into the realm of fairy tales, which Luther already had begun to do when he referred to the Old Testament as fairy tales. And we refer to the loss of revelation as a triumph of the positivism of classical philology: even the psalms are just poetry, at best. They are not promises but just illusions, since over and over they put before us the prospect of reaching some land in which milk and honey flow. And as we have begun to read such writings philologically, we have lost the multidimensionality of language, of words, and of writing. So what do we speak, now? Since our speech has been stolen, the framework of our language seems a quite dull everyday thing – just like the songs we hear on the radio night and day.

What I want to show here, and what remains difficult to understand in the language I am using, is the fact that we have not taken care of our language in philosophy, just as we haven't in science. While theological language is almost completely dried up unless we read aloud from the scriptures, we have instead incorporated the zeitgeist into our thoughts, over and over again. In this we are following the light of the Enlightenment and have welcomed wholeheartedly its consequences in every area of our lives, and have failed to see that we basically ought to have been busy enlightening the Enlightenment. When we don't believe anyone anymore – why should we? – the zeitgeist breaks into our thinking with all its explosive force and is more believable than reality itself, which it created on its own in the first place. The coinage "zeitgeist," which Hegel so deftly slipped into our thought, robbed us of our integrity, of our innocence, of the self-determination of philosophizing. Thanks to "zeitgeist" all thinking proceeds as it were on predetermined tracks. Was it out of bad conscience about our failings that we so easily took refuge in empiricism in our philosophy, as though thereby we would uncover reality once again? And thus we lost our history, we annihilated our unity, for from now on there is a history of law, of race, of art, of postage stamps – it is only the old kind of history that we no longer have. There is no place for people in it any more, except perhaps as an aspect of the history of technology. It was the brave nonsense of the Enlightenment that Voltaire came up with the idea of writing a "philosophy of history," and Jean-Baptiste Lamarck a "philosophy of nature." From these insights descend our eloquent philosophers in

the universities, the rhetoricians that combine misuse and jargon and kill all the
tentative steps of thought as it evolves. Granted, Karl Popper did a good job of
debunking this development and in *The Poverty of Historicism* flagellated this
apostasy, but in his attempt to save philosophizing he remained modest. Had he
tested his falsificationism properly, few of his own viewpoints would have
survived, neither the *Logic of Scientific Discovery*, nor the *Open Society*. The only
attractive point he made was that one is allowed to err and that one can in fact err.
Thus we were freed from the straightjacket of ideology, and yet we had hardly
escaped before the zeitgeist, enmired in positivism, tied us back up. In this,
positivism was at least honest, even if it also became fashionable.

All this changes nothing as to our loss of language. We must admit that we
have always been writing a story, yet we have repressed our motive for doing so,
since the content of the story was always our knowledge about the human soul. It
is mirrored in the story, and yet in the tangled mess of power and splendor, this
mirroring was no longer perceivable. Is Ovid's story of Philemon and Baucis not,
by a large margin, more truly a history than the *Germania* of Tacitus? Isn't
Homer's *Iliad* the definitive interpretation of the true history about which the
Anabasis of Xenophon was a failure, not to mention Polybius?

The Enlightenment was the most efficient attempt to force exactly this kind
of history to be forgotten, and the immediate harvest, historicism, was probably
the wrong direction to go from the beginning. What moved the scholars in the
Enlightenment to think so little about it was that it had been written: "In the
beginning was the Word ...": one could say that the famous short sentence of
Descartes was the exact opposite of this: *cogito ergo sum*. And so his doubting
about the Word drove him to place the natural sciences on a new level, and so
with a vague hope that this was the first step toward bringing about an earthly
paradise. The reversal became most clear in that from now on one had to focus
upon philosophy historically, when one started viewing the work of Augustine as
the first example of a history of philosophy. But it was never the Church Father's
intention to become a second Livy. From this turnaround all the hypotheses are
derived – all the wild interpretations that discover an actual logic embodied within
history. This in the end allowed the close connection of the logos with the spirit
to be loosened, and indeed to break utterly, so that it could be eliminated from the
consciousness of mankind for once and for all. We are now facing the results,
facing the madness of every possible frenzy, and facing the destruction of nature
all the way up to the destruction of the self.

We have not noticed all this. We have more pressing concerns, as we try to
puzzle out whether we can still understand each other and think everything is
alright as long as our telephone works. We have lost any consolation from ancient
philosophy and yet feel no loss for that. We can't even define serenity any longer,
nor composure, and so we cannot answer the question what ought to be our
relation to this world. We know only our right to plunder the "planet." And so the
earth is not being conserved, and flora and fauna are perishing. Too late, perhaps,
have we perceived that this world has only been given to us on loan, and only for
the duration of our lifetimes. At this point in time language floats off into a

separate sphere so as to make up for all that it enabled us to name. This was likely begun by Nietzsche and had its continuation in Martin Heidegger. Language is now to become the absolute, whether it be in poetry or in philosophy, and to have a world of its own, now that the other world is no place to be. The silence of matter joins up with a conceptionless mysticism of language. I believe that in this labyrinth of language we will have a hard time finding our way given our sciences of language. We will however try. And a yearning once again to recover language – to find it intact in the holy scriptures – will continue to draw us, as the zeitgeist becomes ever more disgusting, ever more evil, gruesome, and bloody. Our whole disgust with speech, which again and again serves up abominations to us, is still not great enough to make us finally stop writing such things, which are only new and tedious versions of examples ranging from Bernard Mandeville's *Fable of the Bees* to Marquis de Sade's *Philosophy in the Bedroom*.

This entire constellation you read about here presents the zeitgeist at a safe distance, this hard-to-pin-down phenomenon that spreads itself recklessly throughout our life-world and hinders us from stopping what is killing us. Granted, there are authors, about whom indeed I have been thinking in the course of writing this, who paddled upstream, against the current and "the times," and not at all in vain; but if it is no longer people who are doing the paddling, we will no longer need to worry about having a future. That means, of course, that such perspectives do still exist, but they will not come into view through democratization, but rather through in a change of heart in each of us!

All the best, yours R.

53.
Theater and Politics

Dear Nina, Dear Julian, Marie, and Vicky,

After my lecture today I am really exhausted. Our on-line conference lasted from 1:15 in the afternoon until 6:00 in the evening. There were ten or eleven "viewers" who for most of the session kept to themselves and listened "muted," which made my presentation even more difficult. Some of them said they were very impressed by my letters. For the first time they claimed to have understood my "propaedeutic" to philosophy. So you can see what a high opinion I have of you, that students who were then much older think they have understood something for the first time. This hardly makes me proud or arrogant, since these letters are for you – first and foremost for you – to understand. Now you might ask yourselves, what is one to do with these letters, after all? There are two answers, at least two. If the letters are nothing more than a private writing exercise that my computer makes it easy for me to send, then this writing project is basically inconsequential. It is at best the testimony of an old man who is trying to express himself in writing and is dealing with themes that concern him. Such would amount to off-hand remarks, and basically would lose the importance I secretly hoped they would have – namely that they might be a document for our times. You have already learned of diaries, often those belonging to dramatic times in which important personages have written about how decisions were being reached. Often it was a matter of serendipity, but in another case it was about a dark hour in which the important persons failed to find each other. For example, if the famous Julius Caesar had believed the blind seer – a "handicapped" man, that is, when nobody in Rome at the time would have believed half of what he said – he would have escaped assassination. Being a careful reader, Julian would immediately recall that in Greek tragedy the blind seer plays a crucial role in the discovery of truth! From that event it was important for me that I did not follow Shakespeare's lead and fall in with his own political preference: instead, I slowly came to adopt the position that the historic attempt of Brutus to murder the tyrant was the more important decision. Needless to say I don't like murder at all, and there in the theatre I was outraged that someone could dispense with his leader in this way, but the error in my opinion became more and more clear to me. The most important source for my skepticism was Cicero, who as an unlucky participant in political affairs, as a righteous jurist and at the time a quite clumsy representative of the Republic, may very well have pulled the strings to drive Caesar's opponents toward the "putsch." For me Shakespeare's version has always been a stimulus for thinking politically. Though Cicero doesn't even come in to the story, the future imperial dictatorship of Augustus is cleverly integrated into the plot and Cicero was nevertheless an instigator of the monarchic absolutism to come. It was necessary that Caesar be murdered illegally because James I, the King of Scotland, had cleverly seized the English crown. As a court-poet Shakespeare had to give due attention to this shift of power. And he guessed that certain successors like Charles I and Charles II were on the way to establishing an absolutism. This interrupted the "Glorious Revolution" but in the end could not stop it.

As in the theatre so also in the public view, the murder of Caesar was illegal, and in particular a violation of political succession. So Cicero was basically on the outside, as a spectator from the Senate whose political position was only tolerated. Maybe his own vanity played a role, but as the last upstanding defender of the Republic he was little more than a right-winger fighting relentlessly against corruption, unable to make any friends. So the tragedy of Caesar is even more the tragedy of Cicero. Still, this play is an important political document. Just as Cicero had not been able to become involved, which the court society in London's Globe Theatre surely did not take into consideration, so Brutus had to be depicted as a ruthless character. He is a teachable example of how noble political motives can lead to committing murder, and how a respectable moral duty – to save a Republic – can end in a treacherous assassination. It is no wonder that the "Mark Antony" as we see him in Shakespeare's play, then succeeded to initiate the transition to monarchy.

In a nutshell Shakespeare's play is a showcase for the common political mutation from the principate of a Pompey to the monarchy of a Caesar. And in fact this corresponded with the transformation of Renaissance cities of upper Italy into principates, and into vassals of the papal states. The prediction that Niccolò Machiavelli had very pessimistically formulated, around 1500 in *The Prince*, seems at this point to have come true. He derived his political acuteness out of a more bitter irony – in fact he suggested that one day the Medici's would not only rule the city but soon would become partners with the French crown and the papacy. Twice he was tortured to force him to expose his confidants, and twice Machiavelli withstood the agony and remained silent. And nobody noticed or came to understand why he dedicated his acute political treatises to the *Princes*, his tormenters! A more damning objection he was unable to write. And of all things this book became the "director's manual" for absolutism. So even irony can lead to misunderstandings!

Shakespeare had indeed recognized the signs of the times, but he was no opportunist. His conception had nothing to do with the huge Flemish still-lifes like the *Feast of a Bean King*. His work could much better be compared with the extraordinary paintings of Pieter Brueghel. There is sectarian madness in *The Fight Between Carnival and Lent*, there is evil murder in *The Massacre of the Innocents*, and the haughtiness of the powerful in the *Tower of Babel*. The list of paintings is long, as long as the list of Shakespeare's historical plays, which the King from the royal box of the "World Theater" – the Globe Theater, that is – had to watch without voicing any objections. He had to behold the infamy, the murderousness, the violations, and intrigues of his predecessors, too, and received the bitter message that he was the successor to those benighted excesses. William Shakespeare is a wonderful poet who placed "modern" politics onto the stage, the hypocrisy of the rulers and the insatiable madness of desire among the elites.

To get back to Caesar, it was he who brought the Republic to its final collapse. Though formerly the partisan of the people, he suddenly came to be of divine origin, counting Venus herself as his forebear, and approached his political options with the strategic prowess of a general. But even his killing could not bring the political change to a halt. If it couldn't be Caesar, it would turn out to be Augustus. In this, two phenomena are particularly bitter. On the one hand the old institutions of the Republic continued to function, from the Senate to the institutionalized worship of political virtues according to the state religion, without being able to effect any change in the absolutism of the government; on the other, the political transformation was the foundation for a politics of colonization, an enormous expansion into a world empire. In the course of analyzing this, a book happened to come into my hands that impressed me greatly. Right off, the foreword was devoted to an hypothesis which at the time hardly anyone could understand. And one would not at all have wanted to understand it, either! More than a hundred years ago the Roman historian, Eduard Meyer, wrote on Caesar's capture of power and thought that the USA would do a comparable thing: that rising aspirations of world-power would weaken the traditional lawful foundation of a republic and corrupt democratic institutions from the inside. It had become clear to Meyer, in 1902, not only that the USA would go in this direction, but in addition he dealt point by point with the criteria that on the one hand allow the empire to become a world power, but on the other hand – in the rights and tolerances that derive from it, and later virtual liberties – how a gradual weakening of world empire would at the same time become possible. This was published at almost at the same time as the reflections of Max Weber on the decline of the Roman Empire, admittedly more sharply formulated by Weber: that the peculiar strengths of the Empire become the cause of its gradual weakening. It taught me that "no empire of this world" can last forever.

When I said in the last letter that there are in fact two forms of history, I mentioned finally the one that is described as the genuine and effective one, the one we can reconstruct according to the sequence of the soldier-emperors on all the coins, and in which at the same time we must come to see that even the most extreme and brutal measures will not rescue the situation. Up until the Renaissance ancient Rome remained in ruins. One must imagine that in the Middle Ages, when the emperors had to present themselves at Rome to be coronated they rode through the rubble and ruins to the old basilica that stood like an island stronghold in the midst of them. Up until the 19th century cows pastured in the *Forum Romanum* and understood as little as a Roman shepherd what had happened beneath the grass they were feeding on. Granted, the restoration of these mighty buildings can give us a sense of "what was then;" granted, the reconstruction is important, for now one knows where the great orators had stood, how political opinion would circulate through the maze of streets; but more important – far more important – is the legacy of this "state:" the homogeneity of the rulers, and the genuine stabilization of the manifold societies, cultures, and religions under Roman Law. It was as consequential in general European history as the Roman brick in our architecture, for it made construction of the dome of the Pantheon possible – and the basilica Santa Maria sopra Minerva. Had these two edifices not come into being, Rome's history would hardly have survived.

I started with Shakespeare's *Julius Caesar*. He was in fact the turning point of Roman politics. And I want to conclude on that subject with this: I once went to the Burgtheater for Shakespeare and *Julius Caesar*. I looked forward to being "enlightened" about Roman history just as I had earlier learned about the history of Northern Italy in Friedrich Schiller's *Fiesco*. But right at the beginning it was clear that the director had something else in mind – not Shakespeare, nor even *Julius Caesar*. Before the lights went down the hall was filled with a loud voice. In a pre-recorded audio the crowd of people was being asked what they were looking for here, and why they came. Some were advised to leave: what was about to follow would be an old and uninteresting piece. "Leave while you still have a chance." "There is nothing worth waiting for here!" "What do you want to get from this theater?" "Get out before the subway closes!" After this little episode the hall was darkened, the curtain rose, and on an empty stage one heard only a whisper. Spectators called out for them to speak louder: "Louder please!" "We can't understand what is being said!" Would I not after all be getting insight from this performance why Caesar was murdered? and why of all people Brutus was to be the murderer? and why in the end the ghost of Caesar would still appear in Brutus's camp? Was it the idea of the director himself to treat the piece as an authoritarian, and so to treat the audience also, so as to warn them against absolute power, against the seizure of power, against fascism and Mussolini – in 1995?

Here I want to close. I wanted to make you aware with this disturbing experience how we are consciously misrepresenting topics, giving arbitrary misrepresentations of history, as if the entire import of history leads only to a vision culminating in the night of the Nazi pogrom. The contrived denial of these gruesome horrors in artworks itself becomes, in the end, a message of sympathy for power and terror.

I hope that you will no longer have this sort of *Regie-Theater*, by which all the treasures of drama are being disfigured.

All the best to all of you, your R.

54.
From Cultural Competence to Knowledge

Dear Nina, Dear Julian and Marie and Vicky,

When I think of your everyday regime I imagine it's centered around attending school. Once you have finished the daily lectures you are not left free since the afternoon consists of studying, doing homework, and then there must be some free-time activities, whether it be playing the piano or developing your own ideas or just reading. These activities show your individuality: Julian and Marie have to practice their next piano piece, Nina reads her umpteenth book, and Vicky still has that bit of freedom to do whatever she wants – to play. I would add a nuance to these guesses about your everyday life, that it is at school that cultural competence and knowledge are instilled in you. The teachers teach you insights and opinions, and you are being guided toward attitudes among which you are to make your own evaluation or choice. Since in our civilization education is lasting longer and longer and using up more and more of our lifetime, one's release into adulthood comes quite late. You must imagine that the life expectancy of people in the Middle Ages was on average comparable to the amount of life we spend simply completing our education. Social historians have concluded that with the significant lengthening of the time spent on education, sexual maturation also is delayed. If we leaf through the relevant specialist literature, it was not until the middle of the 18th century that we were able to distinguish between childhood and adolescence as periods of life the way we now commonly do. This is not at all what I set out to write you, but the opportunity affords itself to remind you that phases of life are now greatly lengthened, and with this, that certain forms of life come into view that could not even exist three or four hundred years ago.

Already you know that in all likelihood you will continue your education past school. And you will observe that you must make your own decision. This will be the case every day. As you encounter schoolmates you will judge them according to their appearance and their comportment and will form an opinion about them. This complicated process is completed in just a few seconds. And because it is so complicated one will rely all the more on the judgment of others. Now and then you will think their judgment to be correct. But what about times when it isn't? Then you must form your own judgment. You put it together out of your actual perceptions and life experience. You will not readily grant – in your own minds at least – that this life experience also includes the knowledge and insights you gained at school. My point is, though you will "shoot from the hip" in your answers to many questions, you will be able to remember that you had heard it in school. And now the question arises, to whom does this knowledge belong that you at some point acquired? Since for many years you have known what 2x2 makes, the correct answer has basically has come to be your own. Basically, all the school knowledge we can remember has come to be our own possession. Thus Goethe composed the maxim, "Get hold of what you have inherited from your father to make it your own."

Have we then solved the problem? Can we carry on in our lives under these circumstances, more or less possessing extensive agglomerations of knowledges that we have made our own over the years? Can I still really say that once I am able to add up a column of figures that I have come to possess adequate mathematical knowledge? It would be somewhat arrogant for me to call myself a mathematician on that basis. And yet far worse if I should boast, in company and at an advanced hour, that I of course know the works of Goethe and Schiller. Have I really read all of it? That's not possible even for a Germanist. If then I think I know Goethe, have I merely recited the judgment I received during my school days? Or have I continued with my education and have read, in addition, *Wilhelm Meister* or even *Hermann and Dorothea*? That will lead us into a more heated debate in still later hours, but nobody will think also about justifying the way he reaches judgments nor whether he has in the meanwhile revised his old ideas about Goethe. Entirely thoughtless, we babble on and think nothing of it – and we think not at all about Goethe either – at a wine bar.

You can already guess where this path of thinking should lead. Let's take an example from any current collection of paintings. Quickly you will observe in yourselves that your encounter with paintings begins with an effort to find some characteristic of the painting, and here your memory should help you. You have learned that there is such a thing as style, ways of representation that correspond to each period in painting; and the name of the painter aids you in classifying the period. In this you are reproducing more impressions that are not really your own. Do you now have the leisure and curiosity, in regard to painting, to gather together your own impressions and to formulate your own interpretation? It will not be so easy to get out from under the heap of things under which your willingness to experience has been buried. Most people are so lazy they allow themselves to be guided through the painting gallery: instead of using their own eyes, they allow the explanations of a leisurely guide to wash over them – and to take selfies, with or without the painting. That is, one wants never to be at risk of seeing nothing at first – nothing special or unique. Since we paid the entry price we are sure we will be encountering art, even if we cannot see it. It would be a fraud, after all, if one had paid for the ticket and was not able to see any art anywhere. Thanks to the stampede of tourist groups one's view of the art is considerably obstructed, but perhaps we have changed our habits of viewing, anyway, so that we are viewing the original not in the museum but only later on the screen of our cellphones when we get home, thanks to the facilitation of technological media.

At least in one way the school lessons were completely successful. When one observes these countless graduates, they appear to have heard above all about the "seriousness of life" and now themselves are frozen in seriousness. Joyfulness is among the rarest qualities, which in the context of our society is hardly widespread. And if I may bring up William Shakespeare again, it was always his fools who revealed the truth through their jokes, and were first to reveal what was at stake in the action of the drama. They show in *King Lear* his melancholy seriousness, and in *Othello* his catastrophic madness, which is why neither of these can be overcome since these characters lack joyful openness. The whole corpus of the German classics lacks humor, and what is meant to be comedy rarely gets a laugh. It is perhaps a tragedy that the dramas of the Germans, a people already humorless, always confront the audience with the seriousness of life and recommend that they attend the play with a serious countenance. Nothing is handled there with a light touch; one would prefer above all to escape into Franz Grillparzer, who in the famous great speech of Ottokar von Horneck, in *King Ottokar's Rise and Fall*, wrote these verses: "Thus is the Austrian happy and candid, / Bears his faults, bears frankly his pleasures, / Feels no envy, sooner prefers to be envied."

If I may go back, I opened this letter by trying to describe the structure of prejudice, though I had not called it such. At the risk of being rude at any price, school can be the first source of prejudice without one suspecting it – who after all claims that the values preached in school will be permanent? Too often, in the 20th century, one experienced how the zeitgeist changed and the highest value was given to whatever was in vogue, politically, and whoever didn't praise it would soon be visited by the police. It has unfortunately not remained as Grillparzer made Ottokar Horneck say it was – candid and free. In a further step the question was raised as to who is the true owner of intellectual property. In the 20th century wasn't it dangerous to claim something as one's own that was perhaps thought up by Jews? Indeed great thoughts and enormous literary accomplishments were marked as being Jewish, and therefore to adopt them into one's own knowledge was strictly forbidden. Even their music was discriminated against. And so it was easy to recognize that, with this exception, we do not have to think so very often, since in our everyday life we already have everything laid out before us cut and dried. And this stock of experiences is accrued predominantly from our success at learning. I could almost have taken all this lying down if a certain *daimonion* did not come to me "who always said no." And with this, one needs some guidance about skepticism. On this very point I should have told you more, and this shortcoming I must now repair. One very soon can realize that he must be skeptical about skepticism. Skepticism is often the shield of the stiff-necked ignoramus, protecting him against adopting any insights. Often skepticism expresses nothing but ignorance, or even convenience. Dietrich Bonhoeffer wrote that it is an indication of stupidity though the skeptic sometimes looks as if he is reflecting more, and thinking about things a little more, and thus would be more conscientious. Inimitably clear was Kant's remark, that skepticism "is a resting place, but not at all a place for reason to dwell." To contradict an attitude I need more in my quiver than just the arrow of skepticism. I need concrete knowledge. For this, skepticism can indeed lend methods but cannot be a substitute for creative thinking.

In all these considerations the next step of progress took quite long to master. It began with difficulty. Take for example how we read "classics." I found out that on the one hand we are simply repeating an "alien" knowledge; on the other hand the effort to fill in any possible gaps has become equally alien. Though Friedrich Nietzsche once thought that it is a sign of its obsolescence when world literature is always being taken up into "younger hands," one must contradict him and ask at what age should and can one recommend the prose of Adalbert Stifter to an inquisitive reader? In school one read *From the Portfolio of my Great-Grandfather* at age twelve, and yet what has remained of it? Had the teacher said that we will only be reaching an overview of literature, it remains for us to read a work of Stifter later on; or if he said that Goethe's *Götz of Berlichingen* is quite impressive in the fifth grade, one should still look back at this drama in mature years since by then one has a different well of experience. But school mostly neglects exactly this. Once, while at school, I passionately criticized Goethe, and this prejudice of mine later led me to inquire into the critical literature on Goethe. There I encountered Hermann Bahr, and much later Daniel Wilson, whom the department head, Kurt Haslinger, had recommended to me. Even without Wilson and his 1991 book, *Geheimräte gegen Geheimbünde* ("Secret Councils against Secret Societies," not translated into English – ed.), the teacher in the German class countenanced my defiant interjections not at all. Of course Hermann Bahr was hardly on the same plane as Goethe but if one understands that it was through Goethe of all persons that the "German essence" was being taught in the schools, upon which the "healing of the world" was to follow, Bahr's claim of Austrian independence in literature over 120 years earlier was of inestimable importance. Even worse, that famous work *Faust* due to its use in school became the popular philosophy of the half-educated, and completely undermined thinking in general. Every gym-teacher in a provincial high school was advised to see true philosophy in Faust's coquettish pseudo-intelligence with its suicidal tendencies, and failed to see the total irresponsibility of Faust's lifestyle. Goethe was now taken, with his theatrical piece, to be drenching the German intelligentsia with biting irony –

yet this was basically misunderstood, if indeed it was his intention. As a sort of minister of the interior in Weimar, he kept a watchful eye on its "intelligentsia," on these "do-gooders" and their overheated tempers.

But this doesn't really matter, except for what it led to. For in the next step, one abstains from every judgment and encounters the most significant artistic treasures of Europe with the indifference of an ignoramus. One must only look at the herds of city-tourists in order to see immediately that no interest drives them to the city center, nor any curiosity. Bored, they plod along through the side-streets whose meaning they do not know; soon fatigued, they whine for something to eat or drink at a bar, and they wander with no respect into the churches or the cathedrals, or into the art collections. Proper respect is shown only by the smokers who stay outside, reminding us at the same time that nothing beats a cigarette. In all likelihood the cattle in the Roman Forum were more sensitive, since they avoided defecating on the inscribed tablets. With dignified observance the cows would step through the Arch of Titus and make their way through the bushes toward the Temple of the Vestal Virgins. Conversely, the storm of Mongols, through their city tourism, have destroyed a city's urbane intimacy and robbed it of its secret charm; and their demands led to inescapable extortions requiring every entrance to be made passable and accessible for the sake of mere visitors. Next these nomads are standing before priceless works of art and before looking at them they photograph them. Apparently everyone has become Japanese – though these in aforetimes had at least stood farther back.

Actually, I wanted to communicate something entirely different. In the description of the encounter with paintings I have advised you first to form your own judgment. Whatever it looks like is the result of your own impression. Your evaluation counts, even if it might be incorrect, and for every subsequent conversation over the painting this is your basis for discussion. If you want the discussion to proceed along an orderly path, then you ought to have a look at *Principles of Art History* some time, the book by Heinrich Wölfflin. The system of this great art historian will greatly help you characterize a work of art. But of course you mustn't cheat! You mustn't begin with Wölfflin and then act as though you thought it up yourselves. Rather, the prerequisite is that you see the artwork with your own eyes and interpret it with your own perceptions before you call for any help.

I greatly hope that you will take my advice to heart. Only when one has used his own sight enough that he can basically weigh carefully what he has seen, and test this and study this – only then will you begin to recognize the value of these collections.

All the best, your R.

55.
An Excursion through European History

Dear Nina, Dear Julian, Marie, and Vicky,

It was a beautiful surprise to see you in the courtyard, Nina, and have a chat with you. As always an encounter with you is a bright joy and brings to mind how painful it is not to bump into my other grandchildren in the same casual way.

Today I want to write about a problem that carries through the entire history of the 20th century and has basically come to no satisfying solution. To the contrary. As one reviews this period it was in fact a century-long passage through a vale of blood and tears. I have now reached insights that I believe ought to be seriously weighed and debated, but in the first place understood in terms of their motive! When we go forward from the opening of this century, in the evaluation of the problem the first question to ask is whether the Scandinavian, Dutch, and Belgian and even the Italian monarchies would have survived under comparable conditions. Would these, at the end of the World War in 1918, be superseded as both empires of Central Europe had been? The Czar had in any case not survived, just as the Sovereign of the Ottoman Empire had not, a little later. At least this caesura is most commonly recognized by us, and we have relatively reasonable interpretations of it. The situation in the 19th century is not unfamiliar: Otto von Bismarck had blocked the abdication of the King of Prussia in 1862, and thus maintained the continuity that had outlasted the Napoleonic wars, though with hardships and efforts. The response to Bismarck was that in this tricky situation the King would be beheaded, and his unperturbed reply was, "So what?"

One must immediately raise the question, whether these important princes were really a hindrance against the peace treaty of 1919. One could logically infer that the occupation of the Rhine-Ruhr area by French troops in order to force the paying of reparations, and the simultaneous election of Hindenburg in 1923 as President of the German state, would make the abdication of the princes completely senseless. They were referred to in the propaganda of England as "War Lords," but this was not at all correct. If one of them had been, he would have sometime earlier reacted to the hopelessness of victory and paradoxically enough would have hoped all the more visibly for peace. The sovereigns, almost all of them, will have been aware that further sacrifices for this world war were senseless. Whereas the crown prince had forced the German Kaiser (Wilhelm II) to break off the war, military leaders and some parliamentarians came to this conviction only at its end, if at all – though they could have known that with this the function of a Kaiser would expire, and they were eager to "sacrifice the Kaiser" in order to be able finally to be free to act. They subsequently became the masterminds for the Weimar Republic.

The rash demands in England that the Kaiser be hanged were merely overheated theater for the people, but in their implication were unwise and needlessly provocative. Such an approach would even more quickly have brought on a mystification: the Kaiser would "at home" have become a martyr and the political situation in Germany would have resembled more closely that of Russia. Following the Treaty of Brest-Litovsk in 1917, the subversion of the German soldiers was intensified and along with this the way of Lenin seemed a preferable alternative to a good number of people.

As far as the German "elites" were concerned the princes, after the "unification of the empire" in 1871, identified themselves less and less with their political function. The "people" had identified with Germany as an "empire" more than was expected – perhaps with the exception of Bavaria – but Bismarck overestimated their leaning since he believed the "people" would cling to their sentimental connection with the emperor in Berlin and would probably not risk the step toward a republic. In only a few days these old connections between the people and the emperor were erased. Although the enthusiasm was meagre, as it was in Vienna, the proclamation of the republic still felt as if it were a salvation, a long desired new beginning in the eyes of the "left" and liberal party. At this point the future development of Central Europe in particular was outlined. The political form of a republic was accorded a life-span of fourteen years and ended, rather surprisingly, not with the restoration of an "*ancien régime*" as in France in 1815, but with the dictatorship. Although the nobility were still present in full strength, which was no longer the case in Russia, they did not play a role, although this option was taken very seriously in Austria, in particular. Your great grandfather was briefly a sort of teacher and mentor for the son of the last emperor, for Otto Habsburg-Lothringen, around 1930. The Weimar Republic as well as the Austrian one were replaced by "fascist" dictatorships. This was a surprise since one believed that by this political form a military expansion would stabilize the new "Third Reich" and would create an easily managed structure for police, a secret state police, a security force, or for other miscellaneous organizations, for the purposes of spying. Both these fascist systems, in Austria and in Germany, came to an end in five years and after the occupation of Austria it became "Greater Germany." This political perversion of German unity lasted for seven years, of which, contrary to assurances, only one year was peaceful: it soon became a radical dictatorship incomparable to anything that had ever been seen before. Politically the unifying bond was the bringing together of the German lands into Germany, which would not have held for long if they had not plunged into the world war.

In this dictatorship all historical wishes, options, plans, decisions, and necessary changes come to an end in 1945 with one fell swoop, just as at the end of the First World War. Hence it is an outrageous falsification to attribute to this regime, of all things, the futile idea of a renewed attempt to found a German republic, in the manner of the 1848 parliament at the Church of St. Paul in Frankfurt.

In the face of this development, the histories of the time formulate questions that are not very worthwhile. It was perhaps not their task to answer the pressing questions, how it could come to this or how this horrible episode was to be overcome. Everywhere one hears how it was easily possible for the parliamentary republic to be thrown from the saddle, that the constitutions did not control what one had euphemistically believed they were "controlling," why it could come to such brutality, genocide, and total dictatorship. Basically there was a lack of historical research to trace the sequelae of the political attitudes that had developed in the 19th century, unless they are seen overall in the narrowing of political goals during the French Revolution. The answer to the questions of contemporary history is relatively easy and at the same time meaningless: the years after 1918 encouraged this collapse throughout Europe.

One must say, at the very start, though it is not to be taken as "downplaying" the path to dictatorship, that at the time there was a boom in authoritarian systems in Europe. There was no dearth of authoritarian regimes or one-party dictatorships. Germany and Austria were no exception, but counted as appearances that were taken as "normal," from Spain to Poland, from Italy to Hungary, from Latin America to Turkey. What then, in the German situation of 1933, aroused a greater mistrust than in the situation of Italy or Croatia?

One must also add that the renewal of Germany as a "family of the folk" as it would be presented in Geneva, was untimely. Moreover no political consensus, either in "Weimar" or in Vienna, was to be expected. Because of the abdications of both the emperors the traditional social ties were just as invalid as the old enemies of the monarchs were unwilling to be associated with them. In all likelihood Karl Renner was the exception. Whatever was happening at the peace talks in the suburbs of Paris – completely disrespectful of the representatives of Germany, Austria, Hungary – it was a breeding ground for the complete destabilization of the things all Europe held in common, which through an unbelievably grotesque mythologization of "war guilt lies" appeared at the time to be entirely obsolete. The result was that very irritated states had to "find" themselves, to develop their political identity, but at the same time had to pay reparations. Those who knew how to take advantage of this and were able to cobble together a clever mixture of history and half-truths, made a successful gambit in a controversial relationship of the parties with parliamentary democracy, of all things. Moreover the horrible economic situation in Central Europe fostered a hope for a leader in this area – and it did not remain limited to this area. The thought of an economic democracy, which Karl Renner always supported, and the participation of the social partners in a political process of decision-making had no general support, either from the left or the right.

One must compare this political constellation with previous ones, though it is seldom done. Basically what happened in Austria, as in Germany, was "nothing different" from what happened in the overthrow of democracy in ancient Athens. Athens also went over to tyranny. It was tyranny that increased the nationalistic military enthusiasm, and declared "every Athenian" to be a patriot, and on this basis issued the call to save, to protect, to battle, or to defend anything and everything. With the additional evocation of a military conflict a tremendous integrated force came to be developed. A similar kind of excitement was stirred up during the French Revolution and there were "pictures" to be seen on the leaflets and which could be seen in films about the Nuremberg Party Congress or the Reichstag in Berlin. That is, the repertoire for staging things returned in exactly the same form, and in this way were the radical republicanisms taken over from 1789, in which, admittedly, the succession to bonapartism was already visible. Indeed it was not long before the "consulate for life" was invented, which was a marked reference to Roman history and the process of political transformation at the time of Caesar. You can remember the letter in which I wrote about Caesar's power grab as seen from the point of view of Shakespeare. This sort of thing was now in play, and Napoleon had displayed his talent as a chameleon, to rule as emperor over France and at the same time to spread abroad the blessings of the Civil Code. Over and over again this ambivalence shows up in France, for Napoleon III wanted to continue in this style. And even after 1870-71, one sought a renewed bonapartism, like an operetta, almost laughable, embodied in General Boulanger in 1887-89, whose name meant "baker." In accordance with his self-presentation he saw it almost as a duty to shoot himself at the grave of his beloved.

We owe to the analysis of Leon Trotsky that such bonapartist systems cannot last for long without some "basis." He recognized "at a glance" that without a party, without this support of leadership and ideology, a regime cannot be sustained. The united party allows even a continuation of previously republican institutions, and goes on to occupy the seats of the former administrators in full strength. This perspective was copied from France and served as a paradigm for 20th century totalitarianism. Thus, two systems could run concurrently: a Jacobin-communistic one and a national socialistic one. If already in Vienna one witnessed a grotesquely theatrical Caesarism, brought forth by Engelbert Dolfuss who almost died like Caesar, the soviet version had become rigid instead, like an icon, full of secrecy and lacking transparency.

The political legacy for Austria and Germany after 1918, was surely not a democracy supported by a constitutional monarchy, as in England; instead the French republican model was adopted, and this required that there be a head of state. This new president, somewhat in imitation of the US President, possessed special plenary powers in restless times, means for political influence and the function as arbitrator to settle disagreements. This completely fell through in Austria in 1934, and before that in Germany under different circumstances. In Berlin there was the presidential cabinet which acted like a shadow regime on behalf of Hindenburg. The error was that a president elected by the people had to mediate party squabbles. This is how the grass-roots democracy was imagined, but this vision has nothing to do with having an appropriate personality. One has recently seen in Austria, in 2018, that if the candidates have no convincing reputation to offer, almost everything can falter. At the time, in the Weimar Republic one sought someone as both a military leader and a political genius. In 1932, the alternative before them was Hindenburg or Hitler. The field marshal was victorious but he was not without his drawbacks. Basically Hindenburg had the reputation of a member of the military dictatorship in the last two years of the war, of being passive in the matter of the German "revolution," and not opposing the abdication of the Kaiser. This "transitional model" was also informally operating in Austria.

Leaving aside Charlie Chaplin's excellent parody of Hitler, he is the opposite of a field marshal: the "simple soldier," just the proletarian looking like "Gunner, Rank A," who lacks the talent for the humor of the "good soldier Schweik" of Jaroslav Haske, nor the sovereignty of the Hamburg patrician who keeps appearing in the novels of Thomas Mann. Hitler, I'd say, was only good at playing the role of the "savior" which he switched out at the end of his life into a theatrically acted out role as victim. His allure was bonapartian, with the effect of uniting behind him radicals, the military elite, and the citizens; and it functioned as a German jacobism and a Girondist bourgeoisie. In Paris the citizen-general had turned into an emperor, but Hitler turned into a tyrant.

But now I must bring in the question, why did the political vocabulary so quickly take on this word "Führer" or "Duce?" We know that in political philosophy since around 1770 this idea was ventilated in literature, that it lurked here and there and soon even became popular. At least in the 17th century the question of righteous rule emerged, whether legitimate or illegitimate, legal or illegal. In the Spanish theory of natural right not only despotism but even tyranny played a large role; the question was also aired as to whether the murder of a tyrant could be morally justified. Suárez was not the only teacher who supported tyrannicide. In light of the English Revolution it was no wonder that one might think long and hard about this. The Enlightenment studied the same problem, although not from the standpoint of ethics. It had already been transformed into a sociological issue: how does tyranny come about? That Machiavelli would here be brought in as a source goes without saying. So one browsed through history and found the appropriate case to investigate in Roman history. What is always overlooked is the Scottish moral philosophy with its economic ideas of a division of labor and profit, which sees in a Caesar the largest stumbling block to socio-economic growth. Caesar is indeed the political measure of all things and thence a Caesarism is established that of course also wants to take control of managing the economy. In 1767, Adam Ferguson expressed his worry that if only Caesars should be rulers, one after the other, they would not long manage their various tasks fairly. The same theme inspired Fichte's 1813 lecture, *Staatslehre, oder Das Verhältnis des Urstaates zum Vernunftreiche* ("The Relationship of the Primitive State to Reasonableness," untranslated – ed.). And with this we have turned the page. In his chapter on Rome he saw the advent of the "Second Monarchy" as consisting in political "ingenuity." Fichte dreamed of a rule by astuteness in place of a theocracy under which political culture is weakened and becomes evil. After the weakening of the elites, after the civil war and the collapse of the state, comes the dawn of an "ingenuity of individuals." Thus it was a "stimulus of ingenuity" that drove Rome to world power: "The genius that knows how to rule alone, also wants to do so alone" (*Staatslehre*, 171 = *Sammtliche Werke*, 4.518).

In his *Philosophy of History*, Hegel came close to the idea of a geniocracy in his notion of "individual talent." In Caesar he of course saw a "world-historic individual" in which what is special is not so much genius as being a practical, political man. He must know what is timely – that is, have the gift of naming the ideas in a timely way that are in the signs of the times, and to manage things in accordance with these. "For the advanced Spirit is the inner soul of all individuals, but an unconscious inwardness that the great men bring into consciousness" (from the *Introduction*). And this applies also in his homage to the great figures of world history. They are the "men who do the business of the World Spirit" (*ibid.*) for whom, of course, no happy end is vouchsafed: "To a restful enjoyment they did not come, their entire life was work and toil, their entire nature was ardor. If their goal is reached they fall away, like the empty husk of the kernel. They die early, like Alexander, they are murdered like Caesar, or like Napoleon they are exiled to St. Helena" (*ibid.*). That in Hegel's eyes Cicero is not included among them is no surprise. In particular Cicero lacked the consciousness of the Roman state. Many German philologists followed Hegel in this criticism, above all Theodor Mommsen, for in Cicero he detected a scent of republican moralism, which in the period of Bismarck was a thing not highly prized. Seneca likewise is not appreciated for he was the first person to doubt the talent of Alexander. In his glorification that youthful hero and world-conqueror was not as suitable as being what he actually was: *ferina ista rabies*, said Seneca ("this madness is bestial" – *de Clementia* 25.1): this glamor-boy was often overcome with animal rage, loss of restraint, irascibility. For the philologians this was no way to write about Alexander!

One must now mention that this Caesar-Napoleon myth found many admirers among the Romantics, as we indeed see in the case of Beethoven. And it is immediately obvious that the more dangerous the situations become, so much more does this attitude intensify. It is taken further in the case of the "great man," a creation from the beginning of the 18th century. To him, halls of fame and groves were dedicated, and busts were placed there, which one took as a testimony to his greatness. At the Pantheon in Paris are the Great Frenchmen, and so in the Walhalla in Regensburg on the Danube, and on a more humble scale Parkfrieder's Heldenberg Memorial with Radetzky buried right in the middle. And one had the belief that one needs the "greats," since they are men unleashed representing an unleashed mankind. That the "great men" then made their way into art is natural. Museums basically had in mind at their inception to be documentarian, to be the mediators between the genius and the people.

Now I believe that here all the life-patterns for the "statesman" come into view, although I will not mention also the "soldierly model" with whose help politics shows its belligerent side. Those are the military dictators – the generals in South America, Asia, Africa. It is important that we recognize the path of the historical process, that in fact with the revolution of 1789 the paradigms of the "political" were set for us, and so they were bonapartist, caesarist, and later perronist, each one coming forth out of political ruptures. The foundation was always jacobinism, which became the indispensable "driving mechanism" for the moderns, unfortunately, and which, though it is denied by many, produced republicanism and democracy but also fascism, National Socialism, and communism.

I hope that I have set out a structure for your historical understanding, which in all likelihood is important for your coming to understand your own past. You will seldom hear such a thing as this anywhere: after all we must continually revisit our history to some extent. That is why I am always taking swipes at our so-called contemporary history, since in the form in which we encounter it it helps us not at all truly to overcome our past, though it is always demanding just this of us, and demanding it so loudly…

Wholehearted greetings, your R.

56.
You Can Always Resist!

Dear Nina, Dear Julek, Marie, and Vicky,

Just imagine: I had prepared my thoughts about *William Tell* and for unknowable reasons everything was gone. What does that mean, "gone?" It was all gone. If I had not kept a backup file I would no longer even have the base document. Although I do "save" as I go, it has already happened to me twice that an entire text has simply disappeared. This has not strengthened my trust for these new media. Now two pages on Schiller's *William Tell* are gone.

The purpose of this presentation was to write a counterweight to tyranny. Switzerland, as is well known, went its own way since the Battle at Morgarten in 1315, and it was something of a miracle that the Swiss landscape has in a way maintained its independence. For Austrians it is amusing that the old Swiss family of high nobility was successful since the emigration and then brought an embittered but unsuccessful war against their erstwhile home. I am speaking of the Habsburgs, who were more and more important for European history and finally ruled in the land neighboring Switzerland, but never ruled Switzerland! Friedrich Dürrenmatt once described the difference between Austria and Switzerland. He thought Switzerland was a miniature painting in a slim and humble frame, whereas Austria a painting no larger but in a giant bombastic frame so flashy one sees almost nothing of the miniature painting mounted within.

This of course had nothing to do with my presentation about *Tell*. As the play goes on things come to a climax. Wilhelm Tell keeps returning to the foreground in order to break down the tyranny of a mediocre administrative dictatorship. What Schiller could not have foreseen was what could have served as the frame within which opposition against the regime was justified, meaning it could be carried out, and whether an assassination was justified. And Schiller could not know that of all things it would have a special application to Germany. In any case there would have been a Wilhelm Tell, 600 years later, one with that "gruff implacability" that is characteristic of the people who live in the Alps.

Since all my preparations for the report on "William Tell's Schiller" were erased from my computer, we can have recourse only to associations, and so we must focus on the scandal that for the most part the arbitrary behavior of the tyrant is found to be more acceptable than the courageous readiness of Tell to shoot the apple off his son's head, despite the cruel desire of the tyrant that he try to do so. I once debated with a member of the Academy of Sciences about how one should have survived the Nazi period, and I was shocked that the man saw no problem in merely obeying the one set of laws and then the other. This false interpretation, both outrageous and commonplace, of the famous passage from Matthew – "Render unto Caesar what is Caesar's, and unto the Lord what is the Lord's" – is the usual excuse of the cowardly and fainthearted for their being duty-bound to nothing. Though a country family in Mauthausen hid Russian officers in order to save them from being murdered after their escape from the concentration camp, this courage was hardly present at all in the bourgeois milieu. I was told how your great-grandfather faced some danger in "freeing" soldiers from military service at the beginning of 1945 by carrying forged papers from one office to the next. He had always thought this was the least he could do to resist the regime, but was neither proud of it nor felt himself a hero. This was his contribution to the resistance, within the measure of what was available to him. Likewise it was not common in our family to brag after 1945 about taking part in the resistance. To the contrary we simply resumed the way of life we took to be the normal continuation of our true roles in this world.

Totalitarianism robbed people of their self-determination and blackmailed them at random. A barely perceptible deviation would lead to dreaded visits from the Gestapo. One can follow a large literature that has as its theme the ugly and extortionary dilemma, how one can manage to lay claim to a small and modest life without having to lose one's self-respect. Always I turn to Manès Sperber for this, who was truly the only and the last person to repeat, often, the humble demand that one should never give up righteousness in one's private life – under any circumstances. He criticized even highly placed politicians for having forsworn this rectitude lightheartedly. This was surely one of the important points in his *Sieben Fragen zur Gewalt* ("Seven Questions on Violence" [1978], not translated into English – ed.) that particularly impressed me. What it means is that heroism is not required, just as Eric Voegelin's point was valid: "I am not forced to allow myself to be hanged." – but in such a stance we are still miles away from having become fellow travelers, or thinking with the man from the Academy of Sciences that the Nazi laws were reached by a formally correct way so that he had the duty to act in accordance with them. And by the way, I do not understand why he would go to Stephansdom on St. Stephens's Day, since that Roman officer did not "do his duty" but to the contrary re-affirmed his faith while he was being stoned to death.

What I want to set into relief here is this little honored duty, the duty to protect righteousness. Though it is not too much to require, it is not nothing. Of course one runs the risk of martyrdom, which a hundred communist functionaries took upon themselves, but it was not fundamental in the turn against totalitarianism.

As long as anarchist relations do not prevail, in which murdering spreads like a contagion – let us remember Kristallnacht – one has sufficient wiggle room in which to establish his own personal accent as something different from what the mentality of the time, a diseased time, requires.

This reminds me of many later discussions at the Institute. In the time of the 70's there was nothing to fear – or nothing to look forward to! With the new organization of the university the high time for the opportunists had arrived. In full force they managed the representative duties in the committees and soon after complained about their powerlessness. Even worse were those who thought they had to vote for measures that in their hearts they basically did not believe in. They gave themselves up as victims to duty. It was laughable. Their justification reminded me of the Nazi period, when such arguments were almost commonplace. The perpetrators always made themselves out to be the true victims and conveyed the impression that the victims – those who were shot, gassed, burned and tortured to death – had suffered a lighter loss than these nameless pigs! It made one sick to the stomach to have to hear such arguments. Individual identity was reduced to nothing, to a nullity, though still there was enough of it left for murdering someone. This is what made totalitarianism unendurable, that it institutionalized gruesomeness and denunciation and arbitrary suspicion as democratic processes. This was evident in committee meetings at the Institute. High-ranking elected representatives called in sick when there was a vote in which they would have had to defend colleagues. When they heard that a member of the Institute's board did not support the extension of an assistant's period of service, they ducked out and preferred not to be seen – like mice. As our great reformer, Hertha Firnberg, had one-third parity introduced in the university, it was celebrated merely as a project in democratization. In truth all sat at conferences with their lawbooks open and claimed, with greater or lesser imagination, that nothing is to be decided unless so-and-so – or only if so-and-so then so-and-so – or everything was left hanging. With the democratization, a new power-structure was established whose guiding light was a characterless and inferior opportunism. After that, the intentions of the university were altered and its goals were reformulated. And what is the current outcome? Today, in 2020, minimum prerequisites in the representative fields of study are no longer expected from a graduate – such as spelling, grammar, and the logical structure of a sentence. The beneficiaries of this decline in the university now sit in positions of high importance, in the ministries of law and science. No ordinance works any more, no law can stay in place, and even during the pandemic, implementations for the protection of public safety have to be formulated over and over, in special sessions of the Parliament. Nobody any more is able to do what once was expected. We have arrived at the phase in which the educational outcome of the policies of the 80's and 90's are finally coming into view.

Where was I? At the point where opportunism became acceptable. My beloved Grandchildren! You will be paying for these deficiencies! In all likelihood you will need to found universities anew, design kindergarten anew, and form schools anew. This means that the frustration grows to such a strength that the pleasant words of your highest institutions are finally exposed to be lies, in the light of day. Then there will come an historic opportunity, not unlike the movement of Josephinism, not unlike the politics of reconciliation with Hungary after 1867. I can only hope that in its way it will succeed – through you!

So often you are on my mind! With love, your R.

PS. In order to answer a request for clarification of a problem for which I was bitterly criticized, I make here a comment about Letter 55. The Church of St. Paul in Frankfurt was, during 1848-9, the center of a new "libertarianism," and thus one had the idea of putting the German lands into a framework of republican democracy. This failed, not least because of the power-politics of Bismarck in 1866 and 1870. "Today Germany is ours, and tomorrow the whole world!"

Also I append Bismarck's dates – 1815 to 1898. Someone took it that in my account Bismarck also played a role in 1914. Of course this is not so; after him came Caprivi, I think; and then things rapidly went downhill ... .

57.
Can a University be Reformed?

Dear Nina, Dear Julek, Marie, and Vicky,

The telephone call from Nina was very pleasant. She announced her visit and we will make vanilla crescents together. At the same time I had a video-message from Julian, once again at the piano, playing the famous Opus 10 Number 3 of Chopin. Both contacts made me very happy! Perhaps Marie and Vicky also are able to make similar contacts!

In the last letter I provided a critique that you will probably not completely understand. And yet I will not continue with this, since already in 1990 I wrote a little book on the situation of the university, which I think is still correct today. I entitled it *Uni im Out* ("University on the Outs" – not translated into English – ed.), and yet I am not disappointed that it had no practical effect. I remember well that on the occasion of the "600th Anniversary of the University of Vienna," in 1965, one was able for the first time to recognize that a great loss of love for the university was taking place. During the festivities the very university personalities were invited though the agency of whom the committee had the opinion that the university out of its negligence had simply not taken account of important topics – since 1945. Of all things, the institution that is called upon to interpret history and the present day, has since the 30's lacked such quick wittedness. Thus Rudolf Augstein, the editor-in-chief of *Der Spiegel*, was invited, and also the philosopher Ernst Bloch, and many others. The tenor of the criticism was that there was no department or institute dedicated to Marxism, and that the conveying of knowledge had no sense of relevance to praxis. It was still the case that too few "workers' children" were able to study. The list of shortcomings in knowledge as well as ethics was long and the University left a sorry impression of incompetence.

In any case this celebration brought about a change no one anticipated. Somewhat conservative students turned out to be "rebels" but had not only brought into question their contacts with the new "people's party" and with the reformed ORF (radio and television) but even intensified it. With this "thrust" the people's party in 1966 won an absolute majority in Parliament, before Bruno Kreisky overcame it in 1970-71.

In 1972-3, with the new UOG (University Organization Law), one had probably made the mistake "in politics" of seeing the one-third parity as a democratization, although no democratic types held positions in the committees. The old full professors were indignant, would not negotiate, and simply played out the remainder of their privileged positions; and the scholars were not able to reach consensus. The scholars showed a political behavior more reminiscent of a soviet republic and there was hardly any consistent agreement in the faculty meetings, in conferences of the Institute, or in commissions. "Middle management" generally acted opportunistically, or procrastinated. Within that group, representatives used words that would have been more appropriate on the other side of the Iron Curtain. No sooner were their tirades put to the test than the ladies and gentlemen who were the representatives were nowhere to be found. The way one behaved in such committees was a poor model for subsequent representatives. The fact that this was corrected again, shortly after 2000, was not a wise decision either. From history one should have been able to learn that usually the best way in previous institutions was to find the people appropriate and capable of coming to a consensus. This idea, nobody had in mind.

Basically the goal of the university had fallen out of sight. That alternatives were possible, that they were necessary, is proven by the establishment of "private" universities or new colleges since 1990. In all likelihood we only added to the problem, since with the programs of the European Union in the so-called Bologna Process, not only had the fields of study been agreed to in the curricula but also making the teaching uniform. This didn't even work in the Josephinism of the 17th century. There, the "national" strengths of individual universities was weakened, especially in human and cultural studies, but what was not noticed was that "internationalization" was being sought at any price. The first step toward the test of "internationality" was taken in the field of study called "International Business Administration."

One must say at the outset that the respective claim that universities have a high position in the social context does not correspond to reality. At one special moment this was the case, in France. In 1870-71, one was convinced that France's defeat in the war against the "German empire" was to be traced back to the superiority of the universities. This of course is the plainest of nonsense. And yet Emile Durkheim the famous French sociologist believed it, and because he did he continued his studies in Germany. Far more likely, it was the incredible freedom in the several areas of research, especially in the natural sciences as well as in the new areas of technological training which were also successful.

Such a thing will not be taking place in Austria in the near future after 2020, for in large part one is working with "third party funding," and is compromised by conditions that always have consequences for one's work. Since it is now the rule that research projects cannot go on without selection processes that have this third party funding or will be paid for by the anticipated outcome of the research, there will be no worthwhile innovations but, predominantly, a reduplication of knowledge already on hand. The institutes have "out-sourced" their most important function and with this have confirmed that their mission in teaching is not compatible with their mission in research. When I recall the reviews in the "Bases for the Advancement of Scientific Research" it was always required in the submittal, in the anthropological and humanistic sciences, not only that one present a description of the project but also sketch out the anticipated results. The applications were often rich scientific treatises in themselves, that one could have described as completed projects. I once had denied such an application for renewal on the grounds that in the supporting documentation, outcomes were already set forth and so the continuation of such a research project was to my mind unjustified. Naturally the majority was of a different opinion and the project received the support. It was in the psychological field of "stimulus-response research." It was meant to measure that the subject under investigation reacts differently to the picture of a human than to the sight of a tractor.

This is not a matter of my own value judgments: rather, that the professorial style changed. Surely you can hardly imagine what you are to understand by this. I will provide as an example something that once was usual in the conduct of seminars at the university. The announcement of the seminar usually came at least a half year before the seminar began. The participants had enough time to read the recommended books. Roughly speaking the professor hardly had better knowledge about it than the participants. The seminar was thought of as a forum for discussion which the professor was meant to lead, and surely in some areas possessed greater knowledge than the usual participant. The idea was a technical discussion among "informed" persons. The seminar of today is quite far from that. The teacher was the discussion leader and the source of information, and these roles required him to develop a style.

Most people at the university are now partisans of empiricism. So what one needs to think about has predominantly to do with one's experience with methods, the evaluation of results, and perhaps also a debate about the "questionnaire construction." This means that with this "automation" of the production of social scientific results, the interests of research either took refuge in a "romanticist" style in their self-description and ran off to the Frankfurt School, starting in 1968; or in empirical research on the other hand the so-called facts are immediately and always "on the table" and thus speak for themselves in any case: having to think could consciously be swept aside. An "import" from American science that was partly able to free itself from the complex of positivism and redirect social research toward the empirical, called for an "ahistorical theory," as the historian

Peter Burke characterized it. This design for research very soon after 1945 played a role in the build-up of social and human sciences. The entire humanistic tradition of sociology, for example, was discredited, and was suspected – sometimes rightly – of being close to the Nazi regime, excepting the work of Max Weber. Its analyses of societies could only hold sway as long as there was social homogeneity in the societies, which because of the Iron Curtain became possible. With the reunification of Germany in 1989 this homogeneous social milieu of the European societies completely changed. The socio-empirical style was ideally suited to this homogeneity, but could one still maintain the sovereignty of interpretation? Moreover, after the attempt at a "revolution" in Hungary in 1956 and in the Czech Republic in 1968, the migratory movements got bigger and bigger and soon included people from the Eastern Mediterranean regions as well. The concept of an "empire" in the historical sense would have been more serviceable during this increase in multiculturalism than the "racism of the citizen-state," which had long continued to function as the criterion for nationality in Europe. This was the durable achievement of the French Revolution, and soon narrowed more and more the available resources for solidarity. For the longest time the universities remained unaffected by such pressing problems. Because of the changeover to the Kreisky regime one hoped to change the reputation of the university: indeed the dominant sense was that universities should mirror the bourgeois milieu. In addition the university came to be stigmatized as "unworldly."

The question about students from the sector of the working class getting into the university was of course a pressing problem for the social democrats, or at least achieving social equality for this group. The question was rightly raised as to what social mission the university was to fulfill. And it became clear, especially after revelations of the shameless loss of character among those who belonged to the university in the totalitarian period, that the university could not justify the special privileges accorded its teachers and students. This demand for more "worker children" at the university was given a fundamentally false justification. The fact that later, in a similar way, a higher proportion of women in all possible professions was also incorrectly promoted, shows only that an uninspired program of specious ideologizations had caught on. The universities were the first institutions in which the criterion of biopolitics prevailed and to this day – 2020 – it is decisive as to the university's goals and ambitions.

(Forgive me for the very low level example of "biopolitics": after the relocation of the sociology department into a former office building in Roosevelt-Platz, one of the first decisions of the conference of the department was to make men's toilets available to female personnel. And in the main building the men's toilets were simply refurbished to become women's toilets.)

But now we must turn to more serious things. What knowledge is it that should be shared with as many people as possible at the university? And how is it constituted? Opening the university to "workers' children" or female students is not a question for the university to resolve, but is the business of the state and its social policies. If one had argued as "realistic" that all people must become educated who are today being educated there, the state would have the duty to take this on and provide what is necessary to make it possible. One cannot address such topics with compromises that merely disturb the inner operation or even burden it with negative moods. The opposite was the case. The "state" forced a program for the "children's situation" and forced upon the university certain solutions which are inappropriate for learning institutions. One left it to the universities to make a "political" decision about equal rights, which was clearly too much to ask. The state has to answer the question of who needs a "higher education" and for what purpose. If the universities are to be equipped to educate for the intellectual professions, then some provision for those fields of study must be put in place. But up until now it is not in place. The idea that using universities of applied studies to take care of this social problem would likely entail a diminution of quality.

The universities must concern themselves with educating and advancing the next generation of scientists. Ever since the model of the university from Wilhelm von Humboldt, science and research was established as one of the two pillars. With the transformation of the university they are clearly not fulfilling this duty. Here, too, a "lazy compromise" was adopted in which "research institutions" came to be affiliated with the Institute. Suddenly the director of an institute was no longer only a professor of his specialty but at the same time was involved in an additional institute – the "Boltzmann-Institute" or in Germany the "Max Planck-Institute" – in which he could research, act, and direct, without interference and outside the rules governing his institute. Here he could hire colleagues according to his own plans, and pay them or fire them. With this came the outsourcing of the institute's research. Universities avoided this traditional task because due to outsourcing they did not need to oppose the reforms of the laws about assistants and the new forms of the professions. Today it is impossible to start a clear-cut scientific career, since after an extension of the appointment, at best, the post must be abolished. Systematically, the functions that are creative and that advance the sciences are being reduced, so that the depletion of the society's reserves only accelerates.

One can now follow out the thought whether universities ought to perform the function of professional education and at the same time the promotion of young scientists – and whether they are able to. One can leave it to the colleges, and yet why not achieve a combination of the two? Why, that is, does the very necessary instruction in theoretical knowledge and the guarantee of its inward development remain with the universities, whereas preparation for the professions is the responsibility of the colleges? After all, combining them would likely vitalize university studies and clearly would deepen the materials of knowledge.

Within this debate the concepts of "education," "training," and "general education" need to be clarified. This well-worn inventory of concepts stems from the 19th century, and blurs the fact that neither in physics nor in chemistry or mathematics does one become "educated" but rather comes to possess knowledge, even becomes "learned" – which does not at all to say it is a lesser thing. "Education" is used predominantly of the humanistic sciences, and one could characterize "general education" with the ironical byword, "An idle mind is the devil's playground."

One must realize that when universities were founded in the Middle Ages, they were not meant to provide training in our sense, but rather a systematic representation of the world, of the contents of faith, of the position of mankind, of the philosophy of nature and its "powers" and history. At the center were problems from which the spirit of the Reformation gradually emerged: Which belief was to guide human existence? and What is the basis for philosophy according to Aristotle? Those were the medieval questions and were not attached to any prospect of professional education. Much later, in the period of absolutism and the Enlightenment, professional training came into view as part of the "growth of the state" – the modernization of state administration, of law, and of medicine. The idea around the 18th century was not only to represent a documentable knowledge more and more, but at the same time to bring "order" into the world which is to be achieved through "education." In the French version "education" is a "formatting," a distinct imprinting whereby to achieve a unified compatibility among the "educated." To get an idea of the nature of a university during the Enlightenment you must think of it as being like training musicians to serve in an orchestra. All the necessary voices and timbres are significant and it should produce a harmonic whole, exactly so as to be able to make music together. This was the theme in the 17th and 18th centuries. However it was only gradually that knowledge came to be concentrated, as an "Academy of Sciences." They always had their own way of dealing with science that stood in a special relationship with the interests of the state. A counterweight to the universities had been created that was to act in the state's interest, sometimes more quickly than a university could, and sometimes better able protect its own independence.

There surprisingly came to be a generally different educational canon in the 19th century, which created a fictional "world of education" out of evaluations and functional cooperation, and what it produced was a sort of educated citizenry. The telling sign of this was an ever-diminishing compliance with the political demands of the time; indeed what it had read and had acquired was neither strong enough nor seemed suited to produce any resistance against the pursuits of totalitarianism, for example.

Of course I must scold myself for writing you such a long letter. It may be that this description will be of no interest in twenty years, since it may be the case that the institutes will in the meanwhile be radically altered and the system of education improved. This would be a plus and your own views on the procedures of education might have undergone a change. If such transformations however are not introduced, you could learn from what I am writing to you a history of how the stolidness in our education system arises. I spent the greatest part of my professional life at the university and you likely can read between the lines a certain pessimism operating in my description – how I experienced that opportunities were being wasted, and are being wasted. I said right at the beginning that I observed a "loss of love" vis-à-vis the university, since a whole series of former colleagues quit the university forever, never again to give a lecture and no longer to take part in discussions at the department: this is surely a withdrawal of love! And if it is not a disease that is the cause, it leaves us with the alternative picture that the work of an "academic teacher" is only a job. Was this what was going on during my professional career? I fear so…

All the best, I remain your R.

58.
Science – the "Second Nature"

Dear Nina, Dear Julian, and Marie, and Vicky,

The last letter requires some familiarity with the situation of the Austrian universities, which was shaped by two time periods. The one goes from 1945 to 1965, and the other basically began with the attempt at reform in 1972, which was halfway achieved up until 1995. Despite the war coming to an end, the operations continued uninterrupted, incriminated personnel continued to be employed, the operations in teaching and research remained unchanged, and so the subsequent reform had little effect. Granted, it was hardly a reform that could measure up to the earlier ones dating from the 19th century. The reform installed a socio-political imagined wish, against which there was only one objection: whether the means required to achieve it were able to increase in strength to keep up with the increase in the number of students. This of course was not the case. So the reform during the 70's of the foregoing century only reduced the absurdities. If this was achieved through carrying out the laws of higher education, it was a grueling victory in the one-third parity committees. The distribution of budgetary means at the Institute, the battle over the state of the library, the fights over the financing of bureaucratic and administrative operations, the embittered squabbles over the distribution of copier paper and toilet paper, constituted the usual agenda for the committees. Since an executive board member, no less, had to be present at each of these meetings, out of his own interest, in his case his research work was interrupted.

If I may turn to something more meaningful, it is the ancient metaphor we owe to Heraclitus: everything is flowing. If this declaration of Heraclitus is a description of the elemental way of things, then countless connections between "everything" and "flowing" are thinkable. It can refer to the flow of history, the permanent and continuous trickling of a spring. If viewed that way we see that historical processes show a similar course of movement as a spring that flows continuously. We can linger with this remark of Heraclitus, musing whether both are described as the manner of nature, whether the explanation for history would be taken only from nature, or instead that nature itself possesses relationships impenetrable by us and which we ourselves are unable to unravel even with our methods. We must decide for ourselves whether we should just be washed along on the "flow of time" rather than swimming "against the flow."

Swimming upstream is strenuous. Though it may even be pleasant to be in tune with the flow, doesn't curiosity drive us all the more to ask how it might be to take up a position opposed to the flow? Of course a man is exhausted after a certain amount of time. And so are they right, those who have always claimed that swimming against the flow doesn't pay off? The exhausted person does not, however, see himself as unsuccessful. In his own eyes it has indeed paid off.

If we apply Heraclitus's metaphor to current times we will soon learn that we owe our success to the circumstance that we have succeeded to use the flow, to have moved forward with it quite well. We have learned basic facts of nature, have understood and have used them well enough to perfect a successful exploitation of them. Every sailboat teaches us that we sail along with the current of the winds. And from the beginning of the modern era we moved even quicker when we exploited the Gulf Stream to be carried almost all the way to our destination. That has become our reality. The currents available to us are an adequate proof how the powers of nature are to be used. According to the science of the Late Renaissance, we must follow the laws and powers of nature in order to draw our advantage from nature itself. This was the proclamation of modernity. Nature itself is what has placed us into the position of mastery over nature. This was now a different outlook, in comparison with before when we conquered lands with slash and burn, wanting to show we were masters of the world and of its nature by the annihilation of agricultural fields. Modernity has decoded the structure of nature and all its secrets, and it was the success of the sciences that they were able to wrest from nature, with ever finer methods, not only its secrets but also its "unconsciously" silent powers. We advanced to the point of splitting the atom and this allowed us to feel that we now we were the demiurge in person. Granted, the spirit of science taught us that we cannot exploit nature endlessly. Mastery of nature also includes that we deal with this bounty of nature in a rational way. We run the risk of sawing off the limb we are sitting on. This is how Thomas Bernhard would often put it, and in fact the laugh stuck in our throats. However we did not reckon how the restoration of an "equilibrium" between modernization and protecting nature would take too long to achieve. Actually, everyone that was swimming with the current carefree, should have gotten the idea, now and then at least, to fight against it in order, against the Heraclitean view, to still the flow. Ludwig von Bertalanffy spoke of an equilibrium in flow, that can immediately set in so as to give the flux a certain stability.

This teaches us that our borrowings from nature up to our time have met with a very conditional success. Surely our many hydropower plants have refuted our notion that perpetual streams constitute energy sources of which the flow is unconscious, but we do know what is here be given to us. It is our cunning of reason to have deceived nature. Still the question may be asked, can we perpetually lead nature down the garden path? The water-flows driving the power plants are not powerful enough to avoid desertification. Alluvial lands, which are basically nature's source of energy for protecting of the biodiversity of flora and fauna, are modified into a futile park landscape that cannot restore its previous functions. The regulation of river flows produces unexpected floods and yet we push far from view a "natural" logic of natural transformations. The water does flow, it causes the wheels of the machinery to rotate, people gather and settle around the factories and create a landscape of industry and commercial activity.

It would make Francis Bacon happy to see us, since he thought we must extract our sources of energy from the inner structure of nature. It is not enough to wonder at the anomaly of water, at the enormous power that a tiny drop in temperature will unleash, splitting rocks and undermining walls. We must create parallel natural effects – simulations, imitations – and we will see that this twin of nature itself will put that superpower into the shade. These are the bold hopes presented in every futuristic novel – that we could bring paradise before our eyes and that all is ready within reach; except that in each of these novels the ordering principle is a dictatorship. This is disastrous. As soon as we have our electronic equipment and our boundless ability to communicate, they are overshadowed by authoritarian political powers. Modern technology and democracy split apart. The dream explodes.

This remarkable story is what I wanted to tell you this time.

All the best, I remain, your R.

59.
A Second Gift: Life

Dear Nina, Dear Julian, Marie, and also Vicky,

I am increasingly concerned that nobody is interested in my letters. Nevertheless I will continue writing, for the very worthlessness of the lines I write counts toward the image of my character. The only person that gave me his full attention was my father. Let it be that he overestimated me, let it be that he had no comparable contact with my brothers: still, after so many years – 60 years! – it is very touching that he would take me along to his lectures even as a child, would discuss things with me, and would refer me to authors who seemed important to him. You must imagine that immediately before my bicycle accident I was writing my memoirs and completed them in time to survive that absurd accident, which took place the following day. I had that often-described near death experience, that bright flash, which made me unbelievably curious, followed by the helplessness of letting things happen that I was not able to do. It was a painful experience that has shaped my life ever since. Still and again I think back to the time when Nina was allowed to visit me for the first time. I had just been let out of intensive care. I remember that you, dear Nina, were not exactly aware of how one is to treat an accident victim. You were very embarrassed, it was an alien atmosphere, and then this pitiable accident ward, which was the worst phase in my so-called recovery. Of course you would know that visiting patients in the hospital is important. In my case it was different. I got along quite well all by myself, and was not unhappy about being alone: that way one is not forced to smile against all pain, and doesn't have to entertain anybody. It has been eight years, and I was led to make compromises about my life. Surely I cannot write you that I had other wishes, which would depress you too much: pain, shortness of breath, and loss of movement reduced me to the existence of a mummy. There was only one essential condition for mummification that I had not fulfilled. Then I went to Bad Pirawarth, with a walker. This was a good learning experience since at that point I had learned how to stand on my own two feet, literally. It is a normal condition for human beings. I learned equanimity – late perhaps, but I learned it. And I counted it a talent of mine that I could create a little mirth, both in the dining hall and also during the exercise hour. If I was not to die I wanted to begin laughing like an Etruscan at the prospect of death, to experience happiness in pain, and my wine merchant supported me as much as he could. Thus the evening mood was provided for, the patients were kindly and to the surprise of the nurses silence during the night was never disturbed. The time of my rehabilitation was also a beautiful time. This was followed by stays in Baden and in Sauerbrunn. In the Burgenland the little railroad brought me to Ödenburg and went along a road that my aunt had told me she loved as a child. These stop-overs went quickly – too quickly since they were always amusing. Above all, with my attractive penchant for the macabre there was always a new acquaintance at hand. Thus, in Sauerbrunn, instead of the usual allowance of one glass of wine, I was permitted two.

Now I must turn to something more serious in this letter to you. I have to think hard about what laughing really is. The worst explanation is the one once given by Konrad Lorenz, who claimed that laughing is the inversion of aggression. I do not see it that way. The muscle that indicates a mimic expression of laughing in the raising of the upper lip, is the "zygomaticus major." The assumption of the older anatomy that it is the "musculus risorius" – the "laughing muscle" – is nothing but a misnomer.

So a little bit of the history of science has sneaked into my lines. In any case the false reference teaches us something about the medicine of antiquity. And history does not stop there. Ever since "Homeric laughter" there have been amusing moments, and it is also needful, since laughter can neutralize any fear. And laughter is often also an opportunity to comment on something surprising. The famous Thracian maid could only laugh when Thales of Miletus, observing the stars, fell into the well. It must have surprised her that so learned a man was not paying attention to where he was stepping.

It matters to me to recognize that philological research has led us onto entirely the wrong path. Out of the similarity of an expression – in this case, "*Lachen*" (= laughing) – astonishingly incorrect conclusions were drawn. *Lachen* (laughing) and *Lächeln* (smiling) have ever since been thought to overlap in their meaning. Once again this is old-fashioned nonsense. We began by connecting humor with smiling or with the comical. This is false from the get-go. To the Greeks no less than the Romans, humor was completely unknown. Yes, they had a feeling for the comical but not for humor. Surely Seneca had sneered at things in the composing satire for the first time in history – he described the transformation of Emperor Claudius into a pumpkin, in his *Apocolocyntosis divii Claudii*. This however had far less to do with humor: Seneca was "dead serious." He wanted to make the dreadful emperor laughable, in the sense of the *geloion* of Greek, and only much later did we think that this could be referred to as humor.

If one checks into the little word "humor" it has been passed from one culture to the next and so one has always treated it as a loan word and shied away from keeping it as an essential characteristic. Basically "humor" derives from the theory of the humors, and denotes a fluid that the bodily organs should have; and for a long time "humor" was only to be found in connection with that, up until Paracelsus. Sometime in the 17th century humor made its way into literature and was explained as characteristic of the British: Lessing discovered "humor" in the novels of Jonathan Swift and Laurence Sterne and thus it remained an English quality. Nevertheless the literary world of London wanted to export the word to France and, as is well known, it was taken up nicely by Jean Baptiste Molière. Last but not least it was laid at the feet of the Germans. Christoph Martin Wieland, in 1733, gratefully accepted responsibility for this though without having written anything humorous. To the contrary, Goethe made fun of him and deftly wrote *Gods, Heroes and Wieland* in mockery. And so the only poet in Germany who dealt with humor was Jean Paul. He was notable for defining humor theoretically and in all seriousness, and in the end he classed it as something near foolishness. It may well be that certain passages of Hans Jakob Grimmelshausen's, *Simplicius Simplicissimus* raised a few laughs, but his manner was very clumsy and was more aimed at the grotesque.

There is also smiling, which does not need to be triggered by a suitable object, but from an unusual "subject," in one's perception or observation about it. It is also not smiling that a joke provokes. So if I see one of you, a "smile comes upon my face" as we say. It comes from encountering a person one prizes and wishes to be near.

However there is also the reflective smile of philosophical humor. It is the smile of wisdom, that has no irony in it, no disdain, but packs into a smile an intuition of the wider world of theory. It is the expression of surprise at something someone had always hoped for. One has learned that the mimetic expression in one's face cannot be translated into words. From laughter we learn that such combinations with language do not proceed as clearly as the ancient perspectives claimed. A sharp glance, and even crying, have muscular reactions similar to those of laughing, and even the expression of disdain and bitterness have such anatomical correlates. This was likely the way Konrad Lorenz came to suspect that laughter was the inverse of aggression. But we must go beyond the body language of bitterness and disdain, and the way to do this is with spontaneous, free humor. Though we can interpret any facial expression, only the humorous expression declares itself: playful expressions are ever dominant. All this has nothing to do with the laughable or with the *geloion.*

I hope you find these little splinters of thought enjoyable …

All the best, your R.

60.
A Grotesque

Dear Nina, Dear Julian and Marie and Vicky,

I promise next time I will get back to discussing a more serious theme that might stimulate you to broader thoughts, but this time I want to report to you an especially amusing incident. It would now be more than twenty-five years ago – or was it forty? A special celebration was scheduled at the Institute. For the combined representatives of sociology and the board of the Institute, Leopold Rosenmayr had finally succeeded to found his own "Boltzmann Institute" for the next focus of his research. It turned out that a very complex name was chosen: "Institute for Sociogerontology and the Advancement of Life," and it turned out he was also the head of the department at the Institute of Sociology. This set up was widely prevalent but at the same time it was an absurdity. With this piggy-backed institute it became possible to bring in research money that the "normal" way of doing business in a university department could not do. In any case it was a great day for the members of the new Institute who were already active in the "old" one, in addition.

The porter was responsible for preparations. He was not only an unmistakably delightful personality, but even seemed to come to the Institute directly out of a play by Johann Nestroy. With a corded velvet cap and a blue working coat he made a fuss of sweeping the whole Institute, constantly in motion so that as if a "Jack of all Trades" he had been given not only a general responsibility but had informally become the head of the Institute. Thus it was to him that the job was assigned to prepare everything for the celebratory meeting. The inaugural gathering was set up in the lecture hall, which however did not offer a representative vision of what it looked like: the ugliest dirt spots on the walls were masked with paper. The lecture hall looked like it was about to be re-painted. The entryway from the house driveway and the winding corridor leading to the lecture hall were also masked with paper to mitigate a dreary impression. The reason was that Madame Federal Minister was expected, in person, invited with high officialness to give the opening speech. And because of Madame Minister a mass of aspidistras had been borrowed, as well as a red carpet and further cardboard panels to dress up certain other embarrassments, so as to spare Mme Minister of the Sciences the view of what was the usual condition of an Institute. For the lecture hall a flower arrangement had been ordered since was said that Mme Minister had an eye for flowers and would notice nothing else.

For two days Anton Amort – our Toni – was busy with this adaptation of the Institute. His most important function was then scheduled for the great day: providing sandwiches, preparing coffee and cakes, mineral water, fruit juice, and (only upon request) white wine. During the hours before the Institute celebration was to begin with Mme Minister's arrival at the driveway, Toni had been busy since the early morning with the preparation of the sandwiches, and was exceptionally nervous and cried out like a reed bunting about what was being asked of him without any indication that his work would ever be rewarded. He had set up a buffet in a small anteroom to the library's storage room: in the middle were the sandwiches, with coffee and cakes on the right and fruit juice and mineral water on the left. Behind, coyly hidden, were a couple bottles of white wine and a good number of glasses. Through mid-morning Toni raced back and forth, between the Institute's little kitchen and the buffet, now here now there, untiringly. But as soon as he left the anteroom, the student representatives and some other rascals in the Institute got the idea to grab one of the freshly made sandwiches at any opportunity. Soon Toni noticed and began to stake his life defending the buffet. Just as he would catch one thief another would sneak up to the table. The wine also was no longer safe. In order to bring the chaos to an end he locked the anteroom and disappeared.

Soon the dignitaries arrived with the *vir spectabilis* in the lead, and the dean, and a series of representatives from the medical faculty, the high respectables of the Ministry, invited guests, and new employees. They all assembled in the driveway, awaiting Madame Federal Minister. And she arrived. She dispersed a cloud of sweet perfume, and clutched in her hand her alligator purse and would not let go of it. The Head of the Institute bowed and scraped before her, murmuring something about honors and distinctions and about how special was this event for science, and that one would owe everything to her, and that like a patron saint of universities she had made the impossible possible. Right behind the Head followed the Dean, so as to be seen by Madame Minister. But by special instruction he was pushed aside by the new employees. He could only turn to one of the section leaders and complain loudly, and ever more loudly, about the meager endowments for his own faculty. In order to end the argument the Head of the Institute asked Madame Federal Minister to allow him to introduce her, too, to the *spectabilis*. Immediately the Dean switched out his protestations and straightaway broke into a hymn of praise. And finally the celebratory procession made its way to the lecture hall and tracked an enormous amount of mud onto the red carpet, since it had rained hard in front of the building. For the celebration only the invited guests were allowed to go in and the door to the lecture hall was locked tight to keep out any eavesdroppers.

Meanwhile Toni had reappeared and started making coffee. He had hardly unlocked his doors and was busy with the coffee machine when the next sandwich was swiped. So he locked himself back in cursing loudly. He would not be misled or distracted. The mood was as solemn in the lecture hall as it was festive in the entryway. The student representatives knocked on Toni's doors, jokingly demanding their share of bread and wine. As this was going on the celebration came to an end and the Head-designate for the Boltzmann Institute invited everyone to coffee and sandwiches: one must fortify oneself for the next lectures during the intermission. And so the captive audience made its way, with subdued chatting, toward the entryway. The Head was anticipating an enthusiastic acknowledgement of the careful preparation of sandwiches and coffee, but the procession went afoul. In the role of Head of the Institute and Professor he stepped forward to open the doors to the buffet. But they were locked. And behind the door someone could be heard saying, loud and clear, that the next person to come through the doors would be having to reckon with a knife to the liver. Toni raged and threatened everyone with a "knife to the liver," as he always did without exception. Only the librarian, who was summoned, was able to unlock the doors to the library storage room. The buffet had by now had fairly wilted – apparently it had been set out a bit too early. Of course most of them had lost their appetite for a snack. Toni went on swearing; he could not be calmed down. The Head of the Institute invited everyone to return to the lecture hall. By now everyone had come to see how difficult it was to run an Institute. This deeply annoyed Madame Federal Minister. She turned on her heel and left. The great celebratory gathering froze. Only Toni's voice could be heard, loud and clear: "You louses, you scum…"

You will not believe me but this celebration really happened, and this was hardly the best start. One must not neglect that such grotesque events do take place in the pursuit of science.

I hope that this story has entertained you and I remain, with best greetings, your R.

61.
Is Art Prophetic?

Dear Nina, Dear Julian, Dear Marie and Vicky,

In historiography one has often asked oneself why such large empires and states, almost as large as sub-continents, collapse inwardly and fall into chaos? After the European catastrophe of the Thirty Years War from 1618 until 1648, during the growing dangers of the Ottoman expansion, and during the War of Spanish Succession, people of course wanted to know how states are able to achieve greater political stability. Thus people studied which factors bring on the collapse of a world empire. If one could avoid these, one would achieve greater political security. The best commentary on this was written by Charles de Montesquieu not only in *The Spirit of Laws*, written in 1748, on the end of the

Roman Empire, but also in his book *Considerations on the Causes of the Greatness of the Romans and their Decline*, written in 1749. These analyses led him to his famous construction of the separation of political powers. So I advise you to study these clever books since you will be living in a time when democracies are threatened. This was also the time, at the beginning of the 18th century, when people began reading Machiavelli's *Prince* again, which the Prussian King Friedrich II had also criticized to the hilt in the margins of his copy. The reason for this was again to learn about the stabilization of a state in *Il Principe*. This was what was being read in every royal court. Finally, Edward Gibbon was the first historian to write about Roman decline in great detail, and this was the inspiration for Theodor Mommsen, Eduard Meyer, and finally Max Weber to continue with this theme in the 19th century.

Why are the books I have listed important for you? Because they represent the best introduction to historico-political thought. It was not my intention in this letter to be teaching you about this: I brought these examples in because we live at a time in which we have come to a very precarious situation in the development of art. And if we take this as a starting point there must be very dangerous elements in politics! We find similarly alienating sorts of phenomena in the environment in which we are living, about which art has now for some time informed us. And yet it remains unclear to us how on the one hand we are developing enormous technologies, can fly to the moon and telephone each other through satellites, and yet a brief visit to a contemporary museum teaches us that the objects we see there have nothing to "say" to us: they alienate us, and do not make us feel well given all the irony and nihilism they display.

We can recognize a similar situation from antiquity. Emperor Diocletian for example was tired of being in office or felt he was no longer in a position to rule the world empire on his own. So around 300AD he divided the empire up, passing on the Western half to Maximianus (Herculeus) and keeping the Eastern half for himself. Soon later they agreed that the political burdens were still too difficult to manage. So they chose as *Augusti*, two "Caesars" to give them support: Constantius Chlorus and Galerius. I tell you this since these "tetrarchs" ruled with unanimity and there was no conflict among them, but fights and wars arose at the time of succession, in which Constantinus was victorious, the son of Constantius Chlorus. Constantinus is better known as Constantine, and with the influence of his daughter he integrated Christianity as the state religion. This is not the only reason for my telling you the story. In Venice you would wonder at the sculpture that shows these tetrarchs. It is made out of porphyry, and is important because of the four rulers it depicts. But looking at this sculpture the question comes to mind what happened to the Roman sculptural tradition? The proportion of the bodies is not correct, the legs are too small, it is overall a schematic representation, and it is stiff and lacks fluidity. You can see it in front of the Palace of the Doges in Venice, as "booty" from the overthrow of Byzantium in 1206.

There is a very interesting hypothesis of André Malraux, the famous philosopher of culture, according to which, in general terms, a weariness with beauty contributed to the decline. So, in every change of the times this phenomenon shows up, first in the area of art, and then it gets hold of everyday culture and in the wake of a noticeable weakening of the economy the regnant political doctrine is called into question. Whether such feelings are correct or not, in every case the dignity of artistic execution falls far from the quality of earlier works of sculpture – I will even call it sloppiness. In our observation of such developments we have developed a certain expertise. As I said before, we enter a museum these days with certain "mental reservations." It is seldom that we have "experiences," impressions, and admiration comparable to those we experience in the Villa Borghese in Rome, standing before the works of Gian Lorenzo Bernini or Antonio Canova. As much as the great works of Käthe Kollwitz or Ernst Barlach are just as impressive, they have no successors in spirit – or at least none are known to me. Must we then in connection with the development of art in our times bring up the same question as Montesquieu once raised? Is it a sign of decadence that we encounter in the middle of a room of a museum a bucket of rubble, old bricks, sand and gravel, an old armchair – as in the Stuttgart Staatsgalerie? Has our art become primitive, then? Already Ernst Bloch in his first book, *The Spirit of Utopia*, in 1918 (latest Eng. tr., 2000 – ed.), pointed out about architecture that the tradition of craftsmanship no longer exists, that everything looks "like a washable wall." Have artistic values declined? From Roman antiquity we know that art ran aground in times of war, distress, or anarchy. With some dissatisfaction we refer to that time as the period of the "migration of peoples," basically a migratory movement not unlike the one in our own times, which pillaged, destroyed, and annihilated the legacy of antiquity. In a bit more than a hundred years, between 340 and 480AD, the high culture of antiquity almost totally disappeared. All that would be left were the small communities of Benedictine monks to act as trustees of the past.

Of course, the Saxon emperors and the Salian emperors of the Middle Ages sought to follow the Roman way, and yet what of that was still available to them? Was one to study the letters of Cicero? Did one study the philosophical works of Marcus Aurelius, who persecuted the Christians? Thus it has become our own trauma, as when in the 18th century we set about creating enduring political "bodies," an enlightened "state," and with the policy of Josephinism a reliable administration and an independent judiciary.

Ever since, we have come feel the loss of art as a bad omen. We know that political deprivation in part makes art affirmative and partly forces it underground. Graphic arts in Poland were never of such high quality as during the time of the German occupation. The witty cartoons of *Asterix* became the voice of the resistance in Paris, in 1940, and their quality as subversive criticism was never again attained. Compare that with the satirical periodical *Charlie Hebdo*, to ascertain the level of culture on which we move today! And it was not long ago, measuring according to previous historical processes, that insane criminals wanted utterly to annihilate so-called "degenerate art" – and to burn books by Jews and other authors who were out of favor. It is not long ago that we had to observe how we come to be cut off from our history. And different from other cultures, in addition to these barbarities we have lost our sense of history and our consciousness of time.

Since 1980 we seem to have buried modernity. If one believes Charles Jencks, Postmodernity in its first architectural designs came to life like a phoenix rising from its ashes – among the works of Ricardo Bofill, James Stirling and Hans Hollein. Nevertheless enthusiasm was not aroused. In painting the situation *per se* is bad; and in sculpture even worse. More and more often one encounters shrugging shoulders at the exhibits, unbelieving stares, incomprehension. The descriptions of the objects are on the one hand infantile – as if the reader cannot count to three – and on the other hand esoteric. Taken together the basic mood is melancholy, resignation, and a loss of orientation.

If one looks at it in a sociological way, in Postmodernity there is no longer any avant-garde – as there had been in the galleries of Paris around 1905. If anything is announced at all it is a demand to take things backward, back to the anarchy of the informal, back to the canonical geometrical forms that smack of authoritarianism, or else toward a new photographical realism. Nor are there any admirers of the sort Viennese Fantastic Realism was able to attract, most recently. Somehow these forms of are nowadays torn apart, unable to hang together, and worthless. Perhaps it's because the officials who organize art – the directors of the collections, the officials in the ministries of culture, and the journalists – have become too interested in gossip, and all too clearly have turned toward pursuing their own interests. Vienna is always a good example of this. The city has an air of being incredibly *au courant*, able to recognize what is going on in our time; and in the end we only see more obscenity, more triviality, and more crap.

Thus at museums we stroll alongside rotting wool, intentionally splashed canvasses, and chocolate that looks like poop, or by a stuffed elk. And now the information plaque is needed, beneath the work, to tell us what we are already seeing. This is not new. Gertrude Stein indeed wrote, "A rose is a rose is a rose." These days that has come to be repeated in many senses. An elk is an elk is an elk; an object is an object. And then comes the claim that brings all this together: because it is in a museum, "This is art." What is going on now is a noteworthy naturalism. One does not hear, around Canova's *Theseus* in the Kunsthistorisches Museum of Vienna, "This is white marble." But now, beneath each picture the material composition is given, from bronze to polyvinyl. Does such chemical expertise hold any interest for us? Is it of any interest what a curator thinks, this opportunist with name recognition in the city that has by now "linked into" the web of interests that constitutes culture politics? Did we really not know what a bronze was? Had we not been able to guess what kind of materials the art work was made of, and which kind of metal it is? Is art an elusive ghost, that at one moment is there but more often can only be guessed at?

In fact it is an indication that the erstwhile solicitation of my "I" by the artwork is now shattered. I am no longer being thought of nor is what I still can imagine when I view the Greek athlete in the Ephesus room of the Vienna Kunsthistorische Museum. Art no longer has as its theme the possibilities I can imagine within myself but instead will confront my open anticipation with shock and ugliness. In modernity there was still a concinnity between the feeling of life and the art object. In the happy 50's in which even our living interiors accepted new forms and the old furniture came to be colorfully painted, one was of the opinion that art was moving in an intellectualist fast lane. Like a traffic jam on the freeway one had then quickly decided to break away and maybe even drove outside the lines. Fashion realized it even faster with hot pants and the first torn jeans. And now one is confronted with a sculpture by Richard Serra. For the first time a feeling creeps into your mind: This enormous cube of steel, two by two by two meters – what is "it" supposed to be? What is it?

You are being invited to play a guessing game. If you guessed that the cube was steel all the way through, it must weigh an enormous amount. The normal visitor, to whom the idea that the thing, luckily located in the basement of the museum, weighs tons, guesses at first this cubical die is hollow, like a lightweight that pretends to be heavy. That is the first error that is to occur in the observer: he mistakes the material in which it consists. Of course this cube received a big award, so that its name on the plaque is all the more strange: "White Dwarf." One could just as well describe a horse as an automobile, a radio as a television, or an electric chair as a comfy armchair. The minimalist manner accords itself the freedom to choose perfectly arbitrary descriptions. The specialist at this was Richard Serra, a pioneer for the next wave of the mundane in art.

Let's go back! We were strolling through the museum. We follow the group of tourists and so we move along utterly unimpressed, through the rooms with the paintings of the school of Florence, of Siena, and of the Flemish and the Dutch, and the representatives of Spanish baroque, and after a few stairs the group leads us into the collection of antiquities. We observe the visitors and they are unimpressed, they follow the tour guide, and during her comments many are looking into their art books while others are taking pictures, making selfies, and smiling brightly when they then look at the nice photo. Most are entirely blasé, afford the paintings hardly a glance, and after the fourth room they start hoping for a rest, a pause, or they have seen quite enough. One has no choice but to describe this in such a bitter way.

I myself was stopped by one painting: the portrait of Cardinal Albergati by Jan van Eyck. I would linger at this painting. In the picture was an old man, a Cardinal, and his clear gaze bespoke erudition, strength, and discipline. Perhaps now and then he was pious. He was the top diplomat for the negotiations after the French-English conflict. Laboriously, cleverly, successfully he got them to sue for peace. Who still knows of this Cardinal today? And I noticed on the portrait, in the slight turning of the upper body and in the somewhat too strict haircut, that only clarity in the evaluation of the warring parties can create peace. This is a rare talent, which found a worthy painter for its portrayal. I stayed for a long time with the portrait. And flocks of people were wandering by, blabbering in French and English, Russian and also German. What is it worth anyway, to have brought about peace? Did the Cardinal deserve to be included in a selfie? The picture is too small. The old fellow is not impressive. These are our judgments today. Nobody took the time to recognize the information that emanates from this grand painting. Can we ever achieve an overview of European painting and art, from epoch to epoch?? The art historians have taken this from us. We can only thank them for not having to think about paintings anymore!

My dears, I would so enjoy going through a museum with you! As we recently did in Berlin. I happily remember having approached that enormous painting, that bombastic story: the Kaiser appeared in person at the unveiling of a monument to Richard Wagner. All the honorable persons had shown up. Only twenty years later, the world war would sweep them all away. I chatted with Julian and Marie about this fleeting moment. The guard was completely astonished that I stood with you two in front of this almost intolerable painting for such a long time. He admired us. Probably we were the first to look at this picture close up. And I showed you that even at that festive hour with the Wagner monument and the Prussian generals, this political pomp stood on weak footing: here and there one and another infamous criminal was recognizable. This indeed was the message of the painter! This plurality of extraordinary men owe their fame to the police! We counted twenty three police officials according to their uniforms, with their typically conspicuous inconspicuousness!

Perhaps you still remember?

All my love, your R.

PS: I ask you to look up the paintings I have been talking about on the internet!

62.
What is Consciousness?

Dear Nina, Dear Julian, Dear Marie and Dear Vicky,

In the previous letters you were regrettably confronted with a "buzz word" that now must be investigated somewhat more closely. I mean "consciousness." I call it a "buzz word" since in fact we believe that in this term on the one hand all is to be found that constitutes the I, and on the other, that it is the place where the entire inventory of our intellectual life is "brought together." In sociology consciousness also is used to refer to a social substance or at least that of social minorities which from this designation derive a proof of their independence. In Emile Durkheim there is a "collective conscience," something he thought could be treated as a "sociological fact" and thus as a "thing" one puts on like a shirt or a coat. Before that, psychology had rapidly begun its work of colonization and explained our consciousness with successful clarity. For early positivism this posed no problem, as one can learn by reading Wilhelm Wundt and later Ernst Haeckel. Of course such explanations seemed the subject matter par excellence of psychology; but also one should have been astonished that such a simple mechanism as consciousness is built into the human brain. The opposing movement presented descriptions of consciousness according to it a higher competence than our inventory of experience, even though this in fact broadens our consciousness. Fritz Mauthner was right in this connection to have spoken of a superstition about words. With this he showed that science simply invaded consciousness in the manner of an expeditionary army. We have therefore "gained" more mistrust of ourselves, to which we are pleased to refer as objectification and count that as a gain. If I now want to represent an event in consciousness, I will be served a warning from Melchior Palágy, who in his 1908 lectures on natural philosophy reported on the foundations of consciousness in great detail. In time for the development of Husserl's phenomenology, he warned: "Before one takes offence about the unknowability of 'things' in themselves, he first in all seriousness makes a stop before the inscrutable foundation of the phenomena in themselves. The unknowable begins not at all where psychology and Kantianism place it."

From this we must draw the conclusion that the science of the 19th century as a whole undertook to posit "spirit" as a constituent of consciousness. And this enabled a clever attempt to add with the same stroke "I," language, and memory, by which consciousness turns into an ever larger immaterial "continent." The tracks leading to this giant field were offered by the phenomena of memory, experience, and speech, and through them the analysis became the realistic state of affairs. These constituents of our consciousness finally took on the character of faculties and lost their standing as complete and independent in themselves. Since Christian Wolff around 1750 invented the word "consciousness," it has come to denote the entire intellectual inventory, in the sense mentioned above. And one does not believe at all that thereby all the various qualities in our processes of thought could literally be brought together and categorized "under one heading" – as perhaps the "conscious" or the "psychic." This has greatly helped the sciences since we now could begin to generalize, which in fact enabled Hegel to get to his "universal concepts" such as "popular spirit" and "world spirit."

I don't want to investigate further the theories of Emile Durkheim, since for these it is the most obvious thing in the world that there are forms of consciousness that even "molt up" into socializations. This can be traced forward to the "Frankfurt School" and even up to empirical social research where this is a tacitly employed presupposition. In Robert K. Merton there is then a synthesis that consists of the "I," the "me," the "self," and the "generalized other." The combination was now complete, circumscribing a "social consciousness" from psychoanalysis and functionalism, for a social scientific theory that could serve like a factotum to explain social situations.

So I advise you to follow out my observation that such abstract nouns are always up to no good: life, spirit, consciousness. With a glance at the "archaeology" of our knowledge, already set out by Michel Foucault, one could claim that such nouns are already like fossils, an unearthing of a former primitive people. Consciousness is like a petrified horse-tail, and yet we must immediately admit that we need these fossil-guides since otherwise we could not describe our understanding of reality and would not be able to speak or communicate about it. This would not be a big problem if for instance biologists were not trying to make us believe what life is, or psychologists were not giving up the fruitless attempt to explain the soul to us.

What Christian Wolff had in mind when he referred to our intellectual "faculty" as "consciousness" is hard to guess. In the analysis of the word *Bewusstsein* consciousness has something to do with the fact that "being" (*sein*) seems to be more conscious *(bewusste)* to us than before. This indeed chimes with the Enlightenment. And yet the Latin translation is *conscientia*, and we can see even more quickly what has been done to us. The Latin word means conscience (*Gewissen*) *and* consciousness (*Bewusstsein*). So, if we were in the High Middle Ages we would have no difficulties with both German terms. The scholastics thought of *conscientia* always in this double sense of conscience and consciousness. It was with the Enlightenment that they became two. Was this part of the intention of Wolff? In any case, Martin Luther still treated *conscientia* as a moral category, and so also conscience, which in the Reformation took on the decisive role as the principle for the maturation of personal responsibility.

If we think all this through, in the case of "consciousness" we come upon a narrowing of knowledge, which supposedly comes to us "from the outside" and becomes our knowledge. I described this in one of the first letters, how the internalization becomes "my knowledge." Without splitting hairs, this "conscience" (*Gewissen*) comes as knowledge (*Wissen*) out of the process of *sibi conscire*. This, too, is a process of "internalization." It is an invitation toward self-contemplation, which only begins through the call to pay attention to oneself. Is this ultimately the condition that one should declare to be the goal of consciousness, namely, to know something in a prudent way? The best quality in a jurist is being able to judge with calmness and clarity, which relies upon an ethos and a professional ethics that can meld with one's consciousness. In this way consciousness "expresses" itself in an everyday professional life that becomes a "*habitus*." In order that this be recognized one wore a powdered wig, a wide robe, and a gold chain.

To track things down further, we can describe consciousness as an "activity" that establishes, over and over again and without interruption, the relationship between my inner world and the outer world, and vice-versa. Right away the difficulty arises as to whether consciousness (*Bewusstsein*) is a "becoming conscious" (a *Bewusst-Werden*). With this formulation an amusing situation has been observed in science. At first, in his analyses, one interpreted anything he could and wrote it up, in order then to proudly bring everything out of the depths as a result of scientific powers. Can I say that about the "Oedipus Complex" of Freud? Is the murderer of one's father, in the case he is a mailman, *eo ipso* comparable to Oedipus? Would the mailman then enter a relationship with his mother, Jocasta, if he can hardly expect any inheritance that could be compared to the kingship of Thebes? For all his smarts, he failed to see he brought out only what he himself had put in.

If an idea can be articulated, something that consciousness obviously can achieve, then we are dealing with two abilities: something becomes conscious to us, which must have already lain within our consciousness. Here the metaphor that "the scales have fallen from my eyes" is helpful. When this happens these two phenomena begin to complete each other.

So, in remembering my accident, I remember that "consciousness came back again" and unconsciousness came to an end. It was the gruff shaking of the paramedic who wanted to know my name and my address. I was then again "in consciousness." Apparently I gave the correct answer. The continuity of my memory was tentatively available, and carried forward despite diminutions my mental life before the unconsciousness. The emergency doctor then brought this meek condition of my consciousness back to an end. I still heard him say he wanted to send me "into the arms of Morpheus." A day later my consciousness asserted itself with unpleasant accompanying phenomena: the pains were palpable, more and more unbearable, more and more focused. In such an inescapable situation we experience the qualities of our authentic I. One can come to the idea of being able to contemplate an I and a conception of it at the same time. Subject and object are simultaneously present. Subjectively I was in this amazing invention, a hospital bed; objectively I reconstructed the "series of events," as I was driving blissfully along my favorite route through the Lobau. Though the situation might seem schizophrenic such mental operations are possible. One can refer to it as reflection. Just as one during an accidental occurrence can live through the inescapable sequence, so it happens at the same time that one seems to observe oneself doing so: "one sees himself as if he were looking at another man." In this in-between space, the I becomes possible, thinkable, basically it is what connects an individual past event to the spontaneous present. This is always available to the imagination, out of which the I is retrieved. It is only in a distancing from ourselves that we have experience of "our" knowledge, of our feeling, and this we can now call "self-consciousness."

However, in pietism this does not have the best commendation. The step to this creation of one's "self" as a noun is indicated for the first time only in 1696, and is understood in the rigorous Lutheran view as "evil," "sinful," and "depraved." Somehow it had been brought over to German from the "English work on the Bible" – so I guess.

The undiluted demand to consider consciousness as both subject and object is problematic. To do so leads to madness, which we can "see" for the first time in the paintings of Pieter Brueghel. His paintings split reality not only between virtue and vice, between depravity and piety, between nature and civilization (whence his paintings have the same format as "sections" of reality!) but the division is also visible in the way he constructs two opposite vanishing points. The eyes wander back and forth restlessly, and cannot stop on anything. Obviously Goethe consciously wanted to oppose this powerful sermon of Flemish painting and formulated modern realism in his unification of consciousness and conscience: "The actor is always without conscience; nobody has conscience except the observer." Was this a terribly German conclusion? Even in "American pragmatism" such a brusque assertion could not be found.

It is "conscious" to me that we have gotten into philosophy. And yet it is not at all speculation, but rather focusses itself on something specific within "philosophical empiricism." If you apply this method in your thinking, you will finally toss this relativism to the winds. In modernity only this opportunism of the "relative" has been cited against ideology, and therein the greatest error was contained, that this has something to do with tolerance. Such has often been asserted. Given this, even critical rationalism appears to be something of a salvation. And even Marxism benefits from the presumption of innocence ...

All the best I remain, your R.

63.
... if I may start from myself ...

My Dears,

I must immediately apologize for the delay in writing you a letter. There are two reasons: the one is easy to understand. Christmas is just around the corner and there are many things to do. The preparations are dominated by one really necessary accent: the polishing of the silver. Though I will not yet curse my longstanding love of collecting, this time the job was a bit of a strain for me. To stand up for a long time is painful ever since my accident, and I can relax my back only if I rest my head on the kitchen cabinets and so that the muscles of my back become more relaxed. And also I get some help from Novalgin, Seractil, or Ibuprofen. All three taken together do the job. The second reason is of course the question I keep asking myself: Will you sometime read these somewhat difficult letters? Even after a few years it will still be difficult. And on the other hand it was my project to offer you a kaleidoscopic view of my life, so that the thoughts and ideas appear in a colorful sequence. It may seem that some things are outlandish, but you have to put up with that: they had a big meaning in my life. It may also be that you will be surprised if in the midst of philosophical thoughts a reference to painting or to music suddenly intervenes. I explained once before that in the history of political philosophy, pictorial and also musical "thinking" are equal to our usual conception of thinking. Is it correct to assume that the philosopher's competence for interpreting the world is worthy of consideration but Beethoven had no such competence? Did Francisco Goya have less to say than Edmund Husserl? Did he not put the phenomenal structure of the emotions into a "picture" that brings us closer to understanding?

It was always a quirk of mine – if you are willing to call it this – to jump from theme to theme. Max Weber's theory of human behavior is hard to transfer to the stage, but where can one better observe traditional behavior than in *The Mayor of Zalamea* by Pedro Calderón de la Barca, or in Gerhard Hauptmann's *Beaver Coat*? And it is well known that the theory of roles was developed for a good hundred years in view of the theater, and that it was from the stage that the best models were incorporated into the theory. It was because of this that Erving Goffman entitled his book *Wir Alle Spielen Theater* (lit. "We Are All Play-acting"– the title of the Eng.tr. is *The Presentation of Self in Everyday Life* – ed.).

I don't want to bore you with authors that are important for specialists in sociology. Only in its concrete references did the theory become really "embodied," become tangible and visible; and moreover we learned in this way to distinguish between constants in behavior and variable phenomena. The constants can be the basis for inferring elemental anthropological characteristics but the variables are already well-known during the course of the ages. Is my description understandable? Of course, taking in this information depends upon whether you are interested in it. If one of you is to study mathematics, such studies will probably be uninteresting. Anyway, mathematicians in a social context often exhibit behavior that is still basically infantile, just as conversely social scientists for their part act as if their own understanding of human behavior and action is the master key for understanding "the world." These foolish debates are always going on and remind me of the "Planing Song" from Ferdinand Raimund's *Spendthrift*. Even if Raimund places the carpenter Valentin into the center as a man "as good as gold," one should not overlook the political message that is contained in this. The musical accompaniment to the song, composed by Conradin Kreutzer, detracts from the message, but the piece itself is a touching rendition of the peaceful reign of Emperor Franz II (I). Of course this is not well received in current historical research so that Raimund suffers an unjust treatment, since one takes his theatrical pieces to be mere fairy tales. In this the irritating term "all the same" is the starting point for measuring the realization of opportunities: "Fate brings on the planer, and it planes all things the same ..."

Now I have again bought you an example that merely mentioning social roles leads to theatrical plays, so as to encounter an unexpected political judgment in Raimund. This case ought not distract us from sociological role-theory – assuming you are interested – though it is "brought to life" but also given a "politicization" that within the tradition of this theory often remains attenuated. It is always a matter of attempting to restore to the "world" the individual segments that have undergone theoretical treatment, so as to avoid their treatment in isolation. Focusing on this may also be important because the "cyclopean" view of science, as Kant had called it, comes to be equipped with a "second eye." We know that because we have two eyes we are able to see in three dimensions, and can estimate distance, and thereby perceive the three-dimensionality of objects. This is also true for theories. Max Weber and Emile Durkheim set up the sociological canon, the one the theory of management and administration and the other the method that enables one to grasp social facts. The essential positions of this science surely go back to these two scholars, though this may mean nothing to you now. What is wonderful in Max Weber is that his theoretical concepts are supported with a stupendous knowledge of historical materials, whereas with Durkheim things are more difficult. His "facts" are derived from a series of abstractions so that the abstraction can be handled as if it were a "material thing." Thus his concept of solidarity, which we at first observe as merely an emotional kind of behavior between men, has become a fixed ingredient in the work-world and immediately became the theme of trade-unions, an "intellectual" creation which in turn has become a phenomenon to be empirically quantified. So! I have done enough "talking shop" which might help one or another of you to know at least a little before you get into the complexity of a theory.

I would like again to mention something I have already taken up before. It has to do with the fact that you and I encounter each other in the letters. Thus my experience, which belongs to the past, is made to stand over against the future space of your experience, of the next generation, and the first job is to choose which recommendations from yesterday to bring back and apply at a later time. In this sense, you encounter me as you do a shopkeeper. You will already have observed that at a shop there are wares that you have never yet bought. You haven't eaten each and every one of the foods for sale; but the merchant will teach you to recommend his wares to other customers than yourselves! As far as you are concerned the merchant only needs to offer you chocolate and Coca-Cola. He could not make a living that way, for how often will you be buying that? Thus a business has countless wares that will satisfy a broad spectrum of demands. This is how it is when one has reached an advanced age. If one could practice a profession in which, like a decathlete, he must achieve mediocre competence in a variety of disciplines, this surely has the disadvantage that he will achieve in each only an average success, and yet still success noteworthy for the plurality of ten areas. In the 100 meters, one is only a second slower than the world record, and in the high jump only 5 cm under the world record, and in the pole vault only 40 cm. And if the world champion pole vaulter had to run the 100 meters he would probably be 3 seconds slower than the decathlete, which in the athletics of today is an eternity.

An older man, like a merchant, has a widest variety of "wares" to offer. Unfortunately the tradition of craftsmen is worse off that it was before. I often heard an old craftsman say that nobody shows any interest in what he knows though he has a great deal to show and hand down. Because of this, an enormous amount of knowledge and many craftsman skills have been forgotten. In the "intellectual" realm one notices that the loss is less at first. The situation in the humanities is a little different, since such losses usually have an "effect" much later. The clearest example would be old manuscripts: anything that was composed more than a hundred years ago can no longer be read. Of course you have never learned the Gothic *kurrent* script, which is why you will not be reading my father's diaries. Your only opportunity to read these would be for an archivist who had learned this script to read it to you.

In my own case I owe a good number of advantages to the Gothic script. In my appeal against an administrative fine – I had been faulted for the place I parked my car – I wrote the appeal in Gothic. Nobody would admit he was unable to read it, and nothing more than a warning was issued. The officer asked me to read my letter to him and since he recognized that I was "skilled" in this script he waived the fine. Additionally, writing in the *kurrent* happened to spare me the job of "secretary" in conferences. Keeping minutes is a laborious procedure carried out in "appointment negotiations" at the university for the selection of a new professor out of a plurality of candidates. The minutes must accompany the invitation and are sent along to the ministry. The then Federal President served as chairman of the commission. He let me know that he had to have the minutes rewritten because he could not read them. So at the time I was relieved the duty of being the secretary – so once again my *kurrent* came to good use.

Many will now think, why the *kurrent*? Or why Latin? Why Greek or why education in "pictorial arts," as it was once called? It is always a bad sign when a ministry of education thinks that it can drop something from the curriculum. The theme of "useless knowledge" I have already spoken about once – and you might not believe I could even use that term! One can choose ways to organize science, one can choose another focus, but the argument that one is justified to withhold knowledge from young people cannot be sufficient. The problem is that today only a few possess an overview of a subject. One is always hearing that it is impossible to have an overview of the natural sciences. I do not believe this, since a scholar who has only dealt in chemistry will be able to indicate fairly well what area of chemistry is important for an eleventh grader. Likewise, a Nobelist in physics can say what a fifteen year old needs to know in physics. 120 years ago it was quite a distinction for a great scholar to have written a basic textbook on his subject at the end of his career. Today, one would edit a collection of articles contributed by thirty or so physicists, chemists, biologists, geneticists in order to represent the state of the field, as if in itself this would be perfectly helpful, since even a "beginner" in school at least gets an approximation of the necessary information: no more is necessary. But no! The debate goes on, and in the wrong direction. One will sooner seek to cut "fine arts" subjects in order to offer "Computational Systems." Earlier, it was possible for a person to seem to be "struck by stupidity." Today it is possible that we will be struck *with* stupidity. In such a context the punishment of bygone times, for the teacher to strike the student's hand with a ruler could be called relatively harmless.

It annoys me not only that it occurs to them to drop fields of study, but also that they replace them with computer studies, while this is the most pressing time, given "globalization," to add Indian, Chinese, and Japanese history to the curriculum instead. Also worth pursuing are questions as to why the high culture of India perished. Such an argument is met with doubt: one would claim in defense of dropping such a subject that in any case this is a vanished culture. But in fact such a study is the prerequisite for bringing our own consciousness up to date!

Meanwhile I remain, with my best greetings, your R.

64.
Remarks on Beethoven

Dear Nina, Dear Julian, and Marie, and Vicky,

Just because this is the baptism day of Beethoven, I want to write you a note. Just now I am listening to the *C-minor Symphony*, Opus 67 written in 1808 if I remember correctly.

The conductor Daniel Barenboim is in the Second Movement of the symphony, which wants to begin in such a heroic way. On the way to the mausoleum the parade guard falls out of step and the soldiers seem to stumble. The French horns and trumpets continue above them, the basses try to maintain the seriousness of the hour, but already the hero has become mortal. And in the middle of the movement a sort of polka intrudes forcibly and makes the drama all the more lopsided, which is not made any better by the allure of the flutes and clarinets. These are my impressions during listening, though I know that one ought not think in such a way since the music stands on its own. These images break into the light of day as the sounds break the silence.

And in the Third Movement the trumpets and horns return, mostly the horns, the rhythmic signals which lead one to think there will be an attack. But who would be attacked? Meanwhile you are struck by the beating of the timpani. They are strokes of fate. Most of them come from beyond, from far away. And then the contrabasses embark on a fugato. This is driven forward, utterly inexorable like life, and hastens toward its end, to the closing resolution that will admit no resistance. Then once again comes the impressive restfulness: beneath the surface lurks the restlessness of reality. And during this the "woodwinds" stutter – the bassoon, oboe, clarinets. The light strokes of the notes. In the midst, the violas, those lame ducks.

Yet now the percussion emerges from out of nowhere, and breaks in as a C-major chord, like an outcry, announcing the Fourth Movement. It is a soothing outcry, based on the children's song "A, A, A, the Winter is Here." That song has never sounded so heroic! And now it is deconstructed into different instrument groups. Soon it will sound like Mozart, then it will revert into the greediness of the Romantic, in the manner of Schumann. But the Fourth Movement phase by phase returns to the contemplative, and leaves to the flutes the message of happiness, and then calls again for the other – not victory but the radiance of another world. But what is this anyway, a "world?" Indeed one ought finally to get out of this old skin. *Per aspera ad astra*! The orchestra builds up into an inexplicable unreality which then will be caught up again with stops and starts, wonders and hopes. Yet in the orchestra's *tutti* the C-major chord comes back, like a glacier under a blue sky. And in the backward walk of a crab, the children's song, it is renewed with the assertion that another time has now arrived. Hark! The new time is here! Everything is wiped away, annihilated. I do not want to write the names of what is wiped away. It is the memory of the Reich, which is still there in the Fourth Movement, huge, colossal, despite Napoleon's invasion in 1806, and the closing fugue says it loud and clear: The past is real. The English horn can only agree, and the woodwinds, its loyal tone-companions, are the peaceable ones who lead the "dance in the round" that leads to the ovation at the close.

This is what I wanted to write you – on Beethoven's 250th baptism day.

(I wrote these lines while the symphony was being performed. In the swiftness of writing I was chasing after the structure of the piece, and could barely keep up with and was always behind, though I know the piece by heart in almost all its phases. A special homage to Beethoven! I recommend his trios – as well as his compositions for piano and cello...)

All the best, R.

65.
On Pitch, Sound, and Silence

Let's reverse it for once: Dear Vicky and Marie, Dear Julian and Nina!

The early onset of darkness in December facilitates a wide flight of thoughts. According to yesterday's commentary on Beethoven's *Fifth Symphony* I want to continue in an orderly course; and for that it is necessary to understand the role played by a given sound – for instance that of a violin – in the logic of composition. If I may repeat: sound, like our own voices, is what brings a proposition into expression. "Proposition" here denotes what is essentially being said, but there is a difference as to whether it is spoken by a woman or by a child or by a man. A voice in the soprano register has a different "standing" than a deep voice or a child's voice. But it is the same proposition, and achieves in its timbre its expressive power and becomes audible. This is significant for our contemporary music, since too often a greater significance is accorded to the sound than to the thematic content of the composition. The elementary forms in electronic music are very catchy, where modulations by technical means can produce moods for which one might think such tones in themselves suffice as pure physical sounds. Of course we can find exceptions to this that ultimately get beyond such experimentation. One of the first examples can be heard in Ernst Krenek's *Pfingstoratorium* – and then later in John Cage. In the latter's composition, *I Ching*, the binary number system from the Chinese wisdom book *I Ching* is produced in a musical transformation. This results in strict patterns of a sort similarly used in the twelve-tone music. Cage was the pioneer of serial music, minimal music, and experimental music, and meant for music something similar to what Andy Warhol meant for pictorial art.

It is important to dare to take this step, also, in our listening so as not to become overwhelmed by the musical heritage. An even greater pressure is wielded by contemporary entertainment music, which unfortunately seduces our ears with false harmonies that lead to a skewed understanding of music. For exactly this reason I was never able to enjoy The Beatles. They were always unpleasant for me and later I got a confirmation of my judgment. On their first record cover they chose pictures of assorted political figures – and there was Hitler, right in the middle. This first edition was withdrawn by the manager, who, "half informed" about the Nazi time no longer wanted the thrill of having Hitler on the cover.

All the more did I enjoy the recording I received of Julian at the piano. He was playing a piece by Bela Bartok. About Bartok there would be a whole lot to write – on his *Wonderful Mandarin*, on his symphonic works, his quartets – but more on that, later. First and more fundamental is that Bartok was almost entirely banned from the concert venues. Instead, one "experiences" performances of the living "representatives" in the famous philharmonic subscription concerts in Vienna – which are always weak, and uneventful, and having nothing attractive in them. The names need not be mentioned …

If I may continue with Cage, he was especially interested in giving silence a special place in music. You will laugh, but without silence music is unthinkable. Silence in music is comparable with the empty canvas in painting. You have surely seen paintings where areas are left "unpainted" so as to elevate expressivity. Similarly John Cage brought silence into his way of expression and waited to hear what noises "take place" in the concert hall, during this silence. This began with experiments and ultimately reached programmatic expression in his works. In any case it is always this way with experiments, that they remain vital only when they are novel and are no longer so once they are being reproduced.

In this connection I want to vent a biting remark. On Sunday the cultural elite of Vienna comes to the famous Musikverein for concerts. It is always at 11:00 AM. Once the ringing from Karlskirche fades away the conductor comes to the podium. The musicians, the world-famous Vienna Philharmonic, together stand half way up to greet him formally – it is a symbolic gesture often reported in sociology – and then relax back into their chairs, leaning back and carefully gazing toward the conductor. Will he start? Very well. And when the second movement, marked "slow," then follows, the Viennese cultural elite is bored to death. Only the Japanese visitors are watching, through their opera glasses. The Viennese on the other hand are leafing through their programs and reading, or fan themselves some fresh air with them. And it is when the pianissimo tries to render the most intimate passage that Cage's counter-program arrives, with coughs and nose blowing. Others search uncertainly through their handbags for a cough drop. Still others, in the balcony, lean back into a deep sleep. In the intermission one learns that the second movement was not terribly impressive. Much more interesting are the goings-on for lunch at the Hotel Imperial. Conversely in the third movement one is even able to tolerate Gustav Mahler, when a cast of 120 men gradually mount a fortissimo. As if on command all the men in the cultural elite on the balcony stand up the better to observe this bravura deed. In Munich's Circus Krone it is mostly the children that do this, to let off the tension that has built up in their bodies. But the criticism of the conductor during the break is always the same: once again the Philharmonic musicians have saved the conductor.

So, to return:

Beethoven was the first to use this brief silence, to strengthen enormously the expressiveness of the first measures of his *Third Symphony*. You will certainly hear his famous "*Eroica*" symphony someday. It is in E-minor, Opus 55, and you will not immediately notice that it begins with a quarter-note rest. The purpose for this is to give the theme the impression of being "rushed": one finds oneself quickly out of breath since that lost bit of time needs to be made up. And the music strengthens this unsettling rush with its time signature in 3/4. If you want to make a test of this, take your index finger, draw a triangle in the air, and imagine that the first side of the triangle is silence and the orchestra comes in only with the second side of the triangle. Once you have this symphony in your ear you will notice how difficult it is to have keep the first beat silent.

Now I must go back. We began by mentioning the relation between sound and composition. In sound our fantasy is spoken to – and therefore special mastery of the craft is needed to appeal to the imagination of the listener, to connect them as it were, in their privately experienced imagination, with the composition. Nowhere is this better done than in the *Third Symphony* of Johannes Brahms, especially in the Third Movement, which takes us into a rich landscape of memories and perhaps also of yearning. There are of course some lyric poets who are also able to do this, perhaps with greater difficulty in language since a voice must in their case fill out the volume for communicating that in music calls for an orchestra.

If then the mastery of the craft is damaged, we are confronted directly with the question how we can determine the worth of a composition. Is a subjective arbitrariness the dominating factor from now on? In painting we can immediately get an answer to this. If in a casual way, colors are thrown onto a wall, it may be delightful during the process to watch the colors slowly run down the canvas. It may be enjoyable to observe the very conflictual confrontation of the colors, that they have different chemical composition and thus almost battle against each other: natural colors against wild colors or against colors with a metallic base: ocher against creamy white, which comes from zinc. This can likewise take place in music, when the trumpet abuses the viola or the piccolo mistreats a violin. This is likely the largest problem in modern art in general, that between the spiritual and the material the greatest of mismatches has set in. One can refer to this as the "collapse of values," whether as too great a demand or too little a demand placed upon one ingredient or the other. When modern art, seduced by the technology of our world, thinks that the creature can arbitrarily set his own devices against the creation, what is really going on is a mortal sin against spirit and against nature.

If you will, even Richard Wagner had an inkling of this, since in the *Meistersinger* Hans Sachs attributes the prize song to Walther so that he can win the bride. This song is stolen by Beckmesser, who then performs it very objectionably. But here charlatanry is at work and this does not stop with Beckmesser. Nobody knows more about that than Pablo Picasso. He declared in an interview in 1957, "As soon as art ceases to be the nourishment of the best minds, the artist can employ all the tricks of the intellectual charlatan. Today, most people no longer expect comfort and edification from art. The refined, the rich, the professional do-nothings, the distillers of quintessences, hope only for the unusual, the sensational, the eccentric, the scandalous, in modern art. And since the days of cubism I have been feeding these guys what they are looking for. ... I have understood my times and have profited from the stupidity, the vanity, the greediness of my contemporaries ...." Soon after, Salvador Dali seconded him: "Since we live in a time of the imbeciles in an entirely consumerist society, I would be stupid if I did not serve my own advantage. I would be stupid if I did not succeed to exploit the imbeciles to make even more money for myself."

I hardly want to confront these assertions with Hans Jonas's "ethics of responsibility!" Didn't both painters have the duty to oppose these pseudo-elites and vulgar businessmen? Shouldn't they have taken as their example the pioneer of modernity, namely Francisco Goya?

I have just now mentioned Bartok in reference to Julian. He embodied the opposite of these world-famous painters. After emigrating to New York he almost starved. In his development one finds the paradigm of the composer who in his works has reached the apex of his powers of expression, and finally comes into a period of maturity. This hard work has no other focus than to pursue unconditionally the goal of mastering to perfection the materials of music. If I again may compare spirit and matter, in Bartok the tonal material was his means to a spiritual goal.

You have not yet had enough experience with music to understand right away the pair of questions I think every composer has to ask himself: as far as composition is concerned, he must always ask himself what he wants to say – in music this means, "How should it sound?" The other question is, "What does the instrument say?" If I think for example about the *Bolero* of Maurice Ravel, the total of over a hundred instruments becomes a gigantic sound and yet retains the shape of a dance-step. It may surprise you that the *Bolero* always reminds me of the *Rhinoceros* of Eugène Ionesco. The more the music gets a hold of you – the more it is borne in one's body – the more have I been given insight, through my ears, that this is how a dictatorship comes to take hold.

All music depends upon the instrument, what the dialogue of the instruments brings about, and how the "musical" element thereby achieves its distinctiveness. Instrumentation therefore means that each instrument has its own normative substance, whether an interrogative or regulative or a productive content. This corresponds with the old meaning of the word "concert," namely *concertare* (to contend, to fight).

I could now sing a lament, I could bewail the situation that through the system of electronic components a perfection in the reproduction of music has been reached that partly depresses the "normal musician" and partly forces him to give up making music. The media then support the so-called "preferred" works: a selection process is established that makes the well-known compositions still more well known. One will almost never hear the beautiful *Metamorphoses* – the grandiose composition of Carl Ditters von Dittersdorf, after Ovid. One will also no longer hear the *Grand Macabre* of György Ligeti, composed in 1974, nor Alfred Schnittke's opera *Life with an Idiot* from 1980. The latter is a devastating caricature of Lenin. All this is hardly even known, since perfect recordings of the great piano concertos, featuring star conductors and star pianists, dominate the standard landscape of music. The conductor Wilhelm Furtwängler may almost have been right to say, "There is nothing more for today's person that would really be decisive for him and dedicated to him, that really addresses him, in the face of which and in which he recognizes himself. The prophecy of his fate no longer confronts him in art. But art thereby has become superfluous from within. It has come to an end ...."

His conclusion does not convince me at all. It will be the case that after the glory days of music, which basically were confined to Europe, there followed a period of "reduced" significance. We must always realize that the glory consisted of four centuries of music history, that it was in four centuries that all this powerful music was composed and performed. This period is no way at an end. Demand for music has not become weaker, but different. If one thinks of the musical compositions of West Africa that the Kronos Quartet has played, one can become far more optimistic about what Furtwängler was unwilling to believe. Granted, the senseless art industry cannot be sustained, this focus of intrigue and vanity like the courts of the Roman soldier emperor, this pitiful creature that pops up between opera and New Year's Concert, all these violent crimes against music under the supervision of the so-called cultural elites – and there must be other plans in the offing. There will be, just as there always have been, times in the arts in which new beginnings are made. In music we recognize our need for them; but even the Word we get "in the beginning" can turn into something bad.

At the end of his novel *Crime and Punishment*, Fyodor Dostoevsky concludes that there can never be an end to a story. Even the good-for-nothing Nechayev, who was the model for the novel and during the meeting of the First International in Kiev drove a wedge between Marx and Mikhail Bakunin to the point of splitting them up, was not in a position to take control of history, despite the assassinations at the Apraksin Dvor in St. Petersburg and despite the conspiracies. And so Dostoevsky wrote, "But here a new story begins, the story of the gradual renewal of a man, the story of his gradual rebirth, of the gradual transition from one world to the other, the acquaintance with a new reality that had been completely unknown to him. This could provide the theme for a new story, but our present one has come to an end."

All this must be conveyed to you. You should not simply stumble into the world as into a carnival full of the seductions of all possible sorts of charlatans. We will be able to avoid it in deathless joy, as with measure and eagerness we always seek to make the other actual – over and over again, and always accompanied by hope.

This reads almost like a New Year's resolution. Take it along with you to Guatemala and may it help Nina lighten the period of the pandemic here in Vienna.

Heartful hugs, your R.

66.
What is To Be Painted?

Dear Nina, Dear Julian and Marie and Vicky,

Today is a special day for the building we live in. Six hundred twenty-five years ago, on this day, 19 December, the small church was sanctified and since then has belonged to the Teutonic Order. And five hundred years ago, in 1520, the Gothic winged-alter arrived from Bohemia. We held an especially dignified celebration, which despite the pandemic was able to offer some musical surprises. Most impressive to me was the *Song of Mary* by Johannes Brahms (Op. 22, No.4, marked *Allegro ma non troppo*). The form of the song, in four voices, had a strong echo of the Renaissance, of Carlo Gesualdo, who lived in the second half of the 16th century. But I don't want to write again about music. Equally admirable is the high altar, which was built in the 15th century. It shows important moments in the life of Jesus and therefore has a strongly narrative character.

You will already have heard that *biblia pauperum* were created, to give the common people a conception of the things their faith was about. In their manner of narration, a famous art historian, Ernst Gombrich, thought that these medieval representations consist in the same concept as modern cartoons, or "Mickey Mouse." Like the word-balloons that give words to the mice and the ducks, so also the speech-banners tell the suffering of Christ. Gombrich pushed this comparison in order to emphasize the dialogical character, which one can follow by reading the word-balloons as well as the speech-banners. He didn't care about the old saying, "Though two are doing the same thing it is not the same." The art historian simply ignored the difference in their significance. This is surprising since for some time before, art historians were hesitant to make such comparisons.

In any case modernity is not devoid of written references in its ways of representation. If we think of the early phase of cubism – the paintings of Juan Gris or Georges Braque – the references are unavoidable. The object is named with bold stenciling, even though one can identify what it is without this "clarification." We can assume that in the spirit of "two is better than one," an emphatic certainty about the object is being sought. And perhaps Gombrich should only be criticized for disrespect if he compares the ways of certifying objects or assertions with the "core elements" of the message of salvation. Out of fear that the "contents" being represented will not be deciphered one thinks he must introduce writing in order to achieve an unambiguous designation of the reality, something like the Q.E.D. of mathematics. Clearly, one distances oneself from reality when he uses for instance naturalism or realism as its criterion, but all the more in modernity one is struggling with authenticity. Everything that distracts from the object or that by dint of the manner of depiction allows the object to be understood in a new way must be eliminated, for with this the object will have lost its authentic uniqueness. This ideological orientation then becomes heightened in the case of historical painting which presents lies and a pseudo-heroism. In the sculpture program for the new city boulevards such gestures are even more embarrassing, for the "great" people appear in antique clothing, role models that cannot be modelled, given the social mixture of a megalopolis.

Now I note that I am struggling with a single point, the Archimedean point for modernity: I cannot unambiguously determine how it came about. Might the answer lie in the fact that the pioneers of modern painting – Paul Cezanne, Vincent van Gogh, Paul Gauguin – in their letters and writings were interested in different objects for representation than all the painters before them? The French Realists like Courbet or Corot painted realistic enough interpretations of reality, and repeated this over and over, and their success forced painting into the shadows, between 1780 and 1820. In the gray of everyday life miserable people stand around without a clue, victims of the Industrial Revolution, and these painters provide a witness of their cluelessness. The pioneers, on the other hand, study the physiological properties of seeing and general brain physiology; they do research on the secrets of optics and how the wind alters natural coloring; they move over to the field of philosophy and are surprised that in the course of their excursions the professors of philosophy rebuke them for doing so. Eugène Delacroix was invited into the seminars and soon removed himself. In his eyes philosophy does not do what it ought to do, namely, contemplate the conditions of human existence, the preconditions of the world, the force of nature, and political protest. The letters of van Gogh are a copious testimony of his observations of nature and his interpretations of it, and are records of his painful experiences that slowly took on a psychological cast in a way that corresponds closely with the times.

Although around 1900 the pioneers were dead or were no longer able to paint – for example Monet, Renoir, Degas – the wheel could not be reversed. The impetus of Expressionism continued, and soon came Cubism and Fauvism and the baby-steps of abstract painting in Wassily Kandinsky.

I am not going to retell the history of art, but it was here that one began to ask why "from this point on" this other sense of painting became meaningful. If art up until then had represented the visible, from now on it would make visible what had long been invisible. This change, which Heinrich Wölfflin chose as the starting point for his art history, was not entirely new, but now had to do with what we now could see, that had for a long time been unseen. As medieval painting made the invisibility of the Holy visible, and the unseeable seeable, the moderns do the same but now the object is not the Mystical, not the Holy, but the "inward life" of men and of objects. In *Scream*, Edvard Munch gave the best example that we "from now on" could see what this distress looks like, this fear, this horror – and we can see it, indeed.

Twenty-five hundred years ago Plato wrote about how Leontius the son of Aglaion was coming back up to Athens from the Piraeus. In *The Republic* he describes the shiver Leontius felt when at the base of the wall of Athens he caught sight of the corpses, near where the hangman lived. And Plato tells us Leontius could not decide whether to cast his eyes over there in dismay or cover his head with his wide robe; and that despite the shiver he could not avoid taking looks at the pitiable dead men, whose bodies showed all the effects of torture. Suddenly a horror came upon the man. Similarly, at the end of the 19th century painting aspires to make us look back at the horror once again. Within the horror lies the reality that the world war soon revealed. And this was only the prelude to the horror in painting. Oskar Kokoschka painted the cadaver of an animal; Egon Schiele painted Gustav Klimt dead in the morgue.

I think I've made my point by now. I can appreciate Gombrich's disrespect in not shying away from comparing a cartoon with the Passion of Christ, on a formal level and for art-historical purposes. The horror to be seen on the huge altars of the Gothic period, the murdering of the Lord, has because of the Resurrection redeemed this horrid final moment, has cancelled it, has annihilated it, and has confirmed that our spiritual existence is eternal. It is the great secret of faith that we do not end up mere ash and dust. In modernity this certainty of faith no longer prevails. A horror is a horror is a horror, one could say with Gertrude Stein. Horror, ultimately, is the response to our existence. In an extraordinary way this transformation was fulfilled at Dachau. In the 19th century Dachau was the center for nature painting, the painting of idylls, the broad landscape of moors with the delicate green of the birches along with farmers hard at work. A few years later, with its concentration camp, it was to be the location of horror, of torture and contempt for human beings … a strange coincidence.

Surely the painting of Central Europe was far ahead of the rest, so that only here an early awareness of the coming horror was to be seen. In any aquarelle of Egon Schiele the decrepitude of man is the theme, the pitiableness of existence, and yet with the same whiff of the inclination toward voyeurism. We experience in the aquarelles of Schiele the same dilemma Leontius felt. Should we cover our heads in the sight of this horrible pitiableness and the anonymous suffering, or instead do we risk a glance at the thing which, completely contrary to our will mutates into something erotic? In these aquarelles our gaze loses its innocence, and we cannot help it.

I can already predict that I will take up this theme again.

Now however I've given you some strong tobacco! I can only ask you not to wrestle with my thoughts now, but just to grasp that in these thoughts we have the dilemma of our times. Will we someday overcome this dilemma, defeat it, end it? This lies with you! Even when you become adults you hardly know that your primary task will be to redress this forgetfulness of being. In any case you have in the last two centuries of painting the best documentation of the problem in which we are entangled. I will not speak further now, but surely I will present this again in another letter to you.

I wish you pleasant days leading up to Christmas.... Your R.

67.

Language between the Dyslexic and the Infantile

Dear Nina, Dear Julian, Marie and Vicky,

An entirely different theme appears to have the same importance as economics, art, health, and law. Adults are racing through the streets on E-Scooters. This form of locomotion seems socially desirable, for it reduces automobile traffic within the city center, and just as the case of the folding bicycle is taken to be the beginning of a turnaround in traffic. From the political side potentials have long been in sight for "calming" the traffic in the city. This is done in the very paltry language of the proclamations and announcements. Somehow the language took on the same form as the childish passion for adult scooter-riding. Already twenty years ago it appears to have been a concern to bring out a dictionary that would moderate the dialogue between people. "Dyslexia First!" This noble undertaking bases its charitable efforts on an obvious weakening of the German language among German speakers. It will enable people who have a reading deficiency and suffer learning or speech disorders to take part in social life. Though it has since become honorable to look after people whose "background" shows a deficiency of one kind or another, so also has it become foolish merely to build bridges over these gaps in understanding in one direction only and see the amelioration and mitigation only from the point of a better comprehensibility in accordance with, and for the purpose of, a "barrier free" ability to take part in basic communication. What makes better sense is to find paths of communication for pre-linguistically deaf persons, just as one had come up with braille for the blind. The progress was remarkable and was greatly welcomed.

You will quickly understand my objection: I claim that the now commonplace plea for easier comprehensibility arises not so much out of a regard for those of lesser gifts but is an infamous pillaging of our language of all these forms of expression that contain any complexity at all.

It all begins so harmlessly! At first the sense is, "Anything can be said with simple words! One must formulate statements that will be comprehensible, generally and universally." From the very beginning, in 2017, a writer noticed that "Language Light" is about to become language par excellence. And that is a problem.

From my professional experience I can report that the written works of my students are indeed in a perfect condition, optically – everything is "properly formatted," foreign words in italics, paragraphs properly margined according to the style guide, important items underlined, citations in red font – and yet as for grammar, in every third sentence one encounters grave errors, incorrect tense sequences, and orthographic errors. The difference between *dass* and *das* has faded since the comma required before *dass* is missing. Since in English there are almost no punctuation marks, which makes reading much harder since not everything can be subordinated into the relative clause, one has to manage the word order with care. "Language Light" is the apparently urgent concern of our school authorities with English as a model, so as to erase for once and for all the distinction between "educated" and "uneducated." Today the graduates of this indoctrination in the changes of written expression have been incredibly docile pupils, male and female (*SchülerInnen*, with *Binnen-I*: see below – ed.). This change has existed now for forty years.

Though it was people in the USA who were in the vanguard for creating "political correctness" they have found enthusiastic followers in Central Europe. But still, a standardization like the one that has for a long time been in place in English has not been introduced into our language. Thus, in the USA one can say "student" and it remains gender neutral – conversely, in German, "*Studenten*" (masc. noun), meaning persons who are studying, always refers to the male sex, and even the plural cannot obliterate which sex one belongs to: we have "*Studenten*" (masc. pl.) and we have just as many "*Studentinnen*" (fem. pl.). Since they do not feel properly addressed as "*Studenten*," they must have for themselves the phallic "medial I," and so there is "*StudentInnen*" (denoting students, male or female) just as "*SteuerzahlerInnen*" (tax-payers, male or female), who as "*ArbeiterInnen*" (workers, male or female) fill out the set. Whether this made things any easier remains questionable. In any case there are Germanists who, it seems, successfully completed their endless psychoanalytic conferences and in the end remarked that discrimination against the woman already begins with the plural. And yet this mandatory ruling is still not observed consistently: in the case of assassinations we hear nothing of "*Attentäterinnen*" (assassins, fem. noun form), and in the case of murder or manslaughter only the "*Mörder*" (murderer, masc. noun form) is used, as if he had already been arrested, but never also the suggested "*Mörderin*" (murderer, fem. noun form [invented]). In this way the rule of equality is only appropriate if the good benefit from it. The bad, the evil, the brutal continue as if they belong to the masculine domain and show how far we still are from the full implementation of emancipatory adjustments. The *Lehrer* (teachers, masc. in form), which one earlier spoke of in all cases "without specifying," need their *Lehrerinnen* (teachers, fem. form) just as the Singers in opera need their Singerettes. Probably *der Sessel* (the chair, masc. form) will no longer work since that calls for *die Sesselin,* although the same does not apply to "*Esel*" (donkey), when this term is used of a bad student.

We could happily tarry a long time with such stupidities, if at the same time the intention here was not to abuse sexual membership with the "Language Light" according to the hallmark of the plural. In the future even jumbo jets will be too small to take on the seateds as well as the seatedettes, who will then be served coffette or coffee depending upon their gender. We've gotten into a sorry situation if we have now to pay attention to these novel speech constraints in normal social situations. I experienced a most amusing example when in a gathering of people an unsuccessful merchant was referred to as "Negerant." Both young women immediately expressed their indignation and criticized the entire table for being racist. And it helped me not at all to give the derivation of this word from the old language and from Viennese – out of *néga* (from *Neige*, decline) and taught them that it has unexceptionally nothing to do with "Neger" (which is the German equivalent of "the n word" in English). This is just what Reinhard Fendrich meant when he sang, "I am a Negerant, Madame." Conversely, "Neger" was a borrowing from Spanish by Wilhelm Busch (1897), itself borrowed before from the Latin for black. If one says I am "neger" (using it as an adjective not a noun), it means not that I am black but that I have no money.

Today none of this matters. The indiscriminate destruction of language that is ready to deprive us of our individuality, our personal color, has an impact in two ways: the one is the illimitable increase of gender-specific ways of writing, and the other is the harsh judgment, delivered as a juridical declaration, that difficulty in understanding is no longer basically the responsibility of the listener or the reader but exclusively that of the author. The new language will thus always be directed to women and men, who are to be taken separately, for it must literally be inculcated into every person that there is no longer a policeman who is not accompanied by a policewoman and that a priest is not permitted to exist unless he is in company with a priestess – as in the old cult of Cybele.

Bastian Sick in his booklet, *The Dative is the Death of the Genitive*, correctly brought before our eyes not only that this sexualization of language has come into being – as if one discovered the woman in social life only in the 70's of the last century – but that "Language Light" is ironically the embodiment of what Sick called *Dummdreistigkeit* ("bold stupidity") in his little volume. Even the state parliament of Schleswig-Holstein allowed itself in 2007 to be harassed into "demanding that the leaders of public office introduce Language Light more resolutely and increase their competence for using it in the formulation of written documents." With the well-known process of "trickling down," a similar movement will also be visited upon Austria. However, the vanguard is already actively in place, since the decrees of the education ministry about the measures to be taken against the pandemic in the schools called for the text to be revised three times, since over and over again, misleading and erroneous formulations had replaced earlier ones.

These straitjackets for language would not succeed if they had not found a humorless diffusion among embittered academicians (and acadamiciennes), which itself entails a reduction in the perception of reality. Let us choose as an example a text in the German Historical Museum in Berlin, "In the year 1517 there occurred a reformation of the church. Reformation means renewal. The ideas of the Reformation came from Martin Luther. What was new in the ideas of Martin Luther? Every person ought to take responsibility for himself. For example, as to what consequences his behavior has for his own life in the future. And for the life of other people. In the Catholic Church there was a different opinion." Let's analyze what verbs are available for the museum to use: *give, mean, come, be, have*. Out of a similar inventory political speeches are composed. The politicians are already learned students in Language Light. So one speaks to the voters (and voterettes) as if both were stupid. Since when has there been a right to be protected from difficult formulations and complex contents? What is amusing about it is that using Language Light in fact renders the officials unable to describe the consequences of the measures against the pandemic, and therefore to formulate guidelines that will generally be understood. So we are dealing with a "vicious circle": the fear of complication diminishes the ability to express a fact. Thomas Bernhard put a point on it with his ironic formula, "simply complicated."

If then a wealth of the problems caused by the weakening of the vocabulary and of grammar can no longer be expressed in one's language, one can be relieved since such problems seemed never to have existed, but all the worse they will come back upon one's head later. If culture can be understood as a capacity to solve problems, then Language Light is an inappropriate help. The way when writing rapidly one gives his reaction to what he has just written by adding an emoji after it – happy, surprised, angry, furious, crying – brings to light a process of emotional infantilization.

So I am writing an earnest warning to you, to remain extremely vigilant especially in matters of language. You must take care that regarding the reports and communications that have made their way into your hands you take command of them, quickly and correctly, and resist this almost pre-ordained infantilization. It is dominant already in the high bureaucracy, today; it controls the language of people in charge, so anything is possible. Whether we will still be in a position to maintain the quality of our rule of law in the face of this loss of language is an open question. And we have no Karl Kraus on hand, who pled relentlessly on behalf of our old language, was vigilant on its behalf, and gave it a kind of attention one seldom encounters today.

If you know the prologue to the *Gospel of John*: "In the beginning was the Word and the Word was with God and the Word was God," you can get a rough idea what is ultimately at stake. You are deliberately being prevented from moving within this area. Everything will be undertaken to keep you from coming into this language, which alone opens the world to you, which shows you the wonder of this world and frees you from galamatias (the linguistic chaos Thomas Mann often wrote about).

All the best. I remain, your R.

68.
Christmas as Rebirth

Dear Nina, Dear Julian, Marie, and Vicky,

In the days before Christmas, running the usual errands is not important – all that shopping one thinks of as acknowledging and evidencing one's commitment; it is also not important whether the Christmas Tree reaches all the way to the ceiling or whether the candles are lit in time. And especially this is no time to travel. Far more important is it that we begin reading the great texts in the dark of early morning. It is important to read the psalms. It is important to have read the declaration of love from the *Song of Songs,* the rejoicing over the homecoming of the bride. Christmas has not only the peculiarity that the idea of redemption or redeemability of the world is set forth and receives a concrete embodiment. At the same time that God becomes human, we conversely receive the grace of belonging to him. Every man is now brought into this special status, is brought into the very presence of the Lord. The special thing about Christmas is the great promise of the Lord that from now on the Lord Himself is giving his Son as a pledge of the covenant from of old. And if the census of Augustus Caesar had any meaning it was less in the counting of the tax collector, less in the overview of the economic power of the empire, but that within his census-taking the Son was already included. With this he actually counts as a human being. And over the next few weeks we will learn about the life of this child and young man, about the many signs and tokens, and we may actually come to know that here a new era is breaking forth, which even Karl Jaspers remarked to be a change in time, to be an "axis-time!" But now all such remarks are moot. A miracle has occurred, an event that takes place in the midst of our lives, over and over again, and not just once a year.

Yes, my writing to you wants to make you aware that here the great gift of the Lord to Israel took place, and it is more than this. The Lord, who reconstructed the advent of the Son in three times fourteen generations and rooted it in history, is giving us to understand thereby that it is at this point that our history begins, which we should and may make our own just as we are the likeness of Christ. Christmas is not a festival for the sake of falling for a childish schema from ethology with which to indulge our sentimentalities. Rather, it is the second attempt made by the Lord to speak directly to us. "Hear O Israel!" we often read in the scriptures, and we know how hard it is to hear, these days. And yet, Hear O Israel! Christmas is the invitation to hear. From now on there is this voice worth hearing. Of course it is not louder than the voice of reason which according to Sigmund Freud itself is quiet. Were it not for the cruelties surrounding the appearance of the Lord we would hardly notice and be curious why in the Lord's passing through this world, a trail of blood follows. We know that we possess an earthshaking knowledge, which even goes beyond theology. Christmas is not merely a theological construct. Rather it is the unique realization that we are being born again – with Him. With Him, we are new people.

All my love, your R.

69.
Troubles with Technology

Dear Nina, Julian, Marie and Vicky,

Today I have to send a "zero message." I have tried to specify exactly the term "peace" on the occasion of Christmas. For reasons unknown to me, the four pages on a history of peace are gone. Simply gone. All in vain. This had to happen, when between cooking, preparing, trimming the tree, and making dinner I was completely overwhelmed, and was describing this topic in the midst of all that. Why a machine would do this is beyond me. On the one track "Letters to Nina" are all deleted! Let no one tell me there such things do not happen! These PCs are an infamous machinery and supposedly they never err. That in fact is just what is inhuman about it. Can it be that a text of almost 200 pages is gone? It seems so. That's why I hate these devices. Their ubiquity, their supposed ease of use, is a lie to deceive us. We become trustful because of the ease of functions and what they offer, while in truth they are lousy deceptions.

So I am sending you this letter anyway.

I started it in memory of my father, who died on December 24, 1963. These thoughts about him are also gone...It is analogous to the power of death. The extinction. Even memory, barely present, becomes a victim of the machine that continues the work of death taking it over with a disconcerting matter-of-factness. Reconstructing all that I wanted to tell you about peace, from the Privilegium minus *of 1156 to who knows where – is all gone. If the window were not sealed, I would throw this whole apparatus out of it.*

I am angry!

I do not know how to say goodbye to you – in anger!

The above lines, directed in anger against technological devices, are not really suitable for a letter to you, but I repeat them here nevertheless because they might show you that my letters are also authentic signs of life – but never mind! Why should I remove an expression of my anger from this collection of letters? It's part of the work of writing that things sometimes go wrong. In the past an inkwell would spill all over the paper, or there was no way to make a sheet for writing out of a tanned donkey skin. Yes, there are many obstacles that threaten even things that have already been written!

As a substitute for the letter that disappeared I here report something new that seems to be affecting us more and more. I have outlined these thoughts before, but at some point I put them aside. They fit very well with Christmas and with the days after Christmas that were once thought of as days for contemplation. I'm afraid that hardly anyone is contemplative, today! If that were the case our world would not be in the state it is in. So I offer you this criticism as a substitute for the other. Even if this 69th letter has turned out a little badly at least my intention was to redeem my anger with a warning. Yes, really, I feel like the chief of some North American Indian tribe who had made a comparable appeal to his descendants more than a hundred years ago. And so I would like to take a clue from the old chief.

So once again, *da capo*:

"Dear Nina, Dear Julian and Marie and Vicky,"

I am certainly aware that my letters are difficult to read – sometimes even unreadable – as well as uninteresting since they are yesterday's snow. Seldom are they encouraging, nor terribly illuminating, and basically unneeded. That is how a reader, these days, would put it. Why? Because he lives in the conception that everything he hears and everything he reads was written and said exactly and only for himself. Of course, letters are a peculiar literary form. For they are written *for* someone. Are they comparable to the letters Lord Chesterfield wrote to his son? Does correspondence even exist anymore, nowadays? It did exist, once! Sigmund Freud corresponded with Albert Einstein. Could it also exist today? I have the impression that the "dear" addresses would rather keep their heads down, as if during a war. They do not want to expose themselves. This has less to do with you, since you would be too inexperienced and too young to act that way. Today it is usual to trudge along under a mandate of silence. The first person to speak becomes the loser. It is like a social game. This is how meetings work these days. The only contribution one can make in a meeting is to be silent. And if you break the silence you face character assassination. The more a person might be loquacious on Facebook – this shameless mechanism for unsolicited utterances – the less does the person say to one's face. Facebook has created a recrudescence of the self-accusation people suffered under Stalinism. The chatterboxes are unaware that they are putting their necks on the line before the open public. This is the end of dialogue. If the user's interlocutor is a machine the words simply flow from his lips. Logorrhea becomes the protocol for one's confession of guilt.

This is only the other side of the coin. I find much more annoying the current outlook that nothing has any meaning, in the sense that nothing is capable of upsetting the balance. This new "serenity" is just as important a symptom as the old irritability. Overwhelmingly, young people are sending out the signal that no matter what it is, is it doesn't matter to them.

Immediately my remarks will be met with opposition! The opposition however is hardly well founded. The beneficiaries of the stock market, the winners at speculation, laugh themselves to death when they hear about climate change. Any concern raised about worldwide tourism is received as a betrayal. In their view those they are exploiting should not be allowed a vacation to the Caribbean, to Marbella, to Koh Samui in the first place. Tourism will be the last cultural activity in our world. Once we are finished with that, there will be nothing more to see. People don't like to walk through historic centers in smog. In the heat waves one is driven to cool down somewhere where clean water can be found. But where is there any clean water? The Adriatic now stands out on satellite photos since two thirds of it is brown. Here, in the vicinity of Dubrovnik, is where the noble cruise ships empty themselves out. Meanwhile the owners of these enterprises vigorously and prominently serve on the committees that protect water.

I am afraid that you won't be happy with what we are passing down to you: the world as a garbage dump and a sewer. Just look at the heroes who prevented everything so far. It was a victory easily won, since one could accuse every protest as only a plot to foment leftist chaos.

It is not going well with our earth! The daily weather report for 28 December 2020 was typical: "In the year now ending the temperature in Antarctica was 8° C. too high... ."

So I must confront you especially with this: Will you bring about a change?

All my love, your R.

70.
An Etymology of Peace

Dear Nina, Dear Julian, Marie and Vicky,

Now I must see whether I can once again assemble my thoughts on peace. I still remember a Christmas Eve more than seventy years ago, in 1944. The war was finally in the final round, violence being wreaked by the regime that had nearly destroyed Europe once and for all. It was less a matter of historical things being destroyed which by now would have been destroyed anyway under peaceful conditions. Rather, the loss of blood in the populace, the suffering, the weakening of the important social-political institutions constituted far greater damage. With the end of the World War the world woke up again and the first business was to secure peace, right at the threshold of the Cold War between the USA and the Soviet Union.

Let's begin with some real stories: During the First World War it was said that at least on Christmas Eve there was a truce: one sang Christmas carols for the enemies and vice-versa. In the Second World War, even food would be exchanged, or at least that it would be given to anyone who had already been hungry for days.

I have said I would contribute some ideas about peace, but it is more difficult for me to do this than I thought. One must always observe that a substantial correspondence between "our" notion of peace (*Friede*) and the Latin notion, *pax*, only became possible at the time of the Renaissance. The reason for the long lasting difference lay in the difference between the two words. "Peace" (*Friede*), derived from Indo-European, includes verbs ranging from "to love" and "to spare." This explains how between the most different "social unities" – that is, between families, towns, regions, and lands – special sympathies exist and strengthen peaceful concord. "Sparing" can exonerate the loser, after the end of the conflict, from the consequences of losing.

Throughout the entire Middle Ages this philological "constellation" of connotations connected with "peace" was dispositive. Thus the condition of "peace in the land" was always looked upon as desirable. Indeed the names of the emperor – as for instance of the Hohenstaufens – reflected this political program: Friedrich. The best known was Friedrich I, Barbarossa. Unfortunately his reform of the empire was not realized after he died. We have him to thank, in the course of the reform, for the *Privilegium minus* of 1156, just as Bamberg also through him received a new city charter. But who still knows this? In Austria relatively few know this – if anybody at all. I owe knowing it to the American historian of law, Harold Berman, and his *Law and Revolution*.

It was in the last phase of the Middle Ages that the Latin and West-European sense of *pax* received greater and greater attention in the Empire. *Pax* was not only taken over into English (*peace*) but also into French (*paix*), and this concept of peace soon grew, in the theology of the early Middle Ages. It clearly played a part in the foundation of medieval political theory. Thus for Western Europe – England, France, and Spain, and even the Papacy – questions of peace were based on a juristic paradigm taken from the Roman tradition. In the first instance peace meant "internal" peace and security. Peace was to apply to the commonwealths, to the settlements and cities, to the trading posts, and to municipal governments that still existed. So also did one conceive of it during the medieval tensions, in "France" as also in "England." (I put these terms from political geography into quotes since at the time these lands did not exist in the form the terms now refer to them). Initially the concept was copied from the "order of peace" of the cities of Upper Italy which saw themselves to be in the Roman administrative tradition; soon enough one became interested in this sort of "city-wide peace" since it fostered powerful economic growth, which was recognized to be dependent upon internal security.

Later, in the 17th century, Thomas Hobbes altered this "traditional" and still Roman notion of peace into a notion of domination. This is easier to write than to say. We have to regard the "great arc" as our goal in historiography, by which we mean a coherent common theme from beginning to the end, since only under this condition can we think we have any grasp at all on history. Given such we have no doubt whether there exists a structure of order arising in a factual way in the respective historical processes. And exactly this was gradually introduced with the *pax civilis*. It was always fundamentally a part of law. And so law was a "modernizing factor" all through the Middle Ages: it governed the relationship of the king with later versions of the parliament or standing assembly, and it even confirmed political freedom against the barons, the representatives of feudalism, in the *Magna Carta Libertatum* of 1215.

The *pax civilis* was, especially in England, the leading motive for a "state law" since maintaining tranquility and security was a central issue for this "political land" (after all, external enemies were for England something of a rarity, except for the expeditions of Julius Caesar up to the time of Vespasian, and the Hundred Years' War with France in the 14th and 15th centuries). In the late Middle Ages, Augustinian and Aristotelian elements came to be incorporated in the conceptions of peace, and so "conclusions of peace" were agreements which were unthinkable without the concepts of law and legality. From Augustine came the special form of *justitia* in which there is even a right for the faithful that derives from the faith. At the same time, a natural right independent of the grace of God could be derived from it, which led to the development of a "natural justice." However the conviction remained in the back of people's minds that between the Christians and the pagans there could be no "peace agreement" – only a *pax vera*, so-called. Thus the *pax Christiana* appeared as a special binding duty for "Europe" which because of the Reformation would unavoidably become necessary for bringing the divided confessions into a "dialogue."

With the beginning of modern times peace came to be a matter entirely determined by law. And yet *justitia* in the sense of material legality was radically divorced from the concept of peace. This brings to mind Thomas Hobbes, who treated legality and peace as fundamentally separate orders. He operated under the impression that the old standpoint of political "doctrine" according to which truth, peace, and legality are interdependent, causes wars of religion and that only by separating them can political tranquility and security be reached. He made the point laconically: *Auctoritas non veritas facit legem* ("It is the state's authority, not truth, that makes law). And after this peace becomes further "specified." In the wake of Hobbes it is asserted in the *Teutschen Staats-Recht* of 1764 (*German Constitutional Law* by Johann Möser) that a "*pax civilis*" no longer has to do with attitudes, and no longer bears an influence upon them, but rather that behaviors stipulated in the "peace agreement" serve as the criterion. In contrast, Martin Luther had not yet reached such sharp distinctions. He was still root and branch in the scholastic tradition and saw peace as a spiritual virtue internalized in one's disposition for action. By the time of the Enlightenment this mystical concept no longer had any standing. The political realism of Hobbes had won the day.

If we want to evaluate this debate, which lasted many years, we notice in the concept of peace not only the increasing tendency toward secularization. At the same time peace becomes a "politically intramural" prerequisite for enabling the development of the country and expediting its economic progress. In the end this means that peace becomes a political command and is far from being the ideal that would be welcomed by the Enlightenment. In his *Dictionarium morale* the

Benedictine monk Petrus Berchorius wrote something hardly flattering about peace: "*Pax imperata ... est pax quam principes et magnates imperant subditis suis; nolunt enim quod rebellent contra eos sed quod pacifice portent tyrannides quas imponunt. Ista est pax violenta ... .*" ("Compulsory peace is the peace that princes and those in power impose upon their subjects: for they want them not to rebel against them but peacefully bear up under the tyrannical measures they impose. This kind of peace is violent...").

This passage is worth mentioning, since from Thomas Hobbes we have derived that the task of the state is to foster tranquility and at the same time to protect the peace of the citizens. The monk sees completely clearly that an "enforced-peace" (*pax imperata*) was lurking beneath that notion, a political dictate that the princes and people in power employ in order to coerce their subjects or serfs. This peace cannot hold.

Peace took on its own meaning as a category of "foreign policy" in the 18th century and had therewith become systematically separated from the old *pax civilis*, and rose to become a category unto itself. That a *pax civilis* was able to keep itself in place for so long was also due to the circumstance that the old "Roman Empire" had somehow survived a good number of wars but these were basically a component of a "domestic imperial politics." Only the Silesian wars between Austria and Prussia, three in number, slowly acquired the character of an embittered "interstate" confrontation, so that a new unstable entity emerged – in the middle of Central Europe. And yet the idea always remained dominant that peace is primarily involved with the already existing pre-civil "societies" in the sense of the conception in public law, which consequently described itself as a "science of policing."

The French Revolution brought this constellation to an end. Peace now permanently became a theme in "foreign policy," immediately in the aftermath of the Napoleonic Wars. Had Immanuel Kant still been able to claim that peace is a product of cultural politics, thinking nothing of a "natural peace" whose attractiveness had lain only in the literary conceit of Arcadia since Vergil, so also had the realistic assumptions derived from the social *pax civilis* receded into the background. For the Enlightenment, as for Kant, peace had to be a consequence of political reason, since no war could lead to progress comparable to the sort of progress peace could almost automatically bring about. In Kant the very political form of a republic tended naturally toward peace, since any alternative lay outside a realistic concept of trading interests and of the welfare state. For Immanuel Kant the first step toward "perpetual peace" was to overcome the discord between men by means of a general concord. Of course, it was clear to him that peace agreements after 1648 were just temporary armistices. Not only were they a matter of catching breath before the next war, but the notion that peace is a morally and theologically sanctioned duty was a perversion of the previous foundations of political peace. It had continued to hold, since the Middle Ages, but had lost any sort of "internalization" among the political actors in the 18th century. By then it hardly functioned at all as a seriously incriminating factor within Napoleon's conscience.

In the 19th century peace was almost everywhere an interstate relation. One can easily see this from any lexical entry, whether from the Brockhaus or from the *Meyers Konversations-lexicon*. Peace was not much more than the armistice mentioned above, limited to a time and area, at the discretion of the political calculations of a "power-state" – and there were some of those in Europe. It was a so-called "bellicism," which drove the politics of the European powers in the 19th century. Peace was almost considered a sign of weakness, an acknowledgment of incompetence in political action. In all likelihood, at this time the only land in Europe that could bear this stigma with a light heart was Switzerland. In the perennial conflict between Germany and France one had clearly agreed, without having formulated it explicitly, that Switzerland ought to remain exempt from the political aspirations of the several powers. The assurance for this was one of few positive results of the Congress of Vienna in 1815. Thus Switzerland became a haven of peace.

However, in the second half of the 19th century the aforementioned weakening of the concept of peace came about, since it was plain to see that war had "overcome" previous categories of moral evaluation and overshadowed them. Even children would play at being soldiers or would stage a war with their toy soldiers. Thus there was no proverb more often quoted than *Si vis pacem para bellum* ("If you want peace prepare for war"). It is an abbreviated quotation from the *De Re Militari* of Publius Flavius Vegetius Renatus from the 4th or 5th century, which in the original reads, "*Igitur qui desiderat pacem praeparet bellum.*" It was under the influence of Napoleon that one sharpened the formula into "*Si vis bellum para pacem*," in the spirit of bellicism – according to the historian Louis Fauvelet.

Either way, this formula for foreign policy with its strong military inflection came into greater contrast with the wish for a social peace for which the arising social democracies had given an entirely specific political version as an alternative. This was followed by the peace movement in Europe around 1900: in Austria-Hungary there was Berta von Suttner and Alfred Hermann Fried, in England Richard Cobden, and in France a similar group gathered around Jean Jaurès. Henry Dunant also belonged to this movement. Robert Musil commented with great accuracy even before 1914, "In Europe one talks only about peace, anymore: we are on the brink of war."

These positions were in the end too weak to countervail against the idea that the powers of a *Volk* would be strengthened in the "steel bath" of war. And it was not long before this conviction became widespread in the fascism of Italy. This "military state of mind" was expressed in most European newspapers, in which a contrast would be drawn between "rotten peace and fresh and joyful war." The most important protagonist for the overall healing effect of a war against the decadence and decline of culture was Georges Sorel. The "War of States" involuntarily turns into a "War of Ideas," and vice-versa. At this point preparations for military conflict almost took on the character of a national crusade that would finally give the respective belligerents a "following wind" to take on the much larger role of a world power. It was the first step toward a "globalization" of such overheated ideas, and in the 20th century the wars were not only a consciously condoned destruction of humanity but also rose to the level of "genocide."

Were we any more successful in our politics of peace, after 1945? Did dropping the atomic bombs on Hiroshima and Nagasaki create for us this vulnerable international order of peace? Looking back you will be able to recognize that we have since "lived through" a mess of wars, even in Europe. There was not only the "interstate" war between the component republics of Yugoslavia, but also the war over Crimea between Russia and Ukraine, and the war between Azerbaijan and the region of Nagorno-Karabakh which had earlier been occupied by the Armenians.

I hope you will have the patience someday to come to recognize, as to the derivation and evolution of "peace" from late antiquity, Christendom, and the Middle Ages, the difficulty that other cultures have had in following our understanding of this, even if we should further formalize our order of international law. What will we do if a young power wants to be a world power and therewith wishes to risk war? Is this then the next world war, after the failure of a world peace?

These are horrifying thoughts…

I have sketched out the theme because of Christmas and hope that this treatment does not ruin the Peace of your Christmas – in whatever year the Peace of Christmas may still exist…

A wish to you, rather belatedly, for a blessed Christmas in 2020!

Your R.

71.
The Lodge: a Mysterious Organization

Dear Nina, and You, my Dears, Julian, Marie, and Vicky,

My presentation on "peace" of course focused upon European history. This points to a "Eurocentricity" that according to my presentation was then adapted by the two superpowers, the USA and the Soviet Union, into a two-sided attempt for peace. On the one hand there was the founding of the United Nations, and on the other, as its counterpart, the Sovietophile World Peace Council. It was not clever to locate the United Nations in New York, in contrast with the League of Nations located in Geneva before the Second World War. Maybe the ambience on the East River is more attractive, but it was surely not pleasant for the contending parties to carry on discussions in a major center of the arch-enemy's territory. It was clear in most of the conferences that "*pax civilis*" underwent a continuation in the mandate of the UN. Conversely, in the initiatives for disarmament at the WPC the social situation of the states was hardly taken into consideration. In any case the attempts to keep peace were mostly a matter of international policy and foreign policy, even if this meant that democracy and the right to freedoms remained unavailable for many societies – as for example in East Europe.

I want now to turn to another theme, which ought to bring us closer to sociology. In all likelihood you will hear in a couple of years about "social movements" in school. This expression was chosen during the first halting steps of social science, for many reasons. On the one hand there were, in fact, new ideas among new "conglomerations" of intellectuals – among religious groups that at the time embraced the Enlightenment and among "societies" and "clubs" – ideas directed against the absolutism of princes. The best known "tributary" was the Lodges of the Freemasons in the 18th century, scattered all through Europe, which branched out into the cultural, scientific, and then even the political elites. One of the most interesting treatments is Daniel Wilson's *Geheimräte gegen Geheimbünde* ("Secret Councils versus Secret Societies" [1991], not tr. into Eng. – ed.), in which thanks to the opening of the archive materials returned from Russia the political activity of Goethe, for instance, is placed in a completely new light. Among other things, Goethe was probably only half-heartedly interested in the Enlightenment, and, as a quasi "Minister of the Interior" in Weimar he looked upon the rebellious attitude in the circle of intellectuals with displeasure. This was his reason that the representatives of the literary *Sturm und Drang* movement" had to leave Weimar overnight. Fichte had to abandon his chair in Jena, and here also Goethe had a hand in it, just as he caused Friedrich Hölderlin to be investigated.

I am telling you this story discovered by Daniel Wilson because it is an exciting event and also because of its importance for cultural history.

These circles of a new intellectuality also provided the premise for a theater piece, *The Robbers* by Friedrich Schiller, in particular for the controversy within the play between Karl and Franz Moor. Schiller was inspired by the "nomad" students, a movement around Christoph Kaufmann that fostered unrest in southern Germany and can be seen as the first hippie movement. This fit into the image of the Enlightenment, the freeing up of thought. Perhaps Josephinism, the political concept of Joseph II, would have been a better alternative than the revolution in Paris, since the political transformation would likely have proceeded along more orderly paths – without the murderous excesses of the "white" and the "red" terrors along with the murder of the French king.

You know that in history one must not think in terms of "if-then," nor employ such counterfactual evasions as "if that had happened then blablabla," nor even with pipe-dreams to see the course of history dominated by secret forces. And yet it happens to be difficult to give up such thoughts. It is a romantic element within historicism to indulge in such thoughts despite the fact that they contradict events, and likely it is out of this predisposition within historical thinking that intellectual history was born.

This suggestion provides me my segue to go into the many "movements." I already mentioned that at first August Comte described his early social sketches as a social physics. And in the further interpretation, the mobility of social forces came to be dubbed a "movement." From the "movement of ideas" to the "mass movements" at the end of the 19th century, society came to be seen within this metaphor of social dynamics. The most important interpreter of social movements after the French Revolution was Lorenz von Stein, who later was appointed by the University of Vienna. Thus, just as historicism preferred the history of "great men and heroes" and integrated the new popularity of biographies into historiography, so also did the interpreters of social movements want to describe a general history, as well as the factors that constitute a "flow of history." What ideas *moved* people toward their actions? So the controversy of the 19th century was clear: to place the emphasis more on the role of concepts in history and even on ideas – which were surely operable in nationalism, liberalism, socialism – or on the continuity of historical factors that would assert themselves in domination, political order, economy, and the traditional view of the world. In the end both were accused of being somewhat anemic as "historical theory," for expressing themselves through a process of mythologization. The one had become a mythology of concepts, as for example in Marxism "capitalism" was fundamentally the cause of mistaken or inhumane history; the other made the state absolute like something of a national church to which for the fulfillment of its mission was granted all power to carry out political measures. With Bismarck this model became objectified. It dominated the Prussian political nomenclature. This line of thinking in historiography resulted in a history without God. The old political theology of the Middle Ages was replaced by the Hegelian spirit. This spirit brings itself into a manifestation in history, whether as the spirit of the world or as the spirit of the time or even as the spirit of the people – all abstractions from Hegel's *Phenomenology of Spirit*.

With the increase in the degree of collective performance capacity achieved by industrialization, a "soul-secularization" of consciousness came onto the horizon. Out of this, ultimately, was materialism formulated. For social philosophy and sociology this came later; it enabled sociologists to "isolate" the driving forces of society so well that they could get to the bottom of things through empirical analyses. Thus one conceived of having an overall explanation for social processes the same way one already had an explanation of the movement of the heavenly bodies in astronomy. From this point on one could make the pedantic boast that society itself came to be as an invention of sociological thinking. From now on sociology defined social phenomena, provided that one supported it as having a basis in reality with an empiricism that took its cue from the economic structures and phenomena of transformation. The standardized forms of socialization aided in this purpose, for they were able to give a fairly homogeneous picture of society. Industrial society was about to come into being, though by the two world wars it would be interrupted. And society had to pay a high price for that. The colorfulness of the world was almost completely blotted out.

I did not intend to end on such a melancholy note. And young people will not be able to comprehend this. Their world is this world, and the world has in their eyes the colorfulness which I thought I was lucky to enjoy before the world became colorless – to me. In all likelihood this difference of perception conceals the change, the alteration, the manifold shifts of reference that keep us on our toes all along. No longer are there moments of calm. The time is past when people wrote meditatively. Or else we take no time to do this: What are we supposed to meditate about? This is perhaps the greatest failure of our present times. Perhaps you will sometime come to think that one should again turn to thinking far-reaching thoughts – about God and the world...

Pardon me as I lapse into these almost trivial musings. I become aware more and more often – whenever I take a walk – that we do not indulge each other in the old poetry of a city. We are destroying the old concepts that would give us harmony because we realized that we may not, cannot, will not live in harmony. That was the intention of Otto Wagner or Adolf Loos – the idea of the better world through urban planning. Today we destroy these ideas intentionally and restlessly, since we are powerless to stop wanting to disturb each other. Nobody is permitted to be in peace. Only to be. Behind it all is the neurotic obsession that in some way or other everyone must be a refugee.

It is you who must bring this to an end!

All the best, your R.

72.
Does Information Change Anything?

Dear Ones,

In the last letter I have confronted you with an idea that prophesied the difficulties you will face that are caused by the generations that came before you. A bit of optimism accompanied this picture, that if you assess the situation in time you might be able to find the necessary answers. And very soon I realized that I failed to tell you where you must find your alternatives. As I see it, you have to protect your respective life-worlds or living spaces so that you can see fulfilled in them all the wishes for your lives you hold to be important. In short: it isn't acceptable to destroy some habitat just for the sake of the enjoyment of your recreation there, which inadvertently harms it. One drives and travels in a place where "nature" still exists, or all other things which you have been helping to destroy. If we are successful – you, that is – at preserving your own little world in harmony and fruitfulness, then it might also succeed elsewhere and perhaps the healing of the terrible wounds which nature has undergone can begin. As things are, this will unfortunately not take place. In the year 2020 now coming to an end, the temperature of the Antarctic was on average 8°C. too high: it should be perfectly clear to us that we may not continue in our present ways. If clear-cutting in South America should continue, we will shortly have problems about the supply of oxygen. And notice at the same time that despite the "lockdown" and the pandemic, stock prices rose by 30% over the year. Obscenity is alive and well.

Obviously we will have to deal more prudently with our resources. So my optimism is connected with the expectation that you will develop an ability to live more ascetically, and to use more consciously the gifts of nature and also use them in a very controlled way. Askesis does not here mean eating less but generally being conscientious about whether one can still do what leads to using up necessary resources and what deteriorates ecological systems. One wants to introduce stronger and stronger environmental protection into the law, but at the same time out of economic considerations one is allowing those who sin against the environment to do whatever they want. They determine the conditions of life in the future according to their liking and do not give a damn whether there will no longer be what in the past was the normal condition of nature.

I don't want to continue with this topic. Perhaps it supports our opinion that what we have achieved in understanding has been replaced by the "social status of happiness" – especially in Europe – by the regime of freedom and of the indestructibility of my I. Thus philosophy has been expelled from the terrain where it had been needed. One can mark the decline of philosophy in the way it deals with people. In distinction from medicine, philosophy asks about the reason we suffer. Mustn't it have a "higher" meaning? Unthinkingly comes the spontaneous answer: How does one prevent suffering? This has now become the most important area in philosophy. Because of this, philosophy shows itself to be weary, dried up, clueless. There can no longer be any serious cognition. As to the objects studied by philosophy in the classic sense, we are now supposed to believe that it had merely been indulging in unrestrained speculation. This infamous accusation from the pen of the positivists had the goal of determining what is real rather than what is true.

This is an old story. Already in Greek antiquity one thought that we can all experience truth, "me," "you," and "us." This was at the time of the decline and the occupation of Greece. The recommendation of Epicurus at the time was that one must seek not truth but calmness and prudence, and seek an antidote against anxiety. Epicurus was the first psychotherapist. Aren't his representations comparable with Freud's *Civilization and Its Discontents*? Did he not have a comparable evaluation of happiness? So, philosophy turns into therapy. The proverb showed up in Athens at the time: "Physician heal thyself!" And where does health come from? Epicurus knew the symptoms second to none – at least he thought so: it is the fear of death, the fear of God. And yet Epicurus was not so prudent. He was not the serene philosopher in view of whom one wanted to be an Epicurean: He was, on the contrary, hypersensitive, easily pained, and generally resentful. He who chooses to reject the sciences is usually one who has experienced mortifications because of them. They were able to identify in him the truth of his infirmities. Epicurus had already lost any sense of humor in this regard. Most of the theoreticians of happiness, not only Jeremy Bentham and those touching positivists with their enthusiasm for republicanism up until 1933-4, have been psychologically unstable, soon plagued by hypomania, and soon depression. I would not be surprised if today's advocates of happiness make themselves vomit several times a day and suffer from anorexia. One sees this in every fashion model, who wants to hold out the promise to us that happiness is a physical state, bisexual constructions that they are. As an Epicurean, Epicurus wanted to close his eyes to the face of reality. He would never have been able to tender a proclamation of happiness if he remembered any of his anxious dreams from the night before. He repressed them all. He was left with only a modicum of joy. Even this he owed to his paltry talent for irony. And his students took it at face value. They came out of the school, they reported enthusiastically that the master was above it all. Even today one is puzzled why Cicero fell for it. How was that possible? Cicero was a learned jurist, a brilliant prosecutor and a defender of the republic. Could such a man think himself an Epicurean? Even today we hang our illusions on such people. What has happened to us – that we claim we are not understood when a better order already lies within us? Herewith I throw down the gauntlet against all indifferent persons who take themselves to be the philosopher's stone. Indifferent people are a crumbling stone of consciousness. If I may vary the dictum of Grillparzer: From Epicureanism through Indifferentism the road leads straight to Opportunism.

Unusually dogmatic assertions? Ought I write this way "henceforth"? Perhaps. Do you then understand me better? Do you understand what I am trying to do, here? I await your word!!

I love you – your R.

73.
Is It All Meaningless?

Dear Nina, Dear Julian, Dear Marie, and Dear Vicky,

I hope you were not annoyed by that performance. I thought you might be since you are young.

Last Tuesday Nina's presence here was enjoyable: I listened with one ear to the huge crime story that you came up with. I think at least thirty characters were involved in this story, and one of them was a representative of the law and the police. In comprehensive detail you picked apart the alibis of the suspects. I heard your story from the next room, but who in the end was found to be the perpetrator was not altogether clear to me. I thought along the way that almost all of them seemed suspicious and even the role of the policeman at the very least raised questions. Then I got the idea that this is how one might imagine original sin: although in Nina's drama there were no deaths or murders, it seemed all of them turned out to be perpetrators. This is something that bizarre stories have in common: they often open up access to a truth that before had not even been a subject of debate.

This then brought me to the idea that one must take with a grain of salt the usual talk at the beginning of the new year about the meaning of life. Everybody knows that when visiting wine bars in the late hours the question will be heard whether our life situation, the way of the world, and the universe basically make sense. And indeed people quickly agree that there is no meaning to be discovered, that everything we think about it we have just made up ourselves. Of course we also can come up with stories on this topic that in their outline seem quite plausible. These declarations or assumptions lead in general to the unanimous opinion that even life itself is devoid of any meaning. Most shared this attitude, but overall they did not reflect on their agreement very much longer.

But then a sole objection came, as a surprise though it was not immediately recognized as such, namely that one cannot deny a blanket opinion, no matter how realistic it might seem. At first no notice was made of this objection. In any event the argument was clearly to be heard that the lack of meaning makes it necessary that one at least make up a meaning for oneself. Nobody is bothered by the fact that there may be no recognizable structure of meaning for God and the world, but all around the table nobody will be found who wants to accept that this loss of meaning extends as far as his own personal life.

After one more glass, one becomes convinced that this self-interpretation, that one provides a meaning for himself, cannot in any way be brought in line with the world as a whole. Every thought about that question has lost itself in sheer and empty speculation. If someone at the happy table were to question the meaning of existence based merely on one's profession or income or status, the whole group at the table would immediately attack him. You don't allow your personal career successes to be spoiled so easily! This does not at all disturb the assumption that the overall structure of the world, of the universe, may still be represented as devoid of meaning: that has nothing to do with one's personal life-plan. Surely there was a sense of purpose at work, since it had worked so well to get up the ladder of success so quickly. One cannot 'uestion this. The need to investigate this sense of purpose was ideally suited to succeeding. So one gladly tolerates the contradiction without a second thought: a universe without meaning, but meaning in one's professional success. Each person around the table was of the same mind, namely, to conceive of himself as an exception: indeed one could designate the universe and everything around him as meaningless, and yet this did not apply to those around this table. Each of their actions had always had a meaning. They would not have exerted themselves so much if it were meaningless. How else could one have been successful? This sounded something like the surprising discovery of individualism. Nobody got the idea that the loss of meaning in the universe will come after each one of them and track them all down like a curse. To find that all one's own successes and accomplishments – even one's own ego – are worthless would have been an unbearable atrocity.

Life seems in our present times still to labor under a disappearance of meaning and purpose. Only a few reflect within themselves that the assumptions around the table apply also to oneself. The implication of the thought will be cut off just in time before it reaches any of them. Hence there is a consensus at the table, to everyone's surprise, about the search for meaning – even if it is found in consumerism. And this is what is remarkable in our present way of life, that we do not see through to our futility should we not want to seek the meaning of life outside ourselves.

Prosit 2021.

Your R.

74.
A Political Miscellany

My Dears,

After a pause of four days I ought to return to my correspondence. The first day of the new year always calls on us to look into the future, always confronts everyone with an almost compulsory duty to make resolutions about what one ought to do differently. The future becomes just as constraining as the past. And in such situations we most often decide that things will be as they always were – or so one thinks. Indeed it is amusing that we think we are unable to see into the future and yet we regret it. Would we really do anything different if we knew what was coming upon us? I am convinced that we would change nothing in our intentions. In fact we would make no new plans nor would we set aside our old projects. We even judge that threatening dark clouds will soon pass by and so we go right out into the weather.

Just recently I saw a film about tourism on Mount Everest. Shockingly, those on the adventure scrambled right past others who had died. And even they were being stalked by death. Still, they had no thought of turning back. They had to get their money's worth! One third of the group died and those who were frozen to death were left at the side of the trail.

In any case we are not at all able to shape the future despite our remarkable technologies, since we do not understand our past. History has indicated where we are at present; history has created the environment in which we live, and the facts gained from history would offer a foundation for our extrapolations into the future. But of course if one no longer knows these facts or has forgotten them, one will no longer be able to distinguish between innovation, progress, and tradition: instead everything inexplicably flows into the unknown. For this blind numb-headedness there is a good example from Austrian history. As is well known, the infamous Colonel Redl leaked the plans for the expedition against Russia before

1914. With the apprehension of this scoundrel the plans obviously should have been changed. For a dozen reasons, partly out of vanity and partly out of suppression of this terrible betrayal, the General Staff neglected to make any change. Thus a high number of officers and enlisted men died in the very first year of the war, on the Russian front. I believe that in our own behavior we are no wiser than the Austrian General Staff. The more obscure our situation the more we stick to what is familiar to us. It seems plausible and reasonable, and yet it can be quite the opposite.

In my own analysis of the European Union I have always drawn on my knowledge of imperial history after 1648 so as to recognize that *pari passu* the European Union is approaching a similar powerlessness – or already finds itself there. The lack of consensus, the demand for political action, the increasing split between imperial and domestic power for which the Habsburgs were responsible, had weakened the cohesiveness of the empire and it was finally brought to an end by Napoleon. In citing this I want to offer the thought that in the present case it is unbelievably simple to speculate about the future of the EU. This little giant is barely standing, and standing on feet of clay, yet after all in which direction could it tip over? Officially, the traditional enmities in Europe do not exist, and so the EU is careful in what it says about the areas of conflict within Europe. Ukraine? Nagorno-Karabakh? Azerbaijan? More and more obviously we would have to ask ourselves the question: Who are we, at all? If we knew from history that Europe owes its political name to a 17th century periodical called "The European Theatre" (*Theatrum Europaeum*, a politico-historical "periodical" founded by Matthäus Merian, that ran from 1633 to 1738), we would be more prudent in our evaluation of the current scene in Europe.

When I compare this diagnosis of a "past future" with the present, what comes to me first of all is that in the Western world we are suffering under the excesses of a civilization of the uncivilized. It would be an enormous misunderstanding to take this statement as being aimed at the "small peoples" – at those who already live in the shadows and seem to be happy if only they can somehow manage to stay alive. I consider individual representatives of political parties and the majority of the representatives of economy and science who at some point become conspicuously active in public, to be uncivilized groups. In Austria one encounters them now and then in the lawcourts.

I don't want to start this new year by plowing the same furrow as last year. What I am saying will become obvious soon enough; and yet I ought to include the hint that, probably, with the present political personnel in Europe no adequate political focus can be reached. With the exit of England from the EU the question of the EU's future course awaits determination by a number of stress tests. One can already repeat the assertion that any prognostication for the future is empty. The future continues to be a blackout, like 2020; it is like a radio-silence decreed by the pandemic. And the optimistic announcements of a return to normal just as soon as possible are likely the wrong approach to meet the new and coming demands.

I think one can only advise you to keep your eyes and ears open. It is far more difficult than before. If one starts from the basic proposition that everything must be looked at, that one can resist and overcome the reluctance to face things, it is also true that nobody can keep you from seeing reality in the long run. With this I allude to developments in the electronics of information that are ever more clearly getting their grip on the person, that constrain him to the modes of perception they provide, and want to make him in fact an X before a U. This is why you also need your ears. Often there is a strained tenor in the voice: the story of *Little Red Riding Hood* comes back to the fore, where the wolf uses chalk to make his voice as true to life as that of the grandmother. And so this is my advice for the new year.

We are just now experiencing how a United States President provokes a daring conflict with the media and thereby thinks of risking the constitutional establishment of the USA. This constellation tells us a lot. Donald Trump's electoral defeat has caused a narcissistic illness in him which he brings fully into play, and he is ready to endanger everything, even the stability of the US.

This is an important message for you. It is a teachable moment, that one ought to remember even years from now. So quickly can a democracy be destabilized...

All the best, your R.

75.
What Can Be Known?

Dear Nina, Dear Julian and also Marie and Vicky,

Now I must write about a current event that will perhaps remain important for a long time. It is difficult to assess whether on 6 January 2021 a break in American history took place. In any case what happened was unusual enough that it is important to attempt an interpretation. I have two motives to do it: Might my interpretation hold up under a later historical account? This is important because if so my letters would generally achieve more credibility. That is a risky hope. The second motive is that because of what happened in Washington, it is necessary to measure how stable democracy now is in America.

Since Donald Trump's taking office, on the basis of information from my friend Kenneth Quandt, I had favored the Republican position over the new version of the Democrat position in the form of Hillary Clinton. From San Francisco I received many well-founded arguments all of them connected with the hope that a Republican president would set in motion a renewal of America. The election made it clear that almost a third of American society was party resentful, partly frustrated, and partly bitter and angry with the state of the country. US foreign policy in the Near East under Madeleine Albright had been detrimental to the European Union, causing a continual increase in migration into Central Europe. The reaction in the US was that the trade war with China and the relocation of industries outside the US was the cause of the continuous decline in the prosperity of the middle and lower classes. This increased the irrational anger. When Trump then was placed in the White House he was perhaps successful in partially refurbishing the key industries, but his continual vulgar attempts at self-promotion were tasteless, as was his arbitrary disregard of the current state of problems.

The pre-history of yesterday's event is easy to reconstruct. It confirms above all the often mentioned "split" in the nation that is spoken of in quite general terms without further detail – that the President's supporters consist of those who have been left behind by modernization. This is also a warning for the societies of Europe, which also have more and more people affected by modernization; and additionally tensions are increasing between those who are being left behind and immigrant families.

The President repeatedly asserted that his loss in the election was due to election fraud; this is of course difficult to judge from here. At a distance of seven thousand kilometers one can judge only with difficulty whether there was fraud or everything was done correctly. In fact the first question is, which reports can one trust? When I was present in the USA for the election of Barack Obama, I accompanied my friend to the local voting place. The kind lady would gladly have allowed me to vote and wasn't much interested in a photo-ID.

A distinguishing feature of the Trump Administration will remain: All political discourse was driven by the new media, with more and less believable claims being broadcast constantly. It was the success story of the new media that relatively easily they were able to influence the already frazzled minds of the people, or else led many of them to the blanket conclusion that everybody was lying.

This situation is perhaps the most problematic evidence of mistrust in democracy. Over against it stands the problem Manès Sperber wrote about, of political actors losing a personal sense of uprightness. This infects consciousness with the worst sort of demoralization which then undermines any respect for democratic institutions.

Here one must say that in an incorrect understanding of Marxism it is often heard that ethics and "consciousness" are just mirrors of social processes. The etymon of that word is seductively concise: what is the case (*sein*) determines what one is conscious of *(Bewusstsein)*. Ludwig Feuerbach gave it a more vulgar formulation: *Man ist was man isst* (one is what one eats). In a society the conflict among classes can therefore provide only a morality of power, not a private morality nor a personal sense of uprightness. On can directly conclude from this that bad times produce bad men, and good times hopefully good men; but when might times be good? Bertolt Brecht wonderfully brought this problem to the stage in *The Good Man from Szechuan*. Locating political morality according to the political situation became a usual formulation in social criticism and ever since this has destroyed responsibility, consciousness, integrity, and righteousness.

If I may go back to the event: Trump wanted not to resolve the general desperation, but only fomented it many times over. All he succeeded to do was to bind the "masses" to his own person. It was almost unbelievable that he could become a charismatic figure for the "declassed" – for anybody who fell under the political category of the "plebeians" of Roman history. He supplied these with a lot of material by means of his self-presentation in extravagant television appearances. At the same time he fostered a savaging of language, of expression, and of politeness.

With the election loss, he was stricken with a narcissistic illness. This was a low blow he could not get over. Instead, he stepped up his aggressive posture, took action with his cabinet like a madman, and used every opportunity to alter the result of the election after the fact. He sought to plan a final climax on the day the final election results reached by the electors were to be certified by Congress in the Capitol. He organized an open-air stage, delivered a speech, and persuaded thousands of supporters to be present for this event. He repeated the well-known objections about the brazen manipulation of the voting, how voting fraud had been committed, that his office had been stolen from him by fraud. He stressed that he had been wronged in every way and that the theft was basically an insult to those who voted for him. Finally he demanded that the excited crowd march to the Capitol in order to demonstrate the anger of the people on the steps of the Capitol, the house of the Congress. This sounded like Mussolini's call for the march on Rome in 1922! The "mass" began to move. But no leader led them. And thus there was no way to stop the way the march proceeded. The "people" overwhelmed the small number of policemen who were on duty to furnish protection for the session in the Capitol. Extremists forced their way in and ravaged everything they could. The members of congress were forced to flee. The session was quickly adjourned. The television picture showed security guards with drawn pistols. Other pictures showed the police in flight.

I remain skeptical about all these events, whether the pictures I saw represented the reality or were excerpted in a tendentious way. Are the reports of the German correspondents to be taken on face value? The more the media intrude into our lives the more certainly we must acknowledge that basically one has seen nothing real, although it was given out that everything happened in plain sight – and yet one can only repeat the assertion that one knows nothing any more. The media delude people about reality, and fool our sense-perception, and we can only repeat that we really know nothing for sure.

So, what does one know? Apparently the Capitol was stormed. One could refer to this storming as a putsch. One could think back to the past and the putsch attempt of Cataline, which Cicero discovered in time. Had Trump possessed more courage, he would have accompanied his "mob" to the steps of the Capitol. Instead he sat completely safe in the Oval Office waiting and hoping things would go in his direction. So he comported himself just as Anton Rintelen had once done during the attack on Engelbert Dolfuss. Instead of himself personally accompanying the attackers in the Nazi Putsch in July 1934, and standing in like a hero for victory or defeat, Rintelen remained in the Hotel Imperial in his room and waited for the report of success. When this failed, he decided to kill himself. And in the excitement even this failed. Although Cicero stood up against Cataline personally, and although the front defending the Republic in the senate was able to hold thanks to his rousting, analogous "heroes" in history merely schemed and sent others out in their place to avoid placing themselves in the front lines. So we can compare Trump with Rintelen. The President had acted in the same way. It was lucky for the US democracy that Trump did not want to be personally responsible for a putsch. He probably hoped to rise from ashes like a phoenix, if the thwarting of the representatives of democracy had been successful. Like Salvestro de' Medici acting as delegate to the textile workers during the wool-workers revolt of 1378 in Florence, he would have surrendered his own companions to the knife after gaining power, and would have had a high mass performed in the National Cathedral of Washington, in thanks for the salvation of the USA. As great as the desire may have grown which had animated him to deliver this speech "before the people," his fear won out in the end, fear that the shining hero would be accused of having led a lowly putsch.

So Trump did not possess the courage of Caesar to overthrow the republic of the United States in a systematic way. He had begun with his party, which he subjugated to himself, and for this he had, in the weeks before, set aside two hundred million dollars, with which he financed also the approach to the Capitol, something he also imposed on his cabinet as the policy they must adopt. Anyone who would not play along would be left behind.

It is known that Caesar had won out over his previous co-regents, Pompey and Crassus: he booted them out of the power struggle, while he also completely openly drove the republic toward a "monarchy." Did Trump have similar plans? The plans of Caesar are today well known. He took up the battle with strong resolve and knew that the smartest thing to do was to leave all the other institutions of the republic unscathed. In the short term Cicero was impressed, without forgetting his underlying suspicion of Caesar. Trump was far from that – from making a play for power with astuteness. Instead, all of his actions were arbitrary and moody. It was not from a silk thread that democracy hung, but from a string not much thicker. If he had had the calculating scrupulosity of Caesar he would have been able to overturn democracy in the USA. With the putsch attempt at the steps of the Capitol he ceased to be comparable to Caesar who had led his troops personally into the battle of the senate and stood in person in the senate for his intrigue, and he nearly pulled it off – had it not been for Brutus.

Trump remains a media hero. He was chatty on Twitter like young people in puberty. What was beloved was his boundless vulgarity which played into the hands of the media. His illiteracy he turned to his benefit through aggression and his penchant for power. In his economic initiatives he was successful suffering at most a black eye. This strengthened his dare-devil plans. In politics also did it need to be handled this way? He probably confused world politics with real estate speculation, and his estimate of Israel was based on his estimate of Jews.

And yet the republic in the USA somehow won. It was no accident. In their personal righteousness Republican representatives were able to foresee the enormous danger. Nobody wanted this. The objections against the results of the election were withdrawn. Obviously they did not want their party to be overtaken by Trump.

Was the short-lived political success of Caesar the reason that his accounts of the Gallic War are the general subject of instruction in Latin? In all likelihood it was hardly a clever decision by the school administrators to choose that Caesar's *Gallic Wars* should be read by students of Latin if they wanted to educate students for democracy.

Let's hope Trump's tweets don't become the texts of civics classes. Democracy was saved and yet the concern remains that it could have come out otherwise with a slightly more clever person...

I hope you find it entertaining to read this brief stroll through the history of attempted putsches.

I remain, with the best of greetings, your R.

76.
A Shock in Washington

My Dear Grandchildren,

Through the events in Washington on 6 January 2021, an example was brought to us how quickly a system of rule can be brought into question. It was of course astonishing that a US President sought at the last moment of his term to continue in office nevertheless. This demand in itself shows his attitude toward democracy. He sought, therewith, in an astonishing attempt, to hinder the transfer of power. He tried to do the same thing as Slobodan Milosevic had done in 1990. The latter had rejected the agreed-upon restoration of the office of president in the Confederation of Yugoslavia to the next federal state, and wanted to make his power "permanent."

If Donald Trump had wanted to keep power – and we should aver that he did – he made the decisive mistake on the one hand not to wait for the veto against the final confirmation of the new president, but instead to encourage the demonstration to march to the Capitol during the confirmation session. One had to realize that with an outbreak of hostilities, objections to the election of the new president would be overshadowed. Moreover Trump hereby disavowed his Republican congressmen. Breaking into the Capitol is to be viewed as a half-hearted putsch attempt. After all, five people died.

The next mistake was that Trump did not personally lead the movement against the Capitol. This would have required some guts, but the risk had to be taken. He had placed his intention to retain power in the hands of others. Perhaps he would have been able to moderate the violent acts. In any case he caused a chaotic situation which could only end on the downside for him. Apparently it was not clear to him at the decisive moment during his speech what concrete goal the marchers he provoked would pursue, and how the further "organization" of the enraged manifestations of will would inevitably play out. If he wanted to be a conspirator in his own interests, then he had wretchedly failed at the very thing he had shown to be his strongest point during his term in office: acting on impulse.

In history we must in many cases speak of conspiracies. In general, they pursue the goal of ending a configuration of order and taking the power to oneself. As can already be seen in the shadowy early history of Egypt the goal of conspiracies was to manipulate the dynasty, and to make the "Pharaoh-Gods" act according to their will – if necessary, by murder. The conspiracy in the harem of Ramses III in 1962BC is famous. From that point on, conspiracies became something of a sport and even in the time of the Ptolemies such overthrows were central features in political behavior – up until the fall of the Egyptian empire. And probably Julius Caesar, too, was surprised, when his life came to an end, that he had not recognized in time the attack of the republicans and the supporters of his own party. Surely if he had taken a "conspiracy theory" seriously, he would have gotten out of the sessions of the senate alive.

The most successful conspiracy, on the other hand, should be attributed to the Carolingians. They composed an "intergenerational" intrigue against the Merovingians in the years 747 to 771, so as to overthrow the Merovingian followers of Clovis and put themselves in their place. Very soon after they summoned their chief candidate Charles – soon Charlemagne – for the coronation in Rome, on Christmas 800, and dedicated in his honor the Palatine Chapel in Aachen – the famous central building which served as the symbol of the Empire until 1806.

Looking back, our specialists always viewed these conspiracies as child's play. I do not want to know how they would evaluate the Carolingian intrigues and their agreements with the other Frankish "majors of the palace," had they been alive at the time – whether this was mere child's play.

The problem we have, the Carolingians did not have. In particular it had become normal practice to confine the heirs of the Merovingians within the walls of a cloister, since they were required to become pious monks.

In a conspiracy it is always a matter of seizing total power. For this many conspirators have risked their lives. For the historian the evaluation is quite difficult. It comes down to the question which political system he gives the higher rank. The alleged conspiracy of the students who were opposed to National Socialism, the "white rose" of the Sisters Scholl, was far from being a conspiracy; conversely the murder of the Austrian heir to the throne at Sarajevo in 1914 was a hastily planned initiative of the Serbian opposition in Bosnia – *Mlada Bosnia* – and Gavrilo Princip had no clue what his attack was going to bring about.

Generally conspiracies are double edged. It was a lucky turn that the Greek tyrant Abantidas of Sicyon was brought down by his enemies, but that doesn't mean that the new men in power would be more humane, fairer, or more philanthropic. Conspiracy means leaving behind the knowledge that Mirabeau succeeded to keep in mind. He knew that his road to the scaffold was as long as the road that a senator would have to travel to the Tarpeian Rock if he was condemned to death for high treason. The revolutionaries of 1789 also traveled this road when as "conspirators against the revolution" the National Assembly caused them to be transported to the guillotine at the Place de la Concorde.

Conspiracy is always somewhere between overthrowing tyranny and saving freedom, between the rules of state and common murder. This is also how the revolt in the Netherlands against Philip II took place. In the Spanish tradition up to the illustrious General Franco, it remained a standard political practice. The doctrine had been recognized since the opposition of Egmont had been brought to an end by the falling knife, in 1568.

Of course, religious conscience legitimates a violent act against the state. The foundations for such actions are trysts and plans. The Hussites in Prague and the Catholics in London gathered together against the power of the state and were partly successful – their pleas came to be recognized – though partly they ended in shameful defeat. Such tactics as these have in our present times been completely organized by Islam and have now waxed into a bloody reality.

We hold in honored remembrance all those who set themselves against tyranny. Just so, the representatives of the city of Vienna decided to fight the arrogant acts of the Habsburg dukes and were executed – in the square before Palais Lobkowitz. The mayor, Konrad Vorlauf, and the councilors Rampersdorffer and Rockh were beheaded in 1408. It is in our eyes a tragedy that the tradition of a bourgeois city administration should be put down the way the Decembrist opposition was in Russia in 1820. However, conspirators remain unbelievably vivid in the memory of the Republic, since they were seen as the godfathers of Germany. And while we are looking closely at such stories, let us remark that Fiesco's conspiracy in Genoa was an exciting revelation of conceivable political alternatives.

In this review of history one sees how pathetic and reprehensible was Trump's idea of shaking the USA to its foundations. He saw himself as a victim of conspiracy and was himself not ready to be an instrument in his own conspiratorial plans. After all, he was flirting like a late medieval prince with everything, from Russia to Israel … .

Thus, conspiracy is on one hand the destabilization of power and on the other a defensive weapon against power; it always undergoes its own demise – in success and in failure, as historians know so well. And conspiracy has the historical role that in creating a moment of shock, it brings a diversity of political possibilities or alternatives briefly into view.

I wish for you God's blessings for the new year…

Your R.

77.
On the End of Emperors and the Sultan

Dear Nina, Dear Julian, Marie, and Vicky,

Finally Julian has written me a letter from Berlin. He is in quarantine, having returned from Guatemala. In any case he has not been affected by the virus and has survived his days in South America perfectly well.

I want to bring into focus for you, briefly, a special problem in European history. However it was that the current constellation of European history developed, we rarely pay attention to the fact that each region in Europe has its own particular history. The large processes of unification have so thoroughly ground down the contours of the regions and political landscapes that we now have the sense that the states in Europe always have had the same shape as shown in the political geography map of a middle-school atlas. There we still see the uniting movements of the 19th century, which could destroy the old "empires" – Austria-Hungary, Russia, the Ottoman Empire – we derive this modernization as a consequence of the French Revolution and we attach to this political explosion the incredible waves of modernization that with the industrial revolution changed every aspect of everyday life in Europe bit by bit. Surely these almost 300 years of European history are an important period: they determined the character of our present situation. Nevertheless, despite the efforts for European unity, we are also dealing with historical fault lines that we largely underestimate. We ask ourselves far too seldom why, in the work for unification of the European Union, Hungary, Czech and Poland do not want to participate to the degree that we might wish.

Once again, it is the historical particulars of religious and church history from which the contours are derived. These boundary lines, which divide Europe more than they do any other region, are still present up to today, as East and West and as North and South. Just as earlier boundaries were carved into the landscape according to the Roman Empire and its system of roads, so later came the Carolingian Empire which became the foil for Western Europe as the papacy had been the foil for southern Central Europe and Southern Europe. And the sphere of influence of Byzantium extended up to eastern Central Europe – at least until the fall of Constantinople in 1453, after which it was inherited by the Russian tsar.

Another new boundary was created by the "Religious Peace Treaty" of Münster and Osnabrück in 1648, right through the middle of Europe and the German lands. To this day, even after the enlightenment and secularization, a "religion border" can be felt between Reformed Christians and the old "Catholic" and "Roman" church. That Prussia could finally come into being was thanks to the fact that the Headmaster of the Teutonic Order in 1526 went over to the Lutheran confession and thereupon the entire realm of the Order up to Marienburg – i.e., Livland, and the Masurian Lake District and what later became

Prussia and part of Poland – were secularized, one by one. In Prussia all that remained was the colors of the Order's coat of arms, a black cross on a white ground, and the eagle of the Order is today the eagle of the Federal Republic of Germany. This is how Prussia, once a land within the Order, became the nucleus of Germany.

The first step of the Reformation took place in Prague. The protestant Jan Hus, with his burning at the stake in Konstanz, in 1415, set an example that turned out to influence Europe up to the 17th century. The controversy was about participating in the eucharist "under both kinds" – both bread and wine. It was one of the first signs of life of the University of Vienna, founded in 1365, that it pleaded for the execution of Jan Hus, in its representation of Vienna and the University at the Council. And this line can be traced to the founder of the Czech Republic, Thomas Masaryk, who in his confession belonged to the protestant "Bohemian Brethren." When he emigrated to the USA he met with Woodrow Wilson, who also belonged to the American version of the same institution, called the "Unity of Brethren." Masaryk's plan to found an independent and sovereign Czech Republic was supported by Wilson, in conversation. That was in 1918. Wilson had published his plan for Central Europe, and the German version, published in 1914, was called *Die neue Freiheit* ("The New Freedom"). One should not have been surprised to see the division of the Danubian Monarchy.

To go back: Leopold von Ranke in his history had written as his final conclusion, "Finally, now that Hus was dead, he came to life." Four years after the death of Hus in 1419 a revolution broke out that completely altered the situation in Bohemia, Moravia, Lusatia, and Silesia. The resulting conflicts which began with the prosecution of the Hussites weakened Bohemia, which as a monarchy was absorbed step by step into the Habsburg "Empire" and finally in the 17th century under Ferdinand II in the wake of the bloody Counter-Reformation was thought to have become unimportant. A noticeable indication of this was that the administrative center was relocated from Prague to Vienna, so that the Czech-Bohemian and the Bohemian-German intelligentsia were removed from the country. From then on the "Chancellery of Bohemia" was located in Vienna and ruled over the Bohemians from there harshly and unjustly.

As late as the Reformation period during the 16th century, there was some thought about joining Lower and Upper Austria with the Bohemian Confederation. This confederation, which had existed rather briefly up until 1618, was constructed on the Dutch (and English) model – so in our current sense it was modern and innovative. The Bohemian nobility stood behind this political project and came together under the motto "*Hussus redivivus.*" The best expression of the rebellion against the Habsburgs was the notorious "Defenestration in Prague," in 1618. Although the three victims survived – thanks to dung heaps in front of the building beneath the windows – this event was a harbinger for the terrible Thirty Years' War.

The cause of the protest of the Hussian rebellion was the revocation of privileges in 1611 which had been secured for the Hussites by Rudolph II, the predecessor of Emperor Matthias. It was the first, though subsequently revoked, example of religious freedom. It had become obvious that it was now a matter of the "Catholic World" – the absolute monarchies of France, Spain, and the southern half of Central Europe – over against the "proto-parliamentary" systems of patrician councils in the north and the northwest. In these, one had taken England and the States General of the Netherlands as their example. In these, the right of the individual was at least nominally declared; out of the English root were formulated the "human rights" that were then associated with the revolutions in North America and France. These achievements became topics of conversation – in Moravia and Silesia; and they provided the Bohemian Enlightenment with its orientation. With the demise of Bohemian-Czech-German sophistication located in Prague, these projects were extinguished.

With the disenfranchisement of Bohemia and the "mediatization" of Prague, a Prussian-Austrian dualism within the empire became possible for the first time. The Bohemians could have been a *"pouvoir intermediare,"* which however only Rudolph II had understood, though his brother Matthias soon did not – and Ferdinand II treated Bohemia like a colony. After the judicial murder of Hus under Emperor Sigismund in 1415, the fatal consequences followed: from the 17th century on the Bohemians had to remain in subordination.

For Czech history, in the midst of all this, defenestration became a common practice. Not only did the first defenestration against the Catholic councilors take place in 1419, but in 1483 the mayor of Prague was thrown out a window in order to thwart a Catholic conspiracy. In 1618 came the so-called second defenestration. And finally in 1948 Jan Masaryk was pushed out a window, though it was claimed by the Stalinist regime that he committed suicide. It marked the end of the Czechoslovakian Republic – up until the Prague Spring and then November 1989. The victory over the communist party and the end of dependency from the already dissolving Soviet Union was the achievement of Vaclav Havel. In his programmatic piece, "Try to Live in Freedom" (1978), he speaks to us even today.

I want to recommend this little book to you. The call for self-determination, the immunization against manipulation and propaganda provide, especially in our times, precious support for the sense of personal independence and freedom. I once traveled, in 1988, through our "lands" with Havel's book: I offered several readings in Vienna, Graz, and Salzburg, and hoped to find the path forward for what was still the Czechoslovakian Republic.

I was very proud to perform these readings and recommend you read it, too.

All the best, I remain your: R.

78.
How Rare is Political Virtue?

Dear Nina, Dear Julian, Marie, and Vicky

Now we have the true cold of winter, and you will be glad to receive your lessons through "home-screening": the pandemic has its good side!

In order not to compete with your teachers I want to indicate a position on a topic has to do only with discussions that take place outside your lessons. The school lessons in general must be objective, and as much as possible can answer political questions only on an "institutional" level; thus for the young, the experience of politics is ultimately within the province of the media to determine. The students will repeat opinions or commentaries either from television or newspapers, in addition to the opinions of their parents. If this is the case, a debate during breaks between lessons is almost pre-programmed. I mentioned this once before: during my school years a group that followed the National Socialist outlook ruled the class. The shaping of the reigning opinion will not be much different today. I fear that the acceptance of children "with a migration background" will sink even further, that discrimination of all kinds will dominate the classes at school. A revealing indication is the rising popularity of private schools. Since going there depends upon paying a tuition, the parents hope for at least a more orderly instruction than in the public schools. While the confrontations between different grades of politicization in the public schools are brought to an end by the ringing of the school bell at the end of the break, in private schools a controversy of this kind is expected not even to arise.

This way that the "politicization" of the young accords to where they are points to something that was commonplace in antiquity. Among the "Greeks" or the "Romans" only those who belonged to the political classes practiced politics. Only these persons determined the action of the city-states through history, in matters of war and peace, cult and art. Politics at that time had the quality that all the areas of life were integrated in it, and so its function was "politicized," as every temple shows. When such integration or instrumentalization was absent so also the political meaning of the cultic or artistic works was lost. The acropolis in Athens as well as the Forum in Rome emphatically show that the whole ensemble of buildings and the close connection among all objects, embody a political myth. And so the functions of the buildings were brought together into a tight space and because of this design had almost the character of a political ghetto. The haunts of the political delegates, the senators, and the members of the agora corresponded with their institutions. They all communicated with one another, daily and at all hours. In this one can recognize the difference from the moderns, since neither liberalism nor modern democracy possess such a tightly unified political class – nor did they intend to. In sociology one learns that it is the political bureaucracy and the administrations that had to carry out political plans, or design the political system or at least maintain the political dimension of life. From this point on a question about "the political" could no longer be expressed, just as no one could any longer answer it, either. The time was past in which one could claim the state to be his own, as Louis XIV had, as if embodying it in his very person. Participation in the political became completely opaque. In all likelihood one can count it a political paradox that democracy has the participation of all citizens in mind, but with that the political involvement of a whole population decays into anonymity. This was then the subject of information and disinformation, and of mentality and socialization. It finally became a topic of philosophy, in particular the discrepancy between everyday life, increasing complexity, and a problematic interpretation of existence in a secular society.

Our ideas are now facing a test. From the 19th century the valorization of the "born politician" is still intact, and usually such a person was an exponent of the "power state idea" from Napoleon to Otto von Bismarck, which turned out to be a misplaced hope after 1918. Then, almost everywhere Europe saw in fascism a higher political competence than in democracy. And now, in the form of democratic state consisting in a multiplicity of parties, a "friend vs. foe" relationship developed between the actors that was detrimental to the consensus democracy needs. In the monarchy the Emperor had the job of maintaining balance in order to protect social calm. The Weimar Republic also ran aground for the lack of an Emperor, as had the First Republic in Austria. The case of other states received less attention, in which there were takeovers by Mussolini and by Caudillo Francisco Franco. Similar transformations were forced upon Hungary by Miklos Horthy, upon Poland by Joszef Pilsudski, and upon Portugal by Antonio Salazar.

These individuals, to whom those in South America should be added, were in the end not only infected with fascism but saw themselves justified, given their conception of the "power-state," to impose this alternative style of democracy. This is what makes the schema of "friend vs. foe" as formulated by Carl Schmitt so important. There was now no longer a dialogue and political conversation, which once Leopold von Ranke along with Friedrich von Savigny the historian of law had brought to attention in 1820, but instead the basic assertion: who is not for me is against me. Although after 1918 a democratic constitution was more than recommended by everyone, battle won out over compromise and discord over concord.

Carl Schmitt made a decisive contribution to this, and his form of constitution was extraordinarily attractive – namely, to fight out the question of the constitution bitterly in parliament. So the concept of the political, based upon victory or defeat, became tyrannical. Moreover the institutions of a republic are generally not amenable to interpretation in these controversialist terms. The courts, in their modern understanding of law, do not basically judge according to the criteria of friend and foe. Quite the contrary. Many aspects of law plea for a moderated balance – from managing bankruptcy or compensation to the attempt in criminal law to bring about a reconciliation between the perpetrator and the victim. A radicalism in the theory of law, of all things, became attractive during the first years of the 20th century, and found also a counterpart in a similar radicalism in philosophy – whether it be Bolshevism or the peculiar radicalism of Heidegger.

Agnes Heller diagnosed an "existentialist radicalism" in both Heidegger and Georg Lukács. What she meant by this was that both, in their years of political involvement, saw their life-situation, the situation of their country, to be in a decisive political period. Just as Lukács, as the commissar of Bela Kun's soviet government in Hungary, carried out a political function in 1922-3 which he thought he had no choice but to employ, in a battle against revisionism and reaction, so also Heidegger bore up under his own compliancy regarding the new men in power after 1933. Both saw themselves at an existential crossroads and subordinated their "selves" to the dictates of the political. Following the ideas of Max Weber one might conceive the challenge which both found themselves to be facing as a personal situation in which they recognize its ontological contingency but in the face of that bond, being also a matter of life and death, they must now make a decision that bears absolutely upon their own person. It was literally fateful. This would have remained only personal for the two persons if both of them had not derived from it a radical political philosophy.

The overture of a political philosophy during the 1920's was on the one hand the invention of a political heroism. With 1918, greatness and heroism were no longer readily possible without something further. Both of these were condemned and destroyed. In political philosophy a new chimera was seeming more and more to be real: the blessed and gifted existential collective. With this, destiny could now be defined, which now usurped the role of history. And it will be by destiny that the proof of selection and of exceptionalism and deselection will succeed. In Lukács it was the empirical proletariat; in Heidegger the romantic concept of a *Volk*. At first it was indeed the nation – the German nation! Granted, the German nation had not been recognized as an empire except in the imagination – until in 1806 it collapsed. The last dukes to become princes were certainly the only people who could still warm to the empire – in particular, the Esterhazy or Windischgrätz princes. Now, in political philosophy, the birth of the "New German" takes place, in its revolution, in the removal of the shameless emperor, and in the proclamation of the republic.

For the Marxists it was more complicated. Before the self-liberation and "sublation of oneself" into the stature of an autonomous *Volk* which was the case in Germany, according to Marxism-Leninism the salvation of the proletariat required world revolution. Whatever the positions were, they had in common the thought of a self-salvation as the prerequisite to a new political reality, devoutly to be wished.

Both positions were inspired by illusions, which seemed to have unavoidable defeat written into their DNA. Hannah Arendt, in her political analysis of totalitarianism, was the only philosopher who maintained a clear view during the 30's. Not only would this fantasy of salvation not come about politically, but she shared with Ortega y Gasset the view that the enormous weakening of the political elite would not favor democracy. Arendt was concerned about the foreseeable situation that politics would become banal in the hands of philistines, that then the survivors of this shipwreck would for better or worse become the collective. A new political myth was brought into service, which established its liturgy in Nuremberg, where ultimately it also came to its end.

Arendt conceived of an alternative which she had observed in American communitarianism. She saw this as a more amiable variant that could also awaken democracy. This hypothesis included a dialectical unity of the normative claim with empirical consciousness. Both together are the prerequisites for political philosophy. However, the current philosophy of politics, so rich in ideological motifs, is not at all compatible with this. In modernity it had become normal to think that though philosophy was committed to truth, this truth is not real. What was taken to be just has nothing to do with justice since everything we see around us has more to do with justice than does law and judicial procedure.

However we wish to conceive it, we will realize we need a new concept of the political, which seems more and more paradoxical. Today we know that there are no longer those two prerequisites: there is no longer an authentic political class regardless how it is constituted; and at the same time politics is more opaque to us than ever before. If politics defines the tension between the "is" and the "ought," with which the politician must deal every day, a third component is missing – the characterization of politics as truly belonging to modernity in the first place. It is the ethical component that structures the area of the "ought." If within the interplay of the "is" and the "ought" a prohibition against "individualization" becomes possible – i.e., the lying that leads to gaining power and money – so also the rather undeveloped ethical category has to fulfill social aspirations. Hence the categorial imperative "falls short," since it determines only the norm of the ought that I myself must respect. In politics we must rely on something more, on political virtue, the thing about which there was so much talk in antiquity. It seems this came to be replaced in our times by our concept of freedom, which we now believe must be taken into account and protected and defended in all our spheres of life. It can be the banal freedom to travel and follow whims, it can be the freedom of speech in public and of civil rights (all still succinct); but it can also be the freedom that enables us to recognize its limits. We learn of the freedom *not* to do something! To what extent we here become involved in the dilemma between the elements of political freedom and the new forms of technology that hold our economy in their grip, may remain an open question. In any case our political freedom will be determined by this tension. Thus, the concept of the political is always both normative and empirical...

I started with the small discussion groups of the young that in conversation during recess deal with current topics. Whether the topic be the consequences of a natural catastrophe or the latest incidents of corruption, the evaluations they reach are always according to a criterion whose origin is unclear to them or unknown. At first the judgment is driven by sympathy, then a bit later skepticism, and finally a unanimous judgment is reached that politics as a whole is a crooked business.

That politics should not be this way was the reason that I have given this complicated account, namely in order to oppose such resignation. Less politically aware commentators are able to make declarations about politics since they see the results, but since they do not see the causes and motives the lack of political philosophy is all the more severe …

I hope it doesn't get colder!

Remain healthy!

Your R.

79.
Is There Social Politics After All?

My Dear Grandchildren,

In the last letter I brought up the problem of "the political." If I might summarize it briefly, it should now be obvious that we are still stuck in a previous and "outmoded" version of politics. Especially in times of a crisis such as has now been brought about by the pandemic, we would prefer politicians who can "rise to the occasion," who show much more human qualities than merely those of a manager. This means that this crisis is not only a great burden upon us, but makes all the more clear what questions and problems we were trying to postpone, and about which we have by now been basically clueless for years. We have reacted much less than we should in regard to the worldwide migration, which is the largest in world history. In Europe we have in general not improved the politics of education: social politics in Europe has come to be seen as merely a sub-function of a flourishing economy. The tendency went more in the "American" direction: that everyone ought to take care of himself. I am not of the opinion that one can treat these developments in Europe as due to neo-liberalism: far more notable is the complete take-over of the democratic parties by the "bourgeoisie," the silence of the unions over the "liberalization" of the labor market, and the way those who are completely committed to opportunism in the spirit of the times consider themselves conservative. Niklas Luhmann was completely right to note, in his *Gesellschaft der Gesellschaft* (Eng. tr. *Theory of Society*, 2012-3), that although politics today is a fully elaborated system it is accorded no more importance than sports, subscriptions at symphony halls, and beautification committees. The societies of the industrial countries have become fragmented, so that even basic constitutional consensus is no longer commonly recognized. All these questions appear to be answered by popular opinion as represented by the opinion of one fifth of the European populace. In the USA one is still able to choose a president, so far at least. So we are in the midst of a crisis of a democracy made up of representative parties. The old political power configuration formed by the parties has come to an end; a new configuration has been established in the administration, in the management, in the operations of the authorities. This however increasingly lacks the traditional sort of political legitimacy. As a result the public-political sphere has taken on the appearance of a technocracy that understands how to get things done better than the old officers and their bureaucratic labyrinth.

My letter intended to make this situation clear. Everyone should realize that we are on the brink of a significant change in politics. It is not certain that democratic institutions will survive: at least their foundation is now a sort of economic rationalism that the runs circles around what politics had been. And should someone ask me how the development of India or China looks, what the future of the countries of South America will be, or of black Africa or of Asia Minor, I would answer with some irony that these are probably quite far along, whereas Europe is on the way to becoming India or Brasilia, or like Belarus or Turkey. That the classical criteria of democracy should continue to be valued is what we must wish for. And the wish that human rights will also be honored, will hardly remain a wish but an urgent demand.

I have proceeded from the view that the dogma that democracy is basically the political destiny of our history, though this is heard more and more, cannot be correct. One underestimates history if he believes history can no longer "leapfrog." Quite the contrary. If democracy is not in fact the final way the political realm will be organized, it becomes more important for us to think hard about what will replace it. A break from democracy does not have to end in tyranny. In particular, the renovation of a system can employ the equipment supplied us by Kant and Hegel. The radical philosophy of the 18th century knew the criteria of freedom, just as it knew those of revolution. It is up to us to bring about a peaceful mixture in which both of these are included. The revolutionary element does not need to end in ugliness the way it did in Paris 230 years ago; but the insistence on freedom is a revolutionary element though it is not something that can instigated, and not something that erupts like a volcano or is some widespread event. Rather the revolution of freedom is to be an event that will be durable and simply remain the case in an ongoing way. Freedom is established. It includes an insistence that freedom and everyday life can work together. The everyday life of humans ought to be accompanied by it and take place with it. This is completely thinkable within the philosophical world of Kant and Hegel. Of course to talk this way might sound like a "new historicism," and yet there won't be much else for us to say. We aren't going to adopt China's system, are we? And perhaps China will have carried through the revision and maintained it. To conceive this would be an unbelievable broadening of our political imagination. At this moment we are running the risk of treating freedom as an esthetic value, of finding it in the arts or even in the elegance of fashion or the perfection of technique. This would constitute a fatal curtailment of the political. If art – especially the performing arts – take the liberty to show us the way to un-freedom, this says a lot about an art that no longer knows how to use the freedom it already has been accorded, but only knows how to abuse it.

This is surely an indication that we are "stuck" in a change, a change about which art provides us a message, though it no longer wants to be the herald for freedom that it was, once before. Again and again I am reminded of *Liberty Leading the People*, that great painting of Eugène Delacroix. Do *we* still let freedom inspire us and lead us? Will art in the future raise us to the level where Florestan in *Fidelio* set forth his great aria, "To freedom! To freedom! To the heavenly realm…" I am afraid that art no longer has in mind this kind of liberation into freedom! It is currently the product of a mendacious intrigue of worldwide politics: disinformation, disintegration, disorientation playing the role as expressions of esthetic freedom…

About this I will tell you more, later!

All the best, your R.

80.
Looking Back on a Lecture

Dear Nina, Dear Julek, Dear Marie and Vicky,

On the day after my first lecture of the new year I recognize quite well that I need some time to return to my topic. "Sociology of Mechanization" is what I have called it and I wanted to show what is the difference between technology, technicity, and mechanization. The first term refers in a general way to a phenomenon derived from traditional mechanics. *Technicity* basically means that out of a principle of design things can be further developed without the basic model undergoing a modification. For instance, such different machines as a steam-powered loom and a steam engine or a steam locomotive are comparable, although the purposes of the machines based on steam are very different. And third, *mechanization* denotes an alteration of our life-world, the way it is reshaped more and more by technological achievements and ultimately becomes dominated by technology. Actually one must infer from this that technology, like a prosthesis added to nature, realizes many things humans conceive of, and could even come to be nature's twin sister. We spend more and more time within this "world of technological objects," for longer and longer periods, and even our daily planning is taken over by it. The dream of Leonardo becomes an actuality: he once had the idea that where conditions appear to overwhelm us and the powers of nature seem to overcome the intentions of our civilization, one must build a bridge or create possibilities to overcome these barriers. This was the paradigmatic expression of Renaissance Humanism and optimism! In the copper etchings of Giovanni Baptista Piranesi we can view this unbelievable widening of the possibilities open to us; his classical baroque prints show a rising optimism that also influenced the political thinking of the Enlightenment.

Technology "made its own way." If we think of Thomas Alva Edison, he was an amateur genius – like many others – who began playing in a naively creative way with an "erector set." With the founding of "polytechnic" schools, the first of them in Paris (1794) and then later in Nuremberg (1804) or Karlsruhe, such amateurism was systematically eclipsed. The education of the technical schools was now able to surpass amateurism. At the end of the 19th century there were already technical colleges, which we not so long ago even turned into universities.

I still remember very well the ten lectures of Friedrich Nietzsche who in his merciless criticism of teaching institutions complained about the way people are altered as a result of technical-scientific training. The position was very clearly argued that in this kind of education we are dealing with a system that either makes the student a "pushover," compliant and without any opinions of his own, or that gradually represses one's sense that one needs to reflect upon the question of his professional calling. Of course one did not listen to Nietzsche but disregarded his clairvoyant insight, and just continued to ride on the successful the wave of mechanization. The First World War, an obvious catastrophe, brought into being an unforeseen increase in the forms of mechanization. Here we saw tanks, the first use of airplanes, the first use of military uniforms that camouflage soldiers and enable them to dig their trenches protected by steel helmets, and it brought an end once and for all to the picturesque manner of battle commonplace a hundred years earlier.

In still further developments, a more particular transformation within technology arose. In the 50's, Heinz Zemanek built, in the Technical College of Vienna, the *Mailürftel*, which was the first computer. He often would tell me about it when I went shopping with him on Saturdays. Here was the pioneer in electronics walking beside me, and as I remember he brought up, over and over, the danger we were bringing upon ourselves. This was not the talk of some purist but the warning voice of a man in the know, even though he could not know the current state of communication technology. He had given me to understand not only that these techniques were growing exponentially from decade to decade with a simultaneous decrease in the size of the devices, but also that they were invading our life-world ever more significantly, the way water in a flood makes its way into every crack and cranny. While we would be buying our vegetables, our celery and spinach, we exchanged our concerns about what comes with the mechanization of our life-world. This was not a matter of pessimism: instead we took issue with the lack of "awareness" among the users who were unreservedly surrendering themselves to this world.

I was touched by Heinz Zemanek's shyness, his humble resignation about his insights into the new world of technology. He did not want to undo anything that was happening, not an iota should be taken back from his inventions: he only warned that our reflection about it should substantially be heightened. He himself had soldered together a thousand relays, had tested the operation of his computer a thousand times, and had become sufficiently aware that here lay the foundation of artificial intelligence; and yet at the same time he knew that this expansion of what we had access to, which today we thoughtlessly employ through Google, would be a temptation. There would evolve a sudden acquisition of knowledge without any test of its plausibility. Thanks to these expansions of communication technology we now broaden our knowledge almost at will, without however knowing at the same time whether the things we are assuming to be true are correct or even confirmable.

I do not want to continue with this point. In my course of lectures I am not trying to ostracize technology but to articulate how it is altering our lives and bring to light that twenty years ago we behaved differently, and used our time differently, and formulated our interests differently. Today everyone sits with his iPhone or mobile phone in the subway, and as the social environment around him and around her fades away and recedes into nothingness, this becomes one's actual reality.

I need make no further commentary. What we see clearly before us is the world of the future: A "surveillance capitalism" is in the offing, a strange control over our social world. Shoshana Zuboff has eloquently described the way that comprehensively technological dreams have been realized. It begins with this: every keystroke one types in a search submitted to Google is a piece of information for producing his personal profile. The intention is that everyone become a "see-through person." The project is facilitated by psychology, neurology, and artificial intelligence, and the huge server companies provide the capital. Zuboff has clearly described how renowned scientists are ready to break the vows they made when they received their diplomas. An ethics of science is nearly unknown in their circles.

Suddenly, such utopias as we know from George Orwell become factual descriptions of our coming world. One is struck dumb just thinking of these consequences. We are hardly able to realize how much we are bringing about our own "incarceration." Mechanization creeps into our world in velvet slippers and replaces what had been burdensome for us before, compensates for what had so long seemed too complicated to us, takes over the position of what we a short time earlier had thought to be our individual identity.

As to Zuboff I remember reading how she describes these giant companies that are more and more resolutely devoted to our wishes and to fulfilling them. All the data that can be drawn from us make their way through their algorithms and finally we have become "see-through," and we become the object of our ill-conceived wishes. It seems to be a devil's system, and yet we no longer notice. We stand at the apogee of the modern world and at the same time the nadir of our individuality.

How will this play out? What role will people still play? This remains completely undetermined. This is not the "open society" we had in mind. Open it has indeed become, but in the direction of unlimited surveillance on us, of controlling us, of "domesticating" us. Will anyone pursue this line of thought any further? Will it be one of you?

I am afraid to think about it.

I would wish I could stay with you, to instill courage and confidence in you, when the world seems so grey and dim and when The Power comes in its next disguise and forces you in such a disreputable way to choose where you will stand, between complicity and coercion.

With love, your R.

81.
Does our Present Have Historical Substance?

Dear Grandchildren,

A report about Julian's success at school has reached me. It makes me very happy. Likewise Nina's performances are very fine and promising which has always been the case with her. Unfortunately I lack any similar information about either Marie or Vicky. Vicky will still find it hard to write – indeed, starting to do anything is hard, especially in First Grade.

In the last letter I introduced the topic of mechanization and gave a little information about how mechanization invades our daily life. It seems politics can only achieve independent competence if it plunges itself into the midst of the dilemma between formalism and formlessness and thinks that in this way it will become what democracy needs it to be. Under the pressures of authorities who enforce laws, under the pressures of daily problems of life, and under the competing internal pressures of the respective opposing parties, it seems that an innovative politics is unthinkable. While briefly watching a meeting of the parliament of Vienna on television I was quite shocked by the subjects of deliberation and how they were being treated. Banality set the tone. Basically, it is a kind of griping one knows from one's household when one doesn't empty the garbage, doesn't close the door to the closet, or leaves a light on. It may make the political hacks happy who see in this that the only truly substantial life-questions are being dealt with. It can be that this politicization of life – or de-politization, if you will – is pleasing, which then reaches its ultimate banalization in opinion polls. But it cannot be what it needs to be: given the dramatic problems of migration, hunger, and the destruction of human rights, the issues of world politics deserve much greater attention.

Given Hegel's way of thinking of the Absolute Spirit becoming realized in the present, and in another sense that it expresses itself in its representations from the past, one is then justified in asking whether in the here and now something or other is lodged in our memory that can represent for us a knowledge for the founding of democracy. Currently, democracy in Europe seems to be in the situation that we no longer have a fundamental text for our current political form, nor even is there anyone to interpret it. Thus not only does the current politics make no sense, but its past also is disintegrating and disappearing. We no longer have a clear sense of how the foundations of democracy were laid. For this we would have to find a place in our hearts, the very way we do through music with a symphony of Beethoven or Mozart. Once one has heard the *Haffner Symphony* of Mozart, K. 385 – *Symphony no.35* in D major – which Mozart wrote in Vienna in 1782, its stormy beginning and sweeping continuation with timpani and trumpets, and then in the second theme the melodious violins, one will never forget it. Exactly this feeling I still have when I see the old photographs of the signing of the constitution at Belvedere in 1955, but I have the sense that the members of parliament, our current representatives of democracy, "have nothing to do" with this remarkable history. So often it is said that democracy is so well established that nothing can bring it down, and in fact fully a third of the members of parliament feign a "noble" condescension for democracy, or will tolerate it only until they are able to bring about a political change. The same is going on in Germany where out of the swamp parties have emerged and are to be seen as sympathetic, but likewise have "nothing to do" with democracy. The representations belonging to democracy's past – in the Hegelian manner – no longer constitute a consensus, in our "democracy of parties," and one knows of no consensual way to deal with the problem.

When I stroll through the Vienna Volksgarten, I always stop in front of the great rose bush at the exit that leads to the Chancellery. It came from the garden of the home of Karl Renner in Untertannowitz. It is probably a remnant of Renner's childhood. The house itself, which was the home of a small farmer, was rebuilt in a ghastly way making a disgrace in the midst of a Moravian enclave. Any and all memories were wiped away so that the Absolute Spirit could no longer dwell here in peace. What representation of the past could here find a place? To the contrary it is banality that has found a place, a very desire for disgrace. It was in the aftermath of this that I wrote about the Czech Republic a few letters ago.

The way we now build our houses, or rebuild them as in the case of Karl Renner's birthplace, or the way we sell "Mozart Balls" in the basement of his birthplace in Salzburg as though the true legacy of that musician were melting in one's mouth – this all shows us that we have become placeless. On the one hand we could be at home anywhere – and at the same time, nowhere. Our "world-industrial culture," along with surrealism, has gotten hold of everything, has cooked it and eaten it, and so people can no longer find their personal niche any more than their culture can. This is why ten people cannot communicate: they have read ten different books and not one together. And a hundred people will have read a hundred different books and not a single one together. Literature is no longer a shared dwelling place as it was before, even if it only consisted of "Goethe, Schiller, Lessing."

I write this because one can recognize in this that all we hold in common as a unifying bond is political strife. Today these very different reading habits or ways of living have a remarkable correspondence with the form of our diets and fashions. Even menus no longer offer us a home, in offering us Kassel ribs with potatoes salad, or pizza when we are in Bombay. Menus are an interpretation of the present, and they change every week. This is how we experience this strange certainty of being home in an "absolute" present – thanks to the menu. We order Coca Cola and, satisfied, look over at the burned cathedral in Paris. And who can dissuade us we aren't sitting by the ruins of the Memorial Church of Berlin?

If democracy now wants to offer us a home, it would certainly do so by imitating the architectural style of North America. It was only a short time ago that we thought we were seeing before us a paradigm that claimed historical authenticity: with the march against the capitol on 6 January 2021, reminiscent of

Mussolini's march against Rome, even this political myth evaporated. And so, few people still feel at home in democracy. Most of them are almost ready to take the whole thing as a laughable house of cards. In all likelihood the guards were quite ready to open the doors of the Capitol since they had formed the notion, given the run-up of recent years, that they didn't want to stand in the way of the future.

For the longest time we have lived in the belief that democracy and modernity were fraternal twins, that they would be our political environment for the duration. From North America we took up the notion that a democracy can also embrace national pride. The military snap to attention before the Stars and Stripes always made it seem genuine, offered a view of orderly attentive soldiers – and finally the camera would pan to the Lincoln Memorial, the White House, and the Capitol. One thought this was somehow a new Rome, and the stability of the institutions was greater than those of Roman antiquity. The view of the past was dominated by the US Constitution. It was the project of John Jay, Alexander Hamilton, and James Madison, in the *Federalist Papers* – to give the constitution of the thirteen states an orderly basis. This has changed. But what we generally have not seen was the grotesque political situation of the World War, the way it presented itself in political parties, whether in covert or open obscenity: the participation in elections continued to issue a clear message until finally the Clinton clan was no longer a representation of the good old USA but corrupt instead; and then, conversely, Trump in his vulgarity embodied an open obscenity – indeed he was quite honest about it – and thereby captured the support of the masses.

Where have the times gone when one could understand the USA so well? Alexis de Tocqueville admired the special character of its politics, laws, administration and its liberality, back in 1850. Above all he praised the rectitude and the steadfastness of the smaller courts across the United States, which accomplished more for the unity of the states than the victory in the war of the "North" against the "South." And in the classic movies about the Wild West it was always a matter of violence and anarchy versus law. And the "outlaw" that happened to ride into town on his horse, as represented by John Wayne, fought for, embodied, and restored, the rule of law. It became a political myth that natural and liberal justice was alive and well in any "cowboy" and was defended with his courage and marksmanship. This was the model of an older USA which would be able to decide two World Wars.

We must now ask whether this USA still exists. The US revolution was akin to the French Revolution, though luckily it lacked the doctrinaire element and knew no fanatics who would raise the cry *"tertium non datur."* The guillotine played no part in the American Revolution. Over a period of time they overcame their crises in the 1930's with Franklin Roosevelt's "New Deal;" after 1945 they had cured the exhaustion of Europe with the Marshall Plan and ERP credit, and a few years later everything was better than it was before the war. As in the Wild West movies the USA was the moral authority, and the way-shower to a democratic and prosperous future. However this reputation was squandered, piece by piece. The second Iraq war, the devastating foreign policy of Madeleine Albright, Condoleezza Rice, and Hillary Clinton had obviously turned into sanctions against Europe. And "helpless" Europe, as Robert Musil had called it, had to allow Turkey to be a louse in its fur because of the US intervention.

Complaining will do not good. Europe is destroyed, like a colony of Greece after it allied itself with Hannibal in 220BC. The end of Hannibal is well known, but less well known is that thereby the sovereignty of the city-states of Athens, Corinth, Thebes, and Sparta was virtually destroyed. Because of the short-term successes of the European unification we were strongly convinced that we would become the U.S.E. – the United States of Europe. One was still able to believe this in the 1980's. One had not yet read the little book of Hermann Lübbe or else did not take it seriously: there will not be a United States of Europe.

The problem remained. The characteristic of our existence is loss of place. Just as the USA was lost as a place of refuge, so also the places of democracy are teetering. The smallest storm regularly pushes us to the edge of our existence. We have chosen neo-liberalism as our life-raft. So once again we have lost the memory that liberalism cannot be a home. The basic principle is, Survival of the Fittest: Herbert Spencer and Charles Darwin reborn…

Once again, a bitter letter.

I am writing it since it may be that naming this phenomenon can also banish it. That was the goal of the Absolute Spirit (in Hegel) – that with the envisioning comes also a mastering of the path …

Your R.

82.
What Kind of a Present Do We Have?

Dear Nina, Dear Julek, Dear Marie and Vicky,

For once I do not want to write about politics. You know that the present is not favorable for politics. China has finally become a "global player" on the same level as others and the USA will be happy just to keep up with them. Russian foreign policy under Putin is doing more than taking a "creative pause." Because of the American foreign policy, if it deserves the name, Russia's influence in the Middle East has been strengthened and at the same time – despite the antagonisms – reached an accord of common interests with Turkey under Erdogan. Things could even become so grotesque that in the conflict between Azerbaijan and Armenia Putin would come to be treated as the prince of peace, despite Ukraine and Crimea. He brought the military confrontation to an end and now the new question arises, whether the region of Nagorno-Karabakh will remain under the "re-conqueror" or not... . What I am saying needs greatly to be supplemented if one really wants to have insight into the present situation. What has become of Libya? Will the small countries along the Himalayas somehow survive, given the pressures of China and India? What will become of Central America? Questions upon questions...

As I said at the beginning I want for once to drop that. One can perfectly well think that even this constellation of affairs will be washed away by the rivers of time. Time flows and passes by. Out of the past a stronger flow comes upon us, and yet its narrowest choking point is the present. From here it broadens back out into the unknown – into the future.

Time is already felt to be past with the next thought. The little blip of the present, which one would so much like to expand, is at the same time a unique source of miscalculations. One believes that right now everything is important or fearsome; one believes that something unsurpassable is going on right now. A diary, if one writes one, is a treasure trove of overstatements and miscalculations. Most things are actually irretrievable – gone forever – and yet writing them down is a process that weakens our memory, and even robs it of its meaning. The diary, which even as it is written becomes part of the past, does place something objective before our eyes, but at the same time it hobbles memory which already has its own objectifying power. It was probably a wise decision not to keep a diary, since if it is not eloquent in a literary way its predominant effect is to devalue the moments of time that it takes note of. Diaries call for truth; remembering calls for fantasy. The homogeneity of remembering lives on the malleability of the flow of thoughts. And that's how it will always be.

I have consciously chosen to talk of these splinters of things and I am almost certain, in myself, that more important little things will make the events of the world seem laughable. Perhaps it would work, here, to set forth a proportion: between meaning and internalization we have understood more about the way of the world than the knowledge of all the dates of all the major events. In this connection I think of the phenomenological historiography of Jürgen Osterhammel. In his colossal work on the 19th century (*The Transformation of the World*) he begins his first chapter with an account of photography. For him it is the most significant characteristic of that century. We may forget many a name, but in the end the newness of taking pictures gave us, at that time, a permanent grip on the real.

Perhaps I will tell you about the remarkable connection between naturalism and photography. You must give me time to organize my thoughts ...

Julian I want to thank for his letter, which I will next be answering.

All my love, Your R.

83.
Another Look at Vienna

My Dears!

For the sake of loosening up our correspondence – though I am doing most of the writing! – I'd like to tell you about an incident in our history that you surely did not hear or read about anywhere. The last time it was described was in 1909, more than a hundred years ago. As you one day will read, the history of porcelain in Europe is extraordinarily important. I suspect that you have already encountered porcelain: surely this was the case for Nina this Christmas. This year we ate our Christmas dinner off Bohemian "Birkenhammer" porcelain, which by now is easily 110 years old. I would have enjoyed the English service better, called "pottery" as usual in England, but by now it is a good 140 years old and reminds me of my grandmother, to whom it belonged. The service I inherited was only for six. I always admired the similarly blue "Cauldron" stoneware in memory of your great-great-grandmother, at the home of the political commentator Charlotte Teuber-Weckersdorff who also happened to own a set; this set also I inherited. Now I have service for about 40 persons with all the "trimmings." The small green Bohemian "Ellenbogen" service (1840) is the most impressive of all because of its two terrines and the supplemental pieces. And finally, there is a "Davenport" tea service from 1840.

This introduction shows you that I have always had a preference for porcelain or "earthenware." And now I read, in a very early summary of the history of Viennese porcelain, that it was founded by the Dutchman, Claudius Du Paquier in 1714. There were older companies in Sèvres, France and Meissen in Saxony (it was in Sèvres that the peace treaty with Turkey was signed, in 1919...). The reason for this craze of founding porcelain factories in Europe was that the production of porcelain was at first a part of the "weapons industry." The earliest grenades were made of porcelain, and were shaped like an egg, were filled with black powder and furnished with a small fuse. There was a special troop of grenadiers equipped with these "porcelain eggs," hanging from two leather belts they wore across their chest. And when peace returned, one soon had the idea of making other objects out of porcelain: plates, cups, bowls, and dishes.

Even today the Porzellangasse bears witness to where porcelain manufacture took place at the time. It was erected on land owned by the princes of Lichtenstein, for one reason because the land was given free for this use, and for another because one needed the water of the Alserbach, a stream nearby one can no longer see. Up until now Porzellangasse is an informal border of the city: as the city developed, the area around the princes' castle became a noble bourgeois residential address, whereas the other side of the street (of Porzellangasse), became a workers' quarter, one of the earliest in Vienna. After important victories over the Ottoman Empire not only had the famous Prince Eugene dispelled this danger from Vienna and driven the Sultan out of Eastern Europe, but now the development of the city beyond the city's walls became possible for the first time.

I must quickly insert a story. As you have probably noticed already, the Ringstrasse of Vienna was set up as a gorgeous street. – according to the design of Camillo Sitte, the father of modern urban design. Emperor Franz Joseph decided to remove the more or less ruined city wall, around 1855-60. During Napoleon's attack on Vienna, in November 1805, the French artillery had left the venerable city walls in ashes and rubble. We had the city walls thanks to the sizeable ransom that had been won by Leopold V of Babenberg. He had detained the English King Richard I (Lionheart) in Dürnstein after a quarrel during the Third Crusade, and then delivered him to Emperor Henry II. The ransom came to twenty-four tons of silver coins, today worth four billion Euro. With the money Vienna was newly fortified and the casemates had since held up against two "Turkish assaults."

And if I might tell a more recent story, Viktor Adler, the founder of Austrian Social Democracy at the party convention of Hainfeld in 1888-9, had lived in the "Porcelain Quarter" on Berggasse. Since Viktor Adler preferred to live in a workers' quarter he – also a physician – traded his residence in Berggasse with Sigmund Freud… .

The founder of the porcelain factory, Du Paquier, was not particularly successful. He had stolen the "know how" from Meissen and had used a design of Johann Friedrich Böttger for his first products – unpainted and white. The first porcelain experiments in Meissen initially produced only black porcelain, which looked like stoneware from "Wedgewood." Much later, around 1800, Conrad Sorgenthal brought in painting, in the "Indian Pattern" and in the rose decoration that was then fashionable, and for the first time brought some success to Viennese porcelain. However, the years after the founding of the factory did not show a profit. Thus Charles VI, the Emperor at the time, assigned Count Kinski and later Count Chotek to run the factory. Both of these sat on a mountain of defective and unsalable product, many pieces showing defects in the painting decoration due to incorrect firing or other faults. In their "storehouse" lay porcelain that should have brought in 70,000 guilders. The Counts came up with the idea of arranging a lottery. They put up 6000 raffle tickets for sale at one ducat apiece. The buyers could each take home one item per ticket. Only about 2500 tickets were sold, which covered only part of the production costs. (Today, these faulty objects are much sought-after collectors' items and they command an "astronomical" price). As to the production costs, one must know that the workers and porcelain painters were well paid, but also the wood needed for the kiln commanded a high price. The products became more and more precious and expensive according to the fashion of baroque court life, and were far from being something that could be mass produced, as it later would be in the 19th century. And thus the Viennese manufacture of porcelain came to an end in 1864, and was succeeded by the factories in Bohemia.

Viennese porcelain was also called upon to protect the good name of the "Austrian House" at the Congress of Vienna, in 1815. Because of the war the imperial serving equipment had almost entirely been melted down. The store of historic utensils and table decorations had been completely exhausted to pay military expenditures! So the manufacturers were called upon to produce porcelain table service that was fully gilded as a substitute, in order to give the impression that the empire of the imperial court remained intact despite the war against Napoleon. Now, with the "remodeling" of the "Hof- und Silber-kammer" (The Court and Silver Chamber) in the Hofburg of Vienna, which had been maintained unaltered until a few years ago, this "inventory" is no longer on display, or can only be viewed as individual pieces.

The lottery of the unpurchased products was an unusual scheme for covering the outstanding bills. Indeed, Austrian economic history has always seen unusual ideas. Perhaps I will tell you sometime about the adventurer Glave-Kolbielski, who after getting his doctorate under Kant (!) was, among other things, a secret financial advisor to Emperor Franz I, to help him get through the horrible inflation and the crisis in currency and finance for the young empire in 1811. Or about the finance minister Emil Steinbach, who played a role incredibly worth observing, after 1873, when he managed so perfectly the change of currency policy for the entire Danube Monarchy, which produced stability in the economic life of the later monarchy. He was the son of a Jewish goldsmith from Galicia and a perfect example of an amazing career. He was the only imperial minister at whose funeral, conducted in the Scot's Church in Vienna, the Emperor participated in person.

So, in this letter I have brought you a taste of how history can also be. I hope this very different kind of narration amuses you. It is important for you to note how much one story goes over into another, regarding something else that happened in about the same place. What you can read here is all within walking distance in the 9th District. And you must know that you can still feel its aftermath in the streets. This is why I wrote about time in the previous letter, how it seems to come to a head only briefly in our "present." I would so enjoy taking you by the hand and wandering through these alleys and streets, by which it is not just reminiscence and nostalgia are the main themes but a realization that we here can gather the witness of formative forces that over and over again have effects far beyond us.

It would be a false impression for you to understand these incidents merely as history, only as things of the past, over and done with. No: it is the essentials of living, the documentation of lives, that speaks to us across hundreds of years. Forgive me that I must at this point also bring up that terror, evil, violence, extermination, through war and genocide is always bound up with an intention to bring this story of life to an end, or even to cut it off suddenly and brutally. That is what constitutes the monstrosity of National Socialism, its desire to rob us of the life we lived up until now. And if we want to understand it in a nutshell and how it could succeed, I recommend to you Bert Brecht's "The Resistible Rise of Arturo Ui" – or else take up Hermann Broch's *Sleepwalkers*!

An unforeseeably bitter turn has come into the letter. I had to do it: with this you do not rest with a sugary frosting on history, but still will continue to keep hold of my main thread.

With love, your R.

84.
How Prussia Became "Germany"

Dear Nina, Dear Julian, Vicky, and Marie,

The last letter included a variety of information and should be read as a potpourri. It is an example of how, today, stories come from history, and it is apparently the only form that our "we" find readable. Thus the most ridiculous and at the same time most hysterical figure from Bavaria – our "Sisi" – in the history of Habsburg-Lorraine became the symbol of the Danube Monarchy, which itself is then represented only with kitsch and operetta. "Sisi," anorexic and egomaniacal, becomes a pattern for understanding a period which will never really be understandable on those terms; as soon as one leaves the pleasantries of kitsch and operetta behind, the reader becomes skeptical, dubious, and even loses interest. Were I to tell about the Council Hall of Goslar in 1189, about the mortification of Henry the Lion by the Emperor, this has an enormous importance for the Middle Ages; yet that's where readers begin to shake their heads. If I should start constructing a story around a theme, for instance about law or about fashion, or the organization of power, or about religion, I would probably encounter more resistance: then they would say, "I don't really want to know the details all that closely." And this is a problem in the human sciences. While it will be accepted that some knowledge is needed for the understanding of the natural sciences – or, to put it more amusingly, that one ought to master the multiplication tables, the reason there is gravity, the phases of the moon, and the coming and going of the tide – one thinks that for the humanities no background knowledge is needed. As is well known I find it annoying when comprehensibility is then demanded for such a complicated matter as the "Imperial Recess" of 1803 in Regensburg! The much-traveled gentlemen who so eagerly traipse through the holy states of the world with their backpacks, in athletic shoes, showing no respect and taking pictures instead of opening their eyes, hold this remarkable event in Regensburg to be something they can neglect, though it saved the empire.

In reality this last and perhaps most important decision made at the end of the "Holy Roman Empire" affected some five million people. It amounted to the loss of the territorial possessions of the princes on the left bank of the Rhine, which through secularization of church property and of smaller noble estates became available and had to be dealt with. The area from left bank of the Rhine went over to France and the old holy electors from Cologne to Trier lost their positions and their lands; on top of that the local cloisters in that area, the allodial lands, and the Dominican estates fell as compensation for the new regime (You can some time look up in the lexicon what these concepts from the history of law mean!).

I described before how grotesque it was that at the end of the Napoleonic Wars many parts of the area on the right bank of the Rhine were unattached to any empire. Metternich made the unfortunate decision, and had it ratified through the Congress of Vienna, to give these lands to Prussia. Since then there is a "West

Prussia" that fits in with Prussia neither culturally nor in its religious confession. Later an opportunity arose to virtually equate Prussia with Germany.

I do not want to bother you with such details. But still, the knowledge of this complicated history is basic for understanding the "goods gone awry" as Thomas Mann once put it in his characterization of Germany after 1918. He clearly foresaw the danger and the actual tragedy in his daily notices that with this, Prussia "died into" Germany, with the founding of the German Reich in 1872 and with the proclamation of the King of Prussia as the Emperor of Germany, in Versailles. So wrote Eugen Rosenstock-Huessy also, in 1919, and he was correct, rightly lamenting the demise of the old fabric of Germany. It was at the expense of the "liberty" of the Rhineland, at the expense of the "good old law" in Baden-Württemberg as embodied by Ludwig Uhland, for which Hegel wrote its own separate constitution – at the cost of the great history of Saxony and Bavaria, and at the cost of the Hanseatic cities of Hannover and Saxony-Coburg, which would have become a guarantee for the relationship with England. This is how a transformation in the concept of Germany came about. Germany was a "land" with most highly diverse cultures and local laws. That the kings allowed themselves to be bribed by von Bismarck so that he could secure the foundation for the Reich was the end of what had been "the Germans" for the sake of the new "German Reich" – with all that would follow...

I will not fall back into the old lament that finally Austria had to be excluded from what was formerly a federation so that the structureless "colony city" of Berlin could be declared the center. The placelessness and lack of relation about which Berlin today boasts as being a special beacon for the next generation fed directly into the middle of the arbitrariness of a city that does not even have a history comparable to that of Chicago or New York, or San Francisco or Boston. In a sense the Berlin Wall, as the boundary of the GDR from the "West," turns out to be the first structural measure in Berlin's urban development! And were it not for its world famous museums the city would have no shape at all. But the fact that museums in a city always constitute only a depersonalized aestheticization as a sort of cosmetic, they cannot make up for the absence of a genetic evolution. Today Potsdamer Platz is a world-class example of a non-place, and serves as the paradigm of a loss of integration. Every building in this square says only one thing: Forget your neighbors! Of course Albert Speer recognized right off that a city had to create a fabric, had to create relationships, in order to make the "city scape" seem to be city-like; but everything fell under the influence of the madness of National Socialist usurpation. And today Prussia is no longer even a name!

Moreover one immediately notices the influence of Berlin upon Vienna, in the all-pervasive copying of its architecture, a mixture of Bauhaus and Post-National Socialism. The basis for this was the 1939 urban development plan of Vienna, which was set forth by Hanns Dustmann from his office in Berlin. To this day that concept has apparently remained the controlling concept for the urban development of Vienna. The centerpiece of Dustmann's project was the reconfiguration of the Heldenplatz to accommodate the parades of the NSDAP and the army. Apparently, with the erection of both the new buildings in the

Heldenplatz, this concept finally began to be realized in 2017. It is the perfect ruination of a square. After the parliament returns to the old building on the Ring, the buildings and the structures underground will probably be turned over to the package distribution industry, which for some time already has wanted a location in the center of the city for convenient transport connections. And so the destruction of the city of Vienna is the result of this serious political and totalitarian confusion, which would now be easier to overcome if murder had not been canonized as a duty. Paul Celan correctly remarked that "Death is a master from Germany." Only a poet could say such a thing: he grew up in a fundamental distance from this history and nevertheless experienced it, suffered from it, and yet did not let himself to be taken a hostage of his own German history.

Now I have gotten involved in "structure-history." It is because of the lectures of Giulio Argan, *Storia dell' arte come storia della città* ("The History of Art as the History of the City," 1983 – no Eng. tr. – ed.) who years ago, as an art historian, made me aware how to read the secret meaning in the pattern of city layouts. We have the misfortune of continually being confronted with totalitarianism, even now: it is in no way an edifying story. In brief, the project of Dustmann was always on the agenda of urban development in the municipal council, and the more memory was wiped out, the more quickly had one fixed on his plan. The new central train station is right where Dustmann wanted it to be; the new structure of Lastenstrasse between Landesgericht to the Secession of Josef Olbrich, with its continuation over Karlsplatz to the Stadtpark, was foreseen in the 1939 plan – even the new museum quarter behind the two former main museums. The "UNO City" is located right where Dustmann had planned the center for managing south-east Europe, and new residential developments can be found on his plan where today the Per Albin Hansson housing project is located, built in the 50's. This has made land-speculation enormously easier, since thanks to the overall project, one could anticipate that a given city project would be built right where Dustmann would have placed it. Whether also the destruction of the old Praterstern was part of Dustmann's intention I cannot say. In any case the current look of Praterstern can be compared with that of Potsdamer Platz in Berlin.

These sorry reports are not only based on my own feelings. It seems to be the case that for more than a hundred years, urban planning and urban development in Central Europe has the look of people trying to make their hatred of the city reflected in the planning. Again and again I am reminded, for example in looking at the court in front of the once noble Western Train Station of the 50's, that the sense of the architecture which we can recognize as due to Otto Wagner in the circle of Adolf Loos, connected with the efforts of the Bauhaus School in Dessau – that this standard is deliberately disregarded in order to give people the feeling, even with architecture, that harmony and tranquility and contemplativeness is something they do not deserve. This is a remote effect of National Socialism, which has persevered, despite all the vows made in celebratory speeches and inaugural ceremonies for new buildings. Still palpable is a certain hatred of cities which the botanist Patrick Geddes formulated when he raised his voice against the "suburbs" and urban slums. In striking harmony with the National Socialist ideology of a movement for garden cities, a style of urban planning was advanced against cities. Geddes saw urban planning as a way not to ameliorate the unsatisfactory quarters in cities, but to motivate residents to move to the outskirts. His ideal vision of housing was half-urban, half-rural. And even more irritating was the idea that nature's ideal forms ought to be the pattern for design of residential areas – for instance the pattern of snow crystals or of the structure of chlorophyll. His disciple was Lewis Mumford, the forefather of the "green movement" and theoretician of breaking up urban structures. This then went beyond being a program for cities in America, only. I see "hatred of the city" even today, in the new buildings in the heart of the city, which are consciously meant to be foreign bodies, and to confront the history of cities with deeper contempt. And the excuses for this are building costs, economizing, an almost insuperable population demand, and an ascetic aesthetics in planning programs. Alexander Mitscherlich had already diagnosed this in the 1960's as the "inhospitable" character of our cities.

I do not want to bring back the old "*lamentelli.*" I only wanted to tell you that the politics by which construction within the city is being perverted has not escaped me. Maybe in fifty years you will become interested, in an attempt to reconstruct a lost life-world, in finding out at what point things began to go so wrong. At the start, the postmoderns with Charles Jencks and others undertook such researches of this kind, but soon they got involved in the vortex of the fetishistic planning of those in charge of the city and of economic interests – as for instance the misnomer for the building Hans Hollein designed for Stephansplatz in Vienna, the "Haas House."

All the best, I remain, your R.

85.
Social Reality in a Crime Novel

Dear Nina, Dear Julian, Dear Marie, and Dear Vicky,

Both my last letters were more or less entertaining, though one ought to detect the serious undertone throughout. I have often emphasized that architecture especially is a perfect rendering of the social situation – or can be, at least. I have often indicated that in architecture the will and the competence of a society become visible, or in the negative cases of the shacks and barracks in the poor districts and "apartment houses," we witness scorn for the human being, for the lower strata of society.

I want now to turn to a different story. Over and over I remember the clever and pointed representation of Gilbert Keith Chesterton in his *Verteidigung des Unsinns, der Demut, des Schundromans und anderer missachteter Dinge*, an essay published in German in 1917 ("Defense of Nonsense, Cowardice, Trashy Novels, and Other Disreputable Things" – German title of a translation of *A Defense of Nonsense and Other Essays* [New York 1911]). He became famous because of his detective novels in which Father Brown, a clever and ever wily Catholic priest solves the most difficult cases of crime and regularly dupes the police. With this as my "study-template" I became forever a more skillful reader of crime novels, from Jerry Cotton to Agatha Christie.

If I were to select two examples form the rich store of such novels, it would be Jerry Cotton's *The Tiger of Manhattan* and *Aktion Schwarzer Tod*. Perceptive readers of my letters have surely realized already that for me an old "Wild West" film is not simply a "shoot 'em up" movie: so also a crime novel is not only a sort of literature for when you have the flu or a headache. Both the novels I named open with a dangerous situation. It is literally a matter of saving the right. In the one case, if the Tiger should succeed in his last great attack, law and order would be destroyed and society would fall into anarchy. Jerry Cotton is operating within the stable rule of law. As we have known since St. Augustine, this makes for a state that is orderly, albeit in different ways. If the *latrocinium magnum* should succeed, the entire community is transformed into a gang of thugs. We know of it on a smaller scale in Hollywood films, where a village, usually, is in the hands of an unscrupulous villain. Imagine that the state monopoly on power turns into an illegal force: this in any event is the situation in which Jerry Cotton must now assert himself. The Tiger has the opportunity to take over the power of the state. This is not something unknown in European history; and on 6 January 2021 this almost came about in Washington.

In *Aktion Schwarzer Tod*, basically the opposite is the case. Righteous fanatics want to get the power for once and for all, so as to put into effect the sort of justice Theseus practiced when, imitating Heracles, he killed the blacksmith Procrustes who tried to bring about "equality" in his smithy on Mount Cordallos. The smith could not be dissuaded from believing that equality could only be reached by stretching those who were short or cutting off the legs of those who were tall. The fanatics of righteousness likewise bring the basic order into question and have to be stopped. It is interesting that in the novels thugs and killers, and the underground fanatics of righteousness, are all put on the same level. All of them endanger the legal order since their primary, though not ultimate, way of proceeding is to gain power through violence. None of these groups shy away from violent deeds. And for this purpose a pretty little list of crimes can be brought on board: extortion, coercion, torture, murder, disruption of the social order, terror.

Their goal can be distinguished in terms of the desires that the several groups pursue. The criminal wants to achieve his position of power through acts of force and wipes out anybody who gets in his way. He wants to bring on a regime of terror. The goal of the underground looks totally different. They strive for power by means of terror, and yet they think that if they should finally achieve power in the state, a peaceful community would "automatically" result – that justice will dominate, as well as "*sophrosyne*" (peaceable conciliation), the political virtue we know of from Plato. Once the last enemy is driven out all will be resolved. It is important that in the novel, fanaticism about power is likened to fanaticism about righteousness, that both of them destabilize civil behavior of the community.

The arrival of our hero onto the scene is not simply a matter "here's the wrong-doing" and "here's the danger:" to the contrary he must from the beginning already understand the social situation. A sociologist who "understands" must be clued in on the inherently "conflictual" structure of the community. And in American society such internal contradictions are sharper than elsewhere. The conflict between rich and poor, white and black, is nearly irreconcilable and insoluble. The social "stalemate" might seem calm, but this is far from true. The daughter of one of the "super-rich" declares to the detective, "We are people like everybody else." She receives the ironic answer that there is just one little difference: having 50 million dollars is not like other people. The super-rich will not be visiting a supermarket, they will just skim off the profits it beings in. The well-off live in their palatial estates; they take walks on the grounds of their mansions, and think only of their own welfare. They live in brilliance and luxury; the others live in the poor quarter, in dreary studio apartments, and run out of money on the tenth of every month. In the novel we encounter both these worlds, these different kinds of people, and we accompany the cop with his special power in a world that moves between them – for there do exist between these two worlds certain dark connections.

We do not have to pick up a crime novel to know that between wealth and crime there can be a deep connection. Also we know that crime can create wealth. And it is thought paradoxical that the criminal's most devout wish is to "launder" his ill-gotten gains. There are two ways to do this, and they are familiar to us, too: one must either "control a market," as for instance by trading in land or the necessities of life. And then there is the "underworld structure" of power, the bordellos and gambling dens. This is how the in-between world is created, in which the millionaire and the criminal can meet, often by accident. The millionaire Fremont bumps into Nelson, the "Tiger of Manhattan." And one word leads to another. The millionaire wants to build a weapon factory on a piece of land that belongs to Nelson. It is no wonder that because of his interest, Nelson is invited to the millionaire's home, where only the "best" of society might be met. Any "social update" show on TV conveys such impressions. Among the supposed elite we encounter shady characters. From even the most glamorous events – like the Opera Ball in Vienna – the criminal element is not absent. It is not necessary for the big-time criminal to make this solicitation, which might wreck his "cred": but he still needs to give a signal to the others, poor and déclassé, to achieve his ends.

In the novel poverty is sharpened since it is a stigma first and foremost that marks the "Afro-Americans": the economic contrast is further intensified by the "racial" one. It is above all an imaginary disparity since neither a rich black man becomes white, nor does a poor white man become black. It is this irrational anger that Donald Trump was also able to exploit. However, the poor blacks are the poorest.

We know that the protests since the 1950's have not had a lasting influence. Even in the case of Martin Luther King no lasting relaxation in the tension of this social problem was achieved. And the "assassinations" of blacks by the police, in the last two years, revealed not only the deep insecurity of an authority that thinks it can only enforce its will with firearms but also the widespread frustration of the socially excluded classes. The results are forcible acts, assaults, and sudden explosions of protest that smack of civil war – and yet the results are barren and superficial.

The excluded opposition does not remain inactive. Grand initiatives and plans are floated. Plague-bacteria are cultured that will infect everyone and will spread the "black death" all across the USA. These days it is not so far from a James Bond movie. In the 30's it only had to do with the USA and yet with Bond it always has to do with the whole world. In the earlier Jerry Cotton novels it was only about blackmailing a city. If rats are able to bring New York to a standstill, city institutions will be forced to negotiate with the criminals. And that is the character of the new dimension of crime. It is a question of doom or capitulation, of the infamous element surviving or being annihilated. The righteous want to win and they stand on the brink of victory.

The "plot" of *Tiger of Manhattan* is not essentially different. This fellow Nelson succeeded to get his hands on atomic weapons. And he, too, threatened New York with destruction. The alternative comes to the fore: capitulation or doom. If "Tiger" wins, the illegal becomes legal, order becomes terror. Nelson directs these criminal exploits dressed in hunter's clothes. He is loose, relaxed, and is counting the minutes before his takeover of power.

We read that "Tiger" not only has murders carried out but becomes a murderer himself. In the conflict Nelson's girlfriend is strangled. For "security" he tosses her into the swimming pool in his great villa. A woman next door just happens to observe this. After thinking things over she decides to turn him in. So Tiger gets arrested. At the police station everybody recognizes that the life of the key witness is in danger. She is taken off and hidden in a nearby country house by the sheriff.

This same sheriff reveals the witness's whereabouts for $250,000.00. Although Cotton accompanies her to the court she falls into the hands of the killers. As usual the murder of the witness is a cat and mouse game. And so the court cannot try the charges. Without a witness the accused must be freed. If one wants to analyze it further, right in the midst of the American enforcement of law the court becomes dysfunctional: because of a single corrupt policeman the whole structure of criminal law falls to the ground like a house of cards.

The version presented in the crime novel reveals how shaky the situation is for one who would protect the law. Partly, the police are corrupt, and the court is not really motivated to tangle with "Tiger" – in fact it is the concern for oneself that predominates. Who freely chooses to play the hero? One or two shots from an ambush and the whole affair turns into a blank piece of paper. On the other hand, the civil laws become in a paradoxical way a Magna Carta for the criminal. There is no countervailing force. Who will raise his voice in the parliament? Will the president say anything? Who will speak out against the worst assault on democracy? We know by now that a strange community of interests among the economy, criminality, and politics is not only proving to be durable but that it has brought about a new style of politics. Gradually one comes to recognize the weakening of social policy. Gradually we perceive that art, science, and the media are all collaborators in this project. Maybe it is at the Opera Ball that still larger ambitions might be hatched. The dismantling of the American Constitution looms on the horizon.

And that is the reassuring "feint" in the crime novel: Jerry Cotton and his team are not giving up on this country! One mustn't make it so easy for the enemy! The FBI man begins to look for clues. Soon he notices that the law has been trampled underfoot. He is righteously indignant. He is convinced he will be victorious, but if he wants to win he must be unusually clever. He is backed up by a team of specialists. They belong to all "races" – black, Indian, trappers, farmers, and city dwellers. The special investigation is managed by Mr. High. Along with the men and women of the FBI he embodies the spirit of the American Constitution. This coup by the "Tiger of Manhattan" cannot go unpunished.

The FBI man fulfills all our fantasies of "can-do." High and Cotton together embody the beneficence of America. As an FBI man he cuts a figure slender but sinewy, large but rangy, courageous and fit, sportive but tender when he needs to be. He gets into brawls but soon finds himself back on his feet. So he has a heart ready for any possibility, but no patience. Our hero is shocked about how the National Guard handles a protest of Afro-Americans and has a feeling for the needs of the poor. His special attribute is that he lives strictly by the law and does nothing extralegal but always stays within the law. Very important, given the current situation of the police, is Cotton's decision never to be guilty of assault. There is to be no sort of "legitimate illegality," even if the opposition is throwing cobblestones or Molotov cocktails. So he is glad to be accused of being a square whose hands are clean. For him the Constitution is sacred, and likewise for him morality and law are set in stone.

Our evaluation of the novel's hero is now put to a special test, for the state stands on the brink of devastation. This does not keep him from obeying the law. It is clear to him that there can be no universal righteousness ever since the laws were invented, but they must nevertheless be followed and defended. That's what men like him are for.

The faithful conviction of Jerry Cotton is not at all naïve nor an illusion. He understands that the political situation forces one to cast aside any optimistic liberalism. Some sort of world-encompassing harmony is not in the cards, and probably a social Darwinism in the manner of Herbert Spencer is a more realistic attitude in which he could take part. He sees himself as a skeptic, a cautious man who puts no trust in the promises of a theoretical man. He sees this very clearly, as soon as he compares everyday life to what goes on in a police station. He could even laugh about that if it wasn't so sad. If only a little of this ideal is to be realized, it would need administration and organization. So the administrative state is the goal of any community. If it works as so many theoreticians of the state think, then we would come into the political order consisting of *homines bonae voluntatis*. But in reality this is the naïve dream of a madman. And once again we come upon a division of labor. The police must justify their institution with a defense against danger. They can do nothing more! Conversely, he, with his "special" rights at the edge of legality, must at least keep the evil before himself, front and center.

In a change of scene Jerry Cotton appears in person. Again there is an invitation to the weapons manufacturer's. The elite arrive and leave, and he feels out of place. Already for some time the honorable men have made their "peace" with the criminal. In "society" the tables have turned: Jerry Cotton is the outsider, not Nelson. The FBI man nevertheless consciously goes up to the evening's main characters, and greets the weapons manufacturer and the criminal. Right out of the blue Cotton launches into accusations: Nelson is accused of doing many things, and there's no use denying it. At this moment his position of power is brought down; one has gathered proof of the murders that had been committed. The Tiger had wanted at first to represent the whole thing as a personal smear campaign, as a nefarious libel: all the testimony against him was sworn out of envy. Soon Nelson recognizes that he is no match for these accusations, and so he will answer the attack with violence. But his attempt goes awry and the top man from the FBI has won.

He is completely drained. The day-long investigations, the many sleepless nights, finally catch up with him. Then the beautiful eyes of the millionaire's daughter straighten him up again. As the most beautiful woman on the East Coast, Caroline can set into motion his last ounce of strength. Her diadem with the Moonlight Diamonds dazzles his eyes, not to mention her "blue eyes flashing like a field of bachelor buttons…" After all he had brought back the diadem of daughter Caroline after Nelson had allowed it to be stolen. The diadem is worth a million and a half – all the guests know it. She offers him a drink and the hero takes it. "Her laughter warmed Braddock Avenue all the way to the end of the block." The end is the beginning and makes all things new: the manufacturer's righteousness, the businesses, New York, and of course the USA. His acceptance of the drink is a conciliation with the corrupt society. So all is back in order once again.

Much later Friedrich Dürrenmatt brought a similarly corrupt relationship onto the stage, in the play *Der Mitmacher* (*The Collaborator*, 1973). Criminals, police, and undertakers share the power. And of course the work must end at the place where Jerry Cotton would have given in, if it were not for the enchanting Caroline, who likewise in Dürrenmatt was the girlfriend of the Chief of Police.

Now, two thoughts are called for: Apparently it is love that breaks the bonds of law, the violent deeds, the political collapse and the social imbalance – for a short time. But this cannot last. The realist Dürrenmatt describes in the foreword to his play the important role that corruption plays in a totalitarian system: it humanizes the mechanisms of repression. In the opposite circumstances it destroys the rule of law. We can choose in which circumstance we find ourselves again, or still, or no longer. Horror stories are quite the best teachers for sociologists.

And with this, God save us! Your R.

86.
Are Crime Novels Frivolous?

Dear Loved Ones,

Probably it is not easy to figure why I made a rather shallow crime story the subject of the previous letter. With this letter I want to give you the explanation. As you will probably hear one day, the first real crime stories were from China. I think it was during the 14th century they were written. The most famous of them, still in the genre of an adventure novel, was *The Outlaws of the Marsh* (also translated *Water Margin*). Mostly they are stories in which the mayor or a higher official of a frontier town has to help maintain law and order. He knows that beyond his borders lurk enemies, as always, who are preparing to invade the city. And spies of all sorts are seeking to destabilize the social condition of the little city. With perspicacity, calm, and clever tactics the official succeeds to turn back the threats against the city until military reinforcements arrive.

When I read those stories years ago, I was struck by the importance accorded to bureaucracy, the hierarchical structure of the families, the awkward courtesies and verbal expressions with which encounters formally begin with an exchange of symbols.

With that I broach a topic that became standard in literature from the 18th century onward. We know of important works that reach into the realm of the crime story, whether *The Picture of Dorian Gray* by Oscar Wilde or Edgar Allen Poe's *Murder in the Rue Morgue*. In the 18th century, Friedrich Schiller made a completely different contribution with his novel, *The Criminal of Lost Honor*.

Over and over I have to remember that nobody knows this tale of Schiller. This has always annoyed me quite a lot since it is a great masterpiece! I have to mention it for two reasons: the first is that here Schiller recounts as it were the story of an unfortunate man who nevertheless did not cease to be aware of his guilt; the second is that Schiller already, before the publication of Kant's Categorical Imperative, puts this canon of duty into the mouth of the evil-doer and has him turn himself in. Whoever can make use of this suggestion ought to do so! In a half hour one learns about the *demi-monde* of an innkeeper who has descended into crime and carries on with his misdeeds, although his feelings of guilt teach him a better way. I would be very happy if any of you have a look at Schiller!

But to go back: Jerry Cotton of course belongs on the lowest literary level. I wanted to quickly note that this "asphalt literature" – thus did Josef Goebbels name the literature about city life, at the beginning of the 20th century – later verged on kitsch. One distinguishing feature of pure kitsch is that the citation of reality in the representation of a social situation undergoes no further elaboration but is presented merely like a photo, or is merely put in a spotlight. For the crime author this is enough. For professional authors the higher challenge would be to describe exactly the hardship of the poor man's measly life, his illusory hopes that collapse into disappointment, but the crime novelist uses him merely as illustration. It serves as the grounding for the description of the horrid criminal situation, something that even politics seeks to exploit to justify its ameliorative measures.

The illustration of the social situation is not "elaborated;" instead the author calls upon the reader for "what he's read in the papers" and erects upon this his desolate story. The "plutocrat," the criminal, and the "policeman," who would also prefer to be living among "better" society, open up the interplay of irregular power and punishable crimes. It should be clear to any "photo-realist" in our current art scene that the depiction of a reality gone off the rails does not yet make a claim to being art. Artistic "elaboration" alters reality at the same time that it raises up the standard of art.

In the crime novel, which can be counted as trivial literature, social reality is a more or less flimsy justification for crime. The "grand architectural ideas" of criminal planning, such as we find in Edgar Wallace, must be used to make it halfway convincing. But at that point it is no longer about credibility but about the duel between the criminalist and the criminals. The entire underworld all along the Thames has to pay for this duel, and the entire "underclass" from Soho and the East End is somehow entangled in the plan.

The attraction and seductiveness of the "whodunit" consists in how the long-anonymous powers get hauled up into the light of day – the same enjoyment of hauling up that produces suspicious accounts which the electronic communications media so quickly circulate that they achieve the rank of "conspiracy theories." Whereas Jerry Cotton was still a simple-minded criminalist who had his own way of defining the boundaries of his investigative methods, James Bond had to become more "direct," had to kill in a battle of "it's you or me" and carry out the intentions of the MI5 of Bletchley Park in unconventional ways. He managed to do so from Korea to Peru and from Sidney to Stockholm.

In all these stories there is a strange affinity with the assumption that with the increase of technology and the accumulation of capital, mysterious powers come to rule the world. All the powerful people in the world are mere puppets, and unconfirmed or even absurd information is just nonsense. As if the power were not already big enough there must be even bigger powers behind it. This began in the detective novels that invented a typical framework for their stories, which is why they included capitalism as an ingredient in the concept of the story, for which their readers did not consult the *Communist Manifesto* – a deeper social analysis by social scientists – but made sense of their world along the lines of

Jerry Cotton or Edgar Wallace. And if we needed a passable interpretation of kitsch we could find it in our interpretation of this literature of entertainment. This is not an expression of disdain, but rather that all the essential aspects of socialization are brought in, processed, and at the same time corrupted by the crime. Chesterton led us to this insight!

The depictions in the crime novels I have pointed to actually begin from the principle that "property is theft." This reproach seems justified when we think of those vulgar people who want nothing less than to rule the world. Pierre-Joseph Proudhon is usually considered the originator of this moral reproach. In truth the principle had been published two generations earlier. The proponent of liberal natural law, the Girondist and propagator of freeing the black slaves – Jacques Pierre Brissot – had published in 1870 *Recherches philosophiques sur le droit de propriété et sur le vol consideré dans sa nature*. And he had been a key player – literally – during the storming of the Bastille, for he handed over to the ringleaders the keys to the prison. He advocated war against Austria, and had a clear scheme for establishing a liberal republic. In 1793 he fell victim to Robespierre's frenzy of murder, and came to his end under the guillotine at the age of 39.

The history of such a slogan as this includes the strangest and most surprising twists and turns. More than 1500 years ago even the little-known Church Father Basil found it difficult to pass off theft as a legitimate acquisition: he wrote κλοπὴ γὰρ ἡ ἰδιάζουσα κτῆσις ("taking possession as an individual [ἰδιάζουσα] is theft"). The term "as an individual" is a real surprise.

This almost forgotten Church Father did not have revolution in mind, as Brissot did and Proudhon after him. In the 4th century natural law was still a rare concept: only by the time of Scholasticism did it became a favored hobby-horse among theologians with ambitions as social philosophers. Basil's intention was to make the order of property within the young monasteries or monastic "societies" communistic. His ideal was the "propertyless" monk – and in many areas at that time the church was using a principle of obedience, poverty, and humility. This completely changed in the early Middle Ages. The many church reforms offer testimony about how a return to poverty might be brought about. Still, the road from the "primitive communism" of the monks to the socialism of Proudhon was a long one.

In the debate about property in the 19th century the analysis made it clear that even a complete transformation of the state and the legal order would only make another state and order possible. Thus, the distribution of property and wealth, as such, would not change one iota. If one will not recognize the state he cannot recognize the law: in particular, the genuine and self-respecting anarchist has no concept of property and thus cannot say anything about property, even that property is theft. This was the evolution of thought from Brissot to Proudhon. Thus the anarchist cannot offer a solution, though this was the special conviction, or illusion, of the Russian anarchists. If property is to be theft, this is not the conclusion of an analysis, or an outcome from social conditions: rather, the statement was always meant as a provocation. Basically it was a smear directed against the rich, and against the propertied.

Now we must return to philology. When Basil used "*idiazousa*" he meant by it a private acquisition of one's own (*eigentumlich*), which the monk must reject. If "property" (*Eigentum*) comes from *proprietas* (lat.), and *proprietas* from *idiotes* (gr.), and from *idios* (gr.), Basil had in mind the accusation that for the monk, his "own property" (*eigenes Eigentum*) would be a theft from the cloister. So now we have to focus on this little word "own" (*eigen*). The Church Father asserted the view that there should not be any *eigenes Eigentum* ("own property"). If Proudhon or Brissot had studied Basil more closely it would have to have occurred to them that their critique, the provocation they used, pertained only to a certain historical definition of property. But they also wanted to stretch theft to apply to the modern definition of property. And this brings up another philological problem: *propriété* (fr.) was primarily land-property, ground. And thus *propriété* would in every case be a matter of theft. In the German language the French slogan ("*La propriété, c'est le vol*") was thoughtlessly repeated without making clear which kind of property is involved. If we translate the insult in German with "property" (*Eigentum*) we are talking about any asset, whether moveable or immobile. With this a difference from the French already creeps in. If we reverse the interpretation of the statement then the only possession that is just is the one that is achieved through labor or the exchange of labor. All the goods of this world, if they do not belong to the storehouse of our biosphere, like air or water, should only be exchanged through labor.

Our investigation is not over. Subsequently, the German and the French senses became assimilated, for in the phase of "ideologization" the subtle differences between *propriété* and *Eigentum* were worn away. The Marxian concept of property soon overcame the legal-historical concept, or brought it under an ideological interpretation. Proudhon did not care about this since he had a legal order for the future in mind, in which such historical differentiations would be erased anyway.

Fritz Mauthner in his very smug way saw through this shift in very important political concepts, for a future society. In particular, in his "futurological" shift, terms are always slipping as if on black ice, lose their connection with history and with philological logic, and find themselves in a no-man's-land between criticism and poetry. In this kind of speech the reference to reality is severely conditioned; and with it one can scold, and call everyone a reactionary; the petit-bourgeois philistine and the pedant reap only ridicule and scorn. In this respect Marx was a model since he called the Romantics like Chateaubriand and Joseph de Maistre sycophants.

And now one must make a rather pointed remark. If property is theft, then the genus of property is theft; but if theft presupposes the concept of property the argument becomes circular. Theft is then always an appropriation and becomes my property. If there were no property in the world then nothing could be stolen. We already have the definition of theft from criminal law. In every state of the world it is the unlawful and deliberate appropriation of someone else's movable thing. One could easily take the definition from criminal law and observe that the robbing of property only occurs if the concept of ownership is a prerequisite for all property crimes. The concept of ownership is also the prerequisite to all rights regarding things. Whoever eliminates property from the world will have to do the same with the concept of theft. One could put it in a nutshell with the comment, where there is no thief there is no plaintiff. Both ought, and both can, no longer exist. It could be that such a society should exist but so far such instances have remained within the frame of an early medieval cloister. It is impossible that a concept spoken by our current language can be dragged into the role of a predicate for a statement that belongs to the future. Proudhon would have had to say: property loses any legal status, forfeits its legal origin as well as its legal implications; and so there can no longer be any theft.

We have made a mistake that was already made by Brissot and Proudhon. We needed the concept of right in order to say what we have said. Even if we ourselves believe in a general accessibility to all assets, that it does not have to be established in law any longer, such an opinion is very poetic. Still, we do not want to drop law completely. This is the poetic principle of the revolutionaries, of the do-gooders, not simply to do without law since they need it in order to maintain their own future order. They need the law for it is and always was the sum of valuable and historical statutes in states and in all communities, of any future and any past configuration. Even the commune of Otto Mühl, in its disregard for any legal order no matter how informal, has only become derelict, if not a terrorist organization. Even socialistic communities need lawful life and the operation of rules. Existing law (*lex lata*) derives property from the objective law, and from property other laws are implied. The *lex lata* derives theft from the concept of property. And so also some laws-to-be (*lex ferenda*) derived from natural law, if a state organization or an order of law is recognized at all, will have to recognize a legal character for property. It is amusing that in the encyclical "*Quadragesimo anno*" the titles to property were only discriminated against when they accrued from "*usura vorax*" – that is, from usury. In principle, a distinction has always been maintained between property and theft.

A reader may well object that this longwinded investigation has only confirmed what he already thought anyway. But if one wants to be committed to a kind of physical positivism, in the manner of Otto Neurath, one must always be ready with a tight explanation of any topic, even one that seems in itself obvious. It ought by now to be clear to us that the famous sentence of Proudhon, despite its glamorous history, despite the murder of Brissot in the Place de la Concorde, despite the idealistic conception of a Church Father, is in itself far from being a logical statement. The logic of law forbids this, nor will political history allow it to stand.

I wanted to tell you this in a most definitive way.

I greet you very warmly. I hope that your progress in school will not be too much disrupted in January of 2021 by the pandemic.

All my love, your R.

87.

Natura naturans, natura naturata

Dear Nina, Dear Julian, Dear Marie and Vicky,

Years before my serious accident, I was already a regular guest at the exercise club "Holmes Place." I was advised to take my impending retirement as an opportunity to basically make a change in my lifestyle: on the one hand cycling, which gave me great pleasure and on the other hand a daily visit to the gymnastics club, would together bring about a meaningful improvement of my condition and physical health.

It was to be expected that I would make completely different acquaintances at Holmes Place. Likewise, I admired the trainers who with iron perseverance wanted to bring about the fitness of their clients, which in some cases succeeded. It was also at Holmes Place that I met Wolfgang Hirt, who came to be integrated into the "Heiner Circle." To this acquaintance in turn I owe finding my physiotherapist, Heidi Goldfarb, later on, who put me back on my feet after my accident. Since I attended the group gymnastics together with my wife in the early morning our squad became a fixture, under Daniela Cook, from which we profited greatly. Daniela Cook was an ambitious exercise teacher who combined exercise with guidance in nutrition. Later she also became my "personal trainer," and not infrequently I groaned under Cook's merciless dictates.

Very quickly at the Holmes Place the social structure came into view. The trainers were the "human capital" of the company. Their being human by no means mitigated the regime to which they were subjected. The permanent employees received very modest pay, and the "freelance" trainers had to pay a hefty "rent" for their opportunity to meet potential candidates for private training. This situation was significantly worsened when a rigorous system of control was exercised within the group of employees and "freelancers." This showed the well-known phenomena often observed in sociology, that there are always some who think they have a better position in the company if they denounce their colleagues or drop negative remarks about each other. Thus, resentment and caution were the prevalent moods within the company. Switching out of personnel took place frequently and caused a distinct insecurity. Only a few of the clients noticed the bad working conditions – they were indifferent to it – but from year to year even those who seemed to be completely blind to such things noticed that the "working atmosphere" was gradually deteriorating. The frequent changes in the management, the attempts by newly appointed club managers to distinguish themselves by changing the gymnastics equipment every six months, and the continuous changes in the various training promotions worsened the climate more and more and stood in strong contrast with the company's advertising, which had been posted all over the place, predictably in English, alluding to Juvenal's famous phrase: "One Life. Live well."

With this echo of *mens sana in corpore sano*, the common but largely incorrect interpretation of Juvenal had been adopted. The poet, for his part, was criticizing people's fear which led them to ask the gods for health, and arguing that precisely for this reason "common sense" should be maintained. The original line was, *orandum est, ut sit mens sana in corpore sano* ("what you should pray for is that you have a sound mind in a sound body" – *Sat*. 10. 356). He is not talking about an interaction between body and mind, but is saying that it is not enough to manage one's physical health since the healthy mind will by no means arise automatically. I describe this situation as a showcase for the observation that working in the same company by no means creates a community. The opposite had occurred. As far as the staff was concerned, their relationship with management was a matter of exploitation, which was well camouflaged as if it were voluntary; as far as the clients were concerned, they were downright indifferent to the arbitrary behavior of management. Even before the onset of the pandemic, because of which the operation had to be closed, the trainers had been almost completely dismissed and thus the "climate" in the club grew palpably worse. Only one trainer was allowed to stay, one who as a master of intrigue had apparently denounced most of her colleagues.

You may find this description interesting for the insight it provides about my everyday life, but for me it was interesting for two other reasons. One was a very good illustration of the difference between the sexes. Most of the female visitors were not so much interested in physical fitness, but to improve their look. Natural anthropological features were to be modified by forcing them to conform with the common ideal of beauty, so the concern was for hips that had become wide, and arm muscles and thighs that were relatively weak. Of course for the younger generation there were also athletic ambitions, which is why they performed their exercises with incredible discipline, even doggedly. Among the ladies one very rarely sees a bit of nonchalance, or of self-irony, or a conscious concentration on the practical goal of "maintenance" in the sense of "One Life. Live it well." In the case of the men, most of the young ones are exceedingly ambitious. Perhaps a childhood dream slumbers within them of someday becoming a world champion in weight training. Quite often one observes with what extraordinary determination the dumbbells are lifted and with what doggedness the torments are overcome, which of course must ever be increased, more and more. When I was still going to Holmes Place regularly there was a sort of "strong young men's club" whose goal was to lift some 200 kilos. If I should happen to meet one of these members today, they would complain about their damaged joints, herniated discs, and other severe impairments. It was only to be expected that this sort of extreme strength-training would have such consequences. The men who have reached retirement are much more relaxed. For them, especially cycling on the "home trainer" constitutes a modest fight against aging. Most of the time they interrupt their training regime and spend more time chatting. Presumably, this is far healthier than lifting 180 kilos. The third group one encounters is the working people who "take a break" from their office routine, hurry to the gym at lunchtime, and get back to work on time. They don't talk. They don't chat. They don't look left or right. Then there are the evening visitors, who are mostly 35-year-old unmarried men who after finishing their exercise set about grooming themselves extensively with various creams and lotions. These have a good dose of narcissism.

I am sure there are other phenomena one could describe. For me, gymnastics suddenly became important because thanks to a good physical condition I had been able to survive the accident. However, I was no longer able to continue with my previous regime in full. Above all, I was deprived of cycling. Because of the contusion of the lungs, I have a considerable undersupply of oxygen and am incapable of sustained exercise, and so I endanger my daily life for I have developed an understandable predilection for quietism. As important as it was to try to continue to follow the conditioning exercises, any enjoyment of them had disappeared. The result was diabetes and its attendant side effects. My beloved cycling had been quite spoiled by back pain and shortness of breath. Now it is only in my mind that I may wander through the Danube floodplains and visit my favorite places there; now and then the pictures stored in my telephone help me. I will probably never have those exciting experiences in the flooded floodplain again, and that silence, and having to push the bike through the water. I remember very well the strange scene when I was walking along a path through the water and a swan swam towards me. Probably we thought to ourselves, what was the other doing there? I stopped, the swan stopped, and we looked at each other in amazement. In the end I turned away and the swan continued on its course, probably enjoying its superiority for being able to swim.

All these experiences, for which I can thank the bicycle, were at the same time a prerequisite for helping me getting through obvious impairments after the accident without psychological damage. At this point memories begin to play an even more important role, which are more than just imaginings. Now in waking dreams I ride along the two large meadows and still see the tender green of the grain and in its midst the glow of the poppies. It was never understood why I preferred to dwell on such views of nature, admiring nature's sovereignty, trying to speak its mysterious language of colors.

It is time to remember that *natura* was the most successful word from the Latin vocabulary. It is time to remember, finally and again, that in spite of the "sympathetic" sides of nature, a regime of necessity and also expediency can be seen in it, and how it determines what we call laws and causes. In our emotional reactions we express what we feel is our "natural" reaction and these possess such certainty that we can only with difficulty reconcile them with this lawfulness of nature. As little as I was able to recognize any essence of nature in gymnastics, its being a kind of movement alien to the nature of man, so much the more was nature familiar to me in the contemplation of the silver poplars near Fischamend or the hidden nut trees in Eckartsau. It was exactly this contrast in remembering more and more clearly that we as humans have distanced ourselves more and more from what is "natural" for us, that on the other hand, through this distance from nature we were able to perceive its beauty, its sublimity, which expresses itself in a single violet popping through the snow in spring.

You will find it difficult to comprehend, but since late antiquity we were only able to "come to terms" with nature when we began to distinguish between *natura naturans* ("nature in process of naturing") and *natura naturata* ("nature already natured"). In the first case, nature gives birth to nature, and has almost that divine quality that the pantheists adore in it: we began to think about *natura naturans* within the framework of mythology, in the perception of its mysterious power about which we know nothing. But in the second case nature, although identical with the first nature, is now an object of our research and knowledge. And it is against precisely this latter nature that we had to oppose *our* history, *our* consciousness, in order to be able to assume the role that we have developed since the Middle Ages: namely, knowing that as human beings we belong to the natural order but at the same time we also lay claim to a place outside of nature. Therefore, our history has been written differently and is something quite other than natural history. Even this thought – which is not old! – only reveals a dilemma, which was raised in the 19th century, with on the one hand Charles Darwin and *The Descent of Species* presenting natural history, while on the other hand Hegel presented an outline of human history. The one history seems to need no morality, whereas the other describes only this.

You must excuse me for touching upon such an important topic only cursorily. I hope that you will forgive me this jumping around and that it will nevertheless stimulate you to think about this carefully. Above all, you must get to know nature anew, in its reality, not at the dissecting table and not in the laboratory where we have cut it up and tortured it. In the meantime, it cries out to us in its dangerous catastrophic events, in the combination of climate change and exceptional meteorological conditions. Just after the pandemic subsided, weather patterns in Central Europe hit us hard, as they did in China, and we don't yet know if we're even ready to recognize the extent of the dangers we face. After all, previous records of weather patterns have been far surpassed and are now more complicated: we face a devastation we do not believe to be possible. Hundreds of hectares are burning in the U.S. and Canada destroying forests, while in Siberia the ground's permafrost is slowly softening. What answer do we have? What answer will we be able to give?

With concerned and perplexed greetings, I remain your R.

88.
Why Property Cannot be Theft

Dear Nina, Dear Julian, Dear Marie and Dear Vicky,

I want to return to a topic from two letters ago (Letter 86). I can understand if this circumstantial analysis puts you off, but it is common that one is confronted with an account that at first glance seems articulate and conclusive, while under closer observation it comes into view that this is not always and absolutely the case. In the construction of relations between two or three propositions, in logic, there is the concept of the *quaternio terminorum*. This means that with the syllogizing of two or three propositions that however do not actually fit together, a further proposition might be yielded that in the end must be declared false. So these two terms (*propriété* and *Eigentum*) well deserve a closer look. Our procedure for doing so can be connected with logical empiricism.

Very often one thinks logical empiricism is much ado about nothing, lots of talk, an occupation for idlers. This is not so. It is the explanation of what is supposedly self-evident. The method applies in a variety of disciplines that are not so easy to unify. I have already pointed out that the French word for property is derived from a Latin root, which in turn is anchored in the ancient legal order. In the mingling of the French with the German from the 18th century on, this idea apparently became detached from the juristic sphere, whether of civil or criminal law. The cause of the confusion is that slogan, which came into public usage due to its idealistic brevity. In addition the time was ripe that such thoughts should be aired and threaten the rich with a "declaration of war." One is reminded of the motto, "Peace for the huts, war against the palaces." Georg Büchner circulated this in his *Hessian Courier* in 1834 and was the "ringleader" for the revolutionary groups. In this state of the public mood, "Property is theft" was on everyone's lips and was a fitting characterization of social relationships in German pre-socialism.

The second step was the logic we always encounter in law that is used as a principle for analyzing the logic underlying this motto. Along with this, one was to take into account as a principle of the historical school – not to expand the field of semantic meaning excessively – but instead to stay within the structure of meanings. Despite the pious church hymn, "Lord I am your property...," one cannot transpose the connection of property with theft into another field – whether it is theological or folkloric, let alone a musical one. Thus the primary instruments for the investigation are philology and the logic of law. By combining these the incompetence in the formulation of the political slogan becomes visible This might be fine for a slogan but it immediately reveals itself as a political impossibility. Enough said.

Next, the merging of logical empiricism with a "social grammar" as it were, became awkward and suffered considerable damage in the general process of ideologization during the 19th century. Overall, this investigation via the history of ideas attempts to reconstruct the linguistic and legal-political reality. This is a fine Austrian tradition which got its start in the philosophical "Vienna Circle."

At a time when, because of the pandemic, behavioral measures for the protection of the public are being decreed but no longer meet with widespread political consensus, such "finger-exercises" as we went through in that previous letter become important. We hear everywhere that since the early part of 2020 the laws protecting freedom have been curtailed in this area, that a state is here using the pandemic as a pretext to recapture authority. It is particularly grotesque to claim that the restriction of public life is causing greater damage than the cases of sickness and death. Opposition groups suddenly seemed empowered to set loose violent protests so that, of all people, those who were inspired by National Socialism act now as if the welfare of the community were near and dear to their hearts. Given their previous history this is almost laughable.

I do not want to deal any further with this worldwide problem. I have already noted that there are two phenomena especially worth observing: the one has to do with the social-political responsibility of a regime. In many countries one has decided to fight the virus with restrictions of public activity and closures. This was not always successful, since with the onset of the second wave of the virus, the carelessness of populaces had significantly increased and warnings were thrown to the winds. The decisions in question by the governments in Europe were of an entirely legal nature, for which not only the governing regime was responsible but also the respective legislatures which agreed with them. From the south to the north of Europe the decisions were legitimately democratic. It may be that here or there it did not go entirely according to the rules, but one still worked on getting the compulsory restrictions approved by parliament even if only *ex post facto*. In some countries opposite decisions were reached, as for example in Sweden. There one believed that the continuation of normal life would cause less damage than the measures we mentioned. A person can hold this position if he is ready to accept four times as many cases of death.

I now see, assuming that this letter is directed to the future, that it is out of step with the sequence of time. The form of the present reverts into the past, and that of the past reverts into the pre-past. So a translation in time becomes necessary, one that will not occur until the 2030's at the earliest.

Now I would like to talk quickly about the second phenomenon, which I have dealt with before. The pandemic is a good opportunity to learn how to understand science better. The general understanding unfortunately sets out from a completely false starting point: one hears more and more that the virologists and the pandemiologists and other specialists do not agree, so that the governments are more or less arbitrarily making one scientific view the basis for their decisions. Seldom will we again hear nonsense of this sort! The basis of this assumption is the naïve notion that the plurality of virologists must have one overarching agreement. What kind of science is it when a scientist in Innsbruck says something different from a colleague in Graz? If that attitude were correct, we would have no need to employ several virologists in a medical faculty or university. It would suffice to have one virologist in Austria, a second in Germany, a third in Italy, and a fourth in France. It is true that there would then be only one understanding of virology for each country, and this would make it relatively easy to decide which opinion one is to follow, since indeed there would be only one opinion. But it is the distinguishing feature of science that there are basically very different and even contradictory outlooks, all of which appear to be more or less well founded.

As I thumb through publications in sociology, I gather that society underwent a change, especially in Europe, from an "educational" society in the 1970's to a "knowledge" society around 1990. This means that the access to knowledge was not only greatly facilitated but also that overall in society the level of knowledge in diverse fields increased. Thus it ought to surprise us that the representation of our knowledge about the organization of science as I just described it, as for instance in the universities, should show such deficiencies. Apparently it is known only by a few that it is a property of the basic structure of science that there be various opinions, and it is the job of the state to allow for different forms of science in the respective fields, once they have undergone some vetting, and also to promote them. One can never know which hypothesis is appropriate for explaining a given fact and which theory interprets a given constellation of phenomena in a satisfactory way, so there must be even more scholars who, while of course they have a basic consensus as for instance that viruses exist, will nevertheless represent how they operate in many ways. And at that stage we are not yet even talking about what method will be applicable for combating it. My criticism is that of all people the very "inmates" of the knowledge society have, in large part, no knowledge of what science is. And instead the "half-educated" now are deciding which interpretation of an epidemic might make sense, which measures appear to be appropriate, and even whether a government can draw correct conclusions about the matter at all. I will not try to play the super knowledgeable or to undermine the opinions of many, but in observing the general evaluation of the assessments of the pandemic one can see very clearly which properties of our precious knowledge society in the meanwhile have been assumed to be true. The "receding" of knowledge is in large part handled the same way as purchasing cleaning agents or vegetables. Depending on the need, one expects to find carrots or cleaning products on the shelves. It is clear without any doubt that knowledge is to be available to society as readily as aspirin or metformin at a pharmacy. Our attitude toward knowledge is like the foot-kneading of puppies when they are feeding. And we are astonished and speechless when we are told that we are confronted here and there with the symptom of a disease about which we are clueless. Our inclination is often to blame such a shortage in knowledge on the incompetence of the researcher or his lack of preparation, or on a conscious policy to withhold research funds.

This means that in the analysis of the pandemic we face the distinct problem that the less and less clear it is to us how knowledge works, the more we have adopted automated ways of reaching it, and that we no longer have a clue about the theoretical prerequisites for doing so. It is peculiar and significant that given the enormous equipment at our disposal for our forms of scientific knowledge, we should no longer know anything about science – although more and more people are attending schools, gaining knowledge, and improving their social competence in supplementary studies.

I am not telling anything new here, but I want to open a path for asking at a later time where this misbegotten demand for knowledge comes from. A department head in a Ministry of Science once declared, around 1985, at the founding of a technical college, that it was not only to be welcomed for advancing access to education but above all that science would here be taught without useless theory. Sitting at that time in the radio studio in Argentinerstrasse I listened to the statements of the high official over and over again, since I could not believe what

I heard. It was not only a stupid thing to say but it expressed an outrageous disrespect for all theoretical work, which made all our current knowledge possible in the first place, from physics to Egyptology. This man was an agent of a knowledge society that views objects of knowledge like consumer goods. What cannot be consumed immediately is useless.

Here, finally, I stop.

Maybe I will write again about the state of our knowledge as I once did some years ago in my little book, *Uni im Out* ("University on the Outs" [Vienna 1992] – no eng. tr.). Unfortunately it did not catch on since in my opinion we have, especially in Europe, degraded our universities into teaching institutions, and therewith have done a disservice to research. This is relatively easy to prove since the natural sciences are always claiming they possess an objective measure of research. The European universities have lost their standing – or: The institutes have long since outsourced research.

All the best: I remain, your R.

89.
The Political Message of Music

Dear Nina, Dear Julian, Marie, and Vicky,

I have heard from Julian that he is about to take an entry exam for a music gymnasium. He is practicing the piano diligently. I remember that he was working on a *Nocturne* of Chopin and a piano piece by Bela Bartok. I was happy he chose Bartok, a composer I value highly. I have already said a few things to you about him and will not repeat them now. He is, after all, part of our contemporary music. Maybe you will have the opportunity to hear the *Miraculous Mandarin* some time. If you would go a little further you ought not forget Zoltán Kodály and also György Kurtág. By Kodály there is the very clever and funny "Háry János Suite" which gives a very entertaining musical portrait of an Hungarian craftsman who is returning home from the Napoleonic Wars. Joy about the advent of freedom and peace accompanies Háry all along his return home. His hope for freedom is not only for himself but rather for his entire nation. In the Hungarian historical context this suite, of which there are two versions, presents of course a subtle reference to the Habsburg domination over Hungary. This subject appeared widely in the literature of 1830, and Kodály called this theme back from memory with his composition, between 1920 and 1930. And so it was an extraordinary success in Budapest. The piece quickly went on to achieve popularity in the concert halls of Barcelona, London, and New York, though not in Vienna.

It is too seldom observed that besides the famous school of Schoenberg and his musical constructivism, there were compositions that understood themselves to be within the tradition of composition, though not by simply reverting to the late romanticism brought to its greatest and most significant potential by Richard Strauss. I was always surprised that the Schoenberg school was able almost completely to eclipse the creative movement in Russian music from Alexander Glazunov to Dmitri Shostakovich as well music from other places. It is well known that the music festivals at Donaueschingen were accorded a more or less binding influence as to what music was to be carried forward and what not. Thus, Arthur Honegger or Paul Hindemith and Werner Egk fell into disrepute. The Music Days in Donaueschingen, founded in 1921, by the 1950's and 60's issued informal decrees about what was to be allowed and what was to be banned in contemporary music. The counterpart of this was embodied by Carl Orff and his "Musical Pedagogy" for teaching children. In this there may have been interesting musical ideas – with the recorder, the triangle, and the guitar. And yet this is not the path I would recommend. The consistently arresting *Carmina Burana* and *Catulli Carmina* were composed with something of a tendency that anticipated the National Socialist musical showcase, and include a naturalism that can sometimes be awkward. The chamber opera *Die Kluge – "The Wise One"* – is no different. Nevertheless his work can stand on its own as musical work and despite criticism can enjoy a permanent place in the repertoire.

Now you will be asking, what can count as political in these compositions? In the history of music there are several examples. Let me begin with Tchaikovsky's *1812 Overture*. The sounds of the *Marseillaise* are mixed in with the bells of the great churches of Moscow. Amidst these contrasts the cannons thunder and scare away Napoleon's troops. (After all, that year of greatest peril was the beginning of Alexander Herzen's career – just by the way! He financed the First International, and his memoirs are a treasure trove of the ups and downs of the history of socialism from Russia to France). The *Preludes* of Franz Liszt were used for the most evil propaganda, without themselves being responsible for this special use. With Carl Orff this was much more obvious, above all when a great clap-board "crashes in" at a fortissimo to emphasize the dramatic climax of the Oedipus story. In case someone in the hall had not realized it, this crash indicates that the shepherd has something important to report. And during the retelling of Oedipus's past, its significance its emphasized when the trumpets play their intervals of a fifth. And the motifs receive no elaboration of the sort we hear in Richard Wagner but are only repeated without any heightening. The music flattens out the drama into a monotony, so as not to distract the audience from the plot.

These days we no longer understand how to listen to music sensitively enough to perceive such problems as these. It is also not clear to me whether I will be understood when I connect this music to a time that is difficult to recognize in music, in contrast with the other arts. In painting and sculpture as in architecture we are familiar with "products" that almost make us feel embarrassed. In sculpture we see heroes and heroines presented "naked," and we want to tell them to go back to the dressing room and put some clothes on. In painting, soulless and indistinguishable faces stare out at us. The feeling is overall military, and our architecture gives it a place to inhabit, as if in barracks fronted by bloated facades.

In music nothing like this is heard. The gap is filled by the grim "Badenweiler March" or the marching bands of the Hitler youth. There is only drumming and whistling, and one can't help but get the sense that the Pied Piper of Hamelin must have used such music as this.

But now I have gone far off track. The *Oedipus Rex* tries to achieve significance, which is why Jocasta's aria is built up to the level of the Carmen role, both in the way it is sung and in the music that accompanies it. And if even this doesn't come across, the utterly "insensitive" listener notices that the key phrase in Friedrich Hölderlin's libretto – "and now the inexorable Fates approach in force" – is nearly ignored by the orchestra, the impending disaster evoking from them only their routine indifference.

To contradict these statements with an alternative artistic representation, we can turn to the work of Shostakovich. He, too, lived in the horrible Stalinist type of totalitarianism, and he, too, had to suffer under institutions similar to those of many artists in Germany. I remember reading in Arthur Miller's "*Time Curves*" that he wished to have a chat with Shostakovich on the occasion of an international congress. Nothing happened, since Shostakovich could not take one step away from those who were accompanying him. Later it became known that during the composer's trip abroad his wife was being "held hostage" as it were back home.

In the music of Shostakovich there is always a gesture of brooding slowness. Shostakovich never approached dissonance in the ideological way but at the same time saw no place for pure joy either: instead he buried himself in monological grumbling. His symphonies always had the swing of Artur Honegger and the introvertness of Hans Pfitzner. In contrast with Orff, Shostakovich never had an "aversion against references" to the modes of music that had been characterized as "romantic" or "epigonal" or "modernist." This makes his symphonies, especially the *Fifth*, lively and full of variety and free. And especially impressive is the *Leningrad Symphony*, which was rehearsed and performed during siege and constant bombardment. When there was a lull in the fighting the soldiers would storm into the concert halls to hear it and then would go back to rejoin the conflict. Such motifs shimmer through the texture of the composition. Nowhere is to be heard the command of Stalin that the composers make their compositions appropriately "Sovietized," whatever that would sound like – perhaps the songs of happy harvest workers in the Kolkhoz or members of a Komsomol with balalaikas?

The film music of Shostakovich remains in one's ears, the grandiose waltzes that surge through the concert hall like a wave only to end somewhere in quiet despair. For a contrast one can listen to the "other political language" of the West, the powerful and confident marches of Edward Elgar, *Pomp and Circumstance 1 – 5*, written from 1901 to 1907.

Now I want to make known to you the third movement of the *Emperor Quartet* of Joseph Haydn. Modesty characterizes the development of the theme, with its perfect charm and refined sensitivity. One almost has forgotten that the "melody" was borrowed from a Croatian folk song, borrowing being not uncommon in Haydn, who "invented" a third movement for quartets. This is why it is unbearable to hear the misuse of the melody from this quartet when it is incorporated into a national anthem. Even if it was not Haydn's intention to make it into a "Hymn to the Emperor," it was nevertheless lovely and calm in its political language, simple and sincere. Once upon a time this suited the typically Austrian quality that Franz Grillparzer had Ottokar von Horneck repeat in his great monologue in *Ottokar's Fortune and End*. This language is still apparent, though barely, in Anton Wildgans's *Oration on Austria*. That this language no longer exists is something we owe to the Institute for Destruction of Speech and Language: the Vienna Burgtheater.

Now we have chatted enough about music. One should take this occasion not to forget the composers of the 20th Century, who hardly get a mention, such as Boris Blacher or Alexander Zemlinsky, and the music *Johnny spielt auf* by Ernst Krenek (the "Johnny" cigarette brand made by Austria Tabak got its name from this operetta).

Recommending all this to you warmly, I remain your R.

90.
A Monument for Johann Strauss

Dear Nina, Dear Julian, Marie, and Vicky,

You all popped into my mind today. In a store window a large English table-service for 12 persons from the 19th century was on display. It is in the well-known iron red with motifs from the English villages. I have the intention to bequeath to each grandchild an appropriate set of dishes, even in face of the danger that one will no longer understand their beauty and richness. In twenty years the recipient will probably be unhappy to have it all in the cabinet. We know that plates and bowls are made today to resist the damage of dishwashers. Nobody can still understand that I wash and dry these dishes by hand, and that I enjoy doing so. I have written somewhere else about the cultural disaster brought about by the dishwasher! The aesthetic impoverishment of our table-wares is staggering. I will stop here, since nobody understands this but easily comes to the opinion that I am cranky for being attached to things that are not appropriate for the dishwasher. I know all these arguments, all of them based on the principle of "practicality." In fact this is a preference for the "abominable." By some stroke of "luck" the store was closed because of the "lock-down."

In the last letter you read an assertion that you might have found jarring, namely that National Socialism can be heard in music and seen in painting and sculpture. During a walk in the Stadtpark today I came upon the monument to Johann Strauss. For the first time ever I stopped, since I could not remember ever having looked at it close-up. One must be gentle in making a judgment, since the sculptor cannot be blamed for the fact that the bronze statue has been gilded – once again, this time at the wish of Helmut Zilk, a mayor of Vienna. In 1939 the gilding of the statue had been removed, probably because it was too provocative. The return to simplicity had been good for the statue. The monument, by Edmund Hellmer, was erected rather recently – in 1921. The idea of the representation is not bad, and so because of the overall "composition" of the monument one pays less attention to its detail. And the "whipped cream arch" that surrounds the composer is pure Viennese kitsch. As if Strauss was to blame for these schmalzy Viennese songs, for these grim acoustical assaults, mermaids and nymphs were added as congenial spirits, their embarrassing nakedness more reminiscent of Felix Salten's "Mutzenbacherin" than of the nobility present but barely in the waltz. Given that it is the most popular place to take "selfies" in Vienna, and for a hundred thousand Japanese is more important than the crown of Otto the First in the *Schatzkammer* – with which of course it should not be compared – one must ask oneself what is so grand about Strauss himself and also about the monument, to which a million make their pilgrimage, take pictures, and disappear again. With the re-gilding, the framing arch again becomes an embarrassment: the life-sized statue was more bearable in the contrast of black and white. In gold it joins together with the sylphs as a statement of kitsch. I will not put in a good word in defense of the Viennese waltzes, yet not one of those waltzes ever deserved a disparagement of this kind. They were all solidly composed, and had nothing else in mind than to make a frivolous and irresponsible elite even more frivolous – which then succeeded: 1914.

That this should have happened is not so strange. This "candy-store" monument has as its logical entailment those "Viennese Uglies" that were gratuitously installed on the stanchions of the bridge across the Vienna River near the Museum for Applied Art. They are human-like faces by Otto Mühl that because of the moulage can hardly be made out – and yet one will correctly guess that given the logical development known in the history of art, the monument is to be connected with a tradition that moves from kitsch to the defacement of the human: both of these do the same thing.

Luckily the best sculpture in the Vienna Stadtpark is paid almost no visits. It is a more or less hidden fountain that connects the park's two levels – the path along the Vienna River and the park itself. We can thank the architect Friedrich Ohmann of Galicia for this installation. In a very poetical way he closed Lothringerstrasse at the concert hall and opened up a sightline to the Stadtpark along the axis of the Vienna River.

The name of this hidden fountain is "The Freeing of the Spring." Two "Titans" are rolling a rock away from a spring so that a small stream can gush forth. The two colossal statues are by Josef Heu, who created them in 1903. The fountain was also erected in 1903 and can be called a stellar piece of sculpture by Viennese standards.

Most of the monuments in the Vienna Stadtpark are "Late Romantic." Hans Makart, who died early at 45, is represented as a prince of art; much more modest and simple is the Friedrich Amerling, who famously painted a very impressive portrait of Emperor Franz I, not at all pompous. Years ago I saw this painting in the Austrian Culture Institute in Paris, only to bump into it thirty years later in the Belvedere. On the occasion of an exhibition of the Romantics it was brought back to Vienna. For the vernissage I was asked to present an introductory lecture but I no longer remember what I said. I suspect that I characterized the exhibition by calling Romanticism an enlightenment of the Enlightenment. This is important since one would not be able to understand the birth of historicism without this connection. This scientific movement in history arrived to play a corrective role. But also at the same time it itself became distorted and took on a nationalistic aspect, and of all things counted languages as the "ultimate argument" for unities and divisions among peoples – thus for the first time projecting a unified body politic for Germany.

To return to the pleasantries of daily life, last night at Wolfgang Hirt's I prepared a delicious codfish in the oven, and a side dish of leaf spinach and a sort of tartar sauce, into which I mixed in some mustard and honey. I brought in a Grüner Veltliner from the Weinviertel. Before this we had a frittata soup. This was the reason I didn't send the letter I wrote yesterday. Today, we are having spinach pancakes with feta, and a salad. It's easy and it is a good thing to make – unfortunately there was no fresh spinach today and so I had to use a package of frozen. That sounds disgraceful and I am totally to blame! For drink I will put a sauvignon blanc on the table, which became delicious in the shade of Bisamberg.

All the best – and to Julian I wish still more success on the piano!

Your R.

91.
Sociology as a Department in Decline

Dear Nina, Dear Julian, Dear Marie and Vicky,

Now the heap of letters has grown considerably, and when I leaf through I realize that surely you are being given no light task, a task easy to carry out. Again and again topics "from out of the blue" suddenly become a letter, and you do not know in what context you are to read them, or understand or classify them. The whole thing has become something of a "dream," as if it had all been written a hundred years ago. You have to know that this impressionistic dreaminess ought to be a method for drawing conclusions from the mass of material, the mass of information. On the one hand the letters are supposed to explain the course of recent decades; on the other hand they are meant to recall things that have probably been forgotten. What is forgotten has a very different quality: when one brings it to mind and retrieves it from oblivion, memories are "awakened" and then comes the difficulty of deciding what significance is to be assigned to the thing that has been remembered. Most memories one has are from childhood, and these faded treasures have a more psychoanalytical meaning and hardly any significance for the course of the world. But a connection between childhood and war would give such memories historical significance.

Again and again I think, in this connection, of the description of Manès Sperber (1905-1984), who reports about his experiences in the First World War when war struck his Galician village like a storm, and then after a quarter hour the scare was gone. In all likelihood bodies lay in the street, windows were broken, and somewhere a house was still burning. Slowly people crawled back out to see what was still intact, and started removing the dead.

He had another experience in a train station. Soldiers were sitting around on the platforms waiting for their next orders. Manès Sperber observed an officer giving an order to a soldier, yelling at him and commanding him to stand up. Slowly the soldier got up and gave the officer a resounding slap on the face. Sperber commented that in his eyes this incident signaled the end of the Danube Monarchy.

Though a connection between childhood and war is one of the themes in these letters, there are only a few of my memories that are connected with turning points, which would make them seem more important. The description of other memories will seem unimportant. For instance, while browsing back I found no significant reference to my work at the Sociology Department. I mentioned one or two grotesque incidents, but other than those there is not a single line. Looking back I find this interesting! About years and years of professional life there is not a remark, not even a hint. It is surprising and yet easy to explain. The climate at the department was not very conducive to scientific work. A strategic silence prevailed at our meetings. The reason was that between a penchant for empiricism and a devotion to ideological prejudices there was little breathing room for a general sociology. The unfortunate tension between the two Ordinarii who, because of the university reforms, were always acting in reaction to criticism; and the "intentions" of some of the colleagues – including men and women as we are now careful to say – could not be brought to a common denominator, neither in administrative affairs nor in the teaching curriculum. The way sociology was able to continue was primarily in "hyphenated" forms. The object of study was determined according to several distinct phenomena in society and was exonerated from giving a comprehensive interpretation of society as a whole, which "classic" sociology had always tried to do. Thus youth-, family-, consumption-sociology, or the sociology of art, of age, and of drugs served up an arena for social explanation almost automatically, with verification coming simply from the empirical access of questionnaires and statistics. Moreover, given the simplified way of defining the subject of research, funding could be obtained on a regular basis, which either made it possible to hire an additional assistant or could be exploited to achieve a "territorial" expansion within the department itself. Thus the discussions in the departmental meetings of the whole were always dominated by the question whether one could commandeer rooms being used by the other group to pursue their projects, or how these contested little rooms could be defended. This sounds extremely childish – and it was. The department suffered for this, but it was not so noticeable because the empirical method used in all the projects preserved an appearance of diligence, with countless printouts and heaps of paper created in cross-tabulation analysis and data processing – though in truth it was the machines that were producing the evidence.

I was able to talk about sociology with Paul Neurath, only. I learned from him early on about the problem of the "greatest migration movement" in world history and its consequences: Neurath very clearly saw contours that became more and more clear only after the settlement of the East-West conflict, and which conjured up new forms of social conflict for study. I myself had gotten my start from the position of Ludwig Gumplowicz, who even before 1900 was convinced that "mixtures" in a population produce equally strong "segregations." The area he studied was Lviv in Galicia, around 1870. It was a very early explanation for the raging anti-Semitism of the time, which then brought on the most terrible consequences in the 20th century.

There would not be much to report about this long period at the department if I had not taken part in editing a history of Austrian philosophy with Michael Benedikt. The project covered the period between 1400 to 2000, and eventually the studies grew to seven volumes, and will probably be an interesting compendium for the curious, fifty years from now. Since Austria consistently made exciting contributions to philosophy – it got in late but more than made up for that – the account was devoted primarily to philosophical empiricism, which emerged from the Austrian way of combining pragmatism with social utopianism. It amounted to years of work.

To return to my "dreamy impressions" – it is easy to understand that the connection between science and art was more than a manifestation of the cultural bourgeoisie, but was always a stimulating experience. I can't remember just now whether I told you how long I would visit the museums as a pupil – or better, as a "pupil who was absent from school." It was in the galleries of contemporary painting, and I created in these rooms a world, my own world. Thanks to the scarcity of visitors at the time I was often the only visitor to the Kunsthistorisches Museum, and could imagine that I was the owner of this colossal collection. I will not elaborate on that now – and how I lived among the paintings of Hans Baldung Grien, Hans Holbein the Younger, Oskar Kokoschka, and Richard Gerstl in the Upper Belvedere.

I will close here. I am aware that I am sending a sketch that is not even half finished, but let's leave it at that. After all this is not the last letter – despite the new threatening English variant of the virus now breaking into Germany, soon to be expected in Austria as well.

All the best, your R.

92.
May One Be a Model Student?

Dear Vicky, Dear Marie and Nina, Dear Julian,

It is generally accepted that what we know from psychology and pedagogics define the potential for a person's development. Although astrology is frowned upon, these two human sciences dare to make forecasts that are taken to be vigorously scientific. The rest of a person's life will be determined by them. If the prognosis is less hopeful the persons concerned will even be happy if they will ever be able to hold any kind of job. Sometimes this can be a source of pride, when their parents had been told their child would hardly be able to support himself. In retrospect the predictions might be found to be wrong, but by then countless years had been spent in worry and sorrow, and in struggling against fate. It is lucky for psychologists and pedagogues that the case histories they wrote long ago are gathering dust somewhere in the archives, and psychometricians of the adolescents seem relatively happy that the lisping and failures at school of their murky early years are finally over.

From my own experience I know the pain the school years bring and how great it can be. If one has the misfortune of not fitting the abstract figure of a student, of not conforming with the teacher's image, one has to run a gauntlet that lasts nearly ten years. Given my own school experience I do not understand people who whine that our children have lost so much because of the pandemic – that they would not become educated, and that the educational goals would suffer a setback. Under the present circumstances I am much more unhappy that the young cannot visit the museums. I am unhappy that the museums have not been opened for children, whereas for adults and for tourists the collections must remain closed on principle. It has been a scandal for some time that the museums are orienting themselves toward adults, that the exhibitions are always planned for them while the young are being neglected. And when they do think of children, they present exhibitions that are artistically infantile, because some supreme mastermind has decided what can be expected from children. Compared to these moronic children's exhibitions the cartoon books of Mickey Mouse and Asterix seem positively sophisticated. As a child I could hardly keep from throwing up when people would say about literature or art that it was "suitable for children." This was a common expression since the human sciences at the time conceived of a dividing line before and after the onset of puberty. Up to this imaginary line, with the key-term "puberty," everything had to be "suitable for children" and just after that these poor students, enrolled under compulsion, were immediately confronted with the German classics. At thirteen they were to read Goethe's *Sorrows of the Young Werther*, the *Portfolio of My Great-Grandfather* by Adalbert Stifter, and *The Poor Minstrel* of Grillparzer. What some weeks before had not been suitable for children was suddenly suitable literature for the young! Both policies had been horrendous nonsense brought upon us by our education authorities. Instead of recommending Erich Kästner, Mark Twain, Joseph Conrad, or Daniel Defoe and Jules Verne, Christian Morgenstern and Joachim Ringelnatz, one put extraordinary works into immature hands. This marks the obsolescence of our most important literature, but also the school administration has herewith brought it about that from now on, *Werther* and *Minstrel* will never be read again at a more mature age. Grillparzer as far as I know did not write for 12- to 14-year-olds, neither did Goethe, so this reading list serves only the vanity of the administration and not the school children. In both cases this pedagogic method serves as an inoculation. From now on most of the youth will be immune to literature. When I think back, the advantage of going to the museum was that I was not talked into anything nor was anything withheld from me. I could consider a painting of Dürer the same way as one of Anthony van Dyck. And if I was not comfortable with that, I would wander into the collection of antiquities. If I wanted to read a novel by Gottfried Keller or Arthur Schnitzler the coin rooms of the Kunsthistorisches were a tranquil place and extremely pleasant – they had a princely atmosphere. In the last room there was a comfortable armchair in which many hours flew by.

I remember knowing already that there was no way that the educational plan made any sense. "Expressions of Culture" were withheld: music, painting, drawing, architecture. Instead there was a dyed-in-the-wool Nazi who taught chemistry and geography. He had four classes a week for our grade! Not a single class was given to theater, to the Albertina, to the Upper Belvedere or Galerie Würthle or the Griechenbeisel. Not a single class per week was dedicated to the most important cultural achievements. Even "physical education" had three classes per week, while there was not one class for first aid. Instead, later, in the "philosophy" class we got the problematic psychology of Hubert Rohracher, which was a materialistic psychology. It is hardly believable that an 18-year-old in a well-known high school in Vienna had heard nothing at all about Sigmund Freud, not a word about Ludwig Wittgenstein, nor an introduction to the fundamentals of our federal constitution. And this is lacking even today!

I am still unable to swallow my anger!

If our human sciences, due to their having been made "positivistic," now behave like natural sciences, slavishly following every empirical refinement, it is no longer a surprise that one believes he can assess a 6-year-old and evaluate noteworthy peculiarities. I can give you a counterexample, one among countless others. I am thinking of a person who was not basically extraordinary. During school he was shy among people and he spoke little. Unfortunately no reports from the teachers of young Paul have survived among the school records. You could say he began painting as a young man as a sort of self-therapy. He himself, in the 19th century, did what Leo Navratil sixty years ago tried to do systematically in the Maria Gugging mental clinic for the psychologically and intellectually disabled. Navratil was of the opinion that one could "relieve" or ease the mental suffering through painting, and bit by bit a humble creativity would be strengthened providing a key to the self. In the publication of his research Navratil described warmly the phases of healing he had been able to observe.

Our "test case" was not immediately successful. Paul seemed ungifted in his early paintings. One could not speak of his having talent. In his first steps in painting a certain perseverance was to be noted, a diligent and almost compulsive sense of personal duty to achieve painterly expression, but nobody would have given a wooden nickel for his efforts. We know of similar attempts by which one might repair his weaknesses. The oldest example could well be Demosthenes, who fought his speech impediment by putting pebbles into his mouth. That he became the greatest orator in Greek history is well known. Gustave Flaubert had an extraordinarily hard time with writing. He corrected his sentences over and over. Finally he developed a method for taking notes which ended up controlling what he had written: he would check the rhythm, sound, and syntax of every sentence. A sentence was perfect once it fulfilled these criteria. At 28, our "Paul" had still not gotten that far. He painted and painted, he wandered through the museums to make copies of the great paintings, and yet his works lacked the naturalness of a light touch. Probably many people would have said that Paul was ruining canvasses and wasting oils.

Paul's zealous effort took an interesting turn. He placed his artistic attempts onto the foundation of a mental plan, and developed a special conception about the meaning of the colors. Since a verbal description of images often gives an inadequate rendering that does not correspond with the content of a painting, it is difficult to retrace the stages that made our "Paul" the famous Cezanne that he was, the father of modern painting. Without him there would have been no Cubism, no Fauvism, nor any strong discipline about composition and the use of colors.

Out of an "empirical" interest I once copied a landscape of Cezanne. I came to realize why he took the sheen out of his colors. Even in his paintings of the major avenues the color could almost fade out. It was dull, as if too much turpentine had been used. In my act of copying, an organization among the feelings associated with the colors came into view. They had not just been taken from the palette according to his emotional mood; rather, just as a geometer might lay out a field, Cezanne had assigned a place for each of the colors to appear. And at the same time he was hoping his colors would produce the rapture and the ecstasy that overshadows the artist himself. It was from this point of view that he viewed his favorite painters, Tintoretto and Veronese, whom he respected because they only aimed at painting well.

What I am here telling you is still shaped by the impression that I got at the great Cezanne exhibit in the Upper Belvedere. At the time, in the 50's, it was the great exhibit of van Gogh, Gauguin, and Cezanne. After going through and almost exhausted, I went up into the gallery past the 19th century in the first floor, and then higher up to Egon Schiele, Gustav Klimt, and Richard Gerstl. The painterly superiority of the Western Europeans was easy to see. It was not the Austrians' "provinciality" that bothered me; rather, their new kind of realism was disturbing, just as it had disturbed me in the music of Richard Strauss's *Heldenleben*, *Till Eulenspiegel*, or *Alpensymphonie*. It was clear to me that Egon Schiele had worked himself into a corner that van Gogh would not have gotten into. If I may be more precise about what I remember, it was as if the one painted real suffering while the other painted "play" suffering. Indeed Schiele in his paintings seemed to me to present an hysterical heightening: it all seemed nervous, which the "realism" of Gauguin did not need, although he did use theatricality in his expression. And how free his use of colors was, if I should compare his manner to that of all the great Austrian painters!

Truly, I have kept in memory all those paintings in the Upper Belvedere. If I should ever see one of them again it would be like encountering a friend. I mentioned this when I told you about the bust of Beethoven that I came across again at a friend's home. Conversely I was sad to see, in Salzburg, the painting of an utterly wonderful painter hanging in a gallery. Henri Joseph Harpignies painted amazingly beautiful landscapes of northern France, and one of them had become quite familiar to me since it was inherited by a friend. Every time I went for a visit I admired the painting's intimate rendering of nature. And now it was for sale in Salzburg. So I could see it again, but had to say goodbye to it forever. I hope the giant historical paintings of Adolf Hirémy-Hirschl will not suffer this fate, including *Hannibal's Crossing the Alps* and also the *Wandering Jew*, which are at the homes of friends.

If I may now go back to the beginning, I have assumed that today Paul Cezanne, on the basis of the "Hamburg-Weschler Intelligence Test," would be advised to apprentice himself to a house painter. There he would be able to enjoy his fancy for painting with colors on pipe clay in semigloss. In all likelihood it was lucky for Cezanne that such studies did not yet exist. We would have no glimpse of Monte St. Victoire, no glimpse of the cork oaks nor of the *Young Man in the Red Vest.*

I am of course aware of the one-sidedness with which I here attack the entire school administration at the time when I was doing my compulsory education. I need not cite the publications that support my point of view, such as Alice Miller's *Drama of the Gifted Child*, or Lloyd de Mause's *Do You Hear the Children Crying?* nor so-called Critical Pedagogics. It is the way, the procedure, and the completely uncritical self-image of the school boards that is causing the weakness of our schools. One cannot avoid this fact, and one can make no improvement on it, since no approach to self-criticism will be recognized by the school board. Günter Grass during a lecture once characterized a meeting of our worthy school principals and counsellors as a gathering of cake-eating furry animals – and apparently this hits the mark.

I would like to conclude with this.

Keep your ears perked up! Your R.

PS.

In describing my professional career I left out the punch line. In the last years of my tenure at the department I registered some courses I would teach for the semester. I received a letter from the Dean telling me to restrict the number of lectures, and I was touched. In my naivete I thought he was concerned about my health and feared I would be overworked. I was about to answer the letter in a conciliatory way when I learned, just in time, that his reason for writing the letter was not his concern for me, but that the many hours I would be using the lecture hall would increase the cost of lighting and heating. Presumably they had also taken into account the use of blackboard chalk. It was a striking example of the transformation of the university into a mediocre administrative ministry.

93.
Florence

Dear Nina, Dear Julian, Marie, and Vicky,

In turning back to a normal sort of correspondence, I want to add an observation to what has been said so far. Members of a tour group hang on the words of the local tour guides. Often I have heard the most amazing things from their reports when they get back home. During the trip the group is led along like a herd and is brought to a halt at fixed points as if to a watering trough. Loudly, with a megaphone, there is an explanation – indeed the guide improvises remarks customized to the country the visitors come from ("Kaiser Wilhelm also visited here!"), only to hurry on to the next stopping point where the same game is played. I do not want to comment on this further. This is just one of countless aspects of tourists being driven through cities like cattle. The result is that the commercial landscape of the city is disappearing and must make room for so-called "fast-food chains." The erstwhile infrastructure of centers that once thrived in Europe is running aground. Instead of specialty manufacturers, tailors, cobblers, cabinet-makers, silversmiths, and potters, there are souvenir stores or – according to the importance of the city – one "flag-store" after another. It seems there is a huge advertising campaign underway when one encounters the same stores and the same brands in Paris, London, Madrid, and Rome. One gets the idea that in any city one can buy a "Rolex" and then go to Burger King and after that walk along the rue Tivoli sipping a latte from Starbuck's out of a paper cup. The refuse – the cardboard box and the paper cup – end up on the sidewalk and the trampled rich red of ketchup testifies that foreign tourism is alive and well.

Obviously one's encounter with art in the widest sense no longer has the character of an amazing experience, but instead that of a guided walk through a city. The tourists are notoriously difficult to move along from the store windows since they are raving about the "demi-tasse" that has the Emperor and Sisi, about the Eiffel Tower in a glass ball of snow, how they have a rosary from Rome that was personally blessed by the Pope, and from London a tea-caddy in the form of those old phone booths. The tourists spend more time with the displays at the souvenir shop than with the *Mona Lisa*. They know her well enough. Why should one stand there admiring the *Mona Lisa* of all things behind a hundred Japanese taking photographs? The *Mona Lisa* is available in all sizes and shapes, mounted on the most diverse objects, from a coffee mug to a shopping bag in the museum shop, where the visitors can purchase a memento of anything in the Louvre they might have missed when they went through.

It is actually the greatest of absurdities, what has come of those first touristic journeys. It was at the end of the 16th century that the Lords of England began searching for the Renaissance, and discovered these paintings and sculptures in the context of their completely "un-neurotic" environment. These were the first collectors; they named the 14th and 15th centuries the "Renaissance," and in the letters of Lord Chesterfield one can see this admiration of *Italy!* which he wanted to impart to his illegitimate son. Benjamin Franklin was no different. On the occasion of his trip to Europe he wrote his children about what was worth seeing. These letters are the most beautiful documents of anyone's admiration for a time, an epoch, and its art. When he was the American ambassador to Paris, Franklin got to know the Old Europe. He learned what could be done better, what one ought to imitate, and which goal to strive for. Lion Feuchtwanger composed a very successful trilogy of novels about Franklin. According to Feuchtwanger Franklin, as the first American ambassador to Paris, carefully stayed away from royal pageantry. He avoided going to Versailles and was more involved with enlightenment types in the city. Thus Franklin hoped his children would garner the blessings of the Enlightenment when they should come to Europe. I'm sorry I cannot verify the details since my copies of Franklin's *Autobiography* and the novels of Feuchtwanger are in the country. You cannot imagine how important it is to be able to verify a memory. It is like a confirmation you have not gone completely daffy. I will call my bookseller tomorrow morning about Feuchtwanger and Franklin – as a Germanist she is my go-to person for this sort of thing. And immediately I will tell you if I have made a mistake.

Now I have to go back to the reason for my remarks. I actually wanted to tell you how important it is to have a spontaneous encounter with art. How important it is to be surprised by it. I can only give you an example from my own memory. In my first visit to Florence I got off the train two stops before the famous Piazza Duomo. I strolled through the narrow alleys of the inner city. I discovered the paper store that produces the delightful notebooks in which I so enjoyed to paint. Indeed I had entirely forgotten the goal of my wandering. Somehow it was especially pleasant to linger in one of the alleys and enjoy the much vaunted "Italianità." I ordered a "stretto" in a tiny store – especially strong coffee. I had completely forgotten the world-famous Duomo – if that is possible. I thought to myself, "It must be miles away – I won't be seeing it today." And that would be my preference, not to have to see the things that get stars in DuMont, but instead to talk with the barista about Fiorentina, one of the soccer clubs that was threatened with being downgraded to a lower league – just as in a café in Rome I had talked about Konsel who had been traded to AS Roma as goalie from the Rapids umpteen years ago. The two of us in Firenze rummaged through our memories about Fiorentina. It finally came time to leave. So I walked through the narrow alleys and enjoyed the sounds of the venders' and the stall owners' calls in Italian, the opening of shutters and the revving mopeds. This was already enough to make it worth being in Florence. The other sounds of the street were beguiling. I recognized them from Luigi Dallapiccola, whose flute sonatas possess the same spirit. Suddenly I noticed that I was at the end of the alley: a daydream invaded my perception. It was this unearthly abstract and giant but still unidentifiable wall. Immediately the fineness of the marble came into focus. I had suddenly approached the side aisle of the Duomo. Higher and higher rose this church above my gaze. It took my breath away. Only later did I learn that this was the path by which one was supposed to approach a Bishop's Church. It is meant to stand out like a precious stone in the midst of a narrow sea of houses – something like the monastery at Strasbourg. Construction of Santa Maria del Fiore began humbly in the 12th century. And then came the wave of architectural projects – until in the end the dome became the firmament and the treasure of Florence. Still, nobody remarks that it was a Habsburg idea to clad the Dome with marble, a bizarre idea of historicism and the most important example of how one really ought not trust his eyes. In the octagon or the Baptistery I heard, over and over, that cladding in marble was a common way of building in the early Renaissance. And of course everyone admires the Cathedral. It is as if its shape were a creation of Florentine painting after Giotto di Bondone, Cimabue (Cenni di Peppo) and Duccio Buoninsegna, which of course it also is, but the uniqueness of the lovely architecture is to be seen in the dome, which is both the Florentine firmament and the protective mantel of the Madonna. Like the Santa Maria Maggiore in Rome, the interior is of an intimate simplicity that silences all the art-historical chit-chat.

With this example I wanted to tell you that the most important events in your lives are these spontaneous and unplanned encounters with our great works of art. You will immediately understand when you first fall in love, when the encounter with this beloved person enters your life as an event that each time feels new and is always surprising; something you await with longing, and yet feels the same as you, as part of what makes you alive. The first sight of a great painting is like the first kiss. Just now I think of many such kisses: the *Helen Fourmet* of Rubens, the *Adam and Eve* of Hans Baldung Grien, *Lot and his Daughters* by Veronese, the *Peasant Wedding* by Pieter Brueghel, the *Venus* of Titian, or the highly desirable wife of Amadeo Modigliani, or *Madame Recamier* by Ingres. I hope that you one day will understand my rapture. Sometime you should to get caught up in this "excessiveness," in which you will experience what it is to be a human being. Truly I wish this for you, from the bottom of my heart.

With love, your R.

94.
The Return of Antiquity and the Gods

Dear Nina, Dear Julek, Dear Marie and Vicky,

In the last writing there were several references to Italy. Although one has to hope that the madness of tourism by itself cannot destroy these great gifts and will not do them permanent damage, one must take the time to understand the many cities, the several regions, or the almost entirely separate political landscapes of Tuscany and Apulia. It takes only one trip to remember the special places where art and politics and history became so closely intertwined and thereby established their unique character. "Italy" is however more a geographical concept than a political one. That it became unified politically was not only the achievement of the "Italian Bismarck," Benso Cavour, in the 19th century, but with the beginning of historicism its manifold achievements were also gathered together, under a supposition that art, science, and politics were all due to the influence of the landscape. More than anything else the birth of "Italy" was fathered by the spirit of art history, resulting from the first travel guides in the 16th century. The first Lords were proud to deliver their accounts: at first noble curiosity induced them to transcribe them, but soon, professional travel writers copied each other and in England every private library came to have on hand detailed accounts of the Italian Renaissance.

I must advise you not to delve deeply just into the history of Florence, or of Rome, or of Venice! It is better that you read three or four historians of this period, and only then begin to dig deeper into the documents and the facts. How about Benedetto Croce? He was a great liberal historian.

If we way turn again to the Renaissance, it was given its unique identity only in the 19th century. As I wrote before (or do I only imagine I did?), it was in Italy that the first modern men appeared, for instance Francesco Petrarca or Torquato Tasso: the representation of "Italy" arrived later, in retrospect. Granted, the reports of Winckelmann and Goethe came earlier than this: it was they who discovered "Italy" for the German speaking world. Johann Joachim Winckelmann was the pioneer and architect of art history. Along the way, interest in the Italian treasures grew so much that Winckelmann was always invited to confer in high-level discussions of the art collections, was permitted to give counsel about specialized areas of collecting, and was even entrusted by the Pope with looking through the collections in the Vatican. His death in Trieste was a tragic story. It appears that a certain Arcangeli, a cook, had become an object of Winckelmann's erotic desire; and also that this perpetrator had seen the full purse Winckelmann had been able to fill rather nicely during his visit with Maria Theresa in Vienna. A knife attack seriously injured the learned man; though he succeeded to defend himself he died a few hours after the attempted murder. Later – according to a wild hypothesis made in 1989 – it was claimed that Winckelmann was murdered in Vienna, but it will certainly have occurred in Trieste, in 1768.

But let's not get distracted. I mentioned Winckelmann not only because he is taken to be the founder of "art history" – but because in saying this we undermine the famous biographies of Giorgio Vasari, who described the lives of the painters as a contemporary of theirs.

What particularly interests us is how it was possible to bring about this incredible cultural achievement in such a small space and in such a short amount of time, with means that previously had hardly been known. The answer can only be that the "Renaissance" was predominantly a myth. There must have been some peculiarity from which this eminent cultural phenomenon stemmed. Names come to mind who "deserve" to be considered the inspiration for the myth. First of all Leon Battista Alberti comes to my mind, a "jack of all trades" in art and erudition – and then of course Michelangelo. One might easily imagine that the world is full of heroes – in Florence, Rome, Bologna, or Venice. And besides these heroes, there were the evil forces of the Borgia papacy aligned against them. Indeed these surpassed in evil anything known before. The anti-hero was impressive for his arbitrary power to make or break a man. The size of the opposition along with such an imperial power-gesture, was simply a fabrication – for the Empire existed no more: this arrogance, which even the emperors admired, was the basis for the myth of the Renaissance. It did not take long that with the Baptistery in Florence and with Brunelleschi and Ghiberti, the personal sovereignty we think of as the characteristic of modern men had grown quite strong alongside it. A foundation for this claim thus became possible, for suddenly all the talk was about renewal, reconstruction of the past, revival and rediscovery.

These terms for the Renaissance were not however new. Hadn't Vergil and Ovid already dreamed of a Golden Age? Or fantasized about an alternative to city life and a carefree Arcadia in the *Bucolics*? And these writers were the literature of education. I remember having read that the young Michelangelo at age thirteen had to spend his lunchtime in the garden of the Medici's, and there must have heard debates – about free will! – between Ficino and Pico della Mirandola. Meanwhile the sculpture apprentices argued their opposing views of free will with punches and kicks. That is how Michelangelo lost the hearing of one ear to a blow from a fist.

Likewise one would read that in this "Renaissance," antiquity was "taken so literally" that a person could think that Christ could be integrated into the pantheon of antiquity. He would appear on the same rank as Apollo, Hercules, or Neptune. How far this went we can tell from the elation of Friedrich Nietzsche, who in his comments celebrated this "antiquitization" as leading to an overcoming of Christianity and its "slave morality," though he bewailed its inability to go on and take the last step – namely, to bury Christianity altogether. Nietzsche got himself into a rage: what appeared next was that "peasant lout" Luther, who brought to an end Nietzsche's retrospective hope.

So we cannot decide whether we invented the Renaissance in retrospect – or had the Renaissance perhaps invented itself? If I think of the *David* of Michelangelo, of the Tomb of Pope Julius in San Pietro in Vincoli, in Rome, of his painting of the Holy Family, and of the "Rotunda" in Florence, then surely a new and unique language had emerged – and with it the modern age, as I already wrote. If by this we only understand the age of industrialization we are stuck sounding like men from Mars, but it was not up to us in the first place: the decisions were already made before our time. We know that the author Leonardi Bruni in 1430 had remarked that Petrarch was not only an exceptional phenomenon but also that he possessed the ability to bring the bygone past back into consciousness. And even the Pope remarked at the time that one is standing near the achievement that with learning and piety antiquity would return. He too was convinced that a Golden Age would soon come upon us again.

This was not a matter of chance: Vasari was convinced that cultures symbolize coming into being and passing away. And the rise of "Italy" was unstoppable.

I think this will be enough for now.

Many greetings, your R.

95.
What Disappears with the Word "modern?"

Dear Julian, Dear Vicky and Marie, Dear Nina,

My recalling the Renaissance was not a matter of recommending it, nor even recommending a trip to Italy – a recommendation Chinese culture would deserve just as well – but because new paradigms were entering into history. And this is something you ought to know about. First, there was this surprising and unusual designation of things as "modern." This was in fact an invention of the Renaissance. It is interesting that around 1526 the homeopathic physician Paracelsus started using the term "modern" a lot to describe things. He meant by this that something had just now come into existence. Just now a "novelty" has been developed. The entry for the word in the *Grimms Dictionary* is surprising. There it is said that "modern" was first used in the 18th century, and thus is not a word from the Renaissance; instead the philological references mention only the German derivation of the word from the French, which itself of course stems from Latin. I don't want to bore you with this, except perhaps to make one more point: in the 19th century there was an explosion in its uses: from "modern technology" to "modern painting."

To get back to the topic, I chose to deal with this period of history in the previous letter because from then on there was not only "modern men," as I mentioned, but a tension between the visualization of antiquity – looking back to the "paganism" of the Romans and Greeks, which was especially surprising in Rome, the seat of the Pope – and an unbelievable creativity that was afoot in dealing with form or composition, and in the technology used in art and architecture. The most impressive symbol for this is the cupola of Florence's cathedral by Filippo Brunelleschi. It is the first "aestheticization" of living space in the European context, initially attempted in magnificent gardens and reaching its apex in the villa design of Andrea Palladio. This was the first step toward a "total aestheticization" of the civilized world which was further intensified in the Baroque. But if one wants to be objective, such great progress was made not only in this period between 1300 and 1550. The retrospective of historicism made it possible to see in the Renaissance an alternative to the rather gloomy history of Europe. One can speak of a mythical picture or of a vogue, according to which the entire Middle Ages was thought to be obliterated in darkness, that a virtual historical darkness prevails from 400 to 800AD. With the rather unpleasant expression "migration period" what one is really lamenting is the destruction of the ancient world. Gradually a new structure comes into being, in the later history of France, along the Rhine, and in the colonization of the Danube region. We are basically to believe that a "leap" in time takes place, from the last emperor Romulus Augustus around 450 to Charlemagne around 800.

But since one can see the golden treasure of the Nagyszentmiklos in the Kunsthistorisches Museum of Vienna, one can no longer join in the usual depreciatory judgment of those centuries. All divisions into periods must be examined in greater detail, and one will surely come to the conclusion that such evaluations, still found in books today, must be revised. What I am trying to say in this long-winded way is that the historical sciences wanted to elevate the Renaissance above its context in order to describe it as a model. One thought that in many ways concepts had there come to light that later would count as the guidelines for modernity: enlightenment, humanism, emancipation from the Roman Church and later also from the emperor. And finally, the Reformation had an enormous influence, in that it not only broke up the German states forever along confessional lines but also brought about a need to compensate politically, culturally, and administratively for the lost unity of "Christianity."

I had nothing else in mind than to save you from a dreamy "postcard" awareness. Of course you ought to admire these enormous achievements, but not at the cost of other successes as for instance when I now think of it the Gothic cathedral, or the great efforts in the building of cities and even our technological successes, though they tend to open up a world to us only in a surreal way. So it is now easy to say goodbye to the hypothesis of the philosophy of history according to which epochs must go through a rise, apex, and decline. In support of this insight I recommend a short essay by Max Weber, "On the Decline of the Roman World Empire." Here you will learn very quickly that the causes of decline are not to be found according to that theory, as it is always said, but that something paradoxical took place. Of all things the phenomena that one had thought to be Rome's strengths or to be its excellent capacities to solve problems also led to its downfall because of their brittleness.

This is the point I wanted to make for you, briefly.

All the best, your R.

96.
What Does a "Fail" at School Mean?

Dear Julian, Dear Granddaughters,

I take the opportunity to write to you about an experience we suffer in life over and over again. I want to set aside the advice of the know-it-alls, for instance that one "gets over" a disappointment, that disappointments can even have a positive effect once one "overcomes" them, or that despite disappointment one ought not to hang his head. I remember also encouraging songs – "After every winter comes the month of May," "After the rain the sun comes out again," "A streak of bad luck never lasts forever." It would be a small disappointment that such schmalz and banality could comfort. In fact a disappointment sinks much lower into our state of mind. After all I had had my anticipations, my more or less justified hopes, that now burst like a bubble. The impact of hitting the floor of reality is harsh.

But I will begin again, since we still find ourselves on the harmless side of the issue we are discussing. Since when have we focused upon our disappointments in such a way as to be indignant at having such experiences? It will have been in the 18th century, through the psychological construct of the enlightened ego. If we are not to mince words, one can place disappointments onto a scale representing the quality of the disappointment, from sharp to bitter to unspeakable. Or one can, with Robert Burton at the beginning of the 17th century, refer to this depressing state as a "variation" in the duration of melancholy. Thus, disappointment is not an objective recognition of a failure; rather, and far more, the insularity of one's own world receives a forceful exposure to actual reality.

Since we currently live in a society that is borne along by the notion that we must at all times test and re-test, we are always having to reckon with tests even in our daily life. It begins during the school years. Moving forward in life depends more and more upon tests: already in kindergarten one is subjected to aptitude tests testing whether one might be able to integrate himself into a group, whether he has reached control of his bodily functions and has developed his linguistic ability to the point of being able make himself understood. During school attendance the tests are more and more common, and then they receive their official evaluation in certificates. We are however unconcerned about how many tests a person is expected to take and to pass. Lurking in the background is a certain suspicion in our society that people are not able to do what they claim they can. This has been taken to the grotesque length in Austria that one tries to garner qualifications by devious means in order to move up to a higher position. That the methods of swindling keep pace with the examination procedures is obvious. Anyone who has read Nikolai Gogol's stage play *The Government Inspector* is well informed about the consequences of attempting to get around the procedures of testing and the corruption that accompanies it. It is much more bitter when children earnestly prepare for such tests, sacrificing a good deal of time they could have been improving their knowledge – and then meet the disappointment of not having reached what they had imagined. The harshest version comes with the use of negative marks. Although it is hard to imagine that a candidate knows nothing at all, it soon comes to light that it was not a lack of knowledge or inability or some kind of laziness in learning that was the cause of the negative evaluation, but rather that marks were being misused as a form of discipline. And since from time to time the student's behavior enters into the evaluation of his performance another kind of disappointment arises, for the persons evaluated in this way had no sense they were so bad or so weak. Such disappointments have become part of the routine one must bear in the daily life of school, because they have become the norm: the students have become used to them. And even a worse disappointment – being kept back for a year – is to be overcome somehow, or perhaps even repressed. This is the accepted way of responding to such a sanction. In this connection one should realize that in the school system of Central Europe the rule is still followed that final marks are to be reached by averaging all previous marks. This is a significant dampening of any motivation. Good work at the end is not indicated in the final mark; instead, through the report card one is to be reminded of the indelible stain of a negative mark years ago! Presumably this is the one consistent practice in school – to disappoint the students consistently with the "elephant memory" of their grading records.

And yes, there are disappointments that go still deeper. In admissions procedures that require that candidates have already reached a certain level – for instance, art colleges requiring candidates to submit appropriate art works of their own to be evaluated by the teachers – one expects not only that his own performance will receive a positive evaluation, but also that an objective and acknowledged standard of previous performances has been established, whether in painting, piano performance, drawing, or sculpture. Not to pass this admission procedure is the most bitter disappointment for those who fail to. Was too little time spent in preparation? Does one lack the talent to deserve any further training? Had one made a false judgment in thinking his work so far was worthy of consideration? But weren't his drawings almost perfect, his piano playing flawless, his paintings appealing and imaginative? Getting a negative decision is like being hit by a club.

After such a devastating blow, which can have a lasting effect on the child's psychological stability, it will be difficult to accept rejection and difficult to come to terms with oneself. The usual method is to repress it. One no longer looks at his cherished works, one stops looking at the sheet music, the brushes remain dry. Must one now decide to set aside and leave behind everything that a few days ago was part of his normal repertoire of activities? Will the affected child, the teenager, now concentrate on other areas? Surely not. The disappointment leads to a danger of lethargy and just to let everything be as it is. It promotes the fatalistic notion that if I am bad at what I thought I was good at, then I will be bad in all areas. The principle one adopts, in the figurative sense, is "If the cow is gone, the calf will be gone, too...." This kind of defeatism can last a long time and undermines the structure of motivation that up until two weeks ago one had kept intact so strongly and carefully

I remind you that I brought up this problem in connection with the development of Paul Cezanne. Given his strong personality he had an inner conviction and he kept on painting. But what should a 12 year-old do who is not 28, like Cezanne? One can only hope that boys and girls find the support they need from their parents, and that the stable affection of one's siblings continues.

If I may insert a critical note, it is that talent can lead to a negative experience. Having talent tempts one to overestimate oneself and can pervert self-confidence into conceit. One begins to deceive oneself about himself. Probably one cannot predict whether a given talent comes to its full potential in cases when it basically disturbs or impairs one's self-assurance. The best protection against a distorted view, against an arrogant view of oneself, is reflection, the silence embraced by self-control – in short, a skepticism about what one had previously prized about himself. Of course, this presupposes personal sovereignty, and maybe one will emerge stronger from this negative experience. That this hoped-for state of affairs also has something to do with luck goes without saying.

I must be careful in what I am saying, since I would find it distasteful to leave any good mark about our school system. I don't know why, but school had such a negative effect on me that I can only reach an objective judgment with difficulty. For years I was plagued with migraines, for years I had every possible sickness, which today I would deem psychosomatic. What bothered me was not only the smell in the schools, the alarming noise, the screams during the breaks: above all it was the narrow minded outlook in each field of study regarding the wider horizons of knowledge. Why after all does a "mathematician" want to teach mathematics? What would he want to say about mathematics? Today I know that to all appearances for these mathematicians in the school their life's content consisted in the threat they wielded on the occasion of giving a negative mark on a test. Again and again this insidiousness could be observed, their enjoyment of erroneous calculations; and day after day the sun rose over their bald heads, for they so treasured rendering an easy judgment against a false result as if the result were a moral failure.

I already described the gaping shortcomings in physics and chemistry. A complete misunderstanding of natural science gave legitimacy and importance to these narrow experts. What they had in view was not teaching, nor to seek an interpretation of the world with mathematics or formal science: no, the majority of them were sadists and they were not interested at all in the world. Being too bad to do physics as a science, too bad to find place for research, too bad for academic teaching, they had taken shelter in the protected little workshop of the school. And all they conveyed was a sadistic lust that students might have as much trouble as they had had in their own education. Probably the literary testimony of Roald Dahl about his time in an English college is the best representation of this sublime cruelty. I recommend it to anyone who feels at a loss out of disappointment: look at Roald Dahl's *Boy*.

I cannot change my spots. These same types were there to be found also in the universities. The great professors who used to open their own textbooks at any page and ask the test-taker to recite from it: no surprise it was a psychologist. Another wanted to hear a reference to his own publications in the response, and a third one did not stick to the assigned material but claimed that his own questions were drawn from the common body of knowledge.

People like this are passing out disappointments? It mustn't be so!

So, Julian – and you others, too! Don't let yourselves be destroyed! Just as it says, in the book of *Genesis*, "I am placing enmity between you and the serpent" (I know I am badly mangling the text – see 3.15!), so do I view the situation in schools, today.

Make no mistake! It is *school* that is at fault, not the honored profession of the teachers!

Just now I've thought of a lecture on pedagogy and erotics by Friedrich Kainz, the philosopher of language. He had the opinion that the students are to be taught a love for the subject – and nothing else. Now where is that to be found?

Now, my dears, I'd better close:

All my love to the four of you, your R.

97.
The Messages of Music

Dear Nina, Dear Julian, Dear Marie and Vicky,

In two of my letters I have tried in different ways to give you an understanding of the Renaissance. Perhaps I have not made clear enough the thing that Hermann Broch criticized about the Renaissance, namely its arrogance toward all other periods. In the meanwhile we have come to know what has become of the discovery of the "modern man," namely the madness of the *Übermensch* – or else the melancholic. For this also Hermann Broch criticized the Renaissance. In both cases European civilization did itself no good service. In the "worship" of the *Übermensch* one loses one's knowledge of other cultures and appreciation for them. Friedrich Schlegel fought against this unavailingly, in his *Universal History*. For all the appreciation of historicism, from Leopold von Ranke to Friedrich von Savigny and the historical school of national economics, the view of Europe had become so parochial that even the harbinger of change from North America, the Declaration of Independence of 1776, was not taken seriously but was merely thought of as an "external event" not important for Europe's future history. The enormous expansion in the colonial politics of the European powers in the 19th century only strengthened an unjustifiable arrogance according to which whole continents and subcontinents were being neglected, such as China, Japan, Brazil, or Argentina.

The meaning of this endeavor of mine is to make it clear to you that for your own future world you must pay attention to the history of the "New World." It is a fatal error to think that making a big trip there can substitute for studying these erstwhile "colonies." It is all the more far-reaching stupidity that such tourists are even worse than the worst of colonial officers. Although the latter introduced a completely irrelevant value-system based on a European military model they brought with them from their "motherlands," this was still better than the irresponsible bigotry of vacationers who enter a Zen-Buddhist temple in a T-shirt, shorts, and sneakers, as if it were the train station in Aschaffenburg. Unfortunately the same charge must be brought against the Arabic world travelers or the Russian snob who is more interested in the display of a jeweler than a Japanese woodblock print. And the more modest imitation of these world cruises – hiring a tour guide – is no better nor any more decent.

I didn't want to rant about this again but only remind you: these "denizens of the underworld" are the visible representation of how the world is being destroyed. Thus, for the first time you are faced with the decision by what means and by what considerations the condition of the world can be preserved. You have received a difficult inheritance for which neither renouncing the bequeathal nor a wishy-washy acceptance of your role will be of any help at all. This inheritance will be your own, in whatever condition you receive it.

And I will again circle back to where I began. In the development of music you can quickly come to know that melancholy becomes more and more predominant. Franz Schubert had once observed that all music is sad, but by the time of the late romantic this became more unmistakably clear. Melancholy weighs heavily in the symphonies of Robert Schumann, Johannes Brahms, or Anton Bruckner. And it is not a characteristic of Central European music alone, since things are the same with Peter Ilyich Tchaikovsky and Hector Berlioz. When makes the medieval man different from us is his despair; as for us we have buried ourselves in melancholy.

Since I have written you that in Petrarch we encounter the first "modern man" I want to quote him, since we are stuck in the same dilemma that he was the first to formulate: "How many things are there, in nature, that we have found no way to refer to yet? How many other things are there that though we do have names for them, human speech has not captured their deepest essential meaning yet? How often did I hear you complain, how often have I seen you fall silent or become completely annoyed, since the thing that was so clear and easy for the thinking soul to recognize could not as easily be expressed by the tongue or by the pen? What is the worth of our language, so limited and so awkward, if it can neither get a hold on all things nor what it does get a hold onto it can nevertheless not master?"

It is apparent that our facility with language is ever more limited since we live in a noisy and raucous world, and just when we are about to say something the media has interrupted with something else. We can hardly establish our own structure, our own inner world, since we no longer have the language with which to do it – our language has been stolen from us. It is to be noted that our language has lost its authenticity and no longer has any authority – of which the current "political correctness" is a salient proof. The theft began with the dictionaries of the Enlightenment, and subsequent thefts were brought to our attention starting with Karl Kraus. Our language was either faulted as being a mere dialect or else we had to buckle under rules of linguistic usage. So it will be a most difficult task for you to reformulate your language, to rediscover it. This cannot be done by means of what is currently our common but faulty surrogate, the English language; rather, it will lie with you to develop your own autochthonous language all over again.

The fact that language and music exhibit an inner relatedness is documented by every song. Thus song is present in the earliest written documents – for example in the book of *Samuel* – as a means of expression that along with a musical instrument gives a special expressiveness to language. From long ago we get this message: "when the spirit of God came over Samuel, David took up his harp and played on it with his hand, and Saul was refreshed, and it was better with him, and the evil spirit departed from him." If this refers to the gloominess of Saul, the song of David wielded a healing power. Plato reports similarly that a thief gave up trying to steal when he heard the music of flutes. Thus it was regular in antiquity to use melodies as therapy, for example against melancholy as the tradition says of the physician Asclepiades. Galen of Pergamon expressed the same idea around 200AD.

But what has happened so that after Mozart this "function" of music for achieving joyfulness and liberation was apparently lost? Only a hundred years later, the overture to *Götterdämmerung* depresses us and troubles us, with the loud beats of the timpani and the dark tones of the tubas and horns. How has it come about that the symphonies based on the *Metamorphoses* of Ovid by Carl Ditters von Dittersdorf, composed around 1780, could be followed by Schubert's *"Unfinished" Symphony* in B-minor as soon as 1822?

This surely means that a transformation of the "purpose" of music came about. It has always been believed, since ancient times, that music has the ability to waken different feelings. It lies within it to cause a conversion in the listener, a call to oneself and to reflection; but it can also effect the opposite. As Soranus of Ephesus stated in his medical treatises around 100AD, music can stimulate madness. That the muse might kiss us when we make music is a notion that belongs more to poetry, but Soranus was convinced that the spirit of God can stir us through sounds – and also the opposite. Music was understood as a means of healing and as a poison. At the end of the Middle Ages one believed, once again, that music according to its tone colors and intensity (as the music of the Church already knew) has an influence similar to that of the celestial constellations. In 1482 Ramos de Paseja, in his *Musica practica*, introduced a method by which music could define specific states of mind. This anticipated the *Well-Tempered Clavier* of Johann Sebastian Bach, who however did not see a mystical element but rather a sensory impression mediated by the sound pattern of the chromatic scale: this was the baroque's demonic variation on the mystical.

The point is that already with the Renaissance there was a suggestion of the demonic power of music, which from then on music cannot be imagined to be without. Although the compositions of Hildegard von Bingen were accused of having a bewitching power that detracted from the divine liturgy, this was only the judgment of the Roman curia. And yet from the Renaissance on, music is no longer a reflection of the divine harmony, but becomes a medium of expression produced by men, that can just as soon be used to seduce. Thus for Ficino, music succeeds to distract one from sad outlooks and the lute is able to dispel one's darker thoughts.

Modern man is accompanied by a history of music that brings on more and more melancholy, from Bruckner to Gustav Mahler to Anton Webern to John Cage. My purpose for bringing in this large perspective is to get some grip on the spirit of modern music. Though in the past it may have produced joy or sadness, today we hear all the more clearly that mere sounds have become music. A complete transformation has taken place, a process analogous to the one that has afflicted our language.

This far-flung treatment has in view to show you, using music as an example, just how the essential state of your culture can change: indeed, the whole system of reference has been "reversed." The earlier godly harmony was no longer followed, and instead men saw their musical compositions as harmonic constructions of their own, subservient to whatever mood they wished. In the 19th century the compensation for God consisted in music, in the "stage consecration play" (thus did Wagner characterize his *Parsifal*); and it was advanced in the high liturgy of operas and festivals: in the Religion of Art (Hegel's formulation).

It is important for you to know that a comparable process in our language has come about. The "confusion about language" was best brought before our eyes by Goethe when he tells us that poor young Werther is no longer reading Vergil, whereas in the second chapter of the novel Werther comes to rely on the great literary swindle – "Ossian." Werther admires the epic as an authentic representation of a terrible reality. Macpherson had hidden his forgery of an early medieval poem beneath some stones so as then to be so lucky as to find the manuscript and present it to the public. As we know, Werther's end in the novel is suicide. It is a description of the results of the destruction of language.

With this drastic example I want to confront you with the problem of guarding your language as being the highest good of your existence. You must interpret the statement of John as being also a warning:

> In the beginning was the Word
> and the Word was with God
> and the Word was God.
> …
> All things were made by the Word,
> and without it nothing was that came into being.
> In it was life …

You are very close to my heart. I remain, with the best of greetings, your R.

98.
Thoughts on the Biosphere

Dear Nina, Dear Julian, Dear Marie and Vicky,

We are now in a tricky situation that will affect you even more than it does my generation. The ongoing damage to our natural order is keeping pace with the long-lasting disturbances of our social order. Very different causes for the disturbances can be adduced. One can point to the revolutions – the Industrial and the French Revolutions – which renewed mankind's fantasies of being all-powerful, given the fact such fantasies had been carried forward from the Renaissance: In the Enlightenment they were brought back to life, and brought about something of a secular mysticism in the natural sciences of the 17th century. It may have to do with the problem that the projects of modernization, supported by powerful technological developments, have not been sufficiently understood by us. Friedrich Tenbruck, a sociologist that I prize most highly, once developed an idea, namely that social scientists were generally deficient in their ability to master intellectually various challenges of social change. They presented us with insights about our social positions and status that we accepted as if they were self-evident, and we applied their insights and then made artificial modifications in the forms of our socializations and in our social institutions. And Tenbruck formulated his conclusion succinctly and forcibly: Modern society is formed by the thought of sociology. With this he opened the path for us to say, analogously, that we have not been able to master intellectually the results reached by the natural sciences, first and foremost in terms of their practical relevance: we have followed these blindly, which then with the advance of technology have found almost limitless application in the technization of our "biosphere." When the great comic poet Johann Nestroy once said from the stage, "Progress is smaller than it looks," he really hit the nail on the head. I recall this delightful quotation since with the increase in technology we never took into consideration the damage that would result. When we build an airplane we think hardly at all about how it might crash; likewise we think little even today about the consequences of our interventions in the flora and fauna of this world. Seldom do we contemplate that we ourselves, whom we consider to be a robust life form, can hardly tolerate a fluctuation of our body temperature more than a single degree centigrade; and when have we hardly risen above 37 degrees we feel sick. A body temperature under 35.5 is described as unnaturally low, which is uncomfortable for us, and under 35 degrees we become hypothermic. Especially among those suffering from carcinoma the body temperature falls precipitously.

These remarks alone will make it clear to you that our lives are sustained within an extraordinarily narrow temperature range, and that similar margins generally obtain in the natural world, also. Thus it is not for nothing that one pays attention to fluctuations in climate. It is deeply amusing that the natural sciences and technology have already changed our lives irreversibly, but at the same time were able to make us aware what boundaries we are bumping into or have already crossed.

The advance of technology is as large a cause of transformation as the Revolutions were. What I noted above is again relevant here: apparently we have not mastered, intellectually, the consequences of technology. True, we laugh a little at the few people who adopt a posture of asceticism and will not drive a car or take a plane, avoiding to cause greenhouse gases, but – without having to turn it into a religion – they have obviously understood more about the demands our lives put upon our earth than the hundreds of thousands of people who seek out the far corners of the world on a cruise ship so as continually to damage them. Such cruises our first explorers never mounted. Dr. David Livingston or Fridtjof Nansen, Roald Amundsen and Walter Scott, and much earlier Marco Polo and later James Cook, traveled the world scrupulously, as our pioneers of geography and natural history. Never did the thought occur that hordes of tourists would one day haunt all parts of the world and more savagely than the most savage barbarians in the history of mankind would annihilate every culture and every natural environment with their culture of rapine and egoistical appetite. In the year of the pandemic, 2020, it was observed out of an airplane for the first time that because the waters were undisturbed due to the shrinkage of shipping, an immeasurably large and stationary brown cesspool became visible in the middle of the Adriatic. It was the result of the "emptying out" of all the garbage from the ships, which is simply dumped into the sea. The refuse of 3,500 tourists from a cruise ship ends up in the sea – everywhere, from the Pacific to the Indian Ocean. Along the beaches of the South Sea islands the plastic refuse has constructed giant islands, which now constitute part of the "landscape." One hundred forty years earlier Paul Gauguin painted his *Idylls* of a more pristine landscape.

I do not want to go into lamentations, which I have a tendency to do in any case, but rather want to make it clear to you that you will be faced with a huge task of repair, for which even more intellectual effort will be needed than has been expended in perfecting the world's technology up until now. Even landing on the moon will have been a lesser task than the removal of all the feces, garbage, and plastic bottles. In the course of "modernization" a collective consciousness was created whose self-understanding was framed as "an abbreviated stay in the present." The sequence of styles in "modern art" along with the modes of fashion are no small indication of a rapid succession of a variety of design concepts, sometimes even contradictory ones. This means that van Gogh and Monet are worlds apart although they were contemporaries, and yet we class both of them as embodiments of modern painting. In citing this I want to illustrate to you that we began to designate and describe our world as new, both politically and aesthetically, and from this drew conclusions and became convinced that we were actually moving into a new and unprecedented future – even according to the very opposite motifs of the paintings of Gauguin and van Gogh. Naturally, as in the case of the possible plane crash we ignore, we have not only failed to talk about the negative consequences of modernization, but also about the various implications of losses due to modernization. Political pundits, professionally very fond of democracy, never became fond of thinking about its opposite. Thus it came about that during the wave of democratization and parliamentarism, totalitarianism also became more attractive. And it also came about that the most evil tyranny swept democracy away and instigated a World War that far outstripped the Thirty Years War in gruesomeness. In the midst of the spread of human rights and an unequivocal commitment to humanity and equality, even if it was only in the legal sphere of society, genocide no less had become possible and the erection of the concentration camps or the Gulag, where thoughtless whim was allowed to decide between life and death. Many have succeeded to ignore the fact that totalitarian tyranny was also a result of modernization, at the same time as the establishment of democracies worldwide.

The concept of "modern/modernity," like most concepts having to do with culture and politics, was established out of the church law of the Fifth Century, and designated innovations in the institutions of the church as "modern" in contrast to previous practices. In the Council of Chalcedon, in 451, the "modern" was formulated for the first time as the contrary of the "old." In the quarrel within the Académie Française something similar was the case, from 1687 on, for the one "party" supported the standpoint that with the perfectibility of the sciences a "modernity" had arrived, against which all that came before could not measure up. Previous knowledge lost its "exemplary" status: from now on, one put his trust only in future knowledge and achievements, and their consequences. Just as a mechanic today cannot repair an automobile unless he has the "electronic key" for the motor, so we do not know how to give an exhaustive definition of modernization. We have largely been surrounded with this maelstrom of change and have not noticed that the progression of modernization does not correspond with the realms that constitute our life-world. This is how the striking mismatch has set in between accelerating modernization over against the largely unchanged conditions within our social, political, and cultural frameworks. With capitalism, of course, these framework conditions were no longer seen as apodictic certainties, but could be expressed concretely in terms of money. In part one saw fit to oppose this capitalistic version of social order with socialism, but at the same time, in compromise, one sought to strengthen it in social democracy. Much later, after 1945, an ideal balance was introduced and came to a halt in the neoliberalism of the 1990's.

Whereas modernization was the result of the aesthetic program based on German classicism and European romanticism, the present "modern age" detached itself from its previous historical context. From here on the little word "modern" came into our vocabulary and thanks to the rise of technology got ever-broader application, quite apart from the inherent sagacity or lack thereof of the objects to which it was applied. This insight is significant because in the full flush of modernity political attempts for integration into the state and its laws are fundamentally postponed. This is an illustration of how modernization circumvents the institutions of democracy. In almost all questions the wide field of administrative law falls behind, and while it may imagine it has a chance to resist by procedures of delay, it must ultimately give in to modernization's overwhelming force. This remark is important for the reason that in case you, my grandchildren, ever want to object to the violent disturbance of your life-world, any hope that this development might be brought to a halt by recourse to law stands on very weak legs. With the rise of technology modernization has become a force in the same way that the law of the strongest once prevailed. The rule of law is becoming relativized: the law is undergoing a strange transformation even though the letter of the law remains unaltered. Courts have long since become servants of hidden interests. And they will become more so in the future. It is very annoying to see these men, enrobed with craftiness, dispense an autocratic justice. And yet who has the money or the patience to wait for an outcome that once could be expected, given the settled stubbornness of the courts? I myself have had negative experiences overall – the problem was not one's standing in society but rather a prevalence of routine indifference among the judges. Under this point of view, one's experience of the administration is a game of chance, except of course in cases of the strongly broadening use of bribery in such procedures. I fear that you all will be confronted with exactly this sort of justice, and so my basic advice is to seek a settlement outside of court.

In the stage-play *The Collaborator*, Friedrich Dürrenmatt already described this change. In a commentary on his play he wrote that corruption humanizes totalitarian systems but ruins constitutional ones. We have already reached the condition of a legal government which, especially in administrative law, seems to confirm this assumption of conforming to precedent. As to gauging the importance of administrative law, we learn by studying it not only the condition of a government of laws but also how stable it is, how the wording of a law is respected without its being allowed to be influenced by partisan interests. One should fear that in Europe we have gotten miles away from the original intention of a law, and that bending the law has become more and more acceptable.

With such examples I want to illustrate a situation that is particularly depressing. Our legal institutions more and more clearly show themselves ready to be viewed as products of social conditions and began quite early to legitimate a certain state of society. A strange mixture has come about. Let me describe it with a contrast: in the positivistic evaluation of the legal rules from 1933 to 1938 and up to 1945 a formal finding was reached that everything "played out" within the frame of legality, that the legal order was adequate for managing political order and that it justified the breaching of obligations to human rights. On the other hand one sees oneself more and more pressured by altered laws of freedom that have almost lost their civil meaning and have turned into demands for individual freedom of movement. Law is apparently taking a course similar to the considerable change language usage has itself undergone. One can see a certain insouciance, a general primitiveness required in the description of facts, which no longer adequately conveys meaning. After Karl Kraus, Thomas Bernhard was a key witness of the loss of language, in documenting the decline of institutions and language in his analysis.

Given these observations one can no longer share the optimism of the political pundits who once fostered the belief that all the countries of the world would change into democracies. The would-be dictators, under the force of what has happened to them and their self-criticism, would regret their errors – and yet very few will read the handwriting on the wall but will only tighten the thumbscrews even more. The miracle of democratization after 1945 will not be repeated.

All these factors are aspects of modernization, which does not stop at accelerations of all kinds, nor with the ancillary devices that are de-professionalizing our crafts, nor with reducing the complexity of everyday problems: instead it has forced our consciousness into a dependency that more and more diminishes our chances of intellectually mastering ever-greater problems. It would be interesting to add up what competencies and kinds of knowledge we have lost since the Industrial Revolution.

Of course I surprise you when I represent these changes in such disastrous terms. I can also imagine that you will see exaggerations in this, predictions that in the end will not come true. But I have had nothing in mind but to bring the old blueprint of a republic developed by Montesquieu into our present situation. You will once remember that the three pillars on which political order rests are the executive, the legislative, and the judiciary. You can now measure what changes this great political construction has undergone. The three pillars of a republic are being required to withstand an earthquake brought upon us by another triad: electronic media, technology, and economics.

These three forces affect your existence, your consciousness, and your behavior. They are by now permanent ingredients in the household of your existence. All this has resulted from the dimension of modernization. It has led to an individualistic anthropology that merely focuses on man's relation to himself. If three hundred years ago Kant wanted to answer the question, "What is man?" he could only partly foresee that the tacit framework of the question is one's relation to his neighbor. Martin Buber introduced his dialogue-philosophy in which man can be represented in his essential relations: his relation to being, to life, to the neighbor, and to himself. To put it pointedly, the loss or the weakening of these forms of relation can only lead to loneliness. This must be overcome. If we could, in the meanwhile, perceive that the allure of technology and media and economy are driving us toward this isolation, overthrowing them would become the task before us if we want to continue as human beings. The new challenge, which stands before you, is to design the life-activity by which aloneness and dependency will be overcome. This opens up, literally, a new world. It will not only have to do with balancing the old tension between individualism and collectivism, where in the former case the face of man is distorted as in the caricatures by Honoré Daumier, and in the latter the face is covered up, as in the portraits by Francis Bacon. Both correspond to the new homelessness of man, both show us that man has been marooned, even become a foundling, and then later isolated. In his writings Michel Houllebecq has dealt with this in a depressing way. At most it would be a computer technician or a computer scientist who would see their isolation as an advantage and think that one must be thankful for such an individualism. Should a prospect of escape come into view it would only be found within these kinds of groups. One can shift one's own responsibility over to them. And as this kind of socialization gets a comprehensive and impermeable hold on man, all the easier will it be for him to fall into a collective. Fear of the world calms down, flight from the world comes to an end. And yet in collectivism the human being is lost, for collectivism is the last barrier man has erected before himself in order not to encounter himself.

As a final result the next generation in its philosophical science of humanity must establish a foundation in reality on the basis of which it can reach an altered understanding of the person, and can develop an altered understanding of community. One such basis was given us by Martin Buber, according to whom "the essence of man, which makes him unique, is directly known ... there is I and Thou in our world only when there is man; and in truth the I first exists out of its relationship with the Thou." This recovery of the Thou will be the most important task in order to master all the countless breakdowns.

This was a long letter. It will not be easy to read. And yet I wish you will. It lies with you to test its assertions someday, and to measure its prospect against reality. Why I wrote it to you, you will understand. Whether however it will have the meaning for you that it has for myself, I cannot know. In any case I hope it does. And you ought to appreciate not only my stated motive for the letter – that would be too little – but also the question of what will guarantee and protect your own future existence and way of life, and the world you live in.

All the best, I remain your R.

99.
The Holy Landscapes:
Jerusalem, Athens, and Rome

Dear Nina, Dear Julian, Marie and Vicky,

In the book – a Christmas present for me – my father wrote a dedication that has stayed with me always: "Jerusalem, Athens, and Rome are the fortresses of our spiritual landscape. Defend them! They are also the foundations of your higher self! – Santa Claus (Dad) – 1957." The book is a collection of comments on Latin proverbs. As far as I can tell it was published in 1957. Today, sixty years later, I can only second that dedication and want you to place it into your hearts. Indeed, from Jerusalem, Athens, and Rome we have received our spiritual guidelines for centuries and millennia. Often we have proved undeserving of them, and have sinned against the spirit of this legacy – so very often. European history can unfortunately be included in this criticism, and yet it is an error to see our history as nothing but a catastrophic failure. Is the whole of it to be seen as a continuation of sinfulness ever since Aaron's dance around the golden calf? Our break with Hellenic humanism is just as scandalous, but don't we know countless counterexamples since Sophocles? Of course we have betrayed the political and juristic tradition of the Roman Republic, but was all of it a betrayal? Mayn't we think of Montesquieu or Hugo Grotius? One can fault everything that happened in every century; and yet we have this other shimmering history, once it is allowed to move on its own according to its own self-understanding, since the *Magna Charta Libertatum* of 1215, which was as it should have been all along. In the counter-examples we discover our spiritual landscape, in which our fortresses stand: Jerusalem, Athens, and Rome.

In fact these three cities remain present not only in history: they also live in our consciousness. Often we are unaware how this spiritual legacy became a part of our consciousness. One needs not travel to Israel to know that this cave in Bethlehem in which Jesus was born and that the Church of the Holy Sepulcher built over Golgotha began to define our history.

However you will view Christianity, which in fact depends upon your own earnest decision, you will never be able to avoid the fact that the "Western World," our world, was formed by it. To whatever church you belong, or from whatever church you wish to leave, you will always be moving within the wake of this powerful historical axis-time. Whether it is the old Roman Papal Church with its work of remembrance, or the Reformed Churches with their staunch focus upon Scripture, or the Orthodox Church and its power for mystical veneration documented by its every icon, they are always present. It may be a lonely church temple, the echoing toll of a bell, an icon on display in a museum: all this keeps this landscape in view within which you move; and you can claim a hundred times that you want to overcome this history – as in the revolts against the spirit of Europe in 1789 and in 1917 or in the most evil frenzy and extermination of all its witnesses – still, this history will not be erased. This basis of all your thinking will not go by the wayside in the history of our earth as did Cro-Magnon Man at the beginning of the Holocene, or Neanderthal Man. We will continue to be puzzled about Stonehenge, but not about the religions of the Scriptures, which have become part of us.

We must ever be clear that according to the Bible, the conception of the end of history was hopeful, as being the end of all ugliness and gruesomeness. It is perhaps the greatest burden of Church History on the one hand that it must proclaim this message of salvation beyond history but on the other hand must make itself set the tone within history. Here, the famous highhanded self-promotion of the Papacy in the Renaissance went to extremes. The situation came about over which Friedrich Nietzsche exulted: the church had finally brought on its own demise. That was why he was so furious about that "peasant lout" Luther, who ended up saving "Western" Christianity with the Reformation.

I want to digress, briefly, to make an historical clarification. The Reformation was an explosion of the "letter" and with it a re-awakening of the Word. The Word will once again to speak out of the Book. A few letters ago I cited the prologue of *John* about the Word. Out of the book, which was to become a special subject for philology, the word comes to the fore, and out of history the gospel comes to the fore. The "Protestants" made the sacrament of the Word the central point of their liturgy, but with this they killed the Eucharist. As a result with the Reformation they did not bring the Word to the Christians, now lonely without communion in the church, but mainly taught reading. And thus one began to read everything, and the Bible once again became an object of study for classical philology.

If we may summarize the history, with the Reformation we brought to an end the "united states" of the West. We have indeed built many bridges through the Treaty of Münster and Osnabrück in 1648, but in the end the decline could not be arrested and nationalism took the place of all the bygone perspectives in Europe. One had to face the fact that Christians became Frenchmen, Spaniards, Italians, Germans, Poles, and Czechs. They stood by their patriotic, nationalist, and even modernizing economical motives, but no longer stood by any religious one.

I have wanted to convey this to you so emphatically since the result, since its numerous errors and failures, must not confuse us: the fortresses of our spiritual landscape remain, as my father wrote to me, Jerusalem, Athens, and Rome.

I will not stop here with recalling history. Out of history much that is new, much that is surprising, and much that is holy, has unfolded. Surely you can be familiar with as many saints as with emperors and kings, tyrants and presidents. You will probably be able to name more saints than popes, which counsels us to be humble, but do you understand the sense of the sacred? In the saints the trace of the Lord makes itself known, throughout our history and throughout our lives. It is my hypothesis that we would not have survived the catastrophes of the 20th century if we had not had these traces pointing to our salvation – in the personages of Edith Stein, Simone Weil, Dietrich Bonhoeffer, Alfred Delp, James Graf Moltke… Without these we could no longer look each other in the face.

I am always drawn to the lectures on the Talmud by Emmanuel Levinas. There we find the way for reconstruction: one must read the holy scriptures not with the purpose of becoming learned, in order to know more, or even to reach a higher rank in the community, but out of the love for Him. For the love of this knowledge one can easily renounce the will to power. These thoughts shimmer bright like gold in the flow of history and yet the gold is not seen. So we must ask the question, Who is all this for?

In my last trip to Rome it became clear: This entire and giant power with all art and refinement only distracts us from what Rome truly suffers from: the crisis of humanism, which has already long been underway. This also was brought up in the dialogues of the Rabbis: "For whom is all this?" It is probably kept for the time in which the Messiah comes. Levinas cites the important passage from *Isaiah*: "one will not store it up (the profits) nor hoard them together, but it will belong to those who sit before the Lord." Everything is bathed in the light of the Messiah. And you will understand that I here am following the words of Levinas since he is one of the few who in our times does not want to let men degenerate, or even dissolve, into sociologism or psychologism. "(The rays) do not leave in darkness the abstract architecture of the numbers and the concepts that rise above our Mediterranean Sea: they in no way neglect it, nor likewise the abundance of so much bread and so many ideas, indispensable for one man as for another and also true, ideas that each man carries and brings with himself. But these rays break the horrid curse of *having*, through which one's Being stiffens into what one *is*."

These thoughts "reform" humanity once again, or at least see it on the brink of reformation in concept. Being will be possible only by an interruption of gathering and heaping up, not by accumulating for that distorts our view of our neighbor. We are forgetting our neighbor! If the heaping up of goods comes to occupy our entire consciousness, as a sort of insistence on that way of being, then all there will be will be the usual institutions – money and banks, and therefore men at war with each other: a "dubious ontology."

Alternatively, to offer up such "having" to God is the adventure that the peoples of the world could engage in, instead: Peace. In the same way that Samuel was offered up to God, the whole people became consecrated to God. From this time on, *Psalm 68* tells us (68: 6-10, 19-21, 28-29), the people of our Lord will live in peace and be saved by the hand of God. He created the land but the people of the Lord must administrate this gift correctly, without sin and war. What is really new is that behind the revenge of God against his enemies, the love of the Lord protects peace. The appearing of God repeats itself, beyond all our theology and our reality. In the increasing difficulties of life, the epiphany of the Lord encompasses all mankind.

I wonder if I will be understood in these thoughts. By this I mean not you, since affection opens itself to the most locked-up of thoughts – in particular, as I have written at greater length above, in love of the Scripture.

All the best, I remain your R.

100.
On Astonishment

Dear Nina, Dear Julian, Marie and Vicky,

The thought presents itself again that I should write on art, in general, to advance its importance and thus to acknowledge its relative rank. Surely we must look upon art as an equal to philosophy and science in what it embodies. This attitude I have presented in all my letters because I want to let you see the whole panorama of my life-world; but the attitude also raises the question, which I formulated once before, whether the present phenomena of reality as we know them can stand as an adequate representation of our times. After all with the help of technology we pass our time in huge undertakings – in a single day we fly from Vienna to Tokyo or Johannesburg. Such feats have become commonplace and we are inured from wondering at them. The last author to speak of astonishment was Jeanne Hersch. She, at least, possessed the personal sovereignty to be able to be astonished. The ability to be astonished requires appropriate humility and sensitivity and sympathy. I fear that we have fairly well lost these qualities.

In order not to bore you again with the defeatism for which I am often criticized, I will present an example, which includes my astonishment to boot. I get criticized for always following in my own ways. It was even "worse" when I went by bicycle, before my accident, since I always went by the same route. I would often hear, "Doesn't this bore you?" Regularly I would give the same answer, that the reason I walk the same paths over and over is because I want to experience "what's happening" in nature as it makes its way as the months go by. And so I chose certain plants and made observations throughout the year. Here, once, was a white dogwood, and there a dog-rose, and among them were trees such as beech or a larch or a maple. These are basically simple things. Who would stop to look at a *cornus alba*? I would marvel up close, in the spring, at the beautiful white blossoms that then in mid-April with a light wind would create something of a snow flurry. I would pay particular attention to places where plants had reclaimed a stony area. Week by week tiny plants followed the hearty dandelion, the false chamomile, and the daisy. This was enough to make me marvel. And how much more ought one marvel in noticing how the reproductive power of nature is able to assert itself against the human madness of concrete and asphalt! And a similar astonishment is appropriate in connection with works of art: architecture, sculpture, music, and painting. If I do not fail to notice the "pale snow rose" (*helleborus niger*) nor the *viburnum bodnantense*, the "winter snow-ball," how could I fail to notice the monument by Antonio Canova in the Augustinian Church in Vienna?

In this description I am giving you an example of the "panorama" which I think should also become the environment of your life-world. When I do this literature may seem to recede a bit into the background. We must absolutely keep it in mind: often it must rush to the aid of philosophy when the latter lacks the experiential basis of a "life-background." I have probably told you that Friedrich Schiller brought the "categorical imperative" closer to us than its "inventor," Immanuel Kant. Often these sorts of cross-overs are needed for the things that are not established by the sciences but by poetry.

It was medieval poetry – the *Nibelungenlied* – that described our political landscapes, while philosophy in the West still stayed far away from the topic of politics. By means of such testimonies we can reconstruct an "archaeo-genealogy" that constitutes a prehistory of our ego. And here I can think of some authors who have developed this new theme. With Michel Foucault and Jacques Lacan, we embarked on a search for our ego – for the formation of the ego – because by now we know that all of psychoanalysis is not able to achieve that. Since then, thanks to "discourse analysis," we have come to understand the testimony of myths differently. We are forced to do so since we are no longer satisfied with our present state of being. It seems empty to us, or, rather, filled – indeed "stuffed" – due to our electronic media and technology. So we neither let ourselves be fobbed off by a permanent avant-gardism, nor by the aridity of a positivism of facts from which to build our concepts. Some think, unimaginatively and for a long time, that history begins only after the zero point of Auschwitz; others think that it ends there – particularly for Europe. For a long time there was no talk of such a search, though Oswald Wiener in the *Improvement of Central Europe* (1969) had already sketched the connection of technology and food as significant characteristics of the ego construction, as a reinterpretation of the history of Central Europe. All this sounds rather confusing; it was also the goal the Wiener Group during the 60's.

I am aware that it will be difficult for you to make sense of my retelling. Though I am sure there will be enormous monographs about the 60's in the coming decades – biographies and analyses that will offer you a complete listing of the events – I have the advantage of being able to report to you even now, and from "experience," yet even that was confusing enough. The reason I am focusing on this now is to try to reproduce a panorama, of which later analyses will be unable to have any idea. Before this general background, events take place like scenes, which you were able to read just now. We are reminded of the metaphor we know from Spanish poetry and Pedro Calderón de la Barca as well as Franz Grillparzer: life is a dream.

Hundreds of times I have struggled with not being able to present you this panorama, in the way the enormous paintings of Pieter Brueghel do. In every detail he brings out his interpretation of the world and its inner schism by the subterfuge of using two vanishing points, so that our eyes have to wander restlessly back and forth. For the specifically Austrian ego formation, I would really have to bring the *Nibelungenlied* into play again. This political narrative from the earliest sources, written down for the first time in the 13th century, does not even make room for Christianization(!) and deliberately avoids to present a worldview, whereas the political motives come to the fore all the more clearly. In the *Nibelungenlied* there is no reference to the descendants of the first martyrs who were Roman officers, no Irish-Scottish mission that came as far as Vienna, nor any mention of the mysterious Great Moravian Empire which the Slavic apostle St. Methodius visited – there are only pagans. On the stage of history these merely legendary and dubious heroes act, but know nothing else than blood relationships, blood thirst, and greed for gold – a criminal story that forebodes the German right: it is characteristic of its politics, and in the later course of our history we will recognize these characteristics in the 20th century.

One is almost tempted to think these motifs could constitute the "historical duration" for Central Europe par excellence - a *longue durée* according to the great historian Fernand Braudel. Of course, it has had its "theorist": the music of Richard Wagner, which imposed this anachronistic framework on us. Promptly our ego formation followed its lead and millions thought they finally had discovered themselves in it: as Teutons, Bavarians, Celts, or Huns. All of that is included in the panorama. In the foreground of this mural my small plants are meticulously painted in. In our understanding, however, in the center of the old representations – as with the "Gothic" masters – the crucifixion is backdrop. Or: Brueghel depicted this event, as it were, as a "minor matter" and puts the curiosity of the "masses" in the center. It is the best example of how prominent historical events are allowed to escape us.

If we return to the way we configure things in our imagination, we continue to see ourselves in the shadow of this story as it was commemorated in its most terrible way in the 20th century. We have extraordinary difficulty finding any other point of reference. Some look to the French Revolution (the Russian one is no longer mentioned); others rave about 1848 and still others about the great reform constitution of the Danube Monarchy in 1867; and others again – mostly in Berlin – are enthusiastic about the proclamation of the Prussian king as German emperor in 1871. The American Revolution is rarely mentioned, though it was perhaps the most important turning point with its formulation of human rights (though they were not extended to the indigenous peoples nor to the pitiable black slaves). We can skim back through century after century and probably will end up with Solon's constitution for Athens around 600BC, or that of the "mythical" Lycurgus for Sparta from the 700's BC – though it is hard to imagine a greater contrast, even if Rousseau favored the Spartan constitution.

So if I should be asked what the "panorama" of my present is like, I will halt and stammer for a moment. The most impressive development will probably be China, and to speak frankly, China has not only abandoned its political "quietism," but has become a gigantic and aggressive economic power. However, its economic strength should also be seen as a weapon for conquering national economies and gaining a foothold in countries that previously knew China only by name. The new Russia under Vladimir Putin is very reluctant to oppose Chinese interests, and is more interested in re-annexing the republics of the Soviet Union that had been released into independence. This is an easy task, even if Ukraine is fighting back, because in all the former vassal states authoritarian governments are in power that cannot even meet the criteria of what was then the "reform communism" under Mikhail Gorbachev. And Europe? In my picture Europe has the importance Athens had at the time of the Roman Empire. There, all the scholars and intellectuals sat and philosophized and turned up their noses at the Roman "government of farmers," totally unaware of their own ridiculousness. The last uprising of "Greece" against Rome was in the time of the third Macedonian war around 173BC. There won't be anything more to be said about the present state of "Europe" in the future: the unification of Central and Western Europe into the European Union did not bring the desired success of turning it into a "power," and the only consistent goal in Europe is to maintain and increase prosperity: no other political perspectives are discernible. Its gradual abdication from history is passed off as a policy for peace.

With Donald Trump gone, the USA has recovered its international recognition – in the media – and will take up again its function as a "world power" with groans and complaints. What consequences this function will have in the future are to be determined by the exchange rate for its dollar, by its adventurous fiscal policy, and by the balancing act between economic interests and its position as the lone guarantor in the world of freedom and democracy.

The prospects for South America are also disheartening. The book about Brazil that Stefan Zweig wrote as an émigré describes that land with warm and bright colors. By doing this good deed for the government he wanted to bring it about that Brazil would allow the immigration of Jews from Europe. He promised this would happen but it did not, and so Stefan Zweig felt compelled to commit suicide because he could not keep his promise – to save a lot of people. These huge states like Argentina or Brazil are populist-governed states. And if such a government should be replaced, it will be by a military dictatorship or a bad copy of Fidel Castro's Cuba.

That's how grim things look in the world. The prophesied triumph of democracy has come to a standstill in the meantime, just as the alignment of political sentiments in some fictitious center is no longer taking place. The notion of political scientists that democracy would be victorious had more the character of stargazing, and lacked any real foundation. The political alternatives appear to be considerably narrowed, and the extremes are more and more radical, arising from various subcultural quarters. A closer relationship between states that do not want to belong to a bloc, that want to assert their sovereignty, that want cooperation among equals, is now a thing of the past. Pandit Nehru had such an alternative in mind, but found as ally in Europe only Josip Broz Tito, in what was then Yugoslavia, who was hardly a paragon of democratic sentiment. Even the European social democratic initiative in the 1960's, by which the Arab states under the leadership of the Baath Party as well as the black African states, were meant to receive concentrated economic aid and even political education in democracy, had never even been noticed in those continents. The pressing issue was to persuade Israel and the "Arab world" to conclude peace. And this did not succeed.

Notably my *tour d'horizon* has no "bright spots" in it – nor did writing it. At the moment it looks gloomy: heavy dark clouds have spread out all over the world. If we are to point to goals, destructive ones preponderate, wanting to continue in a post-revolutionary spirit without considering that given the world's population growth, individual self-realization ceases to be the appropriate issue. One is tempted to shed a tear for beloved old times, but did they ever really exist? At least there were reflections on social ethics, even if ethical hopes were not realized. The currency in which we will have to pay for this civilizational change will be shattered nerves, a jumble of fears, – or intoxication. If ever again the thought is expressed as it once was by John Maynard Keynes, that there can be a world in which one concentrates on ends and not on the means for economic growth and individual profit, the very opposite has become the theme in political concepts: armament policy and the production of ever-newer weapons in the manner of the Star-Wars weapons of the US that had their premiere in Iraq.

From this situation are the themes to be deduced that we must implement to make the survival of civilization possible. I do not even dare to mention such themes: it would only reap ridicule and scorn should I mention the topics of peace, disarmament, social justice, or even climate change and conservation of nature. Probably this will be dismissed as simplistic. But among the people around me I know quite enough who are completely indifferent to all such concerns, even if they have managed to find their way into political positions. I can only laugh in derision when, especially during the pandemic, those who are supposedly so important continue to take airplanes, to ski (in Tyrol, of course), or to hold parties for their children. These people don't care, just as they don't care about the climate; they will pay a bribe for a re-zoning; they will proclaim in taverns that money rules the world as if this were the height of wisdom; and they admire those who have succeeded in protecting their interests with murder and manslaughter – truly contemptible people. They run after any advantage and lurk everywhere in the dark corridors that are the bowels of power, driven only by greed. I have written before that a valorization of individualism prevails, with the media spreading like an infection to poison every consciousness: the result is easy to deduce. The media place their backdrops before our eyes and probably the phenomena we have worried about here are pictured on the backdrops, not as the real and vivid conundrums that they are. These interest us more than the bloom of the dandelion.

With kind regards, I remain, your R.

101.
"How happy it is still to be a child" – Albert Lortzing

Dear Nina, Dear Julian, Marie, and Vicky,

I remember with pleasure our evening meals from that time – I was still going to school (sometimes). My brothers were already students and almost every day their circle of friends would stay for dinner. Two fellow students of my brother Wolfgang were very enthusiastic about music and so the time waiting for dinner always went by very fast with astounding offerings from the piano literature. One time we even had a colleague visiting from the GDR, who of course with all the earnestness you could imagine had once studied the *Well-Tempered Clavier*. For me it was the first time that I had heard a composition by Johann Sebastian Bach. Since the other student always carried around with him piano excerpts from Wagner's operas, no greater contrast could be imagined than that of hearing excerpts of the *Götterdämmerung* after Bach. It was the first time that I had any experience of the sublime, shortly after which I experienced the abysmal with all its indulgence in the dreadful. And so it became clear to me, evening after evening and after the series of evenings, what nuances are available in a sequence of notes on the piano – sincerity, for instance, and on the other hand this impressive emptiness behind the powerful harmonies, this intrusive dramaturgy of a "yearning for death."

At that time, around 1957, the colleague of my brother from the GDR had seemed very German to me, as if he came out of the *Ethnologia Europaea* textbook, blond and blue-eyed, tall and slim, but he did not have everything that would be expected, which I had come to recognize through encounters with West German tourists: full-throated speaking, constantly overbearing, even when one was talking about trivialities. It was noticeable that he was unwilling to say anything about politics and immediately fell silent if one asked him how things were "over there." Usually he would turn to the piano and respond with music, whether by Bach or alternatively by Schumann who at the time was too exhausting for me since it was so confused. My brother could not resist playing Mozart's *C-Minor Fantasy*, but often he would switch without any provocation into the second movement of Beethoven's *Moonlight Sonata* – and then one of his colleagues would force him off the bench and continue brilliantly well with a Mozart sonata. Given all this musical hoopla the colleague from the GDR had completely forgotten his deadline to return to Leipzig, and had overstayed his residence permit for Vienna by two days. He was very anxious and reproached himself for possibly bringing the bright lights of scrutiny onto his family at home and perhaps even endangering them, while in any case he was sure he would encounter a hassle at the border of the GDR.

But my father helped him. He procured a writ from a physician that he was unfit for travel due to high fever and possible pneumonia, which was made all the more credible by confirmation from the "stamp and seal" of the police. A student of my father's had by chance become a police commissioner within the district where he lived, and filled out the "Potemkinesque" form with pleasure. Relieved by having this "excuse" he traveled off: it sticks in my memory how degrading this "Iron Curtain" between East and West was for the population of Central Europe.

The enthusiasm after the end of the Soviet empire also made this fact clear: finally a person from a neighboring city could once again visit a place that had for half a century been visible but unreachable. This hope for normalization benefited European unification. That this general energy has almost completely dissipated after more than twenty years now, in January 2021, is a sad thing, and shows that Western and Central Europe are in a deep political crisis.

In any case, the time while we were waiting for dinner, back then, continued to be shaped with a musical potpourri. Very surprising was also the reception of contemporary music, Johann Nepomuk David, for example, Josef Matthias Hauer, who called himself the "inventor" of twelve-tone music. Before my father arrived – he usually returned from university only in the evening – heated exchanges about music were common: meanwhile my older brother Norbert was hammering away his contemporary pop music on the piano, from Lionel Hampton, to W.C. Handy and Glenn Miller. This is why there was no room for me at the piano. But it also explains that in this juxtaposition between Louis Armstrong or George Gershwin and Mozart, Viennese classical music seemed to me clearly preferable.

My mother finally began to set the table, and Grandmother added her "finishing touches" to the dishes according to her fancy, so it was time to eat. Our father led the conversation at the table. It was always topics of philosophy, sociology, and theology. And should something have seemed unclear during the discussion of a topic, it was saved for the "dessert." By then my father would have fetched the relevant books and with them explained what the problem was, how it came about, and finally whether it could be resolved or explained. It was not every evening, but it was often the case that current topics were discussed at length, over plum turnovers or pudding.

Now you mustn't imagine it was always a terribly serious discussion. Often it all dissolved into hilarity, especially during heated debates about Richard Wagner, whose mention regularly led to the question whether a proto-totalitarian element could be heard in his music, or not. There, the venomous objections of Friedrich Nietzsche against Wagner were always a ready starting point; and naturally I don't remember whether the enormous change of tonality and harmony in Wagner was even mentioned. He took his aesthetic deformations to extremes, and in his modulations had already laid the basis for the theory of twelve-tone music, so the fact that Arnold Schoenberg came up with it should no longer have been so surprising.

Now I want to add an amusing memory of something that took place around 1952, or so I assume. The back story is quite simple. Periodically we would receive "care packages" from an American family: food items, staples, canned goods, fish and candy – Hershey's chocolate! It was a welcome addition to our meagre supply of food after 1945. Every month a package came from Baltimore. Along the way we developed a pen-pal relationship, greatly facilitated by my mother's knowledge of English. Eventually the son of the family announced that he would like to visit Vienna on the occasion of his honeymoon. His proposal was connected with a very naive idea: in his letter he asked whether one can see Munich from the Vienna Woods! We laughed a lot and our answer was certainly disappointing for the Americans: No, from Hermannskogel you cannot see Munich.

The young couple arrived in Europe by plane and soon reached Vienna. Our first walks through the city piqued the amazement of the guests, because on the one hand the devastation of the war was still visible while on the other hand they had no idea that in our country everything you see is three, four, or even five hundred years older than what you see in the USA. Then we planned a trip to Bruck an der Leitha. A former sergeant of my father's had become an innkeeper there. My father thought highly of him. He had become a friend after quite successfully protecting my father from the Nazis in the reserve battalion. As I told you before, the commander of this battalion, Walter Scherhaufer, was murdered just before the end of the war. At that time, and until 1955, there was a Soviet military command stationed in Bruck an der Leitha, filled out by several companies of Russian soldiers. We reached Bruck in the evening. While the car was being parked, we could see a lot of soldiers heading towards the inn. They were armed with the characteristic short submachine guns, were sloppily dressed, and talked loudly, some of them singing, some of them dancing in the street. In the dark, the American newlyweds could not yet tell whose soldiers they were. But when we were able to take a seat at a table in the inn right in the middle of the other tables, all of which were occupied by Soviet soldiers in the midst of the Cold War, our guests' desire to do any further traveling dropped to zero. In fact, the young husband was quite afraid and the wife did not dare to look around. While it was normal everyday life for us to encounter "Russians," it was unimaginable for the poor "Americans." What they could not imagine was that one could sit there without any fear, without reluctance, among people who probably were just as worried as we were that the madness of a new war could break out in Europe. Our guests did not view this as a real possibility: at most they had read something about it or seen it in early television reports. Through the intermediary of the innkeeper, an officer came to our table, greeted the "Amerikanski" and our guests wondered, "Is this really a human being? So this is what *homo sovieticus* looks like."

One must recognize of course that for an officer it was a much bigger risk to greet the "enemy" than it was for our guests to shake hands with a Russian officer. That is also why he did not sit down when we invited him to. For the "comrades" sitting around us it would have been a provocation and one way or another, a political officer would soon receive a report.

After pork roast, sauerkraut, and noodles it was back to Vienna. Our guests were visibly relieved that the 7th District was within the American sector. We lived near its border, in the French sector. A further trip we suggested, to Burgenland, they firmly declined to take.

At that time we were taking our summer vacations in Mitterbach near Mariazell. For Austria it was an enormously important year, since with the signing of the State Treaty on May 15, 1955, occupation by allied troops came to an end. Every foreign soldier had until October 26th to leave the country. That is why we celebrate that day in October as National Day. (Much later, in 1978, it became customary for me to go to the sauna near Wildalpen with my friend Karl Preslmayr and his friends from Sankt Johann and Ternitz. There in the middle of the forest we would cool ourselves at a stream that supplied drinking water to Vienna). Anyway, we also were present in Mitterbach during the departure of the Soviet troops . A rather large detachment of the military was stationed there to guard the border with Styria Very soon we figured out how one could escape from the "Russian" zone into the "English," but this was a well-kept secret in the village. This perhaps explains the relatively severe attempts by the "Russians" to control the border, but never did they find out by which path through the forest one could still cross. But the time had come to leave and the last commando attachment was still housed in what was formerly the Lutheran parsonage. Despite the approaching end of the occupation, two guards patrolled along the river at the border. Two years before, their grim faces had filled us with requisite terror: they grabbed their automatic pistols threateningly and we were well advised to make a run for it. But now a spectacle took place similar to one that Manès Sperber wrote about at the time the KuK Army came to an end. Young "rascals" in the village suddenly mimicked the guard, and made faces or stuck out their tongues at the soldiers, or tried to provoke them in some other way. One could tell they would have loved to beat up the youngsters, but probably had stern orders to endure insults. This reversal of "social reciprocity" amazed me at the time but also taught me that such a reversal could come into effect overnight. Perhaps this was my first sociological experiment in the field of the sociology of power relations. A stroke of the pen by the infamous Soviet Minister of the Exterior, Vyacheslav Molotov, in the ceremonial hall of Upper Belvedere, had simply wiped away any fear for these soldiers, and in an instant they became the despised, the hated.

I hope that I was able to bring you a bit closer to the "atmosphere" of my childhood and youth. We don't always have to confer about philosophy and correspond only about problems, and by writing about a once upon a time present we are able to keep it alive a bit longer through our correspondence.

With love, your R.

102.
What is Politics? Again

Dear Nina, Dear Julian, Dear Marie and Vicky,

It would not be correct to describe these last letters as light reading. The ways of our experience sometimes bring together even contradictory themes. In the last letter I hope I was able to describe how observations that remain in one's mind because of their strangeness or even grotesqueness later become merely factual, since through remembering one connects interpretations to what he underwent that only became possible much later. This presents an interesting link, when an experience is made visualizable only by reading a written account about it. But I don't want to indulge in any further "mystification" of this matter.

At some point I got into a rut writing about politics. I literally floundered over the current political situation in Europe. And so I reached only a very vague assessment. I must admit to you that I do notice an "unpolitical" tendency in myself. This does not mean that I find politics uninteresting, but that I can no longer judge things I earlier thought I could judge easily. I have reaped the strongest of disapprovals in the family circle – Nina especially could not make sense of my "indecisive" attitude about the election of the president in 2016, for I was utterly unable to count myself among the enthusiastic partisans of Hillary Clinton, whereas I was unsure about Donald Trump. The 2018 presidential election in Austria presented a similar situation. The fact that the two major parties at the time shot themselves in the foot had the consequence that it was a choice between the "green" candidate and someone from the Freedom Party. To me it felt I was being coerced. Since I was acquainted with the federal president van der Bellen as dean of the social science faculty, I had my doubts about him regarding his objectivity and his devotion to the constitutional state. Thus I became "unpolitical." I was aware that I had to live with shame and reproach from the family, and thus in such questions I lost all respectability. Indeed back in 1840, being unpolitical became a complaint commonly voiced by the first "leftist" intellectuals. Friedrich Schiller comes to mind, who once mentioned in a fragment from *German Greatness* (1801), "... because the political regime wavered, the spiritual regime became ever more strong and more full."

It was during the supposedly quiet Biedermeier period, of all things, that this criticism by the "leftist" intellectuals was voiced: One must make a decision, not only must one pave the way for political progress, but we are no longer free to decide between the either and the or. As for politics only the "or" is permitted. Later the "undecideds" were even criticized: though being enthusiasts for Bismarck, they had in effect "fallen back into the apoliticism of the age of Goethe."

Apparently this mentality exists again, a mentality which of course is not foreign to me. Casting invalid votes or not voting at all is a sign that we are going in this direction. When Friedrich Naumann formulated his criticism in 1903, he had not recognized in his fervor for "the political" what a skewed and fatal level German politics had reached. And this teaches me, considering the many skewed levels of politics in the present – in the EU, in our country's politics, in questions of the social integration of people "with a migration background" (a gruesome coinage), in questions of educational, social, and cultural politics – that the only people who adopt a position about what according to them is the right thing to do are those whose evaluation of diverse questions is clouded by "an utter absence of knowledge." I always feel the presence of this coercion, which is becoming stronger and stronger, and more and more constricting. More and more often one is subjected to these coercions, which begin with the language of "political correctness," with regulations of speech that so easily brook absurdity, and culminate in one's being required to make a choice between arbitrarily formulated extremes. This culminates in debates about euthanasia, in which one comes across as inhumane if he will not accept this assisted suicide as salvation for suffering persons. Speaking *grosso modo*, in Europe we are not competent to decide which form of schooling would guarantee the best education, and yet to resist the program of euthanasia is castigated as inhumane, as an unacceptable restriction on the free choice of the dying that are being treated with palliatives.

Now I must return to the theme. For 150 years the "unpolitical" man has been put into the role of scapegoat.

Now I must tell you how I myself have been involved in "politics." When I remember that for dozens of reasons I supported Bruno Kreisky for leader in the national parliamentary election of 1975, I did so not out of vanity nor for the purpose of having a career, which would not have been advanced by doing so, but in order finally to overthrow the unbearable arrogance in the standstill under the conservatives. I do not want to go into details here. Very soon I saw myself being forced into kinds of "decisions" of which I deeply disapproved. On what basis could one have decided, without further ado, about the conflict between Simon Wiesenthal and Bruno Kreisky for chancellor? Similarly, on the question of nuclear energy how can one, without further ado, decide for "Zwentendorf" merely because the operators' union and the energy lobby wanted us to take it on faith? Important questions would be politicized around an election but retained no interest afterwards for persons whose politics consisted only in the terms of their party's platform. While it is to be acknowledged that within a political group or party a consensus must be reached, it was never reached from the grassroots level, never with a unanimous conviction of a majority. Instead the so-called "committees" deliberated, decided, and enforced, *in camera*. My own position on this may seem naïve, impractical, and only theoretical, but in the meanwhile politics "itself" had changed and more and more often the hierarchical structure was dispositive – and decisions were made "from the top down." And how and why the decisions were being made from "above" became less and less transparent. Democracy had lost a good deal of trust because of the intentions of the very supporters of democracy.

I must say in advance that the misery of 1945 was almost vital for the development of our democracy. Questions of survival had to be decided; every measure had a cogent purpose and in all political decisions there was a dispositive consensus as a matter of course. As is hardly known today, the strength of the great coalition in Austria lay in the fact that a high degree of consensus politics had been reached. The tide had turned when we settled these life-or-death questions in a positive way.

The current inability of a regime or even the EU to succeed at providing enough vaccine for the population against the pandemic – in February 2021 – would in this form have been unthinkable in 1946 or 1947, since despite the shortages and the hardships the political administration functioned as well as it could. To the extent that there are no life-or-death questions to answer in our times, politics falls into the hands of the arbitrary narratives of the media. By these a mental narrowness is inserted into politics and becomes completely ensnared in the nets of our methods of communication. The last politician who was able to orchestrate public opinion like an organist at the organ was Bruno Kreisky, and maybe also Franz Vranitzky. Both of them had the advantage of not being robbed of their personal and unique identity at the hands of the media.

Surely there are still other aspects worth considering. In the present state of politics, which also probably obtains in Germany, we must observe the influence of multiple negative tendencies that already haunted society before. We know the catchwords from sociology: fragmentation, segmentation, or even singularization in society, which actually reveal the current weakness of social and societal policy. Social phenomena have become entrenched in it and now *any* policy faces the problem that it can hardly embrace "cross-sectarian purposes" since favoring the one fragment disadvantages the other. Because of the disappearance of consensus, the competence to make political decisions in a public way suffers, while at the same time a generalized propagation of resentment increases. Right-wing extremism has become a permanent fixture not only in Europe; in Hungary and Poland it is even sovereign in government in a purified form, while the few "left-wing" governments in South and Central America, Asia and Africa, are tending toward authoritarianism. If we disregard the "Maghreb states" of North Africa, which form a separate type because of their religious history, at present the political developments look as though the future of political systems appears to be split between Bonapartism and Peronism. For the first time, Donald Trump had been far more in line with Peronism precisely because of taking a confrontational stance toward Central and South America. Juan Péron ushered in the pattern of authoritarian social policies: he elevated populism into a political doctrine, and formed a contemporary political model with a slightly leftist tinge. If there can still be a variant of a political system, Trump has chosen the Peronist one, whereas Vladimir Putin prefers Bonapartism.

We are not now in a position to give a "draft" version of a political program. If, in the early enthusiasm for "neo-liberalism," people raved about the "lean state," hoping to liberate it from all kinds of burdens so as to limit it to the basic function of steering society, the pandemic teaches that this lean state had fortunately not yet become so lean. In truth, the real intention was to make the state begin to lose its competence.

The other tendency – to reduce politics to a socio-technical program – was propagated 40 years ago. It had been raved over in those years, in unbelievable ignorance of proper policy. Behind it was the ideal of the "open society" advocated by Karl Popper before the Second World War. One may well object, with a little mischief, that an "open society" might indeed meet the political-moral level of Switzerland but is unsuited for the complexity of politics in all fields. The negative side of Popper's concept probably lies in his belief that his pragmatism would be enough as a political doctrine, which however could at best be realized in the old-German "Thing." Thus we are faced with an ideology that politics must be de-ideologized. This resembles the widespread attitude that the most satisfying version of politics is a depoliticization into entertainment – "bread and circuses," television, and Twitter, Facebook and other such media.

In our "modern" present something is repeated that has long been recognized in mathematics. A mathematical concept remains valid also in its negation. We have developed a non-Euclidean geometry over against the Euclidean, which also satisfies truth claims – and so on. Likewise something that is fundamentally contrary to the self-understanding of the political can also qualify as a politics. In the direct switch from democracy to tyranny one might even ascribe a higher political competence to tyranny because of its power. Although it flatly contradicts the theoretical tradition of politics, and contradicts political philosophy which must always refer to the presupposition of the "polis," tyranny nevertheless will produce "a" politics. It will, however, be confined to the matter of perpetuating power in successions.

I must still finally tell you my own kind of relationship to politics. Perhaps I fulfilled the call to politics in the "classical Greek sense" in my activities in the 1st District of Vienna. Lowering of the sidewalk curbs was a concern for me when I had to manage high curbs pushing the baby strollers along. My idea of lowering the curbs at intersections found the necessary support in the district council and then slowly became a provision for all of Vienna. An incredible victory. Since then, strollers and users of a walker can safely and comfortably cross an intersection. In this I went along with the old kind of politics.

At present, I see not only an increase in complexity – as I have already mentioned in connection with the decision for or against wind turbines – but also a diminution of political responsibility. One can say that politics has given over its own responsibilities to the economic world in general. If capitalism is to be viable, it is only if we keep in mind the disproportion between productive and speculative capital. Thus, substantial areas of social policy-making have been taken up by institutions that seem inaccessible to a democratic quorum. To recall what I said at the beginning, I started with the idea of a deliberate withdrawal from political decision-making processes. On the one hand, this has to do with my age but on the other with the fact that I no longer allow myself to be coerced out of the unclarity of the consequences of problematic situations. It is a decision not to decide. This does not mean to decide on nothing as a universal principle, but first of all to make room for prudence. Presumably equanimity and prudence have become more important political virtues than imagining that one is participating in a political public sphere via the chatter of the media.

I would be very happy to hear from you that you have chosen your political convictions with prudence.

All the best, I remain your R.

103.
The Church's Crisis is Also Our Crisis

Dear Nina, Dear "Berlin" Grandchildren,

Just now my brother has called me from Stuttgart and put the question to me: "What's wrong with the Catholic Church?" What is going on, that such a terrible situation has arisen – which is not restricted to the church in Germany. How can I give an answer measuring up to the problem that would not sound like a mere excuse? I write to you, too, about this problem, which I find so important that I am all the more ashamed by the Church's silence and coverup. A halfway successful excuse would be, for example, that a smaller and smaller number of persons are deciding to become priests, and by default an increasing proportion of applicants to the priesthood hope to get a halfway solid grip on their own uncertainty about sexual relations so as to enter a "society of men" without being detected. And then it just happens. In a misunderstanding of pastoral care comes the discovery of one's sexuality, which can be homosexual, heterosexual, bisexual – and more. Today, depressingly, one can recite again the couplet of Georg Kreisler, "... my secretary no longer knows whether he is a she or a he...."

For a civilization in which sexuality has come to play such a dominant role, in which freedom is sought primarily in sexual relations, it is inordinately difficult to keep the vow to live a celibate life. For centuries one already doubted it was possible – among other places in the *Decameron* of Giovanni Boccaccio around 1350. In the Schwabenspiegel, a rule book written by an unknown Franciscan in 1275, one could already read, "Beware of the front of a woman, the rear of a carriage, and all sides of a priest."

Church and sexuality is an old topic, and the decisions regarding church reform made during the "Investiture Controversy" around 1139 only codified what already since 1073 had been the rule: Priests are not to marry. The reasons for it have been researched often and it is idle to take sides. Some think, rather "materialistically," that the bishop would thereby have better control of his priests; others find clear indications in the text of the Gospel of the advantageousness of celibacy. Paul in fact thought that for those anticipating the end of the world, marriage makes little sense.

Let's approach the problem from the other end. Anyone who has noticed that history can include monkey-business will recognize that even the most pious principles and the most righteous convictions can become perverted in their very basis. If the sins only consisted of acts against the rules they had imposed upon themselves, their behavior was less an insult against the moral canon. It regularly provokes derision to talk about the rich Sisters of the poor child, Jesus; or about fasting, after which the lavish menus of the cloisters are discovered. A sin must always be cast as an offense against a cardinal virtue, such as vanity against modesty, or gluttony against asceticism. One needs only quote the sentence of Simone Weil, who with very good reason said, "Evil is the imitation of the good." One must always be conscious that this remark is particularly pertinent to religions. Where else should evil be found if not in perversion? This ought to be clear without saying. In an analogous way populism is a perversion of democracy.

The outrageous inversion of Christ into the pioneer of German Christianity and even worse things in the Protestant Church; the aid to escape given by Rome to the Nazi murderers; the hypocrisy of preaching water and drinking wine – these are merely the first of a long list of sins and crimes. And they are not new: during the High Middle Ages such was the regular subject matter of the *Ludus de Antichristo*. But with the performance of the play evil was clearly named, and thereby banished. These "techniques" for dealing with evil we no longer recognize: they fell victim to the Enlightenment, by which incantation and exorcism were unmasked as nonsense.

The "church critics," who hold their criticism to be as authoritative as an ecclesiastical *magisterium*, assert that the problem lies in the structure of religious communities, so that the best thing would be to forbid religion itself and prohibit its practice. What is being misunderstood, which however is clear to any ethnologist or ancient historian, is that cults in the first place have as their very substance the forgiveness of guilt. This was the metaphysical or numinous purpose in nature religions, in which one seeks forgiveness even for the killing of an animal; this was also the sense of the Day of the False King in Egypt, who had to atone for the crimes of the Pharaoh, and also in Judaism the many burnt offerings by which one would seek reconciliation with God for crimes that had been committed; and in Christianity forgiveness conceived as a commandment to emulate the infinite goodness and mercifulness of God.

In the 17th century a change took place. With the introduction of archiving under Louis XIV everything was noted down, not just the acts of the sovereign's administration. Any misdeed had its representation in the archives, and remained "present" in them. In most religions pardoning is the most important thing. It plays a large role already in the Jewish religion – "forgive us our trespasses" – and reaches its highest expression in Christ, but the archives leave out any pardon, any penance and atonement. In Austria, Friedrich Wilhelm Haugwitz introduced archiving in the administrative reforms at the time of Maria Theresa, which was typical of the Enlightenment, so that for eternity an alternative reality would be created in which nothing was erased and nothing was forgotten in the giant volume of archives: *quod non est in actis non est in mundo*, or *quod non legitur non creditur*. This basic tenet taken from Roman trial law came to take on fatal importance, in the absolutism from the 17th century onward, as creating a political reality and therewith turning the state into a God of vengeance. Michel Foucault studied the archives of 17th century lawcourts and showed how it became part of the infamy of mankind to be more closely integrated in the king's power by *denouncing* (rather than loving) one's neighbor. And the absolutist regimes relied upon the people's willingness, reckoning that betrayal and denunciation would strengthen the grip of the state and produce compliant citizens. In the pincers effect of police and denunciation society was reduced to a uniform state. It was the end of the wide variety of political landscapes distributed among the feudal lords.

As an outcome of all this we can see that we have a harder and harder time forgiving. Of all things the modern media, which from the beginning called moral norms into question and have most vociferously criticized the "puritanism" of bourgeois society, have since arrogated to themselves the authority of moral judgment, and they determine guilt and innocence even before the indictments and trials take place. Our "guardians of morals" today, through their extensive research, are making countless discoveries how even "great" people were wretched sinners. Our "guardians of morals," are shocked and astonished though they should be aware (as if they weren't) of the misdeeds that went on during the world wars. This artificial indignation about historical personalities has the purpose of destroying the continuity of history, of disturbing the "self-confidence" of societies in order to indoctrinate them with far more questionable objectives. Mercilessly the judgments are churned out, and we should be glad the guillotine is no longer in service. Almost all European examples of a great personality would fall victim to this verdict. Wasn't Maria Theresa an anti-Semite? So, away with the monument in Vienna! Wasn't the French king Charles IX a murderer, who was to blame for the murder of the Huguenots in 1572 on Bartholomew's Night? So, away with any monument to such a king! Wasn't it a betrayal of the Protestant Church when Henry IV simply converted to Catholicism in order to be a king in France as well? How many misdeeds would you have to list to discredit all of

European history? This is the European version of the Cultural Revolution that cost millions of lives in China.

Even if one can repent of his offense and try to make amends, he remains a wrongdoer in the archives – forever. Because of the media anyone who wants to embark on a career in politics must try to keep a clean slate no matter what, which will then include smudges to be discovered by "investigative journalism." Only a clever system of complicity and coercion will enable him to clean them up, at least as long as he is alive. Paradoxically this combination of ambiguity and mendacity was the legacy of the Enlightenment, above all directed against the Church, serving as the telltale proof it is dysfunctional.

This reversal of the question of culpability and guilt does not help to make the scandalous misbehavior any less harmful, and does not intend to "understand" how the misbehavior was possible, but in our case we should rather ask whether the accused did in fact feel remorse for his misdeeds already, a long time ago. His remorse was perhaps not great enough, or an admission of guilt might never have been made, or perhaps the victims suffered long-lasting damage. The reversal only makes clear the ambivalent ethical status our indignations are coming to take on.

Here I would like briefly to borrow a thought from Japanese culture, so as to bring forward how a culture is essentially able to deal with the misbehavior of an individual on a social level, and thereby stabilize the moral disposition of a society. With the Japanese concept of "*amae*" the psychoanalyst Takeo Doi describes a psychological "affliction" according to which a child is deemed to have a behavioral problem if he or she does not rely upon his parents' to forgive him. In our case, I find fault with the fact that although we have adopted a very easy approach to guilt, we do not know any way to approach forgiveness. What kind of compensation could be made by which the victim is made whole and the guilty party is able to return to society? Most likely money will not quite be enough.

One must always keep in mind that a secular society, which protects life less and less, whether from abortion or euthanasia, reformulates the catalog of political freedoms into an individualized kind of freedom, and pushes a tendency towards individualization that weakens the ability of society to carry out politics and locates the identity of a person not in cultural belonging but in exclusion – in particular by making place for extremes. Every talk show on television shows that extreme behavioral dispositions are to be accepted, and that tolerance is replaced by varieties of permissiveness. All these phenomena are familiar to us and we see ourselves more tightly integrated into the secular society than into the old traditional forms of community. The contrast between society and community is becoming increasingly clear to us. As this increases, we will understand less and less the special form of a church let alone comprehend the values it represents.

So far I have followed a sociological approach, which must necessarily be supplemented by another perspective. Might metaphysics still have a place here? When I wrote about how the sacred is constitutive for social self-understanding, a single glance at a full soccer stadium is enough to make one aware of the tremendous force that transforms the encounter between two top teams into a secular high mass. But here we remain only in the realm of the ridiculous.

Now you can see very well how I am literally getting in over my head on behalf of this subject. The church is facing a world court, and the charge against it is arrogance. On such occasions people always mouth the magical nostrum that an ecclesiastical understanding must be reached – in particular, that the vow to improve must be backed by a reform. The problem with reform is that it is always the case that one is undecided whether one may spit out the pit of a cherry and the skin of a gooseberry. What's wrong with the word "reform?" It means either that you want to go back to the way things were, or that you want to try again to make things better. In our case the advice of the media will be hearkened to, that is, to allow the marriage of priests or the ordination of women. The spirit of the times, which pretends to know more about what it means to be human than the Bible or the churches, has the say: in this case, to make a small compromise with the demands of the sexual revolution. One does not notice at all in the case of such demands that they are themselves another kind of abuse and rape. On top of that, what the Christian Church wants to do has not been understood: it neither wants to go back to the original form, even if today an ideal case is guilefully attested for it – the hermits and the first monks – nor does it want to be a passive vessel for folklore with Christmas trees and Easter eggs. Rather, it wants to grow and to flourish. The Church sees itself as a new tree with new fruits, and the giant trees struck by lightning leave it cold. The Church, like nature, needs the processes of becoming and passing away, the seasons and meteorological disasters. In winter, also, one hardly can believe that the snowsludged expanses will become blooming meadows, the black and leafless trees will become blossoming chestnuts.

One of our errors is that we predict the demise of the Church. It will not persevere because people dare not take the risk of enlightenment, nor will it survive merely on the basis of its peculiar attachment to pomp and glory and incense. It is not true that the Catholic man leaves all his worries about Christ and his church to the pope and the bishops. This attitude is completely unknown today, since the media perpetuate Max Weber's error in his sociology of religion, seeing in the Church only the clerical hierarchy, its organization and canon law. It may come as a surprise, but the church is the only place where the world is also understood in terms of a salvific event that goes far beyond what we can imagine. This does not mean that the terrible abuses and their incomprehensible cover-up are to be swept under the table, but it would be a step in the right direction to recognize the Church as the only supra-temporal institution in European history. The outcomes we are seeing cannot be described as perversions or obsolescence or anachronisms: what is happening now is that the Church is being thrown out of its salvation-historical context because of the disproportion between world time, life time, and the present. And many bishops are abettors in this insane course of action, against their will.

Especially when we look at the Christian churches, we should not forget the Islamic faith community, which has an increasing share in the cultural fabric of our society. As far as I can understand, Islam in tandem with the waves of immigration has revitalized in Europe a version of heightened conviction, in accordance with which it does not matter whether a man loses his life in battle, dies in bed, or is killed by a tree: the decisive thing is that the end is predetermined. The Koran says: "The soul does not die except by the permission of God, according to the eternal book which has determined the goal of life." Thus, the endless debate in Christianity about free will is not an issue in Islam. We may recall that it was the primary theological-philosophical issue in the Renaissance. If we want to trace any kind of a similar idea of "inner freedom," as Paul called it, in Islam, it was present for a short time in the flowering of Arabic philosophy in the 12th century. And yet Averroes's famous phrase fits poorly with the "eternal book" when he wrote: "*Deus non cognoscit singularia...*" ("God does not contemplate particulars"). This important philosophical tradition breaks off in the 13th century and the Islamic theologians with their narrow dogmatism triumph over their philosophical rivals. Today we see clearly that what Islam lacks is not so much an "Enlightenment," as is always claimed, but the sharpness in the formulation of theological questions that we see in Christian scholasticism. Without this, philosophy and science would not have been possible. Though the Aristotelian tradition was familiar in the Arabic world, expansionism was there more interesting than a sort of theological disputation that could have opened the door to a contemporary dialogue among the monotheistic religions.

Devotion to fate has remained the hallmark of Muslims in the urban-European slums even today. Even when the religious orientation became weaker – due to a kind of secularization coming with the rise of technology – accepting submission remained, which however can turn almost without provocation into irrational aggression, especially in the third generation of immigrants. The general effect is that an areligious fatalism enters the behavioral profile. Armed with a gun, one plays the heavenly "unmoved mover" on a rampage – holding kismet in his very hand. This differs considerably from the conceptions of God even in the Koran, since these can of course resolve the causality of cause and effect and the fated chain through miracles. This can happen, since Allah knows the destinies of all people and interrupts the immutable sequence in special cases. The Great Book has more a function of bookkeeping according to tradition, recording the incomes and outgoes, and from an overall vantage point it determines the prediction of what the will of God will be. In its influence on the conduct of one's life fatalism has continued to take the leading role and can be relied upon to determine unresolved theological and philosophical questions. Since the theological question touches areas that are beyond our ability to make a further determination, the answer is easy, because there is none. The specific details from the Koran reach far beyond anything available even to the imagination.

"Quieting" the debate on free will in the 13th century strangled the alternatives available in Islamic theology. Perhaps the argument can be made more clear if in our historical reconstruction we say that a desire for an irreconcilable struggle finally takes the place of the profound thinking that once existed in Islam. The drive for this is easy to determine, because with the "counter-movement" after the "Crusades" an attempt to Islamize Central Europe was an attractive goal and basically undermined the disposition of Islamic piety once and for all.

I've gone and fetched a booklet that I remembered just now. It has quite a "history" behind it. Once it was in the possession of the philosopher Alois Dempf, an authority in medieval philosophy and the sociology of knowledge. Friedrich Heer borrowed the book from him, and on every page you can read the scribbled commentary of Heer, who was obviously horrified that he found in the book not a comparison of book-religions as he expected, but instead, according to its choice of citations, a declaration of war against Christianity and Judaism. This militant book was printed in 1979. And as I leafed through it, I got the impression that this distinctive hatred has since become even stronger. The most important point is the change in Islam that dates from the outbreak of the "Islamic Revolution," in particular Ayatollah Khomeini's seizure of power in Iran. There is no doubt that Islam, despite its supposed secularization, has since reversed its self-interpretation and has opted for its tradition of aggression – at least for now.

The religious-sociological picture in Europe involves two world religions: the Christian one is being withdrawn from all aspects of cultural-political self-understanding, while Islam, in a *sura*, calls itself the "chosen people" and lives up to that denomination in every marketplace in Europe, in the desolate poor quarters, and in its houses of prayer. The chances for Islamization to succeed increase when bit by bit Christianity, out of guilt for all the Crusades and in apology for the expulsion of the Moors from Spain, wishes to "settle" the present tension. In Letter 26, I mentioned Shmuel Eisenstadt, who predicted this result 30 years ago: a wave of Islamization was in all likelihood unleashed with the political turnaround in Iran at that time, and it continues to this day though under more difficult conditions. Though Islam as a whole does not present a homogeneous picture, it is the Turkish-Arab version that wants to be the definitive one.

This time I have written you a detailed letter that will perhaps be of importance to you in a few years, one way or the other. I hoped that you would recall the letter in which I sketched out the spiritual landscape, the future of which lies in your hands.

This time I greet you in a contemplative way, and in the hopes that these gruesome witch-hunts of modern times might come to an end.

Your R.

104.
On the University

Dear Nina, Dear Julian, Marie, and Vicky,

In my last writing a miserable topic was the point of departure. I had to deal with it since it is a pressing question that will be with us for a long time.

If I may now take another look at "our" university, the education now given in the theological faculty is closer to "religious studies" than an introduction to the mystery of faith. At present the condition of the European universities mirrors the catastrophic character of the situation in Europe in general. A diagnosis can be based on the observation of Friedrich Nietzsche who already 130 years ago accused the universities and educational institutions overall of only being interested in the "turning out" of "average men." The criterion of education is oriented, above all, toward professional functionality, toward utility, whence Nietzsche wrote that they produce "uptime men." In every European country this job-oriented education is the great goal, and so one invests in education that serves ventures that indirectly foster society's prosperity in return. Measured against the older educational ideals associated with Wilhelm von Humboldt's ideas of reform, our current graduates from the highest educational institutions appear to be uncultivated, since in the best case they have specialized but still lack any competence in interdisciplinary knowledge. If we observe the graduates of our system of education, they have contributed to the problem of our climate, they have taken the leading role in the way our cities look, they have shown a strange attitude about going all over the place. That the graduates of the highest institutions remain unscathed by the crossfire of criticism is due to their excuse that one has simply directed oneself to fulfilling the wishes of society, that one has only met the demands and policies for progress which have caused enormous changes over recent years. Nobody has dared to call our graduates the new barbarians, regardless of the fact that they do qualify as specialists or experts. The engineers, doctors, high bureaucrats, scientists, and technologists are more trained than anyone before them but also less educated.

This unexpected barbarism has a special history in Central Europe. Although we can claim the very best of educations in the 1920's due to the flourishing of the University of Vienna, this same institution then ran straight to National Socialism. Given its intellectual rank one would rightly have expected that the large majority of teachers and students would firmly oppose a dictatorship, and yet the opposite was the case. A minority stood up against this and could easily be shut out, and nary a cock crowed about the displaced persons. Thus one can make the bitter observation that while their scientific rank was high, and in some subjects world-class, this neither hindered them from joining the Nazi party even when it was still illegal nor, after the Anschluss of Austria in 1938, from joining the NSKK, a Nazi motorists' club, out of pressure to conform. For those who belonged to the university to warm up to an auto club was something one can characterize with the proverb, "Wash me but don't get me wet." But still the surprising interest shown must have been puzzling. Even if it bought some protection for some people, the more widespread motive was more likely a kind of opportunism that went on to characterize the graduates from that time until after 1945. And even more surprising is the dissonance between holding to a scientific standard and giving in to conformity.

These "old" stories are not parallel to our contemporary situation, but signify only that this dissonance in the universities is still with us, although the mitigations run differently than they did during the phase of totalitarianism. If one wants to formulate the problem philosophically, the diremption between what we know and what we are is becoming greater and greater. In the Fourth Century BC, Zhuangzi drew a distinction: "How could I speak to a frog about the ocean if he had never left his pond? And how with a migratory bird about ice? And how, with a sage bogged down in his doctrines, about life?"

This observation by a Chinese poet perhaps teaches us why a natural scientist has nothing to do with nature – my own deliberate snub. If one wants to suggest a phenomenological interpretation, the advance of scientific knowledge about nature becomes possible through the botanist's knife or the dissecting table, i.e., after reducing the living organism into dead matter. Meanwhile, once they have finished the required curriculum, we have been giving the students a license to be doctor, jurist, bureaucrat, businessman, social scientist, though we do not know what idea our graduates think about this "physical" view of the world, about the limits of science, and about the ethical implications of knowledge. So one should not be surprised when "things" go awry. If we assume that physics is a fundamental science that also seems to have a view of the world, we would classify it as an indispensable factor for our culture. But have we really examined what influence physics now has on contemporary man? When I attempted to introduce the important lectures of Edmund Husserl on *The Crisis of European Sciences* into a reading circle, I completely failed because social scientists did not want to know anything about a problem from 1936, even if it does remain current. As they proceed through life our graduates are content to repeat and repeat more and more outdated knowledge as if reading from a prayer wheel – even though they are the only ones who believe it. If we were to review even physics as a field of study over the last four centuries we would learn therein the prevailing conceptions of God and society, of matter and anti-matter, and about all possible things in the world. The lack of an organized conception returns man to barbarism, even if he is acknowledged to be an expert or specialist. That is why I mentioned the appearance of our modern cities, the destruction of our landscapes to the farthest corner of the earth, as if this frenzy was the highest of barbaric virtues. And a faulty understanding of history is no longer reckoned a deficit: rather, in the consciousness of history-less people it functions as a distinct legitimation, in the sense that one is exonerated from making value judgments – and thus one is ignorant that Europe stands at a crossroads. Intellectual open-mindedness will awaken the strongest aversion, and will raise distrust since it lacks that barnyard aroma of university orthodoxy you can smell from afar. The thing that was once objectionable about the archivists – namely that they look down their nose at a supplicant petitioning obsequiously to view documents – has for the first time "jumped across" to the art historians like a virus and has basically infected entire faculties of humanities and social science. Just as a librarian used to act as if he knew all the books and saw the lending service as a senseless institution serving only the ignorant, this bad habit has now jumped over to the representatives of the empirical social sciences, and spread into most areas of study that use empirical methods. Laughable results from questionnaires come to be treated as solutions to the problems of the world, and statistics as emanations of insuperable wisdom. Such bad habits as these now set the tone of the university. Basically, what graduates of the universities know is but a fragment. Particularly conspicuous in this regard is "Contemporary History," which has not yet noticed that its subject matter is receding further and further into the distance: in the meantime, it has taken more than seventy years for Contemporary History to define the temporal boundaries of its area of research. The treasure trove of their research is the subcultural currents consisting of neo-Nazis, Identitarians, Reichsbürgers, and other psychologically disturbed fanatics, who pass as a half-legitimate subject matter for being contemporary, and thereby guarantee the survival of the field.

Depending upon your choice of a field of study you will run into the attitude I am describing for you. It would be a matter of individual luck if you should encounter a teacher who asserts himself in the midst of this nonsense and stands at a relative distance from the reigning mentality so that he can still declare the sovereignty of knowledge. I repeat over and over that even the most widely different fields of study must not be alien to you – so that if you can connect physics with music, chemistry with the theory of colors, geometry with cubism, and medicine with sociology you will be going in the right direction toward getting a feel for the fullness of life. People will criticize you, saying you live in a panopticon, but that in any case is better than living in a windowless laboratory, in a dusty accountant's office, or sitting in a real estate company where you can't quite open the window onto the light-well. You will see the conditions of the workplace becoming worse and worse, the hours of work further lengthened, and the demands upon the workers increased. Like the pitiable hamster in his treadmill you will have to work, and less free time will be given you than one got at the time of Josephinism in the 18th century. If you are to succeed you will have studied, you will have allowed your variety of interests to be dismissed, and you will have embraced the sermon for once and for all that only the "expert" achieves success. Only to this person is authenticity granted. The "specialist" is the person who is trusted to make an expert judgment, who draws from knowledge, who is always "hands on" and serviceable. And that is exactly how our world is: perfect and on the very verge of collapse.

I can no longer stand those speeches that are made during academic celebrations for the conferring of academic titles of any kind. A dean dressed up like a magician in a puppet show sermonizes that from now on the world lies open before you, that you can thank the great-hearted support of the university from the state and from business for your education, and that overall you must give thanks for the rest of your life, over and over again, even when you pass by the university on the streetcar. With the titles being conferred – though I no longer remember what they are called – one will permanently be a representative of the so-called *Alma Mater Rudolfina*, to which one now swears an oath. Even physicians swear this oath at the same time as the Hippocratic one, and then think nothing of it when a few months later they perform abortions in the gynecology department or prepare patients for euthanasia in the department of palliative care. In a few months everything will look different from the way it did in the ceremonial hall with the ceiling painted by Gustav Klimt. Directly under the stern gaze of the earlier rectors the graduates blithely swear every holy oath, since they learned in their studies that all this means nothing. And with this they are given one final message, that nothing means anything. This would be the highest insight that one could acquire at a university, if it were not that future income makes this nothing into something after all. My favorite one was the speech of a dean who said goodbye to the graduates with the consoling words that from that day on there would be one hundred more unemployed academics. Of course the parent's and grandmother's joy was palpable, and the dean believed that they had applauded his honesty. The successful candidates receive flowers and kisses, and nobody notices the discrepancy between the architectural surroundings and the pitiable celebration, frozen in conventions. It is the last act by which science is deprived of its dignity.

I must write this to you, not in order to disillusion you but in order to prepare you for the fact that you must pursue your education as autodidacts. You will be given very little. I am reminded of Lorenz von Stein, who said to Karl Grünberg around 1880, "Whoever wants to succeed in science must become an autodidact." I want to lay this into your hearts! Likewise, almost funny is the remark of José Ortega y Gasset, that while the university is the place where people can get along even without dignity, the other side of the coin "is expressed in the assertion that the university is *nevertheless* a place of science."

Now I have bothered you at length with my reproaches. I do not want to convert you to something, nor persuade you: I would count it a success, when in your choice of a field of study and in your obedient compliance with the course of studies you earn your certificate of qualification, if only you remember this letter of mine that had advised you to be very careful about the nature of your studies ...

Warm hugs, you "graduates to be" – your R.

105.
On Reading

Dear Nina, Dear Julian, Marie, and Vicky,

Often I have wondered whether my epistolary statements are in general readable for you. At the moment it is difficult for me to decide since it was always my intention to develop a "problematic" treatment rather than to write about some sort of Sunday outing forty years ago, or a vacation, or what-have-you. You will have recognized, as you take the letters together, that they are a "Table of Contents" of my life. You can judge this as you want, but it would already be a confirmation of my request if you disagreed, for to have a contrary opinion would need already recognize that I am describing a problem-situation.

As to how to handle these letters I have suggested that you read them according to their topics. However there is a difference between reading and reading. I take it that you will find some sentences or assertions strange when you read them. Perhaps you must do the same thing I had to do when, for instance, I wanted to get something out of Hegel's *Phenomenology* – to understand what he said and to take it into my own knowledge. It is not that I want to compare myself with Hegel but I may well ask that you take my formulations seriously, as long as they are correct, and even that you study them. I am allowed to request an examination, aren't I? If you get the impression either that you cannot follow the line of argument or that with all my references to names and things I am only showing my vanity, then either the context was not made clear by me, or the reader is unable to successfully fill in what was lacking. This bridging is not as difficult as one might think, for there are handbooks and study guides, and a reference on the order of a footnote is all that is needed. In these letters I have always been of the opinion that a provocative remark will move the reader in a certain direction – that is, toward becoming independent. Marie or Vicky, Julian or Nina will, I hope, then ask further questions and press on. Once upon a time this was the way a seminar worked: to talk about a topic together in a way where one could not know how things might develop.

In the peculiar way I am making my presentations, I have always set out the widest variety of associations, which did not occur at random but were always taken from the fact that everything visible, everything readable, everything hearable characterizes a given period. Johannes Kepler had guessed in his *Harmonia Mundi* that there was a fixed star located where the dimensions of a tonal system required it to be, and this ominous star was indeed there to be found, though Kepler could not see it at the time since telescopes were not yet available. Following this intuition I once noticed something which not only the Greeks pointed to but also Goethe, when he began his *Faust* with the words "The sun sounds in an old way … ." So there were ideas of sound associated with the planets and the sun was to be heard as the basic tone that is always present like the bass line. And this notion was current in astronomy up through the Renaissance, before Newton tidied things up – for he was guided by a different mysticism. I write you this in order to show you with this tiny example that there are surprising interrelations and once they are put together it is possible to see in them an image of an entire period. This is the basis for my undertakings – about which one may think that after me there will be nobody who would want to go along such a course. If this is not the case, if this curiosity dries up, then basically a world sinks away, as many worlds have already sunk away. It would however be an error to assume that it disappeared without a song and without a sound. The loss of antiquity happened with the violent confusion of the migration of peoples. We can assume as much with a clear conscience, since the historians seek desperately for survivals of a few cultural forms and for archaeological remains. For reasons not entirely clear to me we have searched much less for such things that date after the fall of Byzantium. Then, too, in 1453, the end of a powerful culture was brought on by murder and manslaughter, a genocide of orthodox Christians. Without the fall of Byzantium-Constantinople, Russia could not have come to be with its political theology, which we can see in the traces of iconography from Kiev to Moscow. In writing this I want to say to you, only by the way: Be careful! If you remember the background of Byzantium, you will stand on solid ground if you find Russian history interesting. And if I may continue with Russia, we reach very quickly the Russian contribution to the Enlightenment since the Czarina Catherine, formerly a German princess, bought up the estate of Diderot. And with this purchase Denis Diderot's *Neveu de Rameau* was held in Saint Petersburg. But I will stop with that, since I actually wanted to write about the topic of reading.

I am showing you the byways of distraction, which are nothing but distractions due to knowledge and have nothing to do with arrogance: and yet who is still able to point out this world to you? This world is ready to sink away immediately, at least the European part of it. The two World Wars along with totalitarianism were its death knell. So these letters have the purpose of enabling you to look backstage one more time before the theatre burns down. I have wanted to write you nothing but a plea for pluralism in science. This is meant not as an excuse – mere relativism sounds bad – but I want to show you what I referred to as a "panorama" a few letters back. In a theoretical-scientific discussion, priorities must not be allowed to be imposed from the outside! Do you remember that I began with this topic in the first letters? So now we have come full circle. It is just that we did not stop when we felt secure in our understanding! As fine as it is to know something securely, so also must it be kept in mind that we see only a small part of the Milky Way. Pluralism opens the underlying realms of a subject that have long lain hidden beneath, just as pluralism means ensuring the much touted "freedom of thought" which always seems to me to be threatened by commissioned research. The poignant demand (for freedom) by Marquis de Posa near the end of Verdi's *Don Carlo* is more current today than ever. On the one hand we are threatened by its misuse: I fall aghast when speakers from the AFD in the German parliament raise similar demands and it astounds me that the words do not stick in their mouths; on the other hand we notice the restrictions – above all regarding access to our privacy. Among these I would also count contractual research, which decides which questions will survive. The most important investigations in the history of science would never have been financed by contractual research! As to works that are paid for today you would not be able to read the majority of them since they consist of tables, scales, and ominous curves. In articles from the empirical natural sciences, topics belonging to the human sciences are dealt with and presented as if we were at last to learn what man really is. Most of the time the results are not particularly favorable to humans. That is why there is a hue and cry calling for substitutes and compensations, which in turn makes consigning the question to natural science and technology seem appropriate after all. The so-called imperfectability of man makes it necessary to think of a "prosthesis" of some kind. Such a thing might work for teeth, and may help an amputee, but generally they have much more in mind. If I bring in the meaning of the doll in *Tales of Hoffman* and of the pleasant music of Jacques Offenbach, then I am crossing the line and I am unserious. Those others aren't, to whom it never occurred that in the fashion magazines after the French Revolution the young ladies modelling the clothes were reduced to "mannequins" – literally, "little men." To this day it is said on the occasion of a fashion show that the *dernier cri* is presented by a mannequin. Not even the feminists have ever been irked that the feminine idea is embodied by a "little man."

You see, my thoughts have again flown off course. But isn't it delightful fun, in reading, when one breaks beyond the horizon and a wide new prospect comes into view? Doesn't the pleasure of reading consist exactly in this, when a new land opens up, a verse gives you a new reality, and above all when lyricism brings our language into harmony with our feelings?

In my lectures I have always stressed that one must read aloud what one is writing, especially so as to correct it where one finds oneself left hanging in the recitation or stammers in the flow of speech. Though I no longer demand writerly competence in my students, I must always keep in mind that even when I did demand it my assertions were not taken seriously. That does not alter the situation. I must renew my apologies for I had once learned this method from my professor of the Old Testament, who was of the strong opinion that whatever did not have the "melodious speech" of the Bible – whatever did not harmonize with the Hebrew language – was an insertion, an inauthentic textual variant. According to this method Nivard Schögel (O.Cist.) edited the Old Testament – and was promptly "put on the index." I have much lower ambitions and am not thinking of editing the Bible, but still I found this method of treating ancient texts in itself interesting. It did not seem strange to me at all since I knew of a still stranger alternative. Not a few people in the Jewish community reconstruct the text of the *Books of Moses* with a complex numerical system, whose significance might be known from its misuse in astrology. In Paris there lives a Raw – that is, a pious Jew – who is almost at the rank of a rabbi, in whose circle a specialist in this number-mysticism has solved a thousand textual cruxes, for example in the prophets.

So if I give you the advice to proceed in this way – or have I not already done so? – it is with the ulterior motive that this remarkable mysticism in which an actual reality can be identified from numbers can actually serve as a method to learn more: this is the pluralism in science I have advocated.

So let us return to reading. It is so difficult to force this kind of reading upon you when I know that it is not letters but pictures that define your world. It's sad that the quality of these pictures, coming out of a telephone or a tablet or a PC, are of a more limited quality than those of Altamira or Lascaux, but for our current society they have reached the status of replacing reality. The buffalos or panthers evoked in the paintings were made to survive – similarly, realities are confirmed in the reduced symbolizations of our assertions. Thinking laterally, a thought imposes itself as to whether the amorous symbols of Ernst Klee might have something to do with the cult of hunting at Altamira. I don't yet know!

While you are reading you will always have associations similar to the sort I am presenting to you here. That is what is so fine about reading: getting stuck on a sentence, thinking about it, reading the sentence again and becoming aware that more may lie behind it. And so you read over and over again. An important friend would here object that if one must return to the statement, and if it is as "squishy" as I have described, this far more likely has to do with the writer's inadequacies, i.e., his not having formulated his thought adequately, or his having been overwhelmed by the subject matter. I cannot judge this, as far as I can imagine I have simply reproduced what I was able to experience. At this point I gladly hide behind Adalbert Stifter.

Reading Adalbert Stifter is an experience that always has two sides. In my experience I know persons, especially those very familiar with our current life, who are not pleased with the way he broadens reality. They only got through his *Nachsommer* because I forced them to. I am thinking of my very generous doctor, facing the duty to read the *Nachsommer*. His prose is that of Grillparzer's *A Dream A Life* – without the dream. Will you understand what I mean? Thus my internist is trying to follow these strange traces without as yet knowing about the peculiar hypochondria of Adalbert Stifter. Behind the reading of such pages there is a universe of feelings and fantasies. For my physiotherapist the relaxation in Stifter is unbearable, whence the relaxation is the tension. This bothers her about Stifter. I appreciate her toiling through *Nachsommer* but in all likelihood my recommendation was narcissistic. For myself I cannot decide whether I am the uncle Riesach or the nephew. As I aged I shifted from being the enamored nephew to the resigned uncle.

In reading these lines you know well enough it's high time for earnest interpretation. Perhaps you still have a spark of what I have in mind from that confusing thought of Sigmund Freud, so go ahead! Analyze! I push you consciously into this depth of myself, since now you have your grandfather in your cabinet of specimens. If one peers through the glass of the showcase one can observe without shame or hesitation a mummy, as if it were a model made of wood or stone. During my times in the Egyptian collection I always prayed at the display of the princesses and the persons in the circle of the Pharaoh – they are people (!) and I prayed for them and enjoyed wishing them a requiem from their earthly life – which was never my desire across the way from the Natural History Museum at the Venus of Willendorf and the "sitting graves." Regularly I felt indignant when these showcases would be passed by unnoticed – a disturbance of the peace of the dead! – without commemoration. This was also the reason for my long lingering in the Metropolitan Museum in New York, for I wanted to be able to honor these Egyptian women in silent prayer, which they had surely expected would be done for them after their death. Besides, I was madly in love with the Egyptian women, through these sculptures made of wood. I had as much difficulty tearing myself away from these as from the Dorian Woman in the Villa Borghese.

You must understand my elaboration for surely my reference to the mummies, to the Dorian Woman, to the eagle on the grave painting in the Augustinian Church are revealing to you that these references to love have sunk deep into me and into my awareness. They go back thousands of years! Just this sort of irrational intimacy is also hinted at in reading – over and over again. Does this make my writing unserious? or full of truth? This has nothing to do with necromancy, nor has it anything to do with a perverse desire of necrophilia: rather, the laughter of the Dorian Woman was of a sort that was denied me in my life. The bodily charm of an Egyptian woman was more erotic than all the allegedly realistic reproductions of a woman in our magazines. Perhaps you can understand me? I have written quite openly about my predilections, only to emphasize for you that I am writing as a man of flesh and blood. I was not the unsexual grandfather, as grandchildren mostly assume without saying it... Nay, always in my reading there were these countless images ... .

I wanted to present to you a recommendation to read in this letter. What you do about it will be yours to choose.

Heartful hugs, your R.

106.
Hope Against Hopelessness

Dear Nina, Dear Julian, Vicky, and Marie,

I must briefly bring up another serious topic. One may very well raise the justified objection that I have not only described the decline of the "Western World" but that basically there remains no possibility for you to stop the downward slide or bring it to an end. The arguments that your future can only be painted in black are many and hard to oppose. And yet my own temperament is quite different, and I have an unaltering hope that it does not need to end the way my presentations hitherto have set forth. I advanced this perspective intentionally since I wanted you to know and be immune to the insinuations of those who try to couch everything in rosy terms, and do so in truth for their own benefit and to your own harm. It is in fact theology that encourages you to believe that a surprising reversal might arrive, or is always presenting a scenario of our being saved out of the midst of danger. And truly, we should concern ourselves much more with this salvation. I hinted at this once, when I wrote about the martyrs of the 20th century, about Dietrich Bonhoeffer and Alfred Delp.

When I compare journalistic publications, 70% to 80% will announce the approaching threats, scares, crises and unavoidable catastrophes. Nor unfortunately do current political developments provide occasion for exuberant joy. The prognosis points in the opposite direction from any prospect that democracy will succeed to drive all the competing systems from the field. And yet one can see that the criteria of democracy have remained difficult to establish. Protest movements even when they seem to have no chance, as in Hong Kong, force those in power at least to acknowledge democratic institutions, to model themselves on them and imitate them, and therewith to fall into the embarrassment of keeping such imitations from changing actual voting results.

I once sat in the house of representatives in the Chinese people's congress, in Peking. I sat in the seats that had been provided for Inner Mongolia. If I had wanted to see the person presiding over the parliament I would have needed a telescope. This is how I saw the conductor of the Vienna Philharmonic, Zubin Mehta – as if in miniature. And the musical offering was a series of Strauss waltzes solely to entertain the Chinese audience, who were being offered a sort of New Year's concert. The music itself was amplified by a sound system whose quality was under par. At the time I thought to myself that it cannot be that China is up to date with the best developments in electronic gear. We proceeded from the People's Hall of Music toward the subway where the next surprise was waiting for us. The path down had essentially no steps. One made one's way by a steep ramp through gravel. On the main street there was a killer snarl of traffic. From the hotel window I watched the traffic at the intersection. Streams of traffic interpenetrated each other: first came the bicycles, then the mopeds and the scooters. I was told in advance that crossing at the intersection takes something like 20 minutes. The operation of the stoplights had at best the function of an engaging play of colors in red, orange and green, corresponding to the fact that it takes 20 minutes to cross the street.

I remember Peking well, but is it still the way I saw it then? This fits with my reflection about whether there is a positive side to things. When I wandered away from the main street with its twelve lanes, I discovered the other Peking, only a hundred meters away. It had the character of a village. Men sat before their corrugated iron huts sorting their screws and their nails, tinkering with their bicycles or screwing together some device for the household. Most of them sat on the ground and concentrated on their sorting. A nearby factory was surrounded by a protective wall like a barracks: that's where the coziness stopped. I was convinced that the inner part of the city was innovative, and perfectly mastered life, and lived on with an anonymous equanimity. Will this condition be a sign of the future? Similarly I was sold on Confucian medicine. On a lark I visited an outpatient clinic with the usual haughtiness of a European. I was about to have an operation on my gallbladder and was curious whether a Confucian would guess what I had. And he did: I got a lot of tea, and a special soil that I was to drink. I admit I preferred my Busopan suppositories and yet the diagnosis was correct.

The trip on the train to an area at the Great Wall of China confirmed my judgment that the Chinese infrastructure was still in knee-pants. Probably I would have to revise that judgment now, but it would not be accompanied by positive thoughts. China has emerged from its self-centered regime and has quickly learned how to act like a superpower. It has become aggressive, and they should change their ideogram for China. A vertical line through a rectangle is an inadequate depiction of this country's political intentions.

This recollection – I still know I am supposed to find the positive side – does not hinder me in my attempt to do so. It is positive that we no longer are talking about the hole in the ozone layer. Just a few years ago an increase by enormous proportions loomed as a specter over us; and now the danger seems to be gone. And, truly, it was with international cooperation that we found out what caused this phenomenon, which was allowed for the sun's rays to pass through uninterrupted. It was a coordinated international effort under the aegis of the UNO to avert this danger. It was so successful that, this danger is no longer accorded any importance. One wastes not a word on it and yet it was a positive achievement. The effort to deal with many things through the European community is a positive thing, especially for Europe. If we disregard the weaknesses of the EU, we can say that the first steps toward communal political action have been taken. And one must add that the old principle, followed slavishly by the media, applies more than ever: "bad news is good news."

Maybe I have to take myself by the scruff of the neck and admit that I have blown that same horn myself. Earnestly I blame myself for having participated in this sort of defeatism. I have afflicted you with my depressing reports. How can I make good on these errors?

I should not exaggerate. The positive element that I have endeavored to represent is indeed there to be represented, but I fear it is as rare as an albino in the wild. And yet we ought to hold fast to the positive; and it is important that a generation that sees itself as having no chance will abandon the paradigm and then might find the path to the light. It is my conviction that your generation will attempt this awesome deed. I hope for you that it succeeds!

All my love, your R.

107.
From Painting to Poetry

Dear Vicky, Marie, Nina and Dear Julian,

In my last letter I fulfilled my duty to point out that there is always a chance of avoiding a disaster, an open door by which to get free. Open doors and windows play a large role in paintings. From Naturalism to Late Romanticism this is a major feature. A girl might be sitting at a window reading. It would be too flat an explanation to think that the painter was merely trying to show how light got into the room. Sunlight would of course be a convenient way to present the girl "in the best light;" and moreover, she is reading: This fulfills the commandments of the "educated bourgeois" – which would be complemented by knitting and embroidering. An open door, on the other hand, is more to be found in the paintings of farm life, where hardly a single ray of light makes its way into the dark room but the open door beckons one to go outdoors into the fresh and free air, as if it still were necessary to free the farmers. By Albin Egger, better known as Egger-Lienz, there is a painting in which a Tyrolian farmer is just entering the door, and his massive shape makes everything dark. The farmer takes a touch of the holy water with his knobby right hand rather automatically, which makes the scene not the slightest bit more pleasant. It is a gesture entirely ritualized and therefore meaningless. It's interesting that especially in Expressionist Paintings there is no light – light in the sense of the Impressionists – but only brightness. We can immediately recognize this in van Gogh. For him there can be brightness that dazzles the eye, or for that matter darkness, since even in an afternoon landscape his sky might already be dark blue, though we can still see perfectly well since the cornfields, the cypresses, or a path in the field are bright "in themselves," and therefore "illuminate" the picture by the way they themselves are depicted. Van Gogh needed to repeat these circular color movements or to give the cypresses their windings in accordance with his dynamic way of painting. It would be easy to subject this way of expression with colors to psychoanalysis, but only at the expense of ignoring what is happening on the canvas.

It was among my favorite approaches to deny the descriptions that came with modernism. They loved to ascribe everything to the psychological, and to assume the artist had an idiosyncratic psychological disposition that enabled him to continue with his work. I would judge at the very least that these criteria for evaluating art works reach their culmination in linking genius to madness and impose upon these important decades of modernity an almost inescapable template: that the artist may not be measured by the standard of normalcy nor can he conform to the "oughts" of society. At the culmination, among such French lyric poets as Arthur Rimbaud or Charles Baudelaire, it was rumored that they took drugs, and that they would do their work only under the influence of drugs, which had already been rumored of composers and painters. I always objected, against this rumor, that it is not only a mere insinuation, but that one ought realistically to imagine writing or drawing or composing in an inebriated state. Franz Schubert is a well-known case of one who is supposed to have developed his compositional ideas under the influence of alcohol. This is nonsense! It would have been impossible for him to draw all those black ovals and flags on the five lines of the staff: he had to be quite sober if he wanted to write out his works. Notes on a cuff are imaginable but sheet music requires exactitude and consecutive thought. From this I would draw the conclusion that drugs come into play once the work is done – out of exhaustion! The lyric poets who bring their fragile spinnings of words onto paper need relaxation, a "switching off," and for this perhaps they take drugs.

I always direct this interpretation against the suggestion that a certain set of art works, especially modern ones, came almost "automatically" out of drugs. Further behind this suggestion lurks the aim to locate the intentions of the artist and especially the works of the moderns, also, and thus any of their contemporaries, outside and beyond the "oughts" of society. This is easily explained. The previous intention of art was, to use Schiller's expression, to serve as a moral institution. Especially the "bourgeois drama" saw itself as duty-bound to show society what ethical norms are to be emulated. As soon as art abandons its moral and aesthetic calling, it leaves me behind as an uninterested spectator. Thus in any museum we encounter uninterested spectators, who find themselves spoken to only by the depiction of unique or extraordinary things. Thus it is necessary that there be exceptional exhibitions as an attraction, though one also sees the other paintings in next room that are part of the holdings of the museum, regardless. The uninterested observer also owns a concert subscription. This becomes visible when after the ethical appeal in Mozart's music, and after the final chord, one witnesses a charge on the checkroom with the ensuing conquest of capturing one's coat, with pushing and shoving, though one would have gotten it two minutes later. It regularly surprises me how after a powerful symphony one applauds but then an incomparable haste drives one toward the coat check. I suppose the message of the symphony was to rush to the checkroom.

I have often said it is my most bitter sentiment that with the 19th century, art lost its obligation to criticize society: it no longer stood as documenting the catalogue of human virtues as in the Renaissance, no more spoke of the dignity of man, but became "un-exemplary." This un-exemplarity showed up rather suddenly. Just before, if an artist had anything to show, he would visit the most important exhibitions in Paris, London, or Vienna: but what did they bring with them? What was then preferred were mediocre naturalists, or historicist types who sought out salacious scenes from ancient mythology or from writers we know longer know. Around Montmartre in Paris they would have found what they were looking for if they would only go to a little café instead of the Moulin Rouge. I afford myself this malice, since 150 years ago one would have been able to produce a better picture of the world and society for himself than these romping deer in the dappled light of the forest, these grouses mating among the pines, or still life flowers. The Impressionists celebrated communal life, sometimes in the center of town, sometimes at the baths, but freighted these contents with their experiments having to do with the physiology of the eyes. The paintings would also exploit the way we see, how on the retina we are able to put together optical stimuli into an image. A thousand pointilles, through the operation of our brain, become an image.

The short meaning of this long oration is that multiple divisions occurred in modernity. The contents of the image no longer convey an intention. By this I mean that in viewing it I do not consider the person being represented but the manner of the representation. If you pay attention you can easily perceive the difference. In a search engine you can easily find a portrait of Charles V during the battle of Mühldorf. After refusing two or three times, Titian finally painted this event. You must know that two princes were brought together here, one political, the other a prince of painting. For quite a long time Tiziano Vecelli was uninterested in the emperor's request. It was only because of the "strokes of fate" that he became interesting to him, and he painted him twice. I contrast this portrait with the *Boy in a Red Vest* by Paul Cezanne. You will immediately see that the Cezanne is only incidentally representing a young boy, a person we do not know and we also do not have to know. Cezanne is occupied with the formal criteria of painting, with colors, form, composition, and with how the colors can be made to render the weight of the bodies being depicted. The great art historian Heinrich Wölfflin gave us a very simple key for understanding this: painting either renders what is visible or it makes something visible. Cezanne was only thinking about making something visible. In all likelihood he saw behind everything a geometrical form, a distinct formation of masses. At the same time his paintings forgo presenting a personal or universal message, and instead they document the building blocks of our visible world.

I have set this out in such detail so that you can more easily recognize that the previous and hardly frictionless relations between art and social power stood in a close connection, a relationship that loosened up in bourgeois society and ended, by a second step, in modernity. From now on art understands itself with the borrowed military metaphor of an avant-garde and sees its purpose as something between disturbance and provocation. Its relationship with society becomes contrarian, which is why society fights back and excludes art from its self-understanding. It is no surprise if art turns to the political aspects of culture: it just wants to be left to itself. After all, what can still bind the artists to the mendacity of a bourgeois society that willingly enrolled itself into the madness of the war in 1914? The war was really no business of theirs, and from this we can understand the grief and despair of the First World War expressed by Georg Trakl in his poem, "Grodek":

At evening the autumnal forests resound
With deadly weapons, the golden plains
And blue lakes, above them the sun
Rolls more darkly by; night enfolds
The dying warriors, the wild lament
Of their broken mouths ...

I understand that in the face of this gruesomeness, which as a reality principle turns against the frivolity and decadence of self-appointed elites, art also separated itself from this "fine" society. It did so in Surrealism, in the Dada Movement, in the *Merzbau* of Kurt Schwitters – and also of course in the *Sacre du Printemps* of Igor Stravinsky.

The question now occurs to me, whether at that time society wished to maintain its lack of understanding – exactly in the problematic prettification of everyday life in the Jugendstil – or whether contemporary art abrogated its natural bond with society. In the 20's the latter appeared to be the case. In the Surrealism of Joachim Ringelnatz reality itself had been relocated in unreality, as in the paintings of Giorgio de Chirico. Otto Dix portrayed the decadence, while Emil Nolde migrated inward, contemplating nature.

I do not now mean to be teaching you the history of art. I only want to make it clear that in the midst of these diminutions visible throughout art as in the sculpture of Alberto Giacometti or Hans Arp, the laughable lout was able to succeed: Adolf H. You could see it and you could hear it. We could recognize such cruel and puny spirits in the sketches of George Grosz – and yet I am justified in asking, Who thought this inmate of Vienna's Wurlitzer homeless shelter would go on to such a career? It is another reason why art donned its hat and said good-bye.

And there is the other side of the story. As in the university, the positions of professors in art schools did not remain unoccupied. There were specialists in false heroism, who embarrassingly went head over heels to teach kitsch art, against their own better knowledge. And there was the other case, the better one, who lay low and continued in his service in silence. Because of the dawn of a new era, the entire collection of plaster molds of large sculptures were thrown down from the top story of the Academy of Art into the courtyard. It was an emphatic break with history at large.

What I am here describing for you is the tragic misunderstanding between art and society that had its beginnings in the 19th century. It became more intense in the fatal history of the 20th century and it produced strange results. On the one side opportunism flourished; on the other, there was an avant-gardism camouflaged as protest that never took protest as seriously as it once had pretended. A permanent protest against society soon became the fashion in art and it increased its provocativeness, which culminated in Viennese Actionism. The greatest achievement of the great actionists was defacing a lecture hall at the University. Three of them later became professors. They did not have the decency to decline the positions. And "society" answered their provocations by an infamous means possible only in Vienna, where recognition can be the highest form of disrespect. Already in Robert Musil one could read that in Kakania recognition is the cheapest form of mockery. As for opportunism, I saw this in the Vienna's fantastic realism and could never make heads or tails of it, with its shallow symbolism and with its demand for a prerequisite mythical knowledge that any butcher could figure out who would then go on to flatter himself by purchasing the painting. In this connection I wrote a malicious letter to Friedensreich Hundertwasser, which he at least answered, though with many pages.

I have written this history and I owe you an explanation why. I will give that, now. If art in its contemporary products is a version of our socio-cultural development once-removed, if art is diagnostic for our times, then the exhibits we can see in galleries and in "modern museums" hardly present a reassuring message. They swing back and forth between infantilism, obscenity, vulgarity, and primitivism; and seldom will one bump into a work that will interrupt the procession of the tour. What Vaclav Havel once made a theme in politics has happened in art: try to live in the truth – in his case, to break through enforced silence in Czech; but in the vernissages and in the official openings of the exhibits also, not a word is spoken. After a brief introductory spiel everyone dives into the buffet, relieved to get a hotdog or a sausage and a glass of wine, and stand with their backs to the exposition and chit-chat about their skiing trips. Nobody dares to call what is going on by its name, as if Hans Christian Anderson were right in *The Emperor's New Clothes*.

In my presentation I want only to call to your attention that if my assertion is correct that in art the face of the times is recognizable, things are not going well for us. And now you have another task of reform on your hands.

All my love to the four of you, your R.

108.
What is the Significance of Beauty?

Dear Nina, Dear Julian, Marie, and Vicky,

In the last letter I brought to your attention the problem that despite the complete detachment of the development of art from that of society the question remains whether it continues any longer to mirror the social situation. I do not want to decide this for you, but only ask you to look at current exhibitions with an undistracted and attentive mind. In all likelihood Picasso is the great exception, who succeeded in everything using every artistic technique of representation. Everything he touched sparkled with spirit and wit. Picasso is to be thanked for having a better attitude about our times – I mean my times, the times between Stalin and Adolf H. – than these dictators deserved. He was also a conspicuous opponent of Franco in Spain, and created the powerfully monumental *Guernica* in honor of the victims of the civil war. I was always impressed by the horse in it, which though truly blameless was being ridden to its doom and is rearing up in agony. Never had I been gripped by the suffering of an animal as in the *Guernica*.

This example, which I always want to supplement with Käthe Kollwitz's memorial sculpture for her son (*Mother with her Dead Son*) as together a sufficient indication of the suffering that was brought upon Europe. In the watercolors of Egon Schiele, in the representations of Amadeo Modigliani, we experience the terrible vision that was realized in fact a few years later in the next world war. And the harrowing representation of man confronts us again in the photographs of the survivors from Auschwitz. It is unbearable to look upon the watercolors and photographs that show this unspeakable suffering, this tragedy that political madness had brought to a merciless climax.

This case, which I always and again have in my memory, raises the question whether we can still point to something "beautiful" in art. Nelly Sachs was asked, After Auschwitz can one still write a poem? My question is whether there still is any beauty in the wake of this suffering. The following lines are dedicated to trying to answer this. In particular, we are setting upon a search for beauty. In such a case etymology and philology are always helpful. Of course we know that since Homer, Sophocles, and Phidias that the beautiful is clearly defined. Since Sanzio Raphael and Dante Alighieri, since Leonardo da Vinci, William Shakespeare, and Johann Sebastian Bach, we have turned the beautiful into a

European concern, keeping antiquity in mind. What is more significant is that all the geniuses mentioned worked on the beautiful without knowing anything about aesthetics. All of them as a group couldn't do anything with the Greek word, *kalos*. The *kalokagathon* (the beautiful-and-good) mentioned by Plato, did not penetrate the world of art for a long time, but instead it designated a particular virtue or *areté*. In Homer *kalos* is used of men and of women, of animals, of clothing and weapons. There was a small controversy in Greek antiquity as to whether *kallos* as a noun would primarily mean "beauty." The adjective *kalos* was always connected with adornment – *kosmein* – and the highest ornament was probably referred to by the double meaning of *kosmos*.

The excellent "Dictionary of Philosophy" by Fritz Mauthner from 1910/11 teaches us that Latin designated not only boys and girls, cities and houses with "*pulcher*." Soon the property *pulcher*/beautiful was also applied in intellectual spheres. From now on there were beautiful thoughts, which is why *pulcher* appears in kinship with *fulgere*, a shimmering, a shining. A "shining speech" had first of all to be beautiful! That was the long legacy of Demosthenes, reaching up to the debates of the Roman senate. Before that, in early Latin, the more common word was *bellus* and this was much more successful in the history of language, being the godfather of *beauté* and "beautiful." Likewise, in meaning "cute," or "pretty" it went on to mean "stylish." I can only tell you that the history of the word became more and more adventurous, as Fritz Mauthner mentions, for example, in the letters of the apostle Paul, since the "beauty" of Christ transfigured on the cross is also included. For later times, after 1400, the beautiful is lifted out of the context of the Passion of Christ and begins its new career in the Renaissance.

Basically, in this word-history we experience at the same time an incredibly important spiritual history, in which man first forfeits the beauty given him by God and then the beauty given him by nature, and then takes upon himself the super-human task of determining the beautiful. Beginning with the gift as image and likeness, his sociomorphic interpretation of beauty then devolves into a technomorphic "construction," which for the first time confronts us with the misleading vocabulary of the mannequin. Before this last step, the beautiful had already been eroded in the philosophical reflections on aesthetics in the 18th century, as shown in the subsequent development of the performing arts.

Much later beauty was transferred to the physical exterior of people – to the "beautiful woman," to the "beauties" who attend a party at court, to the "beauty" that vexes all the other women in the village. It was a return of the earlier usage: one had used it this way already in Greece, in the 4th century BC as when one would engrave the name of his beloved on a tree and refer to her as *hé kalé*. "Beautiful" was from the beginning used as a value judgment, and it did not take long that art should also be infected by this usage. Johann Georg Walch in his *Philosophisches Lexikon* (ed.4, 1775) reckoned that beauty is not a mere fantasy, not a chimera, but something full of truth, that forms an order and engenders a harmony. An historian of philosophy knows immediately that he was influenced by the dissertation of Alexander Gottlieb Baumgarten, the founder of the "theory" of aesthetics. Although this dissertation was written as early as 1735 it seeped quite slowly into the learned world and began to have an effect over a long period that regularly displeased later philosophers since for Baumgarten taste remained a criterion for evaluation even beyond the province of art. From him we inherited the judgment of taste – why we are always fighting about who has authority to make it? The Cultural Office of the City of Vienna? The Committee of Art Historians? A Senate or the culture journalists? Artists themselves?

The criticism of Baumgarten has a good foundation and yet the debate ever since has been very controversial since one cannot easily separate the beautiful from a "doctrine of sensory perception." Modernity now announces itself, Baumgarten has been dethroned: it is now set forth that beauty and truth can no longer be united. Aesthetic truths can neither be incorrect nor correct, and so one is forced to relocate both of them (beauty and truth) under the rubric of probability. This is very unsatisfactory since up until then we assigned an aesthetic quality to truth. For Baumgarten this notion was trouble for now one could criticize him that behind his moral philosophy a praise of the beautiful could also be a praise of lies. At the beginning of the 19th century this would become a big topic. Edgar Allen Poe for the first time brought to light this ambiguity within aesthetics in his *Murder in the Rue Morgue*: is the macabre, then, to become part of the picture of the aesthetic?

This "aesthetics" project would nearly have been forgotten before the Revolution, as it has been by now, if it had not been that Kant as a perceptive reader of Baumgarten came to the intuition that there is a transcendental (suprasensual) aesthetics, an "*a priori* science of all principles of sensation." Kant strongly rejected the broadness of Baumgarten's notion of the aesthetic: surely it could not be thought of as belonging to a realm outside the sensory as if a special perception of its own. And yet Kant was inclined to accept this idea since Baumgarten wanted to subordinate the beautiful to principles of reasoning. If this could be done one would have fulfilled the first prerequisites of a scientific and theoretical foundation for the beautiful.

I would like to leave it at that. We are here entering rough territory. Perhaps you can recognize what peculiar assumptions would have to be adopted when reason took on the role as *arbiter elegentiarum* in questions of taste, only to recognize thereupon how much it becomes dependent upon sense perception. Thus taste can no longer be measured according to rules that could serve as a basis for certain laws.

Kant was trying to keep the concept of aesthetics from being used exactly the way we use it today. If we refer to something as "aesthetic," it is immediately beautiful and good. We create "aesthetic" solutions and no longer know that it is almost impossible to give a basis for them. The problem was that Kant did not succeed to bring together the subjective feeling of beauty and the doctrine of purposiveness in nature under the same heading. Somehow the matter of aesthetics got stuck in a limbo.

It was Friedrich Schiller who took the bold step of explaining the aesthetic and the beautiful as identical. From him then stems the specific history of the impact of an aesthetics – particularly a German one. With him this topic came up often, and I do not know whether he did any good service for the wider philosophical development of a judgment about the beautiful. It began with the "aesthetic experience of men" which he took further in his *Kallias, or On Beauty* and in lectures on the topic. Everyone was enthusiastic about Schiller's merging of the two ideas, which is understandable: "Beauty is nothing other than freedom showing through: beauty is nature presented artfully."

Maybe you remember that once before I analyzed an influential saying and showed it to be false – that "Property is theft." So also do I evaluate Schiller's pleasing statement that art is "nothing other than" something. I cannot remember right now but think I have likely referred to this "nothing other than" formulation in philosophy. This was a fashionable formulation from 1890 to 1950, meant to communicate a certainty, usually leading to a flat sort of naturalism and a questionable political anthropology: a classic early instance is to be found in Feuerbach's projective psychology (*Essence of Christianity*). Schiller's proclamation was extraordinarily influential. If we look closer at the statement, we see that art in its service to beauty was freed from any ethical corset. It does not take long before ideological assertions finally take hold in art. Suddenly the national hero gets involved in romanticism, and a heroism like that of the *1812 Overture* of Peter Ilyich Tchaikovsky gets involved in national historiography.

For us it is interesting that Goethe was far more moderate and did not fall in with Schiller's flight of fancy. Goethe basically distrusted philosophy, and abstained from such flights into indeterminate realms. On the other hand he was one of the few who was really versed in art. He was familiar with architecture, painting, sculpture, and music, which likely hindered him from passing judgments about "the beautiful," since how could he find a common denominator among these that could constitute a "concept" in philosophy? The Cathedral of Cologne and the Pantheon in Rome are worlds apart, as are Raphael and Dürer, and Bach and Beethoven, and yet each pair belong to the same art, respectively. Goethe was clever enough not to join in what Schiller thought was his greatest speculation. In comparison with Goethe, Kant had never seen a "world famous" work and had heard no music except for the humble music of Königsberg. In the preface to his *Anthropology* Kant praised Königsberg as his source of empirical knowledge. Everything that served him as a basis for philosophizing took place in Königsberg.

Without now losing sight of beauty, the people who would erect a theory of aesthetics are just the ones who are left unaffected by the great variety of real art works. If you read the painters active in the later phase of early modernity, they are far more advanced, for they possess not only practical experience with color and line – the technical demands of painting – a familiarity which up until today I miss among art historians – but also they made up theories for themselves which they developed in tandem with the natural sciences: theories about perception, seeing, feeling, and the reproduction of sensory impressions. Schiller implored the lyric poet Theodor Körner to send him all sorts of art books, prints of Italian painters, and books on architecture, but he was educated as an autodidact and had an unsettled feeling that his theory of beauty would perhaps fail in connection with the art of music. He closed his eyes to the documents of art history and did not take up the wide variousness of the beautiful, in order still to defend a concept of aesthetics that could explain anything and everything. The tradition of art history remained outside his consideration, which Giorgio Vasari had initiated with the publication of his *Lives of the Artists* between 1550 and 1567.

These ideas from Baumgarten to Schiller took place at a time long after William Hogarth had published his notion of beauty and advocated the intuition that a "history" of beauty could literally be established. *The Analysis of Beauty*, published in 1753, was the first attempt to give an analytic – even positivistic – foundation for the beautiful. But Edmund Burke fundamentally altered these analyses in passing them on in the form later adopted by Schiller. In Burke's *Philosophical Enquiry into the Origin of Our Ideas of the Sublime and Beautiful*, we see his influence upon Schiller, who directly took from Burke the phrase that had already played a role in Kant: "Beauty arouses affection without a desire to possess."

So we have on one hand the foundation for the future ideal of education, while on the other hand a distinction must be seen as to what can be possessed – and what cannot. For example one will have to own a copy of poetry in order to enjoy its treasures. In many cases the editions of piano and violin pieces had to be viewed as something one must come to possess – for how else could one come to study the works of Haydn or Mozart? Clearly the sentence that had been lifted from Burke and Kant implies that this abstinence or "disinterest in possessing" could only apply to pictorial arts. It would not be possible that the giant paintings that were in the palaces would in any likelihood be brought into a bourgeois home of the sort that Stifter describes in such detail in *Nachsommer*. How would one be able to bring a sculpture by Canova into a Biedermeier household? Had these beautiful things been denied to "bourgeois consumers"? This doesn't follow since there were always opportunities to visit collections. Obviously there was "bourgeois art" in Holland in the 17th century: the smaller formats of Vermeer van Delft, Jan Stehen, Adriaen van Ostade easily found a place in the bourgeois parlors of Amsterdam or The Hague.

Schopenhauer thought his greatest contribution was to try to cut this Gordian Knot. But did he? He thought that while delight that comes from the good and the beautiful are surely interested, the pleasure based on a judgment of taste is always disinterested, since all aesthetic judgment is disinterested. Obviously the object itself can arouse interest. This compromise at first looks tenable. Kant had formulated it in a different way: "That is beautiful which necessarily gives disinterested pleasure." I once learned this sentence by heart out of enthusiasm as a young boy so I don't have to look it up – and in my view it is far more correct than the compromise of Schopenhauer. With Schopenhauer the "blurriness" is disturbing, since his plea for a distinct kind of judgment without interest, like his admission of interest for the object itself, contains an impossibility. Is it only an impossibility or is it not in the end a delusion? Beauty underhandedly becomes a noun. If "beauty" seems to characterize the object, we experience the object as beautiful. This perception includes our feeling of "the beautiful." That means before we saw it we had no "attitude" about the thing, which means we were uninterested. If the object were for sale, our interest would have been aroused or disappointed.

Basically the art object has neither an original relation with our will nor an originary relation to our enjoyment. Before this occurs it is a non-thing. It must have been a wonderful time when aesthetics did not exist. We made our judgments on the basis of our feeling. We only know that in the past, too, a non-aesthete found pleasure in a beautiful object, and yet on the basis of what interest? It could have been based on the prospect of robbery, or the humiliation of an inferior, since in the object a higher value was intimated; but it can also be that it was pleasing without interest.

Now we must once again turn to music for help. It is one of the arts that had to be brought into reality by the musician before technical reproductions through sound systems became available. A sonata by Schubert could be found sitting on the piano in various households, but in the absence of a piano the music just lies there as mute notations. All our considerations up to now have been about representational art whereas music is a language. It possesses sense and logic and we can understand it but we cannot translate it. Perhaps we ought to take from this special character of music the hint that with the "scientization" since the 18th century, with psychology and the doctrine of affects and emotions, we have degraded beauty. We degrade beauty if we ascribe semi-divine attributes to the artist, notably in the form of the personalization of the beautiful soloist; we degrade beauty if we raise art to the level of religion, particularly the notorious Art Religion, which becomes as powerful as a prehistoric cult.

There is not a single line to be read in the aestheticians that can communicate the joy that art is able to communicate as well as the breadth our view of the world achieves through the experience of art. It is exactly this that I miss in art today, and more and more, and see instead how it is driven by the contrition industry fashionable today, thoughtlessly going on and on, as if it had not already produced enough products of that kind. Who is it that dominates us with claims that only art is in a position to hold up to us a mirror to society? Which art uses which mirror for which society? This attitude is where obscenity finds its place.

So, don't be seduced!

All my love, your R.

109.
The Calamity of Aesthetics

Dear Nina, Dear Julian, Marie, and Vicky,

In over a hundred letters I have brought up a lot of current problems, and shown you something of the course of events, why they were and still are the reason for lasting conflicts. In the last letter I told you, additionally, about the tensions in defining the beautiful, which was stimulated by art of all things. The philosophers were very quick to call "aesthetics" the general principle of art, and claimed this as their own philosophical discipline; and most philosophers far and wide no longer saw any need to deal concretely deal with any works of art. From Immanuel Kant stemmed this ugly term "*das Kunstschöne*" ("art-beauty"), all one word! The most Kant may have seen was a painting by Lucas van Leyden, and some works of the Danzig painter Anton Möller († 1611), who painted in the style of the German Renaissance, and in the churches he probably saw epitaphs and carvings, if they survived the five horrible fires in Königsberg during Kant's life. These catastrophic fires seem not to have disturbed Kant.

Let us focus once again on the fact that aesthetics made one's access to art more difficult, and that subsequently art history was only partially able to overcome this hindrance. Today, with the art-historically ladened term "aesthetic," we are once again on the verge of making the immediate experience of art more difficult. It is also difficult from the point of view of the art historians to deal with the artworks of the actionists as well as artworks readymade or trouvé, within the continuity of art history, except with incredible and made-up language or by means of descriptions full of fantasy. If I transfer to politics this same constellation of issues it could mean that politics in the same way is seeming to lose its orientation at the moment, and that it entered a phase of decadence at the same time that political science was on the rise. Aesthetics increasingly includes the ugly and thus breaks away from the exemplary character of the beautiful, and with the same stroke conversely presents the unexemplary as being the factual or even the true – a negation par excellence. Politics also seems to show similar twists.

The vitalizing principle of democracy – righteousness – has become weaker, and corruption is disproportionately on the rise. The twist can be described by noting that Russia is currently being ruled like the tin-horn dictatorships of South America, though more efficiently. In the Russian variant the KGB has created its "own" state, whereas in Brazil or Argentina this was not the case, since in both these cases it is instead the traditional military that does so. While the erstwhile US American president Donald Trump unprofessionally and insouciantly instigated a coup with a loose-lipped speech, he probably had in mind the return of Napoleon from Elba far more than a concrete plan to usurp the power of the state. This has been pulled off much better in other states – for instance in Turkey. More and more distinctly, political orientations are moving in the direction either of Bonapartism or of Peronism.

One must say in advance that both of these political "crystallizations" came from ideological positions that stemmed from capitalist liberalism and communism, respectively. In both cases it is a matter of assuming that the problem of human existence in society consists only in the immanent satisfaction of the masses. This evaluation drove the intellectuals toward opportunism, either to decide to adopt laissez-faire, which greatly exacerbated economic inequality; or else to decide to become a sort of communist court theologian. In the interpretation of the political situation they played a role like the Delphic Oracle, although their credibility was greatly strengthened because of their analysis of National Socialism, of all things. While capitalist liberalism had proclaimed the immanent salvation of mankind and society and inaugurated the institutions of the modern state in the 19th century with the political clout it had accrued, communism, the bastard child, was soon able to call into question their catalog of freedoms and to accuse the liberals of mendacity, and declared freedom to be possible only through equalizing the distribution of goods.

If we want to characterize their frameworks, both ideologies have an analogous structure, whether teleological or activist. They stand in a dynamic relation with each other. In the one, variants of progressivism and of a utopia come into being, realized step by step through a mysterious evolutionary and teleological process. Theirs is basically a "rightist" political self-understanding. The activist variant conceives of its development as brought about by force, and thereby shows itself to have a "leftist" self-interpretation. This policy gladly dubs itself revolutionary and from this gets its political definition. Within this spectrum democracy still remains embedded, and must basically "denature" these forces – and thereby institutionalize them as parliamentary powers; or else must take on an impossible contradiction in an attempt to pacify them. Believers from right to left distinguish themselves through personal factors such as temperament, capability for enthusiasm, and perseverance.

We do not notice right off that both these positions are completely detached from history. We know that "Western Society" was not conjured out of a hat: the human rights for instance that are incorporated in the US constitution are drawn from "traditions" that we refer to as "Christianity." In that case traditions were being brought together that have always formed our reality in new and creative ways. The notion of cutting oneself off from this is a good example of the point I made a moment ago, that modern society is borne from the spirit of social philosophy and social science formulated in an unhistorical as well as secular way. Karl Marx himself made the distinction between these two orientations. In his *Critique of the Hegelian Philosophy of Right* he names two kinds of revolution, a "partial" one and a "radical" one. The partial revolution could be instanced in the half-hearted bourgeois revolution of 1848, whereas the radical one was still in Marx's time waiting to occur: the Russian revolution of 1917 could well fill the bill, for a short time at least.

This long report ought to stimulate you to a political interpretation of the last two hundred years, during which liberalism and communism were formed and pursued their different goals. What came to be for the one was a "world economy" – called by Adam Smith, euphemistically, the "Wealth of Nations," in 1776 – and for the other the "world revolution," the leap into a new time with a new society. Between these two "systems" or whatever they are to be called, our political policies oscillate, while at the same time each is bent on the decline of its counterpart. So it was a surprise for both of them that a structure suddenly appeared, although it had "always" been there, since 1820: nationalism, the perfect vessel for each, fitting both outlooks. It had had its best mouthpiece in

Napoleon III, so that the foundation had been laid for the subsequent suicide of Europe in 1918.

Nationalism was at the time the more successful movement. It had even wakened friendly feelings among the Slavs all the way to Russia. Nationalism alone stood in the way of a political universalism which, assuming a generous point of view, the Danube Monarchy still seemed to represent – as did the Ottoman Empire under its Sultan in Istanbul. And nationalism had at the same time become the prerequisite for bringing about the internal corruption of a regime. In the Danube Monarchy it was the elite itself that did not grasp the enormous change involved in being part of "what is German," but soon adopted it as a "national virtue." The proclamation of the German Kaiser carried out in the Hall of Mirrors in Versailles, an imitation of the accession of Napoleon to become emperor of the French, was not taken to be a political burlesque but rather to be the founding of an empire under a radiating Wilhelmism. That was when the German "Bonapartism" emerged, which understood the order of the world even worse than did Napoleon himself.

This part of history you will learn in detail, in which the original error is already included, namely a failure to analyze at all the political nature of the lands of "Old Germany" but instead to act as if Saxony and Bavaria, Hannover and Baden-Württemberg, Brandenburg and the Hanseatic cities, had been a unit: as if they had always been Germany. If these had constituted a unity then this would have taken place, in the venerable Church of St. Paul in Frankfurt, but instead it ran aground in the "question of nationality." How after all was the participation of the Danube Monarchy in the "German League" to be judged?

These are old stories, but viewed under the prism of liberalism and communism they only fomented extremism and drove the contents of those positions toward perversion.

After the two World Wars and after the Cold War between East and West a general paralysis came about. The paralyzing spiritual and moral disturbance of the West kept Soviet communism alive longer than one would have calculated. The pseudo-revolutionary skirmishes in the West during the 70's and an opportunistic wait-and-see attitude due to a leftist civil theology left a completely new political force unnoticed, as it emerged out of the movement of migration into Europe and the USA. A new and immigrant nationalism once again showed itself to be more cogent than either of the political myths that arose from ideology. It would now have become necessary for social science again to call upon the discipline of the intellect to ascertain the structure of reality objectively, and to bring political virtues into the foreground – political wisdom and astuteness – and yet all this was taken to be reactionary and seemed obsolete. In the public sphere the prevailing image of the spiritual life had changed enormously. To subject everything to the verdict of being reactionary may have some merit, but a sheer ignorance about facts, an erroneous construction and falsification of history, irresponsible assertions of opinion taken to be sincere, deculturation, intellectual laziness, and arrogance were soon seen as virtues, with the support of the media, and assured one a career. It came about that all intellectual culture was stamped as reactionary, while moral lassitude counted as progress.

This is why I had to show you through the example of contemporary art, the aspects of our political situation that cannot at all be adequately or authentically represented in briefer compass. I do not know whether this presentation succeeds to produce an overview of the crystalized elements of politics under the concepts of Bonapartism and Peronism. In all likelihood Thomas Hobbes's analysis would be impressive in this connection since he succinctly locates a *libido dominandi* operating behind this misled attempt to find truth in the ideologies, regardless from which religion or sect or lodge. In this case even religious concerns can become a camouflage, or a reform-minded idealism can become perverted. In the end it is only a matter of the corrupting element of passion functioning as religion – or to put it even more clearly, it is about the life of the spirit taken over by existential passion.

In this presentation it is easy to recognize that it is no longer possible to follow the great debate of the parties, since nothing really distinguishes the parties any more. They may be at loggerheads, they may accuse each other of the worst offenses, but all this is merely a pretense to compensate for the absence of any perspective. Politics in the USA became caught up between open and hidden obscenity, since a common failing came to dominate politics through the media, namely *superbia*. This is the "system error" that drives perversion.

Our political dilemma stands and falls with the necessity to answer whether we see democracy as the representation of society and as politically constitutive for a people. In the expression "national state," we have been able to bring together society and people, since there was still a "homogeneous ethnic milieu." In the meanwhile, republics have come to take on a multicultural character held together by no common political system of values, nor by a homogeneous milieu – which Talcott Parsons one asserted is the prerequisite for a meaningful sociology. But since we hardly have that any more, except in states that have taken upon themselves an extreme nationalism, the political fabric has become quite unstable. And how does one regain stability? Take three guesses.

In order to get a firm notion of politics we must keep in mind that we not only gain experiences: we just as quickly lose them. They become repressed, are forgotten, or their symbols no longer convey any understanding. I now have the basic impression that one has currently closed oneself off from experiences. It is what Thomas Bernhard described as a refusal to look. If we grasp that history consists of progress at the same time as regress, of increase in knowledge and loss of knowledge, of a development of a higher sensitivity though at the same time cruelties take place, of intellectual and spiritual sensibilities versus indifference, we will be better able to interpret what sort of times we find ourselves in.

Of course I cannot, as if I were a seer or a visionary, set about trying to determine the political constellation of the future. And yet I believe that it has just now become incumbent upon us to notice a certain movement in the evolving process of democracy that is forcing us into increased isolation as individuals, which we do not even notice because of our technical apparatuses. With this we drop out of the traditional opinion-making process, which already was hardly in satisfactory shape. Our "inner world" no longer sees any need to communicate with an "outer world," but only with the virtual world, which appears to us with a certain plausibility so that we are progressively exchanging it for reality. Even the poor, the homeless, and the urban nomad have switched over to the virtual world, though of course they are directly brought back to reality every day by the fact of hunger. While drugs will surely seduce a person into virtuality, under more "normal circumstances" it is consumer electronics that do so, which have become the access to a "world" that has become immaterial. Accordingly there will be political systems that exhibit mixed forms – i.e., isolated factors of democratization that slowly become detached from the essence of democracy, as represented for instance in the development of political correctness in speech – and factors of "surveillance capitalism," patronizing us with the pretense of enhancing our happiness.

These developments one ought fundamentally to oppose!

With loving hopes that you get through the cold spell in Berlin and also Vienna, I remain,

Your R.

110.
On the Question of Power

Dear Nina, Dear Julian, Marie, and Vicky,

Just as little as one can tell how "your" century will look given the way it began twenty years ago, so, conversely, I *can* say about "my" century with some certainty that it developed out of science. Although art had pushed forward in the *fin de siècle* and remained "better known," the discoveries of Max Planck reported in October and November 1900 were trailblazing; and a little later Albert Einstein published his first outlines of a completely new theory. At the same time came the rediscovery of the Mendelian theory of evolution, in which your great-great uncle was involved and is counted as the rediscoverer (Erich Tschermak-Seysenegg). What was decisive for both physicists was that they started a new movement that because of its origin and continuation and repercussions broke through the boundaries. The paradox about it was that the irreversible alteration of the worldview it brought with it came about at a time when traditional power was firmly founded, and yet in truth this political order was no longer tenable. It was, of all things, in just this phase of politics that the greatest breakthroughs occurred in the scientific view of the world, and the natural sciences came to dominate an essential part of philosophy. It was clear that our view of the world had now to be connected with the new research and that the existential questions about man needed to be discussed on the basis of a new and stronger recognition of science.

The answer being offered in cultural and intellectual history was as false and "old-fashioned" as it was quirky: in the midst of the announcement of the *Decline of the West* by Oswald Spengler in 1918, a version of man was being discovered that was made up by combining history, culture, intellectual life, and technology, a man who only gets his identity through a national attribution. For example Julius Langbehn called himself "a Rembrandt German" in his writings. The race theories of Arthur Gobineau and Houston Stewart Chamberlain jibed with this usage.

In the midst of this historical state of decline, the struggles for power become ever more furious and are generally seen as tests of a country's mettle to prove itself. A recognizable example is the buildup of fleets which brought England and Germany to loggerheads. Obviously, it had not been understood that the goal of the showdown was completely different from what the generals had thought. In 1917 not only had dialectical materialism won out in Russia: in the same year the first American soldier set foot on European soil. It was a world-historic event that can be compared with the landing of the Romans in the Piraeus under Quinctus Flaminius during the Second Macedonian War: the general set foot in Epirus and Corinth as a friend of the Greeks in 195BC and protected the independence of the city-states. Not so did the Spanish with Columbus at Guanahani (now the Bahamas), in 1492.

Obviously, the tide had turned in 1914, even if this could not be judged a "decline of the West." One should devote far more attention to the shift of power centers rather than questions of guilt, and also to technological developments, to new types of power brought about by modern physics and its build-up through the arms race. Forces previously unknown were coming into play to shatter the world, at least as manifested in its history. One knew in retrospect what this led to: "Sir Atom joins Lord Power," read a headline in the *Daily Mail* in 1957. This is likely a correct description of a situation that affected Europe especially. In "my" century it became common to ask the question, "Who has the power?" Too obviously, after the devastation of the war, this power was to be attributed to the Allied Forces. Leopold von Ranke had asked this question near the beginning of the first volume of his *Weltgeschichte – Die Römische Republik und ihre Weltherrschaft* (1881) (*World history: The Roman Republic and Its World Rule*, [1886]), and answered it quite intelligently, as if this were the normal political condition: "Only such a community (*sc.* is powerful) that is suited and experienced in both attack and defense." This was after all a severe criticism, by Ranke, of the notorious Alcibiades, who over 2000 years earlier had insisted that once a power established itself it had to keep growing. Since "my" period after 1945 was defined by the arms race, Alcibiades's doctrine remained in force unaltered throughout the entire period of the Cold War between East and West.

As I look at it today, Europe in the form of the "European Union" does not fulfil the one criterion of Ranke's – namely, "to be practiced in defense." This can become a problem since in all likelihood the other pillar Ranke called for is also not for Europe particularly strong. For him, culture was the most important measure of political stability. In an entirely historicist way he saw living forces acting as a defense. Today we take this as being cultural identity, but along with pointing to our uniqueness we at the same time include having a conception of our position in the rest of the world. This is indeed what we were thinking though one can well doubt that Mozart's operas are quite sufficient to guarantee our political integrity. Of course, communities have preserved their sovereignty over hundreds of years, perhaps exactly because, out of their wisdom and morality and according to the advice of the hermit Nicolaus of Flüe, they took to heart equality and freedom as the strongest ingredients of stability. (He was a much sought-after political adviser at the end of the 15th century and mediated in conflicts in Northern Italy; and his advice was influential in averting the danger of the Swiss Confederation splitting up. On the occasion of his death a great requiem for him was celebrated in the Stephansdom in Vienna).

Especially in the use of power and maintaining it, a dynamic principle is usually favored, the essence of which was embodied in Alcibiades. Less often was the converse taken into consideration, that the height of power was also followed by its opposite – the decline of power. Already Anaximander had figured out this "mechanism": In the translation of Diels, "*Woraus aber das Werden ist den seienden Dingen, in das hinein geschieht auch ihr Vergehen nach der Schuldigkeit* ("Out of the things for which there is coming for beings a coming to be, into these there is destruction also, according to their guilt"). As tedious as the German of the philologist might be, it has preserved these worthwhile and valuable sources and insights – up to our day – and we are well advised to remember it from time to time.

In my case I began to look only late in my life at the powers that surrounded us, although they were a common feature in the Viennese street scene up to 1955. The "quartering of powers" in Austria was still what I was seeing, and the hope of a stable arrangement in the great coalition balancing the "Red" and the "Black" parties. Of course, there were shifts according to the results of elections, but the shifts were marginal; the preservation of the spheres of interest for the party and its clientele was more decisive. This had not changed up to 1966, although it was more and more clear that a variation of the coalition with the Freedom Party was being considered. It was an at least queasy and uneasy political climate, which already seemed quite vulnerable. So it became part of everyday life to ask about the nature of power and about its worth, especially when one had gotten the impression that a coalition like the one up until then would impede progress, and – what was more important – that a "small coalition" would mean a huge disturbance since again and again there was doubt about the Freedom Party's loyalty to the state. The doubts were not unjustified. Unfortunately it was part of the overall concept of morality in Austria to give short shrift to the period from 1938 to 1945: the preference was merely to repress it. In any case this aroused tempers for years, which would express themselves in the charge that one side was filling its jurisdiction with their partisans which immediately was denounced by the others as a lie, who in turn retorted with the same charges in the same way. It was a very cheap power game, for which Austria gained a certain notoriety. At least the coalition regime had brought a mass of advantages to the country – social peace, welfare, and a growing economy. Programs in these areas were accepted in the 50's without misgivings, whereas environmental protection, air pollution control, and climate played no role at all. This gave the impression that it would always go on like that. The post-war recovery was successful and was a not-insignificant driver of an economic upswing.

Now I remember the historian Wolfgang Schivelbusch, who wrote *A Culture of Defeat*. There he reports that every defeat can yield unbelievably fruitful prosperity. He studied this phenomenon in the case of the American Civil War. The defeated states of the South, after losing the war, had an economic upswing that despite their predominantly agricultural economy was significantly stronger than that of the industrialized Northern states. Moreover, the freeing of the slaves had eliminated the need to support black American harvesters and cotton pickers in the South: after they were freed they had to support themselves. This brought on the completely unexpected result of social-political shortfalls that in the end the USA has never been able to "replenish." It is the consequence of an uncritical acceptance of the sociological "theorem" of Herbert Spencer – "Survival of the Fittest." Up until today this has remained the doctrine of social politics in the USA: self-responsibility and self-reliance. It is a completely absurd perpetuation of poverty and becoming socially declassified. Thus public health care, social security, and disability pay during a case of illness are missing. This is part of the political creed, and if these social deficiencies were abolished, the majority of people in the US would think that communism had taken over. In Europe, at least until 20 years ago, such social politics were a part of a "cultural model." I have always thought it was a sign of high culture in a state to mitigate social hardships as much as possible. We will never be able to eliminate them completely, but poverty should not be simply left up to fate. Unfortunately, I must here add that for some time this cultural model has taken some hits, as the social partnership cultivated in Austria between capital and labor weakened – partly after its accession into the European Union, partly due to the consciously fostered emancipation of the economy from any governmental steering policy.

The "culture of defeat" favored France after the war against Prussia-Germany in 1871, just as, conversely, the catastrophe of 1945 turned West Germany into an economic wonderland. A similar thing can also be said about Austria.

Everything I have described up until now is part of the processes of power that have strengthened the welfare of Europe. One must also add that the play of power within democracies is subject to a stringent rule, namely a fundamental division among powers. As long as it keeps a certain economical competence there can be balance of interests, which however is always predicated upon consensus. We will also discover negative sides of the coin that are brought about through unregulated access to power. The largest change in recent years can be observed in this area. And yet with the project of an "internationalization" of everything and everyone, a good argument can be brought for the change, because the outcome of the concentrations reached through this was a decisive transformation able even to outstrip a state. At this point the power structures independent of politics were made possible. It may be that they will feel less and less bound by the customs of a democracy, and so the liberalism I spoke of above creates a completely new foundation for capitalism which sweeps along with it everybody and anybody regardless of their worldview, whether it be China or the Sahel. The new power structure is based on the historical paradox that capitalism has become the most revolutionary force in world history. One must recognize this and because of this adopt a new orientation. The power at work is hard to understand: at one time it is indirect or even anonymous and just gets under your skin, but at another you run into it point blank.

For such questions one wishes one had a simple answer, something like a model that unifies once again the powers I have mentioned here. Perhaps it was the great grace of the Middle Ages that it was able to present the truth of life, of the earthly and the eternal history, in its great paintings and in its Gothic winged altarpieces. When one looked at them, whether educated or illiterate, they agreed they saw that another actuality is being indicated, one that is not only historical, not only to be assigned a place within history, but rather that this body of images is about the visualization of a truth of this world and the world beyond. As one contemplates the painted panel, all thoughts of power are as it were sublated.

If we want to go any further with this topic we must turn to William Shakespeare. He was the expert on power struggles and how much they affect people. He was the expert on the ruthlessness of the hunger for power and knew about the shameless use of power. He knew that a person is ready to terminate any relationship if it enables him to win power. What is surprising about Shakespeare is that he allows none of his own preferences to show through in his dramas: we know nothing about his judgments, nothing about his worldview. We only know that he had a vision of order, which is after all the object of the plays. But this order stands on feet of clay, for the earth itself is insecure. Order can be preserved, at least, if a king really means well and the people consent to his will. This is the central assertion of the *Magna Carta Libertatum* of 1215. Shakespeare depicted the failure of such an order with fearsome images of power on the stage, so that everyone could see them – as in *Macbeth*.

In the play *Henry the Fourth* it is no different. The dying king wants to hear more music and keeps checking to see whether his crown is still beside the bed. His son comes in. He should be saying goodbye to his dying father, but it goes without saying that all he has in mind is the crown, and the father notices the son's intention. The debate about legitimacy and legality becomes a big topic. Henry IV stole the power from Richard II illegitimately arrogating the power of the crown to himself. His son, who wanted to snatch it prematurely, was the legitimate heir to the crown. The point in the drama is the fact that the power changes the new king, just as it had changed the father.

> My father is gone wild into his grave,
> For in his tomb lie my affections.
> And with his spirit sadly I survive …

As in the other plays the problem is that power not only changes the person and alienates him from his circle of friends but that he becomes its very slave in the history of domination. Shakespeare is the most important person who still knows the mystique of the crown, the invisible power that emanates from it, an awareness he owes to his becoming "enlightened." Because his knowledge was matured by this double meaning, power is not only the real force that exhibits itself in its domination over court and country but at the same time is the mystical secret that derives from the inherited right of kings and from consecration, and from the grace of politics and from the word given in the fief, so that power is not evil: in the medieval understanding it comes from God.

It is exactly this legitimation that our current powers do not have. There is only a legal acknowledgment for the exercise of power; the other variants that we learn from Max Weber and his sociology of domination have no role. Instead we now hold the narrow position that only legal power is possible, whereas the arrogations of power, which cannot be derived in any other way, differ in no way from the power of a gang leader or a criminal organization. Awe no longer protects power.

This became clear when Friedrich Klopstock was shocked about the developments in the French Revolution, which he had previously praised, and learned about the murders and about the arbitrariness and the gruesomeness. Thus in 1799 he put the question "Why is God silent?" He, who could wield the power, was silent. Klopstock heard that the leaders of the Revolution had blasphemed God, and had trampled underfoot the rights of man. Had God left the world to them? Power had fallen into the wrong hands. Will this be the case in the future? Just as the demise of art will only be understood as a simultaneous drying up of creative force, so had it happened in the realm of faith and in the structure of values that a bourgeois society, with its erroneous estimates of both liberalism and communism, had shown the points of reference that it had adopted. It is the power of negating what is humane. We seem to be at its mercy.

To overcome this inhumane power will be the task of the 21st century.

To this end I wish you forcefulness, courage, confidence.

All my love, your R.

111.
A Closing Cadence

Dear Ones,

As I have already announced I end my letters to you with this one. There are several reasons for this, but I will mention the most beautiful reason to stop writing letters: it is *Piano Sonata 32*, opus 111 in C minor, by Ludwig van Beethoven. He composed it exactly 200 years ago, in 1821, and it was his last piano sonata. My reference to it is quite enough to indicate how ardently I commend music to your hearts. Since I know at the same time that the greatest seductions lurk in music, I recommend that you avoid the contemporary musical entertainment. Its harmonies both deceive and enervate the listener and if you expose yourselves to this "canned" music you will soon lose your feeling for music, and it will also harm your hearing. I can recommend Alfred Schnittke and his clever satire on Lenin in his opera, *Living with an Idiot*; the surreal opera of György Ligeti, *The Grand Macabre*; the compositions of György Kurtág; and the American composer, William Schuman as contemporary music worth listening to.

Conversely, the seductions of background music lie in wait for you in every street, every retail store, every restaurant, café, and rapid transit train station. They are an intentional disturbance of your peace of mind intruding upon you in order to habituate you to stop being quiet. We have been living in this world for some time now. It no longer applies new discoveries or improved provisions of our life-world to the old purposes, but now focuses them above all to robbing you of your highly private "world" and at the same time to perverting it. Perhaps you have been able to read from my letters that this invasion of your world no longer advances the "widening of your horizon" we had gotten used to in life, but now tries to bind you in dependency. I think I only need to point to the cellphone. When one perceives his social and cultural environment exclusively in electronic gadgets, which is apparently the case if you will only look around in a streetcar, the "real" reality recedes into the background and your own organs for perceiving reality – your eyes and your ears – become less and less suited for objective perception.

Give your conversational partner more attention than your cellphone.

Photograph not everything and all the time but look at things with your own eyes.

Go back to reading books and distrust any gadget that seems to be giving you information.

A corollary to this is that whatever amount of time you devote to textbooks on physics and chemistry, the same amount should be allotted to metaphysics. This is a time when we must contemplate and reflect. Both of these strengthen your intellectual independence.

As for which books you should read, it is difficult to say in advance. Out of my own repertoire of authors I would only recommend those who proved responsible: those who were unperturbed by the times they lived in and quite foreign to opportunism: Manès Sperber, Hermann Broch, Elias Canetti, Robert Musil, Eugen Rosenstock-Huessy, and Emmanuel Levinas. In order to learn about intellectual independence, get hold of the *Diaries* of Franz Grillparzer. I hope there is another edition of his collected works, which I have missed for decades – a tremendous disgrace to our "stewardship" of Austrian literature.

You can acquire an understanding of modernity which is now 200 years old, from Lionel Trilling, *Sincerity and Authenticity*; from Werner Hoffman, *Das entzweite Jahrhundert*; from Allan Bloom, *The Closing of the American Mind*; Eric Voegelin, *Science, Politics, and Gnosticism*; and Hans Jonas, *The Imperative of Responsibility*. A "seismogram" of the individual's state of mind in modernity you will find in J. M. Cioran, *Syllogisms of Bitterness,* or his collected works. The dramatic problem of science and the life-world was investigated by Edmund Husserl in *The Crisis of the European Sciences* (1936). A completely different and thought-provoking perspective can be gotten from Simone Weil, *Letter to a Priest*; and also from Edith Stein, *Finite and Eternal Being*, as well as Dietrich Bonhoeffer, *Letters and Papers from Prison*. An explanation for gruesomeness in the context of a socialized consciousness in the 20th century is offered by Stanislaw Lem's *Provocation*.

On the special topic of European intellectual history and the history of science I recommend to you Jacob Taubes, *Occidental Eschatology*; and Alois Dempf, *Sacrum Imperium* and *Die unsichtbare Bilderwelt*. You can always get a scientifically theoretical and social scientific intellectual history from Hans Blumenberg, for instance *The Legitimacy of the Modern Age*, or *Lebenszeit und Weltzeit*.

If you are interested in being educated in general, select volumes from the *Great Books of the Western World*, in my library. There you will find a representative collection of our intellectual foundations from Homer to Max Weber, in about sixty volumes. Important here is the first volume, which can teach you how to use this work. It helpfully guides you through a ten year course of study, as to what is to be read when, and in which context. You will find among these volumes specialized studies in natural science from Copernicus to Galileo or Newton in their original versions, just as well as Augustine and Ludwig Wittgenstein.

The more difficult question is, according to what criteria is "history" to be studied? From my current knowledge, which is not what yours will be in twenty years, I recommend Jürgen Osterhammel, who for the first time uses a phenomenological method, in *The Transformation of the World*. Always important is Friedrich Meinecke, *Weltbürgertum und Nationalstaat*, as a prerequisite for understanding the European Union; or, for a quick study of European history in three days, Eugen Rosenstock-Huessy, *Out of Revolution*. Always exciting are the two British historians, Peter Burke on the Renaissance or Peter Brown on the first "Christian" centuries, from around 300 to 600AD. An insight into the "decadence" around 1900 is given to you by Barbara Tuchman in *The Proud Tower*. It contains the bitter insight that the catastrophes in Europe were brought about willingly! An overview of political miscalculations is offered in her disturbing book *The March of Folly – From Troy to Vietnam*.

Now you will be thinking whether I have deliberately recommended no poets. This has to do with my one-sidedness, for given the many languages in our world there will be important works in all of them. I can therefore give you no real advice. As far as "my" language is concerned, I advise you to read German lyric poetry which is greatly undervalued and hardly read any more. In the first place I put Georg Trakl. Older poets I will not burden you with, though the ballads of Schiller or Goethe are pearls of the German language. Also I recommend to you, in a kaleidoscopic sequence, Hugo Ball, Joachim Ringelnatz, Gottfried Benn, Bert Brecht, Ernst Jandl, H.C.Artmann, Nelly Sachs, Hilde Domin, Else Lasker-Schüler, Erich Fried. But since I am naming names we must not leave out the *Sonnets* of William Shakespeare, sensitively translated by Karl Kraus.

I recommend that you read only one poem at a time and pay attention to the melody of the language. Especially in our times of linguistic disturbance the approach to lyric poetry is of greater importance and conveys a deeper insight into the flexibility of language and its facility for expression.

In the sciences I can give you only a little help, since I cannot say in advance which science you will study one day or whether you will want to study at all. It would be prudent advice, in addition to your one fundamental study, to consider also other disciplines, and to do so thoughtfully, so as not to come out "one-eyed." Unfortunately, to attend other lectures is hardly possible or part of the programs of study. In Europe, we may thank the abstract schematism of study regulations for this, a schema that is to be adopted in the same form by all universities. This nonsense was institutionalized through the "Bologna Process" and since then this narrowing has become a prerequisite for moving on to specialization! Hence, if one of you for instance studies chemistry, it is difficult for me to recommend a course on ancient philology. But if the opportunity arises I advise you to take it. It makes no difference what specialty you choose: much more important is hearing talk on a different theme and learning about another method or another time period. And the converse is just as important: a classical philologist should have a little mathematics or astronomy – after all the Greeks as seafarers developed a special "relationship" with the stars.

What I wish for you above all is that you might have friendships that are reliable, sincere, and stimulating. You are not yet aware that we are being forced more and more in our social environment into a "singularization" that in addition leads to a narcissism that is becoming stronger all the time. It is now a known fact that young men use more cosmetics than women, a significant indicator of this problematic "self-love." It is among the most conspicuous traits of modernity, which Frank Wedekind thematized for the first time in *Spring Awakening* (1891). It is interesting that friendship, above all things, no longer shows up in sociology, whereas it was still a topic in the 1920's – as in the work of Georg Simmel, Alfred Vierkandt, and Leopold von Wiese. This says a lot, since on the one hand, today, we point to how spontaneous relationships are common, while on the other hand relationships after a few years are in general showing a certain unreliability and little durability. It is not an accident that it says in Schiller's *Ode to Joy*, "… who succeeds in the great feat of being a friend to a friend," – but today this work of art is not performed often enough.

All in all, I wish you may spend your lives in peace and freedom.

Your R.

Afterword

With the 111th letter the correspondence was concluded. It is fitting that there should as many letters as Beethoven's works up to his last piano sonata. It was important to follow his pragmatic idealism. How else could one find one's way in and through the political hall of mirrors? That was already the case years ago when I would leave meetings with Chancellor Bruno Kreisky at his office. All possible perspectives quickly melted away. One underestimates the whisperers, the intriguers, and the jealousy of people. For example, environmental problems were already threatening around the mid-1970s, long before climate conferences and the melting of the polar ice caps. Therefore, the assurances of 2020 are as little credible as was the "Club of Rome," back then. As the years went by it became increasingly clear that the constitutional structure of the democratic state has little competence in existential issues. Economic interests, with the help of technological civilization, have prevailed. The old social contract between capital and labor has been terminated.

Thus, the letters to the grandchildren are like an obituary, the documentation of a world long gone. The "grammar" of politics should be recalled – late as it is. The subject, verb, and predicate of this grammar have been Jerusalem, Athens, and Rome. They are the points of reference in these letters. These three cities are the places that define our spiritual and intellectual world. This had to be called back to mind, precisely because Europe, unfortunately, did not improve – after 1914. The legacy and heritage was taken over by the United States of America. This was also the meaning of Woodrow Wilson's 1913 book *The New Freedom*, published in German in Munich in the very year of 1914! And its meaning was already known to the passengers on the "Mayflower" in 1620: that it lay with them to fulfill an historic task.

In this context I would recall the autobiography of Benjamin Franklin. With humility and perseverance he wanted to build a state emancipated from Europe, free from feudalism and serfdom, free from arbitrariness and conceit. To all appearances, today, it looks as if this "Project USA" is on the verge of failure.

Therefore, the letters may mark a turning point in time. One can still find an inkling of Europe in them, a reconstruction. It was probably difficult for the reader as he read them to recognize that all the subjects actually constitute an epilogue, an obituary of what once was. Likewise, across the ocean, it is to be feared that the United States has lost the optimism of its immigrants. The intellectual legacy imported from Europe is drying up, and the venerable political as well as intellectual institutions in the U.S. are weakening. There is a strange belief that Hollywood, Facebook, Silicon Valley, and artificial intelligence will easily make up for the losses. But they are indications of the current obscenity of politics.

In a starkly visible contradiction, the Statue of Liberty still stands at the entrance to New York harbor. It is not to be taken as a document of art history, nor as a monument to political illusions: freedom and the republic are forever present there.

RK.